CRIMINAL COURTS

Third Edition

CRIMINAL COURTS

STRUCTURE, PROCESS, AND ISSUES

Dean John Champion

Richard D. Hartley
University of Texas San Antonio

Gary A. Rabe
Minot State University

Boston   Columbus   Indianapolis   New York   San Francisco   Upper Saddle River
Amsterdam   Cape Town   Dubai   London   Madrid   Milan   Munich   Paris   Montreal   Toronto
Delhi   Mexico City   Sao Paulo   Sydney   Hong Kong   Seoul   Singapore   Taipei   Tokyo

Editorial Director: Vernon Anthony
Senior Acquisitions Editor: Eric Krassow
Editorial Assistant: Lynda Cramer
Director of Marketing: David Gesell
Senior Marketing Coordinator: Alicia Wozniak
Production Editor: Jessica Sykes
Project Manager: Susan Hannahs
Creative Director: Jayne Conte

Cover Design: Suzanne Behnke
Cover Photo: Fotolia
Full-Service Project Manager: Moganambigai
    Sundaramurthy, Integra Software Services Pvt. Ltd.
Composition: Integra Software Services Pvt. Ltd.
Cover Printer: Lehigh-Phoenix Color
Text Printer and Bindery: Edwards Brothers
Text Font: 10/12, Times

Credits and acknowledgments borrowed from other sources and reproduced, with permission, in this textbook appear on the appropriate page within the text

Library of Congress Cataloging-in-Publication Data

Champion, Dean J.
    Criminal courts : structure, process, and issues / Dean John Champion,
Richard D. Hartley, Gary A. Rabe.—3rd ed.
        p. cm.
    Includes bibliographical references and index.
    ISBN-13: 978-0-13-245779-8 (alk. paper)
    ISBN-10: 0-13-245779-2 (alk. paper)
1. Criminal justice, Administration of—United States.   2. Criminal
courts—United States.   I. Hartley, Richard D.   II. Rabe, Gary A.   III. Title.
    KF8700C47 2010
    345.73'01—dc22
                                                                    2011008604

10 9 8 7 6 5 4 3 2 1

ISBN-10:   0-13-245779-2
ISBN-13: 978-0-13-245779-8

To the memory of Dean John Champion, colleague, coauthor, mentor, and friend to many in the field of criminal justice

CONTENTS

Chapter 8   Pretrial Procedures: Plea Bargaining   181

Chapter 13   Diversion, Alternative Dispute Resolution, and Specialty Courts   290

PREFACE

Criminal Courts: Structure, Process, and Issues (third edition) is about criminal case processing from the point when offenders are arrested and charged with crimes through the sentencing and appeals process. This book provides a comprehensive examination of the United States Criminal Court systems, as well as discussion of discretionary actors within the system. Several chapters also deal with issues confronting the system from historical, philosophical, sociological, and psychological perspectives. Finally, this tome also provides a comparison of court ideals with actual court functioning.

The book begins with an examination of law and its social and political origins. Despite the different periods or eras into which world history has been divided by scholars, the pervasiveness and continuity of law are apparent. Laws have always existed in some form or another, but largely intended to fulfill the same general purposes regardless of the culture we choose to examine. The major functions of law are social control, dispute resolution, and social change. Over time, technological changes have occurred and social ideas have evolved that have contributed to how persons should orient themselves to others.

Laws can be differentiated according to whether they pertain to civil or criminal matters. Statements about what the law says and how we should comport ourselves when in the company of others have to do with substantive law. In less-complex social systems, substantive law tended to be espoused by the courts in the form of common law. Common law is traditional, dependent upon the particular needs and desires of groups of people living together in cities or towns. As our social systems have become increasingly complex, we have devised more elaborate legal schemes and more formal mechanisms to maintain the social order and regulate human conduct. How the law should be applied is the province of procedural law. In the United States, one of the most complex legal systems has been contrived. Today, there are all types of law pertaining to different aspects of our society. These laws are either civil or criminal, and a whole body of law focuses upon administrative law.

It is a legal reality that applications of the law from the beginning of time have favored particular interests over others. Some persons believe that our laws have been created to preserve the status quo for those who possess political and economic power. Thus, there are inherent disparities existing where applications of the law are implemented. Those suffering the most from legal disparities historically have been women, children, and minorities. In recent decades, sociolegal movements have prompted substantial social changes in response to disparate treatment of minorities and women in the courts.

Understanding the laws of the United States begins with a critical examination and description of the dual court system this country possesses. The principal components of the dual court system are federal and state court apparatuses. Chapter 2 describes federal and state court organization, and various functions of these different types of courts. There are diverse court systems, and there is little continuity among the states concerning what these different courts should be called. We do not have a universal nomenclature that can be applied to all state and local courts at various levels. However, there is considerable continuity within the federal court system. Federal and state court jurisdictions are distinguished, and the processes and functions of different types of courts are described and discussed.

The court work group consists of the same types of actors, regardless of whether we are discussing federal or state jurisdictions. The government has created a prosecutorial system that enforces the laws passed by the different legislatures. Whenever one or more of these laws are violated, prosecutors at the state or federal level act against alleged offenders to bring them to justice. Thus, Chapters 3 and 4 examine prosecutors and defense counsels in some detail, identifying their principal functions and duties. The United States Constitution and the Bill of Rights have vested all citizens with particular rights to ensure that they will be treated equally under the law.

All persons who are charged with a criminal offense are entitled to counsel if they are obligated to appear in court to answer criminal charges. Under particular circumstances, anyone may enjoy the right to a jury trial comprised of one's peers. The roles and functions of both prosecutors and defense counsels are examined and discussed.

The judge is often seen as the most important actor in the court system. Judges oversee all court proceedings and make important decisions. Several types of systems are used for judicial selection. These systems are described. While legal backgrounds are strongly recommended for persons functioning as judges, it is not necessarily true that all judges have legal backgrounds or training. Thus, different methods for selecting judges are explained, together with the weaknesses and strengths of these methods. Merit selection of judges seems to be favored in many jurisdictions, although often the best judges do not gravitate into these important posts. There is a segment of the judiciary clearly lacking the qualifications and commitment to make good decisions. Some judges are corrupt and commit deliberate acts, which call their integrity into question. Judicial misconduct of various kinds will be described, and some of the remedies available to the public for recalling bad judges will be examined.

At the heart of our legal system is the jury process. Juries are comprised of persons from the general population. Methods of jury selection vary greatly among jurisdictions. In fact, juries account for only about 10 percent of all criminal cases that are pursued. Nevertheless, considerable time is devoted to examining the jury process and how jurors are selected to judge the conduct of others. Both prosecutors and defense counsel conduct *voir dires* or oral questioning of prospective juries from a list of veniremen or a *venire*. Sometimes experts are used to assist as consultants, since some persons believe that jury selection can enhance the chances of a conviction or an acquittal. Various methods for discharging prospective jurors are examined, including challenges for cause and peremptory challenges. Various standards among the states and the federal system are described to show that there are different criteria applied for determining the appropriate jury size and the process of jury decision making. The decision-making process of juries is examined in some detail, and the important topics of jury nullification and juror misconduct are explored.

For offenders who are prosecuted criminally for violating the law, the arrest and booking process are described in Chapter 7. The issue of bail is also discussed. An overview of bail decision making and bail bondspersons is provided. Bail has always been a controversial issue and critics assert that it is punishment against poor offenders who often cannot afford bail. The purposes and practices of bail, therefore, are also discussed in detail. Changing sentiments in some jurisdictions has led to bail reform in order that bail might be more affordable to all offenders and that jail and detention overcrowding might be alleviated.

The actual trial process is also illustrated. Those charged with crimes may undergo either bench or jury trials, where either a judge will decide their case or a jury will deliberate. The criminal trial process is described in some detail with various fictional scenarios that have paralleled some actual legal cases in the recent past. In any criminal trial, due process requires that we consider any defendant innocent of a crime until proved guilty beyond a reasonable doubt. This is a difficult standard to achieve in many cases. Prosecutors who pursue criminal cases against particular suspects believe that they can convince juries of the defendant's guilt. However, the defendant is represented by counsel who attempts to show that the defendant is innocent. Various witnesses are brought forth and testify, either for or against particular defendants. Some of these witnesses are eyewitnesses, while others are expert witnesses who testify about the quality and significance of collected evidence. Juries deliberate and decide one's guilt or innocence.

One, however, must also keep in mind that the most frequently used resolution strategy for criminal offenders is not a trial but plea bargaining. Plea bargaining is a preconviction agreement between prosecutors, defense counsels, and their clients where guilty pleas are entered to criminal charges in exchange for some type of leniency. Plea bargaining results in a criminal conviction, but the penalties imposed are often less harsh compared with the penalties imposed through trial convictions. Different types of plea bargaining will be discussed. The pros and cons of plea bargaining are listed. Furthermore, some jurisdictions have abolished plea bargaining, and their reasons for doing so will be examined.

Regardless of whether offenders plead guilty through some type of plea bargain or are found guilty at trial, they will have a sentencing hearing. Sentencing hearings are conducted by trial judges and are to some extent replays of the court case originally presented against them. However, sentencing hearings permit victims or relatives of victims to make victim impact statements in either verbal or written form. Others testify on behalf of defendants. Judges are the final arbiters and impose different sentences, depending upon the seriousness of the crime, one's prior record, and other factors. Several different types of sentencing systems are used by U.S. courts today. These will be discussed in some detail, together with their implications for the early release of sentenced offenders. In the event that convicted offenders are dissatisfied with the verdict, they are entitled to appeal their cases to higher courts. The appellate process is discussed. Featured are death penalty cases, which are always automatically appealed. The appeals process is especially lengthy, and even those who are sentenced to death in states with capital punishment laws may not be executed for ten or more years.

A parallel system of justice exists for juvenile offenders. Thus, Chapter 11 and 12 examine the juvenile justice system in some detail, with particular emphasis upon how the juvenile court system is structured and operated. A different language applies to juvenile processing, and various comparisons are made between the juvenile and criminal justice systems. Several important landmark juvenile cases are cited where they have been granted certain constitutional rights by the U.S. Supreme Court. Over time, juvenile courts have taken on the characteristics of criminal courts. Some persons believe that in several years, the juvenile court may be abolished and that a unified court for both juveniles and adults will emerge.

Not all persons charged with crimes are ultimately processed by the criminal justice system. Chapter 13 discusses how some offenders are diverted to civil courts or into civil dispute resolution programs where their cases can be concluded in noncriminal ways. Victims and offenders are often brought together in alternative dispute resolution actions, where victim compensation and restorative justice are sought as remedies for wrongdoing. In some states, various laws are being scrutinized for the purpose of changing them and causing criminal acts to become decriminalized through legislative changes. Thus, the process of alternative dispute resolution, pretrial diversion, and specialty courts will be examined.

Chapter 14 concludes with an examination of how the court process is influenced by the media. As our society has become increasingly complex in a technological sense, we have mastered ways of delivering information to more people through different mediums such as television and the Internet. At the same time that we have been increasingly exposed to what goes on in the courtroom, a major litigation explosion has occurred, where increasing numbers of lawsuits are filed. We have evolved into a very litigious society. One reason for the great increase in litigation is the great publicity derived from courtroom coverage by the media and the sensationalization of particular cases. Media in the courtroom will be explored, and the pros and cons of media coverage will be examined in terms of how public opinion is shaped.

Ancillaries and desirable features of this book include numerous questions at chapter ends for review. Key terms are boldfaced throughout the text and listed at the beginning of the chapter, and a comprehensive glossary of these and other terms is found in an appendix. Suggested readings accompany each chapter so that readers interested in learning more about particular subjects can locate further reading for their edification and education. An up-to-date bibliography of both research publications and legal cases is provided in the end-of-book references to facilitate one's research and general study. A particularly interesting feature is the use of chapter openers and boxed case laws in each chapter. These chapter openers and boxes often contain interesting vignettes adapted from local newspapers and featuring stories and events that complement the text itself. These boxes also summarize landmark court decisions and their impact on criminal justice in action, and the real people and real events that take place in society everyday. They have been placed to heighten student interest in learning more about our court system and to provide them with digestible knowledge about important case law.

While this book is coauthored, it is acknowledged that the final result is the work of many persons. We wish to thank Tim Peyton, Eric Krassow, and Jessica Sykes from Pearson, for their patience and help in getting this third edition together. We are also indebted to the many reviewers who have made helpful suggestions and constructive criticisms for all editions of this work. Finally, special thanks to Shruti Bhakta for her help in finding sources, references, and suggested reading materials.

Dean John Champion
Richard D. Hartley
Gary A. Rabe

ABOUT THE AUTHORS

Dean John Champion (1940–2009) was Professor of Criminal Justice at several univeristies including Texas A&M International University, Minot State University, California State University-Long Beach, and the University of Tennessee-Knoxville. He received his Ph.D. from Purdue University and B.S. and M.A. degrees from Brigham Young University. He also completed several years of law school at the Nashville School of Law. Dr. Champion was a prolific wirter and has over 40 texts and/or edited works to his credit, a few of which were internationally recognized having been translated into Russian, Portuguese, Chinese, and Spanish.

He maintained membership in 11 professional organizations and was a lifetime member of the American Society of Criminology, Academy of Criminal Justice Sciences, and the American Sociological Association. He was a former editor of the Academy of Criminal Justice Sciences/Anderson Publishing Company Series on *Issues in Crime and Justice* and the *Journal of Crime and Justice*, and a contributing author for the *Encarta Encyclopedia 2000* for Microsoft. He was also a former Visiting Scholar for the National Center for Juvenile Justice and president of the Midwestern Criminal Justice Association.

Some of his published books for Prentice-Hall include *Crime Prevention in America* (2007); *Research Methods for Criminal Justice and Criminology 3/e* (2006); *The Juvenile Justice System: Delinquency, Processing, and the Law 5/e* (2007); *Corrections in the United States: A Contemporary Perspective 4/e* (2005); *Probation, Parole, and Community Corrections 5/e* (2008). His specialty interests include juvenile justice, criminal justice administration, corrections, and statistics/methods. Dr. Champion was a great advocate of student education and will be missed by all who knew him. His absence will especially be felt in the classroom and at the association annual meetings.

Richard D. Hartley is an associate professor in the Department of Criminal Justice at the University of Texas at San Antonio. He holds a Ph.D. from the School of Criminology and Criminal Justice at the University of Nebraska at Omaha. He teaches courses relating to criminal courts and the administration of justice, as well as research methods. Dr. Hartley's research interests include prosecutorial and judicial discretion, and race/ethnicity and crime. He has been involved with a number of research projects for which he analyzed sentencing outcomes, especially those for federal narcotics and immigration offenders. He holds professional memberships in the American Society of Criminology and the Academy of Criminal Justice Sciences. Dr. Hartley has given lectures to the Texas National Guard on race, ethnicity and crime, the war on drugs, and the nature of narcotics trafficking on the southwest border. Some of his recent and forthcoming publications appear in *Aggression and Violent Behavior*, *Crime & Delinquency*, *Criminal Justice Review*, *Justice Quarterly*, and *Journal of Pediatrics*.

Gary A. Rabe After serving for five years as the Vice President for Academic Affairs at Minot State University (MSU), Dr. Gary A. Rabe has returned to his academic appointment as a professor within the Department of Criminal Justice.

Dr. Rabe earned a Ph.D. in Criminology from the University Delaware, an M.A. in Criminology and Corrections from Sam Houston State University, and a B.S. in Criminal Justice from MSU. His professional experience includes Executive Director of the Rural Crime and Justice Center (MSU), Department Chair and Associate Professor of the Criminal Justice Center (MSU), Interim Dean of the College of Arts and Sciences (MSU), and Director of the Rural Law Enforcement Education Project at MSU. As Director of the Rural Crime and Justice Center, he was successful in obtaining over $8 million dollars in grants and contracts.

Dr. Rabe's professional memberships and services have included the National Consortium for White Collar Crime Research, the American Society of Criminology, the Law and Society Association, and the Academy of Criminal Justice Sciences. Dr. Rabe has served as a consultant to the Federal Law Enforcement Training Center and the National White Collar Crime Center, and served on the editorial Board for the *Journal of Crime and Justice*. Dr. Rabe was recently reappointed by the Governor to a second consecutive four-year term on the North Dakota Commission on Alternatives to Incarceration. Dr. Rabe's academic areas of specialization include Criminological Theory, Criminal Justice Policy Evaluation, Rural Crime, Criminology, Corporate Crime and Sentencing, Courts, and Sociology of Law. He has coauthored three books and published several book chapters, articles, and technical reports.

CRIMINAL COURTS

CHAPTER **1**

Law

The Legal Battlefield

CHAPTER OBJECTIVES

As a result of reading this chapter, you will have accomplished the following objectives:

1. Understand what the law is and the role it plays in various facets of our daily lives.
2. Describe the different functions of law, including social control, dispute resolution, and social change.
3. Understand the evolution of disputes and the formal resolution of them.
4. Understand the difference between substantive law and procedural law.
5. Understand the different types of law, including common law, civil law, as well as criminal and administrative laws.
6. Describe the different sociological perspectives on law such as sociological jurisprudence, legal realism, critical legal studies, and feminist legal theory.

KEY TERMS

administrative law
beyond a reasonable
    doubt
blaming
civil law
claiming
common law
conflict stage

criminal law
critical legal studies
disputant
dispute resolution
dispute stage
feminist legal studies
grievance
judicial activism

law
law in action
law in books
legal realism
naming
pre-conflict stage
preponderance of the
    evidence

procedural law
process of law
social change
social control
sociological
    jurisprudence
substantive law

Friends and acquaintances were not surprised when they heard the news. They have always suspected that Sheri Novak was a little "crazy." Earlier that day, Sheri was found driving at a very high rate of speed down the local highway. This was a very dangerous trip for the passenger in the car. Passing motorists witnessed on several occasions Sheri would dangle her two-year-old daughter out of the car window. Several calls were made to the police about what was being witnessed by passing motorists. After several minutes passed, Sheri threw her daughter out of the car window onto the busy highway. She immediately stopped and ran to her child. Witnesses heard her screaming that she wanted to save her daughter from the "evils of this world." She was arrested and charged with attempted murder and child abuse. Her daughter was hospitalized suffering numerous broken bones and internal injuries. This was not Sheri's first encounter with law enforcement involving her children. Earlier, she had been investigated for child abuse for taping her daughter's mouth shut because she would not stop crying. What penalties should be imposed for someone who does this to a child? Was the earlier incident of child abuse against Mrs. Novak a warning of a more serious problem? What could state authorities have done to prevent the most recent child abuse incident? If you were the judge, how would you judge Mrs. Novak if she was found guilty of attempted murder and child abuse?

INTRODUCTION

Murder or attempted murder, criminally convicted or civilly liable: The preceding scenario is a real example of a crime. For each crime alleged, there are elements that must be proved beyond a reasonable doubt in a subsequent trial. To be held liable in civil court, there are also facts that have to be shown by a preponderance of the evidence. Being convicted will most likely result in some type of punishment in jail or prison, whereas being held liable will result in the payment of damages (usually monetary) to the injured party. Criminal and civil courts are two separate realms and one can be tried in both for the same crime. The fact is there are several different kinds of laws or rules that attempt to govern our behavior and the way the citizenry conduct their lives. There are laws against many violations we may or may not know exist but are in place to protect us from things that may harm or injure us. Law is dynamic and has many definitions. What is against the law in one place or at one time may not be a violation in another place or at another time. What elements of a crime need to be proved to meet the different evidentiary standards? Different states and the federal government define crimes in particular ways. There is much variation among the states about the nature and seriousness of different types of offenses. There is also variation among different jurisdictions in the application of laws, even if they have the same or similar laws. This is referred to as interdistrict disparity. For example, if two persons commit the same federal narcotics violation and have similar backgrounds, but one is being convicted in district court in Texas and the other in district court in North Dakota, their sentences may be very different because of local court contexts (plea bargaining, departure rates, prison overcrowding) even though they violated the same federal law.

There are also many definitions of criminal law in various places and also at various times. While these definitions are important to learn, it is also important to understand the different functions of law for a society as well as the consistency and inconsistency with which the law is applied. This chapter examines various perspectives regarding the purposes and functions of law. Law can be used as a means to regulate the behavior of society, it can be used to settle disputes between grieving parties, and it can be used to elicit change in current practices or ideas. This chapter also provides a framework for the evolution of disputes and their formal resolution. There are different stages in the evolution of disputes. Persons investigating this evolution are concerned with developing a conceptual framework in order to better understand which disputes will reach the courts for formal resolution. Different types of law are also described—substantive versus procedural law, common law, civil law, administrative law, and criminal law. The final section describes some of the more important contributions of sociolegal scholars like Oliver Wendell Holmes, Roscoe Pound, Karl Llewellyn, and Roberto Unger, as well as some feminist legal theorists who have investigated the interplay between law and society.

WHAT IS LAW?

Law is the body of rules of specific conduct, prescribed by existing, legitimate authority, in a particular jurisdiction, and at a particular point in time. Law has been argued by some as an expression of the needs of the ruling class. Depending on your particular view of the legal system, law might be perceived as either liberating or oppressive, preserving the *status quo*, or providing the means and opportunity to challenge the existing social order. Law has been used to both perpetuate and eliminate slavery, dominate and liberate women, and convict and acquit the innocent. Law is related closely to all of these different definitions (Vago 2006).

The *Dred Scott* Case and the Law

The role of law was very apparent in the *Dred Scott* case, in which the slavery issue was challenged. This case was more about citizenship than slavery. Dred Scott was the slave of an army officer. The officer took Scott from Missouri, to Wisconsin, and eventually to Illinois. When Scott returned to Missouri, he claimed that he was no longer a slave because slavery was not recognized in either Wisconsin or Illinois. Therefore, an important constitutional question arose as to whether citizenship and freedom were vested in former slaves as the result of their relocating in states where slavery was prohibited. The U.S. Supreme Court heard and decided the case in 1857. Recognizing the rights of individual states, the U.S. Supreme Court held that citizenship was not a federal issue. Rather, the issue of slavery was to be determined by the individual states. Thus, according to this decision, Dred Scott was still considered a slave, since the U.S. Supreme Court chose not to interfere in states' rights. This decision encouraged antislave activists to make federal citizenship take priority over state citizenship. Subsequently, the efforts of these antislave activists resulted in the ratification of the Fourteenth Amendment. The Fourteenth Amendment established the primacy of federal citizenship and became the foundation by which many legal and social issues have been addressed by the U.S. Supreme Court (Vago 2006).

Women and the Law

The status and role of women in society have been continually restructured through the law. The law plays a powerful but not an exclusive role in shaping and maintaining women's subordination. The law has operated directly and explicitly to prevent women from attaining independence in the public sphere, thereby reinforcing their dependence upon men. Simultaneously, the law's continued absence from the private sphere where women have been relegated not only has deprived women of formal legal remedies, but has also devalued and discredited women as a class.

The law has also been used to control women's reproduction (*Webster v. Reproductive Services*, 1989), access to professional credentials (*Bradwell v. Illinois*, 1873), and the role of women in the workforce (*Muller v. Oregon*, 1908). The law has been used to redress these inequalities through affirmative action, which provides in part for fair and equitable hiring or promotion practices.

Determining precisely what the law should and should not be has proved to be elusive. Adamson Hoebel (1954, 18) has said that seeking a precise definition of law is like the quest for the Holy Grail. Legislators, prosecutors, defense attorneys, judges, defendants, businesspersons, consumers, parents, students, priests, the wealthy, and the poor all have different perspectives about what the law is and how it should be applied. Despite these diverse views of the law, there are several fundamental assumptions about the functions of law.

THE FUNCTIONS OF LAW

Various legal scholars have studied the functions of law in different social systems and at different points in time. Their many observations about the functions of law can be classified as (1) social control, (2) dispute resolution, and (3) social change.

Social Control

Social control consists of efforts by society to regulate the behavior of its members. The most visible form of social control is the application of the law (e.g., being arrested, prosecuted, and sentenced). For most citizens, this method of control is often the subject matter of the evening news and only happens to other people who we believe deserve to be controlled by the state. We seldom realize that we are subject to these same social controls in our daily lives.

Legal scholars distinguish between informal and formal social controls. Informal social controls are an integral feature of the socialization process. From early childhood, we are constantly taught the norms of behavior that our parents and the social world expect of us. These norms are a product of cultural expectations regarding dress, language, and behavior and our biological capacity to comprehend and adapt to these expectations. These informal social controls are effective because we are rewarded or punished by people who are important to us. Such persons are known as significant others in our lives.

For example, if we do things that offend our parents, close friends, or significant others, the sanctions administered by these people that we have grown to love and respect are very powerful, and we often refrain from engaging in these offensive behaviors. If our grandparents learn that we have been engaging in underage drinking, they issue stern words to us or offer an unapproving glance that will have great influence on our decision to drink again. The usual impact of this informal social pressure is that we frequently refrain from those behaviors that tend to elicit harsh words, warnings, or glares. Gossip is another form of informal social control. Gossip flourishes in offices around the watercooler or during smoking breaks from our office buildings. Gossip also flourishes at weekly bridge games, through conversations with our friends over the telephone, through computer e-mail, and more recently through social networking sites. The effects of gossip are fairly consistent. Our behaviors are influenced significantly by the verbal and nonverbal cues we receive from others, either directly or indirectly. Through these different informal sanctions, we conform with what we believe are social expectations of us.

Dispute Resolution

A second function of law is **dispute resolution**. Persons frequently engage in disputes with others. Spouses might disagree about the division of labor in their household. Employees may disagree with their employers about their work effectiveness and quality. Sometimes disagreements occur among total strangers about how to drive on the interstate highways or how we or our children should behave in shopping centers or stores. Historically, persons involved in disputes have relied on informal methods for dispute resolution. In colonial times, families or individuals relied on their village elders to settle disputes. Not so long ago, disputes about many issues were considered private matters settled in nonlegal ways. In more recent decades, informal nonlegal resolutions of disputes have changed considerably. Increasingly, **disputants** rely on the legal system to resolve issues that once were settled privately. A major change in our social dynamics is largely responsible for this shift. Informal methods for dispute resolution used to be more effective in small, closely knit homogeneous societies. Often, the members of these communities were more closely related either through family ties or economically. Therefore, disputes were quite disruptive to the stability of the community and had to be resolved quickly. It was not deemed necessary to use legal means for resolving disputes because these disputes rarely rose to such formal levels.

One additional benefit of nonlegal methods to resolve disputes is that agreements are usually reached that are satisfactory to both parties. In traditional courtroom litigation, legal dispute resolution results in winners and losers. One side is usually dissatisfied with whatever decision was rendered, but tradition called for accepting that decision without further argument. However, as social systems became increasingly complex and heterogeneous, informal dispute resolution methods were less effective. There was no clear interdependence among the disputants, and the authority attempting to resolve the dispute was unclear. This social evolution generated more formal methods for dispute resolution, which gradually replaced less formal methods. Although formal, legal methods may settle the disputes to the satisfaction of the legal system, this doesn't necessarily mean that the dispute will never recur. It has been claimed, for instance, that a legal resolution of a conflict does not necessarily result in a reduction of tension or antagonism between the aggrieved parties (Vago 2006, 20). However, it is unlikely that most disputes are ever fully resolved; rather, they are temporarily quelled but eventually are resurrected into new conflicts and disputes.

Social Change

Social change is another important function of law. Social change is the process whereby ideas and practices are modified, either actively or passively through natural forces or deliberate social actions. Law is the principal avenue through which social ills and biases are resolved. History is replete with examples of law used to effect social changes of various kinds. State legislatures continually implement new laws to change the existing social order. Legislative actions are diverse and change our lives in various ways. For instance, new laws passed by legislatures may require us to wear seat belts or pay increased taxes, may raise or lower the speed limit, or may declare new national holidays. Judges also create social change through their own interpretations of the law and how it should be applied. Because of greater attention given to police methods by the media, most Americans are aware of their *Miranda* rights during custodial interrogations. Most citizens are aware of their right to counsel if they cannot afford an attorney (*Gideon v. Wainwright*, 1963). The judiciary has been most influential in social change through issuing their decisions in legal cases. Thus, precedents established by judges have formed the bases of changes in various social policies. These changes are the functional equivalent of law-making. Legislators regard this activity as **judicial activism** and are opposed to it, since they believe that legislatures, not the judiciary, should have the exclusive authority to make law. Beyond this, law is also a method by which to initiate broader societal changes.

THE EVOLUTION OF DISPUTES

Disputes occur frequently, perhaps many times a day among individuals. We may have disputes with our spouses, children, coworkers, and bosses; however, we rarely rely on the legal system to resolve or settle these types of disputes. It is important to realize that many disputes follow particular patterns, and that a process for seeking legal remedies only occurs when several important factors converge. Some researchers have conceptualized the dispute process as consisting of various stages.

Naming, Blaming, and Claiming

Felstiner, Abel, and Sarat (1980) identify three stages in the evolution of disputes: (1) naming, (2) blaming, and (3) claiming. These researchers were concerned with developing a conceptual framework to understand the evolution of disputes before they reach the courts for formalized resolution. Their view of disputes starts with classifying injuries into either perceived or unperceived. For instance, sometimes we are victimized or injured but aren't aware that we have been victimized or suffering any loss or injury. If we never realize we have been victimized, then we cannot consider bringing a dispute. Have you ever wondered why all of the gasoline prices are the same in your neighborhood? Perhaps this reflects a free and open market where competition has driven gas prices down as far as the local market forces can sustain. Or maybe, all of the gas station owners have secretly conspired to set fuel prices at fixed levels so that they can all benefit from higher prices. The point is that you never know when this situation actually occurs and whether you are being victimized. Each time you refuel your vehicle, you may be benefitting from the free-market system, or you may be being victimized through price-fixing. Thus, you may be the unwitting victim of a crime. When this occurs, even though you are a victim, no dispute arises. However, when you are able to identify yourself as a victim through **naming**, this is the first stage in formulating a legitimate dispute. The second stage in the dispute process is **blaming**. This stage involves translating your victimization into a formal grievance. In order for this event to occur, you must blame someone else for your victimization. For example, smokers move from naming to blaming when they allege that the tobacco companies have failed to inform them about the hazards of smoking. The final stage in the formulation of disputes is **claiming**. This occurs whenever victims believe that they have been injured, have identified a particular victimizer (someone to blame), and formally express a grievance against the person or organization responsible for their victimization. In most cases, victims seek monetary remedies. These claims ultimately evolve into disputes when the claim is initially rejected by another person or an organization. Not surprisingly, most disputes do not result into formal lawsuits. Most injuries are never perceived, and if they are, it is difficult to identify a particular victimizer. Therefore, the courts are faced with and address only a small fraction of the disputes that evolve into formal complaints and where those involved seek legal remedies.

A similar typology of disputes has been developed by Nader and Todd (1978) and Nader (1979). Like Felstiner, Abel, and Sarat (1980), Nader and Todd describe three stages in the dispute process: (1) the grievance or pre-conflict stage, (2) the conflict stage, and (3) the dispute stage. The **grievance** or **pre-conflict stage** requires that individuals or groups must perceive that they have been involved in an unfair or unjust situation. If the grievance is not resolved at this stage, then it progresses to a **conflict stage** where the victims confront the party they believe is the cause of their victimization. The dispute fully evolves when it reaches the **dispute stage** and the dispute is made public.

TYPES OF LAW

Typologies of law are both important and necessary. Law varies according to who prosecutes, the nature and types of existing penalties, and a law's particular historical origins. A broadly applicable typology is difficult to develop that includes all types of law. A common distinction is made between **substantive law** and **procedural law**.

Substantive Law

Substantive law is the **law in books**. Substantive law is what the law says. Basically this is the compilation of local, state, and federal laws created by legislatures. A law exists that defines when someone is under the influence of alcohol when operating a motor vehicle. All states now have .08 BAC as the intoxication standard. Thus, if a motorist has a BAC of .08 or higher, then the motorist is legally intoxicated. If the motorist has a BAC level of .07 or lower, then the motorist is not legally intoxicated. Persons who take money from others by force commit robbery. If they use a dangerous weapon in order to take money from others by force, they commit armed robbery. Laws exist that define these and other criminal acts. Many additional laws combine to form the substance of substantive law.

Procedural Law

Procedural law or the **process of law** pertains to how the law is applied. Procedural law is also called the **law in action**. Procedural law specifies how police officers must obtain and execute a search warrant. It also details how jurors should be selected, how witnesses should be sworn when testifying in court, and how evidence should be admitted in the courtroom. Procedural law also includes how persons should be sentenced when convicted of one or more crimes. For example, in North Dakota judges are required to consider the following factors to determine the desirability of sentencing an offender to imprisonment:

1. The defendant's criminal conduct neither caused nor threatened serious harm to another person or his property.
2. The defendant did not plan or expect that his criminal conduct would cause or threaten serious harm to another person or his property.
3. The defendant acted under strong provocation.
4. There were substantial grounds that, though insufficient to establish a legal defense, tend to excuse or justify the defendant's conduct.
5. The victim of the defendant's conduct induced to facilitate its commission.
6. The defendant has or will make restitution or reparation to the victim of his conduct for the damage or injury that was sustained.
7. The defendant has no history of prior delinquency or criminal activity, or has led a law-abiding life for a substantial period of time before the commission of the present offense.
8. The defendant's conduct was a result of circumstances unlikely to recur.
9. The character, history, and attitudes of the defendant indicate that he is unlikely to commit another crime.
10. The defendant is particularly likely to respond affirmatively to probationary treatment.
11. The imprisonment of the defendant would entail undue hardship to himself or his dependents.
12. The defendant is elderly or in poor health.
13. The defendant did not abuse a public position of responsibility or trust.
14. The defendant cooperated with law enforcement authorities by bringing other offenders to justice, or otherwise cooperated. (North Dakota Century Code, 12.1-32-04)

Common Law

Another type of law is **common law**. Common law is whatever is prevalent, traditional, or customary in a given jurisdiction. It is the law of precedent. There are no specific statutes that govern particular situations. Judges decide cases by common law on the basis of whatever is customary or traditional, not what is written down or codified.

Common law originated in England. Common law is judicially created law compared with law made by legislatures. English judges would travel to different cities and towns and decide cases on their circuits. Their decisions and the sentences they imposed were a combination of existing precedent and local custom. Because customs vary, common law varies among jurisdictions. For example, a judge in one jurisdiction may find that local residents are very tolerant of political dissent. If a defendant is arrested and charged with political dissent in this jurisdiction, it may be customary for the judge to impose a lenient sentence. The judge will probably not impose a harsh sentence because the citizenry would oppose it. However, in another jurisdiction where political dissension is unpopular, a judge might impose a harsh sentence upon a political dissident and have substantial community approval.

Although American society has become formalized and the laws at all jurisdictional levels are largely codified, it is not the case that common law has ceased to exist. In the United States, more than a few jurisdictions have common law and utilize it. Also, they might supplement their common law with codified statutory law. For example, many urban areas do not condone prostitution, although some prostitution exists and is accepted informally. There is a certain area of town where prostitution exists. If prostitutes are arrested, they are fined a nominal amount and are soon back on the street engaging in more prostitution. In many rural areas of the United States, prostitution might be treated quite differently. If police arrested a prostitute, the prosecutor would be expected by the community to pursue the case against the prostitute as a serious crime. Therefore, certain crimes vary in their seriousness according to jurisdictional variations and prevailing customs and definitions of criminal conduct.

BOX 1.1

Two Examples of Common Law

The Case of Ghen, the Whale Hunter

It happened in Massachusetts Bay. A whale hunter, Ghen, shot a whale with a bomb lance off the coast and the whale swam away and died about 25 miles from where it had been shot. Rich, a wandering beachcomber, came upon the dead whale lying on the beach. He stripped the blubber from the beached whale and converted the fat to oil, which he later sold at a nearby market. Subsequently, he bragged about his luck to others, and eventually, word reached Ghen about where his whale had gone. Ghen tracked down Rich and accused him of converting the whale remains for profit, thus denying Ghen any revenue from the whale he had shot. Rich refused to turn over the money he had received from the whale remains, arguing that he had found the whale, didn't know it was someone else's property, and did a lot of work converting the remains to fat. Ghen sued Rich, seeking to recover damages.

An interesting case was presented to the presiding judge. In the Cape Cod area, there were *no laws* governing whale rights. However, it was customary for those finding whales to alert the whale hunters where the whale had washed ashore so that the whale hunters could obtain the blubber and make valuable oil from the remains. The bomb lances used by different whalers were thus marked distinctively, so that anyone familiar with whaling knew whose lance it was and, thus, who owned the whale. In Massachusetts, the custom was that the original whale hunter who shot a whale possessed it through a type of ownership, regardless of where the whale eventually swam or washed ashore. When Rich found the beached whale, he either knew or should have known the proper procedure to follow regarding turning the whale remains over to the rightful owner. In his case, he ignored custom and precedent and converted the whale remains for his own benefit. Thus, the judge ruled against Rich and in favor of Ghen, who was subsequently reimbursed for his loss by Rich.

The Case of the Bradbury's Dead Sister

Bradbury lived in a large two-story building with his sister, Harriet, in a Maine community. During a particularly severe winter, his sister became ill and died in the apartment. Bradbury had little money and could not afford to pay for a funeral for his sister. Therefore, he concluded, he could dispose of his sister in the large apartment house furnace in the basement. He dragged her body to the basement, where he cremated it in the large furnace. Neighbors detected a foul odor and called police, who investigated. They determined what Bradbury had done and arrested him. At the time, there was no law or written statute prohibiting anyone from disposing of a dead body in an apartment furnace. However, the court determined that Bradbury had violated the common law, which spoke against indecent burials of dead bodies. The fact that Bradbury had indecently disposed of his sister's body and had not given her a decent Christian burial was sufficient to find him in violation of the prevailing common law.

In both the *Ghen* and *Bradbury* cases, no statutes existed during those times that prohibited the specific conduct described. In both cases, judges decided these matters strictly on the basis of prevailing precedent established by common agreement through common law. Today in the United States, many states continue to have common laws, although statutory law has replaced much of it. At the federal level, there is no common law anymore, replaced entirely by statutory law.

Sources: *Ghen v. Rich,* 8 F. 159 (1881) and *State v. Bradbury,* 136 Me. 347 (1939).

Civil Law

Civil law originated in ancient Roman law. Contrasted with common law, civil law stresses codification. Early civil law existed as compilations of rules and laws that were made under the emperor Justinian. Rather than rely on local custom to resolve disputes, common-law judges would refer to the written law when deciding cases. Civil law in America is used to resolve disputes between private parties. Unlike criminal law, the private party originates a case against another person or an organization rather than the prosecutor. The penalties sought are typically monetary. If one party is found to be at fault, damages are assessed. These damages are largely financial. Another feature of civil law is the standard of proof. In a civil case, the plaintiff must prove that the defendant was negligent by a **preponderance of the evidence**, which means more than 50 percent. Most Americans were made aware of this difference in the case of O. J. Simpson. While O. J. Simpson was acquitted of murder charges in a criminal case in California in 1995, subsequently he was found at fault in the wrongful deaths of his former wife, Nicole Brown Simpson, and a friend, Ronald Goldman, in the civil case that followed. The media attributed the different outcomes in the two trials to the different standards of proof required for criminal and civil cases. In O. J. Simpson's criminal case, the more difficult standard of **beyond a reasonable doubt** caused jurors to question the evidence against him and find him not guilty of the crimes. However, in the civil case that followed, another jury believed the plaintiffs who asserted that Simpson was responsible for the two deaths. In the latter case, Simpson's culpability was demonstrated according to the civil standard of the preponderance of evidence or weight of the evidence, not the criminal standard of beyond a reasonable doubt.

Criminal Law

For many citizens, the evening news on television is their primary source of information about how the criminal justice system operates. Television dramas such as *Law and Order*, *CSI*, and *N.Y.P.D. Blue* feature stories about the legal system and do much to shape our views about criminal law. We might see a story where an offender is sentenced in California to life in prison because he stole a pizza, or a story where a serial sex offender released by a parole board subsequently commits a new sex crime. For most people, the efficacy of the justice system is measured by the sound application of criminal laws or the poor application of these laws.

Criminal law is differentiated from civil law according to the following criteria:

	Criminal Law	Civil Law
Who Is the Victim	State	Individual
Who Prosecutes	State	Individual
Possible Punishments	Fine, probation, or imprisonment	Monetary awards

In both civil and criminal laws, the victim is a person or class of persons, such as an aggregate of smokers, inmates in a jail or prison facility, or persons who use marijuana. However, in criminal law the offense is regarded as so disruptive to the social order that society as a whole is the nebulous victim. This is because under criminal law, society is considered harmed by someone's illegal actions. In civil law, someone is the victim and brings suit against the victimizer. Punishments under criminal law are more severe than the punishments prescribed under civil law. Persons convicted of crimes may be fined and/or incarcerated. The most severe form of criminal punishment is the death penalty. In civil cases, however, victimizers who are found liable are not imprisoned or put to death. In most instances, however, they are obligated to compensate victims for their losses and suffering. These penalties are monetary judgments or awards for damages.

Again, the O. J. Simpson case demonstrates this difference. If Simpson had been convicted in that criminal case, he would have been sentenced to prison. In the subsequent civil case against him, Simpson was found liable and ordered to pay damages. He was ordered by the court to pay $25 million in punitive damages, which were intended to punish him for his conduct, and he was further ordered to pay $8.5 million in compensatory damages, which were intended to compensate the families of his victims for their pain and suffering.

Administrative Law

Administrative law is the body of laws, rules, orders, and regulations created by administrative agencies. While the other forms of law may not directly affect us in our daily lives, administrative law is pervasive and affects all of us in various ways. There are over 50 federal regulatory agencies that promulgate and enforce a diverse array of regulations. Other administrative agencies exist at the state and local levels. The result is an overwhelming amount of bureaucratic control. When we travel on an airline, for example, we are subject to the administrative rules developed by the Federal Aviation Administration. The food and drugs we consume are approved and regulated by the Food and Drug Administration (FDA). When we telephone others, this communication is regulated by the Federal Communications Commission. If we purchase a house, our actions are influenced by interest rates, which are indirectly related to the actions of the Federal Reserve.

An interesting example of the high degree of governmental regulation and control is given by Vago (2006). Vago indicates that a couple may be awakened by the buzz of an electronic clock or perhaps by a clock radio. This signals the beginning of a highly regulated existence for them. The clock or radio that wakes them is run by electricity provided by a utility company, regulated by the Federal Energy Regulatory Commission and by the state utility agencies. They listen to the weather report generated by the National Weather Service, part of the Commerce Department. When they go to the bathroom, they use products, such as mouthwash and toothpaste, made by companies regulated by the FDA. The husband might lose his temper trying to open bottle of aspirin with a childproof cap required by the Consumer Product Safety Commission (CPSC). In the kitchen the wife reaches for a box of cereal containing food processed by a firm subject to the regulations of the United States Department of Agriculture (USDA) and required to label its products under regulations of the Federal Trade Commission (FTC). When they get into their car to go to work, they are reminded by a buzzer to fasten their seat belts, compliments of the National Highway Traffic Safety Administration. They paid slightly more for their car than they wanted to, because it contains a catalytic converter and other devices stipulated by the Environmental Protection Agency (EPA) (Vago 2006, 123–124).

SOCIOLEGAL PERSPECTIVES AND THE LAW

Just as there are various types of law, there are also many perspectives about the interaction between society and law. The analysis of the interaction of law and society has its early American roots in the writings of Oliver Wendell Holmes Jr., Louis Brandeis, and Roscoe Pound. These authorities were among the first to criticize classical jurisprudence. Classical jurisprudence was concerned with applying a strict interpretation and application of the law. This formal and mechanical method of jurisprudence did not permit the courts to effect changes in social policy. Holmes, Brandeis, and Pound believed that law should be active and dynamic and useful for changing the social order. The perspective on law proposed by these authorities is **sociological jurisprudence**.

Sociological Jurisprudence

Sociological jurisprudence indicates that a part of law should concern itself with making social or public policy. Today this legal agenda is called judicial activism. Oliver Wendell Holmes believed that law should be responsive to and incorporate changing social conditions, although the legislature should remain the primary method of social change. Holmes said that "for the rational study of the law the black letter man may be seen as the man of the present, but the man of the future is the man of statistics and the master of economics" (Holmes 1897, 457). This statement suggests that law and/or judges should acknowledge and utilize social science to further develop and answer legally relevant questions.

The first person to use social science in litigation was Louis Brandeis. Brandeis embraced sociological jurisprudence and utilized social science to win cases. He often incorporated social science results into briefs to the court to bolster his arguments. One noteworthy case was *Muller v. Oregon* (1908), which involved a dispute about the working hours of women. Two years earlier, the case of *Lochner v. New York* (1905) was decided by the U.S. Supreme Court. The Court declared a statute unconstitutional that limited working hours to 60 per week. Aware of this case and holding, Brandeis believed that he had to show that it was harmful for women to work more than 60 hours per week. To substantiate his claim, Brandeis wrote a brief that included statements arguing that women were deleteriously affected by long hours of work. Brandeis used a variety of sources from labor statistics and statements from international conferences about labor legislation as his scientific sources. Dr. Theodore Wely has added that women bear the following generation whose health is essentially influenced by that of the mothers, and the state has a vital interest in securing itself for future generations capable of living and maintaining it (Wely 1904).

BOX 1.2

On the Possible Legalization of Marijuana

Decriminalization in California

In the November 1996 elections, a California citizen-initiated proposal was put before residents for a vote. Should marijuana for medical purposes be legalized? This is not the first time that states have considered decriminalizing the use of previously controlled or illegal substances. Under federal law (Controlled Substance Act of 1970), marijuana use for any purpose is illegal. Since California first proposed this issue, many states have or are considering putting this issue to a vote, and several states have voted to legalize marijuana for medicinal purposes. The Ninth Circuit Court of Appeals in San Francisco is again set to hear arguments in 2006. They are going to decide the right-to-life issue: Should medical marijuana be allowed in cases where it is needed to keep the patient alive or reduce excruciating pain? As a public policy issue, do you think marijuana should be legalized? How much crime would be eliminated through the legalization of marijuana? Should the same decriminalization be applied to substances such as heroin and cocaine?

Source: Adapted from Associated Press, "Medical Marijuana Issue Returns to Court," *Omaha World Herald,* March 26, 2006.

Breckenridge supported this sentiment by suggesting that the assumption of control over the conditions under which industrial women are employed is one of the most significant features of legislative policy. In many advanced industrial countries, the state not only prescribes minimum standards of decency, safety, and health, but also specifies minimal limits for wage earners. The state also takes cognizance of several ways for distinguishing sex differences and sex relationships. Furthermore, the state sometimes takes cognizance of the peculiarly close relationship that exists between the health of its women citizens and the physical vigor of future generations. It has been declared a matter of public concern that no group of its women workers should be allowed to unfit themselves, by excessive hours of work, by standing, or by other physical strain, for the burden of motherhood, which each of them should be able to assume. He adds that the object of such control is the protection of the physical well-being of the community by setting a limit to the exploitation of the improvident, unworkmanlike, unorganized women who are yet to be mothers, actual or prospective, of the coming generation (Breckenridge 1906).

The U.S. Supreme Court was persuaded by this argument and held that the adverse effects of women working long hours were detrimental to the public interest. There is no doubt that the justices of the U.S. Supreme Court were influenced by the social science evidence provided by Brandeis in his brief. The Court reasoned in *Muller* that a woman's physical structure and the performance of maternal functions place her at a disadvantage in the struggle for subsistence is obvious. This is especially true when the burdens of motherhood are upon her. Even when they are not, by abundant testimony of the medical fraternity, continuance for a long time on her feet at work, repeating this from day to day, tends to have injurious effects on the body, and as healthy mothers are essential to vigorous offspring, the physical well-being of women becomes an object of public care in order to preserve the strength and vigor of the race (*Muller v. Oregon*, 1908).

Roscoe Pound elaborated on the purpose and goal of sociological jurisprudence in several of his essays. He recognized that law was not and could not be autonomous or influenced by social conditions. He wrote that the important part of our system is not the trial judge who dispenses justice to litigants, but rather the judge of the appellate court who uses the litigation as a means of developing the law (Pound 1912, 489). Pound developed five strategies by which sociolegal jurists could distinguish themselves from more traditional jurists. These strategies include the following:

1. They are looking more to the working of the law than to its abstract content.
2. They regard law as a social institution, which may be improved by intelligent human effort, and hold it their duty to discover the best means of furthering and directing such effort.
3. They stress upon the social purposes which law subserves rather than upon sanction.
4. They urge that legal precepts are to be regarded more as guides to results, which are socially just ills less as flexible molds.
5. Their philosophical views are very diverse. (Pound 1912, 489–490)

These three legal scholars and practitioners represented a dramatic change in thinking about the law. They believed that classical jurisprudence and jurists should be the only ones to strictly apply existing law. These jurists believed that law and society were inextricably linked. One influenced the other. One was necessary for the other. Judges cognizant of or trained in sociological jurisprudence realized that one of the major functions of law was social change. Lawyers and jurists should apply law with the idea of fostering social change.

Legal Realism

Sociological jurisprudence provided the foundation for **legal realism**. This perspective is described in the early work of Karl Llewellyn (1931). Llewellyn had a broader agenda than his predecessors. He argued that law was dynamic and often inconsistent. Interestingly, the development of the National Reporter system published by West Publishing Company is believed to have contributed to this perspective. This is because the Reporter system disclosed that similar cases or existing legal precedents were actually applied or interpreted differently, depending upon the jurisdiction. Thus, it was that an appellate judge in California applied a particular legal precedent differently compared with how another appellate court judge in Texas applied the same legal precedent.

Karl Llewellyn also believed that the existing understanding of law was inadequate. He believed that law and society were constantly evolving. Realists also believed that law should be the means to a social end rather than an end in itself. Realists were distrustful of legal rules and the perspectives of rule formation. Rather, they were interested in determining the effects of law (Llewellyn 1931).

Critical Legal Studies

Critical legal studies is one of the most dynamic and controversial perspectives on law. This movement began with a group of junior faculty members and law students at Yale in the late 1960s. In 1977, the group organized itself into the Conference of Critical Legal Studies, which presently has over 400 members and holds annual conferences that attract 1,000 or more participants (Vago 2006, 67).

BOX 1.3

Changing the Law: Lawsuits Against Drug Dealers?

Suing the Dealers?

It happened in Wilmington, North Carolina. Blaire Thompson, daughter of Keith Thompson, was a drug addict. She had struggled with heroin addiction for years, attempting to stop using several times but without success. Blaire was a kindergarten teacher and hid her addiction from her peers and students. Nevertheless, the heroin use affected her work. One last attempt to break free of the drug habit led to a 60-day period of abstinence from heroin. In her moments of clarity, Blaire decided to write a book about the dangers of illegal drugs, including heroin. But Blaire's drug dealer called her one morning and offered her another fix. She succumbed and overdosed and died later that night. She was 26.

In the days following her death, Keith Thompson found Blaire's drug connection and confronted him. But Thompson found that he couldn't persuade authorities to prosecute the man for lack of evidence of his drug dealings. Frustrated, Thompson contacted State Senator Julia Boseman of Wilmington, advising her of his concerns and what had happened to his daughter. Subsequently, Boseman proposed a bill that provided, among other things, that drug dealers can be held responsible for the damages inflicted on their clients, whether it be death or physical or mental impairment. Thompson said, "Drug dealers are parasites in our community. They suck the quality of life from our citizens. We must use any and all means we can to continue this war on drugs."

According to the bill, a dealer does not have to be responsible for the damages. Virtually any person or group, even the state, can sue any convicted drug dealer. Dealers could be forced to pay for injuries, treatment, emotional distress, or loss of employment or companionship suffered by drug users or those in their community. The American Civil Liberties Union (ACLU) of North Carolina opposes the bill, saying that the measure is unconstitutional because the dealer sued doesn't have to be the one who causes the injury. Furthermore, the ACLU claims that lawsuits wouldn't be effective deterrents and it would be difficult to determine any particular dealer's assets. But doing something is better than doing nothing. What do you think? Should drug dealers be liable for the harm they cause to their clients through the use of illicit drugs?

In 2001 Steven Steiner, Jr., overdosed and died in New York. He was in his early twenties. His father, Steven Steiner, Sr., subsequently organized New York–based Dads and Moms Against

(continued)

(*continued*)

Drug Dealers (DMADD). DMADD wants to raise drug awareness, pay cash rewards for information leading to the arrest and conviction of drug dealers, and solicit tips from informants about those who deal drugs of any kind.

Similar initiatives are underway in other states, including Hawaii. In Kalihi, Hawaii, for instance, a particular home has been a drug center for years. Illicit drug sales have transpired on a continuing basis under the noses of law enforcement on Stanley Street. The home is owned by a convicted drug dealer who is serving a prison sentence in Oklahoma on drug-related charges. But his sons are continuing the illicit drug trade. Authorities in Hawaii say that as long as there's a demand for these drugs, there is little they can do to prevent their spread and use. But those who live next door to these drug dealers feel differently. Not only do they feel threatened as unwitting observers of constant illegal activity, but they must also suffer the round-the-clock noise and antisocial activities that are a part of this seedy underground industry.

In recent years, Hawaii has launched several bills aimed at combating the drug trade. Among other provisions, several bills proposed would allow families, individuals, companies, government agencies, and anyone else who can show an injury or financial harm resulting from a person's drug addiction to file lawsuits seeking compensation from drug pushers. Citizens who file complaints would also be protected from drug dealer retaliation in the same way that witnesses are protected who testify against persons in criminal proceedings. Do you believe that lawsuits against drug dealers are an effective way of combatting the dissemination of illegal drugs?

Sources: Adapted from Mike Baker and the Associated Press, "Proposed Bill Would Allow Lawsuits Against Drug Dealers," June 2, 2006; Editorial, "We Can Organize to Ostracize Drug Dealers," *Honolulu Advertiser*, June 20, 2006.

The critical legal studies movement involves a thorough examination of the entire legal system. The theoretical underpinnings of critical legal studies are most often attributed to Roberto Unger. The critical legal studies movement had its origins in legal realism. Similarly, critical legal studies takes issue with formal rational law. Critical legal studies contends that we must recognize that the law is subjective rather than objective.

Critical legal scholars believe that law is not value-free. Essentially these scholars believe that the law serves to preserve existing power relations in society. Law schools are structured to train students for hierarchy. In the classroom students learn their social position during lectures. Law school teachers rely heavily on the Socratic method, whereby teachers ask students about different points of the law. The students, regardless of their responses, are always incorrect. The teacher relies on either lower or higher levels of abstraction to fit particular situations. Law schools justify this method because many law professors believe that it makes students think like lawyers. However, for many law school students, this process is a humiliating experience and serves to reinforce the hierarchy of law.

In order to remedy certain problems associated with acquiring a legal education, a radical restructuring of law school curricula and how law is taught is needed. In an ideal legal education, there would be few legal skills classes (e.g., learning legal rules and the categorization of cases), and the major focus in law school would be upon mastering social and political theory and an analysis of the existing social system (e.g., housing, welfare, and criminal justice).

Feminist Legal Theory

Another perspective on the law has its origins in feminism. The diverse experiences of women and the law have evolved into various perspectives on the relationship between law and gender. The feminist's perspective of the law or **feminist legal studies** ranges from the radical to the pragmatic.

BOX 1.4

On the Legality of Assisted Suicide

The Case of Dr. Jack Kevorkian

His name was Jack Kevorkian. He was a physician. He assisted people who wished to end their lives. He enabled them to commit suicide. Was he a monster? Was he a savior? According to police, prosecutors, and his victims, he was both. Kevorkian was a longtime advocate for euthanasia, a practice of ending one's life when one has a terminal illness and is suffering from intense pain. If there is no hope for survival or a prolonged useful life, many patients in this condition want to end their pain and suffering in the most painless way possible. Kevorkian supplied many terminally ill people with "suicide kits," enabling them to use their own automobiles as their personal death chambers through death by carbon monoxide poisoning.

Kevorkian was in several courtrooms defending himself against various types of murder charges over the years. Testifying in his behalf were many family relatives of those who have terminated their lives with his assistance. Living wills recorded on videotape from victims themselves have absolved Kevorkian from beyond the grave. Yet, prosecutors and state legislators continued to bring Kevorkian into court, attempting to secure a murder conviction.

One dilemma was that Kevorkian took an oath when he became a physician. The oath required him to prolong a person's life, not terminate it. Yet, Kevorkian insisted that in all cases where he assisted the terminally ill, he merely provided the means whereby persons can die with dignity, instead of screaming to death in a lonely hospital bed from unbearable pain from cancer and other diseases.

Kevorkian almost always delivered the bodies of victims to hospitals where they could be properly examined. He insisted that although he was referred to in the media as "Dr. Death," he didn't deserve such an appellation. Rather, he saw his role as alleviating the suffering and pain of terminally ill patients. Other doctors rejected his philosophy and claimed that doctors should do everything they can to prolong life. Kevorkian was indicted and eventually convicted of murder in 1999 in a Michigan court for his role in the assisted suicide of one victim. In 2006 he was serving a 10- to 25-year sentence in a Michigan prison. Do you believe that persons should be allowed to choose whether they live or die, if they are suffering from a terminally ill condition and are suffering and in great pain? How should Dr. Jack Kevorkian have been treated by the criminal justice system? Was he guilty of multiple murders under the guise of assisted suicide? Is this a moral issue? What values are evident in this debate over medically assisted suicide? How should it be resolved? What do you think?

Sources: Adapted from Associated Press, "Kevorkian Assists Suicide No. 33," July 11, 1996; Adapted from the Associated Press, "Kevorkian Denied Parole in Bid for Freedom," May 20, 2006.

Some feminists have examined how the law protects male interests. Some persons have argued that the law treats women as objects of men (Abrams 1995). Other feminists have examined how women have had an impact on the legal system. These investigations include research on the impact of women in law school and as attorneys (Chambers 1989) and as judges. The rationale for this view is that women reason differently from men, and therefore as lawyers and judges, women will use a different type of logic when applying the law. Women may be less adversarial and confrontational compared with men. This is quite possibly a positive result. The confrontational adversarial process has a winner and a loser. Women often express dissatisfaction with the win–lose nature of litigation because the real needs of the litigants are never addressed or accommodated. Rather, female lawyers might advocate a process involving less litigation and more mediation and fewer winner-take-all results (Menkel-Meadow 1986).

Summary

Law has a variety of functions. Law is often used as a method of social control or to regulate our behavior. For instance, the law regulates whether or not females have the right to have an abortion, whether patients can use marijuana for medicinal purposes, and whether physicians can legally assist persons in ending their lives. When someone violates the law, the law is used as a method to punish them for their past behavior and to control their future behavior.

Another function of the law is dispute resolution. The law serves as a guide for resolving disputes. When there is a dispute, the law is often used to resolve that dispute. The law provides for rules of evidence and procedure that are employed to hear and process disputes. For example, the law resolves whether or not a person has violated a property law if their tree grows too far into a neighbor's yard; the law resolves whether or not a toy company has produced a faulty toy that has led to child injury and whether they are responsible to pay damages.

Another function of the law is social change. In the United States that law is often used as an agent of social change. State legislatures are constantly passing laws to change the existing social order. For example, the legislature passes a law allowing narcotics users to sue their dealers, the legislators in various states amend their drinking and driving laws and lower the legal blood alcohol limit to .08, or the Supreme Court decides that the death penalty as administered is unconstitutional. Legislative action or law has changed how we perceive and react to various criminal offenses as a society.

The law can be categorized as either substantive or procedural. Substantive laws are the laws on the books, the laws created by the legislature of federal and state governments and also by local authorities. Therefore, substantive law is what the law says.

Procedural law on the other hand is the process of the law, how the law is applied. Procedural law is sometimes referred to as the law in action. It gives, for instance, officers guidelines on how to get a search warrant. It gives judges guidelines on evidence that is and is not admissible in court. It gives prosecutors and defense attorneys rules for selecting jurors for particular cases. Both substantive and procedural laws are typologies or classifications of the law that tell us what the laws are, as well as how they are to be implemented.

Four types of law were identified. Common law originated in England and was made by judges who traveled in circuits and dispensed justice according to the customs common to the region. For this reason, common laws vary in different jurisdictions. Although in recent years we have tried to make what violates law, and the punishments for those violations more uniform, common law still exists. For example, in certain jurisdictions in the country the punishment for prostitution may amount to what is thought of as a slap on the wrist, where a prostitute is basically arrested, required to pay a fine, and is released back to the street to again engage in prostitution. However, the punishment for a conviction of prostitution in another area of the country may involve aggressive prosecution of prostitutes to send a message and act as a deterrent to going back on the streets. It may depend on the prosecutor's agenda; it may depend on the sentiment from the community. How vigorously certain violations of law will be pursued depends on a number of things; the fact is that this is a form of common law that differs across jurisdictions.

Civil law is codified or written and documented. Civil law originated in ancient Roman law. Unlike common law, judges refer to the written law when deciding cases; these decisions then become law. Civil law is used for dispute resolution amongst private parties. The penalties are typically monetary, and are not crimes against the state. In civil law there is also a different standard of proof to be held liable for your actions; it is by a preponderance of the evidence.

Criminal law is differentiated from other types of law in that the society as a whole is a victim, and the government brings charges against the accused when a criminal law is violated. Punishments under criminal law are more severe than those under civil law, and could include imprisonment. Those convicted have to be found guilty beyond a reasonable doubt as opposed to the preponderance of evidence standard in civil court.

Administrative law is the body of law, rules, orders, and regulations created by administrative agencies. Although we may not think about it too often, administrative law affects our lives almost daily. A number of regulatory agencies at both the federal and state levels exist and impose a lot of bureaucratic control on our lives. Every time you drive down the street, pick up prescriptions from the pharmacy, or take a flight to visit friends and relatives, there are various regulations that you, and others, are adhering to in order to ensure everyone's safety. When you drive your car, rules from the Highway Traffic Safety Commission stipulate that you should fasten your seat belt and be sure your car has had a safety inspection. When you go to the pharmacy, rules from the Food and Drug Administration provide guidelines for how many pills to take and other drugs to avoid because of possible interaction effects.

When you go to the airport, the Federal Aviation Administration mandates that certain items will not be allowed on aircraft. All in all, our daily lives are greatly affected by rules put forth by administrative agencies.

Another important aspect of law is how it is dynamic in that it interacts with society. Four perspectives were presented exploring this interaction. Sociological jurisprudence believes law should be concerned with making social or public policy. Oliver Wendell Holmes and Roscoe Pound were avid proponents of this perspective and believed that the law cannot be uninfluenced by, and must be responsive to, existing social conditions.

Legal realism believes that law should be the means to a social end. Karl Llewellyn believed that law and society were constantly evolving, and that we should be mindful of the effects of law.

Critical legal studies is a rather controversial perspective in that it believes that the law is subjective, not objective, and therefore is not value-free. In other words, Roberto Unger and other proponents believed that the law was used as an instrument to preserve the existing power relations in society.

Feminist legal theory purports that the law is used to protect male interests, or treats women as the objects of men. Feminist theorists believe that women apply a different logic to law, and that the law may better serve society if it was less adversarial and confrontational. Each of these offer different perspectives on the interaction between law and society.

Questions for Review

1. What is law? What are two different types of law? Differentiate between each.
2. What was the significance of the *Dred Scott* case?
3. What are four functions of law?
4. What is the significance of the view containing naming, blaming, and claiming?
5. How does substantive law differ from procedural law? What do these different types of law govern? Explain.
6. What is common law? How do judges decide cases on the basis of common law?
7. What is meant by administrative law? Why is it important for social change?
8. What is sociological jurisprudence? How is sociological jurisprudence related to social change?
9. What is meant by legal realism? How does critical legal studies compare with legal realism?
10. How has feminism affected the development of law in the United States?

Suggested Readings

1. D. E. Altus et al. (2004). "The Birth of a New World: Utopian Visions of Justice in Theory, Practice, and Literature." *Contemporary Justice Review: Issues in Criminal, Social, and Restorative Justice* **7:**267–333.
2. Robert Boyle, Donna R. Newman, and Sam A. Schmidt (2003). "Center for Professional Values and Practice Symposium: Criminal Defense in the Age of Terrorism." *New York Law School Law Review* **48:**3–384.
3. C. S. Cooper (2002). "Drug Courts: Current Issues and Future Perspectives." *Substance Abuse and Misuse* **38:**1671–1711.
4. A. Henneth (2004). "Recognition and Justice: Outline of a Plural Theory of Justice." *Acta Sociologica* **47:**351–364.
5. C. W. Mullins, D. Kauzlarich, and D. Rothe (2004). "The International Criminal Court and the Control of State Crime: Prospects and Problems." *Critical Criminology* **12:**285–308.
6. N. Pithy (2004). "Do New Crimes Need New Laws? Legal Provisions Available for Prosecuting Human Trafficking." *SA Crime Quarterly* **9:**7–10.
7. V. Toscano (2005). "Misguided Retribution: Criminalization of Pregnant Women Who Take Drugs." *Social and Legal Studies* **14:**359–386.
8. Steven Vago (2006). *Law and Society*, 8th ed. Upper Saddle River, NJ: Prentice Hall.

CHAPTER 2

The Structure of American Courts

CHAPTER OBJECTIVES

As a result of reading this chapter, you will have accomplished the following objectives:

1. Understand the different ways to classify American courts such as by jurisdiction, by its dual nature, and by type of court.
2. Describe the different types of jurisdiction like subject matter, geographic, and hierarchical.
3. Understand that the United States has two court structures, a federal structure and a state structure.
4. Describe the difference between trial and appellate courts.
5. Describe the federal court structure including U.S. Magistrate Courts, U.S. District Courts, U.S. Circuit Courts of Appeal, and the U.S. Supreme Court.
6. Describe the state court structure including Courts of Limited Jurisdiction, Courts of General Jurisdiction, Intermediate Courts of Appeal, and Courts of Last Resort.

KEY TERMS

amicus curiae	*en banc*	judicial review	trial courts
appellate courts	Evarts Act	Judiciary Act of 1789	United States Circuit
circuit courts	exclusive jurisdiction	jurisdiction	Courts of Appeal
circuit riders	federal district courts	limited jurisdiction	United States District
concurrent jurisdiction	general jurisdiction	original jurisdiction	Courts
courts of last resort	general sessions courts	Rule of Four	United States magistrates
courts of record	general trial courts	subject matter	United States Supreme
criminal courts	geographic jurisdiction	jurisdiction	Court
dual court system	hierarchical jurisdiction	Supreme Court	writ of *certiorari*

Eric Davidson works long days at the local tire factory and after work has a few beers with his coworkers to unwind and remove the stress of routine assembly line work. Eric was recently married and at first, his wife was upset with him spending money at the bar especially if she was left at home. But as time passed and the evenings of drinking after work became more routine, Eric's wife seemed to care less and less about his behavior. Eric attributed this to his wife adjusting to the traditional housewife role and told his buddies that he was happily married. Unbeknownst to Eric, the source of her bliss was the fact that Eric stayed at the bar and drank after work. For several months, while Eric was at the bar drinking, she had been involved in an illicit affair with someone she met during an online chat. As time passed, Eric became suspicious of his wife's behavior. She seemed to almost encourage him to stay away from home and have fun with his friends. She seemed happier than ever. Eric decided to take some sick days and watch his house and his wife's activities from his car down the block. He began to notice a pattern. Almost every day when he would call and tell his wife he was planning to have a few beers after work, about 20 minutes would pass and a strange car would pull into his driveway and a young man would walk to Eric's front door, unlock it, and enter the house. Eric was immediately confused and angry. Who was this strange man? How did he get a key to Eric's house? Was his wife OK? It was apparently somebody she knew because she never emerged from the house screaming for help because of an intruder. Eric concluded his wife was having an affair and he wanted her and the stranger dead. He went to the local cybercafé and proceeded to search for a hitman. After locating several prospects, he decided to contact the one that appeared to know how to pull off the "hit", but more importantly, was cheap. They met and soon began to plan the best way to get rid of Eric's problem. Unfortunately for Eric, he did not realize that the hitman was an undercover policeman. Eric was subsequently arrested and charged with conspiring to kill his wife. The case gathered regional media coverage and was to be televised by the local television station. Eric refused to any plea agreements because he felt no jury would convict him because they would sympathize with a husband who had been cheated on. The case was set for trial at the Supreme Court. Criminal justice students learned of the case through the media coverage, but could not understand how the case could be tried at the Supreme Court. What can explain why the case was to be tried at this court? What type of jurisdiction does this court have? Is this type of court a court of fact or a court of law?

INTRODUCTION

The American court system is one of the most confusing systems in the world. In many countries, the court structure is a centralized system that is very uniform and easy to understand. For people from other parts of the world, the American public, and even students studying the American court system, it is difficult to understand the structure and operations of U.S. courts. There are 51 different court structures in the United States. Each state and the federal government has its own structure and process for resolving disputes and prosecuting criminals. Some states have indeterminate sentencing; others and the federal system have determinate sentencing systems and sentencing guidelines. There are mandatory minimums, habitual offender statutes, and truth in sentencing laws in various jurisdictions that further complicate the U.S. system of courts and sentencing. Also, acquiring an awareness of only the state and federal court systems ignores other court systems, such as military tribunals, juvenile and family courts, probate courts, tribal courts, chancery courts, drug courts, and housing and land courts.

This chapter examines the structure of the American court system. It is beyond the scope of this book to list and describe all of the subtle differences of every type of court structure. Rather, this chapter will classify these court structures according to different jurisdictions and functions with the hope of providing students a better understanding of the American court system.

This chapter will present three types of jurisdiction—geographic, subject matter, and hierarchical. The chapter also discusses the dual court system, meaning that in the United States there is both a federal court structure and a state court structure. Finally, it will discuss the difference between trial courts and appellate courts, and the functions of each. The federal system is made up of U.S. Magistrate Courts, U.S. District Courts, U.S. Circuit Courts of Appeal, and the U.S. Supreme Court. The state court system is characterized by Courts of Limited Jurisdiction, Courts of General Jurisdiction, Intermediate Courts of Appeal, and Courts of Last Resort. We should not focus strictly on court names, however, since the meaning associated with a particular court name varies among counties and states. For example, it might be assumed that the Supreme Court is an appellate court of last resort at the state and federal levels. Most trial courts are called circuit courts or district courts. However, in New York, felony trials are within the purview of the Supreme Court. New York Supreme Courts are the functional equivalent of criminal courts in other states. They simply use the term "Supreme Court" for this type of court.

CLASSIFYING AMERICA'S COURTS

One way of classifying American courts is by **jurisdiction**. Jurisdiction is the legal authority or power of a court to hear specific kinds of cases. Jurisdiction varies most often according to where the offense occurred, the seriousness of the offense, or whether the case is being heard for the first time or on appeal. There are three types of jurisdiction: (1) subject matter jurisdiction, (2) geographic jurisdiction, and (3) hierarchical jurisdiction.

Subject Matter Jurisdiction

Subject matter jurisdiction refers to the type of case the court has authority to hear. Usually misdemeanors and preliminary hearings are processed or conducted by courts of **limited jurisdiction**. For example, if a person burglarizes a house and steals $499 worth of goods, the case typically will be heard by a court of limited jurisdiction (e.g., municipal court, city court, county court). However, if the same person burglarizes the same house and steals $500 or more worth of goods, this case will likely be heard in a court of **general jurisdiction** (e.g., district court, circuit court, superior court). Thus, the actual dollar value of property stolen determines whether the jurisdiction is limited or general. The greater the dollar value of property stolen, the more likely the case will be heard in a court of general jurisdiction. Courts of limited jurisdiction most often decide petty offenses where minor monetary sums are involved.

In many areas of the country, courts of limited jurisdiction are also responsible for processing the initial stages of felony cases. These courts usually issue warrants, conduct initial appearances, establish bail, and advise felony defendants of their rights and the charges they are facing, together with a date for a preliminary hearing to determine whether probable cause exists.

Geographic Jurisdiction

Geographic jurisdiction is determined by the political boundaries where the crime was committed. Geographic jurisdiction is the clearest type of jurisdiction to understand. A defendant's case will be heard by a court within the political boundary in which the offense occurred. If a crime is committed in a county outside of the city limits, a county court will preside if there is a later trial. However, if the crime occurs in the city, then a city criminal court will preside. In Knoxville, Tennessee, for instance, there are courts of general jurisdiction known as **general sessions courts**. Anyone who commits a crime within the city limits of Knoxville will be tried in one of these courts. However, if the crime is committed in Knox County, where Knoxville is also located, then a different court will hear the case. In this instance, the case will be heard in circuit courts. Tennessee is one of a few states that has retained the circuit court concept. In the early 1800s, circuit court judges would ride the circuit or ride on horseback or in buggies to remote, sparsely populated areas of Tennessee to conduct trials for those charged with crimes. These circuit judges would hold court, probably once a month. Both civil and criminal cases were heard by these circuit judges. In recent times, circuit courts in urban areas of Tennessee hear criminal and civil matters that occur outside of the Knoxville city limits but within Knox County boundaries. Furthermore, Tennessee cities also have **criminal courts** that hear more serious criminal cases that are beyond the jurisdiction of general sessions courts. Thus, Tennessee has a relatively complex and overlapping court system compared with other states.

There are other types of geographic jurisdiction besides the political boundaries of cities and counties. For instance, almost every Native American reservation and military base, fort, or installation is located within a particular state or territory. Thus, if someone commits a crime in Sequoia National Park in California, geography itself would seem to indicate that California would have jurisdiction. However, since Sequoia National Park is a federally protected area, the federal court has jurisdiction. Many offenses occurring in federally protected areas are heard by U.S. magistrates. Also, if a crime is committed by a military member on the premises of Minot Air Force Base in North Dakota, it is not relevant that the crime has occurred within the geographic boundaries of North Dakota. Minot Air Force Base is a federal military installation, and military police and courts will arrest, prosecute, and try criminal defendants. North Dakota state courts do not have jurisdiction in these cases, even though the land upon which Minot Air Force Base rests is centered within the geographical boundaries of North Dakota. Politically, the jurisdiction of North Dakota courts ends at the Minot Air Force Base gates. To make this matter even more complex, if a crime is committed by a civilian on the Minot Air Force Base, the Northwestern North Dakota Judicial District would have jurisdiction over the case. In other words the status of the offender (military or civilian) takes precedence over geographic jurisdiction.

Geographic jurisdiction may also be influenced by the perpetrator and victim (e.g., federal agent or federal property). For instance, in the case of *Morrissette v. United States (1952)*, Morrissette, a civilian, was hunting deer one afternoon on a U.S. Army artillery range in Michigan. Although there were signs stating "Danger—Keep Out—Bombing Range," the area was known as good deer country and Morrissette hunted there anyway. In the course of his hunting, he came across a number of spent copper bomb casings that appeared to be discarded. After a frustrating day of hunting, Morrissette decided if he couldn't find a deer, he would offset some of his trip expenses by taking some of these casings and selling them for their copper value. He was arrested and charged with stealing U.S. government property. He was tried in federal district court and convicted, sentenced to imprisonment for two months, and fined $200. The U.S. Supreme Court reversed Morrissette's conviction, holding that Morrissette had no intention of committing a crime. Furthermore, he did not know that what he was doing was unlawful, and through his good character and openness in the taking of the casings, he demonstrated that his action was not deliberately criminal. It is significant here that Morrissette's case was not heard in a military tribunal. This is because Morrissette was a civilian and not subject to military law and sanctions. If the perpetrator had been a soldier in the U.S. Army, however, the soldier would have been tried by a military court for the criminal trespass offense.

Hierarchical Jurisdiction

Hierarchical jurisdiction is basically the difference between appellate and trial courts. Trial courts are often referred to as courts of fact, while appellate courts are referred to as courts of law. **Trial courts** are courts of fact because they are the forum where a judge or jury listens to the facts presented in the case and determines whether the defendant is guilty or not guilty. Trial courts are also responsible for sentencing the defendant. By contrast, **appellate courts** do not hear testimony or impose sentences. Appellate courts determine if the law was applied correctly. For example, a trial court judge during the course of a trial may make many decisions regarding the admissibility of evidence and testimony. For each of these decisions, the judge relies on his or her understanding of constitutional and procedural laws. When a case is appealed, appellate court judges review whether trial court judges followed constitutional and procedural laws when they made their decisions.

FEDERAL COURT ORGANIZATION

Most courts in the United States trace their roots to the actions of colonists during the Constitutional Convention in the 1780s. Prior to the final vote on the Bill of Rights, convention delegates passed the **Judiciary Act of 1789.** Under the provisions of the Judiciary Act of 1789, three "tiers" of courts were created: (1) 13 **federal district courts**, each presided over by a district judge; (2) three higher-level **circuit courts**, each comprising two justices of the Supreme Court and one district judge; and (3) a **Supreme Court**, consisting of a chief justice and five associate justices.

The federal district courts were given jurisdiction in all civil and criminal cases. The circuit courts reviewed decisions of federal district courts, although they had some limited original jurisdiction. And finally, the Supreme Court was given jurisdiction that included the interpretation of federal legislation and balancing the interests between the state and the nation through the maintenance of the rights and duties of citizens. Figure 2-1 shows the structure of the federal and state court systems.

The court system in the United States can be divided into two separate entities. One court system is at the federal level and consists of the U.S. Supreme Court, the U.S. Circuit Courts of

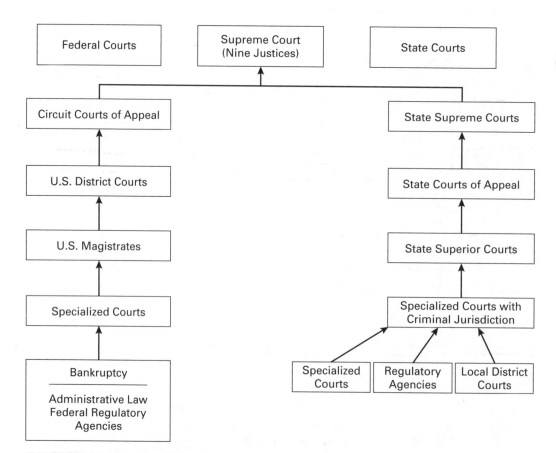

FIGURE 2-1   The Federal and State Court Systems

Appeal, U.S. District Courts, and the U.S. Magistrate Courts. The other court system is established through the authority of the states and consists of state and local courts. These court structures at the state and federal levels are referred to as a **dual court system**. The federal court system has the authority to hear cases identified by the Constitution. Article III, Section 2 of the Constitution identifies disputes that may be heard by federal courts. This includes cases in which the U.S. government or one of its officers is being sued. The Constitution also grants authority to the federal courts to hear cases, in the language of the Constitution, "Controversies between two or more states; between Citizens of the same State claiming land under grants from other states." For example, one state might sue another state for importing hazardous waste. The case is heard at the federal level because the impartiality of the state courts in either state jurisdiction might be questioned.

The Constitution also extends federal court authority to hear cases involving counsels, ambassadors, and other public ministers. The federal courts are also authorized to hear cases involving laws enacted by Congress, treaties and laws related to maritime jurisdiction, and commerce on the high seas. Because of this authority, the federal courts often decide disputes involving interstate commerce. Congress has determined that some of these cases may also be heard by state courts, giving state and federal courts **concurrent jurisdiction**. An example is when a citizen from one state sues a citizen from another state. The case may be heard in the state courts or in a federal district court. However, the case will only be heard at the federal level if the amount of the dispute exceeds $75,000 (Title 28 U.S.C. §1332, 2007). Again, the amount of money involved in a dispute often determines which court will hear the case.

U.S. Magistrate Courts

The lowest court of limited jurisdiction at the federal level is the U.S. Magistrate Courts. In 1968, Congress created the judicial office of federal magistrate. The magistrate's office was created to alleviate the workload of the U.S. District Court judges. In 1990, the position title was changed to magistrate judge. **United States magistrates** are appointed by the district judge and are assigned as either full-time or part-time magistrates depending on the caseload of the district court. Full-time magistrates are appointed to an eight-year term, whereas the terms of part-time magistrates are for four years.

Duties of the magistrate judge are similar to the duties of judges who serve in courts of limited jurisdiction at the state level. Magistrate judges hear disputes involving civil consent matters, misdemeanor trials, and the preliminary stages of felony cases, including preliminary hearing, pretrial motions, and conferences. In 2009, there were 523 full-time magistrate judge positions and 48 part-time magistrates.

U.S. District Courts

At the federal level, **United States District courts** are courts of general jurisdiction. Most civil and criminal cases are tried and disposed of in the U.S. District Courts. Approximately 85 percent of all federal court cases are civil, while 15 percent are criminal. There are 94 district courts in the United States. Each state has at least one federal district court and these courts can also be found in the U.S. territories of Guam, Puerto Rico, the U.S. Virgin Islands, and the Northern Mariana Islands. Thirty-one states and the U.S. territories have only one U.S. District Court with the jurisdiction to hear federal cases. The remaining states have two or more federal district courts.

In 2009, there were 678 federal district judges in practice in the United States within the various circuits (Title 28, U.S.C. Sec. 133, 2007). Federal district judges are also appointed by the president of the United States. They also serve life terms. Federal district judges who serve ten or more years with good behavior are entitled to retire at their option anytime thereafter and receive their annual salary for life. In 2010, the annual salary for a U.S. District Court judge was

$174,000. Although judicial appointments are ideally made without regard to one's race, color, sex, religion, or national origin, these appointments are primarily political and reflect the interests and views of the president. The advice and consent of Congress is required for all such appointments.

THE JURISDICTION OF U.S. DISTRICT COURTS   The jurisdiction of federal district courts is considerable. The federal district court is the major trial court for the United States. All violations of federal criminal laws are tried in the district court. Besides hearing criminal cases, federal district courts have the following jurisdictional authority:

1. To hear all civil actions where the matter exceeds $10,000 and arises under the laws, Constitution, or treaties of the United States;
2. To try diversity of citizenship matters, determine amounts in controversy, and determine costs;
3. To entertain bankruptcy matters and proceedings;
4. To hear interpleaders or third-party complaints;
5. To enforce Interstate Commerce Commission orders;
6. To hear commerce and antitrust suits;
7. To hear cases involving patents, copyrights, trademarks, and charges of unfair commercial competition;
8. To hear internal revenue cases and customs duty matters;
9. To judge tax matters by states;
10. To hear civil rights cases; and
11. To hear matters where the United States is a plaintiff or defendant.

Criminal cases heard in these district courts are commenced in the same way as cases are commenced in local and state courts. Federal law enforcement officers arrest suspects directly, or federal grand juries or federal prosecutors may issue indictments, presentments, or criminal informations against defendants. These defendants appear before magistrates where their bonds are established or where they are released on their own recognizance. Arraignment proceedings at the federal level are conducted in district courts by federal judges. Since arraignments include the entry of a plea by criminal defendants and the determination of a trial date, federal judges and their staffs can best determine an appropriate trial date because of the schedule of events on the federal court docket or calendar.

Federal judgeships are lifetime appointments. There is no mandatory retirement age, and federal district court judges may serve as long as they desire. In the language of the Constitution, they "hold their office during good behavior, and shall at stated Times, receive for their services a compensation, which shall not be diminished during their Continuance in Office." This provision provides for an independent judiciary and allows judges to make decisions without the threat of being removed from office or having their salary reduced.

U.S. Circuit Courts of Appeal

In the early years of the United States, there were only three circuit courts of the United States without any permanent personnel. Two Supreme Court justices and a federal district judge comprised the transient judiciary of the circuit courts. These judges were called **circuit riders**. These judges were obligated to hold 28 courts per year. This created considerable hardship because transportation was poor and it was difficult to travel great distances. Furthermore, since federal district judges were a part of the original circuit judiciary, this placed them in the prejudicial position of reviewing their own decisions.

Over the next two centuries, numerous changes occurred in circuit court structure. Several reforms such as the Judiciary Act of 1891 or **Evarts Act** were introduced to create what is the current scheme for federal appellate review. In 2009, there were 13 **United States Circuit**

TABLE 2-1   The 13 Judicial Circuits, Composition, and Number of Circuit Judges, 2007

Circuits	Composition	Number of Circuit Judges
District of Columbia	District of Columbia	12
First	Maine, Massachusetts, New Hampshire, Puerto Rico, Rhode Island	6
Second	Connecticut, New York, Vermont	13
Third	Delaware, New Jersey, Pennsylvania, Virgin Islands	14
Fourth	Maryland, North Carolina, South Carolina, Virginia, West Virginia	15
Fifth	Canal Zone, Louisiana, Mississippi, Texas	17
Sixth	Kentucky, Michigan, Ohio, Tennessee	16
Seventh	Illinois, Indiana, Wisconsin	11
Eighth	Arkansas, Iowa, Minnesota, Missouri, Nebraska, North Dakota, South Dakota	11
Ninth	Alaska, Arizona, California, Idaho, Montana, Nevada, Guam, Oregon, Washington, Hawaii	28
Tenth	Colorado, Kansas, New Mexico, Oklahoma, Utah, Wyoming	12
Eleventh	Alabama, Florida, Georgia	12
Federal	All Federal Judicial Districts	12
Total		179

Source: Title 28, U.S. Code, Sec. 44, 2007.

Courts of Appeal at the federal level (these include the District of Columbia and Federal Circuits) with 179 circuit court judges in practice. These are shown in Table 2-1. These circuit court geographical boundaries are also shown in Figure 2-2.

Typically, circuit courts hear cases with three-judge panels. In certain circuits, the volume of cases may be such that several three-judge panels may be convened simultaneously. These three-judge panels hear appeals from decisions in U.S. District Courts. On rare occasions, a case may be heard **en banc.** This is where the entire aggregate of judges in the circuit hears and decides the case appeal. Usually, appeals heard *en banc* involve important constitutional issues, and input from a larger number of judges is deemed important.

Like district court judges, appellate judges are appointed for life by the president and confirmed by the Senate. One of these judges is designated as the chief judge. Usually the chief judge is the one with the greatest seniority and who is also under 65 years of age. Chief judges perform additional duties apart from hearing cases, and their maximum terms are seven years. In 2010, the annual salary for a judge on the U.S. Court of Appeals Circuit was $184,000.

Each of the circuit courts of appeal has appellate jurisdiction for all federal district courts in the particular circuit. For instance, the Eleventh Circuit Court of Appeals includes Alabama, Florida, and Georgia. These states are divided into several divisions, each containing one or more federal district courts. When a defendant wishes to appeal a decision of any federal district court within Alabama, Florida, or Georgia, the appeal is directed to the Eleventh United States Circuit Court of Appeals.

While all circuit courts of appeal have appellate jurisdiction from all final decisions from district courts, there are occasions where a direct review may be made by the U.S. Supreme Court.

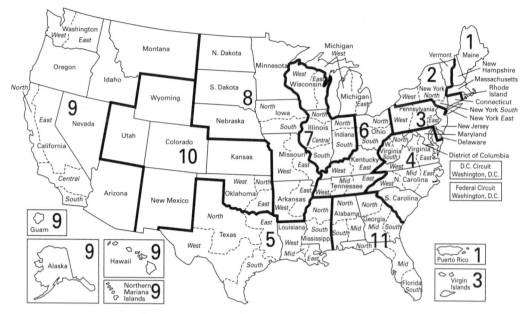

FIGURE 2-2 District and Appellate Court Boundaries

Source: Administrative Office of the United States Courts.

Note: The large numerals indicate the Court of Appeals, and the broken lines represent jurisdiction boundaries of district courts.

Panels of three circuit judges must convene at regular intervals to hear appeals from federal district courts. Of course, if a defendant disagrees with the decision of a circuit court, the U.S. Supreme Court is the court of last resort for appeals.

The U.S. Supreme Court

The court of last resort at the federal level is the **United States Supreme Court**. It is the only court specifically mentioned in Article III, Section 1 of the Constitution. The Constitution states that "the judicial power of the United States, shall be vested in one supreme court, and in such inferior courts as the Congress may from time to time ordain and establish." Like all of the other federal courts, U.S. Supreme Court justices hold their positions for life. They are nominated and appointed by the president, with Senate confirmation. The Supreme Court consists of eight associate justices and one chief justice. The chief justice has the additional responsibility of conducting conferences, supervising the federal judiciary, and assigning the task of writing various case opinions to a member of the judicial majority. Each of the associate justices is assigned to one of the appellate circuits for emergencies, such as death penalty appeals. In 2010, the annual salary of U.S. Supreme Court chief justice was $223,000 and for the associate justices it was $213,000.

The U.S. Supreme Court has both **original jurisdiction** and **exclusive jurisdiction** over (1) all actions or proceedings against ambassadors or public ministers of foreign states; and (2) all controversies between two or more states. Original jurisdiction means the court may recognize a case at its inception, hear that case, and try it without consultation with other courts or authorities. Exclusive jurisdiction means that no other court can decide certain kinds of cases except the court having exclusive jurisdiction. A juvenile court has exclusive jurisdiction over juvenile matters, for example. The adult criminal courts have no juvenile jurisdiction.

THE CASE OF *MARBURY V. MADISON* (1803)   One of the most important decisions that established review powers for the U.S. Supreme Court was the case of *Marbury v. Madison* (1803). This case was a political conflict between the Federalists and anti-Federalists. Outgoing president John Adams made several new circuit court appointments and signed commissions for their appointment on the his last day of office. However, Secretary of State James Madison withheld the processing of these commissions, anticipating a new president and a change in political party where party appointments could be made instead of the old administration appointees. This was an obvious attempt to create additional judicial appointments from party members favorable to the incoming president. One of these appointments was William Marbury, who petitioned the U.S. Supreme Court to force Secretary of State Madison to issue his new appointment. Chief Justice John Marshall ruled in Marbury's favor and issued a *writ of mandamus* to compel the Secretary of State to issue the commissions authorized by ex-president John Adams. Thus, the right of **judicial review** established the power of the U.S. Supreme Court to review and determine the constitutionality of acts of Congress and the executive branch.

The Supreme Court is the ultimate reviewing body regarding decisions made by lower appellate courts or state supreme courts. The Supreme Court is primarily an appellate court, since most of its time is devoted to reviewing decisions of lower courts. It is the final arbiter of lower court decisions unless Congress declares otherwise. Congress may change existing Constitutional Amendments or other Acts. The U.S. Supreme Court meets 36 weeks annually from the first Monday in October until the end of June (U.S. Code, Title 28, Sec. 5, 2007).

The U.S. Supreme Court is in session from the first Monday of October until the preceding day the next year. The year of the annual session is the year when the session is commenced. When the U.S. Supreme Court convenes in October 2010, all cases decided during that term are considered as cases decided during the 2010 term, even though a particular case might not be heard until May or June 2011.

Annually, the court receives between 8,000 and 7,000 case appeals. Most appeals are disposed of when the U.S. Supreme Court decides not to hear the case because of the subject matter, or if it is not significant enough to merit court review. The decision to hear a case is made when the justices meet to review all cases. In order for all of the justices to hear a particular appeal, the case must pass a screening, which is known as the **Rule of Four**. This means that at least four of the nine justices must agree that the case has constitutional merit or national importance and that it should be heard by the entire court. If a case receives four or more votes from the justices, it is placed on the docket and scheduled to be heard. Only about 150 cases annually pass the Rule of Four and are placed on the docket for an opinion.

The primary method that cases reach the Court is through a petition known as a **writ of certiorari**. This is an order issued by the Supreme Court to the lower court to send the record for review. When the Court decides to hear a case, it is scheduled for written and oral arguments by the opposing lawyers. The written arguments are filed with the Court and made available to the public. In some cases other interested parties may file briefs for the Court to hear, on behalf of other parties. These types of filings are called **amicus curiae** briefs. *Amicus curiae* means "a friend of the court," and refers to a broad class of briefs that may be filed by one party on behalf of one or more other parties. For instance, an *amicus curiae* brief was filed on behalf of Gary Gilmore, a convicted murderer in Utah, by Amnesty International, an organization opposed to capital punishment. The brief was on behalf of Gilmore, who was scheduled to be executed. The brief sought relief in the form of a stay of Gilmore's execution, until the U.S. Supreme Court had time to hear and consider new arguments for why the death penalty should not be imposed in Gilmore's case. Although the brief was successful, in that it gave Gilmore several additional weeks, Gilmore did not wish to pursue further appeals. He declared that he wanted to die, and that the state should be allowed to execute him, despite the objections of Gilmore's family and Amnesty International. Gilmore was subsequently executed by a Utah firing squad.

Appearances by attorneys before the U.S. Supreme Court are highly regimented by prevailing protocol. The attorneys for the opposing sides are permitted 30 minutes each to present oral arguments. Green, yellow, and red lights similar to those that regulate automobile traffic flash for the different litigants. A green light means oral argument may proceed. A yellow light flashes when the 30-minute oral argument time limit is approaching. And a red light means that the oral argument terminates. During this time justices are allowed to ask questions of the attorneys presenting the oral arguments. After oral arguments, the justices schedule a meeting, which is called a case conference. In this meeting the justices take an initial position.

Traditionally, if the chief justice is in the majority, this justice assigns the writing of the majority opinion to one of the other majority justices. The senior justice for the minority or dissenting opinion assigns the writing of this opinion to one of the dissenting justices. The writing of the opinion may be quite complicated, especially when the justices on both sides have conflicting opinions about the case. For instance, not all of the majority justices may believe the case should be decided in a given way for the same reasons. Thus, each majority justice may write an independent opinion about why the justice voted a certain way. Accordingly, dissenting justices do not have to agree about why they dissent. Thus, several dissenting justices may write independent opinions about why they dissented. These opinions make for interesting reading for Supreme Court historians and others, since often the personal views of justices are made evident in their opinions.

When the topic of the opinion is controversial, such as a case involving abortion or the death penalty, each justice expresses different views about the issue. For example, in *Furman v. Georgia* (1972), all justices wrote separate opinions. In most cases, the opinion goes through several drafts before it is approved by the majority or dissenting justices, and before it is subsequently made available to the public. Unlike cases heard at the appellate level, the U.S. Supreme Court hears all cases *en banc*. All nine justices hear the case.

There are exceptions. Sometimes, a death or resignation from the U.S. Supreme Court may leave the court with seven or eight members temporarily, until a new justice or justices can be appointed. During the time interval when the Court does not have nine justices, it may still convene and hear and decide appeals. A majority of justices is still required, although a majority is more difficult to achieve. Eight justices may divide equally on a given issue, with a 4–4 vote. Such a vote results in no decision rendered about that particular appeal. Five or more justices are required to support any appeal. When a 4–4 vote occurs, the case is simply discarded and not scheduled for rehearing. The litigants may bring the case before the U.S. Supreme Court again, provided that they raise a different and meaningful issue as the basis for challenging a lower court decision. And the Rule of Four exists for all new case filings, regardless of whether a particular case has been previously heard. Four or more justices must agree to hear the case before it will be docketed.

STATE COURT ORGANIZATION

Studying the American courts would be relatively easy if we didn't have to consider state court organization. But as we have seen, states such as Tennessee provide numerous different court structures and jurisdictions to create some complexity. And each state is different from the others in state court organization and function. Thus, we must add to the federal system the different court systems found in all 50 states. Figure 2-3 shows the federal court system.

The organization and functions of the 50 different state court structures are diverse and complex. For example, Massachusetts has a supreme judicial court, appeals court, superior court, district court, probate/family court, juvenile court, housing court, municipal court, and land court. By contrast, South Dakota has only a two-tiered system with a circuit court and a supreme court. State courts often have overlapping and conflicting jurisdictions. The state courts are also very busy with variable caseloads. Millions of cases are filed and disposed of each year. In 2003, over 100 million disputes were heard by state courts

FIGURE 2-3   The Federal Court System

(Schauffler, Lafountain, Kauder, and Strickland 2004). Most of these cases (about 40 percent) were traffic offenses. Caseloads in all five categories (criminal, civil, domestic relations, juvenile, and traffic) have continued to increase over the past several years (Schauffler et al. 2004). Figure 2-4 shows a basic state court system. Not all states follow this particular diagram, with some states having separate criminal and civil appellate levels. But generally, this model is representative of most state court systems.

A more elaborate type of state court system is referred to as the traditional court model or the Texas Model. This type of court system is illustrated in Figure 2-5. It provides more extensive detail than the state court organization depicted in Figure 2-4.

Other types of court organizational systems have been proposed in past years. For instance, Ezra Pound advocated a simple model, consisting of a supreme court as the highest court, a major trial court, and a minor trial court. The American Bar Association has proposed its own simplified court organizational structure, modifying the Pound Model by adding an intermediate appellate court. A later version of court organization devised by the American Bar Association envisioned a three-tiered system, with a supreme court at the top, an intermediate appellate court in the middle, and a trial court at the bottom. Figure 2-6 shows these three models.

Many jurisdictions do not require that judicial officers have a law degree. In fact, 36 states do not require that judges in a court of limited jurisdiction must be educated in the law. One reason is that many judges are elected rather than appointed or through some other form of merit selection. In short, these judges need to convince the electorate that they have the ability to serve rather than be legal practitioners with professional credentials. The lack of education and knowledge of the judicial process among many state court judges has caused a number of problems. Most of these courts are not courts of record, and so it is difficult to monitor their activities formally. Because many elected judges do not know the limits of their authority or

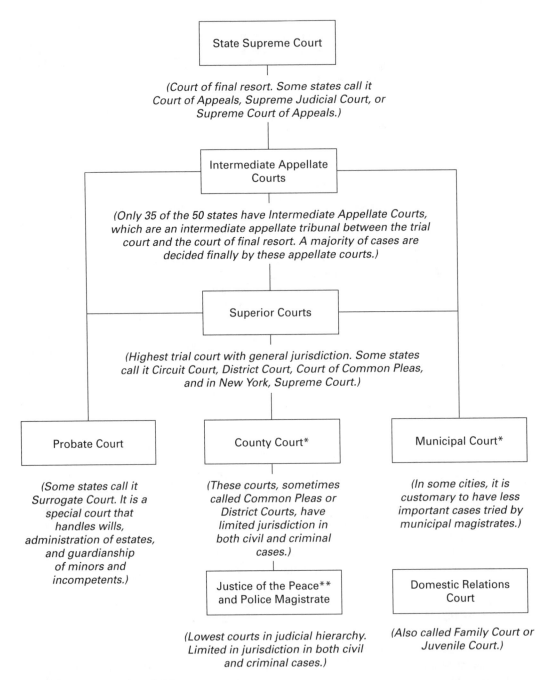

FIGURE 2-4 The State Judicial System

*Courts of special jurisdiction, such as probate, family, or juvenile courts, and the so-called inferior courts, such as courts of common pleas or municipal courts, may be separate courts or part of the trial court of general jurisdiction.

**Justices of the peace do not exist in all states. Where they do exist, their jurisdictions vary greatly from state to state.

are unfamiliar with the processes of the judicial system, many states have established a legal training requirement for newly elected judges. Most of these judges are required to attend a legal training seminar sponsored by the state judicial conference or a committee or program sponsored by the Administrative Office of the U.S. Courts.

Supreme Court
9 justices

Jurisdiction:
• Final appellate jurisdiction in civil and juvenile cases

Court of Criminal Appeals
9 judges

Jurisdiction:
• Final appellate jurisdiction in criminal cases

Courts of Last Resort

Court of Civil Appeals (14)
51 judges

Jurisdiction:
• Civil appeals from trial courts in their respective supreme judicial districts

Intermediate Appellate Court

Civil matters   *Criminal matters*

District Court (310)
310 judges

District Court	**Criminal District Court** (10) 10 judges	**Family District Court**
Jurisdiction: • Original jurisdiction in civil actions over $500, divorce, title to land, contested elections, and probate matters • Original jurisdiction in felony matters • Juvenile matters Appeals de novo in probate Jury trials	Jurisdiction: • Exclusive criminal jurisdiction	Jurisdiction: • Domestic relations, divorce and annulment, birth records, child custody and support • Juvenile delinquency, dependency, and neglect

Civil matters   *Criminal matters*   Court of General Jurisdiction

County Court (260)
360 judges

Constitutional County Court (254) 254 judges	**County Court at Law** (98) 98 judges	**Probate Court** (8) 8 judges
Jurisdiction: • Original jurisdiction in civil actions over $500, divorce, title to land, contested elections, and probate matters • Original jurisdiction in felony matters • Juvenile matters Appeals de novo in probate Jury trials	Jurisdiction: • Civil actions under $5,000, varied limited jurisdiction over civil matters • Limited jurisdiction over criminal matters Appeals de novo Six-person jury trials	Jurisdiction: • Limited probate matters

Courts of Limited Jurisdiction

(Some Municipal and Justice of the Peace Court decisions may be appealed to the District Court.)

Municipal Court (863)
863 judges

Jurisdiction:
• Misdemeanors with fines less than $200
• Exclusive jurisdiction over municipal ordinance violations
Jury trials

Justice of the Peace Court (972)
972 judges

Jurisdiction:
• Civil actions under $200
• Small claims
• Criminal cases with fine less than $200
Preliminary hearings
Jury trials

 indicates route of appeal

FIGURE 2-5   The Traditional Court Model (Texas Model)

FIGURE 2-6   Pound's Model, the ABA Model of 1962, and the ABA Model of 1974

Despite provisions for the legal training of new judges in most jurisdictions, research about courts of limited jurisdiction has revealed that more than few inequities exist. Some of these injustices, such as judicial incompetence, have been highlighted in U.S. Supreme Court cases. For example, the U.S. Supreme Court was confronted with the matter of judicial competence in the case of *North v. Russell* (1976). Judge Russell worked in the coal mines of Kentucky after he dropped out of high school. Later he was elected as a judge and presided over the case of

---

BOX 2.1

The Power of the U.S. Supreme Court

The 2004–2005 Term

The U.S. Supreme Court decides many important cases annually. Most of the cases involve constitutional issues. Compared with Congress, the country's law-making body, the U.S. Supreme Court interprets the law and how the law should be applied. For instance during the 2004–2005 term, they made decisions on many important matters. At issue was whether or not the monument of the Ten Commandments at the state capitol in Austin, Texas, violates the Establishment Clause; whether or not companies that produce file-sharing services allowing the illegal downloading of music are in violation of copyright infringement laws; and whether or not executing individuals who commit crimes before their eighteenth birthday is in violation of the Eighth Amendment against cruel and unusual punishment. What did the Supreme Court decide?

First, the monument of the Ten Commandments can remain on the ground of the capitol in Austin, Texas. The monument has been there for about 40 years and simply having religious content does not violate the Establishment Clause. Second, the Court ruled, in a unanimous decision, that companies making software enabling illegal downloads are in violation of copyright infringement because they acted with a purpose to cause copyright violations. Third, the Court decided that execution of those who committed crimes before their eighteenth birthday does constitute cruel and unusual punishment because the United States is the only country that allows the execution of juveniles.

In other decisions, the U.S. Supreme Court ruled the federal sentencing guidelines unconstitutional and discretionary instead of mandatory. The Court also expanded the criteria for age discrimination lawsuits, ruled in favor of religion in prisons, and overturned the conviction against the accounting firm of Arthur Andersen. Do you think these powers are within the scope of authority originally vested in the U.S. Supreme Court? Should the U.S. Supreme Court be subject to the scrutiny of other bodies, such as the executive branch or Congress? What do you think?

Source: Adapted from the Associated Press, "New Order in the Court," *Los Angeles Times,* July 3, 2005.

Lonnie North, who had been accused of drunk driving. Judge Russell denied North's request for a jury trial, did not inform North of his right to counsel, and denied North's right to appeal the subsequent decision. Judge Russell listened only to the arresting officer's version of the incident and did not permit North testify in his own behalf and provide his version of events. Judge Russell sentenced Lonnie North to 30 days in jail when the statute provided a maximum sentence of a fine and no jail time. In this case, North's conviction was set aside by the U.S. Supreme Court and Judge Russell was criticized for his incompetence.

Generally state courts have a four-tiered court structure. These tiers are (1) courts of limited jurisdiction, (2) courts of general jurisdiction, (3) intermediate courts of appeal, and (4) courts of last resort.

Courts of Limited Jurisdiction

Courts of limited jurisdiction have the greatest variability among the states. These courts hear minor offenses such as violations of traffic laws, minor civil cases, and infractions. They also perform other administrative duties. Courts of limited jurisdiction comprise about 80 percent of the total number of state courts. They are the courts with the greatest caseloads in the nation. In 2007, of the over 21 million criminal cases processed in state courts, 14.7 million were disposed of in courts of limited jurisdiction (LaFountain et al. 2009). On the average, they process over 50 percent of all cases brought before the state courts. The District of Columbia, Iowa, South Dakota, Idaho, and Illinois are the only states without courts of limited jurisdiction.

State courts of limited jurisdiction have many different names. Most of these courts are called municipal courts, county courts, city courts, or justice of the peace courts. Other courts are specialized courts of limited jurisdiction. Some of these courts might be called juvenile courts or family

---

BOX 2.2

Technology and Access to the Federal Judiciary

Technological advances have affected all of us in some way. The federal judiciary is not immune to this trend. Since the 1990s the federal court has made available to the public a number of resources to access information about the cases before the Court and the decisions reached by the Court. The service offered allows the public to obtain information about the actions of the Court without ever stepping foot inside the courthouse. Some of the services offered by the Court are as follows:

The U.S. Supreme Court Electronic Bulletin Board System

The U.S. Supreme Court Electronic Bulletin Board System (EBBS) service provides online access to the court docket, opinions, argument calendar, rules, and bar information forms. Additional information includes general and tour information and special notices.

U.S. Supreme Court Clerk's Automated Response Systems (CARS)

The U.S. Supreme Court Clerk's Automated Response System (CARS) provides callers with information about the status of cases by instructing callers to respond to telephone prompts.

Appellate Bulletin Board System (ABBS)

The Appellate Bulletin Board System (ABBS) is a source of information about judicial opinions offered to the public by federal circuit courts of appeal. These courts offer the public access to court decisions, argument calendars, case dockets, reports, notices, and press releases. Information can be downloaded and viewed online by computer users. Currently, there is a $.60 per minute fee for this service.

(continued)

(continued)

Public Access to Court Electronic Records (PACER)

The Public Access to Court Electronic Records (PACER) is a service that allows users to dial into the bankruptcy court computer to access information about cases and decisions. Again there is a $.60 per minute charge. Users must first register with the PACER service center before they can use this service. Many district and circuit courts have established toll-free numbers to users where additional costs of long-distance telephone calls are not incurred.

Party/Case Index

In 1977, the courts started a new service that would allow users to conduct searches of the bankruptcy court by party name or Social Security number. Searches can also be conducted to locate civil or criminal cases or cases beginning to be appealed. The search will retrieve the case filing date and filing location.

Electronic Filing and Attorney Docketing Service

The Electronic Filing and Attorney Docketing Service (EFADS) is another service that is being tested in selected district courts. This service allows attorneys to submit pleadings and other docket entries through the Internet. The case file and official docket can be viewed online or downloaded electronically.

courts, probate courts, and courts of workers compensation. Recent caseload estimates indicate that traffic cases between 1994 and 2003 in municipal courts comprised the largest percentage of incoming cases. These courts continue to be busy with heavy caseloads because of increases in all other types of cases, not just those involving traffic violations (Schauffler et al. 2004).

Courts of General Jurisdiction

Courts of general jurisdiction have jurisdiction over all major civil and criminal cases. These cases would include any felony or misdemeanor cases as well as criminal appeals from limited jurisdiction courts. These courts also differ from courts of limited jurisdiction because they are **courts of record** and **general trial courts**. They are courts of record because a record is made of all of the proceedings. Various methods are used to make records of these proceedings. Court reporters use tape recorders and several other devices to record whatever is said. With a few exceptions, courts of general jurisdiction are called circuit courts, district courts, superior courts, courts of common pleas, and supreme courts. A list of names of these courts for the different states is provided in Table 2-2.

In 2004, state courts processed and sentenced over 1,079,000 adults for felony offenses. This figure does not include civil filings (Bureau of Justice Statistics 2005). Contrary to what is reported and portrayed by the media, criminal jury trials are relatively rare events. This is because over 90 percent of all criminals who are prosecuted are convicted in criminal courts through plea bargaining, where guilty pleas are entered in exchange for some form of leniency from prosecutors and judges. Thus, criminal trials are conducted only for about 10 percent of all criminal cases.

In recent years, the criminal courts have been processing cases more rapidly than in past years. For instance, in 1988, state courts processed 667,366 cases and the average case processing time from arrest to conviction was about seven months. In 1994 the courts processed 872,217 cases and the average time between arrest and conviction was six and a half months (Maguire and Pastore 2005). In 2000, the court processed 924,700 cases with a median time between arrest and sentencing of 5.1 months (Maguire and Pastore 2005). Many factors account for this decrease in processing time. One reason is that courts, faced with increasing caseloads, have learned and incorporated more efficient caseload management processes to reduce court delays. Or courts may realize the increased caseload and deliberately limit the number of delays and continuances that have been allowed in past years. The workload of the court is strongly

TABLE 2-2   Courts of General Jurisdiction for Each State*

Circuit Court

Alabama, Arkansas, Florida, Hawaii, Illinois, Indiana,[1] Kentucky, Maryland, Michigan, Mississippi, Missouri, Oregon, South Carolina, South Dakota, Tennessee, Virginia, West Virginia, Wisconsin

Superior Court

Alaska, Arizona, California, Connecticut, Delaware, District of Colombia, Georgia, Maine, Massachusetts, New Hampshire, New Jersey, North Carolina, Puerto Rico, Rhode Island, Vermont,[2] Washington

District Court

Colorado, Idaho, Iowa, Kansas, Louisiana, Minnesota, Montana, Nebraska, Nevada, New Mexico, North Dakota, Oklahoma, Texas, Utah, Wyoming

Court of Common Pleas

Ohio, Pennsylvania

Supreme Court

New York[3]

*Compiled by authors.

1. Indiana has both circuit courts and superior courts.

2. Vermont has superior courts and district courts.

3. New York also has county courts.

associated with where the court is located. Typically, urban courts have more cases to process than rural courts. For example, Los Angeles, the busiest court system in the nation, processed 50,197 felony cases in 1994 (Maguire and Pastore 2005). This figure is greater than all of the felony cases processed in the entire federal system during that same year.

The demand for court services fluctuates greatly depending upon certain areas of the country. In 2003, for example, South Dakota processed only 26,384 cases in courts of general jurisdiction; this amounts to about 3,452 cases per 100,000 persons. In that same year, however, Wisconsin processed 248,960 cases in courts of general jurisdiction; this amounts to about 4,549 cases per 100,000 persons (Schauffler et al. 2004).

Judges in the courts of general jurisdiction usually have practiced law either as prosecutors or working in a law firm before becoming a judge. However, in Maine and Massachusetts, judges at this level are not required to have a law degree. The only requirement is that they are learned in the law (Rottman, Flango, Cantrell, Hansen, and LaFountain 2000). Most states require some combination of a law degree, being a member of the state bar for five to ten years, as well as local and/or state residency requirements. Some states have age limitations for judges at this level. Usually, the minimum age is 25–30 years and the maximum age is 70–75. The median salary for judges in trial courts is $112,724. Judges in the District of Columbia's general courts were the highest paid in the nation with a salary of $154,700. The lowest-paid trial judges were in New Mexico with a salary of $86,896 (Maguire and Pastore 2005).

Intermediate Courts of Appeal

Eleven states and the District of Columbia do not have intermediate courts of appeal. Most states have developed an intermediate court of appeal to review and screen the caseload on the state supreme court. These intermediate courts of appeal became necessary shortly after 1900. A few states such as Alabama, Tennessee, and Texas have separate appellate courts for civil and criminal cases. North Dakota has a statutory provision providing for an appellate court at this level, although these judges must be called to action by the state's supreme court. Such an event rarely occurs in North Dakota.

TABLE 2-3   Intermediate Courts of Appeal for Different States*

Appeals Court

Massachusetts

Appellate Court

Connecticut, Illinois

Appellate Division of Superior Court

New Jersey

Appellate Division of Supreme Court

New York, West Virginia

Commonwealth Court

Pennsylvania

Courts of Appeal

California, Louisiana, Texas

Court of Civil Appeal

Alabama

Court of Appeals

Alaska, Arizona, Arkansas, Colorado, District of Columbia, Georgia, Idaho, Indiana, Iowa, Kansas, Kentucky, Maryland, Michigan, Minnesota, Mississippi, Missouri, Nebraska,

New Mexico, New York, North Carolina, North Dakota, Ohio, Oklahoma, Oregon, Puerto Rico, South Carolina, Tennessee, Utah, Virginia, Washington, Wisconsin

District Courts of Appeal

Florida

Intermediate Court of Appeals

Hawaii

Superior Court

Pennsylvania

Courts of Appeals

Texas

Court of Civil Appeal

Alabama, Oklahoma

Court of Criminal Appeal

Alabama, Oklahoma, Tennessee, Texas

Court of Special Appeals

Maryland

District Court of Appeals

Florida

*Compiled by authors.

Most cases are heard with a panel of three judges. Unlike the courts of last resort, they do not have discretionary appellate review. Thus, they are required to hear all cases that are properly filed.

Most of the judges at this level are appointed by the governor after being selected by a nominating commission. Appellate court judges make slightly more than their colleagues in the general trial courts. The median salary was $121,697. Appellate court judges in California are paid the most at $164,604 and appellate court judges in New Mexico were paid the least making $91,469 (Maguire and Pastore 2005). Table 2-3 shows the intermediate courts of appeal for different states.

Courts of Last Resort

The highest court structures at the state level are called **courts of last resort**. Usually these are also called supreme courts. In states with an intermediate court of appeals, these courts have discretionary appellate review. This means that they decide which cases they will hear. By refusing to hear a case, they are allowing the decision of the lower court to stand. In states where there is no intermediate court of appeal, the state supreme court has no discretionary authority. Alabama, Oklahoma, and Texas are unique in this regard because they have two courts of last resort. One is designated to hear civil cases, while the other hears only criminal cases. Judges who preside in state supreme courts are usually selected by a nominating commission and appointed by the governor. In order to remain in their position, they must receive a majority vote in a retention election. The median salary for the state's highest court is $125,292. The highest-paid supreme court justices reside in California and make $175,575. The lowest-paid supreme court justices are in West Virginia, where they receive annual salaries of $95,000 (Maguire and Pastore 2005).

Summary

The American court system is one of the most confusing in the world. Each state has its own court structure, and in many cases courts that perform the same functions are referred to by different names. Therefore, in order to understand the American court structure, we must understand how each court functions as well as the kind of matters they can hear. We must also compare these courts among the different states.

The best and easiest way to understand the American court structure is to classify these courts according to their particular jurisdiction. One of these is subject matter jurisdiction, which refers to the type of case a court can hear.

Courts of limited jurisdiction are granted the legal authority to hear misdemeanor cases or the preliminary stages of felony cases.

Courts of general jurisdiction are basically felony trial courts. They are also referred to as courts of fact.

Appellate courts are called courts of law because they do not determine the facts of the case. Rather, they are charged with determining whether the law has been applied correctly. This is a classification known as hierarchical jurisdiction, basically that trial courts decide the case and appellate courts decide if the law was applied correctly in a case.

Geography also defines the limits of a court's authority. A court's legal authority is limited by political boundaries. For example, a state court in Arizona does not have the legal authority to hear a criminal case from Nevada. Many municipalities have their own court systems, and their jurisdiction is limited to cases that occur within the city limits.

With court systems at both the state and federal levels, this scenario is often referred to as the dual court system.

The basic trial courts in the federal system are the U.S. District Courts. Most civil and criminal cases of federal interest are tried and disposed of in these courts. There are 94 district courts in the United States. Federal district court judgeships are lifetime appointments and there is no mandatory retirement age.

The court below the U.S. District Court is the U.S. Magistrate Courts. These courts were created to alleviate the caseload of district court judges. These magistrate judges are appointed by the district judge, and depending on the caseload, they work either full- or part-time. Full-time magistrate judges have an eight-year appointment, whereas part-time magistrate judges have a four-year appointment. Magistrate judges typically will hear misdemeanor cases, or the preliminary hearings, pretrial motions, and conferences of felony cases.

The federal system also has 13 appellate jurisdictions or U.S. Circuit Courts of Appeal. These are the intermediate appellate courts at the federal level. Again these were created to alleviate the rising caseload of the Supreme Court. These courts then hear the appeals from the decisions made by the U.S. District Courts. Like their district court counterparts, judges in federal circuit courts of appeal are appointed for life by the president.

The U.S. Supreme Court is the court of last resort or the highest court in the land. Nine justices accept between 7,000 and 8,000 cases per year and write opinions in about 200 of them. Unlike trial courts, which have no control over what cases are presented to them, most state courts of last resort and the U.S. Supreme Court decide which case appeals they will or will not hear. They do not, however, have the time to hear every case; rather, they marshal their time and use their discretion to hear the most important matters of the time, or matters that involve important federal questions.

The state court structure is a little more confusing. The state court structure is more difficult to understand because the functions and organization of the 50 different state court structures are diverse. The same or similar courts often have different names in different states, and state courts often have overlapping and conflicting jurisdictions.

Many of the state jurisdictions do not require that judges have a law degree; 36 states do not even require education in the law for their limited jurisdiction court judgeships. One of the most likely reasons for this is that these judges are elected rather than appointed. Therefore, they need only convince the electorate that they can serve in the position well. This has caused a number of problems in the past regarding judicial incompetence and knowledge of the law.

The courts in most states have a four-tiered structure. The tiers include courts of limited jurisdiction, courts of general jurisdiction, intermediate courts of appeal, and courts of last resort, or state supreme courts.

The courts of limited jurisdiction are the courts that are the least consistent among the states. These courts hear the most minor of offenses, minor civil cases, and traffic violations and also perform administrative duties. They are the courts with the highest caseloads in the country.

Courts of general jurisdiction hear all major civil and criminal cases. These courts are the general trial courts in the state system and are courts of record. Again, these courts have a fairly high caseload; however, contrary to popular media perceptions, more than 90 percent of these cases are disposed of through a plea bargain. A court's activity, however, varies in different areas of the country. The courts in large urban jurisdictions are obviously busier than those in rural areas. The judges in courts of general jurisdiction are usually more learned in the law than their limited jurisdiction judicial counterparts and have probably practiced law as either a prosecutor or a defense attorney.

The intermediate courts of appeal screen the caseload of the supreme court. Eleven states and the District of Columbia, however, do not have intermediate courts of appeal. States with high appellate caseloads probably have an intermediate court of appeal. Most of these judges, like their state supreme court counterparts, are appointed by the governor. These courts do not, however, have discretionary appellate review, which means that they have to hear all cases that have been properly filed.

Courts of last resort, also called state supreme courts, do have discretionary appellate review in the states that do not have intermediate courts of appeal. These judges are usually selected by a nominating commission, and then appointed by the governor.

The court structure in the United States can be confusing due to the fact that each state has its own structure and many courts performing the same or similar functions are known by different names. In order to make it easier to understand these courts we must classify them according to their functions and hierarchy.

Questions for Review

1. Differentiate between courts of limited and general jurisdiction.
2. What is meant by geographic jurisdiction? What is the power of courts with geographic jurisdiction?
3. Describe the U.S. magistrate and the duties of this particular type of court.
4. What is the basic trial court for the federal system?
5. When a defendant in a U.S. District Court case is found guilty of a crime, where is the appeal directed? What are the jurisdictional limits of the appellate court you have indicated?
6. What is the court of last resort? Why is it called the court of last resort?
7. What are courts of limited jurisdiction? What are some of the functions of courts of limited jurisdiction?
8. Describe intermediate courts of appeal. Are these courts the same in all states? Why or why not?
9. What is meant by *en banc*?
10. What is the function of an *amicus curiae*?

Suggested Readings

1. Annalise Acorn (2004). *Compulsory Compassion: A Critique of Restorative Justice*. Vancouver, CAN: UBC Press.
2. Monica R. Cowart (2004). "Understanding Acts of Consent: Using Speech Act Theory to Help Resolve Moral Dilemmas and Legal Disputes." *Law and Philosophy* 23:495–525.
3. Paula Hannaford-Agor and Nicole Mott (2003). "Research on Self-Represented Litigation: Preliminary Results and Methodological Considerations." *Justice System Journal* 24:163–181.
4. Gordon Hughes (2004). "The Community Governance of Crime, Justice and Safety: Challenges and Lesson-Drawing." *British Journal of Community Service* 2:7–20.

CHAPTER 3

The Prosecution

CHAPTER OBJECTIVES

As a result of reading this chapter, you will have accomplished the following objectives:

1. Understand the criminal court as an adversarial system seeking to determine the guilt or innocence of defendants charged with crimes.
2. Understand the many roles of prosecutors in pursuing cases against criminal suspects including that negotiating plea bargains is the most common method of obtaining a conviction.
3. Depict both exculpatory and inculpatory evidence that may be presented in criminal cases.
4. Describe the process of screening and prioritizing cases for criminal prosecutions.
5. Describe the discretionary power that government prosecutors have as well as what factors influence their decision-making practices.
6. Assess the potential for prosecutorial misconduct or discretionary abuses arising from the extensive powers of prosecutors.

KEY TERMS

adversary system
assistant U.S. attorneys
  (AUSAs)
attorney general
backdooring hearsay
  evidence
criminal informations
defense attorney

defense strategy
deponents
district attorneys
ethical code
exculpatory evidence
harmless error doctrine
inculpatory evidence
indictments

informations
malicious prosecution
prosecutor
prosecutorial bluffing
prosecutorial misconduct
Rules of Criminal
  Procedure
screening cases

state's attorneys
true bills
United States attorney
United States attorney's
  office
venue
witnesses

Recently, prosecutors in many counties across the country have warned the public that budget cuts could result in some criminal cases not being prosecuted due to lack of resources. Denise Lunsford, a commonwealth attorney in Virginia, states that her office may have to stop prosecuting misdemeanors if budget shortfalls cannot be made up somehow. Michael Golden, a prosecutor in Lewis County, Washington, is expecting budget shortfalls of close to half a million dollars. In light of this, he has asked citizens of the county to come together in a meeting to discuss where resources should be allocated. In essence, Golden is admitting that without resources not all cases can be prosecuted. He is therefore asking for citizen input on which types of crimes his office should focus on prosecuting. Some prosecutors have resorted to laying personnel off and even closing their offices for periods of time. Most of the general public believes that criminals should be prosecuted to the fullest extent of the law. The reality is that prosecuting those convicted of crime costs money. In tough economic times prosecutors may have to use their discretion even more wisely to choose which persons are most deserving of prosecution. Should lack of resources govern prosecutorial decision-making practices? What types of crimes are most deserving to be prosecuted fully in a formal criminal trial? Do you think that these crimes might also be the most expensive to prosecute?

Source: Adapted from *The Chronicle* (Centralia, Washington), "Prosecutor Sees Cuts Ahead, Requests Local Input From Citizens," October 24, 2009, and *The Daily Progress* (Charlottesville, Virginia), "Prosecutors Lament Lack of Resources," February 7, 2010.

INTRODUCTION

Trial proceedings in criminal courts in the United States are exclusively adversarial proceedings. Adversarial proceedings mean that opposing sides present evidence and arguments favoring their position, inculpatory versus exculpatory evidence, either to a judge or a jury, in order to convince them that a particular action should be taken. Depending upon the compelling arguments presented favoring these opposing positions, judges or juries are persuaded to find criminal defendants guilty or not guilty.

Persons charged with one or more crimes, defendants, are prosecuted by the government. The interests of defendants are represented by defense counsels, whose job it is to convince judges or juries that insufficient evidence exists to conclude that the defendants are guilty of committing a crime. Criminal proceedings against defendants may be conducted at local, state, or federal levels, and in each case, one or more prosecutors represent the government's interests in pursuing prosecutions.

This chapter begins with a description of the adversarial system of American courts, which is characterized by opposing sides in the search for the truth. In some respects, this adversarial system is like an athletic contest or sporting event, complete with rules of conduct and different strategies calculated to advantage one side or the other in winning the contest. The outcome of a criminal trial is far different from the outcome of an athletic event, however. One or more lives are at stake, and one's freedom within the community may be in jeopardy. Prosecutors present inculpatory evidence to judges and juries. Such evidence shows defendant guilt. By contrast, defense counsels present exculpatory evidence that shows defendant innocence. Usually both sides have such evidence and present it to bolster their arguments for why judges or juries should decide in their favor. The conduct of any criminal case in court, as well as the introduction of both exculpatory and inculpatory evidence, is governed by rules of criminal procedure and evidence. Both state and local court systems have codified these procedures so that trials are uniformly conducted and everyone understands what is and is not permitted.

The next section describes the prosecutorial role. The roles of prosecutors at all levels— local, state, or federal—are very similar. One consistent feature of all prosecutors is that they have many duties and responsibilities. Prosecutors must screen cases for prosecution and decide whether to bring criminal charges against particular suspects. As the chapter-opening scenario suggests, prosecutors must prioritize the cases they prosecute and often monetary and personnel resources influence these decisions. Not everyone who deserves to be prosecuted can be prosecuted; this is especially the case in smaller jurisdictions and in times when resources are limited. Prosecutors, therefore, use their discretion to make decisions about which cases to prosecute. Because of this discretion to prosecute or dismiss a case, many have commented that the prosecutor is the most important gatekeeper into the criminal justice system. U.S. Attorney General and Supreme Court Justice Robert H. Jackson once stated that "The prosecutor has more power over life, liberty, and reputation, than any other person in America." Beyond the power to screen cases for prosecution, prosecutors must devise effective strategies that they believe will enable them to obtain convictions against criminal defendants. In many cases, the inculpatory evidence against many suspects is overwhelming and the prosecutor's strategies are fairly simple and straightforward. Critics argue that because around 90 percent of cases are disposed of through some type of plea agreement, the system might be best characterized as negotiative rather than adversarial. The prosecutor often drafts a plea agreement wherein a defendant enters a guilty plea to one or more criminal charges in exchange for some form of concessions such as sentencing leniency. These plea deals are usually initiated by the prosecutor but must be approved by the judge. The types of plea bargains and the plea bargaining process are discussed in much greater detail in Chapter 8.

Although fewer than 10 percent of all criminal cases proceed to trial, this does not mean that there are few criminal trials. There are many thousands of criminal trials annually. In fact, the incidence of criminal trials is such that there are serious case backlogs in more than a few jurisdictions. Imagine the backlog, however, if everyone prosecuted exercised their right to have their day in court. Interestingly, because there are so many criminal trials to conduct and a limited time period within which to conduct them, this is a major reason why prosecutors must screen their cases and prioritize them for prosecution. It is simply not possible to prosecute everyone who deserves to be prosecuted for a crime. The screening process used by prosecutors to prioritize their cases will be examined and explained.

In larger cities where a much larger volume of criminal cases is generated, government prosecutors, sometimes known as state's attorneys, district attorneys, or U.S. attorneys, will have several assistant prosecutors to handle larger caseloads. Thus, the head prosecutor has the responsibility of assigning cases to various assistant state's attorneys or assistant district attorneys, or assistant U.S. attorneys, and these persons become responsible for prosecuting the cases they are assigned. Among the different responsibilities of prosecutors is interviewing witnesses and conducting depositions that will enable them to build compelling cases against criminal defendants. Prosecutors also work closely with law enforcement officers who have made arrests and/or collected important incriminating evidence. These persons will eventually testify in court or provide information about a defendant's guilt. These interactions between witnesses, law enforcement officers, and prosecutors will be described and explained.

All attorneys, regardless of whether they are prosecutors or defense counsels, are expected to abide by a code of ethics that prescribes a particular conduct that places these persons above reproach. However, more than a few attorneys have violated one or more of these ethical codes by engaging in prosecutorial misconduct. Like any type of misconduct in any profession, there are degrees of misconduct that may occur. Like misdemeanors and felonies, there are less serious and more serious forms of misconduct. Several types of prosecutorial misconduct are examined.

One type of misconduct is encouraging deceit from witnesses who testify against criminal defendants. Most prosecutors do not ask witnesses to lie under oath or commit perjury. But many prosecutors encourage witnesses to slant their testimony in ways that make criminal defendants look like they might be guilty. In many jurisdictions, prosecutors rehearse their witnesses prior to trial, reviewing the types of questions the prosecutors will ask as well as the kinds of questions defense attorneys might ask. Suggestions are given by prosecutors as to what witnesses might say or how they might respond. While rehearsing witnesses before trial is not unethical, it may raise questions about how such testimony might be interpreted by jurors. Some witnesses may exaggerate the significance of their testimony, and prosecutors may allow juries to draw their own conclusions about these exaggerated remarks. Of course, it is expected that good defense attorneys will clarify for jurors what certain witnesses say and how such information should be interpreted.

Another type of prosecutorial misconduct occurs behind closed doors in confidential grand jury proceedings. About half of all states use grand juries to determine whether sufficient evidence exists against particular defendants in order for the case to proceed to trial. Grand jury proceedings are one-sided affairs, where prosecutors present only evidence that they want grand jurors to see. Thus, prosecutors are in absolute control concerning the particular evidence a grand jury will see against a criminal suspect. If the prosecutor knows of any exculpatory evidence that favors the defendant, he/she may withhold such evidence from the grand jury. This is the prosecutor's decision. If the prosecutor has strong feelings about the case and wants the grand jury to indict the defendant, excluding exculpatory evidence from the grand jury will improve the prosecutor's chances of securing an indictment. Ultimately, the exculpatory evidence will come to light in court when the trial is conducted. In the meantime, however, the defendant, who may be innocent, remains charged with a crime through the indictment. Although indictments do not mean that indicted defendants are guilty of anything, many citizens interpret "being indicted" as tantamount to guilt anyway. The trial process will result in a finding of guilt or acquittal in any event.

The process of prosecutorial bluffing will be described. Prosecutors may attempt to bluff their way through a case prior to trial, leading some defendants to believe that they have inculpatory evidence against them when they have no such evidence. Many guilty pleas have been entered by innocent defendants because of prosecutorial bluffing. If defendants believe that the jury will likely convict them of a crime and their sentence will be severe, these defendants may decide to accept a plea agreement offered by the prosecutor, which usually involves considerable leniency in punishment compared with what a judge may have imposed through a jury verdict of guilt. Several types of prosecutorial bluffing will be described, and the implications of prosecutorial bluffing for defendants will be indicated.

More serious forms of prosecutorial misconduct include deliberately withholding exculpatory evidence from defense counsels prior to trial. Another form of misconduct is pursuing a case against a criminal defendant where no basis exists for the criminal charges that have been filed. Sometimes prosecutors may file frivolous charges against defendants where such charges have little or no basis in truth. These malicious prosecutions against innocent defendants are clearly inexcusable, although proving malicious intent on the part of the prosecutor is often difficult.

Although it is not technically a form of misconduct, prosecutors almost always attempt to select jurors who are most likely to convict the defendant. Some prosecutors hire professional jury consultants to assist them in making such juror selections (Clark 2004b). Both prosecutors and defense counsels have several peremptory challenges and an unlimited number of challenges for cause, whereby they can strike any particular prospective juror from sitting on the jury. Defense counsels also attempt to select jurors who will react favorably toward their clients. Sometimes they hire jury consultants to assist them in juror selection. Since the jury selection process is not an exact science, it is questionable whether accurate forecasts can ever be made about how particular jurors will vote once the evidence from both sides has been presented. Another form of prosecutorial misconduct involves backdooring hearsay evidence. Prosecutors and defense counsel are both barred from making certain kinds of statements in front of jurors. But both sides may make occasional improper utterances or statements anyway, only to have the judge instruct the jury to disregard these statements. But once jurors have heard statements they shouldn't hear, it is difficult, if not impossible, for them to forget that they heard these statements. It is impossible to determine how much these improper statements influence juror opinions and voting during juror deliberations. Different types of backdooring hearsay will be described. The chapter concludes with an examination of the ethical norms and guidelines presently in place to regulate prosecutors and their conduct. Only during the last few decades have prosecutors been more carefully scrutinized by the legal profession and others. Prosecutorial codes of conduct or ethics will be described.

THE ADVERSARY SYSTEM

When a crime is committed, law enforcement officers frequently arrest a suspect who is believed to have committed the crime. Criminal suspects become defendants charged with one or more crimes. While all criminal defendants in the United States are entitled to the presumption of innocence before their guilt is established in court beyond a reasonable doubt, they are also entitled to counter the charges against them. Therefore, defendants are represented by defense counsels, whose job it is to defend their clients against these criminal charges. Presumably, defense counsels who represent clients in court are more or less effective according to their training, expertise, and practical trial experience. The system of alleging criminal charges against defendants and defending them against such charges is known as the **adversary system** (Emmelman 2003). This adversarial system is not exclusively a U.S. creation. It is found and used frequently in other countries, such as Canada, England, Italy, and Australia (Ambos 2003).

The adversarial nature of the criminal court is evident by paying attention to the different roles of the **prosecutor** and **defense attorney**. The prosecutor's aim is to prove that the defendant committed a crime, and that the level of such proof should rise to beyond a reasonable doubt. The defense attorney contests any criminal allegations made against his/her client and seeks to dissuade the court or a jury from thinking that the defendant is guilty of a criminal offense.

Recent high-profile white-collar prosecutions for instance have seen defense attorneys submitting testimony and evidence to the jury about client's lack of knowledge of accounting practices and other financial information. Prosecutors on the other hand usually provide memos and/or e-mails as evidence that an employee of the corporation did have knowledge of fraud and other criminal and regulatory violations. Evidence is presented to both sides in these adversarial proceedings to provide compelling arguments for and against guilt. Depending on the jury's interpretation of this evidence and their opinion about whether the defendant was aware of the criminal actions, corporate malfeasance for instance, persons are either found guilty or acquitted.

Comparing the criminal court to a game being played out from beginning to end is not new. The gamelike nature of the courtroom is reinforced by using court-relevant terminology, such as sides and prosecutorial or **defense strategy**. Prosecutors are on one side and use a particular strategy that they believe will enable them to win the game. For prosecutors, a win is a conviction against the accused. For the defense side, a win is the defendant's acquittal. Prosecutors and defense counsels are often labeled as players by different writers who seek to characterize courtroom procedures in certain ways. The law may not always be seen as a normative system where the most moral person wins, but rather where the more skillful player using the better strategy will win the game by defeating the other player (Black 1973; van Koppen and Penrod 2003).

The adversarial system of justice in the United States is rooted in the tradition of English jurisprudence dating back several centuries (Ambos 2003). In U.S. courts, the key players, prosecutors, defense attorneys, and judges, are the courtroom work group (Hoskins, Ruth, and Ruback 2004). They are bound to observe standardized **Rules of Criminal Procedure** as well as a well-defined **ethical code** (Birzer and Tannehill 2003; Boyle, Newman, and Schmidt 2003). Thus, there are specific rules governing the order in which a case is presented against a defendant and the response from defense counsel (DiCristina 2004). Besides following a predetermined pattern or protocol for presenting a case against and for a defendant, other rules exist that govern the nature and types of evidence and witnesses who may be called for either side. Each side attempts to manipulate the evidence presented in ways that enhance their respective arguments. **Witnesses** are examined and cross-examined by the different sides in an effort to bolster their arguments. Ideally, the side with the most persuasive and compelling argument, either against or for the accused, wins. Juries decide the facts in the case before them, and their deliberations most often favor either guilt or acquittal. On rare occasions, juries may not be able to reach agreement as to which side, the prosecution or defense, has the more persuasive argument. In these instances, juries are deadlocked or hung, and mistrials are declared. Subsequently, the adversarial process begins anew with another trial. In each trial proceeding, it is expected that both sides will adhere to an accepted ethical code and conduct themselves accordingly.

Throughout the criminal trial, evidence is presented by both sides for its persuasive effect. Prosecutors usually present **inculpatory evidence**, or testimony or other forms of evidence that tends to show the guilt of the defendant. For instance, the defendant's fingerprints might have been found on the murder weapon, or eyewitnesses may have seen the defendant pull the trigger of the gun that killed the defendant. This evidence would be considered inculpatory, because it shows the guilt of the accused. By contrast, defense counsel introduces **exculpatory evidence**, or testimony and other forms of evidence that show the innocence of the defendant. For example, one or more persons may testify that the defendant was with them at the time the murder was committed. Credit card receipts or video surveillance from restaurants or shopping malls may indicate that the defendant was somewhere else when the crime occurred. Thus, alibis and other relevant information may show that the defendant couldn't have been the one who committed the crime when it occurred (Cossins 2003).

THE PROSECUTION

Besides the judge who makes important rulings in criminal cases and oversees trial proceedings, the prosecutor has perhaps the most powerful position in the criminal justice system (Schoenfeld 2005). Prosecutors are either elected or appointed officials who pursue criminal cases against those charged with crimes. Prosecutors are held to the same standards of ethical conduct as defense counsel (Connell 2004). Depending upon the jurisdiction, prosecutors are known by different names. They may be known as **district attorneys**, **state's attorneys**, **prosecuting attorneys**, or **county prosecutors**. In the federal system, each U.S. District Court has a **United States attorney's office**. The **United States attorney** in each federal district is appointed by the president of the United States with the advice and consent of Congress. The **attorney general** of the United States, also a presidential appointee, appoints one or more **assistant U.S. attorneys (AUSAs)** to serve in each of these district offices. The number of AUSAs varies from district to district, depending upon the civil and criminal caseload. For instance, the Southern District of New York has 220 AUSAs, whereas the Western District of Texas has 129 AUSAs, and the District of Wyoming only has 18 AUSAs (U.S. office of personnel management 2010).

The Roles of Prosecutors

The primary roles of all prosecutors in criminal courts are to represent the government's interests and pursue criminal charges against those alleged to have committed crimes. For state's attorneys or district attorneys, their roles are similar throughout the different U.S. jurisdictions. A summary of these roles is as follows:

1. To screen cases for prosecution
2. To determine the best strategy for prosecuting cases
3. To make case assignments to assistant district attorneys
4. To interview prospective witnesses against the accused
5. To work closely with law enforcement officers to determine the nature of inculpatory evidence against the accused

In the federal system, the U.S. attorney's offices in the various federal districts are charged with the following broad roles:

1. To prosecute all offenses against the United States
2. To prosecute or defend, for the government, all civil actions, suits, or proceedings in which the United States is concerned
3. To appear on behalf of the defendants in civil actions and suits or proceedings pending in the district against collectors or other officers of the revenue or customs for things they have done or for the recovery of any money exacted by or paid to them
4. To institute and prosecute proceedings for the collection of fines, penalties, and forfeitures incurred for violation of any revenue law
5. To report as the attorney general directs

SCREENING CASES   Screening cases means to assign priority to different cases on the basis of which ones are most deserving of prosecution. The screening function of prosecutors is very important as it relates to obtaining guilty pleas from criminal defendants. Most convictions are obtained through plea negotiations between prosecutors and defense counsel, where some form of leniency from the prosecution is extended in exchange for a defendant's guilty plea. Thus, prosecutors have broad discretionary powers concerning which cases to pursue and what types of offers to extend those charged with crimes as inducements for guilty pleas (Forst 2004).

Prosecutors have the power to determine the types of cases that will be prosecuted more vigorously than others. Domestic violence or child abuse cases may receive high priority in certain jurisdictions because of strong interest from community and/or religious leaders. Prosecutors and police officers can assist these leaders in the prevention and deterrence of domestic violence by vigorously prosecuting and seeking maximum penalties in domestic violence cases. Organized or gang-related crime may have high priority for prosecutors in certain large urban jurisdictions.

Prosecutors seek convictions, and prosecutorial effectiveness is often gauged by the number of convictions they obtain (Keller 2005). The greater the number of convictions, the more effective are the prosecutors. Therefore, it is in the prosecutor's interest to select cases for prosecution that are the easiest to prosecute and obtain a conviction. Where clear and convincing evidence exists against an accused, prosecutors are in a stronger position to succeed in obtaining a conviction. More than a few cases, however, have little incriminating evidence and are based purely on circumstantial evidence. A prosecutor's vigor, persistence, and demeanor are often sufficiently convincing for jurors in courtrooms (Rockwell and Hubbard 2004). Prosecutors must decide whether these cases are worth pursuing, where the conviction of the accused is less of a certainty compared with a case with considerable inculpatory evidence.

DETERMINING COURT STRATEGY   Prosecutors must devise their theory of how and why the crime was committed. They must attempt to link the defendant to the crime in such a way that the jury will be convinced beyond a reasonable doubt of the accused's guilt. There are many potential explanations for a defendant's conduct relative to the crime. It is not necessary that the prosecutor selects the true explanation, only a plausible one. The theory of the crime and its commission is often suggested by the nature and quality of the evidence against the defendant. For example, if one's spouse was violently killed and the surviving spouse stands to collect on a $1 million insurance policy, then this fact provides a motive for why the surviving spouse might have committed the murder. However, if there is another person with whom the surviving spouse has had an affair, then the motive for the murder may be love and not money. It is fairly easy to see how different spins can be given to any criminal scenario.

ASSIGNING CASES   Prosecutors in most jurisdictions usually have assistant prosecutors who can handle some of the case workload (Champion 2005a). In fact, most large-city district attorney's offices are bureaucratized to the extent that there are various specialty areas for different types of legal cases. A general civil–criminal distinction exists, where some of the assistant district attorneys may be assigned civil cases, while other assistants are assigned criminal ones. Further subdivisions may be made, depending upon case volume. Criminal cases may be divided according to sex crimes, property crimes, and other logical divisions. Certain prosecutors acquire considerable expertise in selected legal areas, and this expertise enables them to prosecute certain cases involving their expertise more effectively than other prosecutors without this expertise. For instance, prosecutors with substantial experience with forensic evidence, such as DNA testing, may be more skillful at eliciting more compelling testimony from expert witnesses, and they may also do a better job of cross-examining defense experts on the same subject matter. Other prosecutors may have considerable experience and facility with child eyewitnesses. Each case poses certain types of problems for prosecutors, and thus, it is prudent for prosecutors to make strategic case assignments on the basis of which assistant district attorneys can do the best job of prosecuting under the circumstances.

INTERVIEWING WITNESSES   Prosecutors and their assistants must interview persons who have knowledge about the crime. Often, witnesses for both the prosecution and defense are **deposed**. A deposition is a sworn written record of oral testimony. Persons who are deposed are **deponents**. The purpose of a deposition is to have a written record of what one's testimony is as well as an indication of its relevance to the case. When witnesses testify in court later, their depositions can be used to refresh their recollections. Sometimes depositions can be used to impeach witnesses if they are lying or say things that are inconsistent with their earlier depositions (Carey 2001).

Information provided to prosecutors by witnesses can be interpreted in various ways. Witness interviews can help prosecutors to formulate their strategy for prosecuting a case. The state may use expert witnesses to verify whether a defendant is sane or insane, competent or incompetent. If certain defendants are sufficiently incompetent to stand trial, then prosecutors can use this information to seek their commitment indefinitely in a mental hospital (Bullock 2002).

Prosecutors can determine in which order they will present their witnesses against the accused later in court. Thus, they can use witnesses to build their case against defendants. In complex serious criminal cases, there will probably be numerous witnesses called by both sides. It is important, therefore, that some effort should be made to organize the witnesses into an orderly presentation that will create the most convincing case against the accused. Observations of actual criminal trials reveal such orderly presentations of witnesses for both sides.

WORKING CLOSELY WITH LAW ENFORCEMENT OFFICERS   It is important for prosecutors to develop a working rapport with law enforcement officers. Law enforcement officers have direct crime scene experience and can testify about their conversations with the defendant. If a confession has been obtained, or if the defendant has provided police officers with incriminating information, this information can be developed in court to the defendant's disadvantage.

Law enforcement officers are subject to cross-examination by defense counsel. Experienced defense attorneys can seriously impair the state's case against a defendant by evoking responses from officers that show their ineptness. Prosecutors and their assistants can assist officers in learning how to give testimony that will minimize any weaknesses in the state's case.

Police officers also testify about the evidence they collected at the crime scene that incriminates the defendant. Their testimony is quite important in this respect, and it is vital that prosecutors have the trust of these officers when they are questioned under direct examination in court (Leo 1994). In federal district courts, AUSAs work closely with other agents from the FBI, DEA, Border Patrol, and other federal authorities in presenting evidence against those charged with federal crimes. These agents learn to permit AUSAs the latitude of presenting the case against the defendant in a particular way. Federal agents also learn to be adept at giving testimony in certain ways that will heighten the inculpatory or incriminating effect of it. It is up to the defense counsel, therefore, to attempt to get the agents to admit that other less incriminating interpretations might be drawn from the testimony given.

CHANGING THE VENUE FOR TRIALS   The **venue** is the jurisdiction where the case originates. If a crime is committed in San Antonio, Texas, the venue is San Antonio. A judge in San Antonio will most likely hear the case. The jury will be selected from Bexar County, where San Antonio is located. If the case is an especially high-profile one, either the defense or the prosecution may attempt to change the venue where the case is heard. This is because of the substantial publicity given to the case and the possibility that an impartial jury cannot be impaneled to hear it. Jurors in any criminal case are expected to hear all evidence impartially and to render an objective decision as to the guilt or innocence of a defendant. If pretrial publicity is adverse to defendants, defense counsels may make a motion to change the venue for hearing the case to another county. Prosecutors may oppose such motions.

But changes of venue, which are rarely granted, may also be initiated by prosecutors. If the crime occurs in a locality where the defendant is well known and liked by the community, it may be difficult to find an impartial jury that would convict the defendant, despite the compelling evidence favoring a conviction. In these cases, prosecutors may attempt to change the venue to a jurisdiction where the defendant is less well known. Thus, both prosecutors and defense counsels have a stake in determining the best location for where the ensuing trial will be held. Many circumstances, including pretrial publicity and media coverage, influence such decision making as well as which side will request a change in venue (Posey and Dahl 2002). Neither prosecutors nor defense counsels can mandate changes of venue for their cases, but they can make motions for such changes. They must present compelling arguments to judges for venue changes. Unless there are overwhelming circumstances suggesting that defendants would not receive a fair trial in the original venue, motions for changing the venue of the trial are typically not granted.

OBTAINING INDICTMENTS OR FILING CRIMINAL INFORMATIONS   In about half of all states, grand juries are convened to hear evidence against particular defendants. This evidence is presented by prosecutors in most circumstances, and based on the evidence presented, grand juries issue **true bills** or **indictments**. These true bills or indictments are merely declarations by grand juries that sufficient probable cause exists to believe that one or more crimes were committed and that the defendant may have committed the crime(s). Grand juries, therefore, do not decide one's guilt or innocence. Rather, prosecutors work to persuade grand juries to indict defendants so that their cases may proceed to trial (Schmid 2002).

For less-serious offenses, such as misdemeanors, prosecutors may act on their own and file charges against criminal defendants by filing **criminal informations** or simply **informations**. Informations are similar to indictments, except that prosecutors initiate them on their own. Prosecutors believe that probable cause exists that a crime was committed and that a particular defendant committed the crime. Therefore, prosecutors can file an information against any criminal suspect. The result is the same as an indictment. The defendant will face a criminal trial where their guilt can be decided by the judge or jury.

Prosecutorial Misconduct

Whether prosecutors in various jurisdictions are elected or appointed, there are many pressures on them from different sources. First, there is the immediate pressure to win cases and obtain convictions against defendants. Second, there is pressure to make a weak case look like a strong case. This means that the evidence may have to be manipulated or collected in ways that are inconsistent with proper police procedure (White 2002).

Just like there are varying degrees of attorney competence, there are also varying degrees of prosecutorial misconduct (Schoenfeld 2005). Not all forms of misconduct have the same weight or importance. Some misconduct may be trivial, although the cumulative effect of minor or trivial misconduct may arouse juror suspicions to the degree that a guilty verdict is subsequently rendered. Prosecutors may encourage experts to exaggerate their claims or evidence to enhance their case against a defendant; prosecutors may overwhelm grand juries with purely inculpatory evidence and deliberately exclude any exculpatory evidence; prosecutors may bluff with defendants and threaten or intimidate them; prosecutors may suppress certain types of exculpatory evidence from the defense; prosecutors may exclude prospective jurors who have views favorable to defendants; prosecutors may offer inadmissible evidence in court; and prosecutors may engage in malicious prosecutions. While it is presently unknown precisely how much prosecutorial misconduct occurs nationally, it has been reported by the Center for Public Integrity that since 1970, 20 percent of 11,452 appellate-reviewed cases where the defendants claimed prosecutorial misconduct were dismissed, reversed, or reduced from the original sentence partly or wholly because of prosecutorial misconduct (The Center for Public Integrity 2003; Weinberg, Gordon, and Williams 2005).

BOX 3.1

Case Law regarding Prosecutorial Misconduct

Buckley v. Fitzsimmons, 509 U.S. 259 (1993)

Buckley was charged with murder. Prosecutors made various statements surrounding the indictment of Buckley for the murder, including several untrue statements. Subsequently, the charges against Buckley were dropped, and he sued the prosecutors under Title 42 U.S.C. Section 1983, alleging that his civil rights had been violated by this prosecutorial misconduct. The prosecutors sought absolute immunity from this suit and the U.S. Supreme Court heard the case. The U.S. Supreme Court upheld Buckley's right to sue the prosecutor, who only enjoyed qualified immunity from such suits. Prosecutors are liable for statements they make publicly if such statements are false and they result in harm to defendants who are innocent of criminal wrongdoing.

Banks v. Dretke, ___U.S.___, 124 S.Ct. 1256 (2004)

Delma Banks was convicted of capital murder in the death of 16-year-old Richard Whitehead, which occurred in mid-April 1980. Banks was originally implicated in the murder by two associates, Jefferson and Farr, who were working with the county sheriff, Willie Huff, as informants. Unknown to Banks before and during the trial was the allegation that Jefferson and Farr were testifying against Banks in order to avoid drug charges, which were threatened by the sheriff and prosecutor. At the same time, a confidential informant, Cook, also furnished the prosecution with incriminating circumstantial evidence against Banks. This information was also withheld from Banks pursuant to a motion for discovery. Although Banks had no prior criminal record, testimony from Farr and Jefferson provided the jury with innuendo that Banks had an unsavory and criminal past, which was untrue. Banks's efforts to impeach Farr and Jefferson were undermined because of his own witnesses, who were themselves impeached on cross-examination. Banks was sentenced to death and sought postconviction relief, alleging that the prosecution failed to disclose exculpatory evidence as required by *Brady v. Maryland* (1963), including the threats made to Farr and Jefferson as well as the confidential informant, Cook. In its answer, the state claimed that nothing had been kept secret from Banks and no deals had been made with government witnesses, including Cook. In 1993 Banks's postconviction claims were denied outright by an appellate court. Following this loss, Banks filed for *habeas corpus* relief in a U.S. District Court, which granted relief on Banks's death sentence. In 1999 Banks filed discovery and evidentiary hearing motions, both supported by affidavits sworn to by Farr and Jefferson that the prosecution had wrongly withheld crucial exculpatory and impeaching evidence. The federal court determined that the state, indeed, had failed to disclose Farr's informant status during the original discovery phase of Banks's trial. Therefore, a writ of *habeas corpus* was granted to Banks with respect to his death sentence, but not to his conviction. Banks petitioned the U.S. Supreme Court, who heard the case. The U.S. Supreme Court reiterated that under *Brady*, a prosecutorial misconduct claim must establish three things: (1) the evidence at issue must be favorable to the accused, either because it is exculpatory or because it is impeaching; (2) evidence must have been suppressed by the state, either willfully or inadvertently; and (3) prejudice must have ensued. In its response, the state contended that "it can lie and conceal and the prisoner still has the burden to discover the evidence." The U.S. Supreme Court ruled this assertion to be untenable and a violation of Banks's due process rights. Banks presented sufficient evidence to support his *Brady* claim and was thus entitled to a full evidentiary hearing and a certification of appealability.

ENCOURAGING DECEIT FROM EXPERTS AND OTHER TYPES OF WITNESSES   When prosecutors construct their case presentation, they arrange the testimony of various expert witnesses and others who have relevant evidence to present. Often, expert witnesses may be able to provide too much information in court, and prosecutors must work with them to ensure that only selected pieces of information are disclosed about the case (McKimmie et al. 2004). Thus, experts have their testimony shaped and tailored by prosecutors so that it fits more closely with the scenario of the crime and its commission as envisioned by the state. Therefore, much of the prosecutorial melodrama in court is carefully orchestrated in advance. If certain witnesses are considered weak and have little direct inculpatory information against the accused, they may be brought to the witness stand to testify early in the trial, so that the jury can forget about their weaknesses toward the end of the trial.

Seemingly innocent expert witness statements can appear very incriminating. The prosecutor may ask, "Was the blood found on the defendant's shirt consistent with the blood of the victim?" The expert witness says, "Yes, I can say definitely that there was such a consistency." The jury is transfixed by such riveting testimony. However, the defense breaks this bubble by asking the expert witness on cross-examination, "Can you say positively that the blood on the defendant's shirt is the victim's blood?" And the expert witness lowers his head and says, "No, I can't say positively that the blood found is that of the victim's. I can only say that it is consistent with the victim's blood." The defense probes further. "In what respect is the blood found consistent with the victim's blood?" The expert witness says, "It is Type O positive." And the defense asks, "And is it not so that the defendant also has Type O blood?" And the expert says, "Yes, that is true." And the defense asks, "And is it not possible that the blood on the defendant's shirt is the defendant's own blood from a cut on the defendant's arm?" And the expert witness says, "Yes, that is true."

While DNA matching is increasingly important to show precisely whose blood it is that is found at crime scenes, the fact remains that much contamination of blood can occur to make blood typing and identification somewhat unreliable. This does not prevent prosecutors from using this evidence, regardless of its potential unreliability, to the disadvantage of the defendant.

OVERWHELMING GRAND JURIES   When grand juries are convened, prosecutors are interested in obtaining indictments against defendants. Grand juries consider evidence presented by the prosecutor and determine whether there is sufficient probable cause to believe that a crime was committed and that the defendant probably committed it. Grand juries do not determine the guilt or innocence of the accused. They merely determine whether probable cause exists and that a case should go forward to trial for a legal resolution.

Prosecutors are in a unique position relative to grand juries. Prosecutors direct which evidence and testimony will be presented to the grand jury. Thus, if a prosecutor has considerable evidence and numerous witnesses, he/she may decide to present only the most damaging evidence and the most incriminating testimony. Some witnesses interviewed by the prosecutor may actually provide an alibi for the defendant, showing that the defendant may not have been at the place where the crime was committed at the time when it occurred. Prosecutors exercise their discretion here and determine to present only the evidence and witnesses that show the defendant's guilt.

Since grand juries see only one side of the case against an accused person, they may think only the worst about that defendant. Indictments are issued, therefore, when grand juries are convinced that there is sufficient probable cause to believe that the defendant committed the crime. They are not permitted the luxury of a presentation by the defense counsel to rebut whatever was presented by the prosecutor.

Several attempts have been made by different court systems to monitor prosecutorial conduct before grand juries. For instance, in federal grand jury proceedings, tape recordings have been made and reviewed later by federal district court judges. Misconduct before the grand jury has been referred to as pre-indictment impropriety, and it is often detected only by chance. However, recordings of grand jury proceedings can help to uncover any prosecutorial misconduct that is disclosed. Some of these federal judges have recommended that a full disclosure of grand jury proceedings be made available later to defense counsel and others. Presumably, these recommendations are intended to cause prosecutors to engage in more ethical conduct. It is doubtful that such recordings of grand jury proceedings and subsequent disclosures have curbed prosecutorial abuses of discretion in grand jury proceedings, however.

PROSECUTORIAL BLUFFING WITH CRIMINAL DEFENDANTS: THREATS OR INTIMIDATION?
When criminal defendants are not represented by counsel or are represented by weak defense lawyers, and/or when the cases against criminal defendants are weak, prosecutors may engage in **prosecutorial bluffing** (White 2002). Prosecutorial bluffing means to threaten defendants with a lengthy list of charges, each of which carries serious penalties of fines and lengthy incarcerative terms. The intent of prosecutorial bluffing is to cause a defendant to enter a guilty plea to one of the more minor charges in exchange for prosecutorial leniency. For instance, if the defendant pleads guilty to one felony charge, the other 20 felony charges will be dropped. Or maybe the prosecutor will accept the defendant's guilty plea to a misdemeanor, in exchange for a sentence of probation and dropping more serious felony changes.

The Center for Public Integrity (2003) and other organizations have conducted various polls and surveys of prosecutorial misconduct in recent years with some fascinating results. For instance, it has been found that within the 2341 jurisdictions in the United States, local prosecutors in most of these jurisdictions have stretched, bent, or broken the rules to win convictions since 1970. Individual judges and appellate court judges have cited numerous instances of prosecutorial misconduct as a major factor in dismissing many cases, reversing convictions, or reducing sentences in over 2000 cases. Prosecutorial misconduct has been found to warrant reversals of jury verdicts in another 500 cases. In thousands more of these cases, judges have labeled prosecutorial behavior as inappropriate, but they have upheld convictions nevertheless under the doctrine of "harmless error." Misconduct by prosecutors has led to the convictions of many innocent individuals who were later exonerated. Even guilty defendants have had their convictions overturned and were released back out on the streets because of prosecutorial misconduct. Some prosecutors violate the rules more than others. More than a few are cited multiple times for misconduct. These prosecutors give recidivism a new meaning. Prosecutorial bluffing is not limited to criminal defendants. Prosecutors may also threaten or intimidate prospective witnesses.

SUPPRESSING EVIDENCE FROM THE DEFENSE   Prosecutors are able to view all evidence collected from the police and material witnesses in criminal cases. While some of this evidence may tend to show the guilt of the defendant, other evidence may show the defendant's innocence. If a prosecutor has such exculpatory evidence, he/she is obligated to disclose this evidence to the defense for its use. However, evidence suggests that much of the time, exculpatory evidence is deliberately suppressed by prosecutors, even in capital cases (Harmon 2000, 2001).

EXCLUDING PROSPECTIVE JURORS WHO ARE FAVORABLE TO DEFENDANTS   When prospective jurors are being questioned concerning their qualifications and beliefs or prejudices, both the prosecution and defense have an opportunity to challenge them. Particularly in high-profile trials involving well-known persons, a concerted attempt is made by both sides to configure the best jury most favorable to either side. While jury voting cannot be predicted by either side in advance, prosecutors and their associates attempt to select jurors who will be pro-prosecution in their views.

In a capital murder case, for instance, prospective jurors with strong feelings against the death penalty may be excluded because these prospective jurors believe that their own feelings might not permit them to impose the death penalty if they find the defendant is guilty of the capital crime. When prosecutors dismiss these jurors, they narrow the pool of prospective jurors who might be favorably disposed toward the defendant. Frequently, prospective jurors are dismissed by prosecutors since these jurors exhibit other views that are associated with anti-death penalty sentiments. Defense counsel can engage in similar behavior by excluding those who are in favor of capital punishment (Martin and Roberts 2005). Always the number of jurors who can be dismissed by either the prosecution or defense because of the juror's sentiments is limited. Despite these limitations, prosecutors can skillfully maneuver and create a jury composition that they believe is unfavorable to a defendant (Nadeau, Burek, and Williams 2005). Because of the diffuse grounds used to dismiss particular prospective jurors, it is not easy to determine when prosecutors are engaging in this type of misconduct.

OFFERING INADMISSIBLE EVIDENCE IN COURT   A prosecutorial tactic sometimes used in a weak criminal case is to backdoor hearsay evidence. **Backdooring hearsay evidence** means to mention or comment about evidence against the accused that is not admissible evidence. Perhaps the defendant, charged with trafficking in heroin, has been arrested five times in the past for heroin and cocaine possession. However, these arrests have resulted in case dismissals. Insufficient evidence existed to move forward with criminal prosecutions in each of these five arrest situations. In many jurisdictions, prosecutors may only introduce evidence about one's prior criminal convictions. It is not permissible for prosecutors to mention any arrests that never resulted in convictions. But the prosecutor might make a statement in court while questioning the defendant or a witness. "Were you with the defendant when he was arrested for cocaine and heroin possession on five different occasions during the last three years?" the prosecutor might ask. Before the witness can speak, an objection is made by the defense and the judge sustains the objection, admonishing the jury to disregard the prosecutor's question. But the damage has already been done. The question has been raised and heard by the jurors. They now know that the defendant has been arrested in the past for heroin and cocaine possession. More important, the jurors have no way of knowing that these arrests never resulted in prosecutions or convictions on the drug charges. Inadmissible evidence has been admitted through the back door, although the judge has declared that the jury should ignore it. Jurors cannot ignore whatever they have heard.

It is difficult for the court to determine whether the utterances of prosecutors are deliberate or wilful, intentional or unintentional. Prosecutors may claim that they had no intention of violating court rules by mentioning inadmissible evidence, although they may have done so deliberately. Most courts interpret such utterances as harmless error.

MALICIOUS PROSECUTIONS   The pressure on prosecutors to obtain convictions may induce them to file charges against certain defendants who are innocent of any crime. When prosecutors bring charges against the accused with the full knowledge that the accused is innocent of the crimes alleged, this is a **malicious prosecution**.

Misconduct Risks and Sanctions

When prosecutors commit **prosecutorial misconduct**, particularly in the courtroom, there is always the chance that the misconduct will be detected and sanctioned in some way. Prejudicial commentary by the prosecutor will cause defense counsel to object. Judges will sustain these objections, but the harm has already been done. The jury has heard the prejudicial commentary, and despite an admonition from the judge to disregard such prejudicial commentary, the jury cannot forget about it entirely. For instance, a prosecutor may be barred from mentioning a defendant's sexual preferences in a murder trial occurring in a small religious community. However, the prosecutor may allude to a homosexual defendant's gay rights activism, even though this commentary has nothing to do with the case before the court. Defense counsel will object strenuously, and the judge will sustain this objection. But the jury cannot erase from their memories the prosecutor's statement about the defendant's gay rights activities. Jurors may assume that the defendant is gay, and this assumption may be sufficient to prejudice some of them. Because some of the jurors may dislike gays, they may punish the defendant by voting for his guilt, despite the fact that the defendant's guilt has not been established beyond a reasonable doubt. The prosecutor is successful, therefore, in prejudicing jurors against the defendant by alluding to one or more extralegal factors.

ETHICAL NORMS   Prosecutors can get away with their courtroom misconduct largely because of an absence of ethical norms as standards against which to gauge their conduct. In case after case where prosecutorial misconduct is alleged, the U.S. Supreme Court has failed to articulate clear and consistent ethical norms to guide prosecutors.

Interestingly, juries are more inclined to consider inadmissible evidence favorable to defendants than inadmissible evidence unfavorable to defendants. Despite this factor of defense favoritism, prosecutors might be tempted to sway the jury by introducing highly prejudicial inadmissible evidence. By doing so, they risk jeopardizing any resulting conviction. However, the likelihood of having one's conviction overturned in these instances is extremely remote. The most significant reason for the continued presence of prosecutorial misconduct is the **harmless error doctrine**. Under this doctrine, an appellate court can affirm one's conviction despite the presence of serious prosecutorial misconduct during the trial. Thus, the desirability of the doctrine is undermined when the prosecutor is able to commit misconduct himself without fear of sanction (Carter 2001). The harmless error doctrine also can pertain to serious cases where the death penalty can be invoked.

Also, the standards currently used in ruling on motions for retrial based on false testimony fail to strike an acceptable balance between the right of the accused to a fair and impartial trial and the demand for efficient administration of the criminal justice system in court. Ideally, motions for retrial based on false testimony presented by prosecution witnesses should be governed by a standard drawn from newly discovered evidence and prosecutorial misconduct. The proper test for a new trial based on newly discovered evidence of false testimony is whether there is a significant chance that a jury with a knowledge of the false testimony would avoid convicting the defendant.

Summary

Next to the judge who presides over trials, the prosecutor, also known as the state's attorney, the district attorney, or the U.S. attorney or assistant U.S. attorney, is one of the most powerful members of the court.

Prosecutors represent the state's or federal government's interests whenever one or more crimes are alleged against defendants. Prosecutors are often political appointees or elected persons, all of whom have law degrees or other equivalent entitlements that enable them to practice law.

As attorneys, all prosecutors are bound by codes of ethics, depending upon the professional organizations to which they belong. Most attorneys in the United States belong to the American Bar Association (ABA), which has articulated ethical codes and standards over the years for its membership to follow.

Canons of ethics include exhibiting integrity and competence, assisting the legal profession in various ways to bring distinction upon it, assisting in preventing the unauthorized practice of law, preserving confidences of clients and others, representing the government and/or clients competently, representing the government and/or clients zealously within the boundaries of the law, assisting in improving the legal system, and avoiding the appearance of impropriety.

The criminal court is an adversarial system. The adversaries are the prosecutor and defense counsel. These persons are regarded as sides in a form of competition to win. The general goal of the prosecutor is to convict those accused of crimes, while the goal of the defense counsel is to secure an acquittal for his/her client. Deciding which side is right is the judge or jury's role in a bench or jury trial proceeding.

Both sides abide by rules, including state or federal rules of criminal procedure and rules of evidence. These rules regulate virtually all permissible conduct from the beginning of a prosecution to the end of it. Evidentiary matters are also a part of this process; judges make decisions according to various rules that have been established to govern whether certain types of evidence are admissible by either the prosecutor or the defense or both.

Evidence introduced by either side is either inculpatory or exculpatory. Inculpatory evidence shows the defendant's guilt, while exculpatory evidence shows defendant innocence.

Depending upon the jurisdiction, the roles of prosecutors are relatively simple. All prosecutors function to screen which cases to prosecute and which ones not to prosecute. This means that they must prioritize their cases. Thus, prosecutors decide on their own or in groups whether to pursue particular cases. These decisions are often made according to how much evidence exists against particular defendants, the likelihood of winning the case and securing a conviction, the media visibility of the case, and case seriousness.

Prosecutors are responsible for devising the best strategies for winning cases. They must interview witnesses, including victims of crime and those who saw the crime occur. They must work closely with law enforcement officers who made arrests and conducted criminal investigations. They must also work with forensic teams who analyze evidence collected from crime scenes.

The lead prosecutors in any jurisdiction may also assign cases for prosecution to their assistant district attorneys or state's attorneys. At the federal level, U.S. attorneys assign different criminal cases to their group of assistant U.S. attorneys.

Prosecutors have an immense amount of power. In jurisdictions with grand jury systems, prosecutors attempt to secure indictments or charges against those accused of crimes. They make their cases before grand juries and present inculpatory evidence to them. These are largely one-sided proceedings, since defense counsels are not permitted to present exculpatory evidence in favor of their clients.

Prosecutorial misconduct does not typify most prosecutors, although it exists throughout state and federal systems to an uncomfortable degree. Several forms of prosecutorial misconduct have been described. Prosecutors may coach their witnesses by encouraging them to relate what evidentiary information they have in ways that favor the prosecutor's argument that the defendant is guilty of a crime.

In some instances, prosecutors may encourage defendants to commit perjury on the witness stand and say things about the defendant that are not true. This is subornation of perjury and a crime. Prosecutors themselves may be charged with subornation of perjury and be prosecuted for such an offense if it is detected. There is often a diffuse line between the spins sought by prosecutors from witnesses and their statements and subornation of perjury. It is difficult to determine whenever this line is crossed.

Another form of prosecutorial misconduct is malicious prosecution. Malicious prosecution is the prosecution of someone who is innocent of the crime alleged, and this innocence is known or believed by the prosecutor. Nevertheless, the prosecutor moves forward against these defendants anyway.

Prosecutors usually obtain over 90 percent of their convictions against criminal defendants through plea bargaining. While judges must approve all plea bargain agreements, they do not always detect when innocent defendants enter pleas of guilty to crimes they have not committed.

Prosecutors may also engage in prosecutorial bluffing. Prosecutorial bluffing is intended to frighten criminal defendants and their defense counsels into thinking that prosecutors have more inculpatory evidence than they really have. Often prosecutorial bluffing encourages defendants to enter into guilty pleas through plea bargain agreements, especially if defendants are offered light sentences of probation in exchange for guilty pleas to minor charges.

Another form of prosecutorial misconduct is to deliberately withhold exculpatory evidence from defense counsels prior to or during trials. Under discovery rules, certain materials and evidence must be made available to defense counsels. These materials, known as Brady or Jencks materials after their respective U.S. Supreme Court cases that declared certain materials as discoverable, must be disclosed to defense counsels and are often crucial in showing the innocence of their clients.

Finally, prosecutors may backdoor hearsay testimony before juries during trial proceedings. This is clearly an unethical and unwarranted practice, where prosecutors will ask questions of witnesses or make statements during their opening or closing arguments that violate either the rules of criminal procedure or the rules of evidence or both. These statements, which often tend to incriminate defendants or disclose past behaviors that are clearly inadmissible in court, often result in sustained objections from the opposing side, but the jury has heard these statements.

Questions for Review

1. What is meant by the adversary system? Which actors make up the adversary system? What rules govern the adversary system in courts?
2. At the federal and state levels, who are the prosecutors?
3. What are the functions of prosecutors?
4. Under what circumstances might prosecutors engage in misconduct? What are four types of prosecutorial misconduct?
5. How do prosecutors overwhelm grand juries?
6. How do prosecutors perform screening functions in criminal cases?
7. What is meant by prosecutorial bluffing? What are some examples of prosecutorial bluffing?
8. How can prosecutors bias a case in favor of the prosecution? Give some examples.
9. What is meant by backdooring hearsay evidence?
10. What is a malicious prosecution? What are some sanctions the court might use to reprimand district attorneys who engage in malicious prosecutions of suspects?
11. What is meant by the harmless error doctrine?
12. What sanctioning mechanisms should be in place to punish prosecutors who bend the law to fit their own purposes and ensure convictions of innocent defendants?
13. Should those who engage in prosecutorial misconduct be allowed to continue prosecuting cases?

Suggested Readings

1. A. V. Alfieri (2002). "Community Prosecutors." *California Law Review* **90**:1465–1511.
2. D. Beichner and C. Spohn (2005). "Prosecutorial Charging Decisions in Sexual Assault Cases: Examining the Impact of a Specialized Prosecution Unit." *Criminal Justice Policy Review* **16**:461–498.
3. A. Farrell (2004). "Measuring Judicial and Prosecutorial Discretion: Sex and Race Disparities in Departures from the Federal Sentencing Guidelines." *Justice Research and Policy* **6**:45–78.
4. R. D. Hartley, S. Maddan, and C. Spohn (2007). "Prosecutorial Discretion: An Examination of Substantial Assistance Departures in Federal Crack-Cocaine and Powder-Cocaine Cases." *Justice Quarterly* **24**:382–407.
5. B. A. McPhail and D. Dinitto (2005). "Prosecutorial Perspectives on Gender-Bias Hate Crimes." *Violence Against Women* **11**:1162–1185.
6. B. K. Payne, V. Time, and S. Raper (2004). "Regulating Legal Misconduct in the Commonwealth of Virginia: The Gender Influence." *Women and Criminal Justice* **15**:81–95.
7. L. O'Neill Shermer and B. D. Johnson (2010). "Criminal Prosecutions: Examining Prosecutorial Discretion and Charge Reductions in U.S. Federal District Courts." *Justice Quarterly* **27**:394–430.

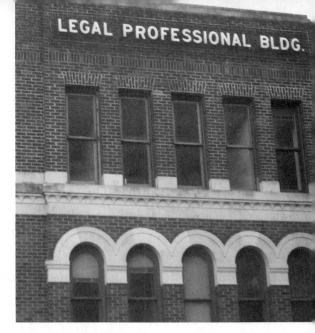

CHAPTER **4**

The Defense

CHAPTER OBJECTIVES

As a result of reading this chapter, you will have accomplished the following objectives:

1. Understand the legal ethics and responsibilities of defense counsels who represent criminal clients.
2. Understand the Sixth Amendment and one's right to counsel regardless of whether the defendant is indigent.
3. Describe the process of self-representation or acting *pro se*.
4. Understand the attorney–client privilege and the confidentiality associated with that relationship.
5. Describe what is meant by ineffective assistance of counsel and learn the criteria used by courts to assess attorney competence.
6. Assess the circumstances under which defendants may request and receive a jury trial.
7. Understand the multidimensional role of defense counsels and the different functions they perform.
8. Describe different types of public defender systems, including the assigned counsel system and the contract system.
9. Understand what is meant by defense misconduct and describe its various forms.
10. Understand the relation between prosecutors and defense counsel and the discovery process.
11. Describe the various affirmative defenses attorneys may raise when representing persons charged with crimes.

KEY TERMS

ABA Model Code of Professional Responsibility
affirmative defenses
alibi
assigned counsel system
attorney competence
attorney–client confidentiality and privilege
automatism
Brady materials
Brady violation

burden of proof
Canons of Professional Ethics
circumstantial evidence
coercion
conclusive evidence
contract system
corroboration
defense of property
demonstrative evidence
derivative evidence
direct evidence

discovery
duress
entrapment
evidence
evidentiary
habeas corpus petition
indigent defendants
ineffective assistance of counsel
intoxication
Jencks materials
jury trial

lie detectors
mistake
necessity
petty offenses
pickpocketing
polygraph tests
pro se
public defender system
self-defense
self-representation
state bar associations
subornation of perjury

55

On June 17, 2010, the National Legal Aid & Defender Association released an evaluation report criticizing the 15th Judicial District's Public Defender Office in Baton Rouge. The report cited that indigent clients were not receiving adequate representation by public defenders. Findings included that almost half of the public defenders had caseloads considered to be excessive by national standards, that new attorneys were sent to court with little training, and that many misdemeanor defendants were not being represented even though they could face jail time. Even though the Sixth Amendment to the Constitution and the Supreme Court ruling in *Gideon v. Wainwright* ensure that indigent defendants are entitled to an attorney, numerous criticisms plague the public defender system. Some of these include that they are overworked and underpaid, that their caseloads are too large to enable them to zealously represent all of their clients, and that they are too quick to bargain away their client's rights. Pedro Gonzalez III, a defendant, says that he could not have survived the yearlong ordeal of being prosecuted, tried, and eventually acquitted of charges, if it were not for his public defender, David Long. Public defenders do not get to select the cases they will represent and they often get few rewards with much less pay than their private practice counterparts. Some, however, argue that public defenders perform a very important duty in our adversarial system of justice; they protect the rights of those accused of crimes and often are able to secure outcomes that are more favorable than those of private defense attorneys. Pedro Gonzalez finished law school two years ago and has decided to enter criminal law. He is happy that a public defender was there to protect his rights and to support and advise him. Instead of sitting in jail he is now a student enrolled in community college and a volunteer firefighter. What do you think? Should more resources be given to public defenders to uphold the Sixth Amendment Right to Counsel? Can you think of any reasons why public defenders might be better than privately retained attorneys despite their large caseloads?

Source: Adapted from The Reading Eagle (Reading, Pennsylvania), "Making a Case for the Defense: Peers Say Public Defenders Deserve Respect for Tackling a Difficult Job that Offers Relatively Few Rewards," August 1, 2010, and The Advocate (Baton Rouge, Louisiana), "Public Defender Blasted," June 17, 2010.

INTRODUCTION

The Sixth Amendment to the U.S. Constitution states that "In all criminal prosecutions, the accused shall enjoy the right to have the assistance of counsel for his defense." The Supreme Court in *Gideon v. Wainwright* recognized that the due process of defendants could not be guaranteed unless they had the assistance of counsel. Today in both state and federal jurisdictions, all persons charged with crimes are entitled to counsel. If a defendant is indigent, and cannot afford an attorney, one will be provided for him/her. This chapter examines the role of defense counsel in great detail. The first section describes one's right to counsel and how it is exercised. Indeed many criminal defendants are indigent and cannot afford to hire counsel. In these cases of indigence, public defenders will be appointed by the court to furnish legal representation to defendants to ensure that their rights are observed. Some defendants wish to represent themselves and reject counsel appointed by the court. These persons proceed on a *pro se* basis, but they are warned by the court that self-representation is a dangerous step and a potentially devastating one. An old adage states that a defendant who represents himself/herself has a fool for a client.

The chapter next examines the attorney–client relationship and the confidentiality associated with it. Whatever conversations pass between an attorney and his/her client cannot be compelled for disclosure to the prosecutor and others. This confidentiality privilege is quite important in preserving the integrity of the criminal justice system, and it protects defendants against self-incrimination. Also examined in this section is the issue of ineffective assistance of counsel. Not all defense counsels are equally gifted in the ways of the law, and from time to time, some defense counsels will fail to act in ways that best represent their clients' interests. When this situation occurs, convicted offenders may challenge their convictions by alleging ineffective assistance of counsel. Subsequently, the U.S. Supreme Court has ruled decisively and determined the criteria used to evaluate whether or not a defense counsel is competent.

For the small percentage of cases that proceed to the trial phase of one's criminal processing, defense attorneys must present convincing cases to judges or juries, whether bench or jury trials are conducted (Zalman 2004). The standards for jury trials have been articulated by the U.S. Supreme Court and will be examined here. For petty offenses and for offenses where the maximum incarceration is six months or less, defendants are not entitled to a jury trial as a matter of right.

The chapter next examines the process whereby indigent defendants have attorneys appointed for them. Different states use one of several types of public defender systems. Some states use several systems simultaneously, but in different counties. These systems include the public defender system, the contract system, and the assigned counsel system. Each system is described, and the advantages and disadvantages of each system for indigent defendants are discussed. The general question of whether private attorneys or public defenders are more effective in representing clients will also be examined. In the chapter-opening scenario, an indigent client is very thankful for the services he received from his public defender. Even though there are numerous criticisms of indigent defense systems, the chapter will provide an in-depth discussion of each of these systems and also explore why perhaps the public defender is able to secure more favorable outcomes for clients than a privately retained criminal defense attorney.

The various functions of defense counsels are also explained and discussed. These functions include faithfully representing clients, attacking vigorously the prosecutor's case against the defendant, counseling with defendants to determine the best defense strategy, negotiating with prosecutors in plea agreement proceedings to configure a plea most favorable for the defendant, vigorously cross-examining prosecution witnesses during trials to undermine their credibility or impeach their veracity, and using any and all legal means at their disposal to defeat the government's case against their defendant. From time to time, defense counsel may confront some ethical issues in their day-to-day duties. Like prosecutors, there are certain ethical guidelines within which defense counsel should conduct their duties and functions. Sometimes they overstep the boundaries between zealous advocacy and unethical behavior.

One important function of defense counsels is to interact with prosecutors and seek discovery of relevant evidentiary information. The discovery process is described as well as its significance for the trial outcome. Discovery has been influenced by several important U.S. Supreme Court cases, which will be described. Materials subject to discovery rules have been variously labeled as Brady materials or Jencks materials, after the major cases where high court rulings were rendered. Much of the discoverable evidence provided to defense counsels is important to the defense's case. Several types of evidence are distinguished and examined, including conclusive evidence, direct evidence, circumstantial evidence, and demonstrative evidence. Defense counsels must decide how and when to use different types of evidence they possess most effectively.

The chapter concludes with an examination about what several of the defense attorneys might use to explain away the conduct of their clients. These are mostly affirmative defenses, and they include automatism or insanity, intoxication, coercion or duress, necessity, alibi, entrapment, defense of property, ignorance or mistake, and self-defense. While this list of defenses is not exhaustive, most affirmative defenses used by defense counsels are presented here. Several examples of these defenses are also discussed.

ON LEGAL ETHICS AND PROFESSIONAL RESPONSIBILITY

Lawyers have been the butt of more than a few jokes. For instance, there's the one which asks what do you throw a drowning lawyer? The answer...his partner! There are several reasons for such jokes. First, some lawyers have engaged in disreputable or dishonest activities. When they have been caught, they often make headlines in their local newspapers. There are hundreds of disbarment proceedings against lawyers every year, where different forms of misconduct have been alleged. The U.S. Supreme Court has rejected most of their appeals for reconsideration. A second reason is that some lawyers have bad reputations for taking advantage of their clients and exploiting them. The public seems to reflect a general mistrust of lawyers as well. Public opinion polls have been taken regarding the honesty of lawyers and other professional persons. In 1997, for instance, lawyers were ranked nineteenth in honesty behind funeral directors, newspaper reporters, dentists, police, and real estate agents (Maguire and Pastore 2005).

In an effort to improve the image of lawyers throughout the United States, various professional associations and organizations have evolved codes of ethics or standards by which lawyers should conduct their behavior. For instance, the American Bar Association (ABA) first adopted its **Canons of Professional Ethics** at a meeting in Seattle, Washington, in 1908. Intended as a means of self-regulation, the Canons of Ethics are a part of the **ABA Model Code of Professional Responsibility**. Attorneys in all U.S. jurisdictions ideally are expected to adhere to this code on a voluntary basis. Whenever violations of this code occur or are alleged, disciplinary rules are invoked to sanction those who are believed to have engaged in unethical conduct. There are nine Canons of Ethics (Morgan 1983, 3) including that

1. A lawyer should assist in maintaining the integrity and competence of the legal profession.
2. A lawyer should assist the legal profession in fulfilling its duty to make legal counsel available.
3. A lawyer should assist in preventing the unauthorized practice of law.
4. A lawyer should preserve the confidences and secrets of a client.
5. A lawyer should exercise independent professional judgment on behalf of a client.
6. A lawyer should represent a client competently.
7. A lawyer should represent a client zealously within the bounds of law.
8. A lawyer should assist in improving the legal system.
9. A lawyer should avoid even the appearance of professional impropriety.

Besides the ABA and its rules and Canons of Ethics, all states have **state bar associations**. These associations are powerful enough to require that all persons who practice law in these states must be approved by these bars in advance. Thus, attorneys who attend law school and graduate with a law degree must first pass one or more state bar examinations in order to qualify as practicing lawyers in those states.

Defense counsels are practicing lawyers and must pass state bar examinations in order to demonstrate their familiarity with local and state laws. Besides passing tests and taking other types of examinations, all lawyers are expected to adhere to codes of ethics and to conduct themselves in a way that will not compromise their integrity. Thus, it is expected that the ABA Canons of Ethics and the ABA Model Code of Professional Responsibility are applicable to virtually all practicing attorneys in the United States. Although not all attorneys in the United States belong to the ABA, the ethical and professional responsibility provisions promulgated by the ABA are generally and implicitly applicable to them anyway.

THE RIGHT TO COUNSEL

The Sixth Amendment says that all defendants shall have the right to a speedy trial by an impartial jury, the right to be informed of the nature of the charges against them, the right to confront their accusers in court, and the right to have assistance of counsel for their defense. Originally, this was interpreted to mean that if a defendant had an attorney, they could bring them to court. Eventually, the Supreme Court, through a series of rulings, rendered the Sixth Amendment's right to counsel clause as mandating provision of counsel to those who could not afford it. While the Sixth Amendment does not declare that counsel must be competent, the Supreme Court handed down a ruling in another case, _Strickland v. Washington_, which provided guidelines with which to gauge attorney effectiveness and competence.

The right to counsel as guaranteed under the Sixth Amendment was not applied to the states until 1963. For many decades, therefore, those accused of crimes were free to hire their own attorneys to represent them (Smith 2004). However, for **indigent defendants**, defendants without the money or means to hire their own counsel, they were often prosecuted, tried, and convicted without benefit of any defense counsel (Cunningham and Vigen 1999). Until the 1960s, indigent defendants in state courts were not entitled to a court-appointed attorney unless they were charged with a capital crime, such as murder. If indigents were charged with noncapital offenses, then they were unable to compel courts to furnish them with an attorney. Without an attorney to defend them, therefore, many indigents were convicted, whether or not they were guilty of the crime(s) alleged. In 1942, the U.S. Supreme Court condoned these state practices. In the case of _Betts v. Brady_ (316 U.S. 455 [1942]), Betts, a robbery suspect, claimed that he was indigent and demanded a court-appointed attorney to defend him on the robbery charge. The court said that Betts could have access to appointed counsel only for rape or murder cases, and his request for an attorney was denied. In felony cases in which life or death was not an issue, the U.S. Supreme Court ruled that the states were not required to furnish counsel to indigent defendants in every case. It should be noted, however, that many states _did_ provide counsel for indigent defendants during this period because it was required by the state legislatures.

EXTENDING THE RIGHT TO COUNSEL TO STATE COURT PROCEEDINGS   In 1963, the U.S. Supreme Court reviewed and decided the case of _Gideon v. Wainwright_ (372 U.S. 335 [1963]). Clarence Gideon broke into a Florida poolroom with the intent to commit larceny. This act was a felony in Florida. Gideon was indigent and asked for a lawyer to represent him. He was advised by the judge that counsel could only be appointed to indigents if they were charged with a capital crime. Since he was denied an attorney, Gideon represented himself. Subsequently, he was convicted and appealed. The U.S. Supreme Court overturned Gideon's conviction, holding that all indigent defendants are entitled to court-appointed counsel in any serious case. The Florida courts interpreted serious case to mean any felony. Thus, the _Gideon_ case established that court-appointed counsel would be provided for any indigent defendant who was charged with a felony. The Supreme Court in _Gideon_ in essence applied the Sixth Amendment right to counsel to the states.

Nine years later, the case of _Argersinger v. Hamlin_ (407 U.S. 25 [1972]) was decided by the U.S. Supreme Court. This also occurred in Florida. Argersinger was an indigent charged with carrying a concealed weapon. This charge was a misdemeanor in Florida and punishable by a fine and six months' imprisonment. Argersinger claimed to be indigent and demanded that the court appoint counsel to represent him. Argersinger's request was denied, because, according to _Gideon_, only felony charges entitled indigent defendants to court-appointed counsel. Argersinger was convicted of the misdemeanor and sentenced to 90 days in jail. He appealed, and the U.S. Supreme Court overturned his misdemeanor conviction. Essentially, the U.S. Supreme Court said that anyone facing possible imprisonment is entitled to court-appointed counsel if they are indigent and cannot afford to hire private counsel.

SELF-REPRESENTATION   Under certain circumstances, defendants may wish to represent themselves in court and not use the services of a defense attorney (Sabelli and Leyton 2000). Any criminal defendant may elect to defend himself/herself and reject court-appointed counsel. When defendants engage in **self-representation**, they are said to be proceeding **_pro se,_** which means "on his or her own behalf" (Arrigo and Bardwell 2000). Defendants who defend themselves do not have to be trained lawyers, nor do they have to be skilled in criminal law or trial techniques. However, in most instances where persons have elected to represent themselves in court, judges have appointed lawyers to assist or advise them anyway, although the roles of these counsels are somewhat passive (Cunningham and Vigen 1999). Self-representation in criminal proceedings is not exclusively an American phenomenon. Other countries, such as England, permit defendants to represent themselves if they request to do so (Tague 1999).

Relatively few persons, however, defend themselves in court. An old adage says that one who represents himself/herself has a fool for a client. At one point in our history, however, indigent defendants were compelled to defend themselves. As we saw earlier in the case of *Gideon v. Wainwright* (1963) (see the section "Case Law Regarding Self-Representation and the Right to Assistance of Counsel"), Clarence Gideon was on trial in Florida for burglary. At the time of Gideon's trial, it was the law in Florida that indigent defendants were not entitled to court-appointed counsel unless they were charged with a capital offense. Gideon defended himself and was subsequently convicted. He appealed, contending that he was entitled to counsel and was denied counsel. The U.S. Supreme Court heard his appeal and overturned his conviction, holding that all indigent criminal defendants are entitled to court-appointed counsel in serious cases or felonies. Subsequently, court-appointed counsel was extended to any person charged with either a misdemeanor or felony (*Argersinger v. Hamlin*, 1972) (see the section "Case Law Regarding Self-Representation and the Right to Assistance of Counsel").

ATTORNEY–CLIENT PRIVILEGE AND CONFIDENTIALITY   Other rules have evolved as well to cover the relation between attorneys and their clients (Canon 4). **Attorney–client confidentiality and privilege** is intended to protect clients from having their attorneys disclose incriminating details of their lives to others, such as prosecutors. If a defense attorney hears a confession from a client, the attorney is vested with considerable legal protection. Prosecutors cannot compel defense counsels to provide them with incriminating information about their clients. The attorney–client privilege is as inviolate as the relation between parishioners and their priests.

BOX 4.1

Case Law Regarding Self-Representation and the Right to Assistance of Counsel

Betts v. Brady, 316 U.S. 455 (1942)

Betts claimed that he was indigent and thus demanded a court-appointed attorney to defend him on a robbery charge. The court said that Betts could have access to appointed counsel only for rape or murder cases, and denied his request. He appealed. The Supreme Court ruled that in felony cases in which life or death is not an issue, the states are not required to furnish counsel in every case; many states at this time, however, provide counsel because it is required by their own constitutions or by court rulings in state courts. This decision was overturned as the result of the ruling in *Gideon v. Wainwright* (1963), in which the U.S. Supreme Court concluded that in all felony cases, state or federal, indigent defendants are entitled to counsel.

White v. Maryland, 373 U.S. 59 (1963)

White, an indigent, was suspected of murder. At his arraignment, he entered a not-guilty plea, but later at a preliminary hearing, he pleaded guilty. He was not represented by counsel at the preliminary hearing, and his guilty plea was introduced later in the trial as evidence against him. He was convicted. White appealed, contending that the preliminary hearing was a critical stage requiring appointment of counsel to represent him. Thus, the guilty plea he entered should have been inadmissible in court later. The U.S. Supreme Court agreed with White and overturned his conviction, saying that preliminary hearings are critical stages in which indigent defendants must be represented by counsel.

Gideon v. Wainwright, 372 U.S. 335 (1963)

Gideon broke into a poolroom allegedly with the intent to commit larceny. This act was regarded as a felony in Florida. Gideon was indigent and asked for a lawyer to represent him. He was advised by the judge that counsel could only be appointed to persons if the offense involved the death penalty. Therefore, Gideon represented himself and was convicted. He appealed. The U.S. Supreme Court overturned his conviction, saying that all indigent defendants are entitled to court-appointed counsel in felony cases. (See *Argersinger v. Hamlin* [1972] for a narrowing of this provision to minor crimes or misdemeanor cases.)

Illinois v. Allen, 397 U.S. 337 (1970)

Allen was charged with robbery. He waived his right to counsel and elected to represent himself. During the jury selection and trial, he was abusive and argued constantly with the trial judge until eventually he was ordered removed from the courtroom. The trial was held anyway and he was convicted. Later, Allen appealed to the U.S. Supreme Court, arguing that his Sixth Amendment right had been violated because he was not present at his own trial when convicted. The U.S. Supreme Court upheld his conviction, saying that repeated warnings to Allen from the judge had had no effect on his conduct, which was so disruptive as to prevent the jurors from properly considering the evidence. Thus, there was nothing unconstitutional about the judge's removing Allen from the courtroom.

Coleman v. Alabama, 399 U.S. 1 (1970)

Several defendants, including Coleman, were accused of assault with intent to commit murder. As indigents, they were denied counsel at their preliminary hearing, with the Alabama judge declaring that nothing that happened at the preliminary hearing would influence the trial later. Coleman was convicted, and he appealed. The U.S. Supreme Court ruled that preliminary hearings are critical stages. Because indigent defendants are entitled to counsel at critical stages, which Coleman had been denied, his conviction was overturned.

Argersinger v. Hamlin, 407 U.S. 25 (1972)

Argersinger was an indigent charged with carrying a concealed weapon. In Florida, this crime is a misdemeanor punishable by imprisonment of up to six months and a $1,000 fine. Argersinger was not allowed to have court-appointed counsel, as required for a *felony*, because his crime was not a felony (see *Gideon v. Wainwright* [1963]). He was convicted of the misdemeanor and sentenced to 90 days in jail. He appealed, and the U.S. Supreme Court overturned his misdemeanor conviction. The U.S. Supreme Court said that any indigent defendant is entitled to counsel for *any* offense involving imprisonment, regardless of the shortness of the length of incarceration. Thus, it extended the *Gideon* decision to include misdemeanor offenses, holding that no sentence involving the loss of liberty (incarceration) can be imposed where there has been a denial of counsel; defendants have a right to counsel when imprisonment might result.

Faretta v. California, 422 U.S. 806 (1975)

Faretta, who was charged with grand theft, desired to represent himself. The judge ruled that he had no constitutional right to represent himself in the case and appointed a public defender to defend him. Faretta was convicted. He appealed, arguing that he had a right to represent himself. The U.S. Supreme Court overturned his conviction, holding that Faretta indeed had a right knowingly and intelligently to waive his right to counsel and represent himself in the criminal proceeding. Thus, he had been denied his constitutional right to act as his own counsel.

Baldasar v. Illinois, 446 U.S. 222 (1980)

Baldasar was convicted in a theft of property not exceeding $150 in value. Although this offense was a misdemeanor, it was Baldasar's second offense, and therefore, it became a felony. He was

(continued)

(continued)

sentenced to one to three years in prison. He appealed, claiming that he had not been represented by counsel at the time of his first conviction. Therefore, the enhanced penalty from the second conviction was not constitutional. The U.S. Supreme Court agreed with Baldasar and overturned his conviction, holding that no indigent criminal defendant shall be sentenced to a term of imprisonment unless the state has afforded him/her the right to assistance of counsel. Baldasar had requested but had been denied counsel in the trial for his original misdemeanor, which became a crucial step in enhancing the penalty resulting from his second conviction.

Godinez v. Moran, 509 U.S. 389 (1993)

Moran was charged with several murders, although he had entered a plea of not guilty by reason of insanity. Several doctors reported test results that indicated Moran was competent to stand trial. Following these psychiatric reports, Moran advised the Nevada court that he wished to dismiss his attorneys and plead guilty to the multiple murders. The court determined that Moran made these guilty pleas knowingly, intelligently, and voluntarily. Further, Moran waived his right to assistance of counsel and other rights associated with guilty pleas. Subsequently, after he was convicted and sentenced to death, he filed a *habeas corpus* petition alleging that even though he had earlier requested to represent himself, he was incompetent to do so. The U.S. Supreme Court upheld the conviction and death sentence, holding that the competency standard for pleading guilty or waiving the right to counsel is the same as the competency standard for standing trial. Moran had been found competent in both instances and had knowingly and intelligently waived the rights he was now alleging had been violated.

Becker v. Montgomery, 532 U.S. 757 (2001)

Becker was an Ohio state prisoner who instituted a *pro se* civil rights action in federal court contesting the conditions of his confinement under Title 42 U.S.C. Section 1983. The federal district court dismissed the complaint because of Becker's failure to state a claim for relief. In a timely manner, within 30 days of the federal court action, Becker appealed, filing a *pro se* notice of appeal with the Sixth Circuit Court of Appeals. However, Becker failed to sign the appeal form. The form contained no requirement indicating that it should be signed. The Sixth Circuit dismissed Becker's appeal because it was unsigned. The Sixth Circuit further declared that Becker's notice of appeal was fatally defective and deemed this defect jurisdictional and therefore not curable outside the time allowed to file the notice of appeal. No court officer had earlier called Becker's attention to the need for a signature. Becker appealed to the U.S. Supreme Court. The Court reversed the Sixth Circuit, holding that when a party files a timely notice of appeal, the failure to sign the appeal does not require the court of appeals to dismiss the appeal. The Court stated further that imperfections in noticing an appeal should not be fatal where no genuine doubt exists about who is appealing, from what judgment, and to which appellate court.

Dodd v. United States, 125 S.Ct. 2478 (2005)

Michael Dodd was convicted of engaging in a continuing criminal enterprise of conspiring with others to possess and distribute marijuana and 16 counts of using and possessing a passport obtained by false statement. He was sentenced in 1993 on most counts and sentenced to 360 months in prison, followed by 5 years of supervised release. Dodd appealed, but his conviction became final in 1997. In 1999 the case of *Richardson v. United States* was decided, which held that a jury must agree unanimously that a defendant is guilty of each of the specific violations that together constitute a continuing criminal enterprise. In April 2001, Dodd filed a *pro se* motion asking that his conviction be set aside, since his jury had not been instructed that they had to agree unanimously on each predicate violation. A one-year statute of limitation existed for filing an appeal based on the subsequent U.S. Supreme Court ruling in the *Richardson* case. The U.S. District Court and the appellate court affirmed Dodd's conviction and rejected his appeal, and he thus sought relief by appealing to the U.S. Supreme Court, where his case was heard. The Court affirmed, holding that the one-year statute of limitation for filing motions to vacate sentences based on newly recognized rights by the Court runs from the date on which the

Court initially recognized the right asserted. Since Dodd had waited beyond one year to file his appeal, the statute of limitation barred him from having his sentence vacated.

Halbert v. Michigan, 125 S.Ct. 2582 (2005)

Antonio Halbert, an indigent defendant, pleaded *nolo contendere* to two counts of second-degree sexual assault involving his stepdaughter and another young girl. When the judge imposed two consecutive sentences, Halbert sought to withdraw his plea, but the court denied his motion. Halbert then filed a *pro se* application for leave to appeal, asserting sentencing error and ineffective assistance of counsel, seeking among other things court-appointed counsel for his appeal. Michigan denied his request for an appellate counsel and rejected his claims. Subsequently, the U.S. Supreme Court heard Halbert's case. Michigan viewed Halbert's initial *nolo* plea as a knowing and intelligent waiver of his right to appeal the convictions and sentences. Michigan also contended that the appointment of counsel for indigents seeking appellate reviews of their sentences is discretionary with trial judges. The U.S. Supreme Court rejected Michigan's views, holding that the due process and equal protection clauses of the Constitution require the appointment of counsel for defendants who are convicted on their pleas, and who seek access to first-tier review in the Michigan Court of Appeals. At the time Halbert entered his *nolo* plea, he had no recognized right to relinquish his entitlement to appellate counsel. Furthermore, the Michigan trial court did not tell Halbert, simply and directly, that in his case, there would be no access to appointed counsel. Halbert's denial of relief by the Michigan Supreme Court was vacated and remanded.

Johnson v. United States, 125 S.Ct. 1571 (2005)

Johnson was convicted in 1994 on federal drug charges and enhanced his sentence because of two previous Georgia drug convictions. In 1998 Johnson succeeded in having his Georgia state drug convictions overturned, which had been used earlier to enhance his federal sentence. Johnson waited almost three years before bringing a *habeas corpus* petition challenging his federal sentence enhancement. Johnson claimed that the delay was attributable to his *pro se* status while filing his appeal and his lack of education. A district court and appellate court affirmed his federal drug conviction and enhanced sentence and the U.S. Supreme Court heard Johnson's appeal. The Court upheld Johnson's conviction and enhanced sentence, holding that Johnson had failed to act in a timely manner in attacking his prior state convictions as the bases for federal sentence enhancements. The U.S. Supreme Court rejected Johnson's *pro se* and "lack of education" arguments.

Kane v. Garcia Espitia, 126 S.Ct. 407 (2006)

Joe Garcia Espitia was convicted in California of carjacking and other offenses. Garcia Espitia rejected court-appointed counsel and elected to represent himself. He requested access to a law library while confined in jail prior to his trial. His repeated requests for law library access were denied. Garcia Espitia proceeded *pro se*. During the trial, he was permitted four hours of law library time just before closing arguments. Following his conviction, he petitioned a federal court with a *habeas corpus* motion, declaring that his Sixth Amendment rights had been violated since he had been denied access to a law library. The district court rejected Garcia Espitia's appeal but the court of appeals reversed. The government appealed and the U.S. Supreme Court heard the case. The U.S. Supreme Court reversed the court of appeals, holding that defendants do not have a clearly established right under federal law to access law libraries while they are in jail awaiting trial as required for federal *habeas corpus* relief. This case is significant because had Garcia Espitia allowed himself to be represented by court-appointed counsel, the defense attorney would have had unlimited access to law libraries and all other legal materials. By knowingly and intelligently waiving his right to counsel, a defendant also relinquishes his right under prevailing federal law to a law library while proceeding *pro se*. This decision does not rule out the possibility that individual states might grant or deny *pro se* defendants access to law libraries and other forms of legal assistance.

(continued)

(continued)

Montejo v. Louisiana, 556 U.S.__(2009)

The case is regarding the issues of uncounseled interrogations. Jesse Montejo was arrested for murder and because he was indigent he was appointed counsel per Sixth Amendment. Prior to meeting with his court-appointed attorney, Montejo gave his consent to be interrogated by police without his attorney present. The government used information from this interrogation against Montejo in court. Montejo appealed under a ruling in a previous case, *Michigan v. Jackson,* 475 U.S. 625 (1986), that once he had been appointed an attorney, he could not be interrogated by police without that attorney. Montejo argued that under the *Jackson* ruling, the government cannot request uncounseled interrogation once a defendant has been appointed counsel. The Louisiana Supreme Court upheld the use of the interrogation evidence stating that *Jackson* was not applicable because Montejo consented to the interrogation and did not state that he wanted his counsel present. Montejo appealed to the Supreme Court and the Court overruled the decision in *Jackson* by a vote of 5–4. The opinion of the court written by Justice Scalia stated that despite the requirement of the *Miranda* warning, defendants are not likely to ignorantly give up their Sixth Amendment rights. Scalia furthered that while the government must ensure that defendants have waived their rights to counsel before interrogations take place, this does not mean that these interrogations cannot occur if a defendant has been appointed counsel but consents to interviews without them present.

ATTORNEY COMPETENCE AND EFFECTIVE ASSISTANCE OF COUNSEL   Probably all attorneys think that they are competent. However, a troubling number of allegations are raised by convicted offenders who believe that their defense counsels are incompetent and ineffective. There is considerable variation among lawyers regarding **attorney competence**; both defense counsel and prosecutors differ in quality and effectiveness. Attorneys of all types vary considerably according to their expertise, years on the job, personal and professional experience, and enthusiasm for defending or prosecuting. However, attorneys are tacitly expected to zealously perform their defense tasks, and in a competent manner (Canons 5, 6, and 7).

Ideally at least, attorneys are expected to do their best, whether they are prosecuting or defending someone on a criminal charge. Counsel competence is difficult to assess objectively. It is more frequently the case that the effectiveness and competence of counsel are assessed subjectively. It is precisely because of the diffuseness of the concepts of effectiveness and competence that more than few challenges are made by convicted offenders where the performance of their attorneys is called into question. These questions pertain to the ineffective assistance of counsel.

The leading case concerning attorney competence is *Strickland v. Washington* (466 U.S. 668 [1984]). Conduct in Strickland's case of whether ineffective assistance of counsel was rendered was measured according to the following standards: (1) Was the counsel's conduct such that it undermined the functioning of the adversarial process that a trial cannot be relied upon to render a just result? (2) Did the counsel's behavior fall below the objective standard of reasonableness? There must be a reasonable probability that, but for counsel's unprofessional errors, the result of the proceedings would be different.

Thus, *Strickland* established the standards of (1) whether counsel's behavior undermined the adversarial process to the degree that the trial outcome is unreliable; and (2) whether counsel's conduct was unreasonable to the degree that the jury verdict would have been different otherwise. This does not mean that all attorney conduct must be flawless and that every stone, large or small, has been overturned in all cases. Most attorneys make one or more mistakes and exercise bad judgment occasionally when defending a client. But many of these mistakes or instances of bad judgment are inconsequential and would not ordinarily affect the trial outcome. There is no obligation on the part of any attorney to raise every nonfrivolous issue in a criminal case (*Jones v. Barnes,* 463 U.S. 745 [1983]; *Murray v. Carrier,* 477 U.S. 478 [1986]) or use a particular defense to criminal conduct (*Knowles v. Mirzayance,* 556 U.S. 07-1315 [2009]).

INEFFECTIVE ASSISTANCE OF COUNSEL   The U.S. Supreme Court has decided instances of **ineffective assistance of counsel** on occasion. For instance, in the case of *Lozada v. Deeds* (498 U.S. 430 [1991]), Jose Lozada was convicted of four crimes relating to narcotics. He was earlier convicted in Nevada on four counts of possession and sale of controlled substances. Following the trial proceedings, Lozada's attorney failed to notify him of his right to appeal, of the procedures and time limitations of an appeal, and of his right to court-appointed counsel. Further, Lozada alleged that his attorney failed to file a notice of appeal or to ensure that Lozada received court-appointed counsel on appeal. Finally, it was alleged that the attorney misled Lozada's sister, and hence, Lozada, when he told her that the case had been forwarded to the public defender's office, which it hadn't. Lower appellate courts dismissed Lozada's subsequent **habeas corpus petition** on the grounds that he had ineffective assistance of counsel as the result of these alleged events. The U.S. Supreme Court found otherwise, however, and reversed his convictions, holding that Lozada had made a substantial showing that he was denied the right to effective assistance of counsel.

Defendants should have a reasonable expectation, therefore, that the counsel representing them is competent and effective. But this expectation should not be that the defense counsel is necessarily the best defense available. The standard of reasonableness is very important, since there are varying degrees of counsel competence and effectiveness that are within the reasonable parameters articulated in *Strickland*. Furthermore, defendants may assume with some confidence that defense counsel will adhere to the ethical codes and manner of professional responsibility articulated by their state bar associations and other professional organizations established to regulate attorney quality and performance.

Recently, the Supreme Court decided in the case of *Vermont v. Brillon*, 556 U.S. _ (2009), that a defendant's Sixth Amendment right to a speedy trial was not violated because his public defender caused delays in his case. Justice Ginsburg, writing for the court, did, however, state that broader problems with a state's public defender system which may cause delays might be in violation of the Sixth Amendment's speedy trial clause.

BOX 4.2

Case Law Regarding Attorney Incompetence

Strickland v. Washington, 466 U.S. 668 (1984)

Conduct in Washington's case of whether ineffective assistance of counsel was rendered was measured according to the following standards: Was the counsel's conduct such that it undermined the functioning of the adversarial process so much that a trial could not be relied on to render a just result? Did the counsel's behavior fall below the objective standard of reasonableness? There must be a reasonable probability that, but for counsel's unprofessional errors, the result of the proceedings would have been different.

Rompilla v. Beard, 125 S.Ct. 2456 (2005)

Ronald Rompilla was convicted in a Pennsylvania court of first-degree murder and other offenses. During the penalty phase, the jury found several aggravating factors that were presented by the prosecution. Rompilla's family provided several mitigating factors. Rompilla's attorney relied upon these mitigating factors and made no effort to discover other mitigating evidence, such as Rompilla's troubled childhood, alcoholism, and mental illness. Rompilla was sentenced to death, therefore, and he appealed, arguing that his counsel was ineffective because he failed to make a reasonable effort to obtain and review evidence of both aggravation and mitigation. The state courts rejected Rompilla's appeals, and ultimately the U.S. Supreme Court heard his case. The U.S. Supreme Court reversed, holding that (1) defense counsel's failure to examine the file on Rompilla's prior convictions for rape and assault at the sentencing phase of his capital murder trial fell below the level of reasonable performance, and (2) such failure was prejudicial to Rompilla, warranting *habeas corpus* relief on grounds of ineffective assistance of counsel.

THE RIGHT TO A TRIAL BY JURY

One of the most significant cases challenging the court's authority to grant or deny a defendant the right to a **jury trial** was *Duncan v. Louisiana* (391 U.S. 145 [1968]). Duncan was convicted in a bench trial of simple battery in a Louisiana court. The crime was a misdemeanor, punishable by a maximum prison term of two years and a fine of $300. However, Duncan was sentenced to only 60 days and fined $150. He appealed, contending that he was denied his constitutional right to a jury trial under the Sixth Amendment. The U.S. Supreme Court agreed with Duncan, saying that any crime carrying a maximum punishment of two years is a serious crime, despite the fact that a jail sentence of only 60 days was imposed. Thus, for serious crimes, under the Sixth Amendment, Duncan was entitled to a jury trial as a matter of right.

Eventually the standard was established whereby criminal defendants are entitled to a jury trial as a matter of right. The standard was set in the case of *Baldwin v. New York*, 399 U.S. 66 (1970). Baldwin was arrested and prosecuted for jostling or **pickpocketing**, a Class A misdemeanor punishable by a maximum term of imprisonment of one year in New York. Baldwin asked for a jury trial, but he was denied one. At the time, New York law defined jostling as a petty offense, one that did not require a jury trial. Baldwin was subsequently convicted and sentenced to 90 days in jail. He appealed. The U.S. Supreme Court heard Baldwin's appeal and declared that **petty offenses** carrying a one-year incarcerative term are *serious* in that jury trials must be provided if requested by defendants. Specifically, the wording of *Baldwin* gives substantial significance to the *months* of imprisonment that defines a serious crime. The U.S. Supreme Court said that a potential sentence in excess of six months of imprisonment is sufficiently severe by itself to take offense out of the category of petty as respects one's right to jury trial (at 1886, 1891). Therefore, the U.S. Supreme Court overturned Baldwin's conviction on these grounds. Presently, jury trials must be granted to any defendant where the possible punishment involves incarceration of beyond six months.

NO JURY TRIALS FOR DEFENDANTS CHARGED WITH PETTY OFFENSES   The U.S. Supreme Court has made clear its position about jury trials and when defendants are entitled to them. According to *Baldwin*, jury trials are available as a matter of right only to defendants charged with serious crimes, where their loss of liberty is beyond six months. Jury trials are not available as a matter of right in other nonserious cases. For instance, in *United States v. Nachtigal* (507 U.S. 1 [1993]), Nachtigal was convicted of drunk driving while operating a motor vehicle in a national park. When he appeared before the U.S. Magistrate, Nachtigal asked for a jury trial but was denied one. His offense carried a maximum incarcerative penalty of six months in jail, and thus it did not qualify for a jury trial. Nachtigal appealed his conviction on the Sixth Amendment grounds that he was denied a jury trial, but the U.S. Supreme Court upheld his conviction, saying that jury trials may not be granted in petty offense cases.

One exception to *Baldwin* is as follows. Sometimes judges will conduct bench trials without juries when a defendant is charged with a serious crime. But these judges will advise the defendant in advance that if the defendant is found guilty, the incarcerative punishment will be six months or less. Judges must keep this promise. Thus, if a defendant is found guilty by the judge later following court proceedings in a bench trial, then the judge cannot impose an incarcerative sentence longer than six months. If a judge were to violate his/her promise to a defendant and sentence him/her to a term of imprisonment of beyond six months, then the convicted offender would have solid grounds to have a higher court review the judge's action and overturn the conviction. Judicial promises made must be kept.

THE DEFENSE

Defense counsel are attorneys who represent those individuals charged with crimes. Defense attorneys adhere to the ABA code of professional responsibility and are obligated to do all that is ethically possible to defend their clients. All criminal defendants are entitled to an attorney as a matter of right. Many defense counsels are retained privately by persons able to afford them.

Yet other defense counsels are appointed by the courts in their jurisdictions to represent clients without money to hire their own attorneys (indigent defendants). Defense counsel who are hired by the state to represent indigent defendants are called public defenders (Maxwell, Dow, and Maxwell 2004).

FORMS OF LEGAL AID FOR INDIGENTS   By 1992 about 80 percent of all criminal defendants charged with felonies were represented by court-appointed counsel. Court-appointed legal representation for indigent criminal defendants plays a critical role in the criminal justice system. About $357,000 was spent on court-appointed counsel for indigents in 1979; $1,336,000 in 1990; and $2.6 million in 1999 (Maguire and Pastore 2005). Table 4-1 shows various types of public defender systems in the United States from a National Prosecutors Survey conducted in 1992. Not every state has the same type of public legal aid for indigent defendants (Smith and DeFrances 1996, 1). Each state is at liberty to establish its own particular form of legal aid services. According to a recent report (Langton and Farole 2010), there were roughly 15,000 attorneys comprising public defender offices around the country. In 2007, these public defender officers represented close to 5.6 million indigent defendants at a cost of roughly 2.3 billion dollars.

Thus, different states have evolved different public defense systems. The most common public defender system used in 28 percent of all U.S. counties is called simply the **public defender system**. This system is state and county funded and serves the needs of numerous persons unable to afford legal aid. The public defender system began in 1914 in Los Angeles, California (Klein and Spangenberg 1993). Public defenders are hired by the state and county to represent indigent clients who are in need of a defense. They draw salaries and are expected to mount the best defense possible, under the limited resources of their agencies. Quite often, their funds for legal defense are limited, and they do not enjoy investigative luxuries and other expenditures that might be available to privately acquired counsel by more affluent defendants.

Two other types of systems are known as the **assigned counsel system** and the **contract system**. The assigned counsel system, used in 23 percent of all local jurisdictions, is used in cities and towns where there aren't many attorneys. Small towns and sparsely populated counties may not have a great many practicing lawyers. Local bar associations function as liaisons between association members and the courts to provide legal services for indigent clients on a voluntary basis. Ordinarily, the local bar association submits a list of attorneys' names to judges who select defense counsel to represent indigent defendants on a case-by-case basis. In most jurisdictions where assigned counsel systems are operative, assigned

TABLE 4-1   Indigent Defense Systems Used by Local Jurisdictions

Type of System	Percentage of Type of Counsel Provided
Public defender program only	28
Assigned counsel system only	23
Assigned counsel and public defender	23
Contract attorney system only	8
Public defender and contract	8
Assigned counsel, public defender, and contract system	6
Assigned counsel and contract system	3
Other	1
Total	100

Source: Steven K. Smith and Carol J, DeFrances. *Indigent Defense,* Washington, DC: U.S. Department of Justice, 1996, 2.

counsel are paid a fixed rate per day for compensation. Compensation may range from $50 to $125 per day for these attorneys, and thus, this is a small sum compared with what an attorney might charge a private client. Actually these per diem rates are more like hourly rates attorneys may charge who are affiliated with small law firms. Some more experienced attorneys in large law firms may bill their clients at the rate of $500 per hour or more. About 23 percent of all local jurisdictions use a combination of the assigned counsel and public defender systems (Weiss 2004).

Because the compensation for indigent client legal services is inadequate, those who furnish their legal services to indigent clients under such a system are not particularly enthusiastic about defending their clients. For many of these attorneys, they merely want to go through the motions of negotiating the best deals for their clients with prosecutors. They often encourage their clients, though innocent, to plead guilty to a lesser criminal charge in exchange for a short jail term or probation. They may persuade their clients to waive their right to a jury trial and opt for a quick plea bargain. The saying "You get what you pay for" is often applicable to attorneys who work as either public defenders or assigned counsel for indigents. The lack of incentives (e.g., monetary remuneration for legal services) causes them to lack the motivation and zeal they should have, in view of the Canons of Ethics and professional responsibility codes they should abide by through the ABA and other state professional legal affiliates.

The contract system involves competitive bidding among different law firms in various jurisdictions for providing legal services to indigent clients. A law firm may submit a bid to represent indigent clients on the basis of a fixed amount of money per hour or per day. The state or county will accept the most attractive bid in order to hold down defense costs. About 8 percent of all U.S. counties use the contract system (Smith and DeFrances 1996, 2). Another 8 percent of all local jurisdictions use a combination of the contract and public defender systems, while another 6 percent use various combinations of all three systems.

One drawback is that the low bidders under the contract system may not be the most competent counsel. A law firm may assign its new and least experienced lawyers to defend indigent clients charged with serious crimes. When the least trained attorneys are expected to defend indigent clients in serious and complex cases, they may not be qualified to perform an adequate defense job. In fact, their defense of indigent clients may be downright incompetent, such that ineffective assistance of counsel charges may be alleged by convicted indigents.

Despite the flaws of these and other defense systems for indigents and others, the fact remains that all criminal defendants are entitled to counsel. The U.S. Supreme Court has never made explicit the exact nature of attorney competence other than what has previously been articulated in *Strickland v. Washington* (1984). In the *Strickland* case, the U.S. Supreme Court declared that an attorney's performance should be such that the adversarial process should not be undermined, or that but for the attorney's conduct, the trial verdict may have been different. The *reasonableness* of attorney conduct was stressed by the Court, although it failed to give precise definition to reasonableness. Therefore, the U.S. Supreme Court has left this determination up to individual state supreme courts and lower courts whenever allegations of attorney incompetence are lodged by convicted offenders.

ARE PUBLIC DEFENDERS AS EFFECTIVE AS PRIVATELY RETAINED COUNSEL?   Under assigned counsel, public defender, and contract systems, states and the federal government set fixed hourly rates for remunerating attorneys who defend indigent clients. These hourly rates, which may range from $25 to $50, are well below the $250 to $500 hourly rates (or higher) charged by private counsel who are hired by more affluent criminals. Many public defenders who work in public defender's offices are fresh out of law school and are interested in acquiring courtroom experience. They are willing to work for low pay in exchange for this experience.

Other public defenders and court-appointed counsel who work on an assigned-counsel basis may be apathetic or hostile toward their clients and the general job of defending criminals. In many of these cases, public defenders will attempt to rush their clients into plea agreements and conclude these low-paying cases quickly, without testing adequately the strength of the case (Weiss 2004).

This rapidity of case processing is particularly prevalent in those jurisdictions with contract systems. A primary consideration in contracting is economizing resources and expediting case processing for maximum efficiency. Such rapid resolution of criminal cases may deprive some defendants of an adequate defense and seriously jeopardize their chances of obtaining equity (Maxwell, Dow, and Maxwell 2004).

At the federal level, the Federal Defender Services program exists, which provides legal counsel for those who cannot afford attorneys. As the number of cases in the federal system increases, so too does the cost to operate the federal public defender system. In 2007, state programs spent a total of $830 million to represent indigent defendants (Langton and Farole 2010).

There is a substantial lack of communication, coordination, and cooperation among the various agencies providing indigent defense services. There is an insufficient number of staff in every category to handle the current caseload and a lack of early representation in the public defender's office. There is virtually no training for public defenders in the office, and little supervision. Salaries are low as well as the morale. Greater use of technology has enabled many jurisdictions to cut their operating costs while maintaining fairly high-quality attorney representation for indigents, however (Spangenberg et al. 1999).

Thus, the general question arises, are court-appointed counsel as effective compared with their privately retained counterparts? Some early research suggests that defense services for indigents in certain jurisdictions such as Hamilton County, Ohio, have been substandard, especially in homicide cases (Steelman and Conti 1987). More extensive continuing education requirements were recommended in order for many of these defense attorneys to improve their criminal law skills. More recent research suggests that inadequate compensation of attorneys for indigents in capital cases produces an increasing number of appeals from convicted offenders who allege ineffective assistance of counsel (Champion 2005a). Despite these criticisms, because 90 percent of cases are disposed of through some type of plea bargain, the public defender works closely with the prosecutor and judge to negotiate appropriate pleas. Some argue therefore that because the system is characterized by negotiation among the courtroom workgroup, public defenders are as effective as privately retained attorneys at securing favorable outcomes for their indigent clients (Hartley, Miller, and Spohn 2010). In short, public defenders offices have been found to be equally effective at defending indigent clients, thus contradicting long-standing criticisms portraying indigent defenders as incompetent, ill-equipped, and poorly trained.

In sum, there is perhaps an element of truth in both views of public defender or assigned-counsel systems. Particularly in larger urban jurisdictions, it is true that public defender's offices are often staffed with new attorneys with little or no criminal trial experience. This fact operates to their disadvantage when relating with prosecutors and configuring plea agreements beneficial to criminal defendants. But in assigned-counsel and contract systems, there are also many seasoned attorneys with considerable criminal law experience. Presently there is great diversity in quality concerning court-appointed legal representation for indigent criminal defendants. At least 80 percent or more of all criminal defendants continue to have court-appointed counsel, and it is likely that this figure will not change substantially in future years (Weiss 2004).

Functions of the Defense

The functions of defense counsel are to (1) represent their clients faithfully, (2) attack the prosecution's case vigorously, (3) counsel with the defendant as to the best course of action in the case, (4) negotiate with prosecutors for a case resolution most favorable to their client, (5) vigorously cross-examine prosecution witnesses to attack and undermine their credibility in front of jurors, and (6) use all legal means to defeat the government's case.

REPRESENTING CLIENTS FAITHFULLY   It is expected that defense counsel will represent their clients faithfully. This means that they will take an active interest in the case rather than a detached passive interest. They will strive to collect relevant exculpatory evidence, interview crucial witnesses, and engage in proper trial preparations. They will consider the defendants' needs and give them every consideration. They will assume that their clients are innocent, even though incriminating evidence might exist to the contrary.

ATTACKING THE PROSECUTION'S CASE VIGOROUSLY   Defense counsel are expected to attack the government's case in a vigorous manner. They should take steps to point out all aspects of the prosecutor's case that are weak or raise reasonable doubt about the defendant's guilt. They should be aggressive and promote their clients' interests to the best of their ability.

COUNSELING WITH DEFENDANTS CONCERNING THE BEST COURSE OF ACTION IN A CASE
It is sometimes the case that defense counsel will be assigned cases where overwhelming direct and conclusive evidence exists about the defendant's guilt. In these types of cases, a vigorous defense should be implemented, designed to provide a plausible explanation for why the crime was committed. One part of the counseling process involves determining the client's view of the case and a disclosure of crime details. This shared information and subsequent defendant disclosures are confidential through attorney–client confidentiality and privilege. Whatever the defendant tells his/her attorney will remain private and confidential. If the defendant admits guilt to his/her attorney, the defense counsel must continue to represent the client with enthusiasm. Defense counsels are in crucial positions to understand the consequences of a trial. In some cases, it may be more prudent to work out deals for clients with prosecutors instead of proceeding with a trial. These bargains often involve some measure of leniency for their clients. The prosecutor may be amenable to reducing more serious charges to less serious ones in exchange for a defendant's guilty plea. If a counsel's client were to reject the bargain offered by the prosecutor and proceed with a trial, a conviction would almost guarantee an increase in the harshness or severity of the penalty imposed by the judge. Therefore, good defense counsels should explain all viable options to their clients and work out what is best for them through close collaboration. Good advice to a client might be to plead guilty to a lesser charge and accept a less severe punishment rather than take a chance in court where a conviction and more severe sentence are imminent.

NEGOTIATING WITH PROSECUTORS FOR A CASE RESOLUTION MOST FAVORABLE TO CLIENTS   Prosecutors determine which charges should be filed against defendants. Defense counsels are expected to negotiate with prosecutors in an effort to reach a compromise with them favorable to their clients. Sometimes, defense counsels may request diversion for their clients, where their cases are temporarily removed from the criminal justice system. Under diversion, clients would be expected to be law-abiding, pay monthly maintenance fees, and perhaps pay restitution to victims or engage in community service. The result of a successful diversion might be that the prosecutor would drop all criminal charges against the defendant or downgrade the charges eventually filed from felonies to misdemeanors. Defense attorneys are key players in facilitating such negotiations between prosecutors and defendants.

VIGOROUSLY CROSS-EXAMINING PROSECUTION WITNESSES AND UNDERMINING THEIR CREDIBILITY   Good defense attorneys engage in vigorous cross-examinations of prosecution witnesses in an effort to undermine their credibility. Often, eyewitness testimony is damaging to defendants, and defense counsels can sometimes cause eyewitnesses to express doubt about what they observed. If defense counsels can encourage prosecution witnesses to admit to uncertainty about what was seen, this strategy undermines the prosecution's case considerably (Bradfield and McQuiston 2004).

USING ALL LEGAL MEANS TO DEFEAT THE GOVERNMENT'S CASE   Within the limits of propriety and the code of ethics that binds together defense counsels throughout the United States, defense attorneys are encouraged to use any and all legal means at their disposal to defeat the government's case against their client. Some of the means may be considered unsavory, although they may be entirely legal. For instance, if a man is suspected of killing his wife and if there are older children or relatives who did not get along with the deceased, it is proper for the defense counsel to suggest to the jury that others might have been motivated to kill. Thus, certain relatives might be named as possible suspects, even though the defense attorney may not believe that they were involved in the woman's death. Rather, the intent of such a strategy is to plant a seed of doubt in the minds of jurors. Someone else may have committed the crime. Others may have had strong motives to kill besides the defendant. If sufficient doubt can be raised by deflecting possible guilt to others, then the jury may acquit the defendant later following their deliberations (Roberts, Gau, and Brody 2004).

One fact that operates to the disadvantage of defense counsels everywhere is that other types of attorneys do not hold criminal defense lawyers in particularly high regard. Defending criminals is viewed by more than a few citizens as an unsavory profession. Defending criminals means having to interact with them. For many attorneys, interacting with criminals is undesirable. Therefore, criminal defense counsels often engage in thankless tasks. They may even be viewed with disdain by their own criminal clients. If they win their cases, they are accused of "getting guilty defendants off" and escaping punishment. If they lose, their clients may appeal and allege that their defense counsels are incompetent or ineffective. Even criminal court judges regard defense counsels with a certain amount of contempt. Thus, for many criminal defense attorneys, considerable stress is generated.

Defense Misconduct

Much of the misconduct that occurs in court is the result of prosecutorial actions or abuses of judicial discretion. However, some misconduct is committed by the defense counsel. While prosecutors are barred from mentioning or admitting into evidence certain types of incriminating information, defense counsels are likewise admonished to avoid saying anything that might prejudice the jury in favor of their client. Certain scientific advancements are such, for instance, that they may not be sufficiently reliable for introduction as evidence in courtrooms (Cook, Arndt, and Lieberman 2004).

For instance, it is widely accepted that testimony about **polygraph tests (lie detectors)** is inadmissible. This is because lie detector results are unreliable and cannot be interpreted with the same degree of precision as fingerprint evidence or other tangible direct evidence. But suppose the defendant submitted to a lie detector test administered by the local police department. Further assume that the defendant passed the lie detector test. The test results would be interpreted to mean that the defendant was telling the truth and that this fact might be considered exculpatory evidence. However, the prosecutor decides to move forward with the prosecution anyway, feeling that the polygraph test results were unreliable. What if the defense counsel asked a police officer who was testifying for the state, "My client took a lie detector test about this crime and passed, didn't he?" The prosecutor would object and the judge would sustain the objection. Just as prosecutors would be guilty of committing harmless errors by backdooring inadmissible evidence, the defense counsel would be equally guilty of backdooring another type of inadmissible evidence, such as the lie detector test results. The judge can order the jury to disregard the defense counsel's question, but can the jury ever forget the question/statement by the defense? No. This is one example of defense misconduct.

Another type of defense misconduct occurs whenever the defense attorney knows that the defendant is guilty. The defendant has confessed his/her crime to the defense counsel, and it is expected that this confession will remain confidential. The privilege of confidentiality exists between an attorney and his/her client, and it is unethical for an attorney to violate this privilege.

While the defense counsel is obligated to defend his/her client despite the confession, the defense counsel is prohibited from advising his/her client to take the stand and lie about the client's role in the crime. Advising one's client, or advising the client's witnesses, to lie is the **subornation of perjury**. Suborning perjury means to encourage someone to lie under oath. If a defense attorney were to suborn perjury, this would constitute defense misconduct. Further, it would be a crime.

INTERACTIONS BETWEEN PROSECUTORS AND DEFENSE ATTORNEYS

Most of us are quite familiar with courtroom drama. We see programs on television such as *Law and Order*. These shows focus on the courtroom as the major contact point between prosecutors and defense counsels. But these programs give us only one dimension of a much larger picture of interaction between the defense and the prosecution. Both prosecutors and defense attorneys are integral parts of the courtroom work group. Actually, their interactions with one another and other members of the courtroom work group are more frequent outside rather than inside the courtroom. For instance, defense attorneys who maintain good relations with various court officers can benefit by being assigned more cases. Defense attorneys, especially recent law graduates, need to earn a living. Being assigned more cases will enable these attorneys to earn more money to support themselves and help to establish their law practices. Defense attorneys with poor attitudes may lose out on various case assignments that are given to more compliant defense counsels.

Defense attorneys consult frequently with prosecutors concerning defendants. Prosecutors work closely with the police and detectives who gather incriminating evidence of crimes, interviews with suspects, and conversations with various experts and eyewitnesses. Some of this information is made available to defense attorneys so that they may advise their clients concerning which course of action is best.

Although the interactions between defense counsels and prosecutors are often characterized as adversarial and antagonistic, the fact is that most of these persons have amicable relations with one another both on and off the job. Most prosecutors are known by defense counsels on a first-name basis. Their relationships are almost always friendly, even though in the courtroom, their respective demeanors might suggest otherwise.

Another consequence of close interactions between prosecutors and defense attorneys is that they both learn about each other's interests and objectives. They are able to assess each other's skills and strategies. Thus, some prosecutors know that they can expect a serious challenge from some defense attorneys who have been successful in garnering acquittals for their clients. This mutual understanding between prosecutors and defense attorneys facilitates the process of whether defendants will enter guilty pleas to certain charges in exchange for leniency.

Also, it is important for both prosecutors and defense counsels to maintain good relations with one another, since they are both interested in ensuring that justice is served when processing defendants. The wheels of justice turn more smoothly to the extent that relations between prosecutors and defense counsels are cordial and cooperative. However, some prosecutors resent having to share case information with defense attorneys. Some defense attorneys are openly antagonistic toward prosecutors. Information exchanges from both sides are slowed and hampered by formality. Under a cooperative scenario, for example, prosecutors would willingly share case information with defense attorneys since it is important for these attorneys to know what they are facing regarding inculpatory evidence against their clients. Under less-cooperative conditions, defense counsels would be obligated to write detailed letters requesting case information to which they are entitled. Prosecutors might drag their feet and delay turning over case materials in a timely manner. Ultimately, however, both sides will exchange information in the process known as discovery.

If the defendant confessed to the crime, and if the confession was videotaped and transcribed, then the defense is entitled to see a copy of the videotape and have a transcription of it for use in the subsequent trial. Accordingly, if the defense has certain types of information, it is also discoverable by the prosecution. Thus, discovery involves an exchange between the prosecution and the defense of relevant information in the case. Both sides must allow each other to see certain types of information they plan to introduce as evidence at the subsequent trial.

THE DISCOVERY PROCESS

Discovery is the procedure or mechanism whereby the prosecution shares information with the defense attorney and the defendant. More than a few countries permit discovery of relevant evidence and materials related to crimes (Gubanski 2004). Specific types of information are made available to the defendant and his/her counsel before trial, including results of any tests conducted, psychiatric reports, transcripts, or tape-recorded statements made by the defendant. Also shared between prosecution and defense is the list of witnesses both sides plan to call to testify at the trial (Gubanski 2004).

BOX 4.3

Case Law Regarding Discovery

Campbell v. United States, 365 U.S. 85 (1961)

Campbell was charged with bank robbery. During the testimony of a government witness, it became known that a previous statement had been made by that witness. The defense sought to obtain that statement, but the court denied them access to it. The government also denied the *existence* of the statement, when, in fact, it actually existed. Campbell was convicted. He appealed, arguing that under the Jencks Act, he was entitled to discovery of the prior statement given by the government witness in order to impeach the witness. The U.S. Supreme Court overturned his conviction and held that under the Jencks Act, such information is discoverable and should be turned over to the defense by government attorneys. Thus, Campbell had been deprived of the right to a fair trial.

United States v. Agurs, 427 U.S. 97 (1976)

Agurs was charged with first-degree murder in the killing of her boyfriend, Sewell. Sewell was known to carry knives. Agurs took one away from him and stabbed him repeatedly. During her trial, information about Sewell's prior criminal record of assault and carrying a deadly weapon and his bad character were excluded from the prosecution's case against Agurs. Agurs was convicted. She appealed, arguing that this information about the victim would have helped her own case. The U.S. Supreme Court upheld Agurs's conviction, holding that the prosecutor was under no constitutional duty to disclose or volunteer any exculpatory information in the case against Agurs. The U.S. Supreme Court adopted a standard for evaluating the materiality of evidence. If such evidence would have been persuasive and produced reasonable doubt about the guilt of the defendant, then it would have been material. Under the circumstances, however, such disclosures would have been irrelevant.

Gardner v. Florida, 430 U.S. 349 (1977)

Gardner was convicted of first-degree murder. Following the conviction, a sentencing hearing was held in which the jury recommended life imprisonment. However, the judge cited aggravating factors and imposed the death penalty. It was important that portions of the presentence investigation relied on by the judge for his knowledge of aggravating factors were not given to the defense under discovery. Apparently, several mitigating factors were cited in the report favorable to Gardner but ignored by the judge. Gardner appealed. The U.S. Supreme Court overturned his conviction, acknowledging that the government had not complied with the discovery law by failing to give Gardner a complete presentence investigation report. The report contained

(continued)

(*continued*)

information to support a life sentence rather than the death penalty. The U.S. Supreme Court declared that the failure of the Florida Supreme Court to consider or even read the confidential portion of the report violated Gardner's right to due process under the Fourteenth Amendment.

Arizona v. Washington, 434 U.S. 497 (1978)

Washington was convicted of murder, but an Arizona court granted him a new trial because the prosecution had withheld exculpatory evidence. At the beginning of the second trial, the defense counsel made various remarks about "hidden" information from the first trial. The prosecutor moved for a mistrial, which was granted. Washington was subsequently convicted in a third trial. Later, as a prison inmate, he filed a *habeas corpus* petition seeking to have his conviction overturned because the second judge's decision to declare a mistrial had been erroneous and had led to his being placed in double jeopardy by a third trial. The U.S. Supreme Court rejected Washington's arguments, holding that the mistrial had been proper. Thus, no previous trial had been concluded with an acquittal and so Washington was not being tried again for the same offense.

Kyles v. Whitley, 514 U.S. 419 (1995)

Kyles was accused in Louisiana of first-degree murder. During the trial, the prosecution failed to disclose to Kyles favorable and exculpatory evidence under discovery. For instance, eyewitness testimony and statements favorable to Kyles were withheld, as were statements made to police by an informant, Beanie. A computer printout of all car license numbers at or near the murder scene, which did not include Kyles's car license number, was in the possession of the prosecution but was not made available to Kyles or his attorney when they demanded discovery. Kyles was convicted and sentenced to death. Appeals by Kyles to higher state courts resulted in affirmation of his original conviction and sentence. Then he sought relief by an appeal to the U.S. Supreme Court. The Court overturned Kyles's conviction, holding that the prosecution had violated Kyles's *Brady* rights (see *Brady v. Maryland* [1963]) to have relevant exculpatory information made available to him by the prosecution. The significance of this case is that it is the constitutional duty of prosecutors to disclose favorable evidence to defendants in criminal prosecutions.

Bracy v. Gramley, 520 U.S. 899 (1997)

Bracy was tried, convicted, and sentenced to death in an Illinois court presided over by Judge Thomas J. Maloney. Maloney was subsequently convicted of taking bribes for fixing other murder cases in Operation Greylord, a federal sting operation intended to detect and prosecute judicial corruption. Bracy appealed his conviction and filed a *habeas corpus* action, arguing that Judge Maloney had a vested interest in Bracy's conviction in order to deflect suspicion that he was taking bribes in other cases. Further, Bracy alleged that Maloney had deliberately suppressed exculpatory evidence that may have mitigated Bracy's sentence. His *habeas corpus* appeals were denied and he appealed directly to the U.S. Supreme Court, where the case was heard. The U.S. Supreme Court reversed Bracy's conviction, holding that Bracy, who was convicted before a judge who was himself later convicted of taking bribes from defendants in criminal cases, showed "good cause" for discovery on his due process claim of actual judicial bias in his own case.

Strickler v. Greene, 527 U.S. 263 (1999)

Strickler was convicted of capital murder in Virginia and sentenced to death. During his trial, Strickler's attorney was permitted to examine prosecutors' files for exculpatory evidence. However, the prosecutor did not advise defense counsel that police files may have contained exculpatory information favorable to Strickler, which may have impeached the veracity of one of the witnesses against Strickler. Strickler filed a *habeas corpus* petition, alleging that the prosecutor had a duty to reveal police documents that may have impeached witnesses against him. Presently, there are three components of a true *Brady* violation: (1) the evidence at issue must be favorable to the accused, either because it is exculpatory or because it is impeaching; (2) the evidence must have been suppressed by the state, either willfully or inadvertently; and (3) prejudice must have ensued. The U.S. Supreme Court heard Strickler's case and decided that although the *Brady* rule had been violated in part, the materiality of the evidence would not have affected the trial outcome. The U.S. Supreme Court held that (1) undisclosed documents impeaching eyewitness testimony as to circumstances about the abduction of the victim were favorable to Strickler for purposes of *Brady*, and (2) Strickler reasonably relied on prosecution's open-file policy and established cause for procedural default in raising a *Brady* claim, but (3) Strickler could not show either materiality under *Brady* or prejudice that would excuse Strickler's procedural default.

Banks v. Dretke, 124 S.Ct. 1256 (2004)

Delma Banks was convicted of capital murder in the death of 16-year-old Richard Whitehead, which occurred in mid-April 1980. Banks was originally implicated in the murder by two associates, Jefferson and Farr, who were working with the county sheriff, Willie Huff, as informants. Unknown to Banks before and during the trial was the allegation that Jefferson and Farr were testifying against Banks in order to avoid drug charges, which were threatened by the sheriff and prosecutor. At the same time, a confidential informant, Cook, also furnished the prosecution with incriminating circumstantial evidence against Banks. This information was also withheld from Banks pursuant to a motion for discovery. Although Banks had no prior criminal record, testimony from Farr and Jefferson provided the jury with innuendo that Banks had an unsavory and criminal past, which was untrue. Banks's efforts to impeach Farr and Jefferson were undermined because of his own witnesses, who were themselves impeached on cross-examination. Banks was sentenced to death and sought postconviction relief, alleging that the prosecution failed to disclose exculpatory evidence as required by *Brady v. Maryland* (1963), including the threats made to Farr and Jefferson as well as the confidential informant, Cook. In its answer, the state claimed that nothing had been kept secret from Banks and no deals had been made with government witnesses, including Cook. In 1993 Banks's postconviction claims were denied outright by an appellate court. Following this loss, Banks filed for *habeas corpus* relief in a U.S. District Court, which granted relief on Banks's death sentence. In 1999 Banks filed discovery and evidentiary hearing motions, both supported by affidavits sworn to by Farr and Jefferson that the prosecution had wrongly withheld crucial exculpatory and impeaching evidence. The federal court determined that the state, indeed, had failed to disclose Farr's informant status during the original discovery phase of Banks's trial. Therefore, a writ of *habeas corpus* was granted to Banks with respect to his death sentence, but not to his conviction. Banks petitioned the U.S. Supreme Court, where the case was heard. The U.S. Supreme Court reiterated that under *Brady*, a prosecutorial misconduct claim must establish three things: (1) that the evidence at issue must be favorable to the accused, either because it is exculpatory, or because it is impeaching; (2) that evidence must have been suppressed by the state, either willfully or inadvertently; and (3) that prejudice must have ensued. In its response, the state contended that "it can lie and conceal and the prisoner still has the burden to discover the evidence." The U.S. Supreme Court ruled this assertion to be untenable and a violation of Banks's due process rights. Banks presented sufficient evidence to support his *Brady* claim and was thus entitled to a full evidentiary hearing and a certification of appealability.

Illinois v. Fisher, 124 S.Ct. 1200 (2004)

Gregory Fisher was arrested for and charged with cocaine possession following a routine traffic stop by police officers in Chicago, Illinois, in September 1988. In October 1988, Fisher filed a motion for discovery, requesting all physical evidence seized by police officers when he was arrested. Prosecutors stated that all evidence would be made available to Fisher at a reasonable date and time upon request and a trial date was set for July 1989. When the trial date occurred, it was discovered that Fisher had fled the jurisdiction, ultimately residing in Tennessee for the next 11 years. An outstanding arrest warrant for Fisher was subsequently executed in September 1999, and Chicago authorities reinstated the 1988 cocaine charges. Fisher renewed his demand to have access to the original evidence seized, but the prosecutor stated that according to established procedures, the substance seized from him had been destroyed after several years of preservation. Fisher moved to have the charges against him dismissed, as the evidence against him no longer existed. The trial court denied his motion and Fisher was convicted by a jury for cocaine possession, based in large part upon police

(continued)

(continued)

testimony and the admission of four laboratory tests that confirmed the substance seized at the time of Fisher's 1988 arrest was cocaine. Fisher was sentenced to one year in prison. Fisher appealed, alleging a violation of his right to due process, since the substance he was accused of possessing had been destroyed by police years earlier, and thus they had framed him for the crime. The appellate court reversed Fisher's conviction, holding that the due process clause required the dismissal of the original charge in the absence of incriminating evidence. The government appealed and the U.S. Supreme Court heard the case. The Supreme Court reversed the Illinois Appellate Court, holding that due process did not require dismissal of cocaine possession charges on the grounds that police, nearly 11 years after Fisher was charged, destroyed the cocaine seized. The Supreme Court held that unless a criminal defendant can show bad faith on the part of police, their failure to preserve potentially useful evidence does not constitute a denial of due process of law. Fisher failed to demonstrate bad faith on the part of police; thus, his claim of a violation of his due process rights was dismissed. There is nothing in the record to indicate that the alleged cocaine was destroyed in bad faith.

The premise upon which discovery is based is that all defendants are entitled to a fair and impartial trial. If the government with its immense resources were to restrict access to various test results and tangible evidence, even oral testimony and reports of experts, this restriction would jeopardize a defendant's right to a fair trial (Schmid 2002). Fundamental fairness is that the defense shall not be deprived of a fair trial. This means that the disclosure of certain types of evidence by the prosecution is mandatory (O'Sullivan 2001).

In several jurisdictions, defense counsel must make a motion for discovery, itemizing the testimony and other evidence it wants. If the defense does not ask for specific items in the possession of the government, the government is not obligated to volunteer them to the defense. This fact is underscored in the case of *Kimmelman v. Morrison* (477 U.S. 365, 1986). In this case, Neil Morrison was convicted of rape in a bench trial in New Jersey. During the trial, a police officer testified about some evidence, a bedsheet found at the crime scene, which had been seized without a proper search warrant. The defense attorney objected and moved to suppress statements about the bedsheet. The judge, however, ruled that it was too late to register such an objection, that the proper time would have been during discovery, when the items seized and to be used as evidence against Morrison were disclosed to him. Following his conviction, Morrison filed a *habeas corpus* petition, alleging ineffective assistance of counsel relating to the bedsheet issue and the motion to suppress it. Because of the defense attorney's incompetence by not raising a motion at an earlier and more proper time, Morrison argued, he was deprived of the effective assistance of counsel, and this problem led to his conviction. An appellate court reversed his conviction on these grounds, and the state appealed to the U.S. Supreme Court. The U.S. Supreme Court heard the case and affirmed the lower appellate court, concluding that Morrison's counsel was ineffective due to his failure to conduct any pretrial discovery and determine what the state had planned to present as incriminating evidence. Further, the counsel clearly failed to make a timely motion to suppress such evidence. On these grounds, Morrison's conviction must be reversed.

It is beyond the scope of this book to list all types of discoverable information. One reason is that there is considerable interstate variation concerning what is or is not discoverable material or statements. Confession statements are always discoverable in all jurisdictions. However, the statements of material witnesses may or may not be immediately discoverable. Usually, when lists of witnesses are exchanged by the prosecution and defense, each side seeks to interview the witnesses to be called. This is to avoid a trial by ambush, where a witness will give testimony unknown to the other side, and the testimony given will influence the trial outcome. Neither side wishes to be surprised by the other.

A leading case about discovery is *Brady v. Maryland* (373 U.S. 83 [1963]). Brady was convicted of murder and sentenced to death. He appealed on the grounds that he was denied access to various statements made by a confederate, Boblit. Actually, Brady took the stand in his own defense and admitted to participating in the crime, but Brady declared that Boblit was the one who actually killed the victim. Various statements had been made to police and prosecution by Boblit. The prosecutor denied the defense access to these statements, alleging confidentiality. Following Brady's conviction, some of this evidence came to light and proved favorable and exculpatory to Brady. He sought an appeal, claiming that he was denied due process by having these important statements withheld during his trial. The U.S. Supreme Court agreed with Brady and overturned his murder conviction, saying that "suppression by prosecution of evidence favorable to an accused upon request violates due process where evidence is material either to guilt or to punishment, irrespective of good faith or bad faith of prosecution." Subsequently, both prosecutors and defense attorneys have referred to discoverable materials and evidence as **Brady materials**. When the prosecutor or defense counsel withholds certain discoverable information, this is called a **Brady violation**.

Actually an earlier case involving a similar issue was *Jencks v. United States* (353 U.S. 651, 1957). The *Jencks* case involved the withholding by prosecutors from the defense of prior inconsistent statements by a key government witness against Jencks. In the *Jencks* case, the U.S. Supreme Court ruled that the government must disclose such inconsistent statements to the defense prior to a criminal trial. In Brady's case, the U.S. Supreme Court overturned his conviction and held that according to ruling in the *Jencks* case, such information is discoverable and should be turned over to the defense by government attorneys. In a way similar to the case of *Brady v. Maryland* (1963), the *Jencks* case has led to discoverable evidence being called **Jencks materials**.

DEFENSE ATTORNEYS AND DEFENSES FOR CRIMINAL CONDUCT

WHO BEARS THE BURDEN OF PROOF IN CRIMINAL PROSECUTIONS?   In any criminal prosecution, it is the responsibility of the state to prove beyond a reasonable doubt that the defendant committed the crime(s) charged. This means that prosecutors must prove beyond a reasonable doubt that (1) a crime was committed and (2) the defendant committed the crime. Thus, the prosecutor bears the **burden of proof** in asserting a criminal charge (Haynes 2000; Schmid 2002). This burden is meant by providing the jury with **evidence** of the crime.

The burden of proof standard, also known as the **evidentiary** standard, in all criminal cases does *not* mean that prosecutors must produce witnesses or victims who can furnish **conclusive evidence** of a defendant's guilt. Conclusive evidence might suffice if several persons watched a defendant commit the crime in plain view. Such evidence is so compelling and strong that it cannot be disputed or contradicted. For instance, a man might shoot his wife, killing her. Then he turns the gun on himself, intending to commit suicide. But somehow he survives the bullet wound and is subsequently tried for his wife's murder. He might have left a highly incriminating suicide note indicating the reasons for why he killed his wife. The suicide note is a type of **derivative evidence**, or written evidence. The weapon he used has his fingerprints on it, his hands have powder residue from firing the weapon, and he is found holding the weapon after his neighbors report the sound of gunshots to police. In this instance, the facts are generally not disputed. District attorneys sometimes prosecute cases with this sort of conclusive evidence (Fisher 1999).

Also, the burden of proof standard does *not* mean that prosecutors must produce any **direct evidence** of the crime. As in the case of conclusive evidence, direct evidence involves incriminating information such as fingerprints or eyewitness testimony (Prentice 2001). Rather, prosecutors may be able to convince a jury that a defendant is guilty of the crime based on **circumstantial evidence** alone. In one New York murder case, for example, a physician, Robert Bierenbaum, was suspected of killing his wife, Gail Katz Bierenbaum, in the summer of 1985. Prosecutors believed that he loaded her body aboard a rented airplane, flew out over the ocean, and dumped her body into the sea. No trace of his wife was ever found. Furthermore, police investigators never found any traces of Bierenbaum's wife's blood in Bierenbaum's automobile trunk or inside the airplane. If such evidence would have been found, this would have been **demonstrative evidence** or derivative evidence, since it is tangible and does not relate to eye-witness testimony. Neighbors reported that they often heard Bierenbaum arguing with his wife. On the day his wife disappeared, Bierenbaum was seen taking off from the airport and flying in the direction of the ocean in a rented airplane, although the police didn't know Bierenbaum had rented the airplane until a year had elapsed. The case was dormant for 15 years, because police didn't have sufficient evidence to charge Bierenbaum with a crime. Subsequently, a check of airport records showed that Bierenbaum had altered his flight log to show that his flight occurred on a different day and time. Also, on the day his wife disappeared, she had spoken with a friend that morning and said that she was leaving Bierenbaum and moving in with a new boyfriend. When the person called her back 40 minutes later, Bierenbaum answered the telephone and told the caller that his wife had just left and he didn't know when she was returning. All of these circumstances and **corroboration** didn't prove that Bierenbaum killed his wife. But prosecutors eventually decided to indict Bierenbaum for his wife's murder in December 1999. He was tried and convicted of murder in New York on October 24, 2000. Despite the fact that the case against Bierenbaum was entirely circumstantial, the jury drew inferences from all of this information and found him guilty of second-degree murder (Rogers, Cotliar, and Erwin 2000, 91).

In another murder case, this time in Atlanta, Georgia, a man was accused of killing his wife and setting his own home on fire to cover up any incriminating evidence. He managed to crawl out of a second-story window of his home while it went up in flames. He told passersby that his wife was inside and had been overcome with smoke. He said that the fire seemed to come from the kitchen in a downstairs area, and that he and his wife were sleeping. He claimed that his wife was too overcome with smoke to assist in her own flight to safety, and that he was too weak to carry her to a window. Thus, he was only able to save himself. Again as in the New York murder, this man had taken out a large life insurance policy on his wife a few months earlier, and he had named himself as the primary beneficiary. It was also found that he was deeply in debt and that his business was failing. Prosecutors surmised that he killed his wife in an effort to save his company from bankruptcy by using the insurance money from her death. The case was purely circumstantial, but the jury was convinced that the man did, indeed, murder his wife and he was convicted of her murder.

Usually, prosecutors must convince a jury that the accused had the means, motive, and opportunity to commit the crime(s) alleged. Since many criminals perform their criminal acts in secret and do not brag about what they have done because they don't want to get caught and convicted, the prosecutor's burden is a somewhat difficult one. Judges will eventually instruct jurors about how they should regard the evidence presented during the trial, and how to weigh that evidence.

The defense is under no obligation to prove anything to the jury. It is not their place to prove their client's innocence. Rather, they may simply offer alternative explanations for how the crime may have occurred. Defense counsels often recommend that their clients should not testify. The fact that defendants do not often testify in their own criminal trials is greatly misunderstood by the public, even many defendants. One of the first things an innocent defendant wants to do is get up on the witness stand and proclaim his/her innocence to the jurors. But prosecutors have many clever ways of distracting and upsetting innocent defendants and twisting their own words to prosecutorial advantage. The defendant's demeanor and self-control are important factors that jurors can observe. On more than one occasion, prosecutors have disturbed defendants so much on the witness stand that they lose their tempers and act guilty, even though they are innocent. It is a fundamental right of defendants, therefore, to remain silent while the prosecution attempts to prove their guilt. This is due process, and all defendants are entitled to it. Some jurors might believe that if the defendant doesn't take the stand and testify, then this is some sort of guilt by omission. That is, if defendants do not declare their innocence on the witness stand, an inference may be drawn that they have something to hide. This is absolutely untrue. While all defendants have the right against self-incrimination, they also have the right to due process, which means in part that if they do not testify, this is *not* a form of incrimination. Ordinarily judges read jury instructions to jurors and highlight this fact so that jurors must not and cannot consider a defendant's refusal to testify as evidence of their guilt. In fact, *no* inferences may be drawn by jurors about the defendant's guilt or innocence when the defendant does not testify.

However, defense attorneys are seldom content to allow the prosecutors' allegations to go unchallenged. A vigorous defense is expected from any competent defense attorney. But most frequently these defenses are designed to explain away the case prosecutors have crafted against the accused. As we have seen, defense attorneys may provide jurors with alternative explanations for why the crime occurred and who might have committed the crime. But when there is direct evidence that a defendant committed the crime, the defense must act aggressively here as well. Under these circumstances when criminal conduct is alleged, the defense attempts to counter the criminal charges with one or more **defenses to criminal conduct**. Defenses to criminal conduct also are called **affirmative defenses**. These defenses include automatism, intoxication, coercion or duress, necessity, alibi, entrapment, defense of property, ignorance or mistake, and self-defense (Fisher 1999).

Automatism and/or Insanity

The defense of **automatism** is that the defendant was incapable of formulating criminal intent because he/she blacked out or was acting unconsciously. For example, someone may sleepwalk and commit the crime of breaking or entering, entering the home of another when they think they are entering their own home. The *mens rea* or guilty mind is eliminated as a criminal element (Jordan and Meyers 2003).

Insanity is occasionally raised in criminal cases. Insanity is defined in different ways among U.S. jurisdictions (Arpey 2003). Usually, it means acting under an irresistible impulse, an inability to conform one's conduct to the requirements of the law, a mental disease or defect, and not knowing the difference between right and wrong (Arpey 2003). If the defendant was not sane when the crime was committed, then the *mens rea* component of a crime can be overcome (Litwack 2003). Therefore, a crime is not committed.

Currently, most states and the federal government have adopted the guilty, but mentally ill plea, where it is no longer the burden of the prosecution to show that one is sane (Mulford et al. 2004). The insanity defense is used in other countries besides the United States. In England, for instance, insanity is used to indicate diminished capacity in criminal cases (Mitchell 2003).

Intoxication

Intoxication is often raised in criminal cases to show that the defendant was not fully capable when the crime was committed. However, intoxication rarely excuses criminal conduct. Intoxication may be used to show that certain elements of the crime may not be present (Brocke et al. 2004). For instance, in premeditated murder cases, the intoxication of the defendant may help the defense to show that the defendant was not capable of premeditating the crime. States differ in the weight given to intoxication as a way of negating criminal intent.

In Tennessee, for instance, Wayne Adkins was charged with and convicted of first-degree murder in the death of Junior Adams (*State v. Adkins*, 1983). Witnesses testifying about what they saw said that Adkins had consumed a case of beer shortly before the shooting and was drunk when he killed Adams. The jury recommended the death penalty nevertheless. The Tennessee State Supreme Court set aside the death penalty, however, and ruled that Adkins was not capable of premeditating the murder as the result of intoxication. This holding is not necessarily indicative of how other state supreme courts might rule on similar issues. Canada and other countries have revised their laws regarding intoxication and whether it can be used as an affirmative defense against criminal conduct (Champion 2005b).

Coercion or Duress

When persons act under **coercion** or **duress**, they feel compelled to act in certain ways in order to avoid harm from others. In youth gang activities, for instance, the gang may pressure younger members of the gang to commit various crimes. The older gang members may intimidate younger gang members by threatening them with bodily harm. "We will beat you up, maybe even kill you, if you don't steal these things from the store," the gang might say to younger gang members. Thus, when the younger gang members commit theft and are caught, they may claim duress. They will allege that the gang made them do it or they would face retribution (Gilbertson 2005).

In another case involving duress, two female inmates held in a California minimum-security prison were charged with escape when they walked away from the prison. They fled the prison when they were threatened by other inmates, lesbians, with physical harm if they did not submit to sexual advances. Later, when the women were free of the prison and the circumstances that might have caused them physical harm, they surrendered themselves to local law enforcement authorities. They claimed duress resulting from the threats of lesbian inmates. They were convicted of escape in a lower California court, but an appellate court set their conviction aside, accepting their defense of duress as valid (*California v. Lovercamp*, 1974). This doesn't mean that prisoners are always entitled to flee from their prison confines if they feel threatened by other prisoners. Each case must be resolved on an individual basis. However, in this *California* case, duress was successfully used. Thus, if a defendant is made to perform conduct that is criminal, duress or coercion may be an affirmative defense to remove it from criminal conduct.

Necessity

In 1996, a man was arrested in Minot, North Dakota, for breaking and entering a car dealership. However, his case was dismissed during trial when he cited necessity as the reason for his actions. In his case, he was driving a car toward Minot from Bismarck when a storm struck. The powerful snow and winds caused a whiteout, where he could not see the road in front of him. During this blizzard, his car slid off the road and he was stranded. He knew that he must seek shelter or die. He walked in the blizzard for about a mile, finally coming to a large automobile dealership on the outskirts of Minot. He broke a window to gain entry into the facility and climbed into an automobile on the showroom floor to keep warm. Employees found him asleep in one of the showroom cars a day later when the storm subsided. They called police and he was arrested. His defense of **necessity** was accepted as valid by the court. He was merely trying to save his life.

Alibi

Whenever a defendant claims an alibi, he/she intends to show that he/she was somewhere else when the crime was committed. Thus, if a crime is committed in St. Louis, Missouri, at 10:00 p.m. on a Monday night, and if the defendant can show that he/she was in New York City at 10:00 p.m. on that same Monday evening, the witnesses who testify in his/her behalf provide him/her with an alibi. Depending upon the veracity or truthfulness of these other witnesses, an **alibi** defense is a strong defense to criminal conduct.

Entrapment

Entrapment occurs whenever a defendant is lulled into criminal conduct by another. Usually, the conduct is something that is extraordinary for the defendant, and not conduct that is normally a routine or practice (Gubanski 2004). Law enforcement officers often seek to induce people to commit a crime so that they can make an arrest. Female officers pose as prostitutes in an effort to arrest those seeking to buy sexual favors. Many prospective customers of prostitutes are thus snared in police stings. However, sometimes the police go out of their way to encourage others to violate the law. They may knock on motel doors until they find someone willing to invite the officer/prostitute in for sex. This aggressive policing often leads to charges of entrapment, where customer/defendants are lured into committing acts that are not ordinarily contemplated by them.

Defense of Property

Defense of property can sometimes be cited as an excuse for criminal conduct. If someone attempts to steal one's car, for example, a defendant is entitled to use reasonable force to deter criminals from committing this crime. Several states have adopted what are referred to as "No Duty to Retreat" or "Castle Doctrine" laws, which allow persons to defend their homes with deadly force. These laws allow homicide to be justifiable under certain circumstances such as when an intruder breaks into someone's residence with intent to steal property or is fleeing the residence with stolen property. Several states have recently expanded or changed their laws to allow deadly defense of one's home or the property therein. The law in Texas, for instance, has even been expanded to include the use of deadly force in defense of a neighbor's property. These laws vary by state and so it depends on where a person lives as to whether deadly force is an acceptable defense of property. The states without the "No Duty to Retreat" laws, however, might allow a defendant to engage in aggravated assault to discourage criminals from stealing his/her valuables or vehicle. Thus, more than a few persons have been acquitted of criminal charges when they have been able to demonstrate that they were merely defending their property when they attacked their attackers.

Ignorance or Mistake

The old adage "ignorance is no excuse" is applicable here to a degree. If someone doesn't know what the law is regarding a certain type of conduct, this fact should reduce the seriousness of whatever they do. Persons who visit foreign countries, for instance, may not know what the laws of the foreign country are. They may unwittingly violate a criminal law by engaging in conduct that might be acceptable in their own country.

In certain cultures, for example, it is customary to perform an operation on all female children to remove their clitoris. This is a ritual that is condoned and socially and religiously approved. However, it is against the law in the United States for such a procedure to be performed. In California and other states, however, some persons have been prosecuted for performing these religious rituals. Thus, the courts have had to weigh the religious and cultural significance of these illegal rituals and their legality in other countries (Tonry 2004). In the United States, however, these rituals are considered illegal and are therefore prohibited.

Mistake or ignorance may be acceptable under other conditions. For example, Morrissette was a hunter who routinely hunted on an army artillery range. It seems that this particular artillery range, although enclosed by a perimeter wire fence, was considered a good deer-hunting area by local hunters. Furthermore, a section of the army post wire fence perimeter had been cut away where private citizens could drive their trucks through and make it easier to hunt deer. One afternoon, Morrissette drove his truck into the military artillery range and hunted deer. After a long unsuccessful afternoon of deer hunting, Morrissette was about to leave when he spied a pile of copper artillery shell casings. Weeds had grown up around the pile of copper shell casings, and it appeared to Morrissette that these casings, some of which were rusting away, had been abandoned. Thus, Morrissette loaded the shell casings into his truck and sold them subsequently at a local flea market for their metal value. With the money, he went to a bar and treated his friends to several rounds of drinks. Nearby enlisted men from the military post overheard Morrissette brag about the copper shell casings he had found and he was reported to police who arrested him for theft of military property. He was convicted, but he appealed, arguing that he didn't know that he was stealing government property when he took the copper shell casings. In this instance, the appellate court believed Morrissette and overturned his conviction. However, this is a relatively rare instance where courts will accept ignorance or mistake as an excuse for otherwise criminal conduct.

Self-Defense

If someone commits a crime and raises the affirmative defense of **self-defense**, it must be shown that the conduct was justified because the defendant believed his/her life was in jeopardy (Hemenway 2004). Self-defense is often raised in homicide cases where one person kills another. If the facts are unclear, a murder charge may be filed against the defendant. Later in court, the defendant raises self-defense as the explanation for the conduct (Hollander 2004). The trial provides the factual forum, where witnesses and others testify about what happened. If the defendant believed that his/her life was in jeopardy and that the only course of action available was to kill the aggressor and eliminate the threat, then the jury will acquit the defendant of the murder charge. Self-defense is always a good defense to this type of criminal conduct if there is sufficient factual information to back up that particular defense (Kaufman 2004).

Summary

In most serious criminal cases, defendants have the right to counsel. When persons are charged with crimes they have counsel appointed (if indigent) or they hire their own counsel. Under certain circumstances, persons may act as their own counsel and represent themselves. This self-representation is called acting *pro se*.

Most defense counsels are members of the American Bar Association (ABA), and many of them belong to local bar associations. These associations have established Canons of Professional Ethics. The ABA has evolved the Model Code of Professional Responsibility. Also, all defense counsels are under an obligation to avoid the appearance of impropriety. Attorneys who violate one or more of these ethical codes are subject to varying degrees of sanctions, including possible loss of membership and disbarment proceedings, depending upon the seriousness and nature of the ethical code violation.

There exists an attorney–client confidentiality privilege between the defendant and his/her counsel, and prosecutors may not seek to violate this confidentiality by any means. Some convicted offenders may challenge their convictions and allege ineffective assistance of counsel. The U.S. Supreme Court has articulated standards governing what conduct rises to the level of incompetence and what conduct doesn't. Under *Strickland v. Washington* (1984), ineffective assistance of counsel occurs whenever counsel's behavior undermines the adversarial process to the extent that the trial outcome is unreliable, and/or if the counsel's conduct is unreasonable to the extent that the jury verdict would have been different otherwise.

Both actions and inactions on the part of defense counsel may rise to the level of ineffective assistance of counsel. These counsels may say or do something to jeopardize one's case, or they may fail to do important tasks with the same result. Most defendants alleging ineffective assistance of counsel find that it is difficult to sustain such charges against their attorneys if convicted of a crime.

The standards governing whether defendants are entitled to a jury trial have been clarified by the U.S. Supreme Court. If defendants are in jeopardy of being incarcerated for a period of beyond six months, they are entitled to a jury trial with one exception. This exception is if the judge assures the defendant that he/she will not suffer loss of liberty of beyond six months if a bench trial is conducted and finds the defendant guilty.

For indigent defendants who cannot afford counsel, each state and the federal government has established methods for assigning defense counsel to such defendants. The most common types of systems include the public defender system, the assigned counsel system, and the contract system. Under the public defender system, state- or county-funded public defender agencies are established and staffed with defense counsels who are assigned to indigent criminal cases.

The assigned counsel system is used in about one-fourth of all states. Often the jurisdictions where the assigned counsel system is operative are sparsely populated and there are few attorneys. The local bar association rotates defense counsel duties among its membership, and the payment for one's services as defense counsel for indigents is modest.

Under the contract system, different law firms in more urban jurisdictions will submit bids to the state or county specifying how much they will charge per client per day to represent indigents. County or state agencies will award contracts to these firms according to varying criteria, most often associated with the lowest cost to the government.

One commonality is that all forms of defense for indigents lack financial sources equivalent to those of private law firms that are retained by more affluent clients.

Lacking financial resources greatly restricts public defenders from conducting their own thorough investigations, and thus, the generalization is frequently made that indigent representation by public defenders or assigned counsel is not as effective as representation by private counsel. The literature suggests that there is often a factual basis for this generalization, given the outcomes of many indigent criminal cases.

Criminal defense attorneys perform various duties and have several important functions. Several of these duties and functions relate closely to the ethical codes of conduct or canons of professional responsibility of their professional organizations. Defense counsels must represent their clients faithfully and vigorously, within the boundaries of the law. They must attack the prosecution's case and do their best to show the innocence of their defendants.

In cases where there is overwhelming evidence of defendant guilt, it is the defense counsel's responsibility to secure the minimum punishment for their clients through plea bargaining (Fisher 2000). This means that defense counsels must consult with prosecutors and agree on a plea and a punishment. Judges approve all plea agreements contemplated between the defense and the prosecution.

Some defense counsels may engage in unethical or illegal practices when defending their clients. While it is permissible to coach clients who will testify in court in their own behalf, it is illegal to suggest to clients that they commit perjury on the witness stand. This is subornation of perjury, and if it is detected, defense counsels may be charged with a crime and prosecuted.

Also, like prosecutors, defense counsels are forbidden from making certain statements in court that are inadmissible and may prejudice the jury (Cook, Arndt, and Lieberman 2004). For instance, it is improper for defense counsels to mention the results of lie detector or polygraph tests administered to their clients by law enforcement personnel, even if those results are exculpatory.

Defense attorneys must be responsible and seek discovery of any and all information about the crime and the defendant in the possession of prosecutors and police. Some of this information is not discoverable, but much of it is. Obtaining this information usually benefits criminal clients in different ways.

Materials subject to discovery include confessions, transcripts of interviews between police interrogators and the defendant, psychological test results, and other materials. These discoverable materials are called Brady materials or Jencks materials after the U.S. Supreme Court cases where such materials were declared discoverable.

Different types of evidence may be presented during a criminal trial. Evidence may be direct or circumstantial. Direct evidence is usually the most damaging, and it is either eyewitness testimony or incriminating fingerprint evidence (Schram, Koons-Witt, and Morash 2004). Circumstantial evidence is less compelling, but it is nevertheless important. In murder cases, for instance, bodies of victims are sometimes never discovered. Nevertheless, there may be substantial circumstantial evidence showing defendant guilt. Evidence may also be corroborated by other persons. This assists prosecutors in building their cases against defendants (Matthews, Pease, and Pease 2001).

Defendants and their attorneys have available to them a variety of defenses to criminal conduct. These defenses are often known as affirmative defenses. One type of affirmative defense is automatism or insanity. The argument is that the defendant was incapable of formulating criminal intent or lacked the *mens rea* to understand what he/she was doing was wrong.

The insanity defense isn't used often, and when it is used, it is often not used successfully. Legislatures have modified the insanity defense standard so that today, many jurisdictions allow defendants to plead guilty but mentally ill. This type of plea usually lessens the harshness of their punishment (McSherry 2004).

Other affirmative defenses include intoxication, coercion or duress, necessity, and alibi. Some defendants claim that they were intoxicated at the time the crime was committed. This is sometimes considered a mitigating circumstance, although most jurisdictions consider intoxication to be a voluntary condition and merely consider it as a minor contributing factor.

Coercion or duress means that the defendant was made to commit the crime by means of a threat. The defense of necessity means that the crime was committed because it was necessary to do so. Someone who breaks into a neighbor's home late at night to put out a fire may claim necessity later if charged with breaking and entering.

Alibi as a defense means that the defendant alleges he/she was elsewhere when the crime was committed. Usually one or more persons will testify as to one's alibi if it is used as an affirmative defense.

Other affirmative defenses include entrapment, defense of property, ignorance or mistake, and self-defense. Entrapment occurs when someone is encouraged to break the law, usually by some law enforcement officer acting in an undercover capacity, and it is not customary for the defendant to engage in such criminal behavior.

Defense of property may be a defense if it can be shown that the defendant was merely defending his/her property from damage, intrusion, or theft by another. Some trespassers have been shot by home owners who later claim defense of property. In certain states, this affirmative defense is successful.

The defense of ignorance or mistake is sometimes used. While ignorance of the law may be claimed, it is usually insufficient to excuse a violation of the law. But sometimes defendants make an honest mistake and violate the law. On income tax returns, for instance, some persons may avoid criminal prosecution for income tax evasion if they are ignorant of the tax laws in some way or if they make a genuine mistake. This situation is almost always a judgment call by either the judge or jury.

Finally, some defendants allege that they were acting in self-defense. Self-defense is usually a good affirmative defense if it can be shown that the victim's behavior was menacing, potentially lethal, and could not be avoided. The use of one or more of these defenses is available to any defense attorney when representing a client in criminal court. In jury trials, juries must decide whether to believe the defendant when such defenses are alleged to account for his/her criminal conduct.

Questions for Review

1. What are five defenses to criminal conduct? Explain in each case how each might be used.
2. What are the general rules governing discovery? What is discovery and what are its purposes?
3. Under what circumstances are criminal defendants entitled to an attorney? Under what circumstances are defendants entitled to a jury trial? What are some leading legal cases having to do with the right to counsel and to jury trials?
4. What is meant by ineffective assistance of counsel? What are some leading cases where ineffectiveness of counsel is defined?
5. What are some major canons of ethics that are a part of the ABA Model Code of Professional Responsibility? Why are they important?
6. What is meant by the courtroom work group and who makes up its key components? Why is it important for defense attorneys to work closely with the courtroom work group?
7. What are several forms of legal aid for indigent defendants?
8. Are court-appointed counsels as effective as privately retained counsel when representing criminal defendants? Why or why not? Explain.
9. Compare the assigned counsel system with the contract system. What are the different benefits of each?
10. What is meant by defense misconduct? What are some different forms of defense misconduct?
11. What is meant by subornation of perjury?
12. What is meant by a Brady violation?
13. Who bears the burden of proof in criminal prosecutions? Under due process, what can be assumed about the guilt or innocence of the accused?
14. Can defendants be convicted of crimes solely on the basis of circumstantial evidence? Why or why not? Explain. Give an example.

Suggested Readings

1. A. Hollander, M. Jacobsson, and S. Sjöström (2007). "Defender, Spokesperson, Therapist: Representing the True Interest of the Client in Therapeutic Law." *International Journal of Social Welfare* **16**:373–381.
2. Robert Boyle, Donna R. Newman, and Sam A. Schmidt (2003). "Center for Professional Values and Practice Symposium: Criminal Defense in the Age of Terrorism." *New York Law School Law Review* **48**:3–384.
3. B. H. Brummer (2009). "The Banality of Excessive Defender Workload: Managing the Systemic Obstruction of Justice." *St. Thomas Law Review* **22**:104–195.
4. Whitley Kaufman (2004). "Is There a 'Right' to Self-Defense?" *Criminal Justice Ethics* **23**:20–32.
5. Daniel A. Krauss and Bruce D. Sales (2001). "The Effects of Clinical and Scientific Expert Testimony on Juror Decision Making in Capital Sentencing." *Psychology, Public Policy and the Law* **7**:267–310.
6. N. L. Piquero and J. L. Davis (2004). "Extralegal Factors and the Sentencing of Organizational Defendants: An Examination of the Federal Sentencing Guidelines." *Journal of Criminal Justice* **32**:643–654.
7. Alison Dundes Rentelm (2004). *The Cultural Defense.* New York: Oxford University Press.
8. John Wooldredge and Amy Thistlewaite (2004). "Bilevel Disparities in Court Dispositions for Intimate Assault." *Criminology* **42**:417–456.

CHAPTER **5**

Judges

CHAPTER OBJECTIVES

As a result of reading this chapter, you will have accomplished the following objectives:

1. Understand the different kinds of judges and the diversity of their powers.
2. Understand the qualifications a judge must have in order to sit on the bench.
3. Describe the different judicial selection methods including partisan and nonpartisan elections, gubernatorial appointment, merit selection, and legislative appointment.
4. Describe the advantages and disadvantages with each type of judicial selection method.
5. Understand which method of selection is best for selection of judges.
6. Describe the different methods of judicial training, and standardization of qualifications.
7. Describe the different types of judicial misconduct and abuses of discretion.
8. Understand some of the current criticisms of judges and the ways in which judges can be removed from office.

KEY TERMS

bureaucracy	incumbents	judicial powers	nonpartisan elections
centralization	interim judges	judicial process	Operation Greylord
confidentiality	judge	Kales Plan	partisan elections
harmful errors	judicial appointments	merit selection	recall election
impeachment	judicial conduct commission	Missouri Plan	reversible errors

It happened in New Mexico. The state supreme court allowed a metropolitan judge to retire, which ended judicial misconduct investigations of her. A host of allegations were lodged against Judge Victoria Grant for putting defendants in jail because they did not hire an attorney, disallowing other defendants to represent themselves, and not allowing a public defender to cross-examine the only witness in a case. When the public defender objected, the Judge retorted "Appeal Me." Grant had been on the bench for 14 years and will retire through an agreement which will end the investigations but stipulate that she cannot run for judicial office ever again. Why would a veteran judge make such outrageous decisions which clearly violate important rules of law? In some jurisdictions, the qualifications to be a judge are very minimal. Should there be more strict requirements for being seated as a judge such as law degrees or some type of prior legal experience? Should there be more judicial training for elected judges who do not have much legal experience?

Source: Adapted from *The Albuquerque Journal*, "Courts Allow Judge to Retire: Misconduct Probe Closed; Rights Violations Alleged," May 15, 2010.

INTRODUCTION

There are many different kinds of judges with diverse amounts of **judicial powers**. The public has several general conceptions about judges and what they are supposed to do. But many of these conceptions are actually misconceptions. For instance, we usually think of a judge as being an ultimate arbiter, a ruler over courtroom proceedings, and the person responsible for meting out punishments. Although a judge is all of these things, in some instances the judge does not have as much education, training, or discretion as we may think.

This chapter examines judges and their qualifications. There is great variation among judges in the United States in their backgrounds, the legal expertise, and how they became judges. Not all judges have the same degree of legal expertise, nor are all judges lawyers or possess law degrees. They differ greatly in their personalities and idiosyncrasies. They have many prejudices and limitations. More than a few persons are interested in how certain persons in our society become judges, and how they come to make decisions. Spohn (2002) speaks of judges sometimes playing a leading role and at other times only a supportive role. Spohn points out that in the sentencing process, for instance, a number of persons are involved. For example, the legislature enacts legislation regarding sentencing, the prosecutor decides which charges to file, a jury may be involved in conviction or acquittal, a probation officer may recommend a sentence to a judge through a presentence investigation report, and then the judge has the responsibility for deciding a sentence. This chapter will describe the judicial selection process in different jurisdictions. Some judges are elected, others are appointed, and still others reach the bench through a merit selection process. This chapter will also discuss the advantages and disadvantages of each of these methods for judicial selection.

The next section of the chapter discusses judicial training. All judges are bound by certain rules that are integral to a court's efficiency and effectiveness. Judges sometimes, however, make decisions that are reversed by a higher court, or sometimes judges allow evidence that should have been inadmissible. The judge decides what is or is not relevant testimony. The judge uses these rules and these decisions to control the trials that come into the courtroom. Some judges are not learned in law; as such, there have been criticisms of some of their decisions, as well as blaming them for court delays. Most jurisdictions now have special training that most judges must go through to make them better able to manage their court caseload.

Because there is great variation in the quality of the judiciary throughout all U.S. jurisdictions, the nature of judicial appointments will be examined. In recent years, the judiciary has come under close scrutiny by various interests and agencies, and some evidence of judicial misconduct has surfaced. Sentiments beginning in the 1980s that judges were too lenient in sentencing have led many jurisdictions to fetter the discretion that some judges enjoy by implementing determinate sentencing and guideline sentencing structures. Some of these abuses of discretionary powers will be presented. Selected criticisms of judges will be provided, together with an examination of several relevant judicial issues.

JUDGES AND THEIR QUALIFICATIONS

In any courtroom, the key figure is the **judge**. Judges make decisions that affect the lives of defendants. All judges have certain rules to follow that are an integral feature of **judicial process**. Sometimes judges make decisions that are reversed by higher courts. A judge may allow the introduction of incriminating evidence against a defendant, or the judge may decide to exclude such evidence. The judge decides what is or is not relevant testimony. The judge controls the conduct of all trials.

It is a common misconception among citizens that all judges are lawyers and have legal expertise. However, in numerous jurisdictions throughout the United States, many judges have no legal training and are not former lawyers. One implication is that in many jurisdictions, judicial selection is more a matter of politics than judicial expertise. The political nature of judicial selection has its roots in seventeenth-century England. In 2004, the minimum age for appellate and trial court judgeships ranged from 18 to 35 years (Rottman and Strickland 2006, 29–32 and 40–45). These minimum-age requirements are somewhat deceptive, since it might appear that an 18-year-old might qualify as an appellate or trial court judge. States with these minimum-age provisions eliminate this possibility by requiring their prospective judges to be members of the state bar association for five or ten years or longer. Thus, it is inconceivable that any 18-year-old would ever hold a judicial post in these states where 18 is the minimum age. Almost every state requires judicial candidates for these posts to be members of the state bar association for specified periods.

About half of the states in 1998 did not require U.S. citizenship for persons to hold appellate or trial judge posts. Furthermore, the years of residence within the state to qualify for a judicial post varied from one year to ten years. More than a few states had no provisions for minimum residence times for either appellate or trial court judges (Maguire and Pastore 2005). Some states specified certain personal characteristics as qualifications, including good moral character, sobriety of manners, integrity, wisdom, and sound legal knowledge. Thus, there is considerable variation among the states about the qualifications of judicial candidates.

The Politicalization of Judicial Selection

The politicalization of the judicial selection process cannot be overstated. When politics is the dominating factor in judicial appointments, one's qualifications for a judgeship are practically irrelevant. Whether a partisan election or a gubernatorial or a presidential appointment leads to one's becoming a judge, the result is often a judicial appointment that reflects party politics rather than one's professional qualities for deciding cases fairly. This doesn't mean that political judicial appointees are incapable of being fair in judging cases, but rather, they are expected to adhere to a fixed political agenda associated with the party placing them in power (Pinello 1995).

Political influence also works to the detriment of women in judicial appointments. Gender bias has been found in more than a few systems whereby judges are appointed by politicians and women are routinely excluded from judicial consideration. Several critics argue that political appointments of judges place too much power in the hands of the appointer, such as the governor or president (Tomasi and Velona 1987). Politically appointed judges have considerably lower levels of accountability, and weak sanctioning mechanisms are in place for the discipline or removal. Those who oppose elections of judges say that voter apathy and disinterest, political influence, and a general lack of information about candidates and their qualifications make this process meaningless.

President Jimmy Carter created nominating commissions for federal circuit courts and district courts. Under Carter's administration, judicial appointees were more likely to have professional experience, age and years at the bar, a legal education, and higher American Bar Association (ABA) ratings compared with subsequent Reagan appointees. Subsequently, President Reagan discontinued the nominating commission method of judicial appointments.

President Clinton appointed the highest percentage of females to the bench; 28.5 percent were female. Clinton also appointed an increased number of racial and ethnic minorities; 17.4 percent were African American and 5.9 percent were Hispanic (Maguire and Pastore 2005, 75). Roughly 67 percent of President George W. Bush's appointees were white males, 8 percent were African American, and 5 percent were Hispanic (Wheeler 2010). President Obama has appointed more female and minority judges thus far with 27 percent of his appointees being white women, 25 percent African American, 7 percent Hispanic, and about 11 percent Asian (Wheeler 2010).

Early research about the qualities of judicial applicants has shown that nominating commissions have identified the following criteria for their judicial selections: age, health, impartiality, integrity, judicial temperament, industry, professional skills, community contacts, social awareness, collegiality, writing ability, and decisiveness and speaking ability (Greenstein and Sampson 2004). However, no precise guidelines have been established to indicate how these qualities should be measured or assessed. There is historical precedent for these ambiguities relevant to the judicial selection process. In early England, for example, much secrecy was involved in the process of selecting judges (Pickles 1987). Judicial selection criteria were purposely diffuse and ambiguous, so that only conservative types of persons could hold judicial posts. These persons were often manipulated by politically influential constituencies (Pickles 1987).

In selected jurisdictions, model guidelines have been generated to assist judges in learning about courtroom protocol and the diverse functions of courtroom personnel. For instance, the National Center for State Courts in Williamsburg, Virginia, has produced a resource manual that is designed to enhance the performance of trial judges (Hewitt 1995). The manual includes a discussion of terminology interpretation, judicial training issues, and general court interpreter services.

Reforms relating to judicial selection are not new. Aggressive court reforms have been undertaken for many decades, as different waves of state and federal judges have manifested characteristics that suggest inexperience and ineffectiveness. Many formal recruitment and judicial selection systems have been proposed, but relatively few have come up with any conclusive data indicating the kinds of qualitative differences that might result from alternative selection systems. Interviews with judges themselves suggest mixed reactions to any type of selection system, whether it is through appointment or election (Johnson 2004).

State Judicial Selection Methods

Judges are either appointed or elected. Alfini (1981, 253) has identified five methods of judicial selection as basic variations on appointments or elections: (1) partisan election, (2) nonpartisan election, (3) gubernatorial appointment, (4) selection through the merit plan, and (5) legislative appointments.

PARTISAN ELECTIONS   **Partisan elections** of judges are the same as elections for other public offices. Democrats, Republicans, and others advance their own slate of candidates for various offices, including judicial vacancies. The public votes for their choice by secret ballot. Persons who win these elections become judges for a fixed term, such as four years. In 2004, the following eight states used partisan elections for selecting the highest appellate judges: Alabama, Illinois, Louisiana, New Mexico, Ohio, Pennsylvania, Texas, and West Virginia (Rottman and Strickland 2006).

NONPARTISAN ELECTIONS   In **nonpartisan elections**, candidates are simply listed to fill judicial vacancies regardless of their political affiliation. In 2004, 14 states used nonpartisan elections to fill the highest appellate court posts. These states included Arkansas, Georgia, Idaho, Kentucky, Michigan, Minnesota, Mississippi, Montana, Nevada, North Carolina, North Dakota, Oregon, Washington, and Wisconsin (Rottman and Strickland 2006, 25–28).

PROBLEMS WITH PARTISAN AND NONPARTISAN ELECTIONS OF JUDGES   There are several problems with electing judges by popular vote. One criticism is whether either partisan or nonpartisan elections actually reflect the people's choices. Usually, some amount of private financing is behind each judicial candidate. The slate of candidates is generated by different political parties and special-interest groups, regardless of whether elections are partisan or nonpartisan. Thus, those persons who are placed on the ballot may not be the persons most likely to represent the interests of the general public.

But despite the partisan nature of judicial voting, there is evidence to indicate that an attentive public is out there who make informed selections of judges in their voting booths. Interestingly, investigations of voter knowledge of the judicial selection process show that while voters may not understand fully the nature of voting reforms, they are informed about the opinions and views of the respective judicial candidates (Pinello 1995).

By contrast, research has shown that depending upon the section of the country where judicial selections are made, there is significant partisanship in public voting. For instance, in the South, the Democratic Party has been successful most of the time in the promotion of partisan judicial candidates. Many incumbents in southern criminal courts have been re-elected repeatedly, reflecting the public's interest in maintaining the status quo for both major and minor judgeships. Other areas of the country exhibit strong differences from the South, such as the moralistic and individualistic political culture of the West. Less money is spent on campaign financing for judicial elections in the West compared with the South. Despite the differential impact of money spent, the overriding variable influencing the outcomes of judicial elections in almost every jurisdiction was the party affiliation.

Perhaps the most significant criticism of using elections for filling judicial vacancies is that the most popular judges may not be the most qualified judges. One's political influence may take precedence over one's competence to be a judge. There are no objective criteria used to evaluate one's judicial qualifications. Most jurisdictions do not require judges to pass tests or engage in any sort of qualifying competition for these important posts. Those elected to judicial positions but who lack judging experience are often sent to schools offering crash courses on how to act like judges. These schools attempt to familiarize judges with the rules of criminal procedure and the rules of evidence associated with their jurisdictions. But it is doubtful that any short course on judge-making can bring an unlearned judge to the point where he/she possesses the competence and experience to make the best decisions in important criminal cases. But for better or worse, partisan and nonpartisan elections are prevalent in most states, and it is unlikely that these states will change their methods of judicial selection in the near future. Other methods for judicial selection, judicial appointments by executives, are equally flawed.

Appointments of Judges by Governors

In 2004, governors made the highest appellate **judicial appointments** in four states: California, Maine, New Hampshire, and New Jersey (Maguire and Pastore 2005, 83). Governors may or may not make use of state and local bar association recommendations for judgeships. Gubernatorial appointments are not necessarily made on the basis of which judges are best qualified to serve. Rather, these judgeships are political appointments. Thus, major contributors to a governor's election campaign make recommendations to the governor for particular judgeships, and quite often, these recommendations result in particular judges being appointed (Pinello 1995).

In many other jurisdictions, persons campaign for judgeships much as candidates run for political offices. In fact, politics is the primary contributing factor that accounts for large numbers of nonlawyers in posts such as municipal judges, justices of the peace, and county court judges. There has been considerable debate about whether judges should be appointed or elected, although no judicial selection method has been found superior to others. Some researchers have observed that gubernatorial judicial appointments in certain jurisdictions result in racial or gender bias in judicial decision making (Pinello 1995).

A study was conducted in 1980–1981 of state supreme court judicial selection according to gubernatorial appointments or merit plans. Questionnaires were mailed to political science professors, judges, and court administrators in each state (Glick and Emmert 1987). On the basis of responses, researchers were able to describe and compare judges selected by different methods. Most judges selected by governors rather than the merit system tended to be born out of state, although these judges were from similar regions (e.g., southern governors tended to appoint southern judges, northern governors tended to appoint northern judges). The merit system, however, resulted in selecting judges who graduated from more prestigious law schools (e.g., Harvard, Yale, Columbia) compared with those who were governor-appointed. Protestant judges were more abundant in southern courts, while Catholic and Jewish judges were more prevalent in northern and eastern courts (Glick and Emmert 1987). One interesting outcome of this study was that merit selection tended to result in fewer appointments of women and minorities as judges. Thus, gubernatorial appointments are more likely to yield selections from women and minorities as political considerations. Tables 5-1 to 5-3 show the method of selection and length and retention terms of the highest state appellate court justices, intermediate appellate court judges, and judges in courts of general jurisdiction.

Table 5-1 shows that of June 2004, 6 states used partisan elections for selecting judges, while 14 states used nonpartisan elections. Twenty-five states used nominating commissions, while governors appointed judges in four states. Only one state used a legislative appointment (Maguire and Pastore 2005, 83–87). Judicial terms for state supreme court justices range from 6 to 15 years, although in three states (Massachusetts, New Hampshire, and Rhode Island), these selections are for life or until age 70 is reached. Most of these states have retention elections following the different judicial terms.

Table 5-2 shows the method of selection, length of term, and retention process for state intermediate appellate court judges. For the most part, the selection methods for intermediate judiciary are the same as for state supreme court justices. However, the terms of intermediate appellate judges are somewhat shorter, ranging from 6 to 12 years with a median. Most of these states also have retention elections following the different judicial terms similar to those held for supreme court justices (Maguire and Pastore 2005, 85).

Table 5-3 shows the method of selection and the length of initial and retention terms for state general jurisdiction judges. Over 30 of these states used partisan or nonpartisan elections for these judges in 1999. The terms of these general jurisdiction judges ranged from 4 to 15 years (Maguire and Pastore 2005, 86–87).

PROBLEMS WITH POLITICALLY APPOINTED JUDGES   Politically appointed judges raise several important issues, however. Some of these issues are the same as those raised in jurisdictions where partisan and nonpartisan elections are used to fill judicial vacancies. Are the most qualified persons selected for the judgeship? An investigation of elected and appointed judges for the California Superior Court from 1959 to 1977 compared their demographic characteristics, educational backgrounds, and pre-judicial career experiences (Dubois 1990). Of the 739 judges investigated, 662 of them had been appointed. Most of these had earlier careers as attorneys or had some previous legal experience. When their decisions were examined for technical accuracy and legal justification, however, no significant differences between elected or appointed judges were found (Dubois 1990). No conclusions could be made about which selection method was best when the quality of their judicial decision making was compared.

TABLE 5-1 Method of Selection and Length of Initial and Retention Terms of the Highest Appellate Court Justices

By state, as of June 2004

| State | Initial Selection | | Retention | |
	Method[a]	Term	Method	Term (in years)
Alabama	Partisan election	6 years	Partisan election	6
Alaska	Nominating commission	Until next general election but not less than 3 years	Retention election	10
Arizona	Nominating commission	Until next general election but not less than 2 years	Retention election	6
Arkansas	Nonpartisan election	8 years	Nonpartisan election	8
California	Appointed by governor	12 years	Retention election	12
Colorado	Nominating commission	Until next general election but not less than 2 years	Retention election	10
Connecticut	Nominating commission	8 years	Commission reviews, governor renominates, legislature confirms	8
Delaware	Nominating commission	12 years	Competitive reapplication to commission, reappointment by governor, Senate confirms	12
District of Columbia[b]	Nominating commission	15 years	Reappointment by judicial tenure commission or the president	15
Florida	Nominating commission	Until next general election but not less than 1 year	Retention election	6
Georgia	Nonpartisan election	6 years	Nonpartisan election	6
Hawaii	Nominating commission	10 years	Reappointment by commission	10
Idaho	Nonpartisan election	6 years	Nonpartisan election	6
Illinois	Partisan election	10 years	Retention election	10
Indiana	Nominating commission	Until next general election but not less than 2 years	Retention election	10
Iowa	Nominating commission	Until next general election but not less than 1 year	Retention election	8
Kansas	Nominating commission	Until next general election but not less than 1 year	Retention election	6
Kentucky	Nonpartisan election	8 years	Nonpartisan election	8
Louisiana[c]	Partisan election	10 years	Partisan election	10
Maine	Appointed by governor	7 years	Reappointment by governor, legislature confirms	7
Maryland[d]	Nominating commission	Until next general election but not less than 1 year	Retention election	10
Massachusetts	Nominating commission	To age 70	X	X
Michigan[e]	Nonpartisan election	8 years	Nonpartisan election	8

(continued)

91

TABLE 5-1 (Continued)

By state, as of June 2004

State	Initial Selection		Retention	
	Method	Term	Method	Term (in years)
Minnesota	Nonpartisan election	6 years	Nonpartisan election	6
Mississippi	Nonpartisan election	8 years	Nonpartisan election	8
Missouri	Nominating commission	Until next general election but not less than 1 year	Retention election	12
Montana	Nonpartisan election	8 years	Nonpartisan election, but if unopposed, retention election	8
Nebraska	Nominating commission	Until next general election but not less than 3 years	Retention election	6
Nevada	Nonpartisan election	6 years	Nonpartisan election	6
New Hampshire	Appointed by governor[f]	To age 70	X	X
New Jersey	Appointed by governor	7 years	Reappointment by governor, with Senate consent	To age 70
New Mexico	Nominating commission	Until next general election	Partisan election the first time; after that, winner runs in retention election	8
New York[d]	Nominating commission	14 years	Competitive reapplication to commission, reappointment by governor, Senate confirms	14
North Carolina	Nonpartisan election	8 years	Nonpartisan election	8
North Dakota	Nonpartisan election	10 years	Nonpartisan election	10
Ohio[g]	Nonpartisan election	6 years	Nonpartisan election	6
Oklahoma[h]	Nominating commission	Until next general election but not less than 1 year	Retention election	6
Oregon	Nonpartisan election	6 years	Nonpartisan election	6
Pennsylvania	Partisan election	10 years	Retention election	10
Rhode Island	Nominating commission	Life tenure	X	X
South Carolina	Nominating commission[i]	10 years	Reappointed by legislature	10
South Dakota	Nominating commission	Until next general election but not less than 3 years	Retention election	8
Tennessee	Nominating commission	Until the biennial general election but not less than 30 days	Retention election	8
Texas[h]	Partisan election	6 years	Partisan election	6
Utah	Nominating commission	Until next general election but not less than 3 years	Retention election	10
Vermont	Nominating commission	6 years	Retained by vote in general assembly	6

Virginia	Appointed by legislature	12 years	Reappointed by legislature	12
Washington	Nonpartisan election	6 years	Nonpartisan election	6
West Virginia	Partisan election	12 years	Partisan election	12
Wisconsin	Nonpartisan election	10 years	Nonpartisan election	10
Wyoming	Nominating commission	Until next general election but not less than 1 year	Retention election	8

Note: These data were compiled through a survey of state statutes; they were then verified by personnel of the American Judicature Society.

"Initial selection" is defined as the constitutional or statutory method by which judges are selected for a full term of office. "Retention" refers to the method used to select judges for subsequent terms of office. "Partisan election" refers to elections in which the constitutional or statutory method by which the judicial candidates' names appear on the ballot with their respective party labels; "nonpartisan election" refers to elections in which no party labels are attached to judicial candidates' names appearing on the ballot. Caution should be used when interpreting partisan and nonpartisan designations as definitions may vary. "Retention election" refers to an election in which a judge runs unopposed on the ballot and the electorate votes solely on the question of the judge's continuation in office. In a retention election, the judge must win a majority of the vote in order to serve a full term, except in Illinois, which requires 60 percent, and New Mexico, which requires 57 percent. "Nominating commission" is a merit selection procedure that refers to the nonpartisan body, composed of lawyers and nonlawyers, which actively recruits, screens, and nominates prospective judicial candidates to the executive for appointment. The nominating commission method of selection was established by executive order in Delaware, Maryland, and Massachusetts and by constitutional or statutory authority in all other jurisdictions. Readers should consult State Constitutions for special provisions and procedures related to issues of premature vacancy (e.g., death, resignation) and other circumstances.

[a]In states that use nominating commissions, selection requirements may vary. The governor may make the appointment solely, with Senate confirmation, or with legislative confirmation.

[b]Initial appointment is made by the president of the United States and confirmed by the Senate. At expiration of term, judge's performance is reviewed by the commission. Those found "well qualified" are automatically reappointed. For those found "qualified," the president may nominate for an additional term, subject to Senate confirmation. If the president does not wish to reappoint the judge, the District of Columbia Nomination Commission compiles a new list of candidates.

[c]Although party affiliation of judicial candidates appears on ballots, judicial primaries are open and candidates generally do not solicit party support. This gives judicial elections a nonpartisan character.

[d]The highest state court is named the Court of Appeals.

[e]Party affiliations of judicial candidates are not listed on the general election ballot, so the election is technically nonpartisan. However, candidates are nominated at party conventions.

[f]Subject to approval of an elected five-member executive council.

[g]Party affiliations of judicial candidates are not listed on the general election ballot, so the election is technically nonpartisan. However, candidates run in partisan primary elections.

[h]Oklahoma and Texas have two courts of final jurisdiction: the supreme court, which has final civil jurisdiction; and the court of criminal appeals, which has final criminal jurisdiction. The selection process is the same for both.

[i]The Judicial Merit Selection Commission screens and then recommends a list of judicial candidates to the legislature. The legislature votes only on the list submitted by the commission. If all candidates on the list are rejected, the process begins again with the commission.

Source: American Judicature Society, *Judicial Selection in the United States: A Compendium of Provisions*, 2nd edition (Chicago: American Judicature Society, 1993), http://www.ajs.org/js/judicialselectioncharts.pdf (January 25, 2005); and data provided by the American Judicature Society.

TABLE 5-2 Method of Selection and Length of Initial and Retention Terms of Intermediate Appellate Court Judges in 39 States

As of June 2004

State	Initial Selection		Retention	
	Method[a]	Term	Method	Term (in years)
Alabama[b]	Partisan election	6 years	Partisan election	6
Alaska	Nominating commission	Until next general election but not less than 3 years	Retention election	8
Arizona	Nominating commission	Until next general election but not less than 2 years	Retention election	6
Arkansas	Nonpartisan election	8 years	Nonpartisan election	8
California	Appointed governor	12 years	Retention election	12
Colorado	Nominating commission	Until next general election but not less than 2 years	Retention election	8
Connecticut	Nominating commission	8 years	Commission reviews, governor renominates, legislature confirms	8
Florida	Nominating commission	Until next general election but not less than 1 year	Retention election	6
Georgia	Nonpartisan election	6 years	Nonpartisan election	6
Hawaii	Nominating commission	10 years	Reappointment by commission	10
Idaho	Nonpartisan election	6 years	Nonpartisan election	6
Illinois	Partisan election	10 years	Retention election	10
Indiana	Nominating commission	Until next general election but not less than 2 years	Retention election	10
Iowa	Nominating commission	Until next general election but not less than 1 year	Retention election	6
Kansas	Nominating commission	Until next general election but not less than 1 year	Retention election	4
Kentucky	Nonpartisan election	8 years	Nonpartisan election	8
Louisiana[c]	Partisan election	10 years	Partisan election	10
Maryland	Nominating commission	Until next general election but not less than 1 year	Retention election	10
Massachusetts	Nominating commission	To age 70	X	X
Michigan	Nonpartisan election	6 years	Nonpartisan election	6
Minnesota	Nonpartisan election	6 years	Nonpartisan election	6
Mississippi	Nonpartisan election	8 years	Nonpartisan election	8
Missouri	Nominating commission	Until next general election but not less than 1 year	Retention election	12
Nebraska	Nominating commission	Until next general election but not less than 3 years	Retention election	6
New Jersey	Appointed by governor	7 years	Reappointment by governor with Senate consent	To age 70

State	Initial selection	Term	Retention	Subsequent term (years)
New Mexico	Nominating commission	Until next general election	Partisan election the first time: after that, winner runs in retention election	8
New York	Nominating commission	5 years	Commission reviews, makes recommendation to governor, governor reappoints	5
North Carolina	Nonpartisan election	8 years	Nonpartisan election	8
Ohio[d]	Nonpartisan election	6 years	Nonpartisan election	6
Oklahoma	Nominating commission	Until next general election but not less than 1 year	Retention election	6
Oregon	Nonpartisan election	6 years	Nonpartisan election	6
Pennsylvania[e]	Partisan election	10 years	Retention election	10
South Carolina	Nominating commission[f]	6 years	Reappointed by legislature	6
Tennessee[b]	Nominating commission	Until the biennial general election but not less than 30 days	Retention election	8
Texas	Partisan election	6 years	Partisan election	6
Utah	Nominating commission	Until next general election but not less than 3 years	Retention election	6
Virginia	Appointed by legislature	8 years	Reappointed by legislature	8
Washington	Nonpartisan election	6 years	Nonpartisan election	6
Wisconsin	Nonpartisan election	6 years	Nonpartisan election	6

Note: States not listed do not have intermediate appellate courts.

[a]In states that use nominating commissions, selection requirements may vary. The governor makes the appointment solely, with Senate confirmation, or with legislative confirmation.

[b]Alabama and Tennessee have two intermediate appellate courts: the court of civil appeals, which has civil jurisdiction, and the court of criminal appeals, which has criminal jurisdiction. The selection process is the same for both.

[c]Although party affiliation of judicial candidates appears on ballots, judicial primaries are open and candidates generally do not solicit party support. This gives judicial elections a nonpartisan character.

[d]Party affiliations of judicial candidates are not listed on the general election ballots, so the election is technically nonpartisan. However, candidates run in partisan primary elections.

[e]Pennsylvania has two intermediate appellate courts; the superior court and the commonwealth court. The selection process is the same for both.

[f]The Judicial Merit Selection Commission screens and then recommends a list of judicial candidates to the legislature. The legislature votes only on the list submitted by the commission. If all candidates on the list are rejected, the process begins again with the commission.

Source: American Judicature Society, *Judicial Selection in the United States: A Compendium of Provisions*, 2nd edition (Chicago: American Judicature Society, 1993), http://www.ajs.org/js/judicialselectioncharts.pdf (January 25, 2005); and data provided by the American Judicature Society. Reprinted by permission.

TABLE 5-3 Method of Selection and Length of Initial and Retention Terms of General Jurisdiction Court Judges

By state and name of court, as of June 2004

State/Name of Court(s)	Initial Selection		Retention	
	Method[a]	Term	Method	Term (in years)
Alabama				
Circuit court	Partisan election	6 years	Partisan election	6
Alaska				
Superior court	Nominating commission	Until next general election but not less than 3 years	Retention election	6
Arizona				
Superior court[b]	Nominating commission	Until next general election but not less than 2 years	Retention election	4
Arkansas				
Circuit court	Nonpartisan election	6 years	Nonpartisan election	6
California				
Superior court	Nonpartisan election or gubernatorial appointment[c]	6 years	Nonpartisan election[d]	6
Colorado				
District court	Nominating commission	Until next general election but not less than 2 years	Retention election	6
Connecticut				
Superior court	Nominating commission	8 years	Commission reviews, governor renominates, legislature confirms	8
Delaware				
Superior court	Nominating commission	12 years	Competitive reapplication to commission, reappointment by governor, Senate confirms	12
District of Columbia				
Superior court[e]	Nominating commission	15 years	Reappointment by judicial tenure commission or the president	15
Florida				
Circuit court[f]	Nonpartisan election	6 years	Nonpartisan election	6

State / Court	Initial selection	Term	Retention	
Georgia				
Superior court	Nonpartisan election	4 years	Nonpartisan election	4
Hawaii				
Circuit court	Nominating commission	10 years	Reappointment by commission	10
Idaho				
District court	Nonpartisan election	4 years	Nonpartisan election	4
Illinois				
Circuit court	Partisan election[g]	6 years	Retention election	6
Indiana				
Circuit court	Partisan election[h]	6 years	Partisan election[h]	6
Superior court	Partisan election[i]	6 years[j]	Partisan election[k]	6
Iowa				
District court	Nominating commission	Until next general election but not less than 1 year	Retention election	6
Kansas				
District court	Nominating commission, partisan election[l]	Until next general election	Retention election[m]	4
Kentucky				
Circuit court	Nonpartisan election	8 years	Nonpartisan election	8
Louisiana[n]				
District court	Partisan election	6 years	Partisan election	6
Maine				
Superior court	Appointed by governor	7 years	Reappointment by governor, legislature confirms	7
Maryland				
Circuit court	Nominating commission	Until next general election but not less than 1 year	Nonpartisan election	15
Massachusetts				
Trial Court of the Commonwealth	Nominating commission	To age 70	X	X
Minnesota				
District court	Nonpartisan election	6 years	Nonpartisan election	6

(continued)

TABLE 5-3 *(Continued)*

By state and name of court, as of June 2004

State/Name of Court(s)	Initial Selection		Retention		Term (in years)
	Method	Term	Method		
Mississippi					
Circuit court	Nonpartisan election	4 years	Nonpartisan election		4
Chancery court	Nonpartisan election	4 years	Nonpartisan election		4
Missouri					
Circuit court	Partisan election[o]	6 years[p]	Partisan election[q]		6
Montana					
District court	Nonpartisan election	6 years	Nonpartisan election, but if unopposed, retention election		6
Nebraska					
District court	Nominating commission	Until next general election but not less than 3 years	Retention election		6
Nevada					
District court	Nonpartisan election	6 years	Nonpartisan election		6
New Hampshire					
Superior court	Appointed by governor[r]	To age 70	X		X
New Jersey					
Superior court	Appointed by governor	7 years	Reappointment by governor with Senate consent		To age 70
New Mexico					
District court	Nominating commission	Until next general election	Partisan election the first time: after that, winner runs in retention election		6
New York					
Supreme court	Partisan election	14 years	Partisan election		14
County court	Partisan election	10 years	Partisan election		10
North Carolina					
Superior court	Nonpartisan election	8 years	Nonpartisan election		8
North Dakota					
District court	Nonpartisan election	6 years	Nonpartisan election		6

State / Court	Initial selection	Term	Retention	
Ohio[s]				
Common pleas court	Nonpartisan election	6 years	Nonpartisan election	6
Oklahoma				
District court	Nonpartisan election	4 years	Nonpartisan election	4
Oregon				
Circuit court	Nonpartisan election	6 years	Nonpartisan election	6
Pennsylvania				
Common Pleas court	Partisan election	10 years	Retention election	10
Rhode Island				
Superior court	Nominating commission	Life tenure	X	X
South Carolina				
Circuit court	Nominating commission[t]	6 years	Reappointed by legislature	6
South Dakota				
Circuit court	Nonpartisan election	8 years	Nonpartisan election	8
Tennessee				
Circuit court	Nominating commission	8 years	Partisan election	8
Texas				
District court	Partisan election	4 years	Partisan election	4
Utah				
District court	Nominating commission	Until next general election but not less than 3 years	Retention election	6
Vermont				
Superior court	Nominating commission	6 years	Retained by vote in general assembly	6
Virginia				
Circuit court	Appointed by legislature	8 years	Reappointed by legislature	8
Washington				
Superior court	Nonpartisan election	4 years	Nonpartisan election	4
West Virginia				
Circuit court	Partisan election	8 years	Partisan election	8

(continued)

TABLE 5-3 (Continued)

	By state and name of court, as of June 2004			
	Initial Selection		**Retention**	
State/Name of Court(s)	**Method**	**Term**	**Method**	**Term (in years)**
Wisconsin				
Circuit court	Nonpartisan election	6 years	Nonpartisan election	6
Wyoming				
District court	Nominating commission	Until next general election but not less than 1 year	Retention election	6

Note: Courts of general jurisdiction are defined as having unlimited civil and criminal jurisdiction (Larry C. Berkson, "Judicial Selection in the United States: A Special Report," *Judicature* 64 (October 1980) p. 178).

[a] In states that use nominating commissions, appointment procedures may vary. The governor may make the appointment solely, with Senate confirmation, or with legislative confirmation.

[b] Counties with populations less than 250,000 select and retain superior court judges in nonpartisan elections for four-year terms.

[c] Local electors can choose either nonpartisan elections or gubernatorial appointment.

[d] Judge must be elected to a full term on a nonpartisan ballot at the next general election. If the election is not contested, the incumbent's name does not appear on the ballot.

[e] Initial appointment is made by the president of the United States and confirmed by the Senate. At expiration of term, judge's performance is reviewed by the commission. Those found "well qualified" are automatically reappointed. For those found "qualified," the president may nominate for an additional term, subject to Senate confirmation. If the president does not wish to reappoint the judge, the District of Columbia Nomination Commission compiles a new list of candidates.

[f] Voters in each circuit may opt for merit selection and retention of circuit court judges.

[g] Circuit court associate judges are appointed by the circuit judges in each circuit for four-year terms, as provided by supreme court rule.

[h] In Vanderburgh County initial selection and retention are by nonpartisan election.

[i] A nominating commission is used for the superior court judges of Lake and St. Joseph Counties. In Allen and Vanderburgh Counties the election is nonpartisan.

[j] In Lake and St. Joseph Counties each appointed judge serves until the next general election but not less than two years.

[k] Nonpartisan elections are used in Allen and Vanderburgh Counties. Retention elections are used in Lake and St. Joseph Counties.

[l] Seventeen of 31 districts use a nominating commission for district judge selection; the remaining 14 select district judges in partisan elections.

[m] Fourteen of 31 districts use partisan elections.

[n] Although party affiliation of judicial candidates appears on ballots, judicial primaries are open and candidates generally do not solicit party support. This gives judicial elections a nonpartisan character.

[o] Nominating commissions are used for selecting circuit court judges in Jackson, Clay, Platte, and St. Louis Counties.

[p] An associate circuit court judge's term is four years; also in counties that use nominating commissions, the appointed judge serves until the next general election but not less than one year.

[q] Retention elections are used in Jackson, Clay, Platte, and St. Louis Counties.

[r] Subject to approval by an elected five-member executive council.

[s] Party affiliations of judicial candidates are not listed on the general election ballot, so the election is technically nonpartisan. However, candidates run in partisan primary elections.

[t] The Judicial Merit Selection Commission screens and then recommends a list of judicial candidates to the legislature. The legislature votes on the list submitted by the commission. If all candidates on the list are rejected, the process begins again with the commission.

Source: American Judicature Society. *Judicial Selection in the United States: A Compendium of Provisions,* 2nd edition (Chicago: American Judicature Society, 1993), http://www.ajs.org/js/judicialselectioncharts.pdf (January 25, 2005); and data provided by the American Judicature Society. Reprinted by permission.

Another issue is whether political appointments contribute to corruption among the judiciary. Judges, because of their powerful positions, may influence trial outcomes, dismiss cases, or find innocent defendants guilty. They can also regulate the harshness of penalties imposed whenever a jury verdict of guilty is rendered. All states have judicial sanctioning boards. These are usually operated through state bar associations, and provisions exist for officially questioning judicial behavior. Studies comparing the qualities of judges elected versus those appointed tend to show little difference in placing high-quality judges on the bench. Judicial accountability versus judicial independence models don't seem to differ significantly as means for improving the quality of judges generally (Blankenship, Sparger, and Janikowski 1994).

Some jurisdictions, such as Pennsylvania, have attempted to hold the governor primarily accountable in instances where political judicial appointments have resulted in the selection of either incompetent or corrupt judges (*Villanova Law Review* 1982). Particularly with respect to gubernatorial appointments of appellate judges, insufficient monitoring methods have historically been used that have resulted in occasional selections of poor judges. Suggested alternative judicial selection methods include a gubernatorial appointment system whereby the records of prospective judicial appointees can be carefully scrutinized by the press and state bar associations. Further, all gubernatorial candidates would have to be approved by the state legislature through some type of confirmation process (*Villanova Law Review* 1982). Perhaps the best method of judicial selection is on the basis of merit.

Merit Selection of Judges

Prior to 1933, no state had any type of **merit selection** plan for filling vacant judgeships. By far the most popular methods of selecting judges involved partisan and nonpartisan elections. Other systems used included gubernatorial or legislative appointments. One reason for the slow adoption of merit systems for judicial appointments is the strong sentiment in predominantly rural communities for the elective process. By the early 1990s, 15 states and the District of Columbia had evolved merit systems for filling judicial vacancies. These included Alaska, Arizona, Colorado, Connecticut, Delaware, Hawaii, Iowa, Kansas, Maryland, Massachusetts, Nebraska, New Mexico, Utah, Vermont, and Wyoming. By 2004, 25 states had nominating commissions to select judges to fill the highest appellate vacancies (Maguire and Pastore 2005, 83).

THE MISSOURI PLAN   A popular method of judicial selection adopted by several states is the **Missouri Plan**. The Missouri Plan was introduced in 1940 and is a method of judicial selection using the merit system for appointments to judgeships (President's Commission on Law Enforcement 1967, 66–67). The essential features of the Missouri Plan are as follows:

1. A nominating committee consisting of lawyers and nonlawyers appointed by the governor and chaired by a judge.
2. A listing of qualified candidates who are nominated by the committee for each judicial vacancy.
3. Each judicial vacancy is filled by the governor by referring to the list of candidates nominated by the committee.
4. Any appointed judge seeking re-election will run only on the issue of whether or not he/she should be retained on the basis of merit.

The Missouri Plan is a version of the 1914 **Kales Plan** (Kales 1914). The Kales Plan has survived in various forms in several states over the years, and its influence on the Missouri Plan is evident. The Kales Plan requires a nonpartisan committee of lawyers, judges, and nonjudicial personnel to draft a list of the most qualified judicial candidates on the basis of their records and expertise. This list is then submitted to the governor to make judicial appointments. Judicial vacancies occur because of death, retirement, or removal because of incompetence. Any choice a governor makes from the approved list would by definition be a good choice. Ideally, politics is removed from such gubernatorial appointments.

But some critics question whether *any* merit plan including both the Kales and Missouri versions can eliminate politics from judicial selection (Blankenship, Sparger, and Janikowski 1994). However, other analysts find the merit plan useful for promoting greater accountability and fairness among judges (Scheb 1988).

One way of making the merit selection plan more palatable to the public is to ensure that the qualification procedures for judicial applicants should be made more rigorous (Dubois 1990). In effect, a thorough screening procedure should be operative as a standard against which to compare different judicial candidates. Thus, when the matter of selecting a judge to fill a judgeship arises, the public knows that all judicial nominees have been thoroughly screened and tested concerning their competency and abilities.

One troubling aspect of merit selection occurs in those states where governors have the power to appoint **interim judges** to fill unexpected vacancies. When a judge dies, becomes infirm, or is unable to perform his/her duties in midterm, governors make temporary judicial appointments without consulting any merit selection committee. Interim judges generally have an easier time as **incumbents** when it comes time to appoint a new judge for a subsequent term. The politicalization of the interim judicial appointment process is furthered by gubernatorial appointments of nominating committee members who convene later to review the credentials of applications for new judicial vacancies.

In some instances, governors have removed themselves entirely from the judicial selection process, even from the process of appointing interim judges to fill temporary vacancies. In New Mexico, for instance, a judicial nominating commission is in place and acts to screen and fill temporary judicial vacancies. The nominating commission submits their recommendations to the governor, and the governor appoints particular persons to vacant judgeships. Thus, the governor is not directly involved in candidate screenings or selecting judges on the basis of his/her own preferences, independent of some nominating commission. Several other states that have nominating commissions include Delaware, Georgia, Maryland, Massachusetts, Minnesota, New York, North Carolina, Pennsylvania, Rhode Island, and West Virginia (Vago 2006).

Under President Jimmy Carter, Executive Order 11972 was issued, establishing the U.S. Circuit Judge Nominating Commission. This commission radically altered the method of selecting federal judges. Carter wanted to devise a system whereby judges would be appointed on the basis of their professional merit and potential for quality service on the bench. Further, he wanted to develop a mechanism that would allow him to place larger numbers of women and minorities in judgeships. One criticism of this method of judicial selection is that Carter may have undermined the merit system in favor of affirmative action considerations. During his presidency, Carter selected 86 percent of the judges from his own Democratic Party. However, he dramatically increased the presence of women and minorities on the federal bench, with 25 percent being women and 29 percent being racial or ethnic minorities. Subsequently, other U.S. presidents have made partisan judicial appointments (Goldman et al. 2003).

Legislative Appointments of Judges

In 2004, only Virginia appointed judges to the highest appellate bench through legislative elections. Nominating committees advance a list of judicial candidates for legislative approval. Legislative voting results in the appointment of judges to benches in various state jurisdictions. Although legislative appointments of judges affect only a small portion of the total federal and state judiciary, the impact of legislatively selected judges has been studied by several researchers. Daniel Pinello (1995) has indicated that where judges have been selected by legislatures compared with those selected by partisan/nonpartisan elections or by gubernatorial appointments, their subsequent performance as judges has been characterized as acquiescent and inactive. Governor-appointed judges tend to choose the interests of individuals over state interests more often than legislatively appointed judges.

Legislative appointments are extremely political and reflect the political leanings of legislators who have been voted into office by the citizens of the state. Thus, a legislature controlled by Democrats might be disposed to appoint Democrat judges, while Republican-dominated legislatures would be expected to appoint Republican judges. Relatively little depends upon the qualifications of those considered to hold judgeships in these jurisdictions. There is a great propensity on the part of state legislators to appoint former legislators to judicial vacancies. Also, any person in the state who has formerly held a political office stands a much greater chance of receiving a judicial appointment from the legislature compared with someone without political experience. Does the legislature appoint the most qualified persons to vacant judgeships? Not if these appointments are based on former political ties to the legislature or other political offices within the state. Virtually the same thing can be said of gubernatorial appointments, which are most often made on the basis that an appointed judge has held one or more state political offices.

ARE MERIT SYSTEMS FOR JUDICIAL SELECTION BETTER THAN ELECTION METHODS?   The debate over which judge selection plan is best is largely dependent upon the assumption that it makes some kind of measurable difference which plan is used—that one plan results in better-qualified judges. However, there are few discernible differences among the various plans in terms of the quality of judges. Partisan elections may not produce better judges than other means of selection, but neither, apparently, do they produce worse ones (Swain 1985). According to one view, the legal profession tends to ignore research findings and blindly and steadfastly adheres to the Missouri merit selection method. One proposed but unlikely modification would be to democratize the Missouri Plan by rectifying some of its major weaknesses (Swain 1985).

For many decades, it has been assumed by the public that judicial selection systems that emphasize merit rather than political interests create greater judicial accountability and independence. Elections are perceived as popularity contests, often rigged to accommodate one vested interest group or another. Gubernatorial selection methods result in the appointment of political hacks as judges who cater to the interests of the governor and the governor's friends. Merit selection, it is argued, results in the most qualified persons performing judicial roles. However, several researchers have raised questions about whether any of these methods is better than the rest. Michael Blankenship, Jerry Sparger, and Richard Janikowski (1994) suggest that the election-merit selection dichotomy is more a myth than fact. They contend that appointive methods for selecting judges are no more effective than the elective process in placing qualified judges on the bench. They add that neither elections nor appointments of judicial candidates succeed in fulfilling the long-range philosophical expectations of judicial accountability and independence.

Federal Judicial Selection Methods

THE NATURE OF U.S. SUPREME COURT APPOINTMENTS   The president of the United States exerts direct influence on the nature of U.S. Supreme Court appointments and judicial appointments to lower federal courts. The president recommends persons for district, circuit, and supreme court judgeships, with the advice and consent of Congress. U.S. Supreme Court appointments have not necessarily depended upon previous judicial experience, however. From 1930 to 1967, there were 23 U.S. Supreme Court justices appointed. Of these, only seven had previous federal judge experience with all but one serving five or fewer years on the federal bench. And only four of these 23 appointments had experience as state judges. Only former justice Cardozo, appointed in 1932, had more than 8 years' experience, having served 18 years in state courts.

U.S. Supreme Court justiceships are appointments by the president of the United States, subject to congressional approval. These are lifetime appointments. In 2008, the salary of a U.S. Supreme Court justice was $208,100 with the chief justice making roughly $217,400 (Schwelme 2008). Because these judgeships are presidential appointments, they often reflect a president's vested interests. Therefore, judges with judicial philosophies consistent with those of the president are appointed instead of other, sometimes more qualified, judges who hold contrary philosophies. When former president George Bush, a Republican, nominated Clarence Thomas, also a Republican, to fill a U.S. Supreme Court vacancy, the nomination was hotly debated by the U.S. Senate Judiciary Committee after examining Thomas's views on various issues. Those most critical of Thomas were Senate Democrats. Political differences were influential in Judge Thomas's eventual acceptance as a Supreme Court justice. Considerable time and attention focused upon sexual harassment allegations against Judge Thomas by Anita Hill, a University of Oklahoma professor who had worked for him. Conflicting testimony before the Judiciary Committee left many persons doubting Hill's accusations, and Judge Thomas's appointment to the U.S. Supreme Court was approved.

During the 1990s, two U.S. Supreme Court justices were appointed by President Bill Clinton, a Democrat. His most significant appointment was Ruth Bader Ginsburg in 1993. She was the first Democrat to serve on the U.S. Supreme Court in 26 years as well as the second woman appointed since Sandra Day O'Connor. Although there have been Jewish U.S. Supreme Court justices in past years, Justice Ginsburg's appointment marked another turning point in the composition of the U.S. Supreme Court as well as the religious composition of it became more diverse. Obama's Supreme Court appointees included the first Hispanic woman on the Supreme Court, Justice Sonia Sotomayor as well as another female Elena Kagan (the fourth female on the Supreme Court), who is Jewish, a woman, and from the academic world; she was the former dean of Harvard Law School.

In 2006, George W. Bush's nomination of Harriet Miers, former White House counsel and longtime advisor to the president, sparked intense debate from both Democrats and Republicans who argued that she didn't have the constitutional or judicial experience necessary for appointment to the bench. Miers subsequently withdrew her nomination after the likelihood of a confirmation seemed slim. President Obama's nominees are currently taking longer to be confirmed than those of previous presidents (Wheeler 2010).

Presidential appointments to the U.S. Supreme Court are also characterized according to whether the appointees are conservative, liberal, or moderate. U.S. Supreme Court justices under Republican administrations have tended to be very conservative or conservative, while justices appointed under Democratic administrations have tended to be moderate or liberal. These philosophical orientations have been very crucial in determining various social policies during the last 50 years. For instance, in the 1960s, the chief justice of the U.S. Supreme Court was Earl Warren, who had been appointed to the high court in 1953 by President Dwight Eisenhower. When Warren became chief justice, the Court became known as the "Warren Court." Under Warren's guidance, the U.S. Supreme Court made a number of rulings that regulated police tactics relative to custodial interrogations and searches and seizures. During Warren's tenure as chief justice, the U.S. Supreme Court seemed to be anti-police, since many of its rulings were viewed by critics as tying the hands of law enforcement officers when investigating crimes. The most notable rulings included *Mapp v. Ohio* (1961), which required police officers to have search warrants before conducting searches of one's premises, and *Miranda v. Arizona* (1966), which required police officers to advise suspects of their right to an attorney prior to being interrogated.

Later U.S. Supreme Courts issued rulings that created various exceptions to warrantless searches and effectively untied the hands of police. Under Warren E. Burger, the chief justice of the U.S. Supreme Court who was appointed by President Richard M. Nixon in 1969, the "Burger Court" established the "totality of circumstances" and "good faith" exceptions to the exclusionary rule, which permitted law enforcement officers considerable latitude when conducting warrantless searches of one's premises, person, and automobile. During the 1990s, the newly configured U.S. Supreme Court presided over by Chief Justice William H. Rehnquist, the "Rehnquist Court," has issued more conservative rulings relating to searches and seizures.

Will the newly appointed chief justice, John Roberts, follow in Rehnquist's footsteps? Roberts was once a clerk for Rehnquist, and Rehnquist's teaching has had an impact on Robert's life and legal career. It is likely that the Court will continue to steer to the right with Roberts at the helm. Thus, the influence of presidential appointments on the composition of the U.S.

Supreme Court cannot be ignored. These appointments, which are highly political, are intended to increase the likelihood of particular social agendas contemplated by those presidents making such appointments. During any election year, a key factor governing one's decision to vote for one presidential candidate or another is what types of Supreme Court justices will be appointed and what will be the nature of their decision making in future years? Since these appointments are lifetime appointments, the long-term social policy implications are quite clear.

CIRCUIT COURT JUDGESHIPS   Judges who serve in Circuit Courts of Appeal are appointed by the president of the United States. Their nomination by the president must be approved by the advice and consent of Congress. As of 2008, the salary of U.S. circuit judges was $179,500 (Schwelme 2008). The Senate Judiciary Committee hears arguments both for and against these presidential appointees and either approves or rejects them. Not all nominated judges are acceptable to the Senate Judiciary Committee. One example of a rejection is the case of Miami U.S. District Court judge Kenneth L. Ryskamp, who had been appointed as a federal district judge by then-president Ronald Reagan in 1986. At that time, the Senate Judiciary Committee recommended his nomination and his appointment was eventually confirmed. However, during the next five years on the federal bench, Judge Ryskamp made numerous disparaging remarks of racial and ethnic minorities. When the Senate Judiciary Committee conducted a subsequent hearing of Ryskamp's qualifications for the Circuit Court of Appeals judgeship in April 1991, committee members called to Ryskamp's attention remarks that he had made once to four blacks who filed suit after being mauled by police dogs. Ryskamp told the four blacks that "It might not be inappropriate to carry around a few scars to remind you of your wrongdoing," even though two of the four were never actually charged with a crime. He also complained from the federal bench that some people were thin-skinned if they took offense at calling a black area "colored town." Judge Ryskamp also belonged to a Miami country club that excluded blacks and Jews. Also while in Washington, Ryskamp failed to follow recommendations from Washington politicians or adhere to advice given to him by his aides. When President George Bush nominated Ryskamp to the Circuit Court of Appeals encompassing Florida, Georgia, and Alabama, there would have been a conservative majority among the judges. While President George Bush had 76 previous confirmation victories and the Senate Judiciary Committee hadn't rejected any Republican president nomination since 1988, they did reject Ryskamp.

Presidential appointments in most cases involve persons who are members of the president's political party. For instance, 95 percent of Democratic president Lyndon Johnson's circuit court judicial appointments were Democrats; 93 percent of Republican president Richard Nixon's appointments were Republicans; 92 percent of Republican president Gerald Ford's appointments were Republicans; 82 percent of Democratic president Jimmy Carter's appointments were Democrats; 96 percent of Republican president Ronald Reagan's appointments were Republicans; 89 percent of Republican president George H. W. Bush's appointments were Republicans; 85 percent of Democratic president Bill Clinton's appointments were Democrats; and 81 percent of George W. Bush's appointments were Republican. The Obama nominees to the federal bench will also surely continue this trend. So far, roughly President Lyndon Johnson's and President Bill Clinton's appointments were regarded by the ABA as exceptionally well qualified as circuit court judges, while President Ford and President Reagan had the lowest ratings of their circuit judgeship appointments, with ratings of 58–59 percent as exceptionally well qualified.

U.S. DISTRICT COURT JUDGES   According the Annual Report of the Director for Judicial Business of the U.S. Courts, there were 678 federal district judges in 2009. Federal district judges are also appointed by the president of the United States. They also serve life terms. Annual salaries of federal district court judges in 2010 were $174,000. Although judicial appointments are ideally made without regard to one's race, color, sex, religion, or national origin, these appointments are primarily political and reflect the interests and views of the president. The advice and consent of Congress is required for all such appointments.

President Jimmy Carter made various appointments that were considered liberal. Investigators examined Carter's appointments to federal circuit courts of appeal and found that he had appointed 56 judges during his tenure as president. Interestingly, of these 56 judicial appointees, 22 were either female or a member of a racial minority. The liberal influence of these judges was tracked over time to see whether there was corresponding liberal decision making on appeals from convicted minority offenders. A study was made of 301 criminal and prisoner's rights cases, 169 sex discrimination cases, and 295 racial discrimination cases. Minority appointees by Carter cast 79 percent of their votes to favor the rights of accused minorities and women compared with only 53 percent of the white male judges he had appointed. Race and gender discrimination cases disclosed more liberal rulings from these judges compared with prisoner's rights cases. Thus, presidential influence in appointing judges at various levels of appeal is not to be underestimated insofar as it influences judicial decision making and social policy relevant to women and minorities.

The pattern of partisanship indicated by presidential appointments to circuit court judgeships was also found for presidential appointees to benches of federal district courts in 2002. Presidential appointments of these judges were very much along party lines, with over 80 percent of all federal district court judges being of the same political party of their appointing president. The ratings of federal district court judges by the ABA were fairly consistent across the different presidencies, regardless of whether the president was a Republican or Democrat. For these different administrations, the ABA ratings ranged from 45 to 69 percent of the federal district judges as exceptionally well qualified (Maguire and Pastore 2005, 76).

Regarding the gender and race/ethnicity of U.S. District Court judge appointments, President Bill Clinton had the largest percentage of females (28.2 percent) appointed, followed by President George W. Bush (20.5 percent) and President George Bush (19.6 percent). President Clinton also had the largest percentage of black appointees (17.4 percent) while President Carter was second (14 percent). All other U.S. presidents have appointed fewer than 8 percent black judges to these district court judgeships. Both President Bush and President Clinton appointed the largest numbers of Hispanic federal district court judges (7.2 and 5.9 percent, respectively).

U.S. MAGISTRATES   U.S. magistrates have jurisdiction over petty federal crimes. They may conduct preliminary stages of felony cases and set bail for criminal defendants. They decide numerous civil cases. They are appointed by U.S. District Court judges and serve terms of either eight or four years, depending upon whether they are full-time or part-time magistrates. The salary of U.S. magistrates in 2005 was $149,132. U.S. magistrate judges have various duties. Besides having jurisdiction over cases involving federal misdemeanors and petty offenses, these magistrates also issue search warrants and arrest warrants/summonses, hold detention hearings, review bail for arrestees, issue seizure warrants, and conduct preliminary examinations. These magistrates also have civil duties as well as criminal ones, although their criminal responsibilities outweigh their civil responsibilities 2 to 1. They hold pretrial conferences, rule on motions, conduct evidentiary hearings, appoint special masterships, and hear some prisoner litigation involving *habeas corpus* petitions and civil rights submissions. Much of their civil work relates to conducting pretrial conferences, ruling on motions, and screening prisoner litigation (Maguire and Pastore 2005, 79).

WHAT DO JUDGES THINK ABOUT DIFFERENT JUDICIAL SELECTION METHODS?   If judges are surveyed, they seem to favor merit plans over elections (Scheb 1988). In 1987, for instance, a national survey of 562 state appellate judges was conducted and their attitudes toward alternative judicial selection methods were solicited. When asked to compare the Missouri Plan of merit selection with the judicial selection methods of political appointment and partisan elections, the judges responded overwhelmingly that the merit plan was the more professional selection method. By this the judges meant that the Missouri merit plan tended to professionalize the courts. Judges selected under the merit system were far less likely to become involved in political causes or debates compared with those judges who were either gubernatorial appointees or elected (Scheb 1988).

In some jurisdictions, such as Texas, judges believe that performance evaluations are made unfairly, since the judicial selection methods used in their state have not been changed since 1891 (Champion 2005a). Thus, creating new jurisdictional divisions among Texas's existing courts could do much to improve case processing efficiency. The performance of judges would be enhanced accordingly with specific organizational reforms. One reform would be to empower presiding judges in different jurisdictions to move other judges to courts on an as-needed basis, and to control court dockets. Restricting the monetary jurisdiction of various criminal and civil courts to $5,000 would also improve court efficiency (Champion 2005a).

JUDICIAL TRAINING

Theories of management and organizations have sometimes been applied in the judicial selection and training process. For instance, **bureaucracy** and its derivative bureaucratic theory emphasize **centralization** of authority in decision making, thus creating a degree of standardization in judicial selection. However, strict adherence to bureaucratic principles may not always result in selections of the most qualified judges in local jurisdictions. A departure from bureaucratic theory would be to decentralize the judicial selection process, to place greater decision-making power in the hands of local commissions for judicial appointments, with some authority given to state supreme courts to oversee the selection process. The legislative electoral process is one way of rationalizing and objectifying the selection process. This would enable local bar elements to recommend those most qualified for judgeships, while the legislature would make the best judicial selections with state supreme court approval.

In the late 1970s, a survey by the American Judicature Society disclosed that there was no uniformity or pattern of organization among different lower courts among state jurisdictions (Knab 1977). The qualifications for state judges were diverse and inconsistent from one jurisdiction to the next. Different standards existed for selecting judges, determining their qualifications to serve in judicial positions, compensation, and retirement or removal of judges.

Several recommendations have been made to improve the quality and accountability of judges in different jurisdictions. For instance, the U.S. Advisory Commission on Intergovernmental Relations (1971) suggested that a set of uniform rules should be established to govern the conduct of judges. Further, procedures for judicial retirement, removal, and discipline should be established with a high degree of uniformity. Finally, a term limit should be established to eliminate the possibility of certain judges serving for long periods. Mandatory retirement ages should be implemented. In order to upgrade and improve the quality of judicial selection, codes of judicial ethics ought to be established, together with explicit judicial compensation and qualification criteria.

Other recommendations for standardizing the qualifications, training, and selection of judges are that judicial elections should be publicly financed and not dependent upon private contributions. A standard amount of money should be available to all judicial candidates for their election campaigns. No private contributions of any kind should be allowed. Further, filing fees should not be required of anyone seeking a judgeship (Beechen 1974). In some county elections, more affluent judges may spend considerably more of their own money on judicial campaigning compared with less affluent candidates. The relative difference in campaign money spent by the different candidates may create the potential for the appearance of improper influence. Further, those candidates of modest means are disadvantaged and may be deterred from seeking public office.

Whether a judicial candidate is an incumbent or one seeking a judgeship for the first time makes a substantial difference in the amount of financial support generated for the campaign. In the 1984 Cook County Circuit Court elections, for instance, judicial incumbents were able to raise substantially more money for their campaigns from lawyer contributions compared with fresh candidates. Even sitting judges who were sure losers were able to generate substantially greater funding compared with more desirable candidates (Nicholson and Weiss 1986).

Subsequent studies of the judicial selection process through partisan elections have revealed that private contributions and frivolous candidate expenditures have raised more than a few questions about judicial ethics and fairness (Keil et al. 1994). Further, the bars of various states have disclosed that they have little influence on the nature of voting for one judicial candidate or another in terms of his/her comparative qualifications (Keil et al. 1994).

Evidence suggests that voters are more attentive to the judicial policy preferences and ideological inclinations of judges than researchers have predicted. Based on a random sample of 1,012 ballots cast in the November 1988, Marion County, Oregon, judicial race, which occurred simultaneously with the Bush–Dukakis presidential campaign, voters were very much aware of the political philosophies and personal ideologies of those competing for judicial vacancies. In nearby Washington State, a survey of voters in a 1986 judicial election indicated that voter knowledge about judicial candidates and their views was critical in their voting participation (Lovrich and Sheldon 1994). In other states such as California, however, voters in judicial elections did not appear to be as informed or educated about the issues involved in other judicial selections (Champion 2005b).

JUDICIAL MISCONDUCT AND ABUSES OF DISCRETION

Judicial conduct is monitored by different persons and organizations among jurisdictions. For instance, in New York, judicial conduct is monitored by the Commission on Judicial Conduct. The commission receives or initiates complaints with respect to the conduct, qualifications, fitness to perform, or performance of official duties of any judge in New York State. After investigation and a hearing, the commission may admonish, censure, remove, or retire a judge. Decisions by the commission may be appealed to the court of appeals.

Forms of Judicial Misconduct

There are several forms of judicial misconduct. However, most misconduct relates to the performance of one's job as judge. A judge is a powerful entity. The courtroom is dominated by the judge. Judges make rulings that have immense influence over trial outcomes.

JUDGES CAN INFLUENCE TRIAL OUTCOMES BY EXHIBITING PREJUDICE IN EVIDENTIARY RULINGS   One of the most frequent types of judicial misconduct is to prejudice the court proceedings in such a way that the trial outcome is favorable to either one side or the other. Such behavior on a judge's part is difficult to detect, however. Simply ruling unfavorably against one side or the other may be explained by numerous frivolous motions filed by that side. Further, most judges can rationalize their conduct if pressed to do so.

JUDGES CAN DELIBERATELY AGGRAVATE OR MITIGATE ONE'S SENTENCE FOLLOWING CONVICTION   When offenders are convicted, judges can deliberately increase or decrease the severity of the sentence imposed. Again, it is difficult for court watchers to detect this form of misconduct whenever judicial intervention is the result of objective decision making or personal vindictiveness.

JUDGES CAN ACCEPT BRIBES FROM VARIOUS PARTIES IN COURT ACTIONS   Judges may also accept bribes from politicians or others where their rulings are influential. Especially in bench trials where judges decide the outcomes of cases, it is easy to decide in favor of someone where a financial bribe has been received. Again, this form of misconduct is difficult to detect. It is not completely undetectable, however. Bribery and judicial corruption were targeted in Operation Greylord in the late 1970s.

CORRUPT JUDGES AND OPERATION GREYLORD   In 1978 one of the largest and most successful investigations of judicial misconduct was launched. The investigation was called

Operation Greylord. It was an FBI undercover sting operation and targeted the judges of Cook County, Illinois (Bensinger 1988). The history of judicial corruption in and around Chicago was notorious and well known throughout the United States. Politically corrupt judges would accept bribes for favorable bench decisions. Organized crime was able to flourish because of judicial participation in illicit activities.

The FBI organized a task force that fabricated a variety of court cases to be heard in Cook County courts. Tape-recorded conversations were made between undercover FBI agents posing as attorneys, defendants, and judges. Electronic surveillance and telephonic wiretaps were installed in different judges' offices in an effort to acquire incriminating information. The results of Operation Greylord were shocking. Over 60 judges and judicial adjuncts were prosecuted and convicted of various forms of judicial misconduct and corruption, including accepting bribes and prejudicing judgments in favor of certain undercover clients. The immediate public reaction to Operation Greylord was a general loss of confidence in the Illinois judiciary, despite the fact that only Chicago and Cook County were targeted. But in later years, public confidence in the judiciary was restored through implementing a series of judicial selection reforms. The Illinois Bar Association and judicial organizations adopted new ethical standards and modes of professional conduct. Merit selections of judges throughout Illinois were the rule rather than the exception. The administration of justice in Cook County was drastically overhauled and revised. While judicial corruption and misconduct have not been entirely eliminated, Operation Greylord did much to reduce its existence (Illinois Supreme Court 1993).

BOX 5.1

Judges Convicted of Crimes

District judge Alan Green was convicted in New Orleans, Louisiana, on two of six counts of mail fraud involving two $5,000 cash payments he took from a bail bonding company. A mistrial was declared on the remaining counts and it is likely that Green will be retried. Green is a former Jefferson Parish prosecutor who became a judge in 1992. He faced up to 20 years of prison on his conviction offenses. Green was accused of taking $20,000 in cash from Louis Marcotte, III, a New Orleans bail bondsman. Bail Bonds Unlimited, operated by Marcotte, enables those charged with crimes to remain jail-free while awaiting their subsequent trials. Marcotte claimed that Green extorted monies from him as a bribe for his court business. Marcotte sent Judge Green two $5,000 checks by mail. Green's attorney claimed that these checks were considered campaign contributions and were later returned to Marcotte. But the prosecution proved otherwise. Green is the first state district judge convicted at trial since 1983, when Judge Roy Price, also of the Jefferson Parish state court, was found guilty in federal court of bank larceny and other crimes. He served 18 months and died in 1989. Under Louisiana law, Green has been convicted of two felonies, sufficient to put him on interim disqualification pending sanctions, including removal from the bench. He was currently suspended without pay.

New Jersey Superior Court judge Stephen W. Thompson, 59, traveled to Russia in September 2002, where he had several sexual encounters with a young teenage boy in a St. Petersburg hotel room. Thompson had his sexual sessions with the boy videotaped by a local pimp. In one of the videotapes showing Thompson having sex with the boy, Thompson is heard telling an unidentified man to ask the child to take off his clothes. Then Thompson is seen climbing into bed nude with the boy and engaging in sexual acts with him. About 40 minutes of sexual footage was recorded. The judge then transported the videotape back to the United States.

Judge Thompson's sexual activities relating to the Russian boy came to light as a result of his affiliation with a group known as the North American Man Boy Love Association (NAMBLA), a group that promotes sexual relations between adult men and children. Apparently an informant tipped off police officers about Thompson's illicit activities, including his possession of an extensive array of child pornography at his home and judicial office. Search warrants were issued subsequently and the following were found: 17 VHS tapes containing child pornography, showing

(continued)

(continued)

children engaging in explicit sexual acts, magazines containing child pornography and child erotica, and materials associated with NAMBLA. More than 300 printed images of child pornography were found; also 57 floppy disks contained over 6,000 images of child pornography. Thompson was charged with multiple counts of having sex with a teenage boy and sexual exploitation of children in a federal district court. He was subsequently convicted of traveling in interstate and foreign commerce with the intent of engaging in sexual conduct with a minor for the purpose of producing a visual depiction of the sexual conduct. His conviction carries a mandatory minimum sentence of ten years in prison. NAMBLA is currently represented by the American Civil Liberties Union.

How much illegal activity is there among judges throughout the United States? While these incidents represent only two cases, how many other undiscovered cases are there involving judges who preside in criminal and civil court matters? What types of investigations are necessary or warranted as the result of various judges convicted of different crimes? What do you think?

Sources: Adapted from the Associated Press, "La. Judge Convicted of Mail Fraud," June 30, 2005; adapted from Jim Douri and the Associated Press, "Superior Court Judge Convicted of Sex Crimes with Boy," October 12, 2005.

CRITICISMS OF JUDGES

SOME JUDGES ARE INCOMPETENT AND INEXPERIENCED   Judicial incompetence is often associated with one's inexperience as a judge. When inexperienced judges rule on motions from the prosecution or defense, these judges may not understand fully the rules of evidence and whether the motion should be granted or denied. Often, inexperienced judges make these decisions on the basis of their emotional sentiment during the trial. Whenever judges make mistakes of judgment in ruling on motions, these are errors. They vary in their importance. Many errors are harmless, meaning that the outcome of the trial would not have been affected if the judge had ruled differently. Other types of errors are **harmful errors** or **reversible errors**.

Harmful errors or reversible errors may result in judicial decisions being overturned by higher appellate courts. But (1) not all errors are detected in a trial; (2) not all *guilty* verdicts are appealed; and (3) not all appeals are heard on their merits by higher courts. The U.S. Supreme Court hears only about 4 percent of the appeals it schedules annually.

For instance, in a murder case, a judge admitted into evidence photographs of the murder victim. These photographs showed the mutilated corpse of the victim, and the photographs had absolutely no bearing on the guilt or innocence of the accused. There were eyewitnesses to the murder, and the defendant's guilt had been proven beyond a reasonable doubt without the photographs. But the photographs obviously inflamed the jury and influenced their decision to impose the death penalty. The murder conviction was appealed, but the verdict was affirmed by the higher court. In that case, the court said there was so much evidence against the accused that the admission of these inflammatory materials into evidence resulted in harmless error. Under other circumstances, however, the admission of inflammatory photographs might be the final element necessary to persuade a jury to render a guilty verdict in an otherwise weak case against the defendant. Again, the trial judge controls the courtroom and influences the general course of the trial as well as the defendant's chances for conviction or acquittal.

It is assumed by all appellate courts that the original judgment or verdict rendered by a lower trial court was the correct one. Therefore, clear and convincing evidence must be presented by the defendant supporting a reversal of a verdict by the trial judge or jury. It is insufficient simply to prove that errors were committed. Even harmful errors are insufficient under certain conditions when attempting to overturn a judge's decision.

SOME JUDGES CONTRIBUTE TO COURT DELAYS AND CLOGGED COURT CALENDARS   Serious court delays are commonplace in most jurisdictions. A study of case processing in New York City, for instance, has revealed that a significant obstacle contributing to court delays is inadequate judicial training. Technology presently exists that facilitates case processing in many modern court systems. However, some New York City judiciary are slow to acquire new technology. Further, courses offered for judges on case management training have relatively low enrollment. Realistic timetables are not adhered to, and more than a few judges inadvertently impede one's right to a speedy trial because of their inefficient case management practices (Correctional Association of New York 1993).

Other factors besides judicial inexperience contribute to case processing delays as well. In some cases, there are attorney appearance conflicts, witness unavailability, attorney unpreparedness, vacations, and illness-precipitated court appearances. Court delays in various jurisdictions are also due to a lack of resources and judicial support staff and equipment. Increasing judicial education through mandatory education programs is one means of facilitating case processing (Clark 2004a).

MANY JUDGES IMPOSE DISPARATE SENTENCES   Judicial discretion in sentencing is often criticized in that judges make decisions primarily on extralegal factors rather than legal ones. Legal factors include one's prior record, seriousness of the current offense, age, and acceptance of responsibility. Extralegal factors refer to race or ethnicity, gender, socioeconomic status, and attitude (Champion 2005b). Sentencing disparities attributable to race, gender, socioeconomic status, and other extralegal factors have plagued judges for years (Champion 2005b). Attempts have been made by commissions and state legislatures to create greater sentencing consistency and bind judges to nonarbitrary standards. Sentencing guidelines have been created in most jurisdictions to make uniform the punishments for various offenses. Some observers question whether structured sentencing guidelines will eliminate disparities in judicial decision making, however. Experiments on various types of sentencing reforms have evidenced some success in improving judicial fairness (Kramer and Ulmer 1996). Other research, however, shows that despite the fact that sentencing guidelines were designed to reduce unwarranted disparity in sentencing, the results of recent research suggest that minorities and the poor may continue to receive harsher treatment because judges find ways to manipulate the reforms, or circumvent them altogether. Additionally, there is evidence of unwarranted disparity in departures from the guidelines (Stith and Cabranes 1998); whites and females more often receive non-prison sentences and downward departures (Kramer and Ulmer 1996).

The recent Supreme Court case of *Blakely v. Washington* (2004) seriously called into question the constitutionality of the federal sentencing guidelines as well as those of nearly a dozen states. Following *Blakely*, the case of *United States v. Booker* (2005) ruled that the Sixth Amendment necessitates that the federal sentencing guidelines be advisory in nature rather than mandatory. This now means that judges are to consult the guidelines when meting out sentences but do not necessarily have to follow them.

REMOVING JUDGES FROM OFFICE

Whenever corrupt or incompetent judges are identified, there are relatively few mechanisms available to remove them from office. In New York, judicial conduct is monitored by the Commission on Judicial Conduct. The commission receives or initiates complaints with respect to the conduct, qualifications, fitness to perform, or performance of official duties of any judge in New York State. After investigation and a hearing, the commission may admonish, censure, remove, or retire a judge. However, decisions made by the commission are directly appealable to the New York Court of Appeals.

The creation of independent commissions to oversee judicial misconduct is not new. The first state to implement a commission to deal with judicial misconduct was California. In 1960 California created a **judicial conduct commission**, which was charged with investigating complaints against judges. Comprised of attorneys, other judges, and politically prestigious others, these commission members function as a part of the California Supreme Court.

They meet in secret and their findings are confidential. They investigate misconduct reports against various California state trial judges and make recommendations to the California Supreme Court. Their array of sanctions includes recommendations for private censure, removal from the bench, or retirement. The California Supreme Court has the final authority concerning recommendations made by the judicial conduct commission.

Unfortunately, the United States has one of the poorest records for sanctioning the behaviors of bad judges. Compared with other nations, such as France, Italy, and England, judicial conduct organizations in the United States institute relatively few cases of judicial sanctioning (Volcansek, DeFranciscis, and Lafron 1996). One reason for this lack of commitment to sanction bad judges is that American judges enjoy near-absolute judicial independence. There is relatively little accountability for judicial misconduct. However, bad judges can be removed through either impeachment or recall elections.

In order to provide some idea about the effectiveness of processing complaints that allege judicial misconduct, during the period for 1999, 12,068 misconduct complaints were received by various state judicial conduct organizations. In the various states anywhere from 71 to 100 percent of these complaints were dismissed outright, while most of the remaining cases were informally disposed of with reprimands, short-term suspensions, and fines. Only 48 cases resulted in judges vacating their offices during the investigation, and only 11 judges were suspended as a final sanction (Maguire and Pastore 2005). Thus, the system is weighed heavily in favor of judges, even bad ones. The likelihood that a complaint against any given judge will be sustained is less than 5 percent. It is even more alarming that there are few provisions for issuing severe sanctions against the worst judges. Thus, while the existence of judicial conduct organizations is commendable, it is also clear that these organizations have relatively little power in administering judicial sanctions.

Impeachment

Impeachment means to allege wrongdoing against a judge or other public official before a legislative or judicial body vested with the authority to remove that judge or public official from office. In order for impeachment to be successful, the allegations must be well founded and upheld by compelling evidence against the accused. In many jurisdictions, the state supreme court is the sanctioning body that hears impeachment allegations against judges and has the power to act to either remove the judge or dismiss the allegations.

For instance, suppose a judge continually fails to safeguard the rights of indigents in criminal cases. A judge might require a defendant to plead without representation by court-appointed counsel. A judge may tell a jury that he believes a defendant is guilty. A judge might set a particularly high and arbitrary bail amount for someone who is not dangerous or likely to flee the jurisdiction. The judge may coerce defendants out of the appeal rights. These forms of disrespect for the law occur from time to time in U.S. courts. However, few mechanisms have existed to remove these persons from office.

In more recent years, procedures have been suggested to systematize the judicial sanctioning process. Certain rules have been promulgated by the Federal Judicial Center, such as rules governing how complaints are filed; the review of complaints by chief judges; the review of the chief judge's disposition of the complaint; an investigation and recommendation by a special committee; rules dealing with **confidentiality**; public availability of decisions rendered; disqualification; and withdrawal of complaints and petitions for review.

Recall Elections

Another mechanism is through a **recall election**. A petition is circulated by interested citizens or by a city council in response to one or more complaints against a judicial official. A special election is held, with alternative candidates presented to fill the judicial post. A popular vote results in the bad judge being removed from office. The election also results in the support of a new judge who replaces the bad one. Recall elections depend heavily on citizen involvement and concern.

One other option is for a bad judge to simply resign. For instance, in Lakewood, Washington, a suburb of Seattle, Lakewood municipal judge Ralph H. Baldwin admitted to drinking beer with a defense lawyer and the prosecutor while the jury deliberated the fate of a defendant facing drunk-driving charges. Even after the case was over and the jury had rendered a verdict of guilty, the judge invited the jury members into his chambers and served them alcoholic beverages. Some jurors were clearly offended by the judge's actions, and his conduct was immediately reported to the Lakewood City Council. The city council confronted Baldwin with the allegations and he admitted them, stating that "I want you to know that none of my words or actions on that evening arose from malice but rather from a misguided sense of congeniality and extremely poor judgment. To each of you, I extend my sincere apologies." Baldwin had only served for 3 months as municipal judge, a $65,000 a year job, when the incident occurred (Associated Press 1998, A2). Baldwin was not available for comment about his resignation when reporters attempted to contact him.

Summary

In any court proceeding, the key official is the judge although, as we have seen, some of the judicial duties such as sentencing can be thought of as a collaborative process. The judge makes decisions about admissibility of evidence, whether or not bail will be set, courtroom administration, in some cases guilt or innocence, and finally punishment.

At the local, state, and federal levels, judges are either elected or appointed.

Among state courts, partisan and nonpartisan elections account for about two-thirds of all judicial positions. State governors and the U.S. president make other judicial appointments. The president selects U.S. District Court judges, U.S. Circuit Court appellate judges, and U.S. Supreme Court justices, subject to congressional approval.

An increasingly popular judicial selection method is judicial appointments on the basis of merit. One of these merit plans is known as the Missouri Plan.

Both partisan and nonpartisan elections are criticized that those on the ballot are not the most qualified, and that voter apathy makes the process meaningless.

Gubernatorial and legislative appointments are criticized that the nominations are too political and again the best candidate is not being appointed.

Merit selection attempts to overcome these criticisms by requiring that a list be drafted of the most qualified judicial candidates based on their expertise or qualifications and then the governor can use this list to make appointments. Judges themselves, when surveyed, seem to favor merit selection over election as a more professional method. Research, however, has shown that really there are few differences in the type of judicial selection method used and the quality of judges on the bench. If you look at the characteristics of presidential appointees to district, appellate, and Supreme Court positions, they overwhelmingly come from the same political party as the president, indicating that the selection process is highly political.

The backgrounds of judges are varied. Many persons performing the judicial role have limited legal experience or expertise, and a large portion lack law degrees.

Demographic qualifications vary as well; for instance, minimum age ranges vary from 18 to 30 years, some states do not require citizenship, and years of residence in a state also vary.

In order to ensure better judicial performance among those less skilled in the law, many judges are required to undergo judicial training. This training familiarizes judges with procedural and evidentiary law, and it socializes them concerning different motions that may be made by prosecutors or defense counsel, as well as how to rule on such motions.

Surveys by the American Judicature Society have shown that there is no uniformity or model of organization in the lower state courts. In virtually every U.S. jurisdiction, there have been instances of judicial misconduct. There is great variation among judges concerning their judicial effectiveness and how their courts are administered or managed.

More than a few judges deliberately engage in various forms of misconduct, which may include influencing trial outcomes because of bribery, or deliberately aggravating or mitigating one's sentence upon conviction. Judges are supposed to be impartial and base their decisions with reference to the facts of the case and the law; however, prejudicing a case can be sometimes difficult to detect and most judges can rationalize their decisions if confronted. Some judges are simply incompetent and make poor decisions that cause appellate courts to reverse their verdicts or sentences. Other judges sentence particular offenders according to extralegal criteria, such as race/ethnicity, socioeconomic status, and/or gender. Again justice is supposed to be blind, but research shows that extralegal factors can and do influence judicial decisions in some instances. Again, in some cases it is difficult to uncover whether the decision was objectively made or was based on some sort of bias. These variations in sentencing are called sentencing disparities and reflect bias or prejudice. There have been many criticisms of judges, not only on the basis of harmful errors; other criticisms have been levied that judges are the reason for court delays and clogged court calendars. This could be due to inefficient case management practices, where again proper training may help alleviate these issues, or factors out of their control like attorney time conflicts, unavailable witnesses, and attorney unpreparedness. In some instances technology could help facilitate case processing; however, judiciary in some states have been reluctant to use this.

Appellate courts can usually more easily manage their caseloads. When appeals are filed by either side following a judgment, appellate courts assume that the original trial judge's decision was the correct one, regardless of whether it was. This presumption is quite difficult to overcome by appellants who must prove by a preponderance of the evidence that the ruling was wrong. Errors are cited by appellants, which may be harmless, harmful, or reversible. Harmless or harmful errors may be insufficient to change the original trial outcome. Reversible errors often result in convictions being set aside or simply overturned. Under these circumstances, prosecutors must decide whether to retry the case and expend scarce resources for a new trial.

For judges who engage in misconduct, it is difficult to recall them and have them removed from office. Various states have judicial conduct commissions, where complaints are heard from different persons, usually convicted offenders, about their treatment in court and how judicial misconduct or abuse of office caused their convictions. While commissions investigate all of these complaints, most complaints are rejected. Hard evidence must be presented in order for particular judges to be sanctioned, and even harder evidence is necessary for judges to be removed from office. In some jurisdictions, judges may be removed from their positions through recall elections. Usually, in response to complaints about an elected official, a special election is held to fill the position. A popular vote will result in removal of the judge from office. Another strategy for removing judges from office is impeachment. Under the rules of impeachment, evidence of a judge's wrongful conduct must be presented to a legislative body. Usually, it is the state supreme court that oversees the impeachment proceedings. Again, a high standard of proof is required in order for particular charges of misconduct against judges to be sustained and to justify the type of sanction taken.

Questions for Review

1. Are there any national qualifications for judges in state courts? What kinds of qualifications would you propose if you could do so?
2. Distinguish between partisan and nonpartisan elections of judges. Is one type of election better than the other? Why or why not?
3. In some states, judges are appointed by governors. What are some criticisms of gubernatorial appointees?
4. How are U.S. Supreme Court justices appointed? Who must approve these appointments?
5. Describe how federal circuit court judges, U.S. District Court judges, and U.S. magistrates are appointed.
6. What is a popular merit method for selecting judges? Why is it favored in various states?
7. Is the merit plan for judicial selection superior to legislative or gubernatorial appointment methods? Why or why not?
8. Differentiate between the Kales and the Missouri plans.
9. What sort of training do judges typically receive before becoming judges?
10. Identify four types of judicial misconduct.
11. How can we sanction judges who engage in misconduct?
12. What are two mechanisms for removing bad judges from the bench? Describe each process briefly.

Suggested Readings

1. D. P. Green and D. Winik (2010). "Using Random Judge Assignments to Estimate the Effects of Incarceration and Probation on Recidivism Among Drug Offenders." *Criminology* **48**:357–387.
2. B. Greg, J. Feinblatt, and S. Glazer (eds.) (2005). *Good Courts: The Case for Problem–Solving Justice*. London, UK: New Press.
3. D. A. Krauss (2004). "Adjusting the Risk of Recidivism: Do Judicial Departures Worsen or Improve Recidivism Prediction Under the Federal Sentencing Guidelines?" *Behavioral Sciences and the Law* **22**:731–750.
4. M. Klatt (2007). "Taking Rights less Seriously. A Structural Analysis of Judicial Discretion." *Ratio Juris* **20**:506–529.

CHAPTER 6

Juries

CHAPTER OBJECTIVES

As a result of reading this chapter, you will have accomplished the following objectives:

1. Understand the history of juries as well as the development of the grand jury and the petit jury.
2. Understand the jury selection process including what the *venire* is as well as the purpose of the *voir dire*.
3. Understand the different ways in which jurors can be excluded including challenges for cause and peremptory challenges.
4. Describe what jury consultants are, and understand the science behind jury selection.
5. Understand the meaning of jury size and whether a verdict has to be unanimous.
6. Understand jury sequestration and other methods of minimizing exposure of the jury to trial publicity.
7. Describe the process of jury decision making and voting.
8. Understand some of the current controversies surrounding jury verdicts.
9. Understand jury nullification.
10. Describe what constitutes jury or juror misconduct.

KEY TERMS

affirmative registration	grand jury	jury sequestration	*venire*
blue-ribbon jury	hung jury	peremptory challenge	venireman list
challenge for cause	juror misconduct	petit jury	verdict-driven jury
evidence-driven jury	jury nullification	scientific jury selection	*voir dire*

It happened in Anchorage, Alaska. Frank W. Turney was convicted of jury tampering in 1994 because he approached prospective jurors at the state courthouse and passed to them information about their rights as jurors. He was the chairman of the Alaska chapter of the Fully Informed Jury Association. Turney attempted to convey information to prospective jurors about their powers in listening to cases and deciding one's guilt or innocence, despite judicial instructions. Turney maintained that he did nothing wrong by attempting to inform prospective jurors about their juror rights under the law. Specifically he gave prospective jurors information about jury nullification, where the term was explained and suggestions for its use were given. Eventually one of the persons Turney contacted became a juror in a case involving a man accused of weapons misconduct. The jury deadlocked when the juror called an 800 number given to him by Turney and the juror decided to vote as he wanted rather than with the other jurors. Subsequently, Turney was charged with and convicted of jury tampering; he was sentenced to 60 days in jail and a $500 fine. He appealed and ultimately exhausted his state remedies. Next he sought relief through the federal court system. He contended that he was merely exercising his right to free speech and did nothing wrong to interfere with the jury process. A three-judge panel with the Ninth Circuit Court of Appeals rejected his most recent appeal in March 2005. Should any person be allowed to distribute information about juror rights to prospective jurors in court-houses or any other public place where trials are held?

Source: Adapted from Amanda Bohman and the Associated Press, "Turney's Jury Tampering Conviction Upheld," March 18, 2005.

It was finally time, time to kill. Time to end the years of abuse and torment. While her common-law husband lay passed out drunk in the pickup, Jane Stafford shot and killed him. When arrested by police, Jane admitted to killing her husband while he was unarmed and unconscious. She was charged with first-degree murder. However, during the trial the jury would hear the alarming details of her husband's abuse for more than five years. The jury learned that many in the community, even law enforcement, feared Jane's husband. He weighed over 250 pounds and had abused and assaulted two previous wives and their children. Jane was also sexually abused by her husband and was even forced to have sex with the family dog. How would the jury decide this case? She had admitted to killing him when he was passed out drunk and no immediate threat to her. To the surprise of everyone, the jury returned a verdict of not guilty. Did the jury return the correct verdict? How could the jury justify this verdict? The murder was obviously not self-defense. Are there any negative aspects of jury nullification? If you were a juror in this case, how would you have voted?

Source: J. Steed, "Will Battered Wife Face a New Murder Trial?" *Toronto Globe and Mail,* February 4, 1983:A1.

INTRODUCTION

Many persons assume that the right to a jury trial has always been an important part of most societies. However, history suggests that using juries to make judgments in disputes is relatively rare. In ancient times, disputes or conflicts were resolved through direct interpersonal violence. The disputants engaged in some form of physical confrontation (e.g., duel or battle), and the winner of the confrontation was also the winner of the dispute. Jurors like judges are supposed to be impartial and hear the facts of the case, and base a decision of guilt or innocence on those facts only.

The next part of the chapter will discuss the history of the jury and relate anecdotes on the development of the grand and petit juries. Being selected for jury duty is an involved process that begins with a list of potential jurors called a *venire*; potential jurors are asked questions relating to their appropriateness to serve; if they answer in the affirmative, they will be asked to further proceed with a process called a *voir dire*. The process is to ensure the appropriateness of persons to sit on a jury but also to ensure a defendant's right to a "speedy and public trial, by an impartial jury in the state and district wherein the crime shall have been committed" (Sixth Amendment). This means trial by a fair jury composed of an adequate cross section of the community. Constructing an adequate cross section of one's peers who are impartial can sometimes be difficult, and there have been many defendants who have appealed their cases based upon a violation of their Sixth Amendment rights. There have been calls that jurors have been removed for no other reason than their gender or their skin color. The Supreme Court has made several rulings relating to the process of jury selection. These decisions will be detailed in this chapter. A number of these have been related to the use of peremptory challenges. These challenges are used by prosecution and defense to remove a juror for no particular reason; these challenges, however, are limited. Another method to remove a juror is a challenge for cause. The prosecution and defense are not limited in the number of these challenges they can request. This type of challenge removes the juror for a particular reason—the person is biased in some way or does not meet the requirements to serve.

The role of the jury has been constantly challenged and revised. A number of cases in the last few decades have caused more than a few critics to question the integrity of the jury system, and have spurred calls for reform. It seems that we are constantly confronted with cases where we believe the defendant is guilty only to have the jury announce a verdict of not guilty and the defendant is freed. Often, we are outraged by reports of juries awarding multimillion dollar damages to plaintiffs where the allegations against defendants have been questionable. It is the idea of excessive jury verdicts, and even calls for jury nullification of the law, that has led to calls for reform. Many legal scholars argue that juries should be replaced with panels of experts who would be more likely to see the merits of a case, understand the law, and not be swayed by emotion (Adler 1995). In fact, we have a system now that is quite the opposite, where experts in the law, law enforcement, professors of law, and members of the medical community are readily excused from sitting on a jury.

THE HISTORY OF JURIES

The jury system in America has not had a direct, linear evolution. The ancient Greeks were the first to rely on certain persons in their community to pass judgment in a variety of cases. At one point the entire population of Athens was required to hear appeals from the magistrates. Thus, it is not surprising that this process became difficult to administer. This process was subsequently replaced with a procedure designed to select jury members drawn from a cross section of the community to work with the magistrate and render decisions in criminal cases. This new jury was called a dicastery.

The ancient Romans also relied on an early form of the jury. In 190 B.C., for instance, magistrates could assemble a jury for certain criminal acts, including forgery, counterfeiting, and embezzlement. The jury was comprised of 35–75 people who decided the guilt of the accused. No provisions for appeals of verdicts were made.

In earlier times, common-law juries had a dual function. They had the responsibility of investigating crimes and conducting trials of accused persons. However, subsequent to the Norman invasion, these two responsibilities were divided into separate functioning units. The grand jury was created to investigate and report crimes, while the petit jury was used to determine a defendant's guilt or innocence. Today, these different jury systems continue to perform the same functions.

THE DEVELOPMENT OF THE GRAND JURY

The earliest forms of the **grand jury** can be traced back to Germanic tribal law and Anglo-Saxon dooms. The earliest versions of the grand jury had its origins in the Assize of Clarendon in 1166. An assize is essentially an order by the king and is binding throughout the kingdom. On this occasion, King Henry II ordered that 12 of every 100 family heads be placed under oath and report offenses or known criminals to the authorities. The most commonly reported offenses were robberies, murders, and theft. This practice was very similar to our contemporary neighborhood watch programs.

In colonial times, since judges traveled in circuits and were only scheduled to visit certain cities or towns every few months, members of the grand jury were responsible for gathering information about known criminal activity and present their information to the authorities whenever they were in town. Most often, when judges heard the cases presented to them by the grand jury, they ordered the defendant banished from the community. In essence, all trials during these early years were bench trials. The judge decided the guilt or innocence of defendants and determined the nature of the punishment. The petit jury or trial jury as we know it did not descend directly from the grand jury. Rather, it gradually replaced trials by ordeal.

THE DEVELOPMENT OF THE PETIT JURY

In medieval England, trials by ordeal were used to determine a defendant's guilt or innocence. The prevailing practice was to have the process blessed by a priest. The belief was that because the proceeding was endorsed by the church and ultimately God, it was also just. The trial participants believed that if a defendant was innocent, God would intervene and protect them from harm. For example, the trial by hot water required that defendants place their hands into a pot of boiling water and remove a rock placed at the bottom. Once the accused placed their hands into the water and removed the rock, their hands were wrapped in bandages. After a specified time, the bandages were removed and if the hands were burned, the defendants were believed to be guilty because God did not intervene and protect the accused from harm. This practice went unchallenged for centuries.

During the Fourth Lateran Council in 1215, the church withdrew its support for the trial by ordeal. This meant that priests would no longer be present to bless the trial. Without the benefit of blessings from priests and the presence of the church, it was also believed that God would not intervene on behalf of innocent defendants. The trial by ordeal was gradually replaced by the **petit jury** or trial jury. Initially, those accused of crimes were reluctant to accept a jury trial because if they were found guilty, they would lose their property and their descendants would lose their inheritance. The same fate would not befall those who opted for the bench trial. Consequently, the initial structure of the jury trial had an additional penalty that was not included in the bench trial.

Another significant event occurred in 1215. King John was forced to sign the Magna Carta. This document provided the foundations for the provisions of due process and the right to a jury trial of one's peers. The section of the Magna Carta that established this concept reads, "No Freeman shall be taken, or imprisoned or be disseized of his Freehold, or Liberties, or Free Customs, or be outlawed, or exiled, or otherwise destroyed; nor will we not pass upon him nor condemn him, but by lawful judgement of his peers, of by (a) the Law of the land. (2) We will sell to no man, (b) we will not deny or defer to any man either Justice or Right" (McCart 1964, 5).

Originally, these rights were extended only to freemen or nobility. This meant that most people were still denied justice and the due process of law. The rights of a jury trial and due process were addressed in the Statute of Westminister of 1275. The relevant portions of this statute mandated that "no City, Borough, nor town nor any maybe amerced [fined or punished arbitrarily] without reasonable cause, and according to the Quality of his Trespass, that is to say, every Freeman saving his Freehold, a Merchant saving his Merchandise, a Villain saving his Gaynage [his rights in agricultural land, his tools and the product thereof] and that by his or their peers" (McCart 1964, 6).

During this same time period, there were no lawyers to act as advocates. To address this deficiency, Parliament authorized 40 men to practice law throughout England. This number was believed adequate to fulfill the needs of the entire country. The trial jury during this period differed in one significant respect from the jury system in America today. The medieval jury was expected to have some knowledge of the case. It was believed that juror knowledge of the case would assist them in determining the guilt or innocence of the accused. Today, our notions of an impartial jury have been used to exclude those who have knowledge of the case. Historically, jurors were considered qualified if they were familiar with the facts of the case. Now jurors are considered more qualified if they have little or no knowledge of the facts of the case.

THE JURY SELECTION PROCESS

Venire

In medieval England jurors were selected by the king and only from the wealthy landowners. Throughout history those who were allowed to serve on juries were few in number. The selection of the **venire** or the **venireman list** of those qualified to serve as jurors has changed dramatically over time. For example, during most of American history, women were excluded from jury service. Some of the most prominent legal scholars of the eighteenth century argued that women should not be allowed to serve on juries. For example, it was believed that women should be excluded from jury service because of the defect of sex. This defect made it impossible for women to engage in intelligent decision making required for jury service. This perspective also existed in the United States. Women were excluded from jury service until 1919, when Utah became the first state to allow women to serve as jurors. The national sentiment against women as prospective jurors changed dramatically after the passage of the Nineteenth Amendment, which gave women the right to vote. When the Nineteenth Amendment was passed, most states allowed women to serve on juries. However, in many jurisdictions, women were not automatically included in the *venire*. As recently as 1966, three states did not permit women to serve on juries. In many other jurisdictions, women had to go to the courthouse and ask to be included in the list of potential jurors. This process was known as **affirmative registration**. In 1966, the U.S. Supreme Court upheld the practice of excluding women from the jury pool when it reasoned, "The legislature has a right to exclude women so they may contribute their services as mothers, wives, homemakers, and also to protect them . . . from the filth, obscenity, and noxious atmosphere...of the courtroom" (*Hoyt v. Florida*, 1961:57). It wasn't until 1975 in the case of *Taylor v. Louisiana* that the U.S. Supreme Court changed its mind and ruled that the affirmative registration process was unconstitutional.

Currently, most jurisdictions use voter registration lists to obtain prospective jurors for the jury pool. Once persons have been drawn from the list, the court sends them a short questionnaire summoning them for jury service and asking then to complete a short questionnaire to determine if they are qualified for jury service. The short questionnaire includes questions that might automatically exclude them from jury service. The standard questions include but are not limited to the following:

1. Are you a U.S. citizen?
2. Are you at least 18 years old?
3. Do you have any mental or physical disability?
4. Have you ever been convicted of a felony?

Answering "yes" or "no" to any of these questions may be sufficient grounds to exclude certain persons from the jury pool. If these persons pass the initial screening, they are sent a letter advising them to appear for jury service at the courthouse on a particular date and time.

Some persons have argued that relying solely on voter registration lists systematically excludes segments of the population. Levin (1988) has estimated that voter registration lists excluded 60 percent of the population. Who does this process exclude? The poor, undereducated, minorities, and women are less likely to register to vote than men, more educated persons, and nonminorities. Most defendants in the criminal court share most of the same characteristics as those who are excluded from jury service. Ultimately, voter registration lists are ineffective for obtaining a cross section of the community. Levin suggests that states must draw upon voter registration lists, tax rolls, public utility records, driver's license records, and the telephone directory to make better prospective juror selections from those groups who are typically bypassed whenever states rely on voter registration lists. In particular, the undereducated, poor, and minorities will most likely drive a car, have a telephone, and use electricity. Relying on these records will increase the representativeness of those who are called to jury service.

Voir Dire

We have the expectation that jurors should be unbiased or impartial when they hear the facts of a case. The process of determining a person's appropriateness or worthiness to serve as a juror is called **voir dire**. *Voir dire* is the opportunity to learn about the existing prejudices of prospective jurors. *Voir dire* means to "speak the truth." *Voir dire* is the crucial process through which attorneys attempt to uncover prospective juror biases, which might prevent certain jurors from providing defendants with a fair and impartial trial. Some persons have argued that while *voir dire* has frequently been called jury selection, this term really is inappropriate. This is because we don't actually select those who sit on a jury as much as we eliminate those who are unsuitable.

The *voir dire* process is described as follows. During *voir dire*, the trial judge and/or attorneys may ask questions of prospective jurors to determine their qualifications for jury service, their knowledge of the defendant and the case, and attitudes toward issues or individuals on the case that bias their views of the trial evidence. For example, questions may be wideranging or more specifically related to the case, depending on what the trial judge allows.

BOX 6.1

A Case of Jury Tampering

Justice takes a while to be concluded. In Frank W. Turney's case, it has taken at least ten years. Turney, a Fairbanks, Alaska, resident, was convicted of jury tampering in 1994. A case was being heard involving a man charged with illegal weapons possession. Turney's method was to approach jurors as they entered and exited the courthouse each day while the trial was in progress and give them information about juror's rights and an 800 number for the Fully Informed Jury Association. Turney was the chairman of the Alaska chapter. Turney also advised several of the jurors in the case that juries have the right to judge the law as well as the facts of a controversy. He told them that jury nullification is one of the checks and balances in our governmental laws, and he advocated that they consider jury nullification as a possible action in the case before them. One of the jurors Turney approached called the 800 number and told them he would vote how he wanted. But the jury deadlocked in the case. Subsequently, Turney's actions came to the attention of the presiding judge, and law enforcement authorities arrested Turney and charged him with jury tampering. He was convicted and sentenced to 60 days in prison and a $500 fine. Turney appealed, and eventually, the Alaska Supreme Court heard the case in 2005. The three-judge panel upheld Turney's conviction. Subsequently, Turney was asked if he was going to appeal to the U.S. Supreme Court. "No," he said. "If there had been one dissenting judge, I would have. But it was a 3–0 slam dunk against me." Turney's attorney argued that Turney had the right of free speech in the case, and that he was only trying to educate the jurors about their rights and responsibilities. The court saw things differently. Should persons have the right to approach jurors in criminal cases and attempt to persuade them to vote in particular ways? Is free speech at issue here? Is "educating" juries about their rights jury tampering? What do you think?

Source: Adapted from Amanda Bohman and the Associated Press, "Turner's Jury Tampering Conviction Upheld," March 18, 2005.

Despite the purpose of the *voir dire* process to remove prospective jurors with biases, many persons have argued that the process actually achieves the opposite result. Both prosecutors and defense attorneys attempt to select jurors who might be sympathetic to their particular position. If one side is successful in soliciting crucial information during *voir dire*, they can use this information to remove unsympathetic jurors and increase jury bias either against or in favor of the defendant. Typically, prosecutors seek prospective jurors who are middle-aged, white, and middle class. It is believed that these persons are more likely to be supportive of the prosecution. However, defense counsels seek to remove prospective jurors with extreme views.

THE ELIMINATION OF JURORS

Challenges for Cause

During the *voir dire* process, the trial judge and attorneys attempt to uncover any biases that might hinder prospective jurors from serving in an impartial manner. There are two methods used to eliminate biased jurors or those considered undesirable by either side for whatever reason. One type of challenge is known as a **challenge for cause** (also a strike for cause). The other type of challenge is called a peremptory challenge. Prospective jurors may be challenged for cause and removed from the jury if they do not meet certain state mandatory requirements (e.g., being underage or not being a U.S. citizen), as well as for a specific bias (e.g., being related by blood or marriage to the accused), or for a nonspecific bias (e.g., expressing prejudice toward the defendant). Either the judge or the attorney may ask these questions. However, when the defense or prosecution wants to have a juror removed through the use of a challenge for cause, they must provide the judge with a compelling reason for doing so. When challenges for cause are used to strike certain prospective jurors, the judge is the final arbiter of whether the juror stays or goes.

For instance, a prominent black Tennessee defense attorney from Nashville, Avon Williams, was noted for his ability to dismiss prospective white jurors for cause whenever he represented black defendants. He would ask these prospective jurors if they were prejudiced toward blacks. Most would answer "No." Then Williams would ask them where they lived and if they belonged to any country clubs. Many of these white jurors lived in all-white neighborhoods, and some belonged to country clubs. He would then ask if these country clubs barred or admitted blacks. These white prospective jurors would become agitated and say that their country clubs and neighborhoods did not include blacks. Williams would then ask the judge to strike these white prospective jurors for cause. The judge usually granted Williams's request, based on the nature of his *voir dire* questioning.

Peremptory Challenges

The second method for removing prospective jurors is by using a **peremptory challenge**. Unlike challenges for cause, peremptory challenges do not require any explanations from attorneys for either side. Both prosecutors and defense counsel are given a limited number of these peremptory challenges. The number of peremptory challenges varies according to the seriousness of the case. In the most serious cases or cases with a significant amount of pretrial publicity, attorneys are given a larger number of challenges. Attorneys involved in less serious cases have fewer peremptory challenges. For instance, in most misdemeanor and less serious felony cases, each side is given six peremptory challenges. For more serious cases such as murder trials, each side is given a dozen or more peremptory challenges. In some jurisdictions, as many as 20 peremptory challenges may be given to each side for their use in striking prospective jurors they don't like, for whatever reason.

How do prosecutors and defense counsels know which prospective jurors to remove? During the *voir dire* process, attorneys usually ask members of the jury pool about their occupation, their attitudes toward law enforcement, and their general perceptions about the offense. For example, it is not uncommon for a defense attorney in a drunk-driving case to ask prospective jurors if it is a crime to drink and drive. Some of the members of the jury pool will say that drinking and driving is a crime. Some defense counsels will use this opportunity to educate the jury pool that drinking and driving is not a crime, and that it only rises to the level of a criminal offense when someone becomes legally intoxicated and drives a vehicle. Attorneys for both sides also use the information gathered from the *voir dire* together with juror demographics (e.g., age, gender, race) to develop a profile of how prospective jurors with similar characteristics feel about certain issues that might arise during the trial.

BOX 6.2

Selected Jury Cases

Batson v. Kentucky, 476 U.S. 79, 106 S.Ct. 1712 (1986)

In Kentucky, a black man, Batson, was convicted by an all-white jury of second-degree burglary. The prosecutor had used all of his peremptory challenges to exclude the few black prospective jurors from the jury pool. Ordinarily, peremptory challenges may be used to strike particular jurors without the prosecutor's having to provide a reason for doing so. In this case, the use of peremptory challenges was rather transparent, and Batson appealed. In a landmark case, the U.S. Supreme Court decided that peremptory challenges may not be used for a racially discriminatory purpose. Thus, creating an all-white jury by deliberately eliminating all prospective black candidates was discriminatory. The U.S. Supreme Court ruled in favor of Batson.

Georgia v. McCollum, 505 U.S. 42, 112 S.Ct. 2348 (1992)

McCollum was indicted on charges of aggravated assault and simple battery. During jury selection, his attorney used his peremptory challenges to strike certain prospective jurors from jury duty because of their race. McCollum was acquitted. The state challenged the use of these peremptory challenges, arguing that they had created a biased jury as in *Batson v. Kentucky* (1986), in which the prosecutor used peremptory challenges for racial-bias purposes. The U.S. Supreme Court agreed with the state and rejected the defendant's attorney's use of peremptory challenges for racial purposes. Thus, according to *Batson* and *McCollum*, neither prosecutors nor defense attorneys may deliberately use their peremptory challenges to excuse jurors on the basis of their race.

Griffith v. Kentucky, 479 U.S. 314, 107 S.Ct. 708 (1987)

Griffith, a black man, was arrested for conspiracy to distribute marijuana. During his 1982 trial in Jefferson County, the prosecutor used four out of five peremptory challenges to strike from jury duty four out of five prospective black jurors. Griffith was convicted. He later appealed, saying that the prosecutor had violated his right to due process by striking from jury duty most of the black candidates. He said the case of *Batson v. Kentucky* (1986) should be retroactively applied to his case. The U.S. Supreme Court overturned his conviction, holding that the *Batson* case, prohibiting prosecutors from using their peremptory challenges to give racial bias to a jury pool, should be retroactively applied where a showing exists that such conduct has occurred. Thus, Griffith's case qualified for a retroactive application of *Batson*. The U.S. Supreme Court held that a new rule for the conduct of criminal prosecutions is to be applied retroactively to all cases, state or federal, pending on direct review or not yet final, with no exception for cases in which the new rule constitutes a "clear break" with the past.

Teague v. Lane, 489 U.S. 288, 109 S.Ct. 1060 (1989)

Teague, a black man, was accused of attempted murder. During jury selection, the prosecutor used all of his ten peremptory challenges to exclude blacks from the jury. He was eventually convicted by an all-white jury. In the meantime, *Batson v. Kentucky* (1986) had recently been decided, which established that blacks could not be excluded from jury duty by use of peremptory challenges.

Teague sought to make this rule retroactive in his case, thus causing his conviction to be overturned and a new trial conducted. The U.S. Supreme Court rejected the retroactive principle relating to *Batson*, holding that convicted offenders are barred from making retroactive claims involving racial discrimination in jury selection. Further, Teague had failed to make a convincing case that the peremptory challenges had been used in a discriminatory fashion.

Hernandez v. New York, 500 U.S. 352, 111 S.Ct. 1859 (1991)

Hernandez was convicted of various crimes. During the selection of his jury, the prosecutor used several peremptory challenges to strike from potential jury duty four Latinos. Following his conviction, Hernandez filed an appeal, alleging that the prosecutor had deliberately deprived him of a fair trial by eliminating persons like Hernandez. The argument was similar to the one made in *Batson v. Kentucky* (1986), in which it was held that peremptory challenges cannot be used to create racially pure juries or to strike off members of a particular race. At the time, objections had been raised by defense counsel, but the prosecutor cited various valid reasons for using these challenges. The U.S. Supreme Court upheld his conviction, holding that an acceptable race-neutral explanation had been provided by the prosecutor for striking the Latino jurors in that case. No evidence to the contrary had been presented.

Powers v. Ohio, 499 U.S. 400, 111 S.Ct. 1364 (1991)

Powers was charged with murder, aggravated murder, and attempted aggravated murder, all with firearm specifications (calling for mandatory minimum sentences). A white man, he objected to the government's use of peremptory challenges to strike seven black prospective jurors from the jury. Subsequently, Powers was convicted. He appealed, alleging that his Fourteenth Amendment right had been violated under the equal-protection clause because of the alleged discriminatory use of peremptory challenges. The matter of excluding prospective black jurors by the use of peremptory challenges had already been decided in *Batson v. Kentucky* (1986), in which it was declared unconstitutional to use peremptory challenges to achieve a racially pure jury. In the *Batson* case, however, the defendant was black, and government prejudice was obvious in the use of these peremptory challenges. In the *Powers* case, the defendant was white, and prospective black jurors had been excluded. The U.S. Supreme Court heard Powers's appeal and overturned his conviction on the same grounds as *Batson*, holding that criminal defendants may object to race-based exclusions of jurors effected through peremptory challenges whether or not defendants and excluded jurors share the same race.

Purkett v. Elem, 514 U.S. 765, 115 S.Ct. 1769 (1995)

Elem, a black man, was accused of second-degree robbery. During the selection of jurors, the prosecutor used one of his peremptory challenges to strike from the jury pool a prospective black juror. Elem appealed, alleging that this use of a peremptory challenge was in violation of a policy set forth in *Batson v. Kentucky* (1986) prohibiting the use of peremptory challenges for racial purposes. The U.S. Supreme Court heard Elem's *habeas corpus* petition and argument. It upheld Elem's conviction when it determined that the prosecutor had used the peremptory challenge in a racially neutral fashion. The reason given for striking this black prospective juror was that the man had long, unkempt hair and a mustache and beard. The U.S. Supreme Court accepted this explanation as being race-neutral. It held that opponents of peremptory challenges must carry the burden of proving that purposeful discrimination has occurred. The explanation given by those exercising their peremptory challenges need not be persuasive or even plausible; rather, these explanations are considered only in determining whether opponents have carried their burden of proof by showing that the peremptory strikes were discriminatory. In this case, the peremptory challenge was satisfactorily explained and Elem's conviction was upheld.

Miller-El v. Cockrell, 537 U.S. 322, 123 S.Ct. 1029 (2003)

Thomas Miller-El, his wife Dorothy, and Kenneth Flowers robbed a Holiday Inn in Dallas, Texas, in 1985. They bound and gagged two employees and then shot them. One employee died, but the other recovered and was able to identify Miller-El and his associates as his assailants.

(continued)

(*continued*)

Subsequently, Miller-El was indicted and tried for capital murder in a Dallas criminal court in February and March 1986. During jury selection, the prosecutor used his peremptory challenges to exclude 10 of the 11 African American prospective jurors, thus creating a largely white jury. Following the jury selection, Miller-El moved to strike the jury on the grounds that the prosecution had violated the equal-protection clause of the Fourteenth Amendment by excluding African Americans through the use of peremptory challenges. Miller-El's motion was denied. Upon his subsequent conviction for murder, Miller-El, a black, was sentenced to death. He began a lengthy series of appeals, contending that blacks had been systematically excluded from the jury. During his appeals, the case of *Batson v. Kentucky* (1986) was decided and established a three-part process for evaluating claims that a prosecutor used peremptory challenges in violation of the equal-protection clause. First, a defendant must make a *prima facie* showing that a peremptory challenge has been exercised on the basis of race. Second, if that showing has been made, the prosecution must offer a race-neutral basis for striking the juror in question. Third, in light of the parties' submissions, the trial court must determine whether the defendant has shown purposeful discrimination. Both Texas appellate courts and the federal Fifth Circuit Court of Appeals denied Miller-El's petitions, citing that insufficient evidence existed to show bias on the part of the prosecutor. The U.S. Supreme Court heard the case and disagreed. The U.S. Supreme Court overturned the circuit court, holding that Miller-El was entitled to appeal the issue of biased jury selection in his original trial, as there was evident unreasonableness associated with how the original jury was selected. Miller-El was entitled to appeal this issue in a Texas court in light of the holding in *Batson v. Kentucky*.

Johnson v. California, ___ U.S. ___, 125 S.Ct. 2410 (2005)

Jay Johnson, a black man, was convicted of second-degree murder in the death of a 19-month-old white child. During jury selection, several prospective jurors were excused for cause. The prosecutor used three peremptory challenges to strike all of the prospective black jurors, thus leaving Johnson to be tried by an all-white jury. These peremptory challenges were opposed by Johnson, but the judge rejected his arguments. The prosecutor failed to explain why he had excused these black prospective jurors, but the judge declared that he (the judge) had reviewed the record and was convinced that the prosecutor's strikes could be justified by race-neutral reasons. Johnson appealed through the California courts, alleging that the exclusion of blacks from the jury deprived him of a fair trial. An appellate court set aside Johnson's conviction but the California Supreme Court reinstated it, acknowledging that although the exclusion of all three black prospective jurors looked suspicious, the court deferred to the judge's ruling and explanation. Johnson therefore appealed to the U.S. Supreme Court, where the case was heard. The U.S. Supreme Court reversed Johnson's conviction, holding that California's standard is an inappropriate yardstick to measure the sufficiency of a *prima facie* case of purposeful discrimination in jury selection. The facts that the trial judge said that the case was close and the California Supreme Court said that it was suspicious that all three black prospective jurors were removed were sufficient bases for a *prima facie* case of discrimination in Johnson's case.

Miller v. Dretke, ___ U.S. ___, 125 S.Ct. 2317 (2005)

Thomas Miller-El, a black man, and Kennard Flowers robbed a Dallas, Texas Holiday Inn in November 1985. During the robbery they bound and gagged two employees and then shot each twice in the back, killing one and seriously injuring the other. Subsequently, Miller-El was charged with capital murder. His trial lasted five weeks. At the beginning of Miller-El's trial during jury selection, 108 persons were selected as the *venire*. Of these, there were 20 blacks. Subsequently, 19 out of 20 blacks were rejected as jurors. Three were dismissed for cause; six were dismissed by parties' agreement; and ten were struck by the prosecutor through the use of peremptory challenges. Miller-El objected to these strikes but his objections were overruled. Miller-El was convicted and sentenced to death. He filed numerous appeals over the years on different grounds. His most recent appeal was a *habeas corpus* action alleging that the prosecutor engaged in purposeful discrimination by striking 10 out of 11 black venirepersons. A U.S. District Court denied the petition and this decision was affirmed by the Fifth Circuit

Court of Appeals. Miller-El appealed to the U.S. Supreme Court, where the case was heard. The U.S. Supreme Court reversed and remanded, holding that the Texas court's factual findings as to the nonpretextual nature of the state's race-neutral explanations for its use of peremptory challenges to excuse 10 of 11 black venirepersons were shown to be wrong by clear and convincing evidence. Based on the totality of relevant facts in Miller-El's case, discriminatory jury selection had been demonstrated. The prosecutors used peremptory challenges to exclude 91 percent of the eligible black venire panelists, a disparity unlikely to have been produced by happenstance.

Rice v. Collins,___U.S.___, 126 S.Ct. 969 (2006)

Steven Collins, an African American, was convicted of cocaine possession, in violation of California's three-strike rule, which would subject him to a harsher sentence. Collins sought postconviction relief on *habeas corpus* grounds, in particular objecting to the peremptory challenge of an African American prospective juror on allegedly race-based grounds (see *Batson v. Kentucky*). The dismissal of this juror, according to Collins, meant that his right to a fair trial by an impartial jury of his peers was violated. A *Batson* challenge, where peremptory challenges of jurors are used to strike prospective jurors on the basis of race, (1) involves a showing that the prosecutor exercised the peremptory challenge on the basis of race; (2) obligated the prosecutor to provide a race-neutral explanation for striking the juror in question; and (3) determined whether the defendant carried the burden of proof in demonstrating that the peremptory challenge was indeed race-based. The prosecutor defended his actions as race-neutral, contending that the prospective juror was struck because (1) she was young and might be too tolerant of drug offenders; (2) she was single and lacked community ties; and (3) she had rolled her eyes when asked certain questions by the court. State appellate courts, including the California Supreme Court, upheld Collins's conviction, but the Ninth Circuit Court of Appeals set aside Collins's conviction on the grounds of an unreasonable factual determination by the prosecutor based on trial information presented. The government appealed and the U.S. Supreme Court heard the case. The U.S. Supreme Court reversed the Ninth Circuit, reinstating Collins's conviction, holding that the Ninth Circuit's grounds for reversal were themselves based on a set of debatable inferences about prosecutorial conduct in jury selection. The U.S. Supreme Court said that while reasonable minds reviewing the record might disagree about the prosecutor's credibility, nothing on the record suffices to supersede the trial court's credibility determination of the prosecutor's actions regarding the peremptory strike of the African American juror and the race-neutral explanation provided.

Social scientists have discovered that often demographic characteristics are quite important and influence one's perceptions and attitudes. For example, Winston and Winston (1980) found that jurors who were opposed to the death penalty were usually under 45 years of age, had a high school education, were employed, and did not watch the news on television. However, those favoring the death penalty tended to be males age 60 and older who had less than a high school education, were unemployed or retired, and watched the news on television. If either the prosecution or defense wish to strike particular prospective jurors, they may simply excuse them by using a peremptory challenge.

Several serious allegations were made about prosecutors who systematically remove minorities from juries where the criminal defendants are also minorities. Some persons have alleged that this has occurred even in the most high-profile cases. For example, Suggs and Sales (1981) describe how prosecutors have used most of their peremptory challenges to remove most blacks from the jury panel where a black defendant is on trial for a serious offense. Defense attorneys have also been accused of using peremptory challenges to remove certain types of persons who they believe would be unsympathetic to their position. For example, in the trial of the Harrisburg Seven, the defense used its 28 challenges to remove those who were wealthy and exhibited conservative views (O'Rourke 1972).

For many decades, the use of peremptory challenges was inviolate. But in 1986, the U.S. Supreme Court decided to review the issue of using peremptory challenges to systematically remove black jurors in the case of *Batson v. Kentucky*. The U.S. Supreme Court found that the peremptory challenges used by the prosecutor were race-based and therefore unconstitutional. In 1991 the Court applied the equal-protection argument to defense counsels (*Georgia v. McCollum*) and in civil cases such as *Edmonson v. Leesville Concrete Co.* (1991). In 2000 the Court in *United States v. Martinez-Salazar* ruled that the use of a peremptory challenge to exclude a juror based solely on their gender, race, or ethnic group is unconstitutional. Lastly, the Third Circuit Court of Appeals in 2003 in the case of *Rico v. Leftridge-Byrd* applied the ruling in *Batson* to Italian American members of the jury because they had been excluded due to their Italian last names.

JURY CONSULTANTS AND SCIENTIFIC JURY SELECTION

F. Lee Bailey and Melvin Belli have been credited as being the first defense attorneys to hire experts to assist them in the jury selection process. However, it wasn't until the Berrigan brothers' trial that **scientific jury selection** became an important trial tactic. Daniel and Philip Berrigan were Catholic priests who had been charged with conspiracy to kidnap then-secretary of state Henry Kissinger, raid draft boards, and bomb tunnels in Washington, D.C. Jay Schulman, a social scientist who sympathized with the defendants, decided to use his skill in social research methods to assist the defendants. He wanted to determine how several demographic characteristics (e.g., age, political philosophy, gender) influenced prospective jurors' perceptions of the issues surrounding the case and their attitudes toward the defendants. He and his colleagues conducted a telephone interview of 840 randomly selected registered voters. These interviews were followed by personal interviews of 262 people. During the face-to-face interviews, the respondents were asked questions in the following areas:

a. Media contact—Respondents were asked of their choice of newspapers, magazines, radio, and television stations and their amount of contact with each.

b. Knowledge of the defendants and their case—The names of the defendants were embedded with the names of other people in the news and respondents were asked if they had heard of the person and what they had heard about them.

c. Greatest American of the past 10 or 15 years (to seek respondent's values).

d. Trust in government—Three questions were asked relating to the governments' decisions and attempts to do what is right.

    1. "How much time do you think you can trust the Government in Washington to do what is right?"

    2. "Do you feel that the people who are running the Government are smart people who usually know what they are doing?"

    3. "Would you say that the Government is pretty much run for a few big interests looking out for themselves, or is it run for the benefit of the people?"

e. Ages and activities of respondents children.

f. Religious attitudes and commitment.

g. Spare time activities.

h. Organizational memberships.

i. Attitudes that were potentially related to the trial. The interviewers sought the extent of agreement with eight statements concerning issues, such as right to private property, support for the government, police use of force, and the like.

j. Scale of acceptable antiwar activities. (Wanamaker 1978, 348)

Using the results of this survey, the researchers were able to determine that conservatives with higher education and who received their news from metropolitan news sources held opinions that were unfavorable to the defendants. Surprisingly, the researchers found that religious

---

BOX 6.3

Can Jury Consultants Select Predictable Juries?

The job of jury consultants is to assist both defense and prosecuting attorneys in figuring out the types of people who will be most likely inclined to find in favor or against particular defendants. Several jury consultant firms have bragged that they have a nearly perfect batting average in picking juries favorable to defendants. However, the job of being a jury consultant is becoming increasingly difficult. This is primarily because of media coverage, particularly in high-profile trials such as those involving key officials at Enron and Adelphia. New stereotypes have formed in the public's mind about company executives and their involvement in company scandals involving possible embezzlement and fraud.

A spokesperson for the jury-consulting firm Zagnoli, McEvoy, and Foley of Chicago has said that it is a rare jury that you talk to now where the majority of people have not lost money in the last couple of years. "Everybody's lost money. That's bad for defendants in trials involving corporate scandals, like Enron." Patricia McEvoy, with Zagnoli, McEvoy, and Foley, has indicated that when allowed by judges, jury-consulting firms can develop questionnaires that seek to draw out potential biases among jurors through a blend of psychology and educated guesswork, but their work to shape a favorable jury panel for a particular defendant is limited. She's not suggesting that corporate executives cannot get a fair trial in America, but it is extremely difficult to select jurors in such cases who will act in predictable ways and vote favorably for certain defendants.

In the case of Credit Suisse First Boston banker Frank P. Quattrone, who was indicted on several counts of fraud, for instance, McEvoy said that the views of prospective jurors about stock market losses and who should be blamed are critical in jury selection. One type of juror targeted by jury consultant firms is the risk taker, the person who understands that rules are flexible and appreciates that executives sometimes have to break them. Therefore, one of the questions McEvoy asks judges to ask prospective jurors is how much of a stickler they are for details and rules. "I don't want someone who thinks they would never do what these guys did," says McEvoy. Sometimes, a hung jury, as was the result in Quattrone's trial, is considered a "victory" of sorts for jury-consulting firms. While it isn't an acquittal, it does give the defense an opportunity to revise its strategy if charges against its clients are brought again. Also, it enables them to see prosecution strategy and hear incriminating evidence. In a subsequent trial, defensive strategy can be tailored to defeat such incriminating evidence.

How good are jury consultants at what they are supposed to do? There are mixed opinions. Phoebe Ellsworth, a professor of law and psychology at the University of Michigan, has conducted a number of studies about jury consultants. She says, "Whether they are any good is a tricky question. Because you never know how the case would have turned out without them." Another expert, Susan Macpherson, the vice president of the midwestern office of the National Jury Project, a consulting group, says that "I think it was all uncharged water pre-Enron. We didn't have a national stereotype in our heads about the types of people who get charged with these kinds of crime."

Can prospective jurors' behaviors be predicted with precision? Will certain types of jurors vote particular ways? How predictable are their behaviors? What do you think?

Source: Adapted from Barry Meier and Jonathan D. Glater, Associated Press, "Picking a Jury for a Case in the Headlines," April 30, 2004.

---

affiliation was an important factor that the defense counsel should consider. Protestant denominations such as Methodists, Presbyterians, and Episcopalians were more likely to condemn the defendants for their actions. The research revealed that from the defendants' perspective, the most favorable type of juror was a female Democrat with no religious preference and employed as a white-collar professional or possibly a skilled blue-collar job (Wanamaker 1978, 349). It is impossible to determine if the information collected was useful in selecting a sympathetic jury for these defendants, but the jury in the actual case voted 10–2 to acquit the defendants.

Had the jury voted to convict them, then the scientific jury selection process engaged in by Schulman and his colleagues would probably have never received much attention. But since the outcome of the trial favored the defendants, the legal community took special notice, and scientific jury selection subsequently became an important component in the jury selection process.

The process of scientific jury selection has evolved into an entirely new professional enterprise. In most of the high-profile criminal cases (e.g., O. J. Simpson, William Kennedy Smith, and Rodney King), jury consultants have been used to assist both prosecutors and defense counsels in their selection of jury members. For example, in the O. J. Simpson criminal trial, the defense team hired Jo-Ellan Dimitrius from Trial Logistics, while the prosecution hired Don Vinson from DecisionQuest to aid in jury selection. Dimitrius and Vinson conducted extensive surveys and relayed this information to their clients during trial strategy sessions. It is interesting to note that Dimitrius assisted during the entire trial. However, Vinson was dismissed by the prosecution after two court appearances (Lafferty 1994).

BOX 6.4

Can the Perfect Jury Be Handpicked?

Jury Selection in North Dakota

How are jurors chosen for criminal trials? How do lawyers choose prospective jurors and what criteria do they use for rejecting certain jurors? Answers to these and other questions have been provided by a jury selection psychologist, Jim Rasicot, a Minneapolis resident. Rasicot was a jury consultant who worked as a defense jury consultant for the Mike Tyson trial in Indiana. He also assisted in the jury selection for the trial on which the movie *Paradise Lost* was based. In addition, he also was in the movie as an "extra."

Rasicot has advised lawyers on how to handle jury selection in a way to make the jurors selected be the most favorable to their case. He said there are several steps in choosing the right jurors. First, the objective is to get rid of those jurors who pose the most danger to the defense. Second, it is important for lawyers to gain rapport with potential jurors and, having done that, to drop the seeds of the case into their minds. This is accomplished while questioning potential jurors about past experiences in an attempt to gain access to their biases that they don't like to talk about. Rasicot said that these things are important because they can cause problems for the defense later on during the trial.

One step in preparing to challenge jurors is to develop the right type of questionnaire and to keep questions short and concise. He said, "Get the information you need (about the potential juror) and get out." Questionnaires for jury trials can be 60 pages or longer. It might take someone several weeks to go through all of the answers. Another important factor in choosing a juror or having one removed for cause is attitude. A lawyer has to consider how the juror's past experiences can affect attitude. He urged lawyers to confirm an attitude the juror might already have, such as "If someone breaks a window, they should have to pay for it, right?"

An important tactic is to get a potential juror to change an attitude. For instance, a juror might have the attitude that the defendant must have done something wrong if he was charged with a crime. "You have to try to change that attitude and create a new one," he said. He added, "Jurors don't want to talk to you, and so your job is to get them to talk. Let them know that there are no right or wrong answers during the jury selection, and to put them at ease." Other tips Rasicot passes along are to include talking to jurors about their occupations and be sure to ask them about any past occupations. One time, he said a potential juror told the lawyer that he was in the sheet metal business and managed the company. Later, during questioning, he said he knew about trial proceedings because he had been a chief of police, and possibly pro-prosecution, before going to work for the sheet metal company. The juror was dismissed from further consideration after that. "It's important to find out about things like that," Rasicot said. "Remember, people might change occupations several times," he added.

Another tip included not insulting any juror. He gave an example of a lawyer who was questioning a female juror who said that she was a housewife. The lawyer said, "Oh, you don't work then." The woman replied curtly, "I work very hard." She didn't serve on that jury. Rasicot said that you need to let the jury know where you are going with the case. Start off with the easy questions about the things they like to talk about, such as occupations and education. Then ease into more controversial subjects that might show juror bias. Can the perfect jury be selected? Do you think jury consultants are effective at selecting the best juries for their clients? Should lawyers be allowed to question prospective jurors at length concerning their qualifications for jury service? Should police officers or former law enforcement officers automatically be excluded as jurors? What do you think?

Source: Adapted from Ken Crites, "Psychologist Discusses Jury Selection Process," June 16, 2000.

Jury consultation has become a big business. This year the American Society of Trial Consultants will celebrate their twenty-fifth anniversary. Despite this rapid growth, much skepticism exists about the quality of scientific jury selection. Litigation Sciences boast a 95 percent success rate, although these success rates may not be attributable to scientific techniques.

Most of the jury consultants were hired in high-profile cases or political trials. In these cases, the defense attorneys are often in the best position to prepare their cases such that acquittal of their clients is more a matter of good lawyering rather than a matter of the advice received from professional jury consultants. Some persons have equated scientific jury selection with jury tampering, and they suggest that the integrity of the jury is undermined or compromised (Enriquez and Clark 2005).

JURY SIZE

Anyone unfamiliar with the court process and who is charged with a felony may be surprised to see only six people sitting as jurors to decide their guilt or innocence. Doesn't the Constitution guarantee them the right to a 12-member jury? What effect will smaller jury sizes have on jury deliberations? Are smaller juries more likely to convict defendants rather than larger juries? These are just some of the questions defendants have raised about smaller jury sizes. These same questions have been asked and researched by legal scholars.

For instance, what is the special significance associated with the number "12"? Why is this number given such importance in our common-law legal history? Are 12 jurors better able to understand the evidence and reach a decision? The reason the number "12" is so deeply ingrained in our perception of the trial process has nothing to do with any scientific or legalistic reasoning. Rather, it has everything to do with historical tradition. Throughout most of the last several centuries, juries were comprised of 12 members.

Several legal scholars have studied the origins of the 12-member jury. Despite their intensive investigative efforts, there is still no definitive conclusion as to the origin of the number "12." Some scholars have traced the 12-member jury to ancient Greek mythology, while others have found antecedents of the 12-member jury in biblical writings (McConville and Mirsky 2005). The most direct lineage of the 12-member jury in America is traced to the Constitution of Clarendon, the Assize of Clarendon, and the Magna Carta.

The Constitution of Clarendon was signed by King Henry II in 1164. This constitution provided that the sheriff was to administer an oath to 12 men of the neighborhood that they would declare the truth and render verdicts in cases brought to them. The Assize of Clarendon was a court created by Henry II to give litigants a legal option to resolve a dispute rather than resolve it in the traditional manner, which was often a duel to the death. If a disputant chose the court rather than the duel, the court would issue a writ to the king to have 4 knights from the region select 12 jurors. The litigants were allowed to challenge the knights' decisions.

This process continued until 12 acceptable jurors were selected. Finally, the Magna Carta, signed by King John, established the constitutional importance of the jury. The right to a 12-member jury remained essentially the same for almost 800 years. This tradition was changed by the U.S. Supreme Court in *Williams v. Florida* (1970).

At the time Johnny Williams was charged with robbery, Florida permitted six-member juries to hear all noncapital criminal cases. Williams argued that his case should be heard by a 12-member jury. His motion was denied and he was tried and convicted by a six-person jury. He was ultimately sentenced to life in prison. He appealed his conviction on the grounds that the Sixth Amendment guaranteed him a right to a 12-member jury. The U.S. Supreme Court held that the Sixth Amendment does not require a 12-person jury. The U.S. Supreme Court majority reasoned that the 12-member jury is a historical accident and unnecessary for the proper functioning of a jury. Justice White said that the essential feature of the jury obviously lies in the interposition between the accused and his accuser of the commonsense judgment of a group of laymen, and in the community participation and shared responsibility that results for the group's determination of guilt or innocence. The performance of this role is not a function of the particular number of the body that makes up the jury (*Williams v. Florida,* 1970).

With authority from the U.S. Supreme Court, many states began to challenge other aspects of the Sixth Amendment. For instance, the use of nonunanimous verdicts was upheld by the U.S. Supreme Court in *Apodaca v. Oregon* (1972) and *Johnson v. Louisiana* (1972) (see the section "On Jury Voting and Unanimity").

In the Apodaca case the U.S. Supreme Court upheld the Oregon statute, which allowed a 10–2 vote for either conviction or acquittal. In Louisiana, the law allowed jury verdicts with a 9–3 vote. The U.S. Supreme Court also accepted this practice as not violating the Sixth Amendment or the Fourteenth Amendment. One year later in *Colgrove v. Battin* (1973), the Court ruled that six-member juries were acceptable in civil cases. In the majority opinion, the Court cited social science evidence they believed indicated that there was no substantial difference between 12-member and 6-member juries. The *Colgrove* court cited four studies they believed provided "convincing empirical evidence of the correctness of the *Williams* conclusion that there is no discernable difference between the results reached by the two different-sized juries" (*Colgrove v. Battin*, 1973:47). With the *Colgrove* decision, the Court seemed to give states the license to decrease their jury sizes. Georgia attempted this. A Georgia statute was passed allowing convictions based on deliberations by five-member juries. This practice was challenged in *Ballew v. Georgia* (1978). Ballew was a theater manager in Atlanta who was charged with violating a Georgia ordinance prohibiting the distribution of obscene material by showing a pornographic and sexually explicit movie starring Marilyn Chambers, *Behind the Green Door.* Ballew appealed his conviction by a five-member jury contending that it violated his Sixth and Fourteenth Amendment rights. Ballew's conviction was set aside after the U.S. Supreme Court declared that five-member juries are too small to constitute a representative cross section of the community. Thus, the minimum jury size was established as six.

BOX 6.5

On Jury Voting and Unanimity

Apodaca v. Oregon, 406 U.S. 404, 92 S.Ct. 1628 (1972)

Apodaca and others were found guilty of various serious crimes by less than unanimous jury verdicts. Oregon has a statute mandating a conviction or acquittal on the basis of a 10–2 vote, or what is referred to by the Oregon legislature as a 10-of-12 vote. In Apodaca's case, the vote favoring conviction was 11–1. Apodaca challenged this vote as not being unanimous, and the U.S. Supreme Court heard the case contemporaneously with the case of *Johnson v. Louisiana* (1972) on an identical issue. In Apodaca's case, the U.S. Supreme Court upheld the constitutionality of the

Oregon jury voting provision, declaring that votes of these kinds do not violate one's right to due process under either the Sixth or the Fourteenth Amendment. The significance of this case is that less than unanimous jury votes among the states are constitutional and do not violate one's right to due process.

Johnson v. Louisiana, 406 U.S. 356, 92 S.Ct. 1620 (1972)

Johnson was arrested without a warrant at his home based on a photograph identification by a robbery victim. He was later subjected to a lineup, where he was identified again. Johnson was represented by counsel. He was subjected to trial by jury for the robbery offense and convicted in a jury vote of 9–3. Johnson appealed, contending that the jury verdict should be unanimous. The U.S. Supreme Court affirmed his conviction, saying, in effect, that states have the right to determine whether conviction requires unanimity of jury votes or only a majority vote. The U.S. Supreme Court concluded by saying that the verdicts rendered by 9 out of 12 jurors are not automatically invalidated by the disagreement of the dissenting 3. Johnson was not deprived of due process or a fair trial because of the 9–3 vote. This U.S. Supreme Court decision applies to states only and does not affect federal juries, who must be unanimous in their verdicts. Federal criminal jury sizes of 12 may be reduced to 11 under special conditions with judicial approval; either size must be unanimous.

Early v. Packer, 537 U.S. 3, 123 S.Ct. 362 (2002)

William Packer was found guilty in a California court of second-degree murder, two counts of attempted murder, two counts of robbery, two counts of assault with a deadly weapon, and one count of assault with a firearm. He was acquitted on ten other counts. The jury had a difficult time in certain of its deliberations, with one juror in particular claiming illness, indecisiveness, and fatigue. At various points during jury deliberations, the trial judge requested information from the jury foreman about the status of jury voting, and he questioned the particular female juror at some length. The judge repeated various instructions to the jury as to their deliberations, including that they should follow the law, determine whether or not the elements of the offense were present, and find unanimously whether Packer was guilty or not guilty of each of those offenses. Subsequently, the jury rendered its verdicts as noted above and Packer appealed, filing a *habeas corpus* petition. The petition alleged that the trial judge coerced the female juror into agreeing with the majority of other jurors in reaching their guilty verdicts on the above counts. Thus, he claimed, he was denied his due process right to a fair and impartial jury. The Ninth Circuit Court of Appeals granted Packer's petition and reversed his convictions. California appealed and the U.S. Supreme Court heard the case. The U.S. Supreme Court reinstated Packer's convictions, holding that the trial judge's remarks and instructions to jurors were not coercive, nor were they unreasonable or contrary to established federal law. Thus, it is not unconstitutional for a trial judge to urge a jury to continue deliberating as long as the judge does not attempt to coerce a particular type of jury verdict. In this instance, all of the judge's remarks clearly admonished jurors to follow and apply the law objectively and to make their decisions about Packer's guilt or innocence consistent with that objectivity.

In all previous U.S. Supreme Court decisions, the justices were reluctant to specify a minimum jury size. But with the *Williams* decision, the Court was faced with a potentially serious dilemma. Again relying on social science, the U.S. Supreme Court argued that their conclusion rested on the assumption there was no difference between 12- and 6-member juries. The Court believed that the deliberative ability, representativeness, verdict reliability, likelihood of conviction, and the minority ability to resist majority pressure were not hindered by decreasing jury size. However, the Court's reading of the literature was seriously flawed. Most of the studies they relied upon evidenced several empirical flaws or limitations. Additionally, where studies were cited that had credibility and were empirically sound, the U.S. Supreme Court misinterpreted some of the results. The U.S. Supreme Court cited a study conducted by Asch (1966), which examined the minority's ability to resist group pressure. Asch found that when the minority position has an ally, it is better able to resist pressure from the majority position. In the context of jury deliberations, this means that in a jury vote of 10–2, the minority jury voters are better able to withstand group pressure more than minority jury voters where the jury vote is 5–1. However, the Court erred in its interpretation and understanding of the social research and concluded that there was no functional difference between the two juries. In any case, a 5–1 jury vote is unconstitutional, inasmuch as all six-member jury voting must be unanimous.

JURY SEQUESTRATION

Historically, **jury sequestration** has been used to isolate jurors from the potential biasing influences of the press and community sentiment. Preventing outside information from reaching jurors allows jurors to be influenced only by the information and evidence presented to them at trial, the instructions of judges, and their fellow jurors. While jury sequestration has many critics, some persons have discovered that sequestration may have some positive effects. Apart from the obvious benefit of not having jurors influenced by outside forces, sequestration, on many occasions, has fostered a group bonding process among the jurors. Following trials, jurors have often referred to themselves as becoming a family who plan to see each other after the trial. Thus, the emotional connection developed as a result of sequestration may have a positive effect on deliberations. Researchers have learned that group communication is enhanced when individuals have formed an interpersonal connection among themselves. Therefore, jurors who have developed relationships with one another are more willing to listen to each other and discuss their differences. When this event occurs, sequestration has enhanced the deliberative process. While these are a few of the positive effects of jury sequestration, these are far outnumbered by criticisms of it.

During sequestration, if the jury develops intergroup rivalries among and animosity toward each other, the deliberative process suffers. People are more likely to gravitate toward people like themselves. This highlights the differences between group members and they begin to resent one other. Alliances are formed between certain jurors, and they form coalitions that become fairly powerful during jury deliberations. Sequestration also puts pressure on jurors who disagree with the majority. The jurors in the minority position see themselves as prolonging the sequestration. If they would only capitulate and agree with the majority, they could all go home and get back to their lives. Jury sequestration is also expensive.

In the O. J. Simpson criminal trial the jury was sequestered for 266 days at a cost to the taxpayers of almost $1 million. Cost was one of the primary reasons the New York courts system eliminated its practice of mandatory sequestration. The cost savings by eliminating mandatory sequestration in criminal trials were almost $4 million each year. Sequestration may also be a primary reason people are trying to get out of jury service. For many jurors, being confined to a hotel and treated like a prisoner in a potentially hostile environment may be one reason why many persons who are called for jury service refuse to answer their calls for such service.

JURY DECISION MAKING AND VOTING

Considerable research has examined jury decision making and voting behavior. For instance, it has been found that women approach jury duty differently, perceive things differently, and often vote differently from men (Fischer 1997). Not only do gender differences influence decision making, but also the type of occupation, ethnicity, and socioeconomic status exerts a profound influence on how people perceive things and process large amounts of evidence and other important information. The differences in juror decision making and final jury verdicts are highlighted the most in civil cases where damages are sought. For example, in the case of *Sterling v. Bechenheimer's Inc.* (1987), a jury awarded Debra Sterling $25,000 in compensatory damages and $1,501,000 in punitive damages after she had been handcuffed and thrown to the ground by a security guard who believed she had stolen a soda worth $1.49. Compare the jury actions in this case with the jury actions in the case of Patricia James. In *James v. K-Mart* (1987), a jury awarded $2 to Mrs. James and $502 to each of her teenage daughters after a security guard had twisted the daughters' arms behind their back and strip-searched them believing the daughters had been shoplifting. Why are there such different jury decisions and monetary awards?

It has been found that several important trial and victim factors influence jury voting behavior. Factors associated with guilty verdicts are physical evidence, a defendant's prior criminal record, and victim attractiveness. Male jurors seem more likely to vote not guilty when the victim puts up some resistance against the offender. Guilty verdicts are also more likely when jurors have had prior jury service. Not guilty verdicts have been associated with offenders being employed, offenders being attractive, and where there has been some degree of victim facilitation (e.g., the victim allows a stranger to take him/her home from a bar). Jurors who have a tendency to blame the victim are also more likely to vote not guilty (Enriquez and Clark 2005).

Another factor is whether jurors are verdict driven or evidence driven. Research indicates that once juries reach the jury room, they commence the decision-making process by following one of two patterns or methods (Champion 2005b). The first pattern is called an **evidence-driven jury**. In evidence-driven cases, juries come together and begin discussing how to proceed. Most jurors or at least a vocal few decide that they should review the evidence as a group before they can contemplate a verdict. With this method, all the evidence is discussed, not simply the evidence individual jurors believe is relevant. However, a **verdict-driven jury** believes that discussing the evidence before a vote is unnecessary. Why debate the evidence when all jurors might vote the same way without a review of the evidence? Using this method, the jury votes first to see how many jurors favor guilt or acquittal. When discussed, evidence is used to support one position or another. Verdict-driven deliberations often take less time than evidence-driven deliberations since there is little or no time taken to review the evidence before jury votes are cast.

Some research shows that the jury deliberation process may not have much impact on the final verdict. In Kalven and Ziesel's (1966) classic study of the jury system, they compared the initial jury vote to the final verdict. They revealed that in the vast majority of cases, the first vote was most often the same as the final verdict. For example, on a 12-person jury, if 7 of the jurors initially voted not guilty, the subsequent verdict tended to be not guilty. However, if the majority of jurors voted guilty, the final verdict would almost always be guilty. Only on rare occasions does the minority succeed in convincing the majority to change their vote. Kalven and Ziesel have said that the real decision is often made before the deliberation begins. The deliberation process might well be likened to what the developer does for an exposed film: A picture is developed, but the outcome is predetermined (1966, 488–489).

JURY VERDICTS

The media always seem willing to report about how the justice system has failed in one respect or another to convict guilty defendants. This most often occurs when we perceive that an obviously guilty person is found not guilty or the jury delivers an excessive damage award to a plaintiff in a civil case. Armed with this anecdotal evidence, more than a few critics have called for reforming the jury system. When we advocate changing the jury system, we have to make two assumptions. First, we have to assume that the jury made a mistake. Second, we have to assume that there is a better alternative. In most cases, advocates for jury reform believe that juries composed of laypersons from the community are often not able to understand or comprehend the complex information presented at trial. This has also been referred to as the complexity exception. Stephen Adler has argued that if a judge doesn't think the jury will understand a particular civil case, he can decide it without a jury (Adler 1995, 143). Adler argues that jury reform should include a return to the **blue-ribbon jury**. During the 1960s and 1970s, blue-ribbon juries were comprised from members of the best-educated or socially placed members of society because it was believed a jury should be composed of such persons. In fact, most persons who serve on juries today would not have been placed on these blue-ribbon juries in past years. In fact, the reverse of the blue-ribbon jury is often practiced in many jurisdictions. New York's judicial rules allow for the automatic exemption of lawyers, doctors, clergy, dentists, optometrists, psychologists, podiatrists, registered and practical nurses, embalmers, police officers, correctional officers, firefighters, sole business owners, and many other professional groups.

In many instances, if we agree with the idea that juries cannot understand the information presented to them and therefore are unable to arrive at a competent verdict, who will replace them? Most critics would shift the responsibility for determining guilt or innocence to the judges themselves. Are juries unable to understand the material presented to them? In an effort to answer this question, Kalven and Ziesel (1966) investigated how juries arrived at verdicts and how these jury verdicts differed from judicial decisions about the same cases. Kalven and Ziesel gathered data from 3,576 trials. In order to compare the differences between judges and juries, the researchers asked that judges say how they would have ruled in the particular case. The research showed that the verdicts of judges and juries were essentially the same in 78 percent of the cases. Conversely, judges and juries disagreed on the outcome in 22 percent of the cases. The data indicate the largest disagreement came where judges said they would have convicted the defendant and the juries said they would acquit the defendant. In essence, judges were more likely to convict than juries. Thus, juries seem to be more lenient than judges in decision making about criminal defendants.

Those critical of the jury system might argue that juries are not more lenient, but rather, the differences in judge and jury case outcomes can be attributed to jury incompetence. They would argue that juries disagreed with judges and acquitted defendants when they should have convicted them, largely because the jurors did not understand the law and the evidence presented to them at trial. In order to address this criticism, Kalven and Ziesel (1966) had the judges rate whether the evidence was difficult or easy to comprehend. If jury incompetence was the reason for the differences, we might expect a higher rate of disagreement in those cases where the judge indicated that the evidence was too difficult to understand. However, the results indicate that judges and juries disagreed equally in both complex and simple cases.

BOX 6.6

Plain English for Jury Instructions?

The judicial counsel of California spent eight years rewriting some of its instructions to juries. They have now approved over 2,000 pages of "plain language" jury instruction in the hopes of helping juries in the future better understand legal terminology so they can make better informed decisions about guilt or innocence. The instructions also did away with many old and rarely used terms, and introduced terms with the cultural sensibilities of today. Many of the legal terms included in California's jury instructions were complicated and not worded in layman's terms. For example, "willfully false" is more simply referred to as "lied," "innocent misrecollection" is now "honestly forgot," and the instructions now include information that not discussing the trial with anyone includes "spiritual advisors and therapists," as well, and that "confidential relationships" are not excluded. These revisions are part of an effort to ease the burden of the jury trial experience in California. California's judicial system, according to officials, is the second largest after the federal system. Do you think that these new instructions will better enable jurors to understand instructions given to them, thereby facilitating less-complex decision making? Should other states consider revising some of their complex legalese to help jurors understand? Does this decrease the seriousness of a court trial, or diminish the authority of the legal system?

Source: Adapted from the Associated Press, "The New Language for Jurors in California: Plain English," *New York Times,* August 28, 2005:A12.

JURY NULLIFICATION

Jury nullification is the refusal of juries to apply the law when they believe following the letter of the law would be a miscarriage of justice. In a criminal trial, the jury is the finder of fact and has the absolute authority to acquit the defendant regardless of the evidence. The jury is also our protection from the oppressive powers of the state. The constitutional protection against double jeopardy makes the jury's acquittal irreversible and the prosecution has no right to appeal the jury verdict. One exception is if there has been jury tampering or some other irregularity that has caused the jury to disregard the evidence against the accused. In a system designed with checks and balances to control state power, the jury system provides ordinary citizens with more power than our highest elected and appointed government officials.

Although we have observed jury nullification in some recent spectacular cases (e.g., Marion Barry, Lorena Bobbit, and John DeLorean), it is not something that is particularly unique to our time. Juries have nullified the law or, more accurately, the actions of the state, for as long as juries have functioned in American and English courts. Jury nullification was common in England during the Bloody Code of the eighteenth and nineteenth centuries. The Bloody Code prescribed over 200 offenses that were punishable by death, including such minor offenses as stealing bread and pickpocketing. Because of the severity of the punishment relative to the offense, juries were reluctant to find defendants guilty of these offenses. The authority of the jury to engage in the practice of nullification was not challenged in England until 1670 in the *Bushell* case, and later in America in the *John Peter Zenger* case.

In 1670, William Penn and William Mead were being tried at the Old Bailey, the Central Criminal Court of England. Penn, subsequently the founder of the Colony of Pennsylvania and a leading proponent of correctional reform, was a Quaker like Mead, and the authorities saw both of them as radicals and extremists. Consequently, they were banned from preaching in the streets. However, this was their only forum because the authorities had barred them from their churches. On one occasion while they were preaching in the street, they were arrested and charged with unlawful assembly. Their fate ultimately rested in the hands of the jurors selected to hear the case. The witnesses included those who testified that Penn and Mead had preached on Gracechurch Street.

BOX 6.7

Are Juries Pro-Police?

The Death of Amadou Diallo. It was a tragic event that occurred in New York City in 1999. An unarmed black man, Amadou Diallo, was shot and killed by four police officers in a small alcove of a dark building, in the aftermath of 41 shots being fired. In February 2000, the four officers went on trial for his murder. The trial was held in Albany, a middle-class, 90 percent white community with a strong Irish Catholic heritage. An Albany defense attorney, Terence Kindlon, said, "If there's a better place to defend a police officer, I haven't heard of it." Another observer, *New York Post* columnist Bob McManus, agreed. He said, "Irish Catholic conservative Albany has a civil service view of the world. They like their cops."

The murder trial of the four police officers charged in Diallo's death was moved to Albany from the Bronx in New York City because, according to authorities, it has a reputation for being hostile to police. It is two-thirds black and Hispanic, and the police have become outsiders. Does it really make a difference where the trial is held?

In January 2000, a jury in Albany was convinced that a well-respected detective actually forged a confession in the murder of an 82-year-old former minister and that police were overzealous in arresting a man who helped an alleged cop shooter to escape. In fact, in that particular case, camouflage-clad police officers were caught on videotape roughing up some store clerks while searching for the alleged shooter. The videotape led to internal disciplinary action against the police officers that once would have been unheard of.

(continued)

(continued)

Some criminal justice experts around the country believe that the location of trials is becoming less important in recent years. More jurors are able to make more sound and fair judgments, according to these observers. One observer, Boston College law professor Robert M. Bloom, said that "Confidence in police around the country is weakening because of such things as the Rodney King beating in Los Angeles and the Abner Louima case in New York City, where a black defendant was sodomized with a broomstick in a police station bathroom."

Amid allegations of pro-police officer bias, there have been numerous incidents around the United States to undermine public confidence in police officers. For example, police officers on highways throughout America have been routinely pulling over blacks in what is known as racial profiling. *Albany Times Union* columnist Fred LeBrun said, "Even in a place like Albany, conservative with an almost Midwestern feel, there is the general feeling that you just can't take a police officer's word anymore."

Echoing these comments and opinions is a law professor from Fordham University, James Cohen. Cohen says, "The feeling is people in power—the white people—tend to treat people without power differently." But there is some concern among those prosecuting the case against the four officers in Albany. In 1999 in Albany, a black basketball player at the College of Saint Rose claimed he was beaten by two off-duty police officers in a police garage following a bar fight. The officers were acquitted. Is it a strong likelihood that juries in one part of the state may be more pro-police than juries in other parts of a state? What about your own state? Is it likely that two different juries in different parts of the state would arrive at different verdicts if police officers were accused of crimes? How can juries be selected in ways that minimize their possible bias and unfair attitudes toward either the prosecutor or defense? What do you think?

Source: Adapted from the Associated Press, "Albany Is a Pro-Police Setting for Murder Trial of N.Y. City Cops," February 8, 2000.

At the conclusion of the testimony, the jury was instructed to retire to the jury room and reach a verdict. When they returned with a verdict of not guilty, they were instructed to return to the jury room and deliberate until they reached a correct verdict. When they returned a second time, they found Penn guilty of speaking at Gracechurch Street but refused to convict him on unlawful assembly charges. The court reacted to this verdict by threatening Edward Bushell, who was identified as the leader of the jury revolt. They were sent back to deliberate once again, and when they returned, they announced that they had again found Penn guilty of speaking at Gracechurch Street, although they persisted and did not find him guilty of unlawful assembly. Additionally, they declared Mead innocent of any wrongdoing. The court was in turmoil. The court announced that Bushell and the rest of the jury would not be dismissed until they reached a verdict acceptable to the court. The judge ordered them locked up without "meat, drink, fire, and tobacco" until they reached an acceptable verdict. Facing this demand, the jury retired to deliberate and returned with an acquittal for Penn. They were ordered to go back and deliberate again, but this time they refused. The judge was outraged. Bushell and the rest of the jurors were fined 40 marks each and sent to jail until they could pay the fine. The jurors filed a *habeas corpus* appeal requesting their release from prison. The appellate court ordered that they be released and declared that the jury had the right to render a verdict according to its belief about the fairness of the law and not act consistent with what the court deemed appropriate.

BOX 6.8

What Happens When Juries Can't Agree on a Verdict?

Victor David, 60, of Marysville, Washington, was married for years to his wife, Linda David, 52. Victor and his wife lived on a sailboat, docked at Everett Marina. The sailboat was filthy, and they shared the boat with seven German Shepherd dogs, some cats, and a wild goose. Eyewitnesses alerted authorities that Linda David had not been seen in several weeks, although they knew that she was aboard the sailboat. Subsequently, a search by law enforcement officers led to the discovery of Linda David laying in a near-comatose condition on the vessel, having suffered brain damage, nearly blinded, and covered with scars. Victor David was charged with felony assault and was placed on trial.

During the trial, evidence of physical abuse came to light through the testimony of physicians who examined Linda and her body. It was also acknowledged that Victor David had obtained money from the state at one point to provide chore services and in-home care for his wife. Several persons who looked after Linda testified about her condition. Prosecutors alleged that Victor David had beaten his wife repeatedly over many years, causing her scars and brain injuries, largely between 1993 and 1997. A state social worker visited Linda in 1997 and reported her case to authorities. She expressed an opinion that Linda had been the victim of Victor David's assault.

But a strong defense was mounted. Victor David proclaimed his innocence and offered other explanations for his wife's injuries, including that she fell repeatedly and struck her head multiple times. He claimed she had a drinking problem and often had difficulty maintaining her balance around the boat.

When the evidence portion of the trial was concluded and prosecutors and defense counsel made closing arguments after three weeks, the jurors began deliberating. Several days of deliberations led to a **hung jury.** After four days, jurors were divided 6–6 on David's guilt. On the fifth day, the vote was 7–5 in favor of acquittal. One juror, John Nichols, was one of the five jurors who had voted for conviction. He said the evidence, including the traumas Linda David had received, swayed him. Linda David had testified against her husband, although her testimony was very difficult to understand. Much of the time it was incoherent and didn't make sense. One juror who voted for acquittal said that the way the prosecution handled her testimony, it sounded like she had been coached, or spoon-fed things, to make her remember events that never happened. Some jurors were troubled that there were no witnesses to the alleged assaults.

Rebecca Roby, regional director of the Pathways for Women, said, "I think the case is a tragedy." She was surprised and saddened by the lack of a verdict. "The emotional scars take a lot longer to heal than a bruise," Roby said. She was not surprised that jurors had trouble with the evidence presented, during the period of the statute of limitations. She sees women every day who don't report abuse until after it's too late for authorities to do anything about it. As far as Victor David is concerned, he considers himself totally innocent of all charges. Juror Kami Cramer said, "There was no verdict because we just couldn't get there with what we had to work with." It was uncertain whether prosecutors would seek a second trial against Victor David.

Can juries be made to agree by presiding judges? How many times should a defendant be tried for a crime before a unanimous decision by a jury can be reached? What inferences should be drawn, if any, from hung juries and the innocence or guilt of defendants? What do you think?

Source: Adapted from Scott North and Jim Haley, "David Jurors Can't Agree," *The Daily Herald,* June 15, 2006.

JURY AND JUROR MISCONDUCT

Juror misconduct falls into categories. The first is engaging in delinquency or lying to avoid jury service. The second is engaging in improper or prohibited behavior while serving as a juror. The first type of behavior is perceived as misconduct largely by those who believe that jury service is a civic duty and that all U.S. citizens are obligated to serve on juries when called to do so. Juror misconduct prior to trials most often involves jurors who lie to avoid jury service. Another problem involves jurors who lie and fail to disclose important information during *voir dire* so that they can remain on the jury. Those who are called to jury service often want to avoid it because of certain hardships jury service would pose. While jurors are compensated for their service, serving on a jury is still regarded by many persons as a financial hardship.

The types of financial hardships for jurors today are quite different from the financial burden on jurors in the 1700s. Jurors were usually compensated one to two dollars per day. However, many jurors had to travel long distances on foot or horseback to the courthouse. Because they could not return home each day, they had to pay for food and lodging. Often, these expenses were considerably more than the amount of their compensation received from the court for their jury service. Today, jurors continue to have the hardship of traveling to the courthouse, although in most instances, they are able to return to their homes each evening. In past centuries, judges routinely refused to feed jurors while they were deliberating in order to starve out a verdict. This is another hazard that contemporary jurors do not endure. The reasons for avoiding jury service have changed over time, although some persons still consider serving on a jury to be a hardship and that jury service is an activity to be avoided.

Another form of juror misconduct is lying. Most often jurors lie to avoid jury duty. In the early 1900s in Cleveland, for example, residents from the wealthiest neighborhoods claimed illnesses more often than those from poorer neighborhoods. Still other persons would fabricate stories about how they were related to defendants in criminal cases simply to be dismissed as jurors. It was later revealed that they had no particular relationship with the accused and that their lies were ruses to avoid jury service (Stalmaster 1931, 74).

Engaging in inappropriate or prohibited behavior while serving as a juror is the most serious form of juror misconduct. While juror misconduct has always plagued the jury system, it is more of a problem today than in the past. Over time, the definition of misconduct has not changed substantially, although what is different today is that jurors of the past had fewer opportunities to engage in inappropriate behavior. For instance, in past decades, it was not uncommon for a felony trial to have only one or two witnesses, and the trial lasted only a few hours. During this time, jurors were closely watched by the bailiff who prevented any misconduct from occurring. Today, trials are much longer and jurors have more unsupervised time. This provides jurors with more opportunities to be exposed to external influences and bribes from a defendant's friends, visiting the crime scene, discussing the evidence and the case prior to final deliberations, drinking alcohol, and reading, listening to, or watching prohibited media.

BOX 6.9

Juror Accepts Bribes from Defendant

Juror Miguel Moya

It happened in Miami. Defendants Augusto "Willie" Falcon and Salvador Magluta were on trial for drug smuggling and large-scale drug dealing. There was overwhelming and persuasive evidence of their guilt presented at trial. But the trial took a peculiar turn when the jury deliberated and came back with an acquittal. Later, jurors said that they had deliberated for three days when they sent a note to the judge that they were "hopelessly deadlocked." The judge ordered them to continue deliberating and "reach a verdict." That's when they decided to throw in the towel and acquit the alleged drug smugglers.

Following the trial, one of the jurors, Miguel Moya, suddenly became wealthy. He bought a $200,000 home in the Florida Keys, jewelry, furniture, vacations, season tickets to the Florida Marlins games, and a sports car. Moya explained that he had recently come into some money from his cousin, Ramon "Ray" Perez, who was also a convicted drug smuggler and former Miami policeman. Perez said that he had given Moya approximately $485,000 as a gift. At about the same time, Moya's parents retired, bought a new home in the Florida Keys, and took a Hawaiian vacation.

Prosecutors were more than a little suspicious about Moya's newfound wealth and they investigated. They discovered that Moya had received nearly $500,000 from Falcon and Magluta following the trial in exchange for his persuasiveness with other jurors in arriving at an acquittal. Prosecutors charged Moya with money laundering, witness tampering, conspiracy, bribery, obstruction of justice, and filing a false tax return. Moya was convicted in July 1999 of the different crimes alleged. He faced 138 years in prison, including substantial fines. His father, Jose, pleaded guilty to witness tampering and was sentenced in October 1999. Falcon and Magluta, reportedly the top drug traffickers in the United States during the 1980s, were charged with smuggling 75 tons of cocaine into the United States and making $2 billion. Their 1996 acquittal was a sound defeat for federal prosecutors, although both men were imprisoned later on lesser unrelated charges. What safeguards should exist to protect juror integrity and insulate jurors from potential bribes from criminal defendants? What policies would you put in place to ensure that jury tampering can be prevented? What do you think?

Source: Adapted from the Associated Press, "Jury: Juror Guilty of Accepting Bribes," July 25, 2000.

BOX 6.10

LAPD in Trouble Again

A Case of Jury Bias?

Three Los Angeles Police Department officers were convicted of conspiracy and other crimes on Wednesday, November 15, 2000, following a lengthy trial. The police officers were part of a police department scandal involving an antigang unit at the police department's Rampart station. It began when former police officer Rafael Perez was caught stealing cocaine from an evidence locker and agreed to become an informant and government witness. Perez told the investigators that other officers framed people, planted evidence, committed perjury, and even shot innocent victims. More than 100 convictions of innocent suspects have been thrown out as the result of the scandal.

When the officers were convicted on November 15, an alternate juror came forward and disclosed to authorities that the jury foreman had decided that the defendants were guilty before any testimony had been presented. Another juror agreed and supported the alternate juror's assertions. Furthermore, the alternate juror said that other jurors often discussed the case outside of court before deliberations began, and that this was in direct violation of the instructions received from the judge. Alternate juror, Wendy Christiansen, 30, who did not participate in deliberations, told the judge that on the day the jurors were selected, she had lunch with another alternate and the jury foreman, Victor Flores. A comment was made that he believed the defendants were guilty. Christiansen said also that throughout the trial, other jurors openly said they thought the prosecution's witnesses were lying when they claimed they didn't remember things. They didn't like the defense attorneys.

When Flores was interviewed by KNBC-TV in Los Angeles, he denied the assertion that he had made up his mind about the defendants before trial and that he absolutely stood by the guilty verdicts. Flores said, "No I did not say that, that wouldn't be something I'd even utter, because the law says they're innocent until proven guilty." In support of Flores, another voting juror, Ingrid Utke, said that Flores had acted appropriately and had not uttered what had been alleged by Christiansen. Utke said, "We pointedly made sure that we never talked about the case. If someone veered toward that, we'd say, 'Anyone see a movie lately?' so we wouldn't talk about it. Also, every time we came back from being out here (in the courtroom), there were lots of comments being made about the defense attorneys. They didn't like the defense attorneys. The person they did like was Joel Isaacson."

Defense attorneys for the convicted police officers were quick to say that this new evidence warranted a new trial. The district attorney's office refused to comment in the case. Sgt. Brian Liddy, Sgt. Edward Ortiz, and Officer Michael Buchanan were convicted of conspiracy and other crimes involving gang members four years earlier in 1996. Barry Levin, one of the officer's attorneys, said, "Whether they like me or not, I could care less. But whether you like an attorney or not, you can't take it out on the client. The crux of the judicial system is you're entitled to 12 unbiased jurors." Should these officers be granted a new trial based on the assertions of juror misconduct made by Christiansen? What safeguards should be in place to prevent jurors from discussing the case before jury deliberations? What do you think?

Source: Adapted from the Associated Press, "Jury Bias Alleged in LAPD Trial," *San Francisco Chronicle,* November 18, 2000:A3.

What are the implications of juror misconduct? For jurors themselves, they are most often held in contempt and are ordered to pay a fine or serve a short jail term. In rare instances they are charged with criminal behavior by the prosecutor. Interestingly, jurors most often charged with misconduct by the prosecutor were members of juries where the result was an acquittal or a mistrial. One of the most common forms of juror misconduct is drinking alcohol during the trial or deliberations. Judges have been reluctant to declare a mistrial when they learn that jurors have been drinking. However, most judges consider drinking during deliberations more serious than drinking during the trial (Stacey and Dayton 1988). In short, it appears that judges believe that jurors must have a clearer head when deliberating the evidence than when hearing the evidence.

Jurors who engage in misconduct are rarely punished. One of the primary reasons for this is that jurors are short-term actors in the criminal justice process. Jurors who engage in misconduct are punished after the trial, and so their fellow jurors are unaware of any punishment. Similarly, new jurors are entering the system everyday. They would typically not have any knowledge of prior punishment of deviant jurors. Therefore, when judges do punish jurors, it has little or no potential deterrent value. Thus, new jurors who elect to engage in misconduct have no knowledge of prior punishments imposed on other jurors. When jurors engage in misconduct, there is always the possibility that the judge will declare a mistrial. In fact, some defendants prefer mistrials, since the likelihood of a successive prosecution is minimized. One way to minimize the adverse effects of juror misconduct is the use of alternative jurors. Judges can replace offending jurors and continue with the trial.

Summary

The role of the jury in the common-law legal system has changed over time. Initially, juries were used very little as disputes were settled using other methods. The ancient Greeks were premiere in using persons from the community to decide on cases, at one time using the entire city of Athens to hear appeals from magistrates. The ancient Romans also used what would be an early form of the jury.

In early England, common-law juries both investigated crimes and decided the trials of accused. Eventually it was decided that two separate units were needed for these tasks and the grand and petit juries were born. The grand jury's sole purpose was to investigate and report on crimes, whereas the petit jury was charged with determining the guilt or innocence of the accused.

Over time, juries were granted more power and autonomy, and they have become an essential component of the American court process. Juries today are made up of cross sections of the community in which the crime has occurred. Indeed juries are an integral part of our court system; as stated in the Sixth Amendment, the accused enjoys the right to a public trial by an impartial jury.

Most attorneys would agree that one of the most important stages in the criminal court process is the selection of the jury. It is during the jury selection process (*voir dire*) that lawyers decide who will hear the case. Both sides in the adversarial process attempt to select jurors who will be impartial. It starts with a list of potential jurors called the *venire*. Traditionally, in medieval England the king would choose wealthy landowners to sit as jurors. Obviously this limited the number of persons eligible to become jurors.

Historically, in the United States, females were excluded from jury service as well. This has changed over time so that today persons chosen to form the *venire* are chosen from voter registration lists in an attempt to draw from a cross section of the community. Once names have been taken from this list of potential jurors, the court will send them a summons to appear for jury service. Questions relating to their citizenship status, their age, whether they suffer from any physical or mental disabilities, and also whether they have been convicted of a felony are asked to ensure they are qualified. Those who pass this initial screening are sent another letter asking them to again appear for jury service. This starts a process known as the *voir dire*. This stage further determines the appropriateness of the person to serve as a juror. *Voir dire* literally means to speak the truth, and it is an opportunity for the prosecution and the defense to learn about any prejudices the potential jurors may have. This determination by both sides of impartiality is necessary to ensure a fair trial for the defendant. Although this has been referred to as jury selection, it is really the opposite where it eliminates those who are not appropriate to serve for jury duty. Some, however, argue that this process is really about the prosecution and defense determining which jurors will be sympathetic with their side. Jurors, who lawyers believe will not be sympathetic to their position, are removed.

Two methods for removing potential jurors from the jury pool include challenges for cause and peremptory challenges. Challenges for cause are used to excuse a person from jury duty for a specific reason. They may be used to eliminate a potential juror because the person does not meet the requirements to serve (underage), has a specific bias (related or an acquaintance of the accused), or has a nonspecific bias (having prejudice toward crimes or criminals). In order to use this type of challenge, the attorney has to provide a convincing reason to the judge for the removal of the juror. Peremptory challenges, unlike challenges for cause, do not require an explanation for the removal of a potential juror. Both sides are given a limited number of these types of challenges depending on the seriousness, or extent of pretrial publicity, of a case. In less serious cases, attorneys may receive 6 of these types of challenges, whereas in murder and other serious felony cases, attorneys may be given 12 or more. Attorneys can gauge the attitudes of a potential juror toward crime, criminals, and even law enforcement officials by asking them certain questions. Attorneys may even have a particular profile of jurors who share certain characteristics that will be more likely to be sympathetic to their position. They can then use this information and their peremptory challenges to eliminate those persons who do not fit this profile. In fact, social science has entered this process on occasion to assist attorneys in the jury selection process. Some question the use of scientific jury selection on ethical grounds that it is jury tampering and that it undermines or compromises the jury's integrity. Nonetheless, it has become big business, with associations boasting memberships in the hundreds, and success rates of 95 percent. There are, however, some who are skeptical about whether this success rate can be attributed to scientific techniques. It should also be noted that the Supreme Court has handed down several decisions regarding the jury selection process, specifically regarding where the pool of potential jurors comes from, the reasons for which a juror can be excluded from sitting on a jury, and jury size.

Jury sequestration is a method to isolate jurors from biases and influences from the media and the community. This is an attempt to prevent them from being subject to outside information that could possibly damage their impartiality. There have been other advantages to sequestration as well. Some believe it fosters a bonding process that better enables the jurors to come to a decision in deliberations. These advocates say that group communication is enhanced with sequestration because the jurors have formed an interpersonal connection with one another. There have, however, been critics who point out that in the same ways that sequestration can foster bonding processes, it can also foster rivalries and animosities to be formed, which would hinder coming to a decision during deliberations.

Although jury deliberations are protected from the public, there have been some studies on how juries make decisions. After the case is given to the jury for deliberations, they usually engage in one of two methods of reaching a decision about the guilt or innocence of the defendant. The first method is the evidence-driven jury where all evidence is examined and discussed before a jury vote is taken. The second form of decision making is the verdict-driven jury. In this scenario, the jury first conducts a vote and then, if needed, the evidence is examined and discussed. However, if all jurors agree on the verdict, their deliberations are concluded. Jury nullification is the process of returning a verdict contrary to the evidence presented in the case. In most cases a jury finds a defendant not guilty although the evidence suggests strongly the defendant's guilt. Finally, juror misconduct can be minor (lying to avoid jury service) or serious (engaging in improper conduct while serving on a jury), but is an ever-present concern, especially since today's trials are much longer, increasing the opportunity for engaging in inappropriate behavior.

Questions for Review

1. Describe the history and development of the grand jury.
2. How has jury size changed over time?
3. What is jury nullification? Do you agree or disagree that juries should have this power?
4. Describe the difference between evidence-driven juries and verdict-driven juries.
5. Should defendants be allowed to spend money to hire scientific jury consultants? If so, does this give them an unfair advantage?
6. What is *voir dire*?
7. What is the relevant case law that has shaped our current constitutional requirement on jury size?
8. What are some of the types of hardships cited by contemporary prospective jurors to avoid jury duty?
9. What are several different forms of juror misconduct?

Suggested Readings

1. T. Brewer (2004). "Race and Jurors' Receptivity to Mitigation in Capital Cases: The Effects of Jurors', Defendants', and Victims' Race in Combination." *Law and Human Behavior* **28:**529–545.

2. D. Graham Burnett (2001). *A Trial by Jury.* New York: Alfred A. Knopf.

3. John Clark (2000). "The Social Psychology of Jury Nullification." *Law and Psychology Review* **24:**39–57.

4. Clay S. Conrad (1998). *Jury Nullification: The Evolution of a Doctrine.* Durham, NC: Carolina Academic Press.

5. E. Finch and V. E. Munro (2005). "Juror Stereotypes and Blame Attribution in Rape Cases Involving Intoxicants." *British Journal of Criminology* **45:**25–38.

6. Norman J. Finkel (2000). "Commonsense Justice and Jury Instructions: Instructive and Reciprocating Connections." *Psychology, Public Policy and Law* **6:**591–628.

7. Shaun L. Gabbidon, Helen Taylor Greene, and Vernetta D. Young (eds.) (2002). *African-American Classics in Criminology and Criminal Justice.* Thousand Oaks, CA: Sage Publications.

8. Valerie P. Hans and Neil Vidmar (1986). *Judging the Jury.* Plenum Publishing Company, New York, NY.

9. Harry Kalven Jr. and Hans Zeisel (1966). *The American Jury.* Little, Brown and Company.

10. Margaret Bull Kovera (ed.) (2004). "Psychology, Law, and the Workplace." *Law and Human Behavior* **28:**1–132.

11. Ana M. Martin, Martin F. Kaplan, and Jose M. Alama (2003). "Discussion Content and Perception of Deliberation in Western European Versus American Juries." *Psychology, Crime and the Law* **9:**247–263.

12. Robert D. Miller (2003). "Testimony by Proxy: The Use of Expert Testimony to Provide Defendant Testimony Without Cross-Examination." *Journal of Psychiatry and Law* **31:**21–41.

13. Judy Sheperd et al. (2002). "Reflections on a Rape Trial: The Role of Rape Myths and Jury Selection in the Outcome of a Trial." *Affilia Journal of Women and Social Work* **17:**69–92.

14. Donna Shestowsky and Leonard M. Horowitz (2004). "How the Need for Cognition Scale Predicts Behavior in Mock Jury Deliberations." *Law and Human Behavior* **28:**305–337.

15. Neil Vidmar (ed.) (2000). *World Jury Systems.* Oxford, UK: Oxford University Press.

16. S. Vollum, Rolando V. del Carmen, and Dennis R. Longmire (2004). "Should Jurors Be Informed about Parole Eligibility in Death Penalty Cases? An Analysis of *Kelly v. South Carolina.*" *The Prison Journal* **84:**395–410.

CHAPTER 7

Pretrial Procedures and the Trial Process

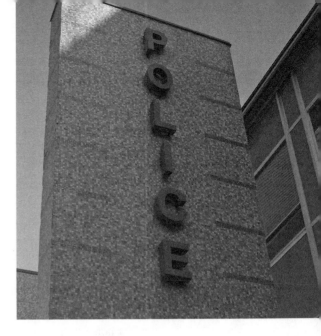

CHAPTER OBJECTIVES

As a result of reading this chapter, you will have accomplished the following objectives:

1. Understand the arrest and booking process, and the initial appearance.
2. Describe bail-granting process and the conditions under which bail may be granted.
3. Understand the Bail Reform Act of 1984 and its implications for clients released on bail.
4. Describe the role of fugitive recovery agents or bounty hunters who track down those who fail to appear or abscond from the jurisdiction to avoid prosecution.
5. Understand the necessity for a speedy trial for a defendant.
6. Understand the difference between bench trials and jury trials.
7. Understand the trial process from indictment through to the judges' instructions to the jury.
8. Describe the different pretrial motions, including motion to suppress, motion for dismissal of charges, motion for discovery, motion for continuance, motion for change of venue, and others.
9. Understand what opening arguments are for, and how the state presents its case.
10. Understand the right to cross-examination and re-cross-examination.
11. Understand the role of eyewitnesses and expert testimony.
12. Describe the process of defense presentation of its case and summation including closing arguments.
13. Understand jury deliberations and whether or not a jury must agree on a verdict.
14. Describe the jury verdict and its aftermath.

KEY TERMS

adversarial proceedings·
alternate jurors
arraignment
arrest
arrestees
bail
bail bond
bail bond companies
bail bondsmen or
 bondspersons
bail recovery agents

Bail Reform Act
Bail Reform Act of 1984
bench trial
booking
bounties, bounty
 hunters
bribery
cash bail bond
criminal informations
cross-examination
direct examination

directed verdict of
 acquittal
excessive bail
exclusionary rule
expert witnesses
eyewitnesses
failure to appear
Federal Rules of Evidence
felony
fruits of the poisonous tree
 doctrine

fugitive recovery agents
grand juries
indictments
informations
initial appearance
jumping bail
jury deliberations
misdemeanor
Misdemeanor Trial Law
motion for a bill of
 particulars

motion for a change of venue
motion for continuance
motion for determination of
  competency
motion for discovery
motion for dismissal of
  charges
motion for intention to
  provide alibi
motion for severance
motion for summary
  judgment

motion for suppression of
  evidence
motions
motions *in limine*
motion to dismiss
motion to suppress
no bill
nolo contendere
objections
not guilty
Philadelphia Experiment
polling jurors

preliminary examinations
preliminary hearings
presentments
pretrial motions
probable cause
re-cross-examination
re-direct examination
reasonable suspicion
release on their own
  recognizance (ROR)
screening
sexual predator laws

Speedy Trial Act of 1974
summation
sworn in
totality of circumstances
trial
trial by the court
trial by the judge
true bill
verdict
victim-witness assistance
  programs
Witnesses

Jim Brookman broke into the home of an elderly woman at 2 a.m. The woman was asleep. While in her home, Jim stole diamond necklaces and bracelets and some rare coins. On his way out he also grabbed a small television set and a gold watch. As Jim was exiting the house through the window, he knocked over a lamp and woke up the woman. As Brookman was driving out of town, a deputy sheriff stopped him for speeding and driving an automobile without any license plates. As the deputy approached the car, he noticed the television in the back seat along with an old gym bag with the zipper partially opened. As he shined his flashlight at the bag he noticed the gleaming reflection of the jewelry. Immediately the deputy suspected foul play. While the deputy was questioning Brookman, the dispatcher came over the radio to report the call of a burglary where a television and some jewelry were taken. Immediately, the deputy placed Brookman under arrest. Later at the station the woman identified the television and jewelry as the items taken from her home. Charges were filed against Brookman and he was booked, fingerprinted, and held without posting bail. Brookman was able to establish he could not afford an attorney and was appointed counsel by the judge. The court-appointed attorney eventually discussed his case with the prosecutor. The defense counsel pointed out that Brookman was a first-time offender who had recently been divorced. He has lost his home and his job. On the night of the burglary, he had been drinking heavily and was depressed and possibly suicidal. The defense counsel argued that Brookman should be treated, not incarcerated. The prosecution was agreeable and advised Brookman to undergo counseling for one year, pay the victim restitution, and perform 400 hours of community service. After one year Brookman had completed all of the conditions of the prosecutor and the charges against him were dropped. Do you agree with prosecutors actions? Should the victim have any say or role in accepting any form of pretrial diversion?

In Louisiana, Mark L. Stephens was on trial for armed robbery and aggravated assault. It was alleged that Stephens had entered a convenience store late at night and pistol-whipped and robbed a clerk. The case was weak and was based primarily on the testimony of three eyewitnesses and the clerk who identified Stephens in a police lineup later. Stephens had been released from prison on parole about six months prior to the robbery, and he had been serving a ten-year sentence for armed robbery and attempted murder. However, Stephens had two alibi witnesses who swore that he was with them all evening in a late-night poker game at the home of one of the witnesses. These witnesses were former offenders themselves, and thus their credibility as witnesses was suspect. When the trial was over, the jury deliberated for four days without reaching a decision. On the fifth day, they returned to the courtroom and advised that 11 of them believed that Stephens was guilty, while the twelfth juror believed Stephens was innocent. The judge accepted the 11–1, nonunanimous jury decision and Stephens was convicted. He was subsequently sentenced to 20 years in prison.

In nearby Mississippi, Roland Abernathy was on trial for armed robbery and aggravated assault. Abernathy had allegedly robbed a convenience store late at night in Biloxi and had shot and wounded the store clerk, making off with over $300 in cash. No one other than the clerk was in the store at the time, and thus the clerk's testimony was the only clear evidence against Abernathy, who had a prior record for three armed robberies. Like Stephens, Abernathy had two alibi witnesses who placed him over 100 miles away from Biloxi at the time of the robbery, claiming that he was drinking with friends at a bar until the early morning hours. The jury heard all of the testimony and when the case was concluded, they deliberated for over five days, failing to reach a verdict. They returned to court on the sixth day and advised the judge that they were not unanimous in reaching a verdict. Of the 12 jurors, 11 voted for guilty, while 1 juror voted for not guilty. The 11–1 vote was questioned by the judge, who asked the jurors if they believed that further deliberation would be helpful in arriving at a unanimous verdict. The jurors said that they were "hopelessly deadlocked" and would "never reach agreement." Therefore, the judge declared a mistrial.

Why was Stephens convicted of armed robbery in Louisiana in an 11–1 jury decision, while Abernathy was not convicted by the same 11–1 jury vote in Mississippi? Under state law, which has been upheld by the U.S. Supreme Court, nonunanimous jury verdicts are constitutional in Louisiana. Under state law in Mississippi, however, jury verdicts must be unanimous. Stephens picked the wrong state to commit his crime.

INTRODUCTION

This chapter is an overview of several crucial pretrial procedures and the trial process. It is important to note that how defendants are processed, from the time they are arrested for an alleged offense until they are convicted, sentenced, and serving time for a crime, may be the basis for an appeal or legal challenge to a higher court. When a crime is committed, it is usually investigated. If one or more suspects are identified, they are arrested. Being arrested begins the criminal justice process. Persons arrested for crimes have allegedly committed misdemeanors, felonies, or both. The use of the term *alleged* is critical because guilt is only established through a trial proceeding or plea bargaining. The chapter opens by discussing arrests and the booking process. Arrested persons are ordinarily taken to local lockups or jails, where they are processed and held. Early in a defendant's processing, he/she will have an initial appearance before a judicial official or magistrate. The initial appearance is important because it is usually during such a proceeding that the matter of bail is raised and settled.

Bail is a surety that guarantees a defendant's subsequent appearance in court for further proceedings, including a criminal trial. The right to bail is examined and discussed. Not everyone is entitled to bail as a matter of right. Normally persons who are likely to flee the jurisdiction or pose a significant danger or risk to others are denied bail. For others, bail is largely discretionary with the judicial official. Many persons are released on their own recognizance, or ROR, and the reasons for such a release are described. Bail bonds and the bonding process are described in some detail. The Bail Reform Act of 1984 is defined and discussed, and its implications for criminal defendants are described. Several bail experiments have been conducted in different jurisdictions, and the results of some of these studies will be presented and evaluated. Whenever persons placed on bail do not appear for additional criminal proceedings later, bounty hunters or fugitive recovery agents are sent after them. The practice of using bounty hunters is examined, and several examples of bounty hunter activities are discussed.

The chapter next examines decriminalization as one way of removing an offense from the category of a crime. Some acts are decriminalized, such as the use of marijuana, where limited uses of this illegal drug have been prescribed for medical purposes. Some states have purportedly moved in the direction of legalizing marijuana generally, although no state has legalized it for the general public to date.

Another pretrial option is pretrial diversion. Diversion programs permit prosecutors to defer prosecution of defendants for specific periods up to one year or longer, while offenders participate in various forms of rehabilitation or therapy. Once the conditions of their diversion program are satisfied, then at the prosecutor's discretion, the case may be dropped. The history, functions, and criticisms of diversion are defined and described.

The chapter also examines several other noncriminal sanctions that may be ordered by judges on the recommendation of prosecutors. For instance, under victim–offender reconciliation, offenders may be required to complete a certain number of hours of community service. The nature of community service varies according to different jurisdictions. Sometimes restitution is ordered, especially where victims have been injured and/or suffered economic losses. Several types of victim compensation programs are described.

Although, as described in previous chapters, the trial process is rare (most cases are processed through some type of plea agreement), there are many different types of trial systems. A trial could involve a judge (bench trial) or a jury of one's peers (jury trial). A jury trial begins with the selection of a 12-member jury. A bench trial is simply a trial by judge, and is usually conducted for defendants charged with petty offenses. In this type of trial, the defendant waives his/her right to a jury trial and the judge hears the evidence, and then decides on the case according to the rules of law. Those persons who are charged with felonies are guaranteed the right to a jury trial. In these cases, the jury will hear the case and decide guilt or innocence based on the facts presented, and then the judge would be responsible for handing out a sentence, if one was mandated. In many jurisdictions, voter registration lists are used to select persons from the community for possible jury service. These persons form the pool from which the jurors will be selected. The jury selection process is important in order to ensure the defendant a fair trial. That process will further be presented in this chapter.

Several constitutional amendments pertain to jury trials and one's right to a trial. The Sixth Amendment guarantees all persons the right to a trial by jury. The Seventh Amendment provides that the right of trial by jury shall be preserved. And finally, the Fourteenth Amendment provides that no state shall make or enforce any law that deprives citizens of their right to due process or of enjoying all privileges or immunities as citizens.

The chapter begins by examining one's right to a speedy trial. The idea of a speedy trial varies among the states and the federal government. Several important speedy trial cases will be presented. According to the federal government, a speedy trial occurs within a 100-day timeline. Probably the longest speedy trial period is in New Mexico, which sets forth a 180-day timeline for a trial. Some states have speedy trial provisions of 90 days. These different definitions of speedy trials will be examined.

Next, bench and jury trials will be distinguished. The process of selecting jurors is described in detail, commencing with the creation of a list of prospective jurors called a *venire* and following through with a **screening** process known as *voir dire*. Once jury members have been selected and the trial commences, judges still serve the function of observing rules of criminal procedure. These rules govern the conduct of trial proceedings. Other rules, such as rules of evidence, govern the nature of evidence that may be introduced or excluded.

Trial proceedings are also accompanied by several pretrial motions. Such motions will be described and explained. Both the prosecution and defense present opening statements. The government presents its case against the defendant, followed by the defense's case. Witnesses from both sides are called in these **adversarial proceedings**. Witnesses could include eyewitnesses, who give an interpretation of the events as they saw them and provide the degree to which the defendant may or may not have been involved, or expert witnesses, who are used by both sides to interpret the meaning of certain types of evidence. Witnesses are cross-examined by each side to determine their veracity and credibility. When the trial is concluded, the prosecution and defense present summations or closing arguments and the jury deliberates. Juries either reach unanimous verdicts or judgments or fail to agree. The process of jury deliberation and voting will be described. Both the federal government and the states have different criteria that govern jury deliberations and voting, either for a defendant's guilt or acquittal. These different scenarios will be described. The chapter concludes with an examination of the aftermath of jury deliberations and verdicts, as well as the judge's role in sentencing.

ARREST AND BOOKING

Arrest

An **arrest** means taking offenders into custody. Usually, arrests of criminal suspects are made by police officers.

Arrested persons are referred to as **arrestees**. Arrests of suspects may be made directly by police officers who observe law violations. Depending upon whether a **misdemeanor** or **felony** is alleged, officers must have at least reasonable suspicion to stop and detain for investigation anyone suspected of committing a felony. If subsequent developments provide the officers with **probable cause** to believe that the suspects they have detained probably committed the alleged offense, the officers can arrest the suspect(s) and take them to jail for further processing and identification. If a misdemeanor is committed and is not directly observed by the officer, the officer may stop suspects and make inquiries. But without **reasonable suspicion** to inquire further, officers are not empowered to arrest possible misdemeanants if the officers lack probable cause (Beger 2003; Stalans et al. 2004).

In a felony case, for instance, officers in a cruiser sitting on the shoulder of Highway 55 may receive a report that a convenience store was just robbed by two men wielding shotguns. The men were described as two black males, one wearing a red cap and the other wearing a green cap. The men were last seen driving east on Highway 55 in a black 1966 Chevrolet van. Just then a black 1966 Chevrolet van driven by a black man in a red cap goes by. The officers give chase and eventually stop the van. The officers cautiously approach and order the suspects to exit from the van. When the suspects are out of the van, the officers observe that the passenger is also black but is wearing a green cap. The officers shine their flashlights into the van's interior and see some money bags on the back seat. These similarities are overwhelming, and thus the officers arrest the two men on suspicion of robbing the convenience store. While these officers didn't see the actual robbery, the descriptions of the fleeing suspects, their vehicle, and the money bags in the van have provided the officers with probable cause to make the arrests.

Booking

Once persons have been arrested, they are usually booked. **Booking** is an administrative procedure obtaining personal background information about arrestees for law enforcement officers (Palermo 2004). Booking includes compiling a file for defendants, including their name, address, telephone number, age, place of work, relatives, and other personal data. The extensiveness of the booking procedure varies among jurisdictions. Most jurisdictions photograph and fingerprint criminal suspects. Sometimes, arrestees are merely detained for several hours and released (Sacks and Pearson 2003). They are usually required to face charges in court later. For example, those arrested for drunk driving may be held temporarily in a local jail overnight. When they are sober in the morning, they are released but must appear before a judge to face DWI charges later. A growing number of jurisdictions are videotaping the entire booking process for individual offenders, in the event that irregular or improper actions are exhibited by jail or police officers as offenders are booked (Schulman 2005). Booking is also a phase of pretrial services. One reason for videotaping this phase is to ensure that discrimination does not occur based on racial, ethnic, gender, or socioeconomic factors (Lobo-Antunes 2004).

INITIAL APPEARANCE

The **initial appearance** of a defendant before a magistrate is a formal proceeding during which a magistrate or other judicial official advises the defendant of the charges. An initial appearance follows the booking process. The magistrate determines from a reading of the charges whether or not they are petty offenses. Petty or minor offenses vary in interpretation among states. Indicators of petty offenses are usually small fines (less than $500) and short sentences (six months or less) associated with the criminal offense. More serious offenses involve larger fines and longer sentences, usually one year or longer in duration (Champion 2005b).

Crime seriousness has been critical in determining whether or not defendants have a right to a jury trial. For instance, the case of *Duncan v. Louisiana* (1968) involved a 19-year-old man who was convicted and sentenced to serve 60 days in jail and pay a $150 fine for simple battery. Duncan requested a jury trial but was denied one. Louisiana claimed that Duncan's crime was a petty offense and thus the offense did not entitle him to a jury trial. The U.S. Supreme Court disagreed. The high court observed that Louisiana's law pertaining to battery, although a misdemeanor or petty offense, carried a two-year maximum sentence and a $300 fine. The U.S. Supreme Court observed that most states define petty offenses as punishable for terms less than one year, and in some jurisdictions, the maximum sentence is no more than six months and a $50 fine. Without defining precisely the meaning of a petty offense, the U.S. Supreme Court said that "We need not . . . settle in this case the exact location of the line between petty offenses and serious crimes. It is sufficient for our purposes to hold that a crime punishable by two years in prison is . . . a serious crime and not a petty offense." Duncan's conviction was overturned.

The Sixth Amendment says that all persons in criminal prosecutions are entitled to the right to a speedy and public trial, by an impartial jury of the state. But this amendment is interpreted differently depending upon the jurisdiction where the petty offenses are committed. Some jurisdictions discourage jury trials to resolve petty offense charges. In a New Jersey case, a defendant was indicted by a federal grand jury on federal misdemeanor charges, and the prosecutor for the government expressed strongly the opinion that the man ought to waive his jury trial rights. The man refused, and so the prosecutor brought new felony charges against the man in retaliation. In this case, the court dismissed all charges against the man as the fair remedy, and the prosecutor was criticized for his misconduct (*United States v. Lippi*, 1977).

When any crime is alleged, it is important for defendants to be advised of the specific charges against them (Nunn 2003). They should also be advised of their rights under the circumstances (Vaughn, Topalli, and Pierre 2004). When persons are arrested by police, their initial appearance before a magistrate, therefore, is a formal proceeding where defendants are advised of the charges against them. At that time, the magistrate advises the defendants of their rights, and bail is considered. This is also the occasion where magistrates determine the date for a preliminary examination or a preliminary hearing to establish whether probable cause exists to move forward toward a trial. Between the time of defendants' initial appearance and the preliminary hearing or examination, defendants can hire defense counsel to represent them (Nunn 2003). If a defendant is indigent, then an attorney will be appointed by the court to represent him or her. Before we examine preliminary examinations or hearings, the bail process will be described.

THE RIGHT TO BAIL

Bail has its roots in New England in the 1690s. Early English common law applicable during that period encompassed many of the guarantees later included in the Bill of Rights, including the right against unreasonable searches and seizures, double jeopardy, compulsory self-incrimination, grand jury indictment, trial by jury, and the right to bail (Hermida 2005; Kuckes 2004). Bail is not unique to the United States. Other countries, such as Australia, have done much to establish bail provisions for criminal defendants and conditions under which bail is granted (Demuth 2003).

RELEASE ON ONE'S OWN RECOGNIZANCE (ROR)   Following one's arrest, a decision is made about whether the defendant will be brought to trial. If a trial is imminent because of case seriousness, most defendants can obtain their temporary release from jail. Many arrestees may not have to post bail, in that they be eligible for **release on their own recognizance (ROR)**. If they have strong community ties and it is unlikely that they will flee from the jurisdiction, they may be freed on their own recognizance (ROR) by the magistrate or judicial officer (Harris and Dagadakis 2004).

BOX 7.1

The Right to Bail

Schilb v. Kuebel, 404 U.S. 357 (1971). In a case in Illinois in which a defendant was ultimately acquitted, 1 percent of the bail amount was forfeited to the bail bond company, which by Illinois law is permitted to make a small amount of money as a commission for posting bail for criminal suspects. Schilb and others filed a class-action suit against the bail bond company as being discriminatory and unconstitutional in its procedures. They further challenged the release-on-own-recognizance scheme as discriminatory. The U.S. Supreme Court upheld the Illinois bail law, saying that its fee of 1 percent of bail was not excessive and that there had been no discrimination between the poor and the rich; in short, the Illinois law did not violate any constitutional amendment.

Stack v. Boyle, 342 U.S. 1 (1951). Stack was charged with conspiracy to commit a crime, and bail was set at $50,000. She protested, saying that the bail was excessive and that no hearing was ever held to determine how much bail should be set. The U.S. Supreme Court agreed with Stack and remanded the case back to the district court, where a hearing could be held on the bail issue. The Court held that bail had not been fixed by proper methods in this case. It did not try to determine or define "proper methods," however.

United States v. Salerno, 481 U.S. 739 (1987). Salerno and others were arrested for several serious crimes and held without bail as dangerous under the Bail Reform Act of 1984. Salerno was convicted and sentenced to 100 years in prison. He appealed, being among the first to challenge the constitutionality of the new Bail Reform Act and its provision that specifies that dangerous persons may be detained prior to trial until such time as their case may be decided. He objected that the new act violated the Eighth Amendment provision against "cruel and unusual" punishment. The Supreme Court upheld the constitutionality of pretrial detention and declared that it did not violate the defendant's rights under the Eighth Amendment if a specific defendant was found to be dangerous.

BAIL BONDS   When the character of the defendant is unknown, or if the offenses alleged are quite serious (e.g., aggravated assault, rape, armed robbery), the magistrate will often set bail or specify a **bail bond**. Bail is a surety to procure the release of those under arrest, to assure that they will appear to face charges in court at a later date. A bail bond is a written guarantee, often accompanied by money or other securities, that the person charged with an offense will remain in the court's jurisdiction to face trial at a time in the future (Demuth 2003).

Motorists may be required to post a **cash bail bond** for minor traffic violations such as speeding or reckless driving. These cash bonds guarantee the motorist's appearance in court later to face charges of violating traffic laws. If the motorist fails to appear, the cash bond is forfeited. The bond set is often the exact amount of the fine for violating the traffic law anyway.

When arrestees do not have the money to post their bail, they may use **bail bond companies**. These companies are usually located near jails. For a fee, they provide the service of posting bail for various offenders. **Bail bondsmen or bondspersons** appear at the jail and post bond for defendants. Defendants are usually required to pay the bonding company a fee for this service, which is 10 percent of the bail bond set by the magistrate. For instance, if the bond set by the magistrate for a particular offense is $25,000, the bonding company may post this bond for the defendant if the defendant is considered a good risk, and if the defendant or an associate of the defendant pays the bonding company a nonrefundable fee of $2,500. If a defendant is unable to pay the fee and no one will pay it for him/her, the defendant must remain in jail until trial is held.

BAIL BONDSMEN AND BONDING COMPANIES

Bail bondsmen are persons who either own or work for bonding companies. Bonding companies are authorized to post bail for various criminal suspects up to a fixed amount. Bonding companies usually have property investments and other capital that they use as a type of insurance with a city or county government. For example, a bonding company may be authorized by a city to post bonds of up to $5 million for various persons charged with crimes. The bonding company owner may have stocks, securities, property, and other assets that he/she has assigned to the city or county as collateral. Thus, the city or county is protected from a potential loss of revenue if the bonding company guarantees the bond amount for the release of a defendant. If the defendant fails to appear later in court, the bonding company forfeits the bond it has posted unless it can produce the defendant later.

If the bonding company is authorized to write bonds of up to $5 million, once this ceiling has been reached, the bonding company can no longer write bonds for defendants. Bonding companies are released from their obligations to cities or counties once defendants have been convicted or acquitted of crimes or the bail bonds are canceled. Bonding companies profit from the 10 percent nonrefundable fees they collect from persons who want to be released from jail before their trials are held. In most jurisdictions, there are several bonding companies that can provide bail for various arrestees.

COMPETING GOALS OF BAIL

EXCESSIVE BAIL　Under the Eighth Amendment, citizens are advised that **excessive bail** shall not be required, nor excessive fines imposed. Some citizens believe that regardless of the offense alleged, bail will be set and defendants will be permitted to remain free until the date of trial. This is not true. Depending upon the circumstances of a particular criminal offense and the evidence obtained, some defendants may have a very high bail, while others may not be granted bail at all. They will be required to remain in jail until trial.

The Eighth Amendment provision against excessive bail means that bail shall not be excessive in those cases where it is proper to grant bail (*United States v. Giangrosso*, 1985). The right to bail is not an absolute one under the Eighth Amendment (*United States v. Bilanzich*, 1985; *United States v. Provenzano*, 1985). In some cases, suspects are detained for trial without bail (*United States v. Acevedo-Ramos*, 1984), while in others, defendants are subject to detention even if they are unable to pay high bail ranging from $25,000 to $1 million (*United States v. Szott*, 1985; *United States v. Jessup*, 1985). If a murder suspect is caught in the act or is a habitual offender, bail will probably be denied. This is because it is probable that such defendants will attempt to flee the jurisdiction to avoid prosecution. Are certain suspects dangerous to others? States vary in permitting judges the discretion for making this decision. In 31 states and the District of Columbia, however, this is a judicial consideration that often results in preventive pretrial detention (Gottlieb 1984).

Whether or not bail is granted is not exclusively determined by whether a crime is violent (Harris and Dagadakis 2004). More than a few defendants who are charged with nonviolent crimes are denied bail. Magistrates consider the **totality of circumstances** in setting bail on a case-by-case basis. A former bank president was denied bail in a case alleging fraudulent manipulation and theft of depositor's funds. While the former bank president had substantial community ties and property interests to protect, he also had a recently acquired passport and travel visas to several foreign countries where he also maintained property and business interests. In addition, $50 million in bank funds were missing as the result of a federal audit. The magistrate considered the bank president to be a poor risk for bail. There was a strong likelihood that the bank president would flee the jurisdiction and live on the embezzled $50 million in some remote location.

Bail provisions of the U.S. Constitution have been challenged by the American Civil Liberties Union and other civil rights organizations. Their efforts as well as the efforts of a variety of special-interest groups have prompted a number of bail reforms over the years. Some of the reasons given for such bail reforms have included the facts that (1) bail is inherently discriminatory against the poor or indigent defendant; (2) those who are unable to post a bail bond and must remain in jail cannot adequately prepare a defense or correspond effectively with their attorneys; (3) there is considerable variation from one jurisdiction to the next and from one case to the next within the same jurisdiction for establishing a bail bond for similar offenses; (4) withholding bail or prescribing prohibitively high bail offends our sense of one's presumption of innocence until guilt is proven in court; and (5) those who pose no risk to the community may suffer loss of job or other benefits from detention as the result of bail. It would seem, therefore, that to deny a defendant bail would be contrary to the presumption of innocence, which is an integral part of due process. Nevertheless, the right to bail is not absolute (Harris and Dagadakis 2004).

Race, gender, and socioeconomic status have been among the variables examined to determine their differential impact on bail decision making. These are extralegal variables and should have absolutely no bearing on whether a defendant is granted bail. However, minorities seem to be at a definite disadvantage in the criminal justice system regarding bail decision making. Racial or gender differences seem to make a difference to judges when making pretrial release and/or bail decisions about particular defendants. For instance, female defendants are granted more lenient pretrial release terms compared with men in many jurisdictions (Jordan 2004a).

Katz and Spohn (1995, 161–163) investigated whether these data might show a pattern of discrimination in bail decision making according to race or gender. The sample of 8,414 defendants was divided according to race and gender. Because of missing information, the sample consisted of 6,625 records for black defendants and 1,005 for white defendants. A small percent of the sample were females. These researchers asked whether it made any difference in the bail decision, as well as the amount of bail, whether defendants were black or white or male or female. When taking offense and prior record into account, race made no difference on the bail decision. However, gender did make a difference. For different types of offenses, female defendants faced significantly lower bail compared with their male counterparts. Regarding pretrial release decision making, however, white defendants were more likely to be released before trial compared with black defendants. Further, females tended to be granted pretrial release more than males. These findings are inclusive, but they suggest that while race and gender may help to explain bail and pretrial release decisions, these variables may not be as important in influencing these pretrial release and bail decisions as was previously thought by other investigators. Other researchers have found similar inconsistencies in bail decision making and race and gender variables (Gallinetti, Redpath, and Sloth-Nielsen 2004).

THE BAIL REFORM ACT OF 1984   The bail reform movement assumes that bail is inherently discriminatory. The **Bail Reform Act** was passed in 1966 and provided that the purpose of this act is to revise the practices relating to bail to assure that all persons, regardless of their financial status, shall not needlessly be detained pending their appearance to answer charges. More recently the **Bail Reform Act of 1984** was passed that vested magistrates and judicial officers with greater autonomy in bail-setting and releasing persons on their own recognizance (Champion 2005b). Presently, bail is available only to those entitled to bail. These are usually persons who do not pose a threat to themselves or others and/or do not pose escape risks. There is nothing inherently unconstitutional about keeping persons jailed prior to their trials, however, under various forms of pretrial detention (*United States v. Salerno*, 1987). Sometimes, pretrial detention of suspects is abused and lawmakers should keep its use within reasonable limits. One reason for this belief is that it is often difficult to forecast accurately who will or will not be dangerous or good candidates for bail (Champion 2007).

Several states have passed **sexual predator laws**, which are targeted at violent sex offenders (Levenson 2004). Washington State, for instance, passed a Sexual Predator Act in 1990 aimed at those likely to engage in future acts of sexual violence. However, the act was soundly criticized because of its failure to cite realistic predictive criteria, which would identify which sex offenders would actually commit future dangerous sexual acts following some type of sex therapy or treatment. Although such laws have drawn criticisms from various civil rights groups, the U.S. Supreme Court upheld the constitutionality of such laws in 1998.

Interestingly, Nebraska passed a sexual predator law concerning a sex offender's right to bail in 1978, 20 years before the U.S. Supreme Court upheld the constitutionality of the Washington State Sexual Predator Act. In 1978, Nebraska amended its constitution to require the denial of bail to defendants charged with forcible sex offenses when the proof is evident and the presumption of guilt is great. Other jurisdictions, such as Texas and California, have enacted similar provisions (Champion 2005b).

OTHER FORMS OF PRETRIAL RELEASE

BAIL EXPERIMENTS   The 1984 Bail Reform Act was innovative in that it contained provisions for judicial officers to release defendants subject to certain conditions, such as (1) complying with a curfew; (2) reporting on a regular basis to a designated law enforcement agency; (3) abiding by specific restrictions on one's personal associations, place of abode, and travel; (4) maintaining or commencing an educational program; and (5) maintaining employment or actively seeking employment if currently unemployed.

Before the Bail Reform Act of 1984 was passed, experiments were conducted to determine the effectiveness of ROR. A National Bail Study was conducted in 20 jurisdictions in the United States (Thomas 1976, 1977) between 1962 and 1971. There was a significant drop in both felony and misdemeanor defendants who were detained in jails during those years, and there was an accompanying increase in the numbers of defendants who were released on their own recognizance (ROR). More judges seemed to be relying on ROR for the pretrial release of defendants, and thus, this meant more limited use of cash bonds, a primary criticism of bail opponents.

Between January 1981 and March 1982, an experiment was conducted concerning bail guidelines in the Philadelphia Municipal Court. This was called the **Philadelphia Experiment** (Goldkamp and Gottfredson 1984). Twenty-two judges were selected for experimentation. One objective of the study was to create visible guidelines for judges to follow in using ROR in lieu of bail in pretrial release decisions. When bail was established, median bail figures for judges not following prescribed guidelines was $2,000, whereas the median bail figure was $1,500 for those judges adhering to the guidelines provided.

Although the findings were inconsistent regarding the use of ROR, the researchers said that the experiment yielded significant improvements in the equity of bail decisions for defendants generally. The study also encouraged greater use of supervised or conditional release programs as outlined within the Bail Reform Act of 1984. As the Philadelphia Experiment suggested, this alternative would provide some degree of relief for jail overcrowding at the very least.

Subsequently, the New York City Department of Correction discharged 611 jail inmates in November 1983 (Gerwitz 1987). Of these, 75 percent were released on bail, while 25 percent were released on their own recognizance. Only four ROR defendants were charged with felonies, while about 75 percent of the bail defendants were similarly charged. Forty percent of the released defendants failed to appear for at least one pretrial hearing. ROR defendants were far more likely than bail-release defendants to fail to appear in court later. Over a third of the ROR defendants were rearrested prior to trial. **Failure to appear** means that persons scheduled for trial and are temporarily released on bail or ROR do not show up in court on their scheduled trial dates. Although obligating defendants to post bail does not necessarily guarantee their subsequent court appearances, it does result in fewer failures to appear compared with those released on ROR.

BOUNTY HUNTERS

BOUNTY HUNTERS AND JUMPING BAIL   It is advantageous for bonding companies if the defendant can post property assets as collateral for the bonding fee. Thus, if a defendant leaves the jurisdiction before trial and jumps bond, the bonding company forfeits the bond it has posted with the court, but it is entitled to seize the defendant's tangible assets or property to cover the cost of the forfeited bond. Defendants may bypass bonding companies altogether by pledging their own real property assets to the court as bond in lieu of confinement. Courts are permitted to accept other types of assets, such as bank deposits, securities, or valuable personal property. When defendants must post their own property as bail, there is a greater likelihood that they will appear later in court compared with those defendants who have bail posted for them by bonding companies. The bail options available to defendants vary among jurisdictions (Dabney, Collins, and Topalli 2004).

When bonding companies provide bond for defendants, they do so on the assumption that bailees will reappear later in court to face the criminal charges against them. Bonding companies avoid furnishing bail to those likely to jump bail and leave the jurisdiction to avoid a subsequent criminal prosecution. **Jumping bail** means to leave the jurisdiction while on bail to avoid prosecution. However, a certain number of defendants leave the jurisdiction and fail to appear later in court. When this happens, the bonding company forfeits its bond to the city or county court. The more bail jumpers a bonding company has, the less bonding funds it has available to use for other defendants. Sizeable profits are lost, at least temporarily, whenever someone jumps bail. For this reason, many bonding companies post **bounties** or monetary incentives to employ **bounty hunters** to track bail jumpers down for a fee and bring them to court. These persons are more recently known as **fugitive recovery agents** and **bail recovery agents** (Dabney, Collins, and Topalli 2004). Unfortunately, we have been unable to devise foolproof mechanisms for predicting which defendants will jump bail and which ones won't jump bail. However, some prediction models work better than others.

In recent years, there have been several incidents involving acts of irresponsibility of bail bondsmen and bounty hunters. Specifically, the wrong persons have been targeted as bail jumpers. As a result, several innocent victims have suffered either serious injuries or deaths as the result of a bounty hunter's actions. Despite these inappropriate and indiscriminate actions by bounty hunters, bondsmen continue to enjoy a broad range of procedural safeguards in surety arrests under both federal and state statutes.

PRELIMINARY HEARINGS

Following an initial appearance and a bail hearing, defendants are entitled to a preliminary hearing. **Preliminary examinations** or **preliminary hearings** are held after defendants have been arrested and have had their initial appearance before a magistrate. Preliminary hearings are conducted by the magistrate or judicial official to determine whether defendants charged with a crime should be held for trial. It is an opportunity for magistrates to determine if probable cause exists that a crime has been committed and the person charged committed it. The preliminary hearing is the first screening of charges against defendants.

The preliminary hearing does not establish the defendant's guilt or innocence at a trial. The government is required to present evidence or proof that (1) a crime has been committed and (2) the defendant committed the crime. If the government fails to present a convincing case to the magistrate, the charges against the defendant will be dismissed.

This option by the magistrate does not preclude the possibility that the prosecutor will take the case to the grand jury for their consideration. In those jurisdictions with grand juries, this is sometimes done. However, if the magistrate believes the case presented by the prosecutor is weak, grand juries probably will not issue indictments either. But there is an important difference in the two strategies. In preliminary hearings, defendants have the right to present facts and evidence supporting their innocence of the crimes alleged. Defendants may even cross-examine witnesses and bring in witnesses supportive of their own position. Again, this is an opportunity for magistrates to determine probable cause that a crime has been committed and the defendant committed it.

In a grand jury proceeding, however, prosecutors present only the government's side of the matter. If magistrates determine that the accused should be released for lack of probable cause, subsequent grand juries may issue indictments or presentments against defendants. In some jurisdictions, preliminary hearings are used instead of grand juries for the purpose of establishing probable cause. Defendants have the right to retain counsel, to be fully informed of the complaint against them and of the general circumstances under which they may secure pretrial release. If the defendant cannot afford counsel, an attorney will be appointed to consult with and represent the defendant.

When the defendant appears before a magistrate, the magistrate will determine whether the defendant wishes to waive the preliminary hearing. With the exception of certain petty offenses, which may be tried by the magistrate directly, the defendant may either (1) waive the right to a preliminary hearing or (2) not waive the right to a preliminary hearing.

The Defendant Waives the Right to Preliminary Hearing

If the defendant waives his/her right to a preliminary hearing, the magistrate or judicial official will bind over the defendant to the grand jury. In those states without grand jury systems, prosecutors may file **informations** or **criminal informations** against defendants. Criminal informations are charges against defendants filed directly by prosecutors. The result of filing a criminal information against a defendant is a subsequent arraignment before a trial judge, one who will usually preside if a trial is forthcoming.

The Defendant Does Not Waive the Right to Preliminary Hearing

If the defendant does not waive the right to a preliminary hearing, then the preliminary hearing is held. The magistrate will determine whether probable cause exists or does not exist. If probable cause does not exist, in the opinion of the magistrate, the defendant is discharged. However, if probable cause exists, again in the opinion of the magistrate, then the defendant will face arraignment on the criminal charges.

Grand Jury Action

Grand juries are bodies of citizens convened to hear criminal charges against suspects. The grand jury will hear evidence from the prosecutor against the defendant and issue either a **true bill** or a **no bill**. If a no bill is issued, the defendant is discharged and the criminal charges are dismissed. If a true bill is issued, defendants face arraignment on the charges against them. About half of all states have grand jury systems.

Sometimes grand juries will be convened for special purposes. These may be investigative grand juries. Perhaps there is a car theft ring operating in several states. Grand juries are convened to hear evidence in these cases. On the basis of evidence collected and examined, these grand juries may issue **presentments**, which are the same thing as **indictments**. The difference is that presentments are not issued as the result of a request from a prosecutor. Rather, the grand jury, on its own, decides that probable cause exists that one or more persons have committed a crime and submit their own true bill. Thus, indictments are the result of requests from prosecutors to charge defendants with one or more crimes, while presentments are independent grand jury actions leading to the same result, but without prosecutor intervention. Prosecutors ordinarily present these charges before grand juries. Federal grand juries consist of 24 persons, while different states have variable numbers of grand jury members.

The result of a charge coming from the grand jury alleging certain criminal offenses on the part of defendants through indictment or presentment brings those defendants to the arraignment stage of the justice process. Thus, the arraignment stage is reached through (1) a finding of probable cause in a preliminary hearing (possibly resulting from a criminal information filed by the prosecutor) or (2) an indictment or presentment from grand jury action.

Arraignments

At the federal level and for many state and local jurisdictions, an **arraignment** is the official proceeding where defendants are informed of the formal criminal charges against them and they enter a plea of (1) guilty, (2) not guilty, or (3) *nolo contendere.* An alternative set of pleas in the state of Kentucky includes (1) not guilty, (2) guilty, and (3) guilty, but mentally ill. Pleas of *nolo contendere* in Kentucky are prohibited, for instance.

If the arraignment stems from grand jury action rather than a preliminary hearing, a copy of the indictment or presentment is given to defendants. In many arraignments, indictments or presentments are read to defendants by either magistrates or clerks of the court.

GUILTY PLEAS   A guilty plea is the equivalent of a confession of guilt in open court. While the procedures vary among jurisdictions, judges usually are expected to inquire of defendants if their plea is voluntary and if they understand the nature of the charge or charges, the mandatory minimum penalty under the law, the possible maximum penalty under the law, and that they are still entitled to an attorney if they have not obtained one. Furthermore, the judge will likely also inquire whether the plea of guilty has been obtained through threats or coercion from anyone, if the defendant understands that the plea can be withdrawn and a plea of not guilty entered, if the defendant understands that they are entitled to a trial if desired, if the defendant understands that they have the right to confront witnesses against them and cross-examine them, as well as that they have the right not to incriminate themselves, and whether there is a factual basis for that plea. In short, the judge usually extends every opportunity to defendants to exercise all possible constitutional rights to which they are entitled.

NOT GUILTY PLEAS   A plea of not guilty obligates the judge to fix a date for trial. The judge also determines whether bail will be continued, if the defendant is currently out of jail on bail. Or the judge may permit defendants to continue ROR if that is their current pretrial release status. Any number of options are available to the judge at this stage. The primary decision reached in an arraignment proceeding after a plea of *not guilty* has been entered is the establishment of a trial date, however.

NOLO CONTENDERE PLEAS   A plea of *nolo contendere* is considered the legal equivalent of a guilty plea. Technically, it is not a plea of guilty, but rather, a plea of no contest. The defendant is not contesting the facts as presented by the prosecution. However, the defendant may take issue with the legality or constitutionality of the law allegedly violated. For instance, the defendant may say, "Yes, your honor, I do not question the facts presented by the prosecution that I possessed two ounces of marijuana, but I also do not believe that the law prohibiting marijuana possession is constitutionally valid."

Sometimes, businesspersons enter pleas of *nolo contendere.* Even though these pleas are treated as the equivalent to guilty pleas in criminal proceedings, they are not considered admissions of guilt in possible future civil proceedings. If a businessman is charged with a criminal offense alleging fraud in the construction of a large building, a plea of *nolo contendere* or "no contest" will result in criminal penalties being invoked. The plea will be treated as though the businessman had actually pled guilty. However, if the building collapses and some persons are injured or killed as a result, they may sue the businessman for damages in a civil action later, but they are prevented from using the *nolo contendere* plea as evidence of an admission of guilt on fraud charges against the businessman. In the case of a guilty plea to the same fraud charges, the businessman could have the plea of guilty used against him in the subsequent civil action as evidence not only of his guilt in the fraud scheme, but also of his negligence. Therefore, a *nolo contendere* plea is sometimes a strategic option for a person wishing to avoid civil liability connected with criminal activities, traffic accidents, or some other law infraction where civil liability may be incurred.

Using a "worst case" scenario, if a defendant enters a not guilty plea, then the arraignment, usually conducted by the trial judge, will accomplish three objectives. As we have seen, arraignments involve entering a plea. They also involve a finalized listing of charges against the defendant. A third objective is to set a trial date. In sum, arraignments are for the purpose of (1) setting forth all charges against a defendant, (2) entering a plea, and (3) setting a trial date. This third feature is significant inasmuch as the trial judge presiding is usually the judge who will eventually hear the case. He/she knows the court docket and schedules the defendant's trial within a relatively short period of time following the arraignment.

TRIAL PROCESS AND PROCEDURES

The Speedy Trial

Many options are available to defendants from the time they are arrested to the time they are arraigned and a trial date is set. In fact, there are many contingencies available to defendants even during the trial and after the conclusion of it.

A plea of **not guilty** by a defendant will obligate the presiding judge to set a trial date and eventually conduct a trial. Normally, this is the case unless some alternative plea is entered, or the prosecution elects to drop charges against the defendant, or if an agreement can be reached between the defendant and prosecutor whereby a formal trial can be avoided. This last contingency is usually referred to as a plea bargain agreement.

Federal courts are bound by law to observe the **Speedy Trial Act of 1974** and its subsequent 1979 and 1984 amendments. The purposes of the Speedy Trial Act are (1) to clarify the rights of defendants, (2) to ensure that (alleged) criminals are brought to justice promptly, and (3) to give effect to a citizen's Sixth Amendment right to a speedy trial (*Klopfer v. North Carolina*, 1967).

According to the provisions of this act, suspects must be charged with a criminal offense within 30 days following their arrest or receipt of a summons. Then the trial should commence not less than 30 days or more than 70 days from the suspect's initial appearance. A 100-day federal provision exists, which is spread out as follows: 30 days from arrest to initial appearance; 10 days from initial appearance to an arraignment; and 60 days from the date of an arraignment to trial.

The leading case relating to a speedy trial is *Klopfer v. North Carolina* (1967). In Klopfer's case, he was charged with criminal trespass. Klopfer eventually went to court and his case resulted in a mistrial. Klopfer then tried to find out if the government intended to prosecute him again for the same crime, but government officials declined to make a commitment. Instead, they formally entered upon the court record a "*nolle prosequi* with leave," which meant that while they were permitting the defendant to be discharged, they were allowing themselves an opportunity to retry Klopfer at a later, unspecified date. This case eventually came before the U.S. Supreme Court, where it was declared that the government violated Klopfer's Sixth and Fourteenth Amendment rights, and that it was unconstitutional to indefinitely postpone his trial without providing an adequate reason. The Supreme Court cited some of the reasons for its decision to endorse a speedy trial provision, which included the facts that (1) witness testimony would be more credible through an early trial; (2) the defendant's pretrial anxiety would be minimized; and (3) the defendant's ability to defend himself/herself and the fairness of the trial would not be jeopardized through extensive, adverse pretrial publicity.

Notwithstanding certain delays for a variety of reasons attributable to the defense, prosecution, or both, the Speedy Trial Act of 1974 provides the following:

1. In a case where a plea of "not guilty" is entered, the trial shall commence within 70 days from the date when an information or indictment has been made public or from the date of the defendant's arraignment, whichever date last occurs.
2. Unless the defendant consents in writing to the contrary, the trial shall not commence less than 30 days from the date on which the defendant first appears through counsel or expressly waives counsel and elects to proceed *pro se* (on his own).

These provisions not only make it possible for a criminal defendant to enjoy the right to a speedy trial, but also eliminate delays otherwise caused by crowded court dockets (*United States v. Nance*, 1982). Some courts have been notorious for their slowness in conducting trial proceedings. Federal judges have considerable power in deciding what evidence to admit and what evidence to exclude, for example. One judge may permit lengthy tape recordings of conversations between an FBI agent and a defendant. These recordings may consume many hours. In another district court, however, the judge may deny the admission of such tape recordings and insist that such materials be presented through more direct and brief testimony from witnesses. With the provisions of the Speedy Trial Act in force, all federal judges are obligated to comply with these provisions in spite of the "general congestion of the court's calendar" (Title 18, U.S.C., Sec. 3161 (h)(8)(C), 2007). Certainly one consequence of this provision is a more rapid trial proceeding.

BOX 7.2

On Speedy Trials

Dickey v. Florida

398 U.S. 30 (1970) Dickey was charged with various crimes in 1968 for crimes allegedly committed in 1960. He made motions to have an immediate trial in several different court appearances, but for various reasons, his trial was delayed until 1968. Between 1960 and 1968, some witnesses died, while others became unavailable for various reasons. Also, some relevant police records were destroyed or misplaced. Following his conviction, he appealed, arguing that his speedy trial rights had been violated. The U.S. Supreme Court overturned his conviction, saying that prompt inquiry is a fundamental right, and the charging authority has a duty to provide a prompt trial to ensure the availability of records, recollection of witnesses, and availability of testimony.

Barker v. Wingo

407 U.S. 514 (1972) Barker and another person were alleged to have shot an elderly couple in July 1958. They were arrested later and a grand jury indicted them in September 1958. Kentucky prosecutors sought 16 continuances to prolong the trial of Barker. Barker's companion, Manning, was subjected to five different trials, where a hung jury was found except in the fifth trial, where Manning was convicted. Then, Barker's trial was scheduled. During these five trials, Barker made no attempt to protest or to encourage a trial on his own behalf. After scheduling and postponing Barker's trial for various reasons, his trial was finally held in October 1963, when he was convicted. He appealed, alleging a violation of his right to a speedy trial. The U.S. Supreme Court heard the case and declared that since, from every apparent factor, Barker did not want a speedy trial, he was not entitled to one. The case significance is that if you want a speedy trial, you must assert your privilege to have one. Defendants must assert their desire to have a speedy trial in order for the speedy trial provision to be invoked and for amendment rights to be enforceable. In Barker's case, the U.S. Supreme Court said that Barker was not deprived of his due process right to a speedy trial, largely because the defendant did not desire one (at 2195).

Strunk v. United States

412 U.S. 434 (1973) Strunk was arrested for a crime and eventually tried ten months later. He was convicted and appealed, arguing that the ten-month delay was a violation of his speedy trial rights. The U.S. Supreme Court heard the case and noted several considerations in determining whether speedy trial rights of suspects have been violated. These considerations are (1) whether there are overcrowded court dockets and understaffed prosecutor's offices; (2) whether there is substantial emotional distress caused to defendants because of long delays; and (3) whether an accused is released pending a trial and whether there is little or no immediate interest in having a trial.

(continued)

(*continued*)

Dillingham v. United States

423 U.S. 64, 96 S.Ct. 303 (1975) Dillingham was arrested for a crime. After a 22-month interval, an indictment was issued against Dillingham, and 12 months after that, Dillingham was brought to trial. Dillingham was convicted and appealed, arguing that the 22-month interval between his arrest and indictment violated his speedy trial rights under the Sixth Amendment. His conviction was overturned and the U.S. Supreme Court declared that invocation of the speedy trial provision thus need not await indictment, information, or other formal charge. Thus, the delay was unreasonable between arrest, indictment, and trial to satisfy Dillingham's speedy trial rights under the Sixth Amendment.

Doggett v. United States

505 U.S. 647, 112 S.Ct. 2686 (1992) Doggett was convicted of conspiracy to distribute cocaine in a U.S. District Court. Because of various delays, mostly caused by the government, Doggett's trial was not held for $8^{1}/_{2}$ years. He appealed his conviction, contending that the $8^{1}/_{2}$-year delay before his case was tried violated his speedy trial rights under the Sixth Amendment. The U.S. Supreme Court overturned Doggett's conviction, concluding that an $8^{1}/_{2}$-year delay in one's trial, largely because of government causes, violates the Sixth Amendment rights of the accused.

Fex v. Michigan

507 U.S. 403, 113 S.Ct. 1085 (1993) Fex, a prisoner in Indiana, was brought to trial in Michigan 196 days following his trial request to Michigan officials and 177 days after the request was received by Michigan prosecutors. Fex was convicted and appealed, alleging that the 180-day speedy trial time period was violated, inasmuch as his trial commenced 196 days after his own request was submitted to Michigan to have a trial. The U.S. Supreme Court heard Fex's appeal and upheld his conviction, noting the detainer warrant phraseology that the statutory 180-day period did not begin until the Michigan prosecutor received his request. The U.S. Supreme Court said that if the warden in Indiana delayed the forwarding of a prisoner's request for a speedy trial, it merely postponed the starting of the 180-day clock. Thus, the receipt of such a notice from a prisoner under a detainer warrant in another state by the state prosecutors triggers the 180-day clock to determine whether one's speedy trial rights are being observed.

The not less than 30 or more than 70 days provision of the Speedy Trial Act applies to the period between one's initial appearance and trial. Ordinarily, there is a ten-day interval between the initial appearance of a defendant and the defendant's arraignment. A federal trial date should be set within 60 days following one's arraignment. The time interval is designed to permit a defendant, together with defense counsel, adequate time to prepare a defense and to spare the defendant any undue delay in coming to trial. If the defendant wishes to consent to an earlier trial date, however, it is the defendant's right to do so under the act.

Many factors affect the 70-day requirement, however. Defendants may discharge one attorney and appoint another. New attorneys will need sufficient time to examine the case and prepare for a defense of their clients (*United States v. Darby*, 1984). The defendant may be ill (*United States v. Savoca*, 1984), or an important witness for either the prosecution or defense must be called and requires additional time to arrive (*United States v. Strong*, 1985). The judge may even request a psychiatric examination of a defendant if, in the judge's opinion, there is reason to believe the defendant is not competent to stand trial (*United States v. Howell*, 1983; *United States v. Crosby*, 1983).

Many local and state jurisdictions follow the federal provisions set forth in the Speedy Trial Act, although they are not bound to do so. For example, North Carolina has a 90-day limit from the time of arrest or arraignment to trial, while New Mexico has a 180-day limit. The "speedy trial" provision of the Sixth Amendment is construed differently from one jurisdiction to the next. Federal courts are bound by the Speedy Trial Act provisions, however.

BENCH TRIALS AND JURY TRIALS CONTRASTED

While the jury system first appeared in the United States in 1607 under a charter granted to the Virginia Company in Jamestown by James I, jury trials existed as early as the eleventh century in England. A criminal trial is an adversarial proceeding within a particular jurisdiction, where a judicial examination and determination of issues can be made and where a criminal defendant's guilt or innocence can be decided impartially by either a judge or jury (Black 1990, 52). There were about 924,900 persons convicted of felonies in state courts in 2000, criminal trials accounted for only 5 percent of these, and the remaining 95 percent were guilty pleas (Maguire and Pastore 2005).

In U.S. District Courts there were 83,530 criminal cases concluded in 2003 (Maguire and Pastore 2005, 426). Federal district judges dismissed 7,957 of these cases (9.5 percent), while less than 1 percent of the defendants were acquitted either by the judge or the jury. There were 74,850 defendants convicted, or about 89 percent. Of these, 96.3 percent (72,110) entered guilty pleas through plea bargaining or by pleading *nolo contendere* or "no contest." In federal criminal trials for the 3,463 defendants whose cases actually went to trial and were not plea bargained, federal juries found 2,413 of these defendants guilty, while judges found 327 defendants guilty. Thus, nearly 80 percent of those who went to trial were convicted.

In both state and federal courts, therefore, trials are comparatively infrequent, inasmuch as plea bargaining is used most of the time to secure convictions. But in approximately 10 percent of all criminal cases, there are trials conducted. These are either (1) bench trials or (2) jury trials.

Bench Trials

A **bench trial**, also known as a **trial by the court** or **trial by the judge**, is conducted either where petty offenses are involved and a jury is not permitted or in cases where defendants waive their right to a jury trial. A judge presides, hears the evidence, and then decides the case, relying on rational principles of law.

Several popular television shows depict bench trials. Television programs such as *Judge Judy* and *Judge Joe Brown* are examples of bench trials. In cases heard by these courts, litigants or parties to the lawsuits have waived their right to a jury trial and have permitted the judge to decide their cases. In criminal courts, defendants often waive their right to a jury trial and permit the judge to decide their cases based on the evidence introduced.

One explanation for waiving one's right to a jury trial is that juries are sometimes more likely to convict persons for felonies than judges. If the crimes alleged are especially heinous or involve emotionally charged issues, defendants will often opt for a bench trial instead of a jury trial, because juries might be more persuaded by emotional appeals and arguments from prosecutors rather than the cold, hard facts of the case. In the early 1990s, for example, the Reverend Moon, known for his indoctrination of children known as "Moonies," was on trial for income tax evasion. Because of the sensationalism associated with his religion and the impact he had on thousands of teenage followers, his defense attorney requested a bench trial, where the judge would decide his guilt or innocence (Wettstein 1992). Other cases involving child abuse in cults have also been decided by judges rather than juries, reflecting the defense counsel's belief that judges can be more impartial when evaluating the factual evidence (Wettstein 1992). Research has also revealed that judges are more likely to impose shorter sentences as the result of a bench trial as opposed to a jury trial, although many other investigations do not support this view (Champion 2005b).

From a purely practical standpoint, bench trials are more efficient than jury trials. If the process of jury selection does not occur, judges can hear evidence and decide a case in less time, since jury deliberations are avoided. For instance, in New York City, a **Misdemeanor Trial Law** was enacted and took effect in 1985. The purpose of this law was to make it possible to reduce the incarcerative punishments for certain types of misdemeanors to six months or less, meaning that jury trials for defendants charged with these misdemeanor offenses could be avoided

(Dynia 1987, 1990). Case backlogs were expedited and overall case processing time greatly decreased. Interestingly, sentencing patterns among judges remained the same both before and after the new law went into effect.

There are several criticisms of bench trials. When judges determine one's guilt or innocence, they may be influenced by extralegal factors, such as one's race, class, ethnicity, and/or gender. Judges are also influenced in their decision making by their own personal feelings about the types of charged offenses. For example, some judges impose more severe sentences upon convicted offenders who commit specific types of heinous offenses, such as child sexual abuse, compared with sentences they might impose for rape, aggravated assault, and murder convictions (Champion 2005b).

When judges decide cases on their own, their susceptibility to corruption is increased. Some judges become susceptible to bribery by influential defendants. In recent years, more than a few judges at the state and federal levels have been charged with corruption and accepting bribes to render decisions favorable to their constituency. **Bribery** is the giving or offering of anything to someone in a position of trust to induce that person to act dishonestly. In 1987, the FBI investigated 105 Pennsylvania judges because of allegations of judicial misconduct. The results of these FBI investigations led the Pennsylvania Supreme Court to temporarily suspend 15 of these judges for bribery. In another FBI investigation, Operation Greylord, a sting operation was conducted against several corrupt judges. Operation Greylord was commenced in 1978 in Cook County, Illinois. FBI agents tapped judges' telephones, recorded conversations, and initiated bogus bribery attempts to induce judges into acting dishonestly in deciding cases. Operation Greylord was successful over the next several years in obtaining convictions against over 60 judges for various criminal misconduct charges, including bribery (Bensinger 1988). Recommendations made by the American Bar Association following Operation Greylord included adopting new ethical requirements for judges and attorneys and the implementation of procedural safeguards to monitor judicial discretion.

Briefly summarizing, the major advantages of bench trials are as follows:

1. Case processing is expedited.
2. Cases are usually decided on the merits of the case rather than on emotionally charged appeals in the case of heinous offenses.
3. Appearances of defendants may be undesirable to jurors, but judges can usually be dissuaded from considering such extralegal factors.
4. In complex cases, judges are often in a better position to evaluate the sufficiency of evidence against the accused and make fairer judgments.
5. Judges are less persuaded by media attention given to high-profile cases where juries might be unduly influenced against defendants.
6. Bench trials are usually cheaper than jury trials, since they don't take as long to complete and require less defense attorney time.

Some of the major disadvantages of bench trials are as follows:

1. Judges may impose more severe punishments on certain defendants, depending upon the crimes they have committed.
2. Judges are more susceptible to corruption when left to their own decision making.
3. Defendants waive their right to a jury trial, where the defendant's situation, appearance, and emotional appeal may work to the defendant's benefit.

Jury Trials

Persons charged with felonies are guaranteed the right to a jury trial in the United States. This guarantee also applies to the states. The landmark case of *Duncan v. Louisiana* (1968) has specified an objective criterion that restricts the right to a jury trial only to those offenses other than petty crimes where the possible punishment of imprisonment of more than six months can be imposed. Other cases such as *Baldwin v. New York* (1970) and *Blanton v. City of North Las Vegas, Nev.* (1989) have upheld this standard.

In the last few decades, the number of trials by jury has increased for both major crimes and the lesser offenses or misdemeanors (Maguire and Pastore 2005). While trials by jury are increasing compared with their frequency in previous years, the trend is that criminal convictions are obtained increasingly through plea bargaining. And in at least one major city, the number of jury trials conducted for all felony arrests has dropped to about 2 percent (Vidmar 2000).

BOX 7.3

U.S. Supreme Court Cases about the Right to Jury Trials

Duncan v. Louisiana

391 U.S. 145 (1968) States must provide jury trials for defendants charged with serious offenses. Duncan was convicted in a bench trial of simple battery in a Louisiana court. The crime was punishable as a misdemeanor, with two years' imprisonment and a fine of $300. In Duncan's case, he was sentenced to only 60 days and a fine of $150. He appealed, saying that he demanded a jury trial and none was provided for him. The U.S. Supreme Court agreed with Duncan, saying that a crime with a potential punishment of two years is a *serious crime*, despite the sentence of 60 days imposed. Thus, for serious crimes, under the Sixth Amendment, Duncan is entitled to a jury trial.

Baldwin v. New York

399 U.S. 66 (1970) Baldwin was arrested and prosecuted for "jostling" (pickpocketing), a Class A misdemeanor punishable by a maximum term of imprisonment of one year in New York. New York law prescribed at the time that this was a petty offense and one not entitling a defendant to a jury trial. Baldwin asked for and was denied a jury trial. The U.S. Supreme Court heard Baldwin's appeal and declared that petty offenses carrying a one-year incarcerative term are *serious* in that jury trials are required if requested. Specifically, the wording of Baldwin attaches great significance to the months of imprisonment constituting *serious* time. The U.S. Supreme Court said that a potential sentence in excess of six months' imprisonment is sufficiently severe by itself to take offense out of category of "petty" as respects right to jury trial (at 1886, 1891). The U.S. Supreme Court overturned Baldwin's conviction and sent the case back to the lower court for a jury trial for Baldwin.

Blanton v. City of North Las Vegas, Nev.

489 U.S. 538 (1989) Melvin Blanton was charged with DUI (driving under the influence). Blanton requested but was denied a jury trial by the North Las Vegas, Nevada Municipal Court. In Nevada, the maximum sentence for a DUI conviction was six months in jail, while the maximum fine was $1,000. Blanton's driver's license was suspended for 90 days and he was ordered to pay court costs and perform 48 hours of community service while dressed in attire identifying him as convicted of a DUI offense. Blanton appealed, contending that he was entitled to a jury trial because the offense, he alleged, was "serious" and not "petty." The U.S. Supreme Court considered his appeal and upheld his DUI bench trial conviction, saying that the most relevant criteria for determining the seriousness of an offense is the severity of the maximum authorized penalty fixed by the legislature. Thus, any offense carrying a maximum prison term of six months or less, as does Nevada's DUI law, is presumed to be petty unless it can be shown that any additional statutory penalties are so severe that they might distinguish the offense as "serious." A further proclamation by the U.S. Supreme Court was that the $1,000 fine did not approach an earlier standard of $5,000 established by Congress in its 1982 definition of "petty" offense, Title 18, U.S.C. Section 1. Thus, the *Blanton* case clearly affirms the earlier holding in *Baldwin* that a defendant is entitled to a jury trial only if the possible incarceration is beyond six months.

THE TRIAL PROCESS

Trial procedures vary greatly among jurisdictions, although the federal district court format is followed most frequently by judges in state and local trial courts. Figure 7-1 shows a diagram of a typical trial from the indictment stage through the judge's instructions to jury members.

Pretrial Motions

Before the start of court proceedings, attorneys for the government or the defense may make **pretrial motions**. Pretrial motions are **motions** *in limine*, and one purpose of such motions is to avoid potentially serious or embarrassing situations that may occur later during trial, such as the attempt by either side to introduce evidence that may be considered prejudicial, inflammatory, or irrelevant. In a brutal murder case, for example, it may be considered inflammatory for the prosecution to introduce photographs of a dismembered body or a mutilated corpse. The jury may be emotionally persuaded to interpret the photographs as conclusive evidence that the defendant committed the crime. Or the photographs may enhance sentencing severity, if additional and overwhelming evidence exists of the defendant's guilt.

In some instances, a defense attorney will make a **motion to suppress** certain evidence from being introduced because it was illegally seized by police at the time the defendant was arrested (Bell 1983). This is known as the **exclusionary rule**, and it provides that where evidence has been obtained in violation of the privileges guaranteed to citizens by the U.S. Constitution, the evidence must be excluded at the trial (Black 1990, 564). Generally, any evidence seized by law enforcement officers as the result of an illegal search would be considered inadmissible in court later. Such evidence would fall within the exclusionary rule, and it would be excluded as evidence against the accused. The leading case in the adoption of the exclusionary rule is *Mapp v. Ohio* (1961). This case involved an illegal search of Ms. Dollree Mapp's premises by police officers in Cleveland, Ohio. Police were searching for a suspect in a bombing incident and believed he was hiding in Mapp's home. They entered her home without a warrant and proceeded to search it. They found nothing incriminating, but in their search, they discovered crude pencil sketches in an old trunk in Ms. Mapp's basement. They considered these drawings

FIGURE 7-1   The Trial Process

as obscene, and they charged Ms. Mapp with violating a Cleveland obscenity ordinance. She was subsequently convicted of possessing obscene materials.

Later, the U.S. Supreme Court overturned Ms. Mapp's conviction because of the illegal search, and they declared that the seizure of the "evidence" by police was unlawful and therefore inadmissible against Mapp. Without the evidence, there was no case against Mapp. The U.S. Supreme Court took that particular opportunity to chide the police officers who conducted the illegal search of Mapp's premises. They warned police officers that in future cases, such misconduct would not be tolerated. Thus, the exclusionary rule was subsequently interpreted by police officers as "tying their hands" and limiting their investigative powers, although the real reason for the rule was to prevent police misconduct relating to warrantless searches.

In another leading case involving narcotics sales, a Chinese suspect, Wong Sun, was arrested by police, charged, and convicted of violating federal narcotics laws (*Wong Sun v. United States*, 1963). Earlier, federal agents had acted on a tip and without a warrant, broke down the door of James Wah Toy's dwelling, and arrested him. They searched his home for narcotics but found none. But Toy told police later under questioning that Johnny Yee was selling narcotics. Yee was arrested and narcotics were taken from his home. Yee, in turn, implicated Wong Sun, who was also arrested. All of the subsequent action against Wong Sun stemmed from an original unlawful search of James Wah Toy's premises and illegally obtained statements from Toy when immediately arrested.

The U.S. Supreme Court overturned Wong Sun's conviction and declared that the statements implicating Wong Sun in narcotics sales were fruits of the poisonous tree. The **fruits of the poisonous tree doctrine** provides that evidence derived from an illegal search or an illegal interrogation is inadmissible against a defendant because it has been tainted. If the tree is poison, then the fruit from the tree will also be poison. Similarly, if a search is illegal and evidence is seized, then the "fruits" of that search or the seized evidence will also be considered illegally seized. Such illegally seized evidence will be excluded later against the accused in court.

Often, a defense attorney will file **motions**, such as a **motion to dismiss**, which is a motion attacking the prosecutor's evidence as insufficient or to signify the absence of a key prosecution witness upon which a conviction depends. Such pretrial motions are ordinarily conducted outside of the presence of the jury. The judge rules on these motions and the trial proceeds. A summary of some of the more frequently used pretrial motions is presented below.

1. **Motion for dismissal of charges** (motion seeking to dismiss the case against an accused based on the failure of the prosecution to state a sufficient case to be prosecuted; alleges critical weaknesses in prosecution's case).
2. **Motion for discovery** (motion to obtain and examine certain documents and evidence collected by the prosecution and the list of the witnesses to be called).
3. **Motion for a bill of particulars** (motion to require the prosecutor to furnish a written statement of charges, outlining the crime(s) alleged, the time and place of crime, and other information).
4. **Motion for continuance** (motion seeks to delay trial proceedings, usually in order to interview additional witnesses and collect additional evidence).
5. **Motion for severance** (if more than one defendant is charged in a conspiracy or crime where several defendants are involved, attorneys for each client may wish to separate the cases so that each defendant can be tried independently in order to avoid any conflict of interest, where one defendant may incriminate other defendants).
6. **Motion for suppression of evidence** (motion seeks to exclude incriminating evidence against the accused, such as any evidence illegally seized from one's premises in violation of Fourth Amendment provisions against unreasonable searches and seizures; in the Denver, Colorado, federal trial of Timothy McVeigh and Terry Nichols, charged with the bombing of the Oklahoma City, Oklahoma, federal building in 1995, for example, several incriminating statements made by Nichols and a receipt for bomb materials with McVeigh's fingerprint on it were the subject of a motion to suppress by their defense attorney).

7. **Motion for determination of competency** (motion seeks to question whether the defendant is competent or sufficiently sane to stand trial; an examination by a psychiatrist might be requested before the trial proceeds).

8. **Motion for a change of venue** (the trial of Timothy McVeigh for the bombing of the Murrah Federal Building in Oklahoma City in 1995 was moved from Oklahoma City to Denver, Colorado, where it was believed that a more impartial jury could be selected, which would be less prejudiced toward McVeigh compared with an Oklahoma jury).

9. **Motion for intention to provide alibi** (motion seeks to demonstrate that the defendant did not commit the offense alleged since the defendant was elsewhere when the crime was committed).

10. **Motion for summary judgment** (motion requesting the judge to order a judgment for the defendant based on the insufficiency of evidence presented by the prosecution to sustain a conviction).

Opening Arguments

Unless both the prosecution and defense attorneys agree to waive their opening statements, the prosecutor makes an opening statement to the jury. Usually, this statement includes the state's theory about the case and why the defendant is guilty. Often, prosecutors will tell the jury what they intend to prove and attempt to persuade them to consider the importance of certain kinds of evidence to be presented later. This outline or summary of the nature of the case is to advise the jury of the facts to be relied upon and the issues involved (Black 1990, 1091).

The defense attorney is also permitted to make an opening statement. The defense is given considerable latitude by the court in addressing the jury. Basically, the defense's statement is intended to undermine the state's case against the defendant and to indicate that in the final analysis, the accused should be acquitted of all charges.

The State Presents its Case

The prosecution begins its case by calling witnesses and presenting evidence that a crime has been committed and that the defendant committed it. Each witness is **sworn in** by a court officer. Being sworn in means that a witness is obliged under the law to be truthful in all subsequent testimony given. This stage is termed **direct examination**. Direct examination is the question–answer exchange between the prosecutor and the prosecutor's witnesses, or between the defense and the defense's witnesses.

The defense has the right to challenge any question asked to a **witness** by the prosecution on direct examination. Usually, defense attorneys raise **objections** to certain questions. Or they may object to an answer given by a witness. The presiding judge rules on such objections and either sustains or grants them or overrules or denies them. The same option is available to defense attorneys whenever evidence is introduced by the prosecution. Objections by either side may be raised at any time, and the judge sustains or overrules these objections. When the defense presents witnesses, prosecutors may also raise objections for the same purposes. Sometimes following an adverse ruling on an objection by the prosecution or defense, the prosecutor or defense counsel will say the word, "exception." The judge will usually say, "Exception noted." This use of "exception" is outmoded in contemporary courtrooms, although some older attorneys continue to use this term. This is because whenever a motion is denied or sustained, this ends further dialogue about the motion. More than anything else, the term is intended to annoy the judge because it is entirely unnecessary. In essence, it is an insulting remark and is intended by either side to chide the judge for whatever ruling is made about the particular motion.

The **Federal Rules of Evidence** contain explicit guidelines for judges and attorneys to follow regarding which types of evidence are admissible and which evidence is inadmissible (Saltzburg and Redden 1994). These are very elaborate and technical rules. If they are not followed by any of the major participants in the trial proceeding, such rule violations could be the basis for overturning a "guilty" verdict on appeal to a higher court. The prosecution is also entitled to appeal a "not guilty" verdict on similar grounds. If certain evidentiary rules were violated, the verdict in favor of the defendant could be reversed on appeal. This scenario actually occurred in the cases of Stacey Koon and Laurence Powell, Los Angeles police officers who were convicted in a federal district court in the Rodney King beating. The federal judge was especially lenient in sentencing Koon and Powell, and the U.S. Attorney's Office appealed the lenient sentences to the Ninth Circuit Court of Appeals. The Ninth Circuit overruled the federal judge. Later, attorneys for Koon and Powell appealed the Ninth Circuit ruling to the U.S. Supreme Court, which rendered a mixed opinion in the matter. The point is that either side may appeal a judge's rulings or particular conduct to a higher court.

The Right of Cross-Examination

After the prosecution has questioned a witness, the defense has the right to ask that same witness questions. This is known as **cross-examination**. The right to cross-examine witnesses is not only a constitutional right, but it also illustrates the adversarial nature of the trial system. The defense attorney attempts to impeach the credibility of the prosecutor's witnesses or to undermine their veracity or truthfulness to the jury (Graham 1985). Sometimes, defense attorneys can use prosecution witnesses to their own advantage and elicit statements from them that are favorable to the defendant.

RE-DIRECT EXAMINATION   Once testimony has been given by a witness from either side, that witness may be cross-examined by the opposition. Once such cross-examination has been completed, additional questioning of the witness may be done by the side who called the witness initially. This questioning is called **re-direct examination**. The purpose of re-direct examination is to clarify certain issues that may be confusing to juries, or to cause the witness to elaborate on points the other side may have introduced, which appear to be incriminating. In contrast with the direct examination, the lawyer conducting the cross-examination is allowed to proceed in a leading fashion. Typically, the lawyer during cross-examination will use short, clear statements that cannot reasonably be denied and that ultimately support the lawyer's version of events. Questions during cross-examination do not seek to disclose new information. Rather, this is an opportunity for the attorney to direct the testimony in support of the position of the questioning party.

For instance, a witness may testify on behalf of the defense in a case where the defendant, Mr. X, a noted sports figure, claimed to have cut his hand *after* a murder had been committed in Denver, Colorado, where the unknown assailant had been injured on the hand. Some blood at the crime scene does not appear to be the victim's blood. In fact, investigators suspect that the blood is from the perpetrator, probably from a cut sustained to his hand from a knife wound during the murder. However, the time interval is such that the defendant claims to have cut his hand on the day following the murder when the unknown assailant's injuries occurred. It is claimed by the defendant, for instance, that he boarded an airplane on the evening of the terrible murder. Investigators have fixed the time of death of the deceased at about 10:00 p.m. At 11:30 p.m., it is known that the defendant boards an airplane and flies to New York. As a passenger on the airline, the defendant sits next to another passenger. The passenger and the defendant converse. The following day, the defendant is notified of the murder and is suspected of it. He flies back to Denver on another airline. He has a cut on his hand. The defendant claims that when he learned of the death of the victim the following day, he smashed his hand down on a table in his hotel room while holding a glass. The glass shattered and the pieces cut his fingers. While on the return flight to Denver, the defendant sits next to another passenger and they converse throughout the trip.

On the witness stand, the passenger who sat next to Mr. X on the first flight is called as a witness for the defendant. The witness is called to confirm that Mr. X did not have a cut hand or fingers later in the evening, after the murder had occurred. The witness is asked some questions by the defense counsel on direct examination.

DEFENSE: "Did you sit next to Mr. X on Flight 161 to New York on the evening of February 26th?"

WITNESS: "Yes."

DEFENSE: "Did you have a conversation with Mr. X during this flight?"

WITNESS: "Yes."

DEFENSE: "Did you notice whether there were any cuts on Mr. X's hands while you were talking with him?"

WITNESS: "I didn't see any cuts on Mr. X's hands."

DEFENSE: "Did you know Mr. X by reputation when you were sitting next to him?"

WITNESS: "Yes, I did."

DEFENSE: "Did you make any special requests of Mr. X?"

WITNESS: "Yes, I asked him to autograph a pad of paper in my pocket."

DEFENSE: "You asked Mr. X for his autograph?"

WITNESS: "Yes, I did."

DEFENSE: "Did he sign something for you?"

WITNESS: "Yes, he signed the paper pad."

DEFENSE: "Where exactly did he sign this pad, you know, did he sign it while holding it in his lap or did he write on some surface?"

WITNESS: "He wrote his autograph on the pull-out tray in front of my seat. He leaned over and signed my paper pad on my pull-out tray."

DEFENSE: "The pull-out tray on *your* seat. OK. And therefore, this gave you a good opportunity to look closely at his hands?"

WITNESS: "Yes, it did."

DEFENSE: "And you didn't see or notice any cuts on his hands or fingers?"

WITNESS: "No, I didn't."

DEFENSE: "And the overhead lights were on when he gave you his autograph?"

WITNESS: "Yes, the lights were on."

DEFENSE: "And you had a clear view of *both* of his hands?"

WITNESS: "Yes, he used one hand to hold the pad and the other to sign his name."

[The prosecutor takes over and cross-examines the witness.]

PROSECUTION: "Sir, could Mr. X have been sitting in such a way so as to hide his hands from you?"

WITNESS: "I don't think so. We talked a lot that evening, and he was quite animated, using his hands."

PROSECUTION: "But you cannot say for certain that there were *no* cuts on his hands when you were talking with him?"

WITNESS: "No, I can't say for certain."

PROSECUTION: "And so if there *were* cuts, it is possible that you just didn't happen to see them that evening."

WITNESS: "That's right. I didn't see any cuts when he gave me his autograph, but maybe I just didn't notice them."

[The defense *re-directs*]

DEFENSE: "Well, you say that you can't say for sure that there were no cuts on Mr. X's hands. Is that right?"

WITNESS:	"Yes, that's right."
DEFENSE:	"But suppose there was a deep gash, or perhaps even several deep gashes on Mr. X's hands? If such gashes were there, they would probably be bloody. Perhaps you would notice, for instance, if Mr. X was wearing some sort of covering to protect such cuts if they were there?"
WITNESS:	"I didn't see any bandages."
DEFENSE:	"But if there was a deep cut, and if it had been made a short time before Mr. X boarded the plane, then you would probably have noticed that, wouldn't you?"
WITNESS:	"Sure, I probably would have noticed that. We were sitting side-by-side in adjacent seats. Lights were on overhead, and I could see both of his hands."
DEFENSE:	"And you saw no cuts?"
WITNESS:	"No, I saw no cuts on his hands. I think I would have seen them if there had been cuts there."
DEFENSE:	"Was there any blood on the paper pad where he signed his autograph?"
WITNESS:	"No. There was no blood on the paper pad. Just his autograph."

Now, suppose we have the second witness on the stand, the one who sat next to Mr. X on his return flight from New York back to Denver. The next witness, also called by the defense, is asked the following questions.

DEFENSE:	"Were you a passenger on Flight 215 from New York to Denver on the day of February 27th?"
WITNESS:	"Yes, I was."
DEFENSE:	"And who did you sit next to while on the airplane, if anyone?"
WITNESS:	"I sat next to Mr. X."
DEFENSE:	"Did you have a conversation with Mr. X while you flew from New York to Denver?"
WITNESS:	"Yes, we talked with one another."
DEFENSE:	"Did you notice Mr. X's hands while you were talking to him?"
WITNESS:	"Yes, I did."
DEFENSE:	"Was there anything unusual or extraordinary about them that you recall?"
WITNESS:	"Yes, there was a big bandage on one of his fingers on his right hand. It looked like it was seeping with blood."
DEFENSE:	"You say the wound was seeping with blood?"
WITNESS:	"That's the way it looked to me."
DEFENSE:	"Did Mr. X tell you how he received that wound?"
WITNESS:	"Yes, he said he cut it on a glass in his hotel room."
DEFENSE:	"Did he say *when* he cut his hand?"
WITNESS:	"Yes. He said he cut it this morning, after he received an upsetting telephone call."

The prosecution cross-examines the second witness:

PROSECUTION:	"When you saw this wound, you don't know precisely *when* the wound was made, do you?"
WITNESS:	"Mr. X says it happened that morning, a few hours before the flight to Denver."
PROSECUTION:	"Yes, but you don't really know for sure *when* that cut was made, do you?"
WITNESS:	"No, I don't."
PROSECUTION:	"It could have been the night before, couldn't it, maybe even around 10:00 p.m. at night?"
WITNESS:	"I suppose so."

| PROSECUTION: | "So you really don't know *when* the cut was made, and that it could perhaps have been made the night before, is that right?" |
| WITNESS: | "That's right." |

The defense re-directs:

DEFENSE:	"Did you actually *see* the cut on Mr. X's hand or just the bandage covering it?"
WITNESS:	"I saw the cut. He changed the bandage once, just before we landed."
DEFENSE:	"When you saw the cut, how did it look to you?"
WITNESS:	"What do you mean?"
DEFENSE:	"Did it look like an old cut or a new one?"
WITNESS:	"It looked like a cut that was made fairly recently."
DEFENSE:	"If a cut like the one you saw had been made the night before you actually saw it, would it still be bleeding like that, as you have described?"
WITNESS:	"I don't think so. It probably would have healed some. I don't know."
DEFENSE:	"And so you are saying that the cut looked entirely consistent with Mr. X's explanation that he had just cut his hand on some glass in his hotel room, is that it?"
WITNESS:	"Yes, that's it."

As can be seen from the above exchange, each side, the defense and prosecution, attempts to use these two witnesses in ways that work to each side's particular advantage. The prosecution wants the jury to think that the cut occurred when Mr. X, believed to be the murderer, used a knife to kill the victim. The defense wants to show that there was no hand or finger cuts when Mr. X left Denver late on the evening of the murder, but that a cut *was* there when Mr. X was seen by others the following day. If it can be established that Mr. X's hand cut occurred the day following the murder, then it couldn't have been made when the murder was committed. The prosecution wants the jury to believe that the cut occurred during the murder, not afterward. Both the defense and prosecution are permitted to engage in re-direct examinations and **re-cross-examinations** of each witness until they feel that they have adequately made their respective points. They are shaping and forming versions of events that make a case for or against Mr. X. We might even consider re-direct and re-cross-examinations as refinements of witness testimony, to know for sure what the witness saw or did not see. The jury listens and decides which version seems most believable.

RE-CROSS-EXAMINATION   While some persons consider re-cross-examination prolonging an otherwise long trial, each side is entitled to re-cross-examine witnesses and recall witnesses to the stand for further questioning. This tactic is particularly important whenever new evidence is revealed from other witnesses. Judges may abbreviate extensive cross-examinations and re-cross-examinations if they believe that attorneys are merely covering previous information disclosed in earlier testimony.

IMPEACHING WITNESSES   Impeachment means to call into question the truthfulness or credibility of a witness. If either the prosecutor or defense attorney can demonstrate that a particular witness may be lying or is otherwise unreliable, then that witness's testimony is called into question. Jury members may not believe such witnesses and the evidentiary information they provide for or against defendants. Of course, defendants themselves are subject to impeachment if they testify.

There are several ways defense attorneys can impeach a witness. Attorneys can obtain inconsistent testimony from the witness or can get the witness to admit confusion over certain facts recalled. Or attorneys can introduce evidence of the untruthfulness of the witness based on previous information acquired through investigative sources. Perhaps a witness previously has been fired from a company because of embezzlement. Embezzlement is one form of dishonesty, and an inference may be made by jurors that if witnesses were dishonest in their employment, they may not be telling the truth on the witness stand even though they may be telling the truth in the present case. Of course, when the defense presents its witnesses, the prosecution has the same cross-examination rights and can make similar attempts to impeach the credibility of the witnesses called in the defendant's behalf.

Eyewitnesses and Expert Witnesses

There are many instances in criminal law where expert testimony is solicited (Penrod, Fulero, and Cutler 1995). Experts can testify and identify blood samples, firearms, and ballistics reports; comment on a defendant's state of mind or sanity; and provide opinions about any number of other pieces of evidence that would link the defendant to the crime. By the same token, defense attorneys can introduce expert testimony of their own to rebut or counter the testimony of the prosecution's experts.

Expert witnesses are used by either side to interpret the meaningfulness of evidence presented by either the prosecution or defense (Ross, Read, and Toglia 1994). Expert witnesses have extensive training and experience in matters of fact that may be introduced as evidence in a trial. Their opinions are given more weight than those of laypersons who do not have such training and experience. Complex issues or topics are clarified for jurors whenever expert testimony is presented (Penrod, Fulero, and Cutler 1995).

Being an expert witness involves certain hazards or risks, however. Some expert witnesses have reported that they were harassed by defendants or their attorneys outside of the courtroom. Particularly in the case of forensic psychiatrists who might testify as to a defendant's sanity or criminal motives, some expert witnesses have reported actually being physically assaulted or threatened with harm (Read, Yuille, and Tollestrup 1992). A majority of cases involving harassment involved criminal cases or where the insanity defense was raised.

Eyewitnesses are also of significant value to both prosecutors and defense attorneys (Davies et al. 1995). They can provide opinions and interpretations of events they actually experienced, and they can provide accounts of the defendant's involvement in the crime alleged. But some researchers have explored the impact of eyewitness testimony on jury verdicts and have suggested strongly that any such testimony should be corroborated with additional supportive evidence in order to be more fully reliable (Champion 2005b).

There has been some criticism and suspicion about the credibility and reliability of eyewitness testimony. Despite these doubts countless hundreds of persons every year are convicted on little more than the testimony of witnesses. This has become a problem for courts that they have yet to resolve in spite of research showing that juries overrate the reliability of witnesses (Loftus 1996).

A major problem faced by prosecutors is obtaining the cooperation of victims or witnesses to testify in court as to pertinent information they might have about a particular case. The courtroom is a frightful experience for many persons, and the thought of enduring questioning on the witness stand is not a desirable one. In an effort to allay fears of victim-witnesses, various victim-witness assistance programs have been initiated, particularly by prosecutors and courts in various jurisdictions.

Victim-witness assistance programs are services that are intended to explain court procedures to various witnesses and to notify them of court dates. Additionally, such programs permit victim-witnesses to feel more comfortable with the criminal justice system generally. One particularly important function performed by such programs is to assist witnesses in providing better and clearer evidence in criminal prosecutions, with the result that a greater number of convictions will be forthcoming where their testimony has been given (Finn and Lee 1985).

CHILDREN AS EYEWITNESSES   One area that has received much attention in recent years is the reliability of the testimony of child witnesses, especially in cases alleging child sexual abuse (Dent and Flin 1992; McGough 1994). The scientific study of child witnesses by psychologists in the United States began during the early 1900s, and some researchers have concluded that children are the most dangerous witnesses of all (McGough 1994). One reason for this view is that a child's memory of an especially traumatic event such as a rape or homicide is often distorted, and that their recall or true impression of what actually occurred is flawed in one respect or another (Dent and Flin 1992; Mason 1991).

A large number of child victims of sexual abuse are under age 12, and nearly a third are under age 6 (McGough 1994). By 1994, half of all states had adopted special hearsay exceptions when children are giving testimony about being abused, however. Of primary concern to the judge and other participants in the courtroom scene is the ability of children to distinguish between real and imagined events (Davies et al. 1995; Whitcomb et al. 1994).

In addition to the obvious trauma of being asked about emotionally disturbing events such as sexual molestation, the parents of sexually abused children are often reluctant to allow their children to testify in court. Some persons have suggested that children be permitted to testify in an isolated location away from the actual courtroom, and that their testimony should be monitored through closed-circuit television (Whitcomb et al. 1994). Under the Sixth Amendment, however, defendants are entitled to a face-to-face confrontation with their accusers (Ceci and Bruck 1995; Zaragoza 1995). Thus, at least for the present, it would seem that the utilization of closed-circuit television in cases such as child sexual abuse will need to be assessed further by the U.S. Supreme Court before it is approved on a national scale.

At the conclusion of the state's case against the defendant, the defense attorney may make a motion for a **directed verdict of acquittal**. A directed verdict of acquittal requests the judge to dismiss the case against the defendant because the prosecution has not proved the defendant's guilt beyond a reasonable doubt. Thus, the defense believes that their client has not been proved guilty and should be freed. No evidence exists to indicate the frequency with which such a verdict is requested, but such a motion is probably made often in many criminal cases. One reason is that it doesn't cost the defense anything to make such a motion. And on occasion, the motion may be granted. In most instances, if the case is being tried by a jury, the presiding judge is reluctant to grant such a motion. The jury is charged with the responsibility of determining one's guilt or innocence. Judges may grant such a motion, however, if they believe that the state has failed to present a compelling case of the defendant's guilt. If the case is a high-profile one, such as the trial of O. J. Simpson, the judge is even less likely to grant such a motion. Such a motion was made in Simpson's trial in early 1996 following the prosecution's case, but presiding Judge Lance Ito denied the motion.

The Defense and Summation

The defense attorney presents all relevant evidence and calls all witnesses who have relevant testimony favorable to the defendant. The prosecutor may object to the introduction of certain witnesses or to any kind of evidence the defense intends to introduce. Defendants may or may not choose to testify in their own behalf. Their right not to testify is guaranteed under the Fifth Amendment of the U.S. Constitution, and no defendants may be compelled to give testimony against themselves. Evidence from defendants themselves may be self-incriminating, and the Fifth Amendment provides for the right against self-incrimination. Of course, if a defendant does not testify, the jury may believe that the defendant has something to hide. It is difficult to make the jury understand that defendants are merely exercising their right not to testify under the Fifth Amendment, and that no inferences should be made by jurors if the defendant elects not to testify in his or her own behalf. It is the responsibility of the state, the prosecution, to prove the case against the defendant beyond a reasonable doubt. The defendant is entitled to a presumption of innocence until guilt is established according to the "beyond a reasonable doubt" standard. The judge is charged with the responsibility of instructing the jury in this regard and acquainting them with the Fifth Amendment protections extended to defendants under the law.

Some persons erroneously claim that if a jury finds a defendant not guilty and votes for acquittal, it doesn't necessarily mean that the defendant is innocent. Thus, the status of being found "not guilty" is not the equivalent of the status of being acquitted of criminal charges. But this erroneous belief undermines the fundamental principles of the U.S. Constitution and the rights it conveys to all citizens, regardless of how guilty they may appear to the public or media. Therefore, if we presume correctly that a defendant is innocent until proved guilty in a court of law, beyond a reasonable doubt, then an acquittal causes the presumption of innocence to remain unchanged. For instance, Fred Graham, a former attorney and expert commentator for *Court TV*, accepted a telephone call from an interested viewer following the O. J. Simpson trial. The caller posed the following question to Graham: "Mr. Graham, the fact that the jury found Simpson not guilty doesn't mean that Simpson is innocent, does it?" Graham answered, "That's right, it doesn't mean he is innocent." Graham was clearly wrong in his response to the anonymous caller. The presumption of innocence continues as a part of our right to due process throughout a trial and its conclusion, unless a guilty verdict is declared by the jury. In the eyes of the law, therefore, O. J. Simpson continues to be viewed as innocent of the crimes previously alleged.

Interestingly, two quite different books appeared in 1996 following the verdict in the murder trial of sports figure O. J. Simpson. A work by Ron Huff, Arye Rattner, and Edward Sagarin, *Convicted But Innocent: Wrongful Conviction and Public Policy*, and another work, *Guilty: The Collapse of Criminal Justice*, by Harold J. Rothwax both address fundamentally different views of jury voting. Jury decisions may result in convictions of innocent persons, while jury decisions may result in acquittals of guilty persons. Rothwax, a former judge, suggests that current laws and procedures handicap the police and prosecutors from apprehending and convicting criminals, and preventing the courts from resolving the primary question of whether the accused committed the crime. He explores various drastic changes in the laws so that the ends of justice might be served more effectively, through more frequent convictions and fewer reversals of convictions on technical grounds. The work by Huff and his colleagues examines various wrongful convictions, where innocent persons were convicted anyway, despite the fact that they were innocent. Presently, we acknowledge that our legal system is flawed, and it is likely that it will always be flawed.

Various interesting scenarios have been portrayed by motion pictures, where a guilty offender is convicted of murder but later his conviction is overturned because evidence is found implicating another offender of the murder. The other offender has murdered several persons, and so it is believed that he is fully capable of murdering one more person. The fact is that the second murderer has entered into an agreement with the first murderer. The agreement is that the second murderer wants his parents killed, and the first murderer (who really is a murderer) agrees to kill the second murderer's parents if the first murderer is freed. Therefore, a plot unfolds where evidence is suddenly discovered that leads to freeing the first murderer. While this convoluted plot seems peculiar, it is no more silly than imagining scenarios where guilty suspects are acquitted and innocent suspects are convicted. In many murder cases, only the real murderers know for sure. While these two books offer criticisms of the criminal justice system that allows for such events to occur, there is no foolproof way of preventing their occurrence, no matter what reforms are implemented.

CAN PROSECUTORS CRITICIZE DEFENDANTS FOR NOT TESTIFYING IN THEIR OWN BEHALF?   The prosecution is forbidden from mentioning a defendant's refusal to testify to the jury (*Griffin v. California*, 1965). For instance, if the prosecutor were to say, "Ladies and gentlemen of the jury, if this defendant were innocent, he would get up here on the stand and say so," this statement would be improper, and the judge would order the statement stricken from the record. In fact, such an utterance by the prosecutor may cause the judge to declare a mistrial. Both prosecutors and defense attorneys alike are bound by legal ethics to comply with court rules when presenting a case or representing a client in the courtroom. But occasionally, some attorneys engage in unethical conduct, either deliberately or inadvertently. Sometimes, such conduct will result in the judge declaring a mistrial, and the case will have to proceed from the beginning in front of a new jury.

Ordinarily, judges will give the jury instructions when it is ready to deliberate and decide the case. These instructions include statements about the rights of the accused and whether any inferences, either positive or negative, may be drawn from an accused's right not to testify in his or her own behalf. The jury is instructed not to consider the fact that a defendant chose not to testify in his own behalf. One reason for this admonition is to remind the jury that it is the prosecutor's burden to show, beyond a reasonable doubt, that the accused is guilty of the crime(s) alleged. It is not the responsibility of the accused to prove himself *innocent* to the jury. While these admonitions may seem self-evident, more than a few jurors have been influenced by the refusal of defendants to testify. We cannot possibly know what impact this refusal to testify will have on jury decision making.

Each side is permitted a **summation** at the conclusion of all evidence presented. Ordinarily, defense attorneys present the final oral argument on behalf of their client. This argument is followed by the closing argument of the prosecuting attorney. Sometimes, with court consent, prosecutors may present a portion of their closing argument, followed by the closing argument of the defense, followed by the remainder of the prosecutor's closing argument. In short, the prosecutor gets in the final remarks to the jury. There is a very good reason for this order of summation. Since the burden of proving guilt beyond a reasonable doubt is so difficult, prosecutors are given the last word. It is assumed that if these prosecutorial remarks are the last words heard by the jury, besides the instructions they receive from presiding judges, then their subsequent deliberations will be tainted initially by these prosecutorial remarks. During jury deliberations, however, a critical examination of all evidence introduced will lead the jury to one conclusion or the other. If the prosecutor has failed to carry the burden of proof in the case, the jury will vote to acquit the defendant.

JURY DELIBERATIONS

After the prosecution and defense have presented their final arguments, the judge instructs the jury on the procedures it must follow in reaching a verdict, and the jury retires to the jury room to consider the evidence and arrive at a verdict. The judge's instructions to the jury often include a recitation of the charges against the defendant, a listing of the elements of the crime the prosecution must prove beyond a reasonable doubt, and a charge for jurors to carefully weigh and consider the evidence and testimony of witnesses.

Again, depending upon whether the case is in federal district court or in a state jurisdiction, the jury must either be unanimous or comply with the particular state rules governing jury verdicts. It will be recalled that federal juries must be unanimous. If a jury of 12 persons fails to agree, a mistrial will be declared by the federal judge. And if one jury member becomes ill, an 11-member federal jury, with court approval, is acceptable and must render a unanimous verdict as well. In states such as Louisiana and Oregon, the particular state rules governing jury verdicts have approved 9–3 or 10–2 majority votes in order for verdicts of guilty to be rendered. In six-person juries, the jury must reach a unanimous decision, according to the U.S. Supreme Court (*Burch v. Louisiana*, 1979).

Jury deliberations and the decision-making process of arriving at particular verdicts have also been targeted for study by social scientists in recent years (Kerr 1994; Kerr and MacCoun 1985). The primary difficulty confronting those interested in studying jury deliberation processes is that such deliberations are conducted in secret. Some investigators have participated as actual jury members in their respective jurisdictions. And the insight gained through such experiences has been instrumental in preparing defense attorneys more adequately in presenting convincing cases to juries on behalf of their clients.

Jury deliberations have often been the subject of feature films and novels. The 1957 drama *Twelve Angry Men*, starring Henry Fonda, epitomized the emotion and anger of jurors in a murder case. In that film, Fonda was the lone juror voting "not guilty" against the other 11 "guilty" votes. The remainder of the film described the jury's attempt to convince Fonda that he was wrong. As it turned out, Fonda convinced the other jurors that *they* were wrong, and the defendant was acquitted. And in a 1996 novel by author/lawyer John Grisham, *The Runaway Jury*, a detailed depiction of jury deliberations is presented, with an incredible amount of interplay among jurors and the ease with which jurors' opinions are changed by particularly dominant jury members.

Jury deliberations such as those occurring in *Twelve Angry Men* are not uncommon. Jurors who differ as to their estimation of the value of particular evidence attempt to persuade the other jurors to side with them. At the outset, jurors may take an informal ballot or vote to see where they stand for conviction or acquittal. More often than not, this initial ballot influences significantly the final verdict by presenting to all jury members the disposition or determination of the majority of jurors favoring guilt or acquittal.

Group pressure is often responsible for changing minority factions in a jury to aligning themselves with the majority opinion. And in jurisdictions where the majority-rule option is in effect, such as Oregon and Louisiana, agreement among jurors is achieved more rapidly than in those states where unanimity of opinion is required. Figure 7-2 shows the jury deliberation task.

When deliberations commence, juries may or may not establish a deliberation agenda. But ordinarily, discussions take place concerning the relevance and importance of particular pieces of evidence and witness testimony. If there is an initial vote and the jury is in disagreement as to the verdict, deliberations continue until a verdict is reached. If the jury simply cannot agree on a verdict, or if the required majority cannot be obtained in those jurisdictions providing for a majority vote for conviction, the judge will likely declare a mistrial.

Must Juries Agree on a Verdict?

JURY VOTING IN U.S. DISTRICT COURTS   In federal district courts, juries consist of 12 persons. The judge may or may not permit the selection of alternate jurors. **Alternate jurors** are used in the event that one or more of the regular jurors become ill during the proceedings. Also, during jury deliberations, if a juror cannot continue to serve, Title 18 U.S.C., Rule 23 (2006) provides that "if the court finds it necessary to excuse a juror for just cause after the jury has retired to consider its verdict, in the discretion of the court a valid verdict may be returned by the remaining 11 jurors" (Title 18, U.S.C., 2006). In federal courts, whether a 12- or 11-member jury hears a case, the decision reached for either guilt or acquittal must be unanimous. If one or more

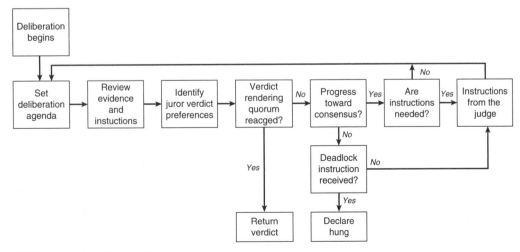

FIGURE 7-2 Jury Deliberations

jurors disagree and persist in their disagreement with the other jurors, the judge declares a hung jury and a mistrial is declared. Mistrials are erroneous, invalid, or nugatory trials (Black 1990, 1002). This means that the entire case will have to be heard again before a new jury later. Mistrials also occur during the trial, especially if irregularities or errors occur to jeopardize a defendant's fair trial rights. Sometimes, inadmissible evidence may be admitted erroneously. A witness may make an utterance which may tend to substantial jury bias. Whenever such trial irregularities and other errors occur, the judge ordinarily grants a motion by either side for a mistrial (Hodge 1986; Institute for Court Management 1983).

JURY VOTING IN STATE COURTS   At the local and state levels, however, the federal rule for jury agreement or unanimity does not always apply. Under existing U.S. Supreme Court guidelines, state juries may vary in size from a minimum of 6 to 12 persons. Actually, the U.S. Supreme Court has established the minimum number of jury members at six in the case of *Williams v. Florida* (1970). However, no such precedent has been established for upper limits of jury sizes. Thus, it is conceivable that a defendant may request a jury consisting of more than 12 persons, such as 25 or 50 jurors. But this would be very unusual. It would also pose severe logistical problems for courtrooms, where it would be difficult to find sufficient seating for all of these jurors. Furthermore, there would be considerable difficulty for all of these jurors to reach agreement about the guilt or innocence of criminal defendants.

Six-member juries must be unanimous in their verdict (*Burch v. Louisiana*, 1979). However, if juries consist of 12 persons, a majority verdict may be acceptable in certain states, unless unanimity is required under state or local laws. For instance, in the cases of *Apodaca v. Oregon* (1972) and *Johnson v. Louisiana* (1972), the respective defendants were convicted by a majority of jurors, but there was no unanimity of agreement. In most states, however, unanimous verdicts are required by statute.

An example of a legitimate nonunanimous verdict is the case of *Johnson v. Louisiana* (1972). In the *Johnson* case, Frank Johnson was arrested, tried, and convicted of armed robbery in 1968. The 12-person jury convicted him by a 9–3 vote (the absolute minimum majority required under Louisiana law). In another case, unanimity of jury voting was not required either. This was the case of *Apodaca v. Oregon* (1972). In Apodaca's case, Robert Apodaca and several other defendants were convicted of assault with a deadly weapon. Apodaca was convicted by an 11–1 jury vote. In Oregon, the minimum vote required by a jury for conviction is 10–2. Their respective appeals were heard by the U.S. Supreme Court. The U.S. Supreme Court upheld both of their convictions and underscored the right of states to utilize the rule of a majority vote in their jury trials. Also some states, such as Tennessee, where the Tennessee State Legislature has copied the Federal Rules of Criminal Procedure, require their 12-member juries to be unanimous in their voting. There are some exceptions to nonunanimous jury voting, however. In capital cases where the death penalty may be imposed, the jury vote for conviction must always be unanimous.

POLLING THE JURORS   Judges will frequently poll jurors once they have rendered their verdict. **Polling jurors** simply refers to asking each juror to state in open court whether the verdict is a true reflection of his/her feelings and how he/she voted. It is unlikely that a jury will vote to acquit a defendant, where a particular juror will say to the judge that he or she did not agree with that vote. In those cases where juries must be unanimous in their decision to convict or acquit defendants, such an event is especially important. In situations such as in Louisiana or Oregon where unanimous votes are not needed, polling individual jury members identifies the specific vote breakdown. However, in the event that one or more jurors disagree with the majority in a state or federal court where the jury vote must be unanimous, judges will send the juries back to deliberate more extensively, until unanimity of voting is reached. Otherwise, if the jury deliberates for an unusually long period and cannot agree on a verdict, a mistrial will be declared and a new trial may be scheduled. Scheduling a new trial is up to the prosecutor. Mistrials are sometimes based on unclear or insufficient evidence. If prosecutors believe that the issues to be resolved in particular criminal cases are so controversial that no jury will likely agree in the future, then no further prosecution against the defendant will be conducted.

THE SELLING OF JURY DELIBERATIONS   During the 1980s and 1990s, increasing interest has been expressed in jury deliberations and the factual accounts of what transpires in jury rooms (Kerr 1994). Juries have become increasingly scrutinized bodies. Individual jury members have exploited their jury membership to their advantage for profit. This phenomenon is not peculiar to the United States. Other countries, such as Australia and Great Britain, have found that jurors in particularly high-profile cases have focused on the profit motive as a primary reason for their jury involvement (Findlay and Duff 1988).

In particularly sensational trials, jury members' opinions about jury deliberations are increasingly marketable products. Several jurors in the murder trial of O. J. Simpson were excused as jurors when it was learned by the judge that the jurors were planning to write books about their experience and actually negotiating with publishers for book contracts. One former juror had been keeping a journal about his experiences as a juror. Keeping such a journal of trial events was forbidden and regarded as juror misconduct. Another juror, a former airline attendant, was excused for a different reason. It was learned that she had been approached by representatives of *Playboy* magazine and had agreed to pose nude for a large sum of money when the trial was completed. Thus, she was exploiting her role as a juror in the high-profile trial. While posing nude for a men's magazine is not against the law, it raises serious questions about the juror's original motives for becoming a juror.

Whenever jurors in any trial consider the potential profits stemming from their roles as jurors, this raises doubts about their veracity or truthfulness when the *voir dire* was originally conducted. If they have hidden agendas, such as writing a book about their experiences, no laws prohibit subsequent expressions of their opinions and views. But it is juror misconduct to keep journals about their jury involvement and observations. If the prosecution or defense learns about such activities or behaviors, then these revelations become grounds to bar these jurors from further jury service.

In one New York City trial, for instance, a highly publicized event occurred in the Howard Beach community. The case involved a racial attack. During the trial, several jurors contacted the media in an attempt to sell their story and give their account of jury deliberations. Some news reporters believed that such conduct by jurors was acceptable and within the boundaries of free speech. The court and prosecution took a different view by condemning those jurors who sought to profit from their experiences as jurors. The jurors were excused (Kleinig 1989).

What if persons seek to become jurors for the purpose of advancing some political view or social cause? Ideally, juries are comprised of persons who will render fair decisions and consider and weigh all factual information presented by both sides during the trial. But if some jurors are sidetracked with collateral issues not directly relevant to the trial proceedings, this may impair their ability to render fair judgments about what they have seen and heard.

THE VERDICT AND ITS AFTERMATH

After deliberating, the jury returns to the courtroom and delivers its **verdict** to either the judge or an officer of the court. The defendant rises and faces the jury, while either the jury foreman or the judge reads the verdict aloud. If the verdict is "not guilty," the defendant is released. In some cases, acquitted defendants may be rearrested for other crimes that have occurred. Ordinarily, an acquittal effectively removes the defendant from the criminal justice system.

BOX 7.4

On Wrongful Convictions

Kenneth Marsh, 50, from San Bernardino County, California, spent nearly 21 years in prison following his conviction for the second-degree murder of his girlfriend's son, 3-year-old Phillip Buell in 1983. Marsh claimed at the time that Buell had fallen from a couch and hit his head on the fireplace hearth. Prosecutors alleged that Marsh had beaten the boy. After many years and appeals, Marsh's case was newly investigated. It was discovered that Buell had been treated at a local hospital following his head injury and that doctors at the hospital treated him with the drug Mannitol, which turned out to be a "substantial factor" in the boy's death. Philip Buell also had an undiagnosed blood disorder that was unknown to physicians at the time. Although he had been stabilized for a time at the local hospital, a physician administered Mannitol to the boy during his recovery, which only served to exacerbate his bleeding and swelling, thus leading to his death. An appellate court overturned Marsh's conviction and freed him. The appellate court ruled that the death of Buell appeared to be an accident, not a deliberate act on Marsh's part. Subsequently, the California State Compensation Board approved $750,000 for Marsh, which amounted to approximately $100 per day that Marsh spent in prison. Marsh says that "Nothing can make up for the time I spent in prison unless they gave me my 21 years back." San Bernardino County Prosecutor Michael Ramos personally apologized to Marsh. Marsh added that Ramos's apology "goes a long way." Marsh has since then filed a $50 million lawsuit in federal court against the doctors and hospital where Buell was treated, alleging malpractice. Lawyers for the hospital and doctors were seeking to have the lawsuit dismissed, since the allegations were "far-fetched."

Ray Krone, 48, was living in Phoenix, Arizona, in 1991 and worked for the U.S. Post Office. He played darts regularly at a Phoenix bar where Kim Ancona, a bartender, worked. Subsequently Ancona was killed under mysterious circumstances, and he was bitten in several places on his body. Ray Krone was called in for investigation and gave police an impression of his teeth for comparison with the bite marks on Ancona's body. Krone was convicted in 1992 of Ancona's murder and sentenced to death, largely on the basis of expert testimony from a forensic pathologist who testified that the bite marks on Ancona's body were made by Krone's teeth. Krone's 1992 conviction was overturned by an appellate court on procedural grounds in 1994, but a new trial resulted in a new conviction and sentence in 1996. This time, Krone was sentenced to life, because the judge said he wasn't sure that Krone was the killer.

In 2002, new DNA testing proved that Krone was definitely not Ancona's killer. Using the FBI database, DNA was matched with a man who was already in prison for another crime. The other man was charged with Ancona's murder and Krone was ordered released and his conviction was expunged. Krone subsequently received $3 million from Maricopa County for his wrongful conviction and imprisonment. Nevertheless, he filed a new lawsuit against Phoenix police who he claims did a shoddy job of investigating the murder and didn't look at other suspects closely enough. His lawsuit alleged that Phoenix authorities used altered and manufactured evidence, and that the forensics expert gave false testimony that he knew to be untrue. Krone also sued Arizona agencies for mental anguish and for the physical pain and suffering he had endured. Also, he was stabbed by another inmate while in prison, had his arm broken, and contracted hepatitis C. In 2006, Krone was living in Dover Township, Pennsylvania, near his family. He currently serves on the Commission on Safety and Abuse in America's Prisons and speaks out against the death penalty. He supports the use of DNA testing in capital cases. In 2005, Krone was on the television show *Extreme Makeover*, where he received extensive dental treatment. During his trial and afterwards, he was dubbed the "snaggletooth killer" for his crooked smile. Now he has a straight row of pearly whites.

How much liability should states or the federal government absorb for wrongful convictions? Should there be limits on the amounts wrongfully convicted persons can recover from their governments following the discovery of new evidence showing their innocence? What do you think?

Sources: Adapted from the Associated Press, "$750K for Man Wrongfully Jailed," January 20, 2006; adapted from Beth DeFalco and the Associated Press, "City Approves $3 Million Settlement for Wrongfully Convicted Man," September 27, 2005.

In the event that a "guilty" verdict is rendered by the jury, the defendant has the right to appeal the verdict. The defense attorney may again request the judge to issue a directed verdict of acquittal despite the jury's decision. The judge may, indeed, exercise this option. However, if the judge sets aside the jury verdict and declares the defendant acquitted, the prosecution may appeal that decision to a higher court.

If the judge does not grant the defense attorney's request, the defendant is sentenced. The appeals process may take many years. In all of the U.S. Supreme Court cases presented in this and previous chapters, the interval of time between the offense, the conviction, and the U.S. Supreme Court decision has been several years. Before a case gets before the U.S. Supreme Court, however, it must be reviewed by higher courts within the particular state jurisdiction where the original judgment was entered against the defendant. This appeals process consumes much time as well. Cases presented before the U.S. Supreme Court usually involve constitutional issues. Were a defendant's constitutional rights violated at any stage of the criminal proceeding? Were there procedural errors committed by different court participants, such as the judge, such that the original conviction might be set aside and a new trial ordered?

Summary

The criminal justice process commences with the commission of a crime. The crime is investigated, and in a proportion of the cases, one or more perpetrators are arrested. An arrest means to take someone into custody. Types of crimes for which persons are arrested include misdemeanors and felonies. Misdemeanors, or minor crimes, are distinguished by the fact that they are punishable by less than one year in a jail or prison, and a possible fine. A felony, or major crime, is punishable by confinement in a jail or prison for one year or longer, and a fine may also be assessed contemporaneous with one's incarceration. Persons are arrested based on probable cause that a crime was committed and the person arrested probably committed it. Subsequently, a trial will decide whether the defendant is innocent or guilty of the crime(s) alleged.

Following an arrest, arrestees are booked, usually at a local jail or police station. Booking is a process whereby law enforcement officers collect detailed information about one's identity, formal criminal record if any, and other relevant information. Those charged with serious offenses are subject to an initial appearance before a magistrate or other judicial official. The purpose of an initial appearance is to advise the defendant of the charges against him/her and determine whether bail should be granted. Bail is a surety, sometimes known as a bail bond, which is usually posted for less serious offenses and permits defendants freedom in the community until they can be tried for the crime(s) alleged.

Bail is not an entitlement to everyone. Under the Eighth Amendment, excessive bail is prohibited, but this does not mean that all persons are eligible for bail. Those denied bail are usually deemed likely to flee the jurisdiction to avoid prosecution, or they pose a serious risk to the community if released temporarily pending trial. Bail bondspersons usually are available to post bail for persons granted it.

For many persons, bail is not necessary, and such persons may be released on their own recognizance (ROR). Under the Bail Reform Act of 1984, greater autonomy was given to magistrates and other judicial officials to determine the amount of bail or whether bail should be required to guarantee one's appearance in court later. Several bail experiments have been conducted over the years with many of these studies showing that persons released on their own recognizance subsequently appear in court. The Philadelphia Experiment was designed to determine bail fairness, and although the results were inconclusive, the equity of bail decision making was greatly improved in Philadelphia and other jurisdictions. ROR is increasingly used instead of cash bonds or other forms of sureties. A totality of circumstances test is usually used to determine which persons should be granted bail and which ones should not be granted it.

When some persons fail to appear in court to face the criminal charges against them or jump bail, fugitive recovery agents or bounty hunters usually are hired to track them down. Bonding companies in various cities usually have a fixed amount of money they may use for posting one's bond, and if someone flees, the bond is forfeited. Bonding companies cannot afford to lose these bonds and thus resort to bounty hunters to recover their funds.

A trial proceeding provides defendants with the opportunity to confront and cross-examine their accusers and to offer exculpatory evidence favoring a verdict of "not guilty." A trial is an adversarial proceeding, where the prosecution attempts to establish a defendant's guilt and the defense attempts to ensure the defendants' rights are not violated.

Trial procedures vary from one jurisdiction to the next. A bench trial could be held where the judge oversees the proceedings and is responsible for hearing the facts of the case and making a judgment based on those facts. Bench trials are usually used for less serious and petty offenses in which the defendant has waived his/her right to a jury trial. Some advantages of a bench trial include the following: case processing is expedited, judges are less likely than juries to consider extralegal factors, judges are usually in a better position to decide the sufficiency of evidence in more complex cases, judges are less persuaded by media attention, and bench trials are usually cheaper than jury trials. Disadvantages, however, include that judges may impose more severe punishments on certain defendants, and defendants waive their right to a jury trial where maybe their appearance, emotional appeal, and situation could have worked to their benefit in front of a jury.

Those defendant's charged with felonies are guaranteed the right to a trial by jury. This guarantee also applies to the states; the case of *Duncan v. Louisiana* specified the right to trial by jury for those charged with offenses other than petty crimes for which the possible punishment imposed could be six months of imprisonment. Where a jury trial is conducted, the number of jurors ranges from 6 to 12. At the federal level, a jury verdict must be unanimous. At the state and local levels, however, a unanimous verdict may or may not be required, depending upon the prevailing laws.

The trial process is varied in the different jurisdictions of the United States. There are many stages that characterize the trial process beginning with the indictment of a defendant through to the judge's instructions to the jury members. There are also a number of motions that may be made, and either granted or denied. Pretrial motions are used to ensure that there are no surprises at trial. For instance, a motion to suppress is used in an attempt to exclude certain evidence from being introduced at trial, evidence that the defense believes has been obtained illegally. The exclusionary rule provides that evidence obtained in violation of certain privileges U.S. citizens enjoy must be excluded at trial. A motion to dismiss may be filed by the defense attorney, stating that he/she does not believe the prosecutor has sufficient evidence to proceed with a trial. A motion for discovery is usually made by the defense, which will enable them to obtain and examine evidence collected by the prosecution as well as the witnesses they plan to call to testify. A motion for continuance is usually made to allow delay of the trial for the purposes of collecting more evidence or interviewing additional witnesses. A motion for determination of competency is made to question if the defendant is competent or sufficiently sane to stand trial. A motion for change of venue is a request to hold the trial elsewhere in the belief that in the current jurisdiction the ability of the defendant to have a fair trial would be difficult. These and many other motions are usually made before a trial begins in order to ensure that the defendant is given a fair trial by an impartial jury.

During the actual trial process itself many procedures are also followed. Each side is permitted to address the jury with an opening statement. Both the prosecution and the defense will make opening arguments where each side will give a preview of what they are going to prove or disprove throughout the trial. The prosecution will usually present their theory of the events and why the defendant is in fact guilty. The defense will try to undermine the state's case saying that the prosecution doesn't have enough evidence to prove the elements of the crime, and that when all is said and done, the jury will see that the defendant should be acquitted. Following opening statements, the prosecution will present its case by presenting evidence and bringing in witnesses that prove a crime has been committed and that the defendant is the one who committed it.

There are federal rules of evidence that judges and the attorneys must follow regarding which types of evidence are admissible or inadmissible. Judges are responsible for determining the relevance of objections and evidence. The defense also has the right to question the prosecution's witnesses; this is known as cross-examination. This is where the defense will attempt to show that the witness is not a credible one. Once cross-examination is finished, the prosecution can then ask additional questions of their witness; this is called re-direct examination. As the trial progresses and new evidence surfaces, prior witnesses can be called to the stand again; this is known as re-cross-examination.

Both sides usually call to the stand eyewitnesses and expert witnesses to give various testimony. Expert witnesses are used to give meaning to the evidence that is presented. Usually, expert witnesses will have extensive training and experience in particular matters. This gives their testimony more influence than the testimony of laypersons. Eyewitnesses can also be of value to both the prosecution and defense. These witnesses provide opinions or interpretations of the events that transpired, and can account for the involvement or lack of involvement of the defendant in the crimes alleged.

After the prosecution has rested, the defense then presents its case, revealing evidence and witness testimony favorable to the defendant. The process continues until both sides are satisfied that the evidence before the jury has been adequately presented.

The final procedure involves a summation by both sides. This time the defense presents its closing arguments first, and the prosecution has the last word to show that it has proven, beyond a reasonable doubt, that the defendant is in fact guilty of the crimes he/she have been charged with.

After summations, the judge will instruct the jury on the procedures to be followed in deliberations. The jury system first emerged in the United Stated around 1607; however, they existed in England as early as the eleventh century. Juries are made up of persons from a cross section of the community or region in which the crime has occurred. The selection of jury members involves questioning them concerning their possible biases or prejudices in the case before the court; whether biases are specific (knowing the defendant) or general (having certain ideas about crime and criminal offenders), a potential juror with either should be excluded from duty so that an impartial jury can be formed. Both prosecution and defense attorneys attempt to select jurors favorable to their particular interests. Jurors are excluded from jury duty for reasons of illness or their occupations, or if they do not meet requirements, and both prosecution and defense attorneys may challenge any juror for cause. Jurors may also be excluded by means of peremptory challenges, as the prosecutor and defense attorney attempt to construct the most favorable jury for their particular position. These peremptory challenges may not be used for purposes of discrimination, however.

The science of jury selection is popular. Many attorneys turn to consulting firms that specialize in the selection of jury members. However, the results of studies investigating particular jury member characteristics and their decision-making inclinations have been inconsistent and disappointing. No one has been able to predict with 100 percent certainty how particular jury members will vote in a given trial. Questions of ethics about scientifically selecting a jury have also been raised.

Jury deliberations are conducted following the presentation of witnesses and evidence from both the prosecution and defense, and a verdict is determined. Jury deliberations are done in secret, meaning that no one other than jury members is allowed in this process. Jurors may attempt to persuade each other to side with their decision. Research has shown that group pressure can cause those in the minority decision to align themselves with the majority. Depending on whether the case is a federal, state, or other trial, the verdict must either be unanimous or in compliance with the jurisdiction's rules regarding verdicts. Federal juries must be unanimous. If the jury cannot agree on a verdict as local, state, or federal law requires, the presiding judge will declare a mistrial. This will require a new trial before a new jury. If a jury finds the defendant guilty of the crime alleged, the judge will sentence the convicted offender, either at the conclusion of the trial or in a separate subsequent proceeding.

After deliberations, the jury returns to the courtroom to give its verdict. The defendant must rise and face the jury, and the foreperson or the judge will read the verdict aloud. If a verdict of guilty is found, the defendant may appeal; appeals can take several years before they are exhausted depending on the seriousness and nature of the appeal. If found guilty, the judge is responsible for handing out a punishment to the defendant. Usually the defendant is remanded to custody and the sentence will be given at a sentencing hearing on a subsequent date.

Questions for Review

1. What are sexual predator laws? What is their significance regarding whether someone is granted bail?
2. Who is a bail bondsman? Is a bail bondsman also a bounty hunter? Distinguish between each.
3. What is a bail bond? How can persons obtain bail?
4. Is everyone entitled to bail? Under what circumstances might one not be entitled to bail?
5. Describe the process of arrest, booking, and an initial appearance.
6. What is a preliminary examination or hearing?
7. What does it mean to release someone on his/her own recognizance?
8. How are failure-to-appear rates affected by whether one is granted bail or is released on his/her own recognizance?
9. What are the competing goals of bail?
10. What were some important provisions of the Bail Reform Act of 1984 in terms of how citizens were treated when arrested?
11. What is a pretrial motion? What is it called? What are some examples of pretrial motions?
12. Differentiate between a "bench trial" and a "jury trial." Is there any evidence to indicate that a defendant is better off having a bench trial as opposed to a jury trial?
13. What is a trial? What are some of the functions of a trial proceeding?
14. Does a criminal defendant have to have a jury trial if he/she is charged with murder? Can the defendant waive his/her right to a jury trial? What constitutional amendment pertains to jury trials?

15. Identify three functions of juries. What U.S. Supreme Court decision pertained to setting lower limits for jury sizes? What was the limit established?

16 In a particular criminal case before a six-person jury, the jury brought back a verdict of guilty, but the vote was 5–1. Evaluate this verdict in view of what you have learned about jury size and unanimity of agreement among jurors.

17. On the basis of some of the research conducted about jury size, is a 12-member jury more representative of community interests compared with a six-person jury? What are some differences between these jury sizes other than the number of jurors?

18. What are five "maxims" believed by many attorneys about juror characteristics and accompanying juror attitudes?

19. What is meant by the "fruit of the poisonous tree"? What does it have to do with evidence? Explain briefly.

20. What is the exclusionary rule?

21. How reliable is the testimony of a child witness? Cite some research that has investigated the competency of child witnesses.

22. What is the purpose of a victim-witness assistance program?

23. Who usually gets the last word and closing argument in a criminal case before a jury?

Suggested Readings

1. Raymond A. Atkins and Paul H. Rubin (2003). "Effects of Criminal Procedure on Crime Rates: Mapping Out the Consequences for the Exclusionary Rule." *Journal of Law and Economics* **46**:157–179.

2. Donald Dripps (2001). "The Case for the Contingent Exclusionary Rule." *American Criminal Law Review* **38**:1–146.

3. O. O. Elechi (2005). "Repairing Harm and Transforming African-American Communities Through Restorative Justice." *Community Safety Journal* **4**:29–36.

4. Alejo Freire et al. (2004). "Lineup Identification by Children: Effects of Clothing Bias." *Law and Human Behavior* **28**:339–354.

5. John C. Goodman and Philip Porter (2002). "Is the Criminal Justice System Just?" *International Review of Law and Economics* **22**:25–39.

6. Jakub Gubanski (2004). "Comparative Criminal Justice: Special Investigation Techniques During the Criminal Trial: Disclosure Issues in Polish and American Legal Systems." *Crime, Law and Social Change: An Interdisciplinary Journal* **41**:15–32.

7. J. L. Herman (2005). "Justice from the Women's Perspective." *Violence Against Women* **11**:571–602.

8. Douglas N. Husak (2004). "Guns and Drugs: Case Studies on the Principled Limits of the Criminal Sanction." *Law and Philosophy* **23**:437–493.

9. Pamela K. Lattimore et al. (2003). "A Comparison of Prebooking and Postbooking Diversion Programs for Mentally Ill Substance-Using Individuals with Justice Involvement." *Journal of Contemporary Criminal Justice* **19**:30–64.

10. Ruth E. Masters (2004). *Counseling Criminal Justice Offenders*. Thousand Oaks, CA: Sage Publications.

11. Thomas N. McInnis (2001). *The Christian Burial Case: An Introduction to Criminal and Judicial Procedure*. Westport, CT: Praeger Publishers.

12. Roger H. Peters and John Petrila (2004). "Co-Occurring Disorders and the Criminal Justice System." *Behavioral Sciences and the Law* **22**:427–610.

13. Robert J. Ramsey (2003). *False Positives in the Criminal Justice Process: An Analysis of Factors Associated with Wrongful Conviction of the Innocent*. Ann Arbor, MI: University Microfilms, Inc.

14. Thomas Trenczek (2002). "Victim-Offender Reconciliation: The Danger of Cooptation and a Useful Reconsideration of Law Theory." *Contemporary Justice Review: Issues in Criminal, Social, and Restorative Justice* **5**:23–34.

15. Tim Valentine, Alan Pickering, and Stephen Darling (2003). "Characteristics of Eyewitness Identification That Predict the Outcome of Real Lineups." *Applied Cognitive Psychology* **17**:969–993.

CHAPTER 8

Pretrial Procedures

Plea Bargaining

CHAPTER OBJECTIVES

As a result of reading this chapter, you will have accomplished the following objectives:

1. Understand what is meant by plea bargaining and the conditions under which it is applied.
2. Describe different forms of plea bargaining, including implicit plea bargaining, charge-reduction bargaining, sentence recommendation bargaining, and judicial plea bargaining.
3. Understand the advantages and disadvantages of plea bargaining both for the criminal justice system and criminal defendants.

4. Understand why plea bargaining has been banned in various U.S. jurisdictions and the reasons for this action.
5. Describe judicial actions when approving plea bargain agreements, including the information required by judges before they can accept guilty pleas from criminal defendants.
6. Understand different sentencing systems used by judges in various jurisdictions at both the state and federal levels, and how these sentencing schemes relate to plea bargaining.

KEY TERMS

charge bargaining
charge reduction
  bargaining
coconspirator
concession givers
determinate sentencing
differential discretion
electronic monitoring
fact-finders
factual basis for the plea

federal misdemeanor
Federal Rules of Criminal
  Procedure
flat time
going rate
guilty plea
habitual offender
  statutes
home confinement
implicit plea bargaining

indeterminate sentencing
intensive supervised
  probation
judicial plea bargaining
judicial privilege
jury waiver system
negotiated guilty pleas
nolle prosequi
presentence investigation
  reports (PSIs)

selective chivalry
self-incrimination
sentence recommendation
  bargaining
three-strikes-and-you're-out
  policies
trial delays
typicality hypothesis
United States Sentencing
  Guidelines

In rural Kentucky, a prosecutor was approached by a defense attorney representing a client charged with possession of methamphetamine with intent to distribute. If convicted, the sentence would amount to ten years in prison and a substantial fine. The defense counsel argued that the woman had only been a mule for her boyfriend who was part of a suspected large methamphetamine manufacturing operation in the state. The prosecutor argued back that she was caught with a large amount of the drug and should do at least three years. The defense attorney pointed out that this was the woman's first offense and she might be willing to testify against her boyfriend in order to stay out of prison and with her two children. He felt she should be placed on one year of probation and complete some community service. The prosecutor agreed and asked the defense counsel to have his client in the prosecutor's office early the next morning so they could draw up the plea agreement and she could start providing testimony against the large-scale methamphetamine operation. Do you agree with the prosecutor's decision? Should the prosecutor have this much power in the court system? What would happen if the judge rejects the plea? Do you think local law enforcement would be happy with the prosecutor's decision? It happened in Bentonville, Arkansas. Two men raped and killed a 13-year-old boy, Jesse Dirkhising, on September 26, 1999. Subsequently they were apprehended. The two men, Davis Don Carpenter, 39, and Joshua Brown, 23, his lover, were linked to the crime by various circumstances. Subsequently, they both gave confessions implicating the other. These are their stories. Brown says that he bound Jesse with duct tape and raped him with various objects, including food, but he never intended for the youth to die. Medical examiners concluded that Jesse died of positional asphyxia, wherein he was unable to breathe because of the way in which he was bound on Brown's bed. He was also given an antidepressant and was too drugged to be moved to a position where he could catch his breath. Brown claimed that Carpenter had directed the assault but did not take part in it. However, in a jailhouse interview later, Brown admitted that Carpenter was actively involved in Jesse's murder. According to Brown, Carpenter had diagrammed how the murder should occur. Carpenter's version of events was that for most of the sexual assault, he was asleep. He claimed that he was awakened by Brown when Brown took a break from the assault to eat a sandwich. However, a witness said that she saw Carpenter buy duct tape at her all-night grocery store in the middle of the night. The prosecutors have surmised that both men were equally culpable in the sexual assault and murder. The state sought the death penalty for both men. However, Brown was subsequently sentenced to life without the possibility of parole for his role in Jesse's murder. Subsequently, Carpenter was allowed to plea bargain and receive the same sentence of life without parole to avoid the death penalty. Many citizens and family members of Jesse Dirkhising were outraged that Carpenter and Brown were not given the death penalty in the case. While the judge was the final arbiter in the case, the prosecutors were the ones who negotiated the life-without-parole sentences with Brown and Carpenter. Is plea bargaining a just way of concluding a heinous crime such as that committed by Brown and Carpenter? Should plea bargaining be permitted in death penalty cases? Do prosecutors have too much power? What do you think?

Source: Adapted from Brian Skoloff and the Associated Press, "Man Pleas to Get Life Sentence," April 19, 2001.

INTRODUCTION

It is difficult to imagine an efficient criminal justice system operating without plea bargaining. This chapter explores plea bargaining in great detail. Plea bargaining is a preconviction agreement or negotiated guilty plea between the government and defendant wherein the government offers some form of leniency, usually a lighter sentence, in exchange for a guilty plea to lesser charges. Thus, through plea bargaining, the state benefits because it avoids a protracted and expensive trial. The defendant benefits in that a sentence is accepted, which is often much shorter and less severe than a sentence that may have been imposed had the case proceeded to trial and the person had been convicted. All plea bargain agreements are subject to judicial approval.

The chapter opens with an examination of plea bargaining generally and the issue of why defendants should enter into plea bargain agreements. A brief history of plea bargaining in the United States is presented. Plea bargaining is not unique to the United States and occurs with some frequency in many other countries. Over 90 percent of all criminal cases are concluded annually through plea bargaining of some kind. This section examines the conditions under which plea bargaining may occur and when it may occur, which is at any time from the point when one is arrested through the jury deliberation process. The coercive aspects of plea bargaining are examined. Also discussed is the matter of promises made by prosecutors to induce defendants to enter guilty pleas. Under all circumstances, these promises from prosecutors must be honored; otherwise, plea agreements are invalidated.

The next section examines several types of plea bargaining. Implicit plea bargaining is examined, where it is generally understood by both prosecutors and defense counsels alike what the **going rate** is for a particular crime charged. Usually agreements are reached between these opposing parties about the type of plea the defendant will enter and the punishment recommended. Another type of plea bargaining is charge reduction bargaining. Where many charges have been filed against criminal defendants, prosecutors may agree to drop most charges if defendants plead guilty to one or more of the lesser charges. A third type of plea bargaining is judicial plea bargaining, where the judge recommends a sentence to a defendant in exchange for a plea of guilty. The fourth type of plea bargaining is sentence recommendation bargaining. Under this type of plea bargaining, the prosecutor recommends a specific sentence to the defendant in exchange for a guilty plea. The weaknesses and strengths of each of these types of plea bargaining are examined.

The chapter next examines a wide array of arguments favoring plea bargaining as well as a lengthy list of arguments opposing it. Arguments in favor of plea bargaining include that it results in fewer trials and trial delays; more convictions are obtained; expensive trials are avoided; and defendants can anticipate some form of leniency in sentencing. Opponents of plea bargaining claim that plea bargaining violates one's right against self-incrimination, since one must admit guilt in order to receive a more lenient sentence or sentence recommendation. Other arguments include that judges lose control over cases that are plea bargained; defendants may be ignorant of the rights they are waiving when entering into plea agreements; guilty pleas may be rejected by the court; habitual offender statutes may be circumvented; some persons may receive more lenient sentences when their crimes deserve harsher penalties; some heinous aspects of crimes are not disclosed through plea agreements; plea agreements may appear to be too routine and rubber-stamped; the potential exists for gender bias in plea bargaining; the jury process may be invalidated; sentencing reforms may be hampered; negotiated guilty pleas are too bureaucratized; and lawyers may be vested with too much authority in the plea bargaining process. In some jurisdictions, plea bargaining has been banned. Despite the ban on plea bargaining, it still exists even in jurisdictions that have banned it. Some of the reasons for banning plea bargaining are listed and discussed.

The chapter next examines the important role of judges in the plea bargaining process. Judges must determine whether defendants wish to waive their right to a trial. They must also determine if there is a factual basis for the guilty plea. More than a few instances have occurred where defendants have been bullied into guilty pleas by aggressive prosecutors where no evidence of defendant guilt exists. Under these circumstances, judges have rejected such plea agreements and acquitted defendants, despite the fact that they entered guilty pleas to various crimes. Also, judges may or may not participate in the plea bargaining process. North Carolina is a state that allows judges to sit in while plea bargaining occurs between prosecutors, defendants, and their attorneys. In most jurisdictions, however, judicial participation in this process is banned.

Furthermore, in some jurisdictions where sentencing guidelines have been established, plea bargaining may pose problems for enforcing these guidelines. Thus, different forms of sentencing may affect the plea bargaining process in a variety of ways (Wooldredge and Griffin 2004).

PLEA BARGAINING: NEGOTIATED GUILTY PLEAS

WHY SHOULD ANY DEFENDANT PLEA BARGAIN?   Ideally, defendants who wish to enter guilty pleas to criminal charges know that they are guilty. There is substantial evidence against them. They have the right to compel the state to try them in a court of law. All criminals have a right to their day in court. However, in cases where one's guilt is not seriously contested, trials are perfunctory rituals with almost absolutely predictable results.

Unfortunately for criminal defendants, trial convictions usually result in more stringent applications of sanctions (Champion 2005a). Judges tend to deal more harshly with convicted offenders who have insisted on trials despite the existence of substantial evidence of their guilt beyond a reasonable doubt. However, pretrial agreements where guilty pleas are entered often result in less severe sanctions or sentences. Early research on the differences in sentences imposed through plea bargaining or trial has highlighted a pattern of judicial sentencing behavior. In more than a few jurisdictions, judges have advised defendants of the sentences judges plan to impose (Cummingham 2005). Judges further advise that if the plea bargain is rejected and the case proceeds to trial, convicted offenders are likely to incur a harsher sentence. Thus, those who contest their guilt compared with those who plead guilty are subjected to established practices whereby judges sentence them more harshly (Kirschner and Galperin 2001). The harsher sentence is imposed as a punishment for burdening the state with the responsibility of proving one's guilty beyond a reasonable doubt.

Plea bargaining usually results in reduced charges for criminal defendants. In some instances, criminal charges may be dropped altogether in exchange for valuable information about a crime. For instance, a man was engaged to a school teacher in a northeastern state during the 1980s. The woman broke off the engagement. Enraged, the man killed the woman and buried her body off an old logging trail about ten miles from her home. The woman's disappearance was quickly noticed, although there was no evidence of foul play. The man was the key suspect in the case, but the prosecutor was helpless. There was no direct or circumstantial evidence of his culpability or anything to suggest that he had harmed her. The man subsequently moved to a western state where he found work and started a new life for himself. After over a decade of searching for the missing woman, the prosecutor contacted the man during the 1990s and said that if the man told him where the body could be found, no charges would be brought against him for the crime. The man entered into an agreement with the prosecutor to disclose details about how the woman came to be missing. The man said that he had killed her in a jealous rage when she had spurned him. And then he carefully concealed the body in a large shower curtain and buried the woman on the logging trail. He led police and the prosecutor to the exact spot where the woman was buried. Her body was recovered and she was given a proper burial by her family members. The man was not prosecuted for this murder and returned to his state to resume his life. The prosecutor was soundly criticized by the public and media for this agreement not to prosecute the man, but the prosecutor stated that unless he had made that agreement, the woman's body never would have been recovered. At least her family had the peace of mind of knowing what had happened.

In less dramatic cases played out in courtrooms throughout the United States, prosecutors and defense counsel attempt to arrive at the most favorable sentences for state interests and for defendant's interests. Depending upon whether offenses alleged are felonies or misdemeanors, negotiations between prosecutors and defense counsel are geared to arrive at an appropriate term of years or months for defendants who wish to enter guilty pleas. The prosecution seeks to maximize these years or months, while the defense seeks to minimize them (Tappan 2005).

For instance, suppose a defendant is charged with burglary and conversion of stolen property. The burglary and conversion of stolen property statutes provide a $5,000 fine and up to five years in prison on each charge. A worst case scenario would result in a jury trial and convictions on both charges, a $10,000 fine, and consecutive sentences of the maximum five years each for a total of ten years. Seeking to avoid both the fine and a ten-year term of imprisonment, the defendant may enter into a plea bargain agreement and plead guilty to one of the charges, such as the burglary. The prosecutor will drop the conversion of stolen property charge and recommend waiver of the $10,000 in fines. The prosecutor may suggest a two- or three-year prison term in exchange for a guilty plea to burglary. While the defendant wishes to avoid prison entirely, he is faced with either accepting the two- or three-year sentence or taking his chances in court. There is a strong likelihood that he would be convicted of both offenses. Further, the judge would likely impose a harsher sentence, such as five or more years. Therefore, a powerful incentive exists for defendants to enter guilty pleas rather than face potentially harsher punishments in courts if they are subsequently convicted.

Fines attached to criminal statutes are imposed, but infrequently. One reason for not imposing fines is the state's inability to collect fines from convicted offenders, who are most frequently unemployed and indigent. Crime may be their only livelihood. When offenders are apprehended, convicted, and incarcerated, they have no means whereby to earn money to pay off fines imposed earlier by judges. An offender's inability to pay fines cannot be used to lengthen his/her sentence. However, if certain defendants have assets, including property, automobiles, or expensive possessions, these items of value may be subject to seizure under asset forfeiture. An embezzler might have purchased property and other material possessions with money stolen from a business. One way of restoring the business's money is to seize the offender's assets and liquidate them. The proceeds from such liquidations are given to the business from which the money was stolen.

In typical property offense cases, however, convicted offenders may be drug or alcohol dependent. Their drug or alcohol habits may cause them to steal and obtain money to purchase more drugs or alcohol. Gambling addiction may drive offenders to steal another's property and convert it to money to satisfy their gambling addiction. Thus, many offenders have no assets and are deeply in debt when arrested by police. Because there are no assets to seize, the government can impose fines of any amount with little or no expectation of ever recovering even a fraction of the fines imposed.

WHY SHOULD PROSECUTORS BARGAIN WITH CRIMINALS?   Are prosecutors obligated to collaborate with defense counsels and work out negotiated guilty pleas for each defendant? No. The U.S. Supreme Court has declared that prosecutors are under no obligation to enter into plea bargain agreements with any criminal defendant (*United States v. Benchimol*, 1985). Plea bargain agreements are sought by both prosecutors and defense counsels. It is to a prosecutor's advantage to resolve criminal cases without formal trial proceedings. Trials involve considerable preparation and state expense. There is no guarantee that juries will convict guilty defendants, regardless of how much evidence exists against them. Plea bargains avoid trials and the often difficult burden of proving defendants guilty beyond a reasonable doubt. Most successfully concluded plea agreements result in convictions. Prosecutors are driven to convict defendants by one means or another. By far, the cheapest and easiest convictions obtained by prosecutors are through plea bargain agreements (Thompson 2005).

The effectiveness of prosecutors is most often evaluated in terms of their record of successful prosecutions. Successful prosecutions are those resulting in convictions. Thus, the more convictions, the more a prosecutor's effectiveness. If some prosecutors have political aspirations, aspire to judgeships, or seek promotions within their own district attorney's offices, their conviction records are direct evidence of their effectiveness as prosecutors (O'Sullivan 2001). Their reputations are enhanced and their careers are furthered to the extent that they are effective at whatever they do (Schram, Koons-Witt, and Morash 2004). It is in the prosecutor's best interests to seek quick convictions through plea bargaining.

POLITICS AND PLEA BARGAINING   Thus, plea bargaining has subsequently emerged as a powerful political tool. It has become an increasingly visible and integral part of the criminal justice process. Within the criminal justice system, plea bargaining has shifted a great deal of power to prosecutors who have become the ultimate decision makers about a defendant's life chances (Boari and Fiorentini 2001; Rose-Ackerman 2002). Prosecutors now perform pivotal roles as they decide which cases should be prosecuted and which cases should be dropped. Prosecutors contemplate particular sentences for defendants charged with various crimes.

It is important also to understand that in most plea bargaining and the hearings that follow, ordinarily judges see only what prosecutors decide to reveal against criminal defendants. Judges may be unaware that other charges against specific defendants were not included in the plea agreement but simply ignored or dropped by the prosecutor in order to elicit a guilty plea. This is not the fault of judges. Usually there are so many plea agreements submitted to judges for their approval that most judges don't have the time to study each agreement in detail. Furthermore, many judges view plea bargaining as a fundamental feature of the criminal justice process, and they cooperate with prosecutors by approving plea agreements that are seen as a reasonable trade-off between crime control and due process (U.S. Sentencing Commission 2003). There are some important exceptions, however.

In an Alabama case, James Smith entered a guilty plea and was convicted of first-degree burglary and rape. Earlier a grand jury had indicted Smith for burglary, rape, sodomy, and assault. In exchange for a 30-year sentence, Smith entered a guilty plea to the burglary and rape charges, provided that the prosecutor dropped the sodomy charge. When the judge approved the plea agreement, he sentenced Smith to two concurrent 30-year sentences. However, a procedural technicality raised later by Smith resulted in a higher court vacating his original 30-year sentences. Subsequently, Smith went to trial on all four charges and was convicted by a jury. This time, the same judge sentenced Smith to life imprisonment on the burglary and sodomy convictions, and 150 years on the rape conviction. The judge explained the different sentences because he had not been fully aware of the circumstances under which these terrible crimes had occurred. The trial disclosed all of these details. Smith appealed unsuccessfully to the U.S. Supreme Court, contending that the judge was deliberately being vindictive with the imposition of these enhanced sentences. Rejecting his appeal, the U.S. Supreme Court said that in cases that go to trial, greater and more detailed information is available to sentencing judges compared with the information contained in a plea bargain agreement. This additional information justifies the court's harsher sentencing decision (*Alabama v. Smith*, 1989).

Ultimately, however, the decision to charge any particular defendant with specific crimes lies with the district attorney's office. Whether prosecutors interact with private counsel or public defenders, these persons wield considerable power in deciding how rigorously certain cases are pursued. Prosecutors have the greatest amount of power in cases where multiple offenses have been committed by a defendant. If a gun was used during the commission of a robbery, for example, prosecutors can decide whether or not to include this charge in a subsequent indictment or information. Usually, plea bargaining will result in some reduction in the number of charges filed. If prosecutors can be persuaded by defense counsel to leave out the fact that a weapon was used during the commission of a felony and charge simple robbery instead of armed robbery, the result will likely be a guilty plea to the lesser charge. This is because when weapons are used during felonies, they often involve mandatory incarcerative penalties. For example, Michigan has a use-a-gun-and-get-two-additional-years provision, meaning that an automatic addition of two years of **flat time** is added to a convicted offender's sentence where a weapon was used during the commission of a felony. It is to the defendant's advantage if the prosecutor decides not to file a weapons-related charge. Thus, this fact becomes a bargaining chip for the prosecutor and can be used strategically to elicit guilty pleas more easily from defendants who have committed weapons-related offenses (Cummingham 2005).

Another factor that affects the prosecutor's decision making about which cases to pursue vigorously is case pressure. In jurisdictions where the volume of cases processed is high, prosecutors may elect to ***nolle prosequi*** or decline to prosecute marginal cases that might have been pursued earlier for a guilty plea. Prosecutorial options under these conditions might include reducing more charges against defendants, recommending lighter sentences, or demanding more severe sentences after a trial.

HOW LONG HAS PLEA BARGAINING BEEN USED IN THE UNITED STATES?   Historians have investigated the use of plea bargaining in the United States. Evidence suggests that plea bargaining occurred in the various states during the period following the Declaration of Independence in 1776. A study of plea bargaining in New York during the period 1800–1865 shows a pattern of plea bargaining usage that escalated during the second half of the nineteenth century (McConville and Mirsky 2005). The use of plea bargaining accompanied the rise in importance of district attorney's offices, the presence of elected judges, the judicialization of magistrates, the reorganization of the police, the marginalization of juries, and politicization of crime.

During the 1800s, plea bargaining was simply referred to as a **guilty plea**. No formal classification of guilty pleas existed. In the early part of the nineteenth century, jury trials were proscribed for almost all criminal offenses. State reliance on jury trials was strong. However, by the mid to late 1800s, the growth of attorney organizations and increasing professionalization of police work modified greatly the art of criminal investigations. At the same time, court dockets became overcrowded and the glut of jury trials worsened. Thus, guilty pleas with one or more prosecutorial concessions gained in popularity as an alternative to formal courtroom trial procedure.

The professionalization of police meant that larger numbers of minor prosecutions were shifted to municipal and police courts, such as those in Boston during the period 1814–1850 (Ferdinand 1992). Data analyzed from over 30,000 cases from the Boston Police Court during the early to mid-1800s showed that between 1814 and 1850, the caseload for police courts doubled. During the same time interval, the municipal court docket load increased by over 1,000 percent. Plea bargaining in Boston became increasingly commonplace as a means of resolving most cases. At the same time, court officers became more professional and formal courtroom procedures grew more intricate (Ferdinand 1992). It was in just such a milieu that the modern criminal court was born. Today's criminal courts are high-volume and multipurpose. The sheer numbers of cases crowding these court dockets made plea bargaining especially appealing, since valuable court time could be saved by out-of-court bargaining between prosecutors and defense attorneys.

BOX 8.1

Plea Bargaining

There is no mention of plea bargaining in the U.S. Constitution. Although the Bill of Rights makes no mention of plea bargaining, this practice has consistently been upheld by different courts, including the U.S. Supreme Court. Over 90 percent of all criminal convictions are obtained through plea bargaining, even in jurisdictions where it has been banned. In most plea-bargained cases, defendants enter guilty pleas to reduce charges in order to avoid more serious penalties. This strategy almost always works to the benefit of both prosecutors and defendants. Michael Kopper, an Enron accountant, and John Walker Lindh, an American Taliban and Afghan fighter against U.S. armed forces, both plea bargained with the government in order to avoid severe penalties during the early 2000s. Lindh entered a "guilty" plea in order to avoid an execution. Kopper entered a guilty plea to avoid exposing security sources.

In the eighteenth century public prosecutions of persons became more pervasive. Prosecutors generally dictated what sentences defendants would receive, although judges controlled and continue to control actual offender sentencing. In some ways, plea bargaining is

(continued)

(continued)

an outgrowth of industrialization and has reduced substantially the courtroom workload. A brief history of plea bargaining is in order:

> 1633: Galileo gets house arrest during the Inquisition in exchange for his reciting penitential psalms weekly and recanting Copernican heresies.
>
> 1931: Al Capone brags about his light sentence for pleading guilty to income tax evasion and Prohibition violations. The judge then declares that he isn't bound by the bargain, and Capone does $7\frac{1}{2}$ years in Alcatraz.
>
> 1969: To avoid execution, James Earl Ray pleads guilty to assassinating Martin Luther King Jr. and gets 99 years.
>
> 1973: Spiro Agnew resigns as vice president and pleads no contest to the charge of failing to report income; he gets three years of probation and a $10,000 fine (roughly one-third of the amount at issue).
>
> 1990: Facing serious federal charges of insider trading, Michael Milken pleads to lesser charges of securities fraud; soon after, his ten-year sentence is reduced to two years.

Although other countries throughout the world have been slow to adopt it, plea bargaining now occurs virtually everywhere, including Japan, where it is officially banned. Italy has legalized it formally; Germany says it is controversial; and Japan says the practice is horrible. Scandinavian countries largely maintain prohibitions against it.

A hypothetical case of why plea bargaining is so successful and widely used in the United States is the district attorney who has 100 cases a year and a budget of $100,000. With only $1,000 to spend investigating and prosecuting each case, half the defendants will be acquitted. But if the prosecutor can get 90 percent of all defendants to enter guilty pleas and avoid expensive investigations and trials, then the prosecutor can concentrate office resources on the 10 percent who refuse, and spend $10,000 on each case and get a conviction rate of 90 percent.

Viewed from the defendant's perspective, plea bargaining makes a lot of sense. In the federal system, the conviction rate of criminal cases that go to trial is over 90 percent, depending on the nature of the offense. If there is a 90 percent chance of being convicted and receiving a severe sentence, most defendants will enter into plea bargains with U.S. attorneys to obtain less severe sentences. Conceivably all defendants would be better off if they rejected offers from prosecutors to plead guilty in exchange for leniency, forcing their cases to trials. But individual rationality does not always lead to group rationality.

Source: Adapted from Dirk Olin, "Plea Bargain," *The New York Times Magazine*, September 29, 2002.

The growth of formal legal education was apparent during this same period. More persons were acquiring formal legal training from newly established law schools, and the numbers of lawyers invading criminal courts to represent growing numbers of clients meant more protracted litigation. A relief valve was plea bargaining. A more educated lawyer contingent made plea bargaining more attractive to criminals as well as to judges, since criminals could bargain their way to lesser penalties without formal trial proceedings (Blackwell 2004). The trend toward greater use of plea bargaining continued into the 1900s. Since the 1960s, plea bargaining has escalated in use to the extent that over 90 percent of all criminal convictions are secured through plea negotiations. Because of the great savings in case processing time, most courts today are able to function with only moderate delays. It is difficult to contemplate what our courts would be like today if plea bargaining were banned outright.

IS PLEA BARGAINING UNIQUE TO THE UNITED STATES?   No. Many countries use some form of plea bargaining as a means of speeding up criminal case processing. Plea bargaining is used frequently in Australia, Canada (Kellough and Wortley 2002), France (Ma 2002), Germany (Ma 2002), Israel (Ajzenstadt and Steinberg 2001; Herzog 2003), Italy (Boari and Fiorentini 2001), and the United Kingdom (Ma 2002). Citizen discontent with plea bargaining in these countries is about the same as it is in the United States. In Canada, for example, a survey of 1,049 citizens revealed that most disapproved of plea bargaining. One primary complaint was that plea bargaining appeared to result in insufficient penalties for criminals. However, these citizen respondents also indicated that if judges were to take a more proactive role in the plea bargaining process to ensure fairness to victims and the punishment process generally, then they would be inclined to be supportive of it (Goodman and Porter 2002). And in Germany, plea bargaining has been evaluated by prosecutors, judges, and defense counsels. They vary in their opinions toward plea bargaining depending upon the various costs and benefits of plea bargaining versus trial (Ma 2002).

HOW MUCH PLEA BARGAINING IS THERE TODAY?   In order to understand both the need for and use of plea bargaining, we must first appreciate the magnitude of federal and state litigation and rapid growth of criminal cases. In the federal system, for example, there were 44,144 criminal prosecutions in U.S. District Courts in 1982. This figure had risen to 64,000 in 1994. There were approximately 49,000 convictions in federal courts in 1994. Judges dismissed or threw out nearly 9,000 cases that same year for various reasons, including insufficiency of evidence. About 92 percent of all federal criminal convictions were obtained through plea bargaining and without an expensive and lengthy trial. At the same time, there were over 500,000 prosecutions in state courts in 1982. By 1994 there were 1.2 million prosecutions in state courts, resulting in 872,217 convictions (Champion 2005b). Of these, 89 percent had entered guilty pleas while the remaining 11 percent were convicted through trials.

The rate of plea bargaining has remained fairly constant during the period 1970–2005 (U.S. Department of Justice 2005). In the 1970s, at least 90 percent of all convictions were obtained through plea bargaining. Even with 90 percent of all guilty pleas in either state or federal courts resulting from plea bargaining, the trial court delays in the criminal justice system today are notorious. Some cases, such as the California murder trials of the Menendez brothers and the O. J. Simpson murder trial, consume several months of court time before they are resolved. In the Menendez case, two brothers were accused of killing their parents. There was considerable incriminating evidence. Nevertheless, the brothers sought and got two juries to hear their cases, only to have both juries deadlocked at the conclusion of the first lengthy trial. A second trial, which resulted in guilty verdicts, took several months to conclude.

But these cases are high-profile and received considerable media attention. But less celebrated cases also consume large amounts of court time. What about the length of time taken to prosecute low-profile cases? In 1995, for instance, federal courts conducted 7,421 criminal trials. Of these, 4,400 were concluded in one or two days, while about 400 took ten or more days. At least 110 of these trials took 20 days or longer. Most of these cases were low-profile and received little media attention (Maguire and Pastore 2005). Despite this inattention, these trials are sufficiently drawn out to underscore the necessity for plea bargaining. Without it, federal and state courts would probably come to a grinding halt. Or at the very least, case backlogs would be such that most scheduled criminal cases could not be heard for at least one or more years. In view of a defendant's right to a speedy trial, these courts would be hard-pressed to comply with this important constitutional provision.

DO ALL JURISDICTIONS USE PLEA BARGAINING?   No. Most jurisdictions use it. In some jurisdictions, plea bargaining has been banned. The most visible jurisdiction prohibiting plea bargaining is Alaska (Champion 2005b). The ban against plea bargaining was announced by the Alaska Judicial Council in 1975. Routine sentence agreements between prosecutors and defense attorneys were virtually eliminated after the ban and have not returned. Presently, most defendants are sentenced by a judge at an open hearing, with participation by the prosecutor, defense, and presentence reporter. Thus, the responsibility for sentencing rests primarily with the judge.

Some jurisdictions, such as Bronx County, New York, have sought to limit plea bargaining to specific phases of criminal processing. Whether a defendant has been indicted is significant here. A pre-indictment period is the time before criminal defendants are formally indicted for specific offenses. A post-indictment period occurs following their indictment. Once indictments have been issued in Bronx County, plea bargaining has been discouraged under a new policy. At the same time, pre-indictment plea bargaining has been openly encouraged.

In El Paso, Texas, a felony plea bargaining ban was implemented in 1975 (Holmes et al. 1992). Researchers investigated the effects of this ban on case processing and dispositions. While the conviction rate was generally unaffected, much greater numbers of cases went to trial. As a result, there was a gradual decrease in the disposition rate. Thus, it was concluded that the plea bargaining ban in El Paso adversely impacted the ability of district courts to move felony case dockets along efficiently.

Later in 1981, the Superior Court of Merrimack County, New Hampshire, banned plea bargaining in response to criticisms of the practice and the perceived decline in public confidence in the judicial system's ability to effectively administer criminal sanctions. Unexpectedly, the quality of indictments against criminal defendants in Merrimack County did not improve. Actual sentence lengths imposed for various criminal offenses have remained unaffected by the ban. Court backlogs were increasing when researchers conducted a two-year follow-up and ban assessment (Champion 2005a).

WHEN CAN PLEA BARGAINING OCCUR?   In most jurisdictions unless otherwise prohibited by either policy or legislative statements, plea bargaining can occur at virtually any stage of a criminal proceeding prior to a finding of guilt. While most plea bargaining occurs before a trial is conducted, plea bargain negotiations may transpire throughout a trial.

In some cases, plea bargains have been struck while a case is in progress or while a jury is deliberating. In September 1997, for example, a television sportscaster, Marv Albert, was accused by a woman of sexual assault. The case went to trial in Virginia. During the trial, the alleged victim described to the jury how Albert attacked her. Later, the defense was able to impeach the woman's credibility with exculpatory evidence of their own. But the prosecution brought forth an additional witness who testified to similar treatment by Albert on another occasion and under different circumstances. Albert's attorney sought to introduce other evidence of an exculpatory nature, including testimony and records of past sexual behavior of the victim. But the judge ruled against the introduction of this evidence. Shortly thereafter, Albert's attorney announced that his client was going to plead guilty to a lesser included offense rather than sit through more disclosures by other witnesses. When the jurors were reconvened, the judge announced the decision of Albert to plead guilty and the jurors were dismissed.

Ironically, one of the jurors said that she didn't think the state had presented a sufficiently strong case to convict Albert, even with the additional witness and her damaging testimony about Albert's alleged actions. No doubt Albert was thinking that if the jurors were persuaded by this later testimony (which they apparently weren't), then he would be convicted and suffer a more severe sentence. In retrospect, Albert probably would have been acquitted of all charges.

Interrupting a criminal trial with a plea bargain has about the same effect of refusing to plea bargain in the pretrial and pre-indictment periods. Considerable expense has been incurred by the state in the defendant's prosecution. Judges are unhappy with events such as these. However, the prosecution bears some of the responsibility by entering into these late plea bargaining negotiations. Perhaps the prosecutor in the Albert trial believed that there was a good chance that Albert would be acquitted. Thus, the plea bargain was attractive since it would guarantee a conviction, even for a lesser included offense. In the Albert case, it seemed that neither side was willing to gamble on the jury outcome in view of the different types of evidence presented.

IS PLEA BARGAINING COERCIVE?   There is no question that plea bargaining is coercive. Almost no offender wants to admit guilt to any wrongdoing. Therefore, when an offer is made by the prosecutor to plead guilty to reduced charges or face prosecution on more serious charges, most defendants find this choice coercive. Even judges think plea bargaining is coercive (Champion 2005a). At the same time, however, judges concede that plea bargaining is a suitable trade-off between due process and crime control. Further, plea bargaining makes life much easier for these judges, prosecutors, defense counsel, and criminals.

The U.S. Supreme Court has ruled in several important cases where coercion relating to plea bargaining has been alleged. Three cases dealing with coercion in eliciting guilty pleas through plea bargaining are *McMann v. Richardson* (1970), *North Carolina v. Alford* (1970), and *Bordenkircher v. Hayes* (1978).

BOX 8.2

The Plea

The Case if Charles Gampero, Jr.

Charles Gampero, Jr., 20, was arrested and charged with second-degree murder in 1994. Gampero insisted that he was innocent of the crime. He admitted to having a fight with the victim outside of a bowling alley on the night the victim died, but he claimed that the victim was very much alive when he left him. There were numerous unanswered questions about the case. The victim's family, for instance, had told police that the victim had been the target of harassment and vandalism by unknown parties during several weeks before his death. Gampero believed that a jury would acquit him if the case went to trial.

During the process of jury selection, however, the judge advised Gampero that if the case went to trial and Gampero were found guilty, the punishment would be a sentence of 25 years to life. But if Gampero pleaded guilty to a lesser charge, then the judge would impose a sentence of only 7–21 years instead. The judge told Gampero's parents point blank, "I will give your son 25 years to life, so you better take the plea, or if you don't take the plea, he's getting it." Charles Gampero, Sr., Gampero's father, encouraged his son to take the plea, believing that his son would only serve seven years. Gampero, Sr., said, "We took the plea agreement, thinking that my son would be home by the time he's 27. It didn't work out."

The Case of Erma Faye Stewart

Erma Faye Stewart was arrested in a major drug sweep based on information provided by a police informant who was later deemed not credible. Stewart, 30, maintained her innocence, but her court-appointed attorney didn't want to hear it. "He was like, pushing me to plead guilty and take probation. He wasn't on my side at all." After spending 25 nights in a crowded jail, Stewart finally agreed to follow her attorney's advice and plead guilty. "Even though I wasn't guilty," she said, "I was willing to plead guilty because I had to get home to my kids. My son was sick." When she accepted the plea bargain and a ten-year probation, Stewart was freed. What she didn't know was that under the terms of her probation, she would be required to pay a monthly fee to the probation department. Her felony conviction also meant that the single mother was banned from the federal food stamps program. Within three years of falling behind in her probation payments, Stewart was evicted from her home. Steve Bright, a defense attorney and law professor with the Southern Center for Human Rights, says of plea bargaining that "One reason a lot of people plead guilty is because they're told that they can go home that day, because they will get probation. What they usually don't take into account is that they are being set up to fail."

The Case of Patsy Kelly Jarrett

In 1973, 23-year-old Patsy Jarrett, a North Carolina resident, drove to New York with a friend for a summer vacation. Three years later, police showed up at her door and she learned that sometime during their New York stay, her friend had robbed a gas station and murdered the

(continued)

(continued)

attendant. The evidence against Jarrett's friend was strong. The only evidence against Jarrett was that an elderly witness said he saw a car at the time of the crime with someone inside. The man did not know, however, whether the person was a man or a woman. To avoid a trial, prosecutors offered Jarrett a plea bargain: If she would plead guilty to the robbery, they would drop the murder charge and give her a 5- to 15-year prison sentence. Jarrett said, "I told my attorney I can't do this." Her attorney said, "Well, my hands are tied. They want to drop the murder charge against you if you plead guilty to the robbery." And Jarrett said, "But I haven't robbed anybody." Convinced that the jury would believe her, Jarrett refused the plea bargain and went to trial. She was subsequently convicted and sentenced to 25 years to life. Jarrett commented after the trial and sentence, "I believed in the American system of justice. I believed that, you know, just tell the truth and the judge and jury will hear you and nothing will happen to you. But I was wrong." Interestingly, 12 years into her prison sentence, Jarrett's case was reversed, but the state appealed the reversal. The state offered her another plea bargain: admit to committing the crimes, and she would be sentenced to time served and released. Jarrett steadfastly maintained her innocence and refused the plea bargain. Her conviction and sentence were reinstated and she has now spent over 30 years in prison for crimes she claims she never committed.

Source: Adapted from "The Plea," *Frontline*, June 17, 2005.

In the case of *McMann v. Richardson* (1970), the defendant entered a guilty plea knowingly and voluntarily and pleaded guilty to murder. He was sentenced to 30 years in prison as the result of the plea bargain agreement. Later, he appealed, contending that his guilty plea had been coerced by the prosecutor. The U.S. Supreme Court heard his argument and ruled that no evidence existed to show that his guilty plea was coerced. Merely alleging coercion is insufficient to succeed on an appeal and have one's conviction overturned.

In the case of *North Carolina v. Alford* (1970), Alford was indicted for first-degree murder and faced the death penalty if convicted. Alford maintained his innocence and that he had murdered no one. Subsequently, he was permitted to enter a *nolo contendere* plea to second-degree murder in exchange for a 30-year sentence, which the judge imposed. *Nolo contendere* pleas are treated the same as guilty pleas, although they technically do not involve admissions of guilt by defendants. Rather, defendants enter such pleas and merely acknowledge the facts as set forth in indictments without actually admitting their guilt. Later, Alford contested the 30-year sentence, arguing that he was coerced into pleading guilty in order to avoid the death penalty, which may have resulted from a subsequent jury verdict. The U.S. Supreme Court was unsympathetic and held that when an accused, such as Alford, enters a plea voluntarily, the accused knowingly and understandingly consents to the imposition of a prison sentence even though he/she is unwilling to admit participation in the crime, or even if his/her guilty plea contains a protestation of innocence, when, as here, he/she intelligently concludes that his/her interests require a guilty plea and the record strongly evidences his/her guilt. Put more simply, plea bargaining is not considered coercive when a defendant chooses a lengthy prison sentence in order to escape the possible imposition of the death penalty (Foley 2003).

The leading case on this specific point is *Brady v. United States* (1970). Brady was a codefendant in a case involving kidnapping. The offense carried the maximum penalty of death. Brady initially pleaded not guilty to the kidnapping charge. However, Brady's codefendant decided to plead guilty to a lesser charge in exchange for his testimony against Brady in a later trial. Brady changed his mind and pleaded guilty to the kidnapping charge in exchange for a 50-year sentence, which was subsequently commuted to 30 years. However, Brady brooded about the lengthy prison term and eventually filed an appeal, alleging that his guilty plea had been coerced. The U.S. Supreme Court heard Brady's appeal and upheld his conviction. The Court held that a plea of guilty is not invalid merely because it is entered to avoid the possibility of the death penalty. The U.S. Supreme Court further noted that although Brady's plea of guilty may well have been motivated in part by a desire to avoid a possible death penalty, we are convinced that his plea was voluntary and intelligently made and we have no reason to doubt that his solemn admission of guilt was truthful.

In a noncapital Kentucky case, _Bordenkircher v. Hayes_ (1978) involved a career criminal, Paul Hayes. Hayes was arrested for check forgery in Fayette County, Kentucky. The possible punishment for check forgery was a prison sentence of two to ten years. Hayes had several prior felony convictions, and thus, he was eligible to be prosecuted under Kentucky's Habitual Offender Statute. Under this statute, Hayes faced a sentence of life imprisonment. The prosecutor offered Hayes a plea bargain, which included a guilty plea to a bad check charge in exchange for a three-year sentence in prison. Hayes rejected the plea bargain and proceeded to trial. Hayes was prosecuted on the forgery charge as well as a habitual offender under the Habitual Offender Statute. He was convicted and sentenced to life imprisonment. Later he appealed to the U.S. Supreme Court and claimed that the prosecutor had attempted to coerce him into pleading guilty to one crime while threatening to prosecute him for another crime. The U.S. Supreme Court concluded that Hayes had not been coerced. If prosecutors have grounds for filing particular criminal charges, then their threats to file such charges if defendants don't plead guilty to lesser charges are not considered coercive. In sum, prosecutors may use additional charges against defendants as leverage to elicit guilty pleas to lesser charges whenever there is probable cause to believe that the additional crimes have been committed by the defendant. There must be a factual basis underlying any criminal charge.

IF PROMISES ARE MADE BY PROSECUTORS TO OBTAIN GUILTY PLEAS FROM DEFENDANTS, ARE PROSECUTORS OBLIGATED TO FULFILL THESE PROMISES? Yes. If a prosecutor promises to recommend leniency or a specific sentence in a plea agreement, then the prosecutor is bound to observe that promise if it is used to elicit a guilty plea. A prosecutor cannot promise a specific form of leniency merely to elicit a guilty plea from a defendant. Prosecutors must follow through on their promises.

In the case of _Santobello v. New York_ (1971), Santobello was charged with two felony counts and pleaded guilty to a lesser-included offense following a prosecutor's promise _not_ to make a sentence recommendation at the plea bargain hearing. However, the plea bargain hearing did not occur for several months. When the proceeding was conducted, a new prosecutor had replaced the earlier one. The new prosecutor, unaware of the earlier prosecutor's promise to Santobello, recommended the maximum sentence under the law, which was imposed by the judge. Santobello appealed, arguing that his guilty plea resulted from a promise by the former prosecutor not to recommend a particular sentence. While the judge himself said that he was unaffected by the new prosecutor's statement to maximize Santobello's sentence, the U.S. Supreme Court saw things differently. Santobello's conviction and sentence were overturned, since a promise had been made to Santobello as a means of inducing him to plead guilty. The U.S. Supreme Court held that the second prosecutor was honor-bound to observe the earlier prosecutor's promise. Santobello was allowed to withdraw his guilty plea. A prosecutor may not make promises to defendants to obtain guilty pleas from them, unless the prosecutor fully intends to keep the promises.

This same idea works both ways. If a prosecutor offers a reduced sentence to a defendant in exchange for that defendant's testimony against another defendant, then the defendant must fulfill his/her promise to testify or the plea bargain and sentence imposed are withdrawn. In the case of _Ricketts v. Adamson_ (1987), Adamson was one of several codefendants charged with first-degree murder. Before his conviction, however, Adamson entered into a plea agreement with prosecutors to testify against his codefendants. In exchange for his testimony against other codefendants in separate trials later, Adamson was permitted to plead guilty to second-degree murder and receive a prison term instead of the death penalty. Adamson was convicted of second-degree murder. Later, when the trials of his codefendants were scheduled, Adamson refused to testify, breaking his earlier promise to prosecutors. The prosecutors appealed

Adamson's conviction and sentence and the Arizona Supreme Court overturned the conviction. New first-degree murder charges were filed against Adamson and he was later convicted of this offense, which carried the maximum penalty. Adamson appealed to the U.S. Supreme Court, alleging that his right against double jeopardy had been violated with the new trial following his earlier conviction. The U.S. Supreme Court upheld his second conviction saying that his breach of the original plea agreement removed the double jeopardy bar that otherwise would prevail, assuming that under state law, second-degree murder is a lesser-included offense of first-degree murder. Therefore, even criminal defendants are obligated to keep their promises in order to make the plea agreement enforceable.

TYPES OF PLEA BARGAINING

There are four types of plea bargaining. These include (1) implicit plea bargaining, (2) charge reduction bargaining, (3) judicial plea bargaining, and (4) sentence recommendation bargaining. These types of plea bargaining are ordinarily distinguished according to which party initiates the bargaining. In three types of plea bargaining discussed below, either judges or prosecutors initiate plea negotiations with defense counsels and their clients. A fourth type of plea bargaining actually occurs through a mutual understanding among parties of what charges will result and what penalties will be expected in exchange for guilty pleas entered (Champion 2005a).

Implicit Plea Bargaining

Implicit plea bargaining is an understanding between defense counsel and the prosecutor that a guilty plea will be entered to a specific offense, which carries a conventional punishment. The expected and contemplated punishment is usually somewhat less than the maximum sentence that could be imposed. The key word in this definition is *understanding*. Much hinges upon what sentences have been imposed for similar offenses in the past, depending upon the jurisdiction. Those who have entered guilty pleas to burglary charges in the past have sustained penalties ranging from straight probation to 48-month prison terms. There are also jurisdictional variations among cities and counties involving identical crimes, even within the same states (Myers and Reid 1995).

In view of one's prior record, age, mental state, and a host of other factors, defense attorneys are generally in a position to know the going rate for specific offenses. For first offenders, the going rate for burglary may be 18 months in prison. Depending upon the circumstances of the burglary (e.g., whether there were victim injuries, the amount of property loss/damage), a defendant may receive probation for a specified period, such as two or three years. In the case of chronic offenders who have multiple convictions for burglary and other crimes, courts are inclined to impose more severe sentences. Maximum sentences may be contemplated. Further, because the defendant is a habitual offender, there is an additional charge that could be filed by prosecutors. Most states have habitual offender statutes, meaning that for habitual offenders, a conviction on a habitual offender charge would lead to life imprisonment or life without parole.

Thus, when defense attorneys consult with their clients, they acquire an intimate familiarity with the defendant's prior record and other background factors. Defense counsels have a fairly good idea of what they can expect from the prosecutor's office regarding a plea bargain for their clients. A knowledge of the going rate for specific offenses enables these defense counsels to advise their clients accordingly and to let them know what they can likely expect from the prosecutor and court.

The practice of implicit plea bargaining begins when a defense counsel advises his/her client that if the client enters a guilty plea to a specific charge, the result will probably be a particular sentence. The defendant is induced to plead guilty based upon the expertise of the defense attorney and his/her familiarity with the legal system. Offers to enter guilty pleas in exchange for particular punishments are attractive to prosecutors, since obtaining guilty pleas relieves them of having to prove the case against the defendant later in court. Because of the defense counsel's knowledge and agreeability of prosecutors, most plea agreement negotiations are completed rather quickly.

Exceptions are high-profile cases or cases that are particularly offensive, such as child sexual abuse, mutilation or torture, or some type of perversion. However, in some types of cases, court policy may dictate that no plea bargains will be struck with certain types of offenders. For instance, a large suburban county in the Midwest enacted a policy of no deals with dope pushers (Church 1976). Those who dealt in illicit drugs knew that they could not plea bargain their way into lenient punishments. Thus, a strong law-and-order stance taken by the courts and prosecutors in this county was intended as a deterrent to drug dealing. Drug dealers knew that if they were arrested, their plea bargaining chances were nonexistent. However, while prosecutors were not permitted to plea bargain drug cases, it did not prevent judges from dispensing with such cases quickly, often without trial. In these instances, judges would dismiss more troublesome cases or make their own sentence recommendations to conclude cases. In short, one form of plea bargaining was replaced with another, as the responsibility for initiating bargains shifted from prosecutors to judges (McConville and Mirsky 2005).

An example and comparison of implicit plea bargaining is illustrated as follows. Suppose we have two criminals, Joe Jones and Phil Smith, both of whom are charged with burglary and larceny. Each has broken into homes and stolen jewelry and other valuables assessed at $2,000. Profiles of the two criminals are highlighted here:

	Joe Jones	Phil Smith
Age	25	24
Education	9th grade	completed high school
Family stability	stable	stable
Marital status	single, never married	divorced, two children
Prior record	three felony convictions for larceny, fraud	none
Employment	unemployed	employed as day laborer
Drug use	yes	no
Alcohol use	yes	yes

This information is often derived from arrest reports and booking documents. It is known both to the defense counsel and the prosecutor. Jones has a more serious criminal record compared with Smith. The most important factor weighing against Jones is his prior record, consisting of three prior felony convictions for larceny and fraud. The most important factor weighing in favor of Smith is his lack of a criminal record. In other respects, compared with Smith, Jones has less education, has less of a chance for holding a steady job, and is involved with both drugs and alcohol. The going rate for Jones in the present case may be five to seven years in prison. The prosecutor may threaten to bring habitual offender charges against him, and these charges would be easily substantiated. In Smith's case, the going rate might be probation or a short jail sentence. The facts that Smith is a first-offender, is employed, has two children from a prior marriage, and has a high school education make him an ideal candidate for some form of probation or leniency.

One point made by this comparison is that the going rate varies depending upon an offender's prior record and general background. The same crime committed is punished differently because of the difference in criminal histories for two otherwise similar offenders. Another feature of implicit plea bargaining is that no specific agreement or bargain is reached between the defendant and prosecutor. Guilty pleas are entered in the hope that leniency will be extended by both the prosecutor and the judge. In most situations, some form of leniency issues from judges in exchange for guilty pleas. However, there are no rules that obligate judges or prosecutors to extend leniency to anyone who enters a plea of guilty to any crime. Judges remind defendants of this very fact before the guilty plea is accepted (Pohlman 1995).

Charge Reduction Bargaining

Charge reduction bargaining or **charge bargaining** is an offer from the prosecutor to minimize the number and seriousness of charges against defendants in exchange for their pleas of guilty to lesser charges. When crimes are perpetrated, often there are multiple offenses arising from the original crime. For instance, Joe Jones and Phil Smith steal a car; enter a convenience store and rob it at gunpoint with automatic weapons; wound two customers who attempt to intervene; shoot and kill the convenience store clerk who attempts to telephone police; elude police who chase them through four counties; cause extensive damage to multiple vehicles during the hot pursuit; engage in a shootout with police and wound several innocent bystanders; and severely wound a police officer before they are subdued and taken into custody. The list of charges against Jones and Smith include murder, attempted murder, armed robbery, menacing, eluding police, firing upon law enforcement officers, resisting arrest, hit-and-run, aggravated assault on the police and bystanders, vehicular theft, and possession of illegal automatic weapons.

Charge reduction bargaining would involve the prosecutor, who would probably suggest a guilty plea to second-degree murder and armed robbery. The punishment sought would be life imprisonment. Without the plea bargain offer, the prosecutor would file all of these charges against these defendants. The death penalty would probably be sought as well. The result might well mean the imposition of the death penalty or consecutive life imprisonment terms. The offer to reduce the charges and the recommended punishment might sound attractive to Jones and Smith. After all, they avoid the death penalty and are parole-eligible. But plea bargaining of this sort is not always one-sided (Worden 1995). Negotiations include counter offers from defense counsels. Thus, charge reduction bargaining and several other forms of plea bargaining are considered episodic, occurring over time and involving multiple defense counsel/prosecutor encounters. Further affecting the use of charge reduction bargaining is the bureaucratization of courts in different jurisdictions. The greater the sheer volume of cases in particular jurisdictions, the greater the use of charge reduction bargaining as a technique to facilitate case processing and move more cases through the system more rapidly (Champion 2005b).

In another case, this time involving two real defendants, two young men were under police surveillance and suspected of dealing drugs. They happened to be members of a nationally recognized football team in a southern state and were quite popular. The city police, county detectives, and state bureau of criminal investigation were involved in a coordinated effort to investigate them and determine the extent of their alleged drug dealing. An informant, another football player, agreed to plant a bug in the telephone of their apartment. Other listening devices were planted throughout the apartment at the order of the local criminal court. Subsequently, the young men were videotaped and telephonically recorded engaging in at least 28 transactions. Each of these 28 transactions involved Class X felonies, which meant life-without-parole sentences on each count or charge. This is because the quantity of drugs (many kilos of cocaine, heroin, and marijuana) was substantial and qualified their crimes as Class X, the most serious felony category in the state.

The young men were eventually arrested. The most prominent criminal defense attorneys were hired for them by the football team's booster's club and other private supporters.

With this formidable defense and the local popularity of these football players, the prosecution knew that despite their clear-cut evidence of criminal conduct and seized drugs, there was a possibility that these men would either be acquitted later or be convicted of some downgraded charge. Thus, the prosecutor approached their attorneys with the following deal: Have your clients plead guilty to simple possession of a controlled substance (cocaine), and get six months' jail time (with time off during days and weekends to play football), and do an additional two years on probation with 400 hours of community service. The plea agreement was concluded quickly and the young men were sentenced to six-month jail terms. Each was permitted to leave during the day for football practice and required to report back to the jail during evening hours at 9:00 p.m. Weekends were spent playing football with the rest of the team.

Many citizens in the community were upset by the excessive leniency extended to these football players by the court. It was believed that their status and popularity as football players overshadowed their otherwise criminal conduct, which under other circumstances would have qualified them for 28 consecutive terms of life without parole. But the prosecutor defended his action by arguing that a jury may have thrown out the case against these defendants, despite the mountain of evidence that had been compiled, the incriminating drug deals videotaped and telephonically recorded, and numerous statements of informants and undercover agents. The final irony of this case is that *both* players failed to comply even with the simplest of conditions associated with their jail terms. They failed to observe their 9:00 p.m. curfew on at least three occasions and the judge invited them back to his courtroom where four-year prison terms were imposed. The football players eventually were sent to the state penitentiary.

Cases such as this have been cited to underscore the ethics of plea bargaining and the morality of prosecutorial discretion in reflecting public interest in honest law enforcement (Connell 2004). Cases in which prosecutorial discretion is flagrantly abused, such as the football player scenario above, do little to foster public perceptions of prosecutorial integrity. In fact, such prosecutorial indiscretions have functioned as platforms for plea bargaining and sentencing reforms in most states (Wilmot and Spohn 2004). Also, plea bargaining may be unethical and counterproductive relative to the court's manifest goals of retribution, deterrence, incapacitation, and rehabilitation.

Judicial Plea Bargaining

Judicial plea bargaining occurs when judges make offers of sentences to defendants in open court in exchange for their guilty pleas. One of the most frequent uses of judicial plea bargaining involves petty offenses, such as public order offenses, such as public intoxication or disturbing the peace. Persons arrested for being drunk and disorderly appear before judges in the morning following their arrest. Very often, they are eager to leave the courtroom and get on about their business. The judge knows that the criminal punishment for their conduct is not especially severe.

In New Orleans, for instance, judges must face thousands of intoxicated arrestees every Mardi Gras. Bourbon Street and the French Quarter generate large numbers of targets inviting arrest by police for public intoxication. While their crime is not especially serious, they may do themselves harm by being out on city streets in their condition. Thus, the drunk tanks of local jails fill rapidly and empty the following morning. Judges bring in 20 or more persons charged with public intoxication and inform them as a group as to the punishment contemplated. They are usually given fines and suspended sentences. Many courts accept credit cards in lieu of cash payments. The proceedings are concluded quickly, as justice is rapidly dispensed through judicial plea bargaining. Anyone wishing to contest the matter can remain jailed and stand trial later, where the outcome will likely be the same (McDonald 1985).

BOX 8.3

Judge Rejects Plea Bargain Agreement

Geraldo Montoya, 19

On October 16, 2001, Daniel Herrera was shot and seriously wounded in Laredo, Texas. He was hit in his upper leg following an argument with another man, Geraldo Montoya, 19. A subsequent investigation by police and a search of Montoya's residence disclosed a sawed-off shotgun, a 9 mm handgun, and several other weapons. Montoya was arrested and charged with two counts of aggravated assault with a deadly weapon. The second charge arose from an earlier incident, where Montoya allegedly pistol-whipped a woman in the face.

Montoya's attorney met with the district attorney later and worked out a plea bargain. According to the terms of the plea bargain, Montoya would plead guilty in exchange for a two-year sentence in a Texas penitentiary. Montoya agreed and pleaded guilty to the charges. However, Judge Manual Flores examined the plea bargain and rejected it. The judge said, "This doesn't sound like a plea bargain I would accept." The implication was that the offer made by the state to Montoya was too lenient. The judge ordered the attorneys back to the bargaining table to craft a more suitable plea agreement, where more time served might be contemplated. The reason given by the judge was that there were deadly weapons involved in both incidents, and that these weapons constituted serious aggravating circumstances.

Should judges have the power to reject plea bargains wherein the state has offered a reduced sentence to a defendant in exchange for his guilty plea? Some people criticize plea bargain agreements as being too lenient on offenders. How does this judge's ruling regarding the original plea agreement counter these criticisms? What sentence do you think would be suitable for Montoya for shooting one man and pistol-whipping a woman?

Source: Adapted from Laurel Almada and the Associated Press, "Judge Denies Plea Bargain Agreement," November 17, 2001.

Judicial plea bargaining is the functional equivalent of a bench trial, but without much of the formality of prosecutorial involvement. In many cases, defense attorneys are not involved. Historically, bench trials such as those described above frequently involve a defendant's waiver of the right to a jury trial. However, defendants who waive this right are rewarded, while those who demand a jury trial are punished (Cohen 2004). Known as the **jury waiver system**, this method of concluding cases is far less restrictive of one's Sixth Amendment rights than plea bargaining per se.

But the frequency with which judicial plea bargaining occurs has certain adverse consequences for defendants. Decisions to plead guilty are encouraged, and the circumstances under which judges offer specific sentences to defendants, even fines, are somewhat coercive and threatening. Many defendants do not take the time to consider their options and frivolously enter guilty pleas, even if there is the possibility that they are innocent. Being rushed into a guilty plea, therefore, compromises due process to an extent. This is especially true regarding indigent defendants. In New York, for instance, data were obtained from 236 indigent defendants involved in 150 felony cases from 1984 to 1985 (McConville and Mirsky 2005). Assignment of counsel to these indigent defendants included showing defendants that they will receive more severe penalties if they fail to plead guilty. Then these defendants are given exactly 15 seconds to accept or reject the pleas and sentences offered by these judges. Almost all defendants acceded to the judge's request for them to plead guilty to the recommended charge and accept the proposed sentences (McConville and Mirsky 2005).

One unfortunate consequence is that once a guilty plea has been entered, even to a minor charge, it cannot ordinarily be withdrawn later. If it is withdrawn successfully later, there is little to prevent prosecutors from using the initial plea of guilty to their advantage in the courtroom later if the case proceeds to trial. Thus, defendants lose in several different ways no matter what their decision might be.

Judicial plea bargaining also results whenever power is removed from prosecutors to strike deals or plea bargains with defendants. If charge reduction or sentence recommendation bargaining is minimized or prohibited, then the responsibility for deciding punishments and negotiating with defendants shifts to judges. When judges are given this additional responsibility, they become **concession givers**, roles previously performed by prosecutors. More than a few judges get bogged down in their docket loads when dealing with defense counsel who seek reassurances for their clients that probation or some minimal jail time will be imposed. Judges who are not prepared to grant probation in certain cases tend to develop docket problems.

Sentence Recommendation Bargaining

The fourth type of plea bargaining is **sentence recommendation bargaining**. Sentence recommendation bargaining occurs when the prosecutor proposes a specific sentence in exchange for the defendant's guilty plea. In one respect, sentence recommendation bargaining is an overt articulation of implicit plea bargaining. A prosecutor informs the defense counsel representing a client as to the contemplated sentence in exchange for a guilty plea. In a take-it-or-leave-it fashion, the defense counsel relays the information to the client, who decides whether the proposed punishment is worth the guilty plea. It usually is.

Sentence recommendation bargaining is not entirely discretionary with the prosecutor. In fact, judges must approve all plea bargain agreements in all jurisdictions (Worden 1995). Therefore, if the prosecutor proposes a punishment that will later be rejected by the judge, it is viewed as a waste of court time, and the prosecutor will be chastised accordingly. Thus, prosecutors must be knowledgeable about what the court will or will not accept. This means that all actors (e.g., prosecutor, defense counsel, and judge) must have a general understanding of the going rate for any crime, given contextual factors and defendant backgrounds, including their criminal histories.

Sentence recommendation bargaining is often finely tuned, depending upon a prosecutor's experience with the system and relationship with the judge. There is a clear relation between a judge's beliefs about the leniency and coerciveness of plea bargaining and the trade-off between crime control and due process, and their own willingness to cooperate with a prosecutor who attempts plea negotiations with defendants (Worden 1995). In the mid-1990s, however, efforts were underway in several jurisdictions to overhaul the architecture of plea bargaining to remove its extralegal properties. Various forms of sentencing classification have been proposed as guidelines in plea negotiations. Of course, this raises the informal nature of plea bargaining to a much more formal and predictable level. Thus, the clear intent of plea bargaining reformers is to structure plea bargaining and eliminate the often protracted interplay between prosecutors and defense attorneys. In many respects, the reform envisioned would be similar to guidelines-based sentencing schemes such as those used in Minnesota and other state jurisdictions, as well as the federal court. Offense-specific charts would be consulted, where one's crimes would be cross-tabulated with one's criminal history. Where the points intersect would define a range of months or years that would determine the latitude of the plea bargainers. Jurisdictions such as Massachusetts have been experimenting with sentencing commissions vested with such powers over plea bargaining and certain sentencing issues (Champion 2005a).

One troubling feature of sentence recommendation bargaining and other plea bargaining forms is gender disparity (Auerhahn 2004). Gender disparity occurs when one gender receives preferential treatment or consideration in plea negotiations and sentencing. Gender disparity studies indicate that females with no prior records are more likely than similar males to receive charge reductions and less severe sentence recommendations from prosecutors (Champion 2005a). The **typicality hypothesis** has been described, which proposes that women are treated with chivalry in criminal processing, but only when their charges are consistent with stereotypes of female offenders. **Selective chivalry** suggests that decision makers extend chivalry disproportionately toward white females. Finally, **differential discretion** suggests that disparity is most likely in informal charge reduction bargaining than in the final sentencing process and sentencing hearing (Champion 2005a). Records of 9,966 felony theft cases and 18,176 felony assault cases were investigated for the year 1988. Given the similarity of prior records, women were more likely than their male counterparts to receive charge reductions and have a greater chance of probation. Such chivalry has been described in other jurisdictions as well, as evidence of gender bias and preferential treatment by courts (Williams, Craig-Moreland, and Cauble 2004).

We have also seen how indigents seem to receive unfair treatment during plea bargaining, especially when they are assigned public defenders who are usually courtroom novices (Weiss 2004). Not only are they assigned less-competent counsel, they also are rushed into accepting reduced sentences from prosecutors and judges in exchange for their guilty pleas. The coerciveness for indigents is that they almost always face the prospect of harsher penalties from a jury trial on more serious charges. Plea bargaining is the symbolic poster child for socioeconomic unfairness in the criminal justice system. The phrase "You get what you pay for" has special significance here.

Unfortunately, there is no easy way to eliminate socioeconomic status as a relevant extralegal variable in the complex plea bargaining equation. This is one reason plea bargaining was banned in Alaska in 1975. However, simply banning something does not mean its informal abandonment. In fact, plea bargaining did not disappear in Alaska following the ban, and it is alive and well now. Prosecutors and defense counsel have simply modified their strategies for circumventing the Alaska plea bargaining ban (Champion 2005b).

But because plea bargaining occurs at the front end of the criminal justice system and affects virtually every stage following it, the potential for disparities attributable to most any variable must be carefully monitored (Ball 2005). While the bureaucratic apparatus is in place to ensure strict compliance with sentences imposed through plea bargains, there is a glaring absence of controls to protect against the unwarranted intrusion of social status variables in any particular plea negotiation.

THE PROS AND CONS OF PLEA BARGAINING

Plea bargaining has its proponents and opponents (Herzog 2004). Below is an extensive list of reasons why plea bargaining is both popular and unpopular with the public and justice experts.

Arguments for Plea Bargaining

REDUCING THE UNCERTAINTIES OF CRIMINAL TRIALS   There are several arguments favoring the use of plea bargaining in the United States. Plea bargaining reduces the uncertainties and risks inherent in a trial for willing participants (Herzog 2004). This means that offenders who decide to plead guilty to one or more criminal charges know with some degree of certainty the nature and extent of their punishment, including about how much time they will serve, either on probation or in jail, and any other conditions contemplated by the prosecutor and approved by the judge. If the case were to go to trial and the defendant were convicted, it is more difficult to predict with certainty what the judge will impose. Case processing time is more rapid through plea bargaining (Greenstein 1994). If cases are plea bargained, case processing time is much faster than if the case were to go to a lengthy trial.

FEWER TRIALS AND TRIAL DELAYS   Plea bargaining also means fewer trials and **trial delays**. Prosecutors do not have to prove critical elements in state's cases against defendants. Trials obligate prosecutors to present arguments to the jury about the defendant's guilt beyond a reasonable doubt. Juries may not be easily convinced. This does not relieve prosecutors from proving one's guilt, however. In any plea agreement, the prosecutor must lay out for the judge in writing what evidence would have been presented to show the defendant's guilt beyond a reasonable doubt if the case had gone to trial. This is called the **factual basis for the plea**. This evidence is often minimal, but it may be sufficient to convince most judges of the soundness of the prosecutor's case against the defendant. It should not be assumed literally that prosecutors do not have to prove anything against the accused in a plea bargain agreement. The prosecutor is obligated to furnish the judge who oversees the plea agreement with sufficient evidence that would have been introduced to show the defendant's guilt, if the case had gone to trial. Some plea bargain agreements have been rejected by judges because of insufficient evidence presented by prosecutors.

PLEA BARGAINING MEANS MORE CONVICTIONS   Plea bargaining results in larger numbers of convictions. Usually the concessions arising from plea bargaining are sufficient to induce most defendants to plead guilty. Ninety percent or more of all convictions are obtained through plea bargaining. Without plea bargaining, trials would determine one's guilt or innocence. With juries deciding many cases, it is likely that there would be fewer convictions, even under conditions where evidence against the accused is strong. There are fewer jail backlogs and less jail and prison overcrowding as the result of plea bargaining. This is because the use of probation and nonincarcerative alternative sentencing options (e.g., **home confinement**, **electronic monitoring**, **intensive supervised probation**) are seriously considered and often imposed as enticements to elicit guilty pleas (Erez and Ibarra 2004).

Plea bargaining involves **negotiated guilty pleas**. Because these guilty pleas are negotiated, they are often better than trials in terms of the deals arranged for guilty defendants. Again, trials are often unpredictable in outcome. And if a defendant is found guilty through a trial, then the punishment is often harsher than if the case had been concluded through plea bargaining. Plea bargaining avoids potential jury bias and emotional influence of adverse evidence. More rational sentencing decision making through bargaining is achieved and the factual circumstances of terrible crimes, such as murder or aggravated rape, are less emotionally charged (Fearn 2004). Juries may be persuaded to find someone guilty of a serious crime because of sympathy generated by the prosecutor for the victim and the victim's survivors (Enriquez and Clark 2005). Emotional persuasion is often strong and overrides sound, cold deliberations that are expected of jurors when both sides have presented their case (Fryling 2005).

Offenders convicted through plea bargaining often avoid the taint of a formal criminal prosecution. They do not spend much time in court, except to participate in the plea agreement hearing. Little fanfare accompanies such hearings, which are not attended by many persons. As opposed to trials, plea agreement hearings are not usually announced to the public. Most plea agreement hearings, although open to the public, are held only with the judge, court reporter and other court officers, the prosecutor, defense counsel, and defendant. Thus, the specter of a lengthy courtroom drama is avoided. Judicial discretion is more limited because of the conditions and concessions outlined in plea agreements (Champion 2005a). Judges reserve the right to reject plea agreements if they feel that plea agreements are too lenient. However, judicial rejection of plea agreements is rare. Most plea agreements are rubber-stamped by most judges in most jurisdictions.

PLEA BARGAINING AND ANTICIPATED LENIENCY   Plea agreements may also soften the impact of sentencing guidelines in states that have them (Barrile and Stone 2005). Guidelines schemes tend to be excessively rigid. Prosecutors may downgrade the seriousness of one's offense or write the plea agreement in such a way so as to subvert the intended impact of guidelines to systematize the sentencing process and create greater uniformity in sentencing (U.S. Sentencing Commission 2003). However, each case is developed and rests on its own merits. Each plea bargain agreement is slightly different from others, even in the same jurisdictions. Their uniqueness is about as varied as personality systems.

REDUCING THE COSTS OF TRIALS   Regarding its cost-effectiveness, plea bargaining is far less expensive than jury trials (Champion 2005b). In jury trials, witnesses must be subpoenaed.

Experts must be obtained. Evidence must be examined in greater detail for use in court. The valuable time of judges, court officers, and other key participants is expensive. Thus, from a pure economic standpoint, plea bargaining is a cheap way of getting a guilty plea. In the federal system, for instance, the U.S. Sentencing Guidelines have severely limited the use of plea bargaining with extremely lenient sentences to less than 20 percent (U.S. Sentencing Commission 2003). Under the pre-guidelines indeterminate sentencing followed by the U.S. District Courts, probation was granted to convicted offenders about 60 percent of the time. Under the **United States Sentencing Guidelines**, which went into effect in October 1987, the use of probation as a sentence in federal courts decreased to about 12 percent. In fact, the U.S. Sentencing Guidelines table provides for probation in only the least serious misdemeanor or felony cases. U.S. probation officers are obligated to file more complete reports under the federal sentencing guidelines. The additional mandatory information to be included negates any attempt by federal prosecutors to leave out details that would intensify one's offense seriousness (Barrile and Stone 2005). Under previous indeterminate sentencing, prosecutors could leave out details, such as the use of a weapon during the commission of the crime, in an attempt to negotiate a more lenient sentence for a federal defendant in exchange for a guilty plea. The fact that federal judges used probation 60 percent of the time under pre-guidelines sentencing is strong evidence that presentence investigation reports were often modified to give judges the impression that they were sentencing defendants who were less serious offenders.

Arguments Against Plea Bargaining

THE SELF-INCRIMINATING NATURE OF PLEA BARGAINING   There is considerable opposition to the use of plea bargaining in negotiating guilty pleas. One argument is that defendants who plea bargain give up their constitutional right to a jury trial. Further, they give up the right to cross-examine their accusers. They also relinquish their right against **self-incrimination**. However, the greater leniency extended to defendants in exchange for giving up these rights is sufficient to justify their waivers of jury trials and insistence of observance of their constitutional rights to full due process. Many convicted offenders are thankful for plea bargaining, since a jury trial would almost certainly have involved harsher punishment for them. As a consequence, there are fewer trials with plea bargaining, and thus, fewer forums are convened where defendants can present the full body of exculpatory evidence showing their innocence (Holmes et al. 1992). More than few experts are bothered by this fact. Their belief is that jury trials mean that all facts will be heard and that the fairest decision will be rendered by the jury hearing all of the evidence.

THE LOSS OF JUDICIAL CONTROL   Plea bargaining may signify a loss of judicial control of courtrooms, giving lawyers free reign to divert jurors from the facts with theories that portray their clients as supposed victims of an unfair criminal justice system (Champion 2005a). Most defendants are more than willing to ride through this loss of judicial control with a relatively lenient plea agreement, however. If a defendant is convicted through a trial, the punishment is almost invariably harsher than whatever had been contemplated in a plea bargain. Once a defendant has entered a guilty plea and a sentence has been imposed by the judge, it is difficult to withdraw the guilty plea. Despite the predictability of plea bargaining, there is always an elusive element. This is **judicial privilege**, which means that judges may accept or reject one or more plea bargain agreement terms and substitute more or less punitive sentences. Thus, although clients have been reassured by their counsel and the prosecutor that entering a plea of guilty to a specific charge will likely result in one type of sentence, another type of sentence may actually be imposed by the judge. Again, judges are not obligated to follow precisely every condition noted in plea agreements.

DEFENDANT IGNORANCE AND PLEA BARGAINING   Ignorance or mistake often leads to guilty pleas. Therefore, the plea agreement process may lack sufficient guarantees to ensure proper application of the law and sentencing options. Many defendants are ignorant of the law. Those with some knowledge of the law may lack the foresight to appreciate and understand the seriousness of the guilty plea they enter. Criminal convictions are serious and often result in a loss of one's job. Or naive defendants may enter into plea agreements with prosecutors not knowing that they have the right to litigate fully any charges against them. Their own attorneys often fail to apprise them of their various legal options. Relevant defense evidence is not presented. Opponents of plea bargaining single out this particular factor as most damaging to defendants. If the accused enters a guilty plea, crucial evidence that may have resulted in an acquittal if the case had gone to trial instead is often overlooked or deliberately ignored. Thus, opponents of plea bargaining argue, the true extent of one's case cannot be known unless it is subjected to a trial proceeding. But many defendants enter into plea agreements hoping that some of the evidence against them will never be heard. They see plea bargaining as a way of slipping through the system with minimal damage. Plea bargains often offer more benefits to the accused than would be forthcoming at a trial, where circumstances could be much worse.

REJECTIONS OF GUILTY PLEAS AND JUDICIAL PAYBACK   Judges are more likely to be more severe with defendants who reject initial plea bargain agreements. Thus, one danger of plea bargaining is that if an offer to a defendant is made to plead guilty in exchange for what the prosecutor (and judge) believe is a reasonable punishment, refusal to accept that agreement and force the case to trial will sometimes disturb the judge. Upon conviction, the judge may exact some revenge by extending one's sentence by one or more years. Judicial intervention is minimized such that the ineffective-assistance-of-counsel issue cannot be adequately explored. When plea agreements are negotiated, there is little, if any, opportunity to ascertain whether one's defense counsel is representing the best interests of the client. Is defense counsel competent? With so many cases being plea bargained, and in fairly standard ways, there is no clear opportunity to evaluate defense competence.

The judge becomes an advocate intent on inducing a defendant to plead guilty, when due process presumes one innocent until proven guilty beyond a reasonable doubt. This particular factor is another sore point with plea bargaining opponents. They do not want judges to engage in a form of bribery by dangling attractive lenient sentences before defendants who would face much worse if they went to trial on the same charges. When plea bargaining is allowed, judges wield a great deal of power in the offers they make through judicial plea bargaining. There is a hint of coercion in plea bargaining, particularly implicit plea bargaining, where threats of greater punishments are implied if guilty pleas are not entered to less serious charges, which may cause some persons to plead guilty to crimes they did not commit. Thus, some innocent people may accept criminal convictions in order to avoid harmful or fatal punishments. Usually, these are cases where innocent defendants are swept into the criminal justice system through suspicious circumstances. Persons who cannot account for their whereabouts when crimes have occurred or appear to be involved may find themselves in the unenviable position of facing harsh punishments if convicted. Death rows throughout the United States have set free occasional convicts who were subsequently determined to be innocent through newly discovered evidence or confessions from the real perpetrators.

CIRCUMVENTING HABITUAL OFFENDER STATUTES   Plea bargaining may circumvent **habitual offender statutes** or **three-strikes-and-you're-out policies**, where mandatory penalties are contemplated. The danger of plea bargaining here is that chronic or persistent offenders with multiple felony convictions can avoid mandatory punishments an unlimited number of times through plea bargaining. However, the purpose of mandatory penalties is to remove chronic and persistent offenders from society by incarcerating them either for life or substantial terms of years. Such punishments are thwarted through plea bargaining, however. Because of plea bargaining, therefore, there is an inconsistent application of mandatory penalties among jurisdictions (Vincent and Hofer 1994). Habitual offender statutes are frequently used as leverage for inducing guilty pleas from defendants. There is no apparent intent on the part of prosecutors to enforce such habitual offender statutes, however. Circumvention of sentencing guidelines is encouraged by plea bargaining (Stemen, Wilson, and Rengifo 2004). Sentencing guidelines are designed to establish fairness in sentencing. Whenever these guidelines are bypassed through plea bargaining, fairness is unevenly applied for those who do not plead guilty but rather, go to trial.

SENTENCING REDUCTIONS FOR THOSE UNDESERVING OF SENTENCING REDUCTIONS   Sentences for many serious offenders are reduced when such sentences shouldn't be reduced (Kramer and Johnson 2004). Sex offenders and child sexual abusers find themselves given sentences that are often far too lenient, given the seriousness of their offending. Often, critical case information may be buried or overlooked in an attempt to get a plea bargain negotiated. Therefore, some very serious offenders may get lighter sentences, when in fact their punishments should be more severe. At the same time, such offenders may avoid helpful counseling and therapy that otherwise might occur through traditional trial convictions (Alexander 2004). Plea bargaining may reduce the sheer volume of criminal prosecutions. There is no reliable evidence, however, that the absolute number of prosecutions is abbreviated because of plea bargaining. We must remember that plea bargaining results from a prosecution. Thus, a decision by a prosecutor to prosecute someone for a crime sets the stage for offers and counteroffers from defense counsels and prosecutors, as plea bargain agreements are negotiated.

CONCEALING HEINOUS ASPECTS OF CRIMES THROUGH PLEA BARGAINING   Prosecutors and others may be able to conceal more serious aspects of a crime from the sentencing judge by withholding certain information from a plea agreement. Some professionals object to this circumstance as ethically wrong. Justice somehow seems politicized by this process (Champion 2005b). Defense lawyers who have cultivated amicable relations with prosecutors over the years are more seasoned and better-prepared to negotiate desirable plea bargains for their clients. New lawyers performing public defender functions are at a disadvantage, since they are often unaware of how the system works in a particular jurisdiction. Where who you know gets you a better deal in the plea agreement process, this is a fairly clear indication that plea bargaining has been politicized.

RUBBER-STAMPING PLEA AGREEMENTS   Judges tend to rubber-stamp plea bargain agreements without doing their jobs effectively. Judges are supposed to determine whether a factual basis exists for a defendant's plea of guilty. Judges must also determine whether guilty pleas are voluntary. Do defendants wish to relinquish critical constitutional rights, such as giving up the right to cross-examine accusers or give evidence in one's own behalf? Because of the glut of court cases in many jurisdictions today, judges are often relieved to merely approve agreements where guilty pleas have been entered. They often are lax when performing their oversight functions. Since plea agreements often result in more lenient treatment for offenders, they tend to acquire a cynical view of the criminal justice system. They may take subsequent chances by committing new crimes, expecting leniency in the future because it had been extended in the past. They are not wrong in their appraisal of the criminal justice system, nor are they wrong in anticipating further leniency from prosecutors.

THE POTENTIAL FOR GENDER BIAS IN PLEA BARGAINING   It is claimed that women tend to benefit to a far greater degree from plea bargaining than men. Women tend to be granted probation more often than men, given the similarity of their prior records, instant offenses, and other salient factors. Because of this less than even-handed application of justice, therefore, the goals of deterrence, incapacitation, and rehabilitation are either undermined or defeated. Another form of discrimination in the use of plea bargaining applies to the poor and those in the lower socioeconomic statuses (McConville and Mirsky 2005). Courts are deluged with thousands of indigent defendants, often drawn into the criminal justice system through police sweeps in drug-infested sections of cities. Much street crime is perpetrated by those who are unemployed. Youthful offenders are drawn into the criminal justice system as well, especially minority youths (Champion 2007). Less affluent defendants are less likely to avail themselves of jury trials, where private counsels are most effective.

DOES PLEA BARGAINING INVALIDATE THE JURY PROCESS?   Some critics say that plea bargaining invalidates the jury system (McConville and Mirsky 2005). By bypassing a jury trial, defendants are dealt with more swiftly and without the benefit of jury trials. However, it is incumbent upon judges to advise defendants of their right to a trial by jury and whether they wish to voluntarily relinquish that right. In more than a few instances, it is disadvantageous to criminal defendants to air their cases before juries, since the details and circumstances of their crimes may offend more sensitive jurors. This, in turn, could lead to more serious criminal convictions with accompanying and commensurate sentencing consequences. Thus, for some offenders at least, jury trials are not desired and for good reason (Enriquez 2005). Plea bargaining encourages more proactive policing and arrests of indigents (McConville and Mirsky 2005). According to this line of thinking, police officers are interested in making increasing numbers of arrests that will result in convictions. Street people, indigents, drug users, and youthful offenders who loiter or act suspiciously are often arrested and charged with assorted offenses. Police officers know that there is a strong likelihood that many of those arrested will be offered plea bargains resulting in probation or charge reductions. Convictions result in greater approval of the actions of law enforcement officers, and thus a self-reinforcing cycle is set in motion with predictable consequences.

HAMPERING EFFORTS TO REFORM SENTENCING   Sentencing reforms are hampered through plea bargaining. If 90 percent or more of all convictions are obtained through plea bargaining, it is more difficult for reformists to convince legislatures of the necessity for sentencing reform. The existence of going rates and other traditional plea bargaining features has become institutionalized nationally. There is no dramatic need to reform a system that seems to be accepted by criminals, prosecutors, defense counsels, and judges. However, plea bargaining is blamed for some amount of sentencing disparity (Park 2005). One obvious disparity resulting from plea bargaining is the difference in sentencing severity between plea-bargained cases and convictions resulting from trials. Another type of disparity occurs that is more difficult to detect. Different attorneys continually network with various assistant state's attorneys or district attorneys to work out agreements for their diverse clientele. All plea bargains are individualized; therefore, there is an inherent inequality that exists. Only judges monitor plea agreements, and little effort is made by these judges to ensure that sentencing uniformity occurs according to the salient factors that should influence sentencing decisions (e.g., prior record or criminal history, instant offense, victim injuries, and other aggravating or mitigating factors) (Johnson 2004). Without any consistent monitoring mechanisms to govern plea bargaining in any particular jurisdiction, sentencing disparity must be assumed to occur. We do not know how much sentencing disparity exists resulting from plea bargaining.

RACIAL DISCRIMINATION AND PLEA BARGAINING   More people of color are discriminated against through plea bargaining. This means that much racial and ethnic discrimination occurs (Clark 2004a). Racial and ethnic discrimination also exists at other stages of criminal justice processing, including imprisonment (Spohn and Keller 2005). Street crimes are given greater attention by police officers, and proactive policing discussed above targets street people most often. These persons are frequently ethnic and racial minorities. These persons, frequently indigent, must accept defense counsel who often lack the experience and expertise of seasoned private attorneys retained by more affluent criminal clients. Efforts are currently being made to upgrade legal services for indigents. But such efforts are sporadic and unevenly applied among jurisdictions. Also, there is no one to monitor the actions of prosecutors. Thus, a serious accountability problem exists. Who should oversee the credibility and quality of case screening and prioritizing? Prosecutors in many jurisdictions have virtually unbridled authority to drop or pursue a case, adjust charges, and make recommendations (Connell 2004). In short, prosecutors have too much decision-making power in charging decisions. Also, shifting greater decision-making power to prosecutors reduces justice system accountability as case decision making is shifted toward the front of system. Rights activists are concerned that due process protections for the accused are jeopardized and that victim participation is minimized under widespread plea bargaining.

THE BUREAUCRATIZATION OF NEGOTIATED GUILTY PLEAS   The perfunctory nature of plea bargaining has certain bureaucratic characteristics. If there is greater reliance on bureaucratization, then there is less individualized attention given to more important cases (Ferdinand 1992). The existing administrative structures of some jurisdictions, such as Pennsylvania, are frequently relied upon by prosecutors so as to ensure consistency in plea bargaining practices. A positive consequence of bureaucratization in plea bargaining is that extralegal factors, such as race, social class, and gender, are less important in negotiating guilty pleas. In **coconspirator** cases, it is more difficult for innocent defendants to separate themselves from guilty defendants (Champion 2005a). If the guilty defendant enters into a plea agreement with prosecutors and agrees to testify against an innocent party named as a coconspirator, the innocent coconspirator is tainted. Thus, if the case comes to trial for the codefendant who does not plead guilty, such circumstances work to the disadvantage of the innocent party.

ARE LAWYERS VESTED WITH TOO MUCH AUTHORITY IN PLEA BARGAINING?   Some critics say that plea bargaining gives too much authority to lawyers. There is little or no weight given to **fact-finders** or juries. Essentially, this is a complaint that jurors are in a better position to determine guilt or innocence and evaluate evidence in contrast to a prosecutor–defense attorney plea agreement where all pertinent facts about the crime may not be disclosed and weighed properly. Plea bargaining is so pervasive that many defense attorneys have become complacent about it. If defense counsel must defend indigents, these attorneys are not paid at rates equivalent to private counsel. Thus, the financial incentives do not exist to work hard for indigent clients. Particularly where indigents are involved, defense counsel are often quick to conclude a case with a plea bargain (Champion 2005a). If cases do go to trial, there are questions about the competence of defense counsel required to represent indigents. Are they enthusiastic enough to present the best defense, or do they go through the motions of defending clients, taking the easiest path that will conclude proceedings?

WHY IS PLEA BARGAINING BANNED IN SOME JURISDICTIONS?

Plea bargaining has been banned in various U.S. jurisdictions, most notably in Alaska. When Alaska announced that it was banning plea bargaining on a statewide basis in 1975, other jurisdictions were apprehensive. Would such a ban mean a glut of trials involving petty offenders? Would the wheels of Alaskan justice come to a grinding halt as more cases were processed without informal plea agreements worked out in advance?

It is important to note that although plea bargaining in Alaska was officially banned, it did not disappear. What occurred is that plea bargaining gave prosecutors considerably greater charging powers. With greater power over charging decision making, prosecutors in Alaska were more careful to screen those cases destined for trials. One result was that there was actually a reduction in the number of criminal prosecutions, as many cases that once were plea bargained were simply dropped. A more significant consequence of the Alaska plea bargaining ban was to create greater charge bargaining. Prosecutors were vested with considerably more authority to decide which charges should be brought against defendants. Subsequent bans of plea bargaining by various jurisdictions, such as New Hampshire, have revealed a similar pattern, with a substantial increase in charge bargaining (Herzog 2004).

At the core of plea bargaining bans is the unfairness inherent in sentencing bargaining. Most plea agreements contemplate a particular punishment. Much of the punishment meted out through plea bargaining is more lenient than traditional punishments associated with trial convictions. Thus, the leniency of plea bargaining concerning sentences received by convicted offenders, often serious offenders, has been objectionable to more than a few citizens and lawmakers.

Reasons for Banning Plea Bargaining

1. Where plea bargaining has been banned, a greater amount of charge reduction bargaining occurs. This has shifted much of the decision-making power to prosecutors and away from judges. Some experts view this shift unfavorably.
2. Under a plea bargaining ban, there is greater likelihood of incarceration. This means that jail and prison overcrowding could be exacerbated by an absence of plea bargaining. On the one hand, those who favor strong get-tough anticrime measures will applaud the elimination of plea bargaining. On the other hand, jail and prison officials may not be pleased with the overcrowding that will likely result.
3. Under a plea bargaining ban, cases are more carefully screened by prosecutors. Thus, only the more serious cases for which strong evidence exists will move forward to criminal trials.
4. Selective bans against bargaining with certain offenses targeted (e.g., no deals with dope pushers) appear to work in selected jurisdictions. Thus, when offense-specific plea bargaining restrictions are implemented, prosecutors are prohibited from accepting reduced-charge guilty pleas from drug dealers. This doesn't necessarily mean that convicted drug dealers will be treated harshly, however. Current sentencing policies in certain jurisdictions are intended to incarcerate more offenders who commit certain types of offenses, such as drug dealing, for longer periods of time (Champion 2005b).
5. Even if plea bargaining is banned, judges and others find ways to get around it (Spohn 2004). It is virtually impossible to eliminate plea bargaining. Informal negotiations will always occur, no matter how stringent the controls or plea bargaining restrictions.

JUDICIAL INSTRUCTIONS FOR ACCEPTING GUILTY PLEAS AND RIGHTS WAIVERS

In most jurisdictions, judges are obligated to determine the factual bases for guilty pleas, encourage frank discussion of the facts of the case, and facilitate further consideration of sentencing alternatives. In federal district courts, for example, judges must observe all of the **Federal Rules of Criminal Procedure** relating to plea bargaining (Ulmer and Burchfield 2004). Specifically, this is 18 U.S.C., Rule 11 (U.S. Code, 2001). Rule 11 outlines with considerable precision whatever judges must do in the process of approving plea agreements. Under Rule 11, federal judges must make sure that defendants who enter guilty pleas to criminal charges understand the following:

1. The nature of the charge(s) to which the plea is offered.
2. The maximum possible penalty provided by law.
3. The mandatory minimum penalty as provided by law.
4. The effect of any special supervised release term and any special provisions for compensating victims.
5. That a defendant who does not have an attorney has a right to one; and if the defendant cannot afford an attorney, one will be appointed at state expense.
6. That the defendant has the right to plead not guilty and to withdraw a guilty plea at any time.

7. That the defendant has the right to a trial by jury and the right to the assistance of counsel at the trial.

8. That the defendant has the right to confront and cross-examine prosecution witnesses.

9. That the defendant has the right not to incriminate himself or herself.

10. That if the plea of guilty or *nolo contendere* is accepted, there will be no further trial of any kind; therefore, the plea is a waiver of the right to a trial.

11. That there is a factual basis for the plea.

12. That the plea is voluntarily given and that it is not the result of force, threats, or coercion apart from a plea agreement.

13. That the judge may accept or reject the plea agreement.

14. That the plea is accurate.

15. If the plea is the result of prior discussions between prosecutors and defendants or their attorney.

Items 11, 12, 13, and 14 are of great significance to defendants. These items are to determine whether the guilty plea entered by a defendant is voluntary. There must be a factual basis for the plea; the judge may accept or reject the plea agreement; and the plea agreement is an accurate summarization of the facts. These provisions seemingly protect defendants from overzealous prosecutors who threaten long sentences and drawn-out prosecutions if guilty pleas are not entered and suggested sentences are not accepted. This is the ideal scenario. It does not always happen this way in the real world.

Federal judges have no special litany for determining these and other facts about a defendant's guilty plea and the nature and terms of the plea agreement. The spirit of the law is that federal judges must ascertain these facts, in open court, by orally addressing the defendant. Each judge uses his or her own style for covering these important items. Thus, Rule 11 provides general guidelines for judges to follow. Past challenges from defendants about whether judges asked them about these items in precise ways have been unsuccessful. That is, federal judges are not compelled by Rule 11 to recite these questions precisely in the context of the rule.

If a federal judge is not satisfied with the evidence proffered by a U.S. attorney or his/her assistant, then the judge is not bound to accept the plea agreement. Judges can throw out charges against defendants if the evidence against them does not or would not support a subsequent conviction if the case proceeded to trial. A case in Tennessee provides a good example.

A man from Chattanooga, Tennessee, was charged with several felonies relating to copyright infringement governing the use of 16mm films and their possession by private film collectors. He had collected feature films as a hobby, but the Motion Picture Association of America (MPAA) and the Film Security Office under the direction of President Jack Valenti instituted a series of legal actions against private collectors to prevent them from trafficking in these motion pictures. The government's theory, at the urging of the MPAA, was that no motion picture had ever been sold to private individuals; therefore, all motion picture 16mm prints in the hands of film collectors must be stolen or obtained in nefarious ways. While there are several flaws in the government's theory about the critical elements of criminal copyright infringement, suffice it to say that the Chattanooga film collector was innocent of any criminal wrongdoing. He had purchased most of his 16mm prints of these motion pictures from film rental companies or from film reclamation services. Thus, he had legal title to these pictures. At the time, film collecting was regarded by the MPAA as jeopardizing the profits of major motion picture film companies. In reality, the number of motion picture collectors was small and the sum of their monetary profits from dealing in motion pictures was trivial. Subsequently, these motion pictures have been made available in DVD format, and any private citizen may now own just about any motion picture sold in this format.

In Chattanooga, Tennessee, however, the defendant was a fairly high-volume trader of motion pictures at the time. While he probably profited from motion picture film trades and sales, he never intended to defraud film companies of any revenue that they might obtain through film rentals or leases. In any event, the assistant U.S. attorney (AUSA) for the federal district court in Chattanooga brought several criminal copyright infringement charges against the film collector. The defendant was in his early fifties and had a heart condition. He was employed only on a part-time basis and supported himself from a portion of the revenue he realized from his film collecting.

The AUSA in Chattanooga approached the defendant with an offer—plead guilty to a **federal misdemeanor** and the AUSA would recommend a three-year probationary term. The defendant, who was assigned a court-appointed attorney, declined any offer to plead guilty to any criminal charge relating to his film-collecting hobby. However, a persuasive public defender pointed out to the defendant that a three-year probationary term wasn't bad compared with the 30 years and $200,000 fine associated with felony convictions on the criminal copyright infringement charges. Reluctantly, the defendant agreed to plead guilty.

On the day of the plea agreement hearing, however, the defendant stood before the federal district court judge and answered the different questions faithfully. When it came to the matter of whether the defendant wanted to plead guilty to this crime, even a federal misdemeanor, the defendant balked. "I never committed any crime, judge," he said. With a frustrated expression on his face, the judge asked the defendant's attorney if he wanted to confer with his client before proceeding. The defense counsel had a lengthy discussion with his client who later went back into court before the judge and entered the guilty plea. Here is where things get interesting.

The judge next asked the AUSA what evidence would have been submitted to show that the criminal elements existed and could have been proved beyond a reasonable doubt. The AUSA said that the evidence was summarized as a part of the plea agreement. The judge asked, "Is that all you have against this man?" The AUSA said, "Yes, your honor." At that point, the judge faced the defendant and said, "You are hereby freed, as I am dismissing all criminal charges against you." Then he turned to the AUSA and chastised him for bringing such a poorly prepared case before him. It was clear to the judge that the defendant had been cajoled into pleading guilty for fear of a harsher prosecution.

Unfortunately for many federal and state criminal defendants, not all judges are as judicious and meticulous in examining federal or state plea agreements and their contents (Johnson 2004). A majority of federal and state court judges "rubber-stamp" these plea agreements, since the court is backlogged with many serious cases to be plea bargained. Many judges give plea agreements only a cursory glance and overview before holding plea agreement hearings. Thus, often their actions relating to accepting plea agreements are perfunctory.

CAN JUDGES PARTICIPATE IN PLEA NEGOTIATIONS BETWEEN PROSECUTORS AND DEFENSE COUNSEL? NO AND YES   At the federal level, district court judges are prohibited from participating in plea agreement negotiations between defense counsels and prosecutors. The policy about judicial participation in plea bargaining negotiations varies among the states. However, most states follow the federal government and prohibit judicial involvement in these negotiations. The primary reason is that where judges are involved in these discussions, it places them in the position of configuring an agreement that they will most certainly approve later. This type of influence is considered unethical and inappropriate in most jurisdictions.

Only a few states, such as North Carolina, permit state court judges to participate in plea negotiations. Thus, defense counsels and prosecutors can confer with judges about what judges will accept or reject as plea agreement terms. Some opponents of judicial participation in plea bargain negotiations rightly note that the adversarial nature of the justice system is substantially removed through judicial intervention of any kind (Worden 1995).

SHOULD JUDGES BE EXCLUDED FROM PLEA BARGAINING NEGOTIATIONS BETWEEN PROSECUTORS AND DEFENSE COUNSELS?   Some researchers believe that judges should be an integral part of the plea bargaining process. Judges can give both parties a clearer idea of what the sentence will be, the specific parameters of plea negotiations, and various correctional options. Essentially, judges can tell prosecutors and defense attorneys, "This is the deal I will accept. Don't bring me anything more lenient than that."

Sometimes judicial concern focuses more on particular offenses, such as those involving drugs. Political sentiment and the judiciary in one jurisdiction, a county in the Midwest, established a policy of "no deals with drug pushers" (Church 1976). In that Midwest jurisdiction, reduced-charge plea bargaining for drug cases was all but eliminated, but trial rates soared. Court dockets were incredibly crowded. Judges were hard-pressed to resolve their court cases quickly. Interestingly, judges became concession givers, a role abandoned in drug cases by the district attorney. Defense counsel shifted their attention to judges and negotiating with them instead of prosecutors. If defense counsel could not obtain probation for their clients charged with various drug offenses, then they would insist on a full-fledged trial, a time-consuming proceeding. Judges were compelled to make concessions, usually by granting probation or short jail terms for a majority of charged drug offenders.

Judicial participation in plea negotiations is sometimes suspect because of the implication that the defendant is guilty. Traditionally and consistent with due process, judges are supposed to assume a stance of neutrality and consider all defendants innocent until their guilt is proven in court beyond a reasonable doubt. Suppose a judge says that he/she will approve a particular guilty plea from Defendant X. Later Defendant X withdraws his guilty plea and goes to trial before the same judge. Can that judge continue to remain neutral and impartial in rulings on motions and other matters during Defendant X's trial? It seems somewhat contradictory for a judge to be an advocate during plea bargaining who encourages the defendant to admit his guilty, and then turn around in the defendant's trial and judge him fairly if he decides to reject the plea bargain agreement.

SENTENCING SYSTEMS AND PLEA BARGAINING

Plea bargaining has been modified in different jurisdictions depending upon the sentencing scheme adopted (Herzog 2004). One purpose of sentencing reform is to reduce sentencing disparities among judges, which are attributable to extralegal factors, such as one's race, age, ethnicity, gender, or socioeconomic status. Sentencing guidelines have been created in most jurisdictions to create sentencing uniformity, although no sentencing guideline scheme has completely eliminated the influence of extralegal factors in sentencing offenders (McManimon 2005b).

SENTENCING GUIDELINES AND RESTRICTIONS ON PLEA BARGAINING
For federal courts, however, the U.S. Sentencing Guidelines have operated to limit the negotiating parameters of prosecutors and defense counsel (Levine 2005). Prior to the establishment of U.S. Sentencing Guidelines, federal prosecutors could tailor their plea agreements in ways that would maximize a defendant's acceptance of the plea agreement terms and encourage more guilty pleas. If a firearm was used in the commission of a robbery, for instance, the prosecutor could leave that fact out of the plea agreement. This omission would enable prosecutors to downgrade more serious felonies to less serious ones and offer defendants more lenient (and acceptable) punishments. Probation was used about 60 percent of the time in most federally plea-bargained cases prior to the establishment of sentencing guidelines.

When the federal sentencing guidelines were established, new rules were instituted requiring U.S. probation officers to include all relevant legal variables in **presentence investigation reports (PSIs)**. Prosecutors were prohibited from omitting these relevant variables. Thus, if a federal defendant used a firearm during the commission of a felony (e.g., robbing a U.S. post office), this fact had to be reported and noted in subsequent plea agreements. Further, the use of probation under the new federal sentencing guidelines (October 1987) dramatically decreased to about 12 percent of all plea-bargained cases. Guidelines tables now exist that restrict the use of probation to only a limited number of minor federal offenses (Ulmer and Burchfield 2004). If federal defendants are recidivists, then the chances for probation as a sentence are eliminated.

Thus, federal prosecutors have lost an important plea bargaining chip in the game of negotiating plea agreements with those charged with federal crimes. Furthermore, under new federal and state sentencing guidelines, penalties for specific types of offenses, such as drug trafficking, have greatly increased (Inciardi et al. 2004).

OTHER SYSTEMS AND PLEA BARGAINING   If a particular offense carries with it a mandatory term, this means that judges must impose a specific sentence as required by law. Their hands are effectively tied. However, under **indeterminate sentencing** or **determinate sentencing** schemes absent any guidelines or other restrictions, judges and prosecutors may operate more or less freely in configuring plea bargain agreements with various defendants. There is considerable jurisdictional variation in this regard. In many jurisdictions without definite guidelines in place for offender sentencing, judges' sentencing practices are often influenced more by their work circumstances, their close relationships with courtroom prosecutors, and an absence of competing recommendations from probation (Worden 1995).

Summary

Over 90 percent of all criminal convictions, both felonies and misdemeanors, are obtained through plea bargaining. Plea bargains or plea bargain agreements are preconviction agreements wherein defendants enter guilty pleas in exchange for some form of sentencing leniency from prosecutors and judges. It is difficult to imagine how the criminal justice system would operate smoothly without plea bargaining, inasmuch as criminal court dockets are notoriously clogged even with plea bargaining eliminating over 90 percent of all criminal trials.

Several advantages for criminal defendants are that plea bargaining generally results in a lesser punishment than one that might have been imposed had the case gone to trial. Plea bargaining thus results in shorter sentences, greater use of probation, and generally greater freedoms for defendants. Prosecutors are advantaged by plea bargaining, since they are spared having to prove their cases against criminal defendants in court beyond a reasonable doubt. The sheer volume of criminal cases is reduced. Prosecutors generate much higher conviction rates and improve their chances of re-election in those areas where their positions are contested by popular vote. Generally, plea bargaining works well for prosecutors who have weak cases and for defendants where evidence against them is strong. Under plea bargain agreements, some of the more serious aspects of one's crime(s) may never be disclosed, since the plea agreement may stipulate such omissions. Plea bargaining has been used to resolve criminal cases for several centuries. Furthermore, plea bargaining exists in many other countries. It is not a uniquely American phenomenon.

Not all state jurisdictions condone plea bargaining in the United States. In Alaska, for instance, plea bargaining has been banned. However, informal forms of plea bargaining continue to exist in Alaska despite the ban. Plea bargaining may occur at almost any stage in offender processing. Plea bargaining is typically attempted before a case comes to trial, in an effort to spare the state the expense of a lengthy trial. If plea bargaining efforts are not successful, plea bargaining may nevertheless occur during a trial as evidence is disclosed against the defendant, and even during jury deliberations. Some persons have labeled plea bargaining as coercive, since prosecutors sometimes overcharge defendants and then offer lenient sentencing options if defendants enter guilty pleas to lesser offenses. Generally, if there is a basis for one or more charges against a defendant, then plea bargaining is not coercive. It only becomes coercive if prosecutors engage in malicious prosecutions or pursue charges against criminal suspects where insufficient evidence exists to convict them. Whenever prosecutors make promises to defendants in order to induce guilty pleas from them, these promises must be kept. Otherwise, plea bargain agreements are invalidated. Judges oversee and approve all plea agreements between prosecutors, defendants, and defense counsels.

Four major types of plea bargaining have been identified. These include implicit plea bargaining, charge reduction plea bargaining, judicial plea bargaining, and sentence recommendation plea bargaining. Implicit plea bargaining is a subtle form of plea bargaining where both prosecutors and defense counsels are familiar with going rates for particular types of offenses. Negotiated guilty pleas generally are close to these going rates associated with particular offenses. An understanding is reached between prosecutors and defense attorneys and a plea agreement is configured that both sides can live with, with judicial approval.

Charge reduction bargaining arises when prosecutors stack multiple charges against defendants. Subsequently, prosecutors offer to drop one or more of the serious charges in exchange for a guilty plea, usually to a lesser charge. Defendants see charge reduction bargaining as beneficial since they will not be prosecuted for other offenses they may have committed. Judicial plea bargaining occurs whenever judges offer defendants a particular sentence in exchange for a guilty plea. Often this type of plea bargaining occurs in misdemeanor cases, where judges may offer defendants fines in exchange for guilty pleas.

Sentence recommendation plea bargaining is initiated by prosecutors. Prosecutors make a recommended sentence known to defense counsels who advise their clients whether to accept it. The pros and cons of the sentence are evaluated, and defendants enter guilty pleas if the offered sentence recommendation is acceptable. Although prosecutors generally initiate sentence recommendation plea bargaining, judicial approval is necessary. Thus, some knowledge about what judges will or will not approve is quite useful when configuring sentences to recommend.

There are several arguments for and against plea bargaining. Arguments in favor of it include that the uncertainty is removed from the outcome of a criminal trial if one were held. It is difficult to anticipate what juries will decide, even if defendants are innocent of the charges against them (Gants 2005). More than a few innocent defendants have been convicted of crimes they have never committed. Also, plea bargaining reduces the sheer number of trials conducted and the delays such trials would cause. Plea bargaining also guarantees more convictions for prosecutors. Plea bargaining generally reduces the harshness of sentences and reduces the costs of criminal trials, since they are essentially avoided.

Arguments against plea bargaining, some of which are used by Alaska where it is banned, include that plea bargaining is self-incriminating. Defendants must admit to crimes they may or may not have committed in order to secure lenient treatment from prosecutors. In this respect, at least, plea bargaining has a coercive dimension. Although judges must approve all plea agreements, some degree of judicial control is relinquished as the interaction between the prosecution and defense becomes more important. Sometimes defendants are ignorant of the full implications of pleading guilty to certain charges. They literally relinquish all of their constitutional rights to a jury trial, to cross-examinations of witnesses against them, and they cannot give statements or testimony in their own behalf. Other rights are also waived voluntarily. In some instances, plea bargains are rejected by judges inasmuch as prosecutors have failed to provide sufficient evidence to support guilty pleas entered by less sophisticated defendants.

Another criticism is that plea bargaining circumvents habitual offender statutes that most often carry mandatory penalties. Habitual offender statutes are designed to remove chronic and dangerous offenders from the streets, but plea bargaining often bypasses these mandatory penalties that would result in an offender's incarceration. Also some heinous aspects of one's crime are not disclosed in plea agreements approved by judges. Thus, some offenders may escape harsher sanctions simply because judges are not aware of the full extent of their crimes and the harm they have caused victims. Plea agreements are often rubber-stamped with little or no effort by judges to ascertain whether a factual basis exists for the plea. Although judges must determine from defendants the voluntariness of their pleas and give close attention to the plea agreements they sign, there are simply too many plea agreements in many jurisdictions for judges to do a proper job in this respect.

Plea bargaining is said to invalidate the jury process, since trials are almost always avoided. But since greater leniency is extended to offenders through plea bargaining compared with what the penalty would be if the case were tried before a jury, most criminal defendants are satisfied with the results of plea agreements and their punishments. Plea bargaining also hampers attempts to reform different types of sentencing systems. If sentencing systems are designed to provide certainty of sentencing as a deterrent, these efforts are more than offset by plea bargaining, which undermines such efforts.

Another criticism of plea bargaining is that it may result in gender and/or racial bias in its application. Often, indigent defendants who cannot afford more competent counsel are pressured into accepting plea agreements without fully understanding their consequences. Guilty pleas are also bureaucratized and streamlined, as both prosecutors and defense counsels seek quick solutions to otherwise lengthy trial proceedings. The matter of power in the hands of lawyers is also a criticism of plea bargaining. Some persons question whether attorneys should have such powers to determine one's fate.

In jurisdictions where plea bargaining has been banned, such as Alaska, authorities have cited several reasons for such a ban. These include that there is a greater likelihood that just deserts and justice will be served and that offenders will have to suffer some loss of liberty through incarceration. At the same time, however, others say that more charge reduction bargaining occurs where greater decision-making power shifts from the judge to prosecutors and attorneys (Connell 2004). In some jurisdictions, selective bans on plea bargaining have targeted particular offenses, such as capital murder or aggravated rape. Ultimately, however, even where plea bargaining has been banned outright, various courtroom actors have found ways to defeat the ban. In short, it is impossible to completely eradicate plea bargaining in any jurisdiction.

All plea agreements are supervised and approved by judges. In most jurisdictions, with exceptions such as North Carolina, judges are prohibited from participating in plea agreement proceedings and exerting undue influence on this process by declaring what they will or will not approve. Judges are obligated in all jurisdictions to determine the voluntariness of one's plea, whether one

wishes to waive the right against self-incrimination, the right to cross-examine one's accuser, and other important due process rights. One of the more important functions of judges in overseeing the plea agreement process is to determine whether a factual basis for the guilty plea has been exhibited. It is incumbent upon prosecutors to demonstrate for judges what evidence would have been presented to show defendant guilt had the case gone to trial. Absent such incriminating evidence, the plea agreement fails, and more than few plea agreements have been rejected by judges and cases against defendants have been dismissed for lack of evidence.

Questions for Review

1. What is plea bargaining? Why is it controversial?
2. Name four types of plea bargaining and differentiate between each. Which one do you prefer and why?
3. What is the nature of judicial participation in plea bargaining for individual states and the federal government?
4. Should plea bargaining be banned? Why or why not?
5. What is meant by the going rate?
6. Briefly outline the history of plea bargaining in the United States.
7. In some jurisdictions, such as Alaska, plea bargaining has been banned. Does plea bargaining still go on in Alaska, even though it has been banned?
8. What is the significance of Federal Rule of Criminal Procedure 11 as it relates to plea bargaining?
9. What specific rights are waived by defendants who enter into plea bargain agreements?
10. How does the type of sentencing scheme influence plea bargaining?

Suggested Readings

1. George Fisher (2000). "Plea Bargaining's Triumph." *Yale Law School Journal* **109:** 868–1086.
2. M. McConville and C. L. Mirsky (eds.) (2005). *Jury Trials and Plea Bargaining: A True History.* Oxford, UK: Hart.
3. S. Herzog (2004). "Plea Bargaining Practices: Less Covert, More Public Support?" *Crime and Delinquency* **50:** 590–614.
4. Susan Rose-Ackerman (2002). "Corruption and the Criminal Law." *Forum on Crime and Society* **2:** 3–21.
5. Yue Ma (2002). "Prosecutorial Discretion and Plea Bargaining in the United States, France, Germany, and Italy: A Comparative Perspective." *International Criminal Justice Review* **12:** 22–52.

CHAPTER 9

Sentencing Goals and Structures

CHAPTER OBJECTIVES

As a result of reading this chapter, you will have accomplished the following objectives:

1. Understand the goals of sentencing, including the punishment philosophies of retribution, deterrence, incapacitation, rehabilitation, and restoration.
2. Understand functions of sentencing such as crime control, reintegration, and prevention.
3. Describe different forms of sentencing, including indeterminate, determinate, guidelines-based or presumptive, and mandatory sentencing and their implications for criminal defendants.
4. Describe habitual offender or chronic offender statutes such as three-strikes laws and their use in different jurisdictions.
5. Understand truth-in-sentencing provisions and how such provisions have evolved.

KEY TERMS

career criminals
chronic offenders
chronic recidivists
court-appointed counsel
Crime Bill of 1994
crime prevention
criminal history
death penalty
deterrence
early release
extralegal factors

flat term
felony property offending
get-tough movement
good time
good-time credit
guidelines-based sentencing
habeas corpus
habitual offenders
incapacitation
life imprisonment
life-without-parole sentence

mandatory sentence
mandatory sentencing
parole board
persistent felony offenders
persistent offender statutes
presumptive sentencing
punishment
rehabilitation
reintegration
sentencing disparity
sentencing guidelines

Sentencing Reform
    Act of 1984
serious felonies
three-strikes-and-you're-out
truth in sentencing
truth-in-sentencing laws
United States Sentencing
    Commission
violent felonies

Recently various states have been looking for ways to reduce their prison populations due to the economic downturn and state budget shortfalls. The federal government, on the other hand, continues to increase the number of prosecutions annually, which has resulted in ever-increasing federal prison population. The number of criminal cases in federal courts has risen from 69,575 in 2005 to 76,655 in 2009. Given that close to 90 percent of federal defendants are incarcerated, the federal prison population continues to rise; the United States Sentencing Commission states that federal prisons are currently 34 percent above their capacity (USSC 2010). Over half of the prisoners are serving time on drug charges, another 10 or so percent for immigration violations, and only about 8 percent are in prison for violent offenses. Some scholars are starting to question the necessity of lengthy prison terms for drug violators especially at the current cost of incarceration. Critics have raised questions about how the federal government is going to continue to pay for this as the Federal Bureau of Prisons already eats up $6.8 billion dollars of the Department of Justice's budget. Another concern comes from the employees of these prisons; another concern that arises from prison overcrowding is the safety of prison guards. There are just over 35,000 federal prison employees and as prison overcrowding increases so do threats to their safety. In 2008, a federal prison guard in California was stabbed to death by two inmates, a homicide that could have been prevented if the prison had the appropriate ratio of guards to prisoners. Further, there have been over 300 assaults on federal prison guards since this deadly incident. What do you think? Do you think that Congress or the voting public considers the safety of prison guards when they sponsor or support tougher criminal penalties. Would you support a politician who is truthful to the public about the consequences for overcrowding and the realities of guard safety that come with enactment of tougher penalties for crime? Do you think that taxpayers are going to want to continue to pay for the increasing costs of locking up drug or immigration offenders?

Source: Adapted from The Crime Report, "The Crunch in Federal Prisons," available online at: thecrimereport.org.

INTRODUCTION

This chapter discusses issues surrounding the sentencing process. Sentencing offenders is not as simple as it may appear. Numerous judges have remarked that if sentencing becomes easy, it is time to step down from the bench. Moral and ethical decision making aside, there are other reasons why sentencing is a rather complex process. There are many different types of schemes under which a defendant can be sentenced and changes are being made in different jurisdictions annually as various forms of sentencing are adopted and practiced. Sentencing is an adjudicatory function where a penalty is imposed on an offender convicted of a crime. This chapter opens with a discussion of the goals of sentencing and describes the different types of punishment philosophies. These philosophies include retribution or just deserts, deterrence, incapacitation, rehabilitation, and restoration. There are also other more generic functions or aims of sentencing such as prevention, crime control, and reintegration. Throughout history, each of these philosophies or functions has waxed and waned as the primary goal of punishment. This is not to say, however, that more than one may be emphasized at the same time. Further, sentencing is often criticized regarding whether a particular function or goal is realized as the result of a particular sentencing scheme used.

Several sentencing forms are examined in the next section. These include indeterminate sentencing, which is the most pervasive sentencing form in the United States. Indeterminate sentences are distinguished as those where parole boards often end up determining how much time in prison the convicted offender will actually serve. The advantages and disadvantages of indeterminate sentencing are presented. Among the criticisms of indeterminate sentencing are that extralegal factors such as age, race/ethnicity, gender, and socioeconomic status often influence early-release decisions by parole boards, and thus, some inmates may serve longer or shorter terms depending on these factors. This causes disparities in sentences according to race/ethnicity and gender; these charges of sentencing disparity are discussed in further detail.

Another sentencing form is determinate sentencing. Determinate sentencing is similar to indeterminate sentencing, except that one's early release from prison is determined by the accumulation of good-time credit and other noteworthy accomplishments. Some states have day-for-day good-time credit meaning that if an inmate's behavior is good, they would get a day taken off of their sentence for every day served. In other words, their good behavior would result in them only serving half of their sentence. During the 1970s and 1980s, a major shift occurred from indeterminate to determinate sentencing. The implications of this sentencing shift for the country's prison populations are discussed.

A third sentencing form is presumptive or guidelines-based sentencing. Almost half of all states along with the federal government have implemented sentencing guidelines to assist judges in determining proper sentences for convicted offenders, where extralegal factors are essentially excluded and have no bearing on sentencing decisions. However, even presumptive sentencing can be abused by judges and others (prosecutors and defense counsel), often through plea bargaining, and thus, equal justice may not be met in all cases. Recently, the U.S. Supreme Court has ruled that the federal sentencing guidelines are only advisory, not presumptive or mandatory as they were prior. This means that federal district court judges must consult the guidelines in determining an appropriate sentence but may hand out sentences that depart from the guidelines recommendation if they wish. Thus, even under federal sentencing guidelines, whose goals were uniformity and disparity amelioration, individualized sentencing has now been allowed by the highest court in the land. The pros and cons of presumptive or guidelines-based sentencing are discussed.

The fourth type of sentencing is mandatory sentencing. Often mandatory sentencing is imposed for specific offenses. Closely associated with mandatory sentencing are habitual offender statutes; these statutes pertain to offenders in certain conditions or circumstances or where certain crimes are committed. For example, if an offender uses a firearm during the commission of a crime, this may result in a mandatory sentence, which varies by jurisdiction. If a gun is used during the commission of a crime in Florida, an additional three-year mandatory term of incarceration is added to one's sentence for the crime itself. In Maryland, a five-year mandatory prison term is imposed for the same scenario. Mandatory sentences have been enacted under the notion that they will deter criminals from using firearms or other dangerous weapons during the commission of other offenses. This deterrent effect, however, has not been found through empirical research studies and critics argue that these laws to not provide deterrence because they are often circumvented by prosecutors in order to obtain pleas bargains (Tonry 1995, 1996).

Some states have evolved statutes that attempt to give a sentence some substance. Under indeterminate sentencing, for instance, offenders may often serve 20–30 percent of their time and are paroled. Citizen reaction to such abbreviated sentences is very negative. Seeking to placate citizens, legislatures have evolved truth-in-sentencing provisions, whereby offenders must serve most of their sentences (up to 85 percent) instead of serving only a portion of them before being paroled (McManimon 2005a). Regardless of the form of sentencing used in any jurisdiction, the goals of these sentencing schemes can easily be defeated. Habitual offender statutes, for instance, where mandatory sentences apply, can be plea bargained away and pose no threat to criminals. Jail and prison overcrowding is out of control in many jurisdictions, and harsh sentencing policies cannot be enforced because there is no space to place convicted criminals. These issues will be examined and discussed.

FUNCTIONS AND GOALS OF SENTENCING

Sentencing offenders serves many different and important functions. Spohn (2009) outlines some of the goals of sentencing or what scholars often refer to as punishment philosophies: (1) retribution or "just deserts," (2) incapacitation, (3) rehabilitation, (4) restoration, and (5) deterrence.

Punishment

Before we discuss these five philosophies of punishment, it is necessary to give a brief introduction to what punishment is. **Punishment** is any sanction imposed following a criminal conviction. The primary function and aim of sentencing is to punish offenders for their crimes. Each crime carries minimum and maximum penalties. When judges or juries find defendants guilty of committing one or more crimes, sentences are imposed that presumably punish offenders (Gants 2005). Considerable variation exists regarding the application of penalties for each crime. Most lawmakers believe that punishments should be proportional to the crime committed or amount of harm done. Depending upon the circumstances and jurisdiction, judges can impose probation for a period of years, or they can require that convicted offenders be incarcerated in either a jail or prison. How harshly or leniently convicted offenders are treated should depend on the crime's seriousness and the prior criminal history of the offender. Ideally, the more serious the crime, the harsher the penalties imposed. In reality, however, it doesn't always work this way. Investigators can always find examples of some rapists, robbers, or even murderers receiving probation instead of prison. Accordingly, some burglars and thieves may receive lengthy sentences in jails or prisons. Likewise, the more lengthy an offender's previous criminal history, the more lengthy or harsh the sentence will probably be, especially in jurisdictions which have adopted habitual offender statutes.

Retribution/"Just Deserts"

The earliest forms of punishment embodied **retribution** or the law of *lex talionis* and were also written in Hebrew scripture as "an eye for an eye, a tooth for a tooth, an arm for an arm, a life for a life." These notions represent the functional idea of retribution; they also imply that there should be proportionality in punishment. The goals of punishment under a retributive ideal are justified because the offender has committed a wrongful act. In other words, an offender engaged in a criminal act has to be punished; he/she deserves to be punished for the wrongdoing. You may have heard someone remark that a particular offender got what he deserved or got his "just deserts." This phrase reveals that the goals of punishment under a retributive philosophy are focused "on what the offender 'deserves' as a result of his criminal behavior" (Spohn 2009, 10).

Hospers (1977) points out that although retribution may seem to focus on the infliction of pain onto an offender equivalent to the injury or harm cause by the crime, it is actually the infliction of punishment for the sake of justice. Although Gandhi once remarked that an eye for an eye will make the whole world blind, most persons when asked why those who have committed crimes should be punished will reply with some notion of retribution as justification for punishment. The other four philosophies that will be discussed are perhaps more in line with Gandhi's sentiments about punishment. Incapacitation, rehabilitation, restoration, and deterrence are all based on utilitarian justifications for punishment, which focus on promoting good (Hospers 1977). In other words, utilitarian justifications for punishment argue that the goal of punishment should be to prevent crime in the future.

Incapacitation

The primary aim of punishment under this philosophy is to incapacitate those convicted of crimes, particularly those who are persistent or chronic offenders. **Career criminals** who make their living from crime are frequently targeted by the criminal justice system to receive the harshest penalties. Special statutes have been written to make it possible to mete out stringent penalties for **chronic recidivists** or **chronic offenders**. It is believed by many state legislatures that if **persistent felony offenders** and chronic recidivists are removed from society for prolonged periods through longer sentences, then they cannot commit new crimes against society while confined in prison. Thus, the system takes these offenders out of circulation for a period of years. **Incapacitation** achieves the goal of preventing crime in the future because the individual offender will be locked up and therefore unable to commit further offenses or victimize others. If such offenders are allowed to remain in their communities through some form of probation, then probation departments maintain surveillance over these clients by monitoring their whereabouts in different ways. Home confinement and electronic monitoring systems are used, together with regular face-to-face visits with probation officers. These forms of managing convicted offenders in their communities don't prevent them from committing new crimes in any absolute sense, but for many of these offenders, there exists some degree of crime prevention depending on the nature of these management methods.

Unfortunately, research has shown that our ability to predict who will reoffend, in other words, which offenders need to be incapacitated, is very poor. In the United States, incapacitation is used a great deal as a punishment for those who have violated the law. As the costs of incarceration continue to increase, some states are rethinking the philosophy of incapacitation, especially for offenders who have not committed violent offenses. A number of jurisdictions are starting to experiment with alternatives to incarceration while at the same time still attempting to achieve crime prevention. This requires some ability to predict or select those who are a low risk to reoffend and divert them away from prison or jail and into some type of community-based correctional program.

Rehabilitation

One intended function of punishment is **rehabilitation**. A high degree of cynicism is prevalent among jurisdictions, however, concerning just how well corrections in any form actually rehabilitates convicted offenders. Rehabilitation is focused on preventing crime in the future by correcting the offender's behaviors, attitudes, or thought processes. Some experts believe that rehabilitation never occurs, while others believe that for many offenders, particularly those incarcerated in prisons, rehabilitative programs have been successful in enabling them to turn their lives around and become law-abiding when they are eventually released back into society. Rehabilitation is sometimes referred to as the medical or treatment model because it aims to "cure" the offender. Critics, however, believe that rehabilitation can only work for those who want to reform. Further, rehabilitation assumes that we know the causes of the offender's bad behavior and can therefore subject him/her to the best cure; judges often may not know the reasons why the person engaged in the wrongful behavior or there may be a number of causes involved that resulted in the criminal offending. Most persons would probably agree that a judge has neither the time nor necessary information to play pathologist at sentencing.

Rehabilitation, however, is present in some form or another in conjunction with other punishment philosophies such as incapacitation. Indeed, most prisons include various vocational/technical/educational programs for offenders who wish to take advantage of these rehabilitative services. Individual and group counseling and other forms of social and psychological assistance are provided to inmates. Some jails and prisons have rules and regulations requiring inmates to participate in certain programs, whether or not they wish to participate. Literacy programs have been established in jurisdictions, such as Virginia, where it is expected that illiterate inmates who are serving long prison terms must learn how to read and write as one condition for their early release. Some authorities question whether voluntary or mandatory participation in any particular prison program is directly responsible for one's rehabilitation over time.

Restoration

Restoration takes a more holistic approach to punishment and prevention of crime in the future. Restorative justice ideals aim at repairing the harm that occurred as a result of the criminal act and focus on including the victim and/or larger community along with the offender in the punishment equation (Braithwaite 1998). Restoration believes that if the true aim is justice and promoting good in the future, then all parties must be involved in the punishment process. Restoration or those who advocate restorative justice believe that in order to prevent crime in the future, all persons affected by the crime, not just the offender, must be involved in restoring the balance back to relationships, communities, and society. Stated another way, if it takes a village to raise a criminal, it also takes the village to reform, restore, or rebuild the lives affected.

For instance, perhaps community service or restitution to the victim of crime better serves justice than simply having the judge place an offender on probation or send them to jail. Often victims may feel a better sense of justice if they are allowed to participate in determining an appropriate punishment, or relaying to the offender how the crime has impacted them, or receiving monetary reparation for the harm or injury they suffered. Obviously, restoration may be better suited for certain types of crime; for especially violent crimes such as homicide, it may be difficult if not impossible to restore the lives of people affected by the harm or injury.

Deterrence

Sentencing is also symbolic, both to convicted offenders and to those who are contemplating committing crimes. When judges impose sentences, there is a tacit expectation that others will consider the harshness of these sentences and refrain from crime because of their fear of punishment. Thus, punishment and sentencing are designed as forms of **crime prevention** and/or **deterrence**. One direct intention of the **get-tough movement** is to mete out harsher penalties for offenders to set examples and deter others from crime. The death penalty is regarded by some persons as an effective deterrent for those who are contemplating capital offenses. No one wants to be executed. Theoretically, if the **death penalty** is the punishment for murder, then fewer murders will be committed. This view has been challenged by experts frequently, and most criminal justicians agree that the death penalty does not necessarily deter some persons from killing others (Robinson and Darley 2004). Deterrence theory requires that punishments be swift, certain, and severe in order for them to have a deterrent effect. Although punishments for certain crimes may be severe, the swiftness and certainty of them are called into question. Even clearance rates for homicide nationally are only about 64 percent (USDOJ 2010); in other words, even for a serious crime like murder, the chances of being caught and punished are not certain. Also, longer prison terms for those who deal in drugs do not prevent drug dealers from carrying out their illicit activities.

Nevertheless, in an ideal world, sentencing is supposed to act as a deterrent and prevent others from committing crime. Largely because of this aim, the sentencing systems of all jurisdictions throughout the United States have been changed to maximize sentencing effectiveness. As we will see in the next section, sentencing reform has yielded several important types of sentencing schemes to further the aim of crime deterrence and prevention. Unfortunately, all forms of sentencing have generated criticism from experts and the general public, with little agreement as to which sentencing scheme is best (Champion 2005b).

Deterrence also assumes that criminals are rational and that they weigh the costs and benefits of committing crimes. When the benefits outweigh the costs, they will commit the crime; detection, prosecution, and punishment therefore are important costs in this equation. Deterrence advocates state that the punishments must outweigh the costs of committing crime in order to deter. Obviously, there are critics who would argue that a lot of criminals are not rational when they commit a crime such as assault or murder; they are crimes of passion or the offender was under the influence of drugs or alcohol at the time of the offense. Further, it might be hard for some persons to imagine criminals conducting a cost–benefit analysis in their heads before deciding whether or not to violate the law; although we may be able to agree that criminals might contemplate odds of getting caught, it is doubtful that they are thinking about the possible punishments for their behaviors.

REINTEGRATION

Related to utilitarian ideals of punishment and the prevention of future crime is the notion of reintegration. Reintegration involves assisting criminals to become readjusted so that they can fit back into their communities and society. This aim is most closely associated with nonincarcerative sentences, including all forms of probation, but many projects have begun that are focused on helping those who have been incarcerated to readjust to live outside of prison. When judges sentence offenders to probation, there are usually several conditions of probation attached. These conditions might include mandatory participation in counseling programs, job placement services, restitution programs, and other activities that will assist offenders in finding employment and becoming self-sufficient without having to return to crime. Particularly for first offenders, community correctional programs are quite helpful in enabling them to remain in society. They may retain contact with their families and receive their social support. Further, these offenders will not have to be exposed to the criminogenic influence of incarceration. For those who are incarcerated, this process may be even more difficult. Adjusting to life outside of the strict routine of prison can often be too difficult for those recently released. Compounding this difficult readjustment is the stigma that society places on those who have been locked up; it may be very difficult to obtain a job or find living arrangements because of some requirements to disclose any criminal convictions on job applications or apartment and housing leases as well as background checks conducted by some employers. Almost all of the states have or are seriously discussing the adoption of reintegration programs that can facilitate adjustment of released offenders back into society. With recidivism rates annually over 60 percent, most legislative officials are realizing the need for reintegration programs to prevent the public from being revictimized in the future as well as to curb the increasingly high costs of incarceration.

FORMS OF SENTENCING

Federal and state judges tend to believe that the toughest part of their jobs is imposing punishments on convicted offenders. There are so many types of offenders with varied backgrounds and criminal histories that the act of sentencing them is one of the most stressful and complex decisions made by these judges (Aas 2004). Assisting judges in their sentencing decision making are various legislatively enacted sentencing schemes. These sentencing schemes provide a rational structure within which to make sentencing decisions. There are generally four main types of sentencing schemes used by various jurisdictions throughout the United States. These are (1) indeterminate sentencing, (2) determinate sentencing, (3) presumptive or guidelines-based sentencing, and (4) mandatory sentencing.

Indeterminate Sentencing

Indeterminate sentencing is a sentence imposed by the judge that includes a minimum term of years and/or months and a maximum term, where the offender's early release from prison is determined by a **parole board**. Thus, the maximum term may or may not be served by any particular offender, depending upon their institutional behavior and other factors (Stemen 2004).

Indeterminate sentencing has its roots in early correctional history from the 1850s and 1860s. Influenced by penal reforms in Ireland, Scotland, and England, the United States was inclined to experiment with indeterminate sentencing as a means of providing incentives for inmates to behave well while confined. Provided that their institutional conduct was acceptable, once inmates had served the minimum portion of their sentences as imposed by judges, they would become eligible for parole or early release or serving their full terms. Parole boards would decide whether to grant **early release** to these parole-eligible inmates. Their institutional conduct would be examined, together with the circumstances and seriousness of their conviction offenses, and the parole board would either grant or deny their parole. Those denied parole on one occasion may apply for it on subsequent occasions, usually at regular intervals such as once a year or every two years. Most paroling authorities in the United States today continue to make such decisions.

However, indeterminate sentencing has been criticized for its potential for discrimination on the basis of race, gender, and/or socioeconomic status (Champion 2005b). Both judges and parole boards have been accused of respectively abusing their sentencing and early-release discretionary authority by making decisions on factors other than legal ones. These **extralegal factors** are most often racially or ethnically based, or related to gender or socioeconomic differences. Convicted offenders of minority groups more often receive longer sentences by judges or are denied early release by parole boards more frequently compared with white offenders who have a similar **criminal history**. Those with private counsel often are treated more leniently in sentencing compared with indigent convicted offenders who are represented by public defenders or **court-appointed counsel** (Weiss 2004). Since these factors should not be considered as significant in such decision making, substantial efforts have been made by different interests to reform state and federal sentencing policies and practices. In some instances, states and the federal government have abolished parole in favor of what they believe to be more equitable sentencing schemes. One noticeable shift among many states has been from indeterminate sentencing to determinate sentencing (Champion 2005b).

Determinate Sentencing

Determinate sentencing is a sentence imposed by the judge involving a fixed minimum term and a fixed maximum term, but where one's early release from prison is determined by the accumulation of **good-time credit**, which is deducted from one's maximum term. **Good time** or good-time credit is a fixed number of days inmates may accumulate based upon the amount of time they serve. A substantial number of states provide that offenders may accumulate up to 30 days for every 30 days they serve. Thus, if an inmate serves one year, he/she may accumulate one year of good-time credit. This credit is deducted from the maximum sentence originally imposed by the judge. It is conceivable, therefore, that inmates sentenced to ten years under a determinate sentencing system may serve only five years, with the accumulated good time deducted from their maximum ten-year sentences. Thus, determinate sentencing is intended to produce greater certainty, proportionality, and rationality in punishment (Champion 2005b).

Determinate sentencing is believed by its proponents to correct the potential for discrimination according to extralegal factors by judges and parole boards. With determinate sentencing, inmates can calculate their own approximate early-release dates. Thus, there is greater release certainty with determinate sentencing compared with indeterminate sentencing. But inmates may jeopardize their good-time credit by misbehaving while confined. They may receive write-ups from correctional officers for fighting or possessing illegal contraband or drugs. Violations of other institutional rules will result in good-time being revoked or cancelled.

Determinate sentencing has received mixed criticisms. Several states, such as Delaware, Colorado, Iowa, Minnesota, and Washington, have used determinate sentencing to replace indeterminate sentencing. Some of these states, including Minnesota and Washington, have opted to implement guidelines-based sentencing after experimenting with determinate sentencing for several years. Despite the promise of significant reform in curing previous ills of discrimination in sentencing, determinate sentencing has not been as successful in this regard as originally projected. Similar to Minnesota and Washington, a few other states have opted for another form of sentencing designed to curb judicial sentencing discretion and the potential for its abuse. In the last few decades, guidelines-based or presumptive sentencing schemes have been proposed and implemented (Champion 2005b).

Presumptive or Guidelines-Based Sentencing

Presumptive sentencing or **guidelines-based sentencing** is the establishment of fixed punishments for each criminal offense, graduated according to offense severity and one's criminal history. Punishments for different offenses are ranged according to months. Punishment range midpoints are the presumptive number of months imposed according to a fixed table. Minnesota was one of the first states to implement **sentencing guidelines** (DeLone and Wilmot 2004; Kramer and Johnson 2004). Subsequently, many other states established their own guidelines, such as Florida, California, and North Carolina (Crow 2004). The federal government established sentencing guidelines as well, following the extensive work of the

United States Sentencing Commission. The U.S. Sentencing Commission originated as the result of the Comprehensive Crime Control Act of 1984 and promulgated punishment guidelines for all federal crimes. These guidelines were implemented in 1987. Federal parole was abolished in 1992 and replaced with supervised release.

An example of guidelines-based or presumptive sentencing is the U.S. Sentencing Guidelines. These guidelines are shown in Table 9-1. Across the top of the table are Criminal History categories. These range from I, where offenders have little or no criminal history, to VI, which reflects persons who have the most extensive and serious criminal histories. Down the left-hand side of the table are offense levels ranging from 1 to 43. There is an offense seriousness level for every federal crime. The more serious the crime, the larger the offense seriousness score. In the body of the table where the criminal history and offense seriousness scores intersect are ranges of months. These are guidelines used by judges when sentencing offenders. Judges must remain within these month ranges in most cases. The midpoint in each month range is considered the presumptive sentence judges must impose, unless certain factors dictate otherwise. For instance, if the month range is 40–50, the presumptive number of months is 45.

TABLE 9-1   U.S. Sentencing Guidelines Grid (Sentence in Months)

Offense Level	Criminal History Category					
	I	II	III	IV	V	VI
	0 or 1	2 or 3	4, 5, 6	7, 8, 9	10, 11, 12	13 or more
1	0–1	0–2	0–3	0–4	0–5	0–6
2	0–2	0–3	0–4	0–5	0–6	1–7
3	0–3	0–4	0–5	0–6	2–8	3–9
4	0–4	0–5	0–6	2–8	4–10	6–12
5	0–5	0–6	1–7	4–10	6–12	9–15
6	0–6	1–7	2–8	6–12	9–15	12–18
7	1–7	2–8	4–10	8–14	12–18	15–21
8	2–8	4–10	6–12	10–16	15–21	18–24
9	4–10	6–12	8–14	12–18	18–24	21–27
10	6–12	8–14	10–16	15–21	21–27	24–30
11	8–14	10–16	12–18	18–24	24–30	27–33
12	10–16	12–18	15–21	21–27	27–33	30–37
13	12–18	15–21	18–24	24–30	30–37	33–41
14	15–21	18–24	21–27	27–33	33–41	37–46
15	18–24	21–27	24–30	30–37	37–46	41–51
16	21–27	24–30	27–33	33–41	41–51	46–57
17	24–30	27–33	30–37	37–46	46–57	51–63
18	27–33	30–37	33–41	41–51	51–63	57–71
19	30–37	33–41	37–46	46–57	57–71	63–78
20	33–41	37–46	41–51	51–63	63–78	70–87
21	37–46	41–51	46–57	57–71	70–87	77–96
22	41–51	46–57	51–63	63–78	77–96	84–105
23	46–57	51–63	57–71	70–87	84–105	92–115
24	51–63	57–71	63–78	77–96	92–115	100–125

25	57–71	63–78	70–87	84–105	100–125	110–137
26	63–78	70–87	78–97	92–115	110–137	120–150
27	70–87	78–97	87–108	100–125	120–150	130–162
28	78–97	87–108	97–121	110–137	130–162	140–175
29	87–108	97–121	108–135	121–151	140–175	151–188
30	97–121	108–135	121–151	135–168	151–188	168–210
31	108–135	121–151	135–168	151–188	168–210	188–235
32	121–151	135–168	151–188	168–210	188–235	210–262
33	135–168	151–188	168–210	188–235	210–262	235–293
34	151–188	168–210	188–235	210–262	235–293	262–327
35	168–210	188–235	210–262	235–293	262–327	292–365
36	188–235	210–262	235–293	262–327	292–365	324–405
37	210–262	235–293	262–327	292–365	324–405	360–life
38	235–293	262–327	292–365	324–405	360–life	360–life
39	262–327	292–365	324–405	360–life	360–life	360–life
40	292–365	324–405	360–life	360–life	360–life	360–life
41	324–405	360–life	360–life	360–life	360–life	360–life
42	360–life	360–life	360–life	360–life	360–life	360–life
43	Life	Life	Life	Life	Life	Life

Source: U.S. Sentencing Commission. U.S. Sentencing Guidelines, Washington, DC: U.S. Government Printing Office, 1997.

If the range is 3–40 months, then 35 would be the presumptive number of months. Judges may move upward or downward within each range, depending upon whether there are aggravating or mitigating circumstances. They may impose sentences outside of any particular month range if they believe there are circumstances to justify such departures (Ulmer 2004). Several recent Supreme Court decisions have altered the presumptiveness of the current federal sentencing guideline structure. In the case of *United States v. Booker* (2005), for instance, the Supreme Court stated that the guidelines were no longer mandatory for judge, only advisory. What this means is that judges still must consider the guidelines in a decision about an appropriate sentence for a given defendant; however, they are no longer required to apply the presumptive guideline sentence. Judges, therefore, now have more discretion to mete out what they believe is an appropriate sentence. (See "Case Law: Sentencing Guidelines No Longer Mandatory" for more on the *Booker* decision.)

According to Kauder and Ostrom (2008), although there is some debate about whether some states are actively using sentencing guidelines, there were 21 states who had adopted presumptive sentencing or guidelines-based schemes. About half of the states adopted what have been characterized as voluntary (meaning judges are not required by law to follow them) guidelines, while the others have mandatory sentencing guidelines. Presumptive sentencing is considered one of the most promising sentencing reforms because of its potential for minimizing sentencing disparities according to extralegal factors, minimizing incarceration rates, and reducing prison overcrowding. Similar conclusions have been reached by those investigating different dispositional schemes for juvenile offenders (Champion 2005b).

Many states have sentencing reform acts to change the ways convicted offenders are sentenced. The federal government passed the **Sentencing Reform Act of 1984**, which led to the creation of the U.S. Sentencing Commission and a revision of the entire federal criminal code. Also in Washington, the state's Sentencing Reform Act of 1981 established determinate sentencing for felonies. But various deficiencies in determinate sentencing laws have caused state officials to modify their existing sentencing policy with a more structured one, a sentencing system that will obligate sentenced offenders to make frugal use of institutional resources in becoming rehabilitated. Thus, with new sentencing guidelines, the Washington Sentencing Guidelines Commission expects to address the following issues: truth in sentencing, prosecution standards, sentencing standards and ranges, juvenile dispositions, and mentally ill offenders (Champion 2005b).

BOX 9.1

CASE LAW: Sentencing Guidelines No Longer Mandatory

Blakely v. Washington 542 U.S. 296 (2004)

Pursuant to a plea bargain agreement in Washington, Ralph Blakely pleaded guilty to kidnapping his estranged wife and was convicted of second-degree kidnapping involving domestic violence and the use of a firearm. In his plea agreement, Blakely admitted to the kidnapping and to limited facts that supported a maximum sentence of 53 months under Washington's guidelines sentencing scheme. However, the judge rejected the prosecutor's recommended 49- to 53-month sentence and instead imposed an exceptional sentence of 90 months, 37 months longer than contemplated by the plea agreement. The judge justified his departure because of "deliberate cruelty" exhibited by Blakely, because the maximum sentence is up to ten years, and because "deliberate cruelty" is an aggravating factor under Washington's Sentencing Reform Act. Blakely appealed, contending that this sentencing procedure denied him the right to have a jury determine all facts legally essential to his sentence. The Washington Supreme Court denied Blakely's appeal and the case was heard by the U.S. Supreme Court. The U.S. Supreme Court invalidated Blakely's 90-month sentence, holding that because the facts supporting Blakely's exceptional sentence were neither admitted in the plea agreement nor found by a jury, the sentence violated his Sixth Amendment right to a trial by jury. The U.S. Supreme Court elaborated, stating the trial judge could not have imposed the exceptional 90-month sentence solely on the basis of the facts admitted in the guilty plea. According to U.S. Supreme Court precedent, statutory maximum sentences are maximum sentences judges may impose solely on the basis of the facts reflected in a jury verdict or admitted by the defendant. The U.S. Supreme Court further noted that this decision does not question Washington's sentencing guidelines scheme or its constitutionality. Rather, it reflects the scope of judicial discretion in sentencing under the circumstances of this case.

United States v. Booker 543 U.S. 220 (2005)

Booker and another defendant in an unrelated case, Fanfan, were convicted in separate jury trials in different federal district courts of cocaine distribution. In Booker's case, a 21-year, 10-month sentence was prescribed for his conviction offense by the U.S. Sentencing Guidelines. However, during the sentencing hearing, the judge found additional facts by a preponderance of the evidence to support a sentence of 360 months to life and gave Booker a 30-year sentence. In Fanfan's case, a judge made a similar finding and imposed a harsher sentence, 16 years instead of the 6 years prescribed by the U.S. Sentencing Guidelines, on Fanfan. Both cases were appealed, Booker's to the Seventh Circuit and Fanfan's to the First Circuit. Both circuit courts overturned these convictions, holding that any fact(s) that increase the penalty for a crime beyond the prescribed statutory maximum must be submitted to a jury and proved beyond a reasonable doubt. The government appealed both cases and the U.S. Supreme Court heard them. The U.S. Supreme Court affirmed the circuit court decisions and vacated the enhanced sentences for both Booker and Fanfan. The U.S. Supreme Court held that the federal sentencing guidelines are subject to Sixth Amendment jury trial requirements, and that if a judge authorizes a punishment on the finding of a fact, that fact, no matter how the judge labels it, must be found by a jury beyond a reasonable doubt.

> ### *United States v. Kimbrough* 552 U.S. 85 (2007)
>
> The *Kimbrough* case has to do with the mandatory minimum trigger ratio between powder and crack cocaine. During the Reagan administration's war on drugs, Congress passed a law requiring a five-year mandatory minimum for those convicted of possession of 500 grams of cocaine powder; the same five-year minimum would apply to someone convicted of possessing only five grams of crack cocaine. This law created a 100–1 disparity in the trigger for the minimum. Kimbrough pleaded guilty to distribution of 50 grams of crack cocaine. Under the federal sentencing guidelines Kimbrough's sentence ranged from 19 to $22^1/_2$ years. The judge in the case believed that this sentence was too harsh and gave Kimbrough 15 years instead citing the ruling in *Booker*. The Court of Appeals for the Fourth Circuit rejected the sentence citing that a judge cannot depart from the guidelines due to disagreement with federal sentencing policy. The Supreme Court in a 7–2 opinion in favor of the judge and Kimbrough reversed the Fourth Circuit stating that because *Booker* made the guidelines advisory, the judge could reasonably depart from the presumptive sentence. This case set precedent for the idea that the district courts can deviate from the 100:1 crack-to-powder cocaine sentencing minimum ratio.

Perhaps the most immediate impact of newly implemented presumptive sentencing guidelines is the reduction of sentencing disparities, where similar offenders receive widely divergent sentences (Davis-Frenzel and Spohn 2004). In Minnesota, for example, a 22 percent decline in **sentencing disparity** was observed to occur in the year following the implementation of guidelines. A 60 percent reduction in sentencing inequality for the length-of-time-in-prison decision was also observed. But even presumptive sentencing guidelines can be circumvented by creative sentencing judges (Geoghagan 2004). One way of seemingly curbing such abuses of discretion is through mandatory sentences where judges must impose specific terms regardless of their own views and prejudices (Piquero and Davis 2004).

Although state sentencing guideline schemes seem to provide more uniform sentences for similarly situated offenders, recent research on the federal sentencing guidelines has shown that disparities according to race/ethnicity and gender still exist especially across district courts. Spohn (2005) for instance found significant sentencing differences across three federal district courts, and Ulmer (2005) and Johnson, Ulmer, and Kramer (2008) found inter-district variation regarding departures from the guidelines. Hartley (2008) likewise found similar interdistrict variation in the sentences given to narcotics offenders in four federal districts in the southwestern United States. The findings from these studies call into question the idea that adopting sentencing guidelines will necessarily result in increased uniformity and amelioration of disparity.

Mandatory Sentencing

Mandatory sentencing is the obligatory imposition of a specified period of years and/or months for specific types of offenses. Judges are bound to impose a **mandatory sentence** for certain types of conviction offenses. For instance, Michigan has a mandatory penalty of two years for using a gun during the commission of a felony and under federal law there are over 60 mandatory minimums that cover over 100 offenses (Tonry 1996). The use-a-gun-and-go-to-prison law in Michigan is added to whatever sentence is imposed when offenders are convicted. Thus, a bank robber might be sentenced in Michigan to 20 years, with an additional 2 years as a mandatory sentence for using a firearm when robbing the bank. When all or part of the offender's 20-year term is served, a mandatory additional 2 years must be served by the offender for the weapons offense. The intent of this mandatory law is to discourage criminals from using weapons when they commit crimes. Weapons-use reductions by criminals usually mean fewer serious injuries or deaths resulting from their crimes. The deterrent effect of Michigan's law and other states with similar laws is presently unknown.

The most important feature of mandatory sentencing is the obligation it places on judges to impose consistent sentences for a variety of convicted offenders, regardless of their gender, race or ethnicity, or socioeconomic status. Under these mandatory sentencing provisions, judges must impose specific sentences as authorized by their state legislatures. However, even mandatory sentencing policies may be circumvented. Prosecutors may choose to ignore those aspects of one's crime that carry mandatory penalties. Larger numbers of plea bargains are obtained if certain facts about one's crime are ignored. Armed robbery may be downgraded to simple robbery, for instance. The fact that a firearm was used in the offense is not mentioned. Even in the presentence investigation report prepared by probation officers, certain facts may be omitted. Thus, sentencing judges may never see the full set of circumstances involving the crime committed. If crimes with mandatory penalties are not included in the prosecutor's information or charges, and if these facts are also omitted in the plea bargain agreement, the judge imposes a sentence consistent with presumptive guidelines or determinate sentencing.

Such a scenario occurs too frequently throughout the United States, according to some critics. Many law-and-order proponents advocate greater truth in sentencing. If someone uses a gun when committing a crime, then this fact ought to be made known to the court. Further, if the convicted offender is a recidivist with prior felony convictions, this information ought to be made known to the court. All states have habitual offender statutes that apply to **habitual offenders** with lengthy criminal records. These persons are in jeopardy of being given a **life-without-parole sentence** as a mandatory sentence for their conviction as habitual offenders.

HABITUAL OFFENDER STATUTES AND TRUTH-IN-SENTENCING LAWS

Habitual Offender Statutes

Chronic, persistent, and violent felony offenders pose the greatest risk to the public. These criminals commit new crimes frequently, and these crimes often result in serious victim injuries and/or deaths. There is also a broad class of chronic and persistent felony offenders who commit property crimes, such as larceny, vehicular theft, and burglary. All types of chronic recidivists have been targeted in recent decades for special and harsher treatment by the criminal justice system. Since the 1970s, virtually every jurisdiction throughout the United States has evolved habitual offender statutes (Champion 2005b). In some jurisdictions, these laws are called **persistent offender statutes**. Habitual offender or persistent offender statutes are laws that proscribe life sentences for those who are convicted of three or more felonies.

The intent of habitual offender statutes is to incapacitate those who persist in committing crimes. If these high-rate offenders are removed from society, then some crime prevention or crime control occurs. The primary problem is that there are so many persistent and chronic felony offenders that there isn't enough prison space to house them for extended terms. Furthermore, more than a few inmates convicted as habitual offenders have filed lawsuits challenging their lengthy prison sentences compared with the nonserious nature of their conviction offenses. These are usually *habeas corpus* actions, where relief is sought in the form of sentence reductions (Fletcher 2004). Also, some experts do not consider these statutes as particularly beneficial as deterrents or methods of crime control (Freedman 2001; Hack 2003).

WHO ARE HABITUAL OFFENDERS?   A key problem confronted by all jurisdictions with habitual offender statutes is defining who are the habitual offenders. Do habitual offenders include all types of offenders, or is the definition limited to those committing only the most serious and violent types of felonies? This problem seems universal in nature. England, for instance, has been vexed by the problem of habitual offender legislation and its inability to provide precise guidance about who qualify as habitual offenders. Are habitual offenders only violent criminals who pose an immediate threat to society, or are they also the bumbling petty thieves and property offenders?

Florida has attempted to refine the habitual offender definition by establishing a limited number of categories and a guideline matrix (Champion 2005b). Thus, not every Florida felon with numerous convictions qualifies as habitual offender. Further, Florida law provides for gradations in offense seriousness and whether certain convicted offenders will be classified as habitual offenders.

A subsequent study of the application of Florida's habitual offender statute has generated an offender database consisting of 25,806 persons eligible for habitualization. Interestingly, only 18 percent or 4,783 persons from this database were actually prosecuted and convicted as habitual offenders (Florida Joint Legislative Management Committee 1992). This finding is consistent with the earlier work of Hunzeker (1985), who found that although every state has habitual offender statutes, relatively few inmates are serving sentences as habitual offenders. In fact, eight states have reported that 2–3 percent of the inmates were serving terms as habitual offenders. Nine states reported that less than 1 percent of their inmate populations were serving terms as habitual offenders.

The consensus is that while all states have habitual offender statutes, most states do not enforce these habitual offender statutes with any consistency (Champion 2005b). More often than not, prosecutors in most jurisdictions use habitual offender statutes as mechanisms of coercion to elicit guilty pleas from persistent offenders. Thus, prosecutors threaten to prosecute particular habitual criminals as habitual offenders unless they agree to plead guilty to other crimes. This sort of leverage is perfectly legal and is not considered coercive by the U.S. Supreme Court (*Bordenkircher v. Hayes*, 1978).

NARROWING THE HABITUAL OFFENDER DEFINITION: THREE-STRIKES-AND-YOU'RE-OUT!   In recent years, the federal government and various states have enacted provisions to punish more serious felons with harsh punishments if they are convicted of three or more felonies. Such legislation is termed **three-strikes-and-you're-out**. Essentially, offenders convicted of three serious felonies are out in that they are sentenced to life terms in prison. The get-tough movement and general public seem supportive of legislation aimed at incapacitating persistent felony offenders (Ueckert 2005).

California is one of several jurisdictions that have passed three-strikes-and-you're-out legislation. California's three-strikes legislation mandates that felons found guilty of a third serious crime must be locked up for 25 years to life. The long-term effects of this legislation on California's correctional population have recently been realized. Most of California's prisons are operating at 150 percent of maximum capacity and some are housing twice as many as they were designed to. With the recent economic downturn, California does not have sufficient prison space to accommodate all of these offenders presently, despite the fact that it has one of the nation's most vigorous prison construction programs (Stephenson-Lang 2005). In 2010, the California legislature along with Governor Schwarzenegger were devising plans to release upwards of 60,000 inmates due to court orders and budget constraints. Clearly, states looking to pass increasingly tough habitual offender statutes will want to look to the California experience and the annual costs incurred by implementing these types of laws.

A FELONY IS A FELONY IS A FELONY ...   Some attempt has been made by California and other states to limit the types of offenses that qualify under the habitual offender statute and three-strikes legislation. Distinctions have been made between those who commit **violent felonies** (rape, murder, aggravated assault, armed robbery), **serious felonies** (robbery, drug dealing), and **felony property offending** (larceny/theft, vehicular theft, burglary). In theory, at least, the most serious persistent felons will be given 25 years to life, while less serious felons will receive shorter sentences. But few states, including California, have found the three-strikes legislation to be effective in reducing violent crime (Ueckert 2005).

Furthermore, three-strikes legislation has sometimes resulted in greater racial and ethnic discrimination by targeting proportionately larger numbers of blacks and others for long mandatory sentences. In California, for instance, blacks are arrested at a rate 4.7 times greater than that of whites; blacks are incarcerated 7.8 times greater than whites; and blacks are incarcerated as habitual offenders at a rate that is 13 times greater than that of whites. California is not an isolated case, however. Disparities in mandatory sentencing laws according to race, gender, socioeconomic status, and ethnicity have been found to exist in other jurisdictions (Champion 2005b).

Use-a-Gun-and-Go-to-Prison Statutes

Not all mandatory penalties involve **life imprisonment** or life without parole. Some mandatory penalties are intended to downgrade the seriousness of violent crimes whenever they are committed. One way of discouraging some violent offenders from using firearms when committing their crimes is to provide mandatory sentences of incarceration whenever firearms are used (Lightfoot and Umbreit 2004). Other types of mandatory penalties are associated with crimes such as repeat-offense driving-while-intoxicated cases.

Michigan has enacted a mandatory penalty for using a firearm during the commission of a felony. This penalty is a **flat term,** a two-year sentence that must be served following whatever other sentence is imposed. Thus, if someone is convicted of armed robbery, a sentence of 10–20 years might be imposed for the armed robbery charge, and then a separate sentence of 2 years will be added on to the original sentence. This second sentence must be served in its entirety. If the offender is parole-eligible after serving 15 years of the 10- to 20-year sentence, then the 2-year sentence commences. No time off for good behavior will be extended to those serving these mandatory sentences. California enacted such a law over a decade before Michigan (Champion 2005b). Presently, most states have such mandatory sentencing provisions for firearms usage whenever felonies are committed.

Many of these mandatory sentences are primarily symbolic, in that they show the public that the legislature and other politicians are concerned about public safety and citizen fear of crime. Frequently, mandatory penalties are circumvented by defense counsel, prosecutors, and judges through plea bargaining, where the violations incurring mandatory penalties are carefully omitted from any reports or written documents. Many presentence investigation reports are doctored by probation officers at the request of prosecutors, so that judges will be more willing to impose variable sentences under indeterminate or determinate sentencing. If judges don't know whether particular defendants used a firearm when a felony was committed, then they cannot be compelled to impose mandatory penalties, even in Michigan. However, more than few jurisdictions have made it increasingly difficult for these mandatory sentencing provisions to be circumvented. The federal sentencing guidelines and changed roles of U.S. probation officers have greatly restricted the degree to which certain aspects of one's crime can be ignored (Champion 2005b).

Truth in Sentencing

The federal Violent Crime Control and Law Enforcement Act of 1994 provided monies to states that changed their sentencing provisions and adopt harsher sanctions known as truth-in-sentencing statutes. **Truth-in-sentencing** statutes were a response to the reality that the actual time an offender serves is prison is always shorter than the time the judge sentenced them to serve. For instance, according to a Bureau of Justice Report, violent offenders released in 1996 served an average of 45 months before being released despite that the average sentence handed out to them was 85 months (Ditton and Wilson 1999). Under truth in sentencing, however, violent offenders admitted to prison in 1996 would serve an average of 88 months in prison, almost double the current time serve for those released in 1996 (Ditton and Wilson 1999). Truth-in-sentencing statutes, therefore, also contribute to prison overcrowding as the average time served is now considerably higher. According the Bureau of Justice about 27 states have adopted the 85 percent minimum time served standard, requiring that all convicted offenders would have to serve at least 85 percent of their maximum sentences before becoming parole-eligible. A few other states like Texas and Nebraska have adopted a 50 percent of sentence standard, and still a few other states like Idaho, Nevada, and New Hampshire have adopted a 100 percent time served minimum. Politicians wanting to look like they are tough on crime and outcry from the public about the fact that inmates in many states have been serving only fractions of their actual sentences have led to reforms such as these.

While truth-in-sentencing laws have been enacted and the public's feelings have been assuaged to a degree, corrections officials have struggled to find more space for those offenders spending longer terms in prison. The direct result of truth in sentencing has been enormous prison population growth. Prison overcrowding is now a characteristic of all U.S. prisons. A significant contributing factor has been the **Crime Bill of 1994**. President Bill Clinton promoted this bill to provide for greater numbers of police officers on city streets as a means of preventing crime. Another provision of this bill was to maximize offender sentences so that convicted persons must serve between 80 and 90 percent of the maximum sentences before being granted early release or parole.

Originally, the intent of truth-in-sentencing provisions was to make sure that inmates would serve a large portion of their prison terms (McManimon 2005a). While this event has occurred in those jurisdictions where it has been mandated by state legislatures, other problems have been created. For instance, in 1994, before the Federal Crime Bill, North Dakota was one of six states without an overcrowding problem. The state prison in Bismarck could house about 650 inmates. Shortly after enacting truth-in-sentencing laws, however, the North Dakota Penitentiary in Bismarck quickly became overcrowded and a new prison facility had to be built in Jamestown. In 1998, North Dakota officials were planning two additional tiers in the Jamestown prison facility as dramatic increases in the inmate population were projected. Thus, North Dakota taxpayers now face unprecedented tax increases to help defray some or all of the new prison construction.

While the public may want tougher laws such as truth in sentencing requiring longer prison terms for inmates, they may not want to pay the dollar cost of new prison construction in order for this policy to remain in place. Most states now have major prison overcrowding problems and state budgets that are too tight to begin any new construction of prison facilities.

Summary

Although sentences for similar offenders may vary across the states and in the federal criminal justice system, goals and functions of sentencing are more or less universal. The goals of punishment include retribution, incapacitation, rehabilitation, restoration, and deterrence.

Punishment is the primary sentencing objective. Persons who have violated the law and been convicted of one or more crimes must be held accountable for these acts in some way. Punishment, usually proportional to the seriousness and nature of the offense, is a suitable measure to be taken against convicted offenders. Punishments are generally restrictive, in that convicted persons are limited in their freedom to move about in their communities. They suffer losses such as the right to vote or to possess firearms.

Retribution focuses on the harm done and what the offender deserves for inflicting that harm. Although the notion of *lex talionis* and an eye for an eye are not applied in reality today, proportionality, or that the punishment should fit the crime, is a major goal of sentencing today.

Incapacitation as a goal of sentencing seeks to remove offenders from society, at least temporarily, so that such offenders cannot commit new crimes against citizens. Prisons and jails in many jurisdictions have been increasingly used to warehouse offenders, to remove them from public view, and to place them in circumstances where they pose no threats to others. This is a form of crime control, since incapacitated persons are not in a position to reoffend. Persons who are career criminals or chronic recidivists and who make their livelihood from crime are especially targeted for incarceration, and for lengthy periods.

Although rehabilitation is a sentencing goal, many persons believe that no type of sentencing or punishment is truly rehabilitative. Although vocational, technical, educational, and other useful programs are offered to persons convicted of crimes and incarcerated or placed under community supervision of some form, high recidivism rates among offenders suggest that only about a third of all convicted persons actually benefit from these programs. For those with addictions or who suffer from psychological problems, individual or group counseling and other treatment programs and therapies exist to assist them. But the benefits of these programs are limited to a small proportion of those willing to utilize these resources effectively. Thus, cynicism often characterizes the public view toward rehabilitation as a correctional goal.

Restoration seeks to repair the harm that was done and is a more holistic approach to justice by including the offender, the victim, and the larger community in decisions about appropriate punishments. Although for some serious and violent crimes this may not be possible, restorative justice seeks to restore relationships or return things to the way they were before the crime occurred, thereby hopefully preventing future criminal events from occurring again.

Sentencing also attempts to send the message that violating the law will have adverse consequences for criminals, and that they will be caught and convicted for their crimes. The severity of their punishment seeks to deter them and others from repeating these acts in the future. But the deterrent effects of sentencing are questionable. It is unknown to what extent sentencing, even tough sentences imposed, actually functions to prevent crime and deter those punished from committing new crimes when they are eventually released.

Reintegration is also important to prevent future offending. Reintegrative programs seek to maintain a convicted person's connection with his/her communities, families, and work. Probation is used as a punishment to foster reintegration, and parole permits incarcerated persons to be released short of serving their full sentences in order to live law-abiding lives through the assistance of parole officers and others.

Several types of sentencing are being used as methods for determining appropriate punishments for offenders. All of these sentencing schemes have been criticized for different reasons, largely because they seem ineffective at accomplishing their various goals and functions. No sentencing system seems to work perfectly in any jurisdiction, and thus considerable experimentation with different sentencing variations has been observed.

Four basic types of sentencing schemes have been described. These include indeterminate sentencing, determinate sentencing, presumptive or guidelines-based sentencing, and mandatory sentencing.

Indeterminate sentencing has been used for over two centuries. This sentencing form specifies a minimum and maximum sentence, with one's early release from incarceration being determined by a paroling authority or equivalent body.

Determinate sentencing is similar to indeterminate sentencing, but early releases of inmates are governed by an accumulation of good-time credits, or days off one's maximum sentence for so many days served. A shift from indeterminate to determinate sentencing occurred during the 1970s. It was believed that parole board discretion was not entirely objective and ineffective. But removing discretionary power over one's early release has raised concerns among citizens and legislators that some inmates may be released automatically when it is believed that they should remain incarcerated for longer periods. There are no easy solutions to these particular sentencing conflicts and problems (Levine 2005).

Presumptive or guidelines-based sentencing has been used for several decades, by both the federal government and different states. Each crime is given a seriousness score, and one's criminal history or prior record and other factors are combined to determine an approximate range of months to be served. The middle number of months of any specified range is the presumptive sentence, and aggravating or mitigating factors can increase or decrease the number of months of incarceration imposed within the recommended range. But the U.S. Supreme Court has declared that at least for the federal government, the sentencing guidelines it created in 1987 are merely recommended sentencing ranges judges must follow. The intended function of sentencing guidelines is to create greater fairness in sentencing, where extralegal factors such as gender, socioeconomic status, race, and/or ethnicity are not serious considerations. The implementation of sentencing guidelines was originally intended to limit or remove sentencing disparities among different judges according to these and other extralegal variables. However, despite the establishment of guidelines, sentencing disparities continue to exist in all jurisdictions.

Mandatory sentences mean that offenders must serve flat time, or full sentences of incarceration without any time deducted from their sentence maximums for good behavior, however significant that behavior may be.

Habitual offender statutes or chronic offender provisions seek to impose mandatory sentences on offenders who have been convicted of three or more felonies. California's three-strikes-and-you're-out law was intended to impose life sentences on persistent dangerous felons. It is believed that these mandatory penalties associated with the use of firearms during the commission of a felony will decrease the incidence of deaths of innocent bystanders and others if deadly weapons use carries mandatory incarcerative penalties. The effectiveness of these measures has been questioned, since deaths of persons from firearms use during crimes have not diminished significantly since such mandatory sentencing laws have gone into effect.

Many states have truth-in-sentencing provisions, where legislatures have acted to provide that convicted persons should serve most of their sentences instead of smaller portions of them. Violations of federal criminal laws require that convicted federal offenders must serve at least 85 percent of their sentences before becoming eligible for early release. Many states have emulated the federal government by passing similar legislation. However, truth-in-sentencing laws have done little to deter violent crime, and in many jurisdictions, mandatory sentencing provisions and truth-in-sentencing laws have been either ignored or circumvented through plea bargaining and other sentencing options (Champion 2005a).

Questions for Review

1. What are four general functions or aims of sentencing?
2. How does indeterminate sentencing differ from determinate sentencing?
3. What constraints are imposed on judges by presumptive or guidelines-based and mandatory sentencing schemes?
4. What is a habitual offender statute? Do most states have such statutes? Are these statutes used frequently by these states? Why or why not? Explain.
5. What is a use-a-gun-and-go-to-prison statute?
6. What is meant by truth in sentencing? How is truth in sentencing achieved?

Suggested Readings

1. J. Austin and J. Irwin (2001). *It's About Time: America's Imprisonment Binge* (3rd ed). Belmont, CA: Wadsworth.
2. M. S. Crow and K. A. Johnson (2008). "Race, Ethnicity, and Habitual Offender Sentencing." *Criminal Justice Policy Review* **19:**63–83.
3. B. D. Johnson, J. T. Ulmer, and J. H. Kramer (2008). "The Social Context of Guidelines Circumvention: The Case of Federal District Courts." *Criminology* **46:**737–783.
4. C. Spohn (2000). *Thirty Years of Sentencing Reform: The Quest for a Racially Neutral Sentencing Process. Policies, Processes, and Decisions of the Criminal Justice System.* Washington, DC: United States Department of Justice.
5. J. T. Ulmer, J. Eisenstein, and B. D. Johnson (2010). "Trial Penalties in Federal Sentencing: Extra-Guidelines Factors and District Variation." *Justice Quarterly* **27:**560–592.
6. M. Zatz (2000). "The Convergence of Race, Ethnicity, Gender, and Class on Court Decisionmaking: Looking Toward the 21st Century." In J. Horney, J. Martin, D. L. MacKenzie, R. D. Peterson, and D. Rosenbaum, *Policies, Processes, and Decisions of the Criminal Justice System: Criminal Justice 2000*, Vol. 3, pp. 503–552. Washington, DC: U. S. Department of Justice.

CHAPTER 10

Judicial Sentencing Options, Sentencing Disparities, and Appeals

CHAPTER OBJECTIVES

As a result of reading this chapter, you will have accomplished the following objectives:

1. Understand the options that judges have at sentencing and that these vary by type of crime and jurisdiction.
2. Understand sentencing disparities and how factors such as race/ethnicity, gender, socioeconomic status, and age affect one's sentence.
3. Describe the sentencing hearing and its various functions.
4. Describe presentence investigation reports, their contents and components, preparation, and usefulness in the sentencing process.

5. Understand victim impact statements, the circumstances under which such statements are appended to presentence investigation reports, and the usefulness of such statements in the sentencing process.
6. Describe the death penalty and bifurcated trials, including the functions of such trial proceedings. Understand the appeals process, who initiates appeals, various bases for appeals, including *habeas corpus* petitions, tort claims, and civil rights Section 1983 actions.

KEY TERMS

Acceptance of
  responsibility
affirm
aggravating circumstances
appeal
appellants
appellees
argument
bifurcated trial
brief
circumstantial evidence

conditions of confinement
death penalty
death row
defendant's sentencing
  memorandum
dissenting opinion
DNA fingerprinting
intermittent sentencing
isolation
jail as a condition of
  probation

mistrial
mitigating circumstances
mixed sentencing
narrative
notice of appeal
opinion
oral argument
pardon
probation officer
reversed and remanded
sentencing hearing

sentencing
  memorandum
shock incarceration
shock parole
shock probation
solitary confinement
split sentencing
stare decisis
warrant
wrongful
  convictions

A judge in Arlington, Virginia, offered defendant Michael Guerra the opportunity to avoid incarceration by joining the military. Guerra could have been sent to jail for up to a year after pleading guilty to aggravated assault. Mr. Guerra's attorney informed the judge on his intent to enlist in the military and the judge offered Guerra a choice, join the military or go to jail. Army spokespersons, however, stated that the military has regulations which disallow those facing criminal charges to enlist. If the judge sentenced Guerra to probation, this would bar him from joining the Army; however, if the judge grants him a conditional discharge with the condition being that he joins the Army, Guerra may be able to enlist. What do you think? Should a judge have the power and discretion to sentence someone to the armed forces? Should the Army have to accept these persons into their ranks? What if the offender doesn't meet the requirements of enlistment? Do you think joining the military is an equitable alternative to incarceration in jail?

Source: Adapted from "Judge said Army or jail, but military doesn't want him," available online at: www.stripes.com.

INTRODUCTION

For most serious crimes, incarceration is an option that judges have when deciding an appropriate sentence. Other options may include probation or some other alternative type of punishment; for those convicted of a capital crime, the **death penalty** is also a punishment option that can be invoked. In the United States the most often used punishments are incarceration and probation. Critics have argued that a just system of sentencing would allow for other options for the sentencing judge, especially those in between prison and probation or what are referred to as intermediate punishments (Morris and Tonry 1990). A discussion of both shock probation and split sentencing is also given. Most convicted felony offenders receive some incarceration time as part of their sentence, whereas convicted misdemeanants most often receive probation with certain conditions attached. A great deal of research has been conducted regarding judicial sentencing decisions and what factors judges consider when meting out appropriate punishments. As justice is supposed to be blind, most of this research focuses on examining whether extralegal factors (race/ethnicity, gender, age, and socioeconomic status) play a role in the decision-making practices of judges. Some of the results of this research are discussed.

A sentencing hearing is held following one's conviction. This hearing is to examine various aggravating and mitigating circumstances that exacerbate one's punishment or lessen it. Usually victims or their relatives speak out against convicted offenders during these hearings, while offenders' relatives and close friends speak out in their behalf. Judges ultimately decide the punishment, which often is codified according to the seriousness of the offense.

The next section examines presentence investigation reports (PSIs), or documents that are usually prepared by probation officers. These reports contain a vast amount of information about the crime one has committed, his/her version of events, the police report, a victim impact statement (VIS), and the background of the defendant. Judges use PSIs in their sentencing decisions, although it is unknown how much credence such reports receive. These reports are also used later in parole decision making when parole boards are considering certain inmates for early release. The format and contents of PSIs are described and discussed. Other sentencing options are included and described, such as shock probation and split sentencing. Their implications for offenders are presented.

In death penalty cases, the U.S. Supreme Court has declared that such proceedings should be conducted in the form of bifurcated trials, where the trials consist of two stages. The first stage is to determine the guilt or innocence of the defendant. If the defendant is guilty, then the jury reconvenes and determines the sentence to be imposed. This sentence may be death or life imprisonment or several other sentencing options.

All convictions may be appealed. The next section of this chapter examines the appeal process. Several important bases for appeals are described. These include *habeas corpus* petitions, which challenge the length, nature, and fact of confinement. Another basis for appeals may be through a tort claim. Finally, inmates may appeal on the basis that their civil rights were violated in some way. This civil rights litigation is through the Fourteenth Amendment and is called a Section 1983 action, since it is found in Title 42, Section 1983, of the U.S. Code. Each of these bases for appeal is described, and examples are provided illustrating their use by inmates.

Appealing a case to higher courts is also described. The U.S. Supreme Court may be petitioned through a writ of *certiorari*, and the appeals process is rather lengthy. It may be several years from the time an appeal is filed before it is eventually heard by the high court. Many cases are not heard at all and are dismissed because they lack merit or are frivolous. The appeals process is discussed and several implications for convicted offenders are indicated.

JUDICIAL OPTIONS AT SENTENCING

Incarceration

Because many jurisdictions have enacted increasingly tougher laws in the last two decades including adopting determinate, guidelines-based, or mandatory sentencing schemes, for certain types of offenders and for certain criminal offenses, incarceration is not an option; it is a requirement (Spohn 2009). In other words, in many jurisdictions, especially for serious and repeat offenders, judges do not have any discretion to decide between prison and probation; the offender must be sent to prison. In some cases, where presumptive guidelines are in place, the judge may have little say in the length of the sentence as well. For less serious cases and jurisdictions that still practice indeterminate sentencing, however, judges have fairly wide discretion to tailor a sentence that they deem appropriate; they have the option to send the offender to prison or give them probation. Sometimes this may depend on whether the convicted offender pleads guilty through some sort of plea agreement; in others, it is left to the judge to decide.

As stated earlier, judges often exercise their right to incarcerate offenders. In fact, the United States has one of the highest incarceration rates in the world. The United States has 5 percent of the world's population, yet we house 25 percent of the world's prisoners (Liptak 2008). Table 10-1 displays the percentage of felony defendants sentenced to prison or jail

TABLE 10-1   Types of Felony Sentences Imposed in State Courts, by Offense, 2006

		Percent of felons sentenced to					
		Incarceration			Nonincarceration		
Most serious conviction offense	Total (%)	Total	Prison	Jail	Total	Probation	Other
All offenses	100	69	41	28	31	27	4
Violent offenses	100	77	54	23	23	20	3
Murder/Nonnegligent manslaughter	100	95	93	2	5	3	2
Sexual assault	100	81	64	18	19	16	3
Rape	100	86	72	15	14	10	4
Other sexual assault[a]	100	77	58	20	23	20	2
Robbery	100	85	71	14	15	13	2
Aggravated assault	100	72	43	30	28	25	3

TABLE 10.1 Continued

Other violent[b]	100	70	39	30	30	26	4
Property offenses	100	67	38	29	33	29	4
Burglary	100	73	49	24	27	24	3
Larceny	100	69	34	34	31	28	3
Motor vehicle theft	100	83	42	41	17	15	2
Fraud/Forgery[c]	100	59	32	27	41	35	6
Drug offenses	100	65	38	28	35	30	4
Possession	100	63	33	31	37	33	4
Trafficking	100	67	41	26	33	29	4
Weapon offenses	100	73	45	28	27	25	2
Other specified offenses[d]	100	70	36	34	30	27	3

Note: For persons receiving a combination of sentences, the sentence designation came from the most severe penalty imposed, with prison being the most severe, followed by jail, probation, and then other sentences, such as a fine, community service, or house arrest. Prison includes death sentences. In this table "probation" is defined as straight probation. Detail may not sum to total because of rounding. Data on sentence type were reported for 98 percent of the estimated total of 1,132,290 convicted felons. Percentages are based on reported data.

[a]Includes offenses such as statutory rape and incest with a minor.

[b]Includes offenses such as negligent manslaughter and kidnapping.

[c]Includes embezzlement.

[d]Comprises nonviolent offenses such as vandalism and receiving stolen property.

Source: Sean P. Rosenmerkel, Mattew R. Durose and Donald J. Farole, Jr. (2009), Bureau of Justice Statistics, National Judicial Reporting Program.

(incarceration) and probation (nonincarceration). As can be seen, for all offenses together about one-third of defendants receive probation and the other two-third are incarcerated; 41 percent are sent to prison and 28 percent are sent to jail. Obviously, incarceration rates increase where the crimes are more serious; for instance, only 3 percent of murderers receive probation, 93 percent are sent to prison, and 2 percent are sent to jail. From this table, it can be seen why the United States has one of the highest incarceration rates in the world, as even the majority of property and drug offenders receive prison or jail time.

With the inception of mandatory minimum statutes and truth-in-sentencing laws, these inmates are also spending longer periods of time incarcerated. It will be interesting to see if the United States can continue this incarceration trend or if there will be a tipping point at which our imprisonment binge (Austin and Irwin 2001) has to stop. Numerous states are experimenting with alternatives to incarceration, especially for those who have committed nonviolent offenses, in order to keep the costs of punishment down as well as to help curb recidivism rates (rehabilitate and reintegrate offenders).

Probation

In Table 10-1 we learned that roughly 27 percent of all offenders receive probationary sentences meaning that they are not required to spend time in prison or jail. Probation allows offenders to remain in the community and keep ties with family, employers, and perhaps even educational institutions. Although they are not subject to the rigorous structure and interaction with other convicted offenders that occurs in prison, probationers are still under the control of the criminal justice system and are thus required to comply with certain conditions. These conditions range from random alcohol and drug testing and vocational and educational training to restitution, community service, and/or other restrictions (curfews, counseling). All probationers are required to obey the law (not reoffend) and maintain contact through face-to-face visits with their probation officer; these may be monthly, weekly, or as frequent as several times per week. If those on probation fail to comply with these conditions, their probation may be revoked and they would have to reappear before a judge who would decide whether to continue them on probation or revoke their probation and send them to either jail or prison (Spohn 2009).

A 2009 Bureau of Justice Statistics report reveals that in 2008 there were nearly 4.3 million persons on probation in the United States (Glaze and Bonczar 2009). The report also shows that in 2008, about 17 percent of probationers were incarcerated due to revocation of probation; another 8 percent had absconded or could not be located. Similar to incarceration rates, 30 states plus District of Columbia reported increases in their probation populations while 20 other states and the federal system reported declines. These incarceration and probation statistics reveal that the number of persons under some type of criminal justice supervision continues to increase annually. Sometimes judges will sentence certain offenders to both incarceration and probation hoping that this will be a greater deterrent effect to reoffending.

Shock Probation and Split Sentencing

Where judges are permitted great latitude in their sentencing discretion, they are inclined to impose probation for many first offenders convicted of minor offenses or less serious felonies. Offenders sentenced to some form of probation are assigned by the judge to a probation department or some community corrections agency where their behavior will be supervised for a period of time (Champion 2005b).

One type of sentence designed to shock or scare convicted offenders, particularly those who have never served time in a prison or jail, is **shock probation**, **shock incarceration**, or **shock parole**. Shock probation and shock parole refer to planned sentences whereby judges order offenders imprisoned for statutory incarceration periods related to their conviction offenses. However, after 30, 60, 90, or 120 days of incarceration, these offenders are taken out of jail or prison and resentenced to probation or parole (Champion 2007). Ohio introduced shock probation for the first time in 1965. Since then, shock probation has spread to almost every U.S. jurisdiction.

The intent of shock probation is to literally shock or frighten convicted offenders through the incarceration experience (Champion 2005b). No one wants to be imprisoned. For those who have never been confined for either short or long terms, the experience of being behind bars for one or more months is sufficiently traumatic to deter them from further criminal activity. Early evidence suggests that the recidivism rates among shock probationers are relatively low compared with other probationers who have not been imprisoned for short periods (Vito 1984).

In several jurisdictions, judges may engage in **split sentencing**. Split sentencing, also known as **mixed sentencing**, **intermittent sentencing**, and **jail as a condition of probation**, are combination sentences imposed by judges, a portion of which includes incarceration and a portion of which includes probation. If an offender has committed more than one offense, then the judge may impose a separate sentence for each offense. One sentence may be one year in jail, while the other sentence for the second offense may be probation. Thus, this mixed sentence means that the offender will spend some time in jail as well as on probation.

Intermittent sentences involve offenders who are sentenced to partial confinement. These offenders may be sentenced to a jail on weekends, but they may be permitted freedom during the week to work at a job and support themselves and their families. Jail as a condition of probation is where the judge orders the offender to serve a specified term of months in a jail before being placed on probation (Vito 1984). The intent of these split sentencing options is to dramatize the seriousness of the offender's crime. Serving some time in jail or prison will make the point that crime is bad and should be avoided. Otherwise, imprisonment will result. This simplistic view underscores the fact that many shock probationers take this experience to heart and never reoffend. The effectiveness of shock probation varies among jurisdictions. Generally, however, shock probationers tend to have lower rates of recidivism compared with other types of offenders (Champion 2005b).

The Death Penalty and Bifurcated Trials

The most serious sentence criminal courts can impose is the **death penalty**. The death penalty is reserved only for those who have committed capital crimes, primarily murder. In recent years, the death penalty has been approved for use in cases where certain federal offenders have been convicted of large-scale drug dealing.

The death penalty is controversial. However, according to a Gallup poll conducted in October 2007, 69 percent of all U.S. citizens support its use as a suitable punishment for capital offenses. Similar polls conducted by Gallup in 2010, however, show weaker support for its use (47 percent) when subjects are given the option of choosing life without parole. In 2010, Ronnie Lee Gardner chose to be executed by firing squad in Utah. Utah is the only state which still allows the offender to choose death by firing squad if they wish; most of the 34 other states which have death penalty statues have lethal injection as the main execution method. The number of death sentences handed out annually has dropped in the last decade from 306 in 1998 to only 109 in 2009, and New Mexico abolished the death penalty in 2009 (Death penalty Information Center, 2010). Because of numerous exonerations of death row inmates, mostly due to DNA evidence, many states and Supreme Court decisions have restricted the instances when a death sentence can be sought.

Furman v. Georgia (1972) and *Gregg v. Georgia* (1976)

The death penalty is used as the maximum punishment in about two-thirds of all states. The minimum age for executing persons in the United States is 18 (*Roper v. Simmons*, 2005). In 1972, the constitutionality of the death penalty in Georgia was challenged. Disproportionately large numbers of blacks were being executed compared with whites, often in cases involving rape or assault. In 1972 the U.S. Supreme Court declared in *Furman v. Georgia* that the death penalty as it was currently being applied in a discriminatory manner in Georgia was unconstitutional. All states temporarily suspended the death penalty until more information could be obtained from the U.S. Supreme Court about the procedural appropriateness of the death penalty and its application.

In 1976, the U.S. Supreme Court held in *Gregg v. Georgia* that the revised procedural application of the death penalty in Georgia was constitutional. States resumed the application of the death penalty shortly thereafter. Gary Gillmore, a Utah murderer, was executed by firing squad in 1979 and was the first person executed after the U.S. Supreme Court approved of Georgia's new method for imposing death penalties on those convicted of capital crimes (Merlo and Benekos 2004). The U.S. Supreme Court approved Georgia's legislative revision of the death penalty statute, which called for a **bifurcated trial** in all capital cases.

Bifurcated Trials

A bifurcated trial is a two-stage proceeding wherein the first stage consists of the main trial, where one's guilt or innocence is established; if an offender is found guilty of the crime, the jury meets in a second stage to consider the punishment and whether the death penalty should be imposed. Aggravating and mitigating factors are weighed by juries, and the death penalty will be recommended to the judge in those instances where the aggravating factors outweigh the mitigating ones (Kremling 2004).

Bifurcated trials are presently commonplace in those states with death penalty provisions. Bifurcated trials permit juries to consider both aggravating and mitigating circumstances (Gants 2005; Levine and Petitt 2005). It is believed that the nature of bifurcated trials overcomes the criticisms of those who believe that the death penalty is applied in a discriminatory manner. One's race is not a factor in these two-stage proceedings. We have already examined the common set of statutory aggravating and mitigating circumstances that juries consider.

Another feature of bifurcated trials is that death penalties can no longer be automatically applied. It used to be the case on some felony murders or when police officers were killed during a crime that those convicted of such crimes would automatically be sentenced to death. The *Gregg* case was significant in causing these automatic death penalty statutes to be declared unconstitutional. The 1980 case of *Woodson v. North Carolina* held that automatic death penalties were unconstitutional anyway, even though the essence of this holding was conveyed in *Gregg* four years earlier. The main reason is that automatic death penalties do not permit juries to weigh any possible aggravating or mitigating circumstances.

THE SENTENCING HEARING

When offenders are convicted, they are sentenced by a judge to a term of years, either on probation or in jail or prison. In most felony cases, before offenders are sentenced, they must have a **sentencing hearing**. A sentencing hearing is a proceeding where evidence and testimony is presented both for and against the offender. The hearing furnishes the sentencing judge with additional information about the offender, the crime, and the victims. In the context of this additional information, judges can make an informed decision about the best sentence to impose. Oral testimony is given by anyone who has relevant information. Usually, testimony is given by the offender and those speaking on his/her behalf. Victims and their families also offer their opinions and tell how they were affected by the offender's actions. This oral testimony is considered by the judge in making the sentencing decision.

Weighing the Aggravating and Mitigating Circumstances

The sentencing hearing is also important because it permits the judge to consider **aggravating circumstances** and **mitigating circumstances**. Aggravating circumstances are those factors that tend to intensify the severity of the punishment. Aggravating factors include whether the crime involved death or serious bodily injury, whether the offender was out on bail or on probation at the time the crime was committed, whether the offender has a prior criminal record, whether there was more than one victim, whether the offender was the leader in the commission of the offense involving two or more offenders, whether the victim was treated with extreme cruelty by the offender, and whether a dangerous weapon was used by the offender when committing the crime (Fryling 2005).

Mitigating circumstances are those that tend to lessen the severity of punishment. Mitigating circumstances include whether the offender was cooperative with police and gave information about others who may have been involved in the crime, whether the offender did not cause serious bodily injury or death to a victim, whether the offender acted under duress or extreme provocation, whether there was any possible justification for the crime, whether the offender was mentally incapacitated or was suffering from some mental illness, whether the offender made restitution to the victim, whether the offender had no previous criminal record, or whether the offender committed the crime to provide necessities for himself/herself or his/her family.

Judges consider these aggravating and mitigating circumstances, and it is determined whether the aggravating circumstances outweigh the mitigating ones. If this is the case, then judges can mete out harsher sentences. However, if the mitigating circumstances outweigh the aggravating ones, then judges can be more lenient with offenders in their sentencing decision (Fryling 2005).

When the jury or judge finds the defendant guilty, a sentence is not imposed immediately. Sentencing hearings are usually scheduled four to six weeks following the trial. Within the context of due process, defendants are presumed innocent of any crime until they are proven guilty beyond a reasonable doubt in court. When this event occurs, most judges wish to gather additional information about the convicted offender, the circumstances surrounding the commission of the crime, and the impact of the crime upon the victim(s). Probation officers are most frequently assigned the task of researching the background of each convicted offender in an effort to furnish judges with a fairly complete package of information. This information is compiled in a PSI. A **probation officer** needs time to gather all relevant information, and thus, this explains the lapse of time between conviction and sentencing. Probation officers interview the offender's employer, relatives, friends, church and school officials, and victims. The offender's criminal history is described as well. All of this information is summarized in the PSI and submitted to the judge. Defendants are also given the opportunity to describe their involvement in the crime and to take responsibility for what they did.

THE PRESENTENCE INVESTIGATION REPORT (PSI): CONTENTS AND FUNCTIONS

A PSI is a written summary of information obtained by probation officers concerning an investigation of the convicted offender's background and other relevant evidence about the nature of the crime's commission and implications of the crime for all relevant parties, including victims.

Most PSIs compile considerable background information on the defendant so that the judge has adequate background information when it comes to making decisions about appropriate sentences. This information may include the name, address, telephone number, marital status, and dependents of defendant; whether home is rented or owned; how long defendant has lived at the address provided; occupation and income; Social Security number; employer and gross monthly income; education, military service record, if any, type of discharge, and general physical condition; prior criminal record; instant offense, seriousness, and offense classification; date of offense and arresting agency; days in custody following arrest; codefendants if any; victim and victim address; defendant's version of crime (offender's **sentencing memorandum**); investigating officer's version of crime or **narrative**; other information including defendant's reputation, attitude, leisure-time activities, associates; comments by probation officer about sentencing alternatives, treatment proposals, community service; and mandatory attachments, including criminal information/complaint, law enforcement investigation report, and VIS (if applicable).

Probation officers sometimes locate school officials and associates of the offender and interview them. Likewise, victims and their families are interviewed. Probation officers summarize this information and make their own recommendations to the judge. Judges consider the PSI in making their sentencing decision. It is important to note that both the sentencing hearing testimony and the contents of the PSI are considered by the judge. None of this information binds the judge to a particular sentence. Prior to the *Booker* case, federal judges were required to sentence within the range recommended in the PSI; now this is only an advisory sentence recommendation. Judges, therefore, may give reference to the sentence recommended in the PSI, but can also consider any additional relevant information before imposing the actual sentence.

The sentencing hearing gives defendants a chance to speak on their own behalf, to apologize, and to accept responsibility for what they have done. Because defendants are not required to testify in their own criminal trials, they may not have had the chance to tell their side of the story until the PSI. **Acceptance of responsibility** for one's crimes is considered important as the first step toward rehabilitation (Champion 2005b). Sometimes judges are persuaded to be more lenient in cases where convicted offenders admit the wrongfulness of their actions and express genuine regret for what happened. However, additional testimony from victims may persuade the judge to deal more harshly with offenders when it is learned how much the lives of others were adversely affected by the offender's crime (Champion 2005b).

Functions of PSIs

The functions of PSIs are to (1) provide information for offender sentencing, (2) aid probation officers in determining the most appropriate treatment or rehabilitative programs for offenders in need of assistance, (3) assist prisons and jails in their efforts to classify offenders effectively, and (4) furnish parole boards with important offender background data to assist them in determining an offender's early release. Probation officers attempt to solicit the most accurate information about the offender and victims. The contents of PSIs are disclosed not only to judges, but to prosecutors and defense counsel as well. This is to ensure that they are accurate reports. Disclosures of the contents of PSIs are usually mandated by legislative provisions for both the states and federal government. Two important components of PSIs are the offender's sentencing memorandum and VISs (Champion 2005b).

The Offender's Sentencing Memorandum

A **defendant's sentencing memorandum** is a document prepared by the convicted offender that describes the crime, why it was committed, and the attitudes and feelings of the offender concerning his/her involvement. The memorandum also provides an opportunity for the offender to accept responsibility for the crime.

In recent years, the phrase *acceptance of responsibility* has become an increasingly important part of the sentencing process. The U.S. Sentencing Commission provided that acceptance of responsibility would enable sentencing judges to possibly mitigate one's sentence. Various states have added acceptance of responsibility to their sentencing provisions. Thus, offenders who make full admissions regarding their crimes and apologize for these crimes in open court during the sentencing hearing may incur some leniency from judges. It is insufficient to merely declare, "Your honor, I'm sorry for what I've done and I accept responsibility for my actions." Much depends on the circumstances and sincerity of the person making such an admission. Many convicted offenders learn to act contrite and make false statements about their acceptance of responsibility. Judicial discretion is accorded great weight here. If the judge is convinced that the offender has truly accepted responsibility for the crime, then the judge may decide to mitigate the harshness of the penalties imposed. Defense counsel are often key players in the sentencing process. They have one final opportunity to summarize the facts as they see them and to make a case for judicial leniency toward their client.

Victim Impact Statements and Victim Input

Another important part of the sentence mosaic is the VIS. VISs are oral and/or written testimony concerning how the victims and their close relatives were affected by the offender's crime. The nature of victim impact is very important, since judges can learn much more than what was originally disclosed about the crime during the trial. Most jurisdictions in the United States permit victims and their relatives to provide written and/or oral evidence of how the offender's crime has affected them. All states allow some type of victim impact information for use at a sentencing hearing. These may be either written or oral, and a majority of states require that this information be in the PSI (National Center for Victims of Crime 1996).

The inclusion of VISs in sentencing hearings is not new. Many states have provided for victim involvement in the sentencing process in past years. Between 1980 and well into the 1990s, victim involvement in sentencing decisions has dramatically increased (Phillips 1997). In 1987 the admissibility of VISs was prohibited by the U.S. Supreme Court in the case of *Booth v. Maryland*. However, by 1992, the U.S. Supreme Court changed its position to allow VISs in most criminal proceedings, including sentencing hearings (*Payne v. Tennessee* 1991).

One reason for increased victim participation in sentencing decisions is that more than a few citizens regard the criminal justice system as far too lenient on offenders, particularly those who have committed violent felonies. Many factors enter into the judge's sentencing decision besides victim impact, however. Sometimes there are logistical constraints, such as chronic prison overcrowding, such that not all convicted felons who deserved to be imprisoned actually are imprisoned. California, for instance, places about 70 percent of its convicted felons on probation annually. This fact disturbs critics of the criminal justice system as well as the general public.

In an effort to make judges more accountable and impose sentences more in line with the seriousness of the offense, victims and their families have attempted to provide information that will cause judges to deal with offenders more harshly. Investigators have studied VISs and whether judicial sentencing practices have been influenced, either one way or another, in different jurisdictions. Little evidence exists today to show a direct correlation between how victims have been affected by one's crime and the severity of sentences imposed by judges (Phillips 1997). However, there is evidence that victim participation in sentencing has a cathartic effect. This means that victims and their families who participate in the sentencing hearing tend to be more satisfied with the sentences imposed by judges. It has been suggested that victim participation may not directly influence judicial sentencing decisions, but victims or their relatives may feel as though their input *was* somehow influential nevertheless. Victim input may also be allowed in jurisdictions that have a more restorative justice orientation where all parties are involved in determining an appropriate outcome for the criminal act.

Experiments have been conducted with mock juries in death penalty proceedings. At North Carolina State University, for example, 99 undergraduate students were asked to place themselves in the position of jurors in a hypothetical death penalty case. Other students acted as victims and gave testimony about a convicted offender who had murdered their relative. Later, the students were polled to determine whether the VISs were influential in any way concerning whether the death penalty would be applied. Significant numbers of students disclosed that the VISs were important in persuading them to vote for the death penalty, where the death penalty or life-without-parole penalties were options. While this experiment involved students reacting to an imaginary scenario, this does provide some evidence of how actual jurors might react to similar testimony from real victims in capital trials. Other researchers have arrived at similar conclusions (Jacoby and Bronson 2004; Unnever and Cullen 2004).

BOX 10.1

Case Law: Victim Impact Statements

Booth v. Maryland 482 U.S. 496, 107 S.Ct. 2529 (1987)

Booth was convicted of first-degree murder in a Baltimore, Maryland court. During his sentencing hearing, a victim impact statement (VIS) was read so that his sentence might be enhanced or intensified. Following the sentence of death, Booth appealed, alleging that the VIS was a violation of his Eighth Amendment right against cruel and unusual punishment. The U.S. Supreme Court agreed and said that during sentencing phases of capital murder trials, the introduction of VISs is unconstitutional. Among its reasons cited for this opinion, the U.S. Supreme Court said that VISs create an unacceptable risk that a jury may impose the death penalty in an arbitrary and capricious manner. At the time, therefore, VISs were considered unacceptable and inadmissible during the sentencing phase of one's trial. The U.S. Supreme Court's position about VISs changed in 1991 in the case of *Payne v. Tennessee*.

Payne v. Tennessee 501 U.S. 808, 111 S.Ct. 2597 (1991)

Payne was convicted of a double murder. At the sentencing hearing, Payne introduced various witnesses on his behalf to avoid the death penalty. During the same hearing, the victims' relatives introduced their VIS, pressing the jury to impose the death penalty on Payne. The death penalty was imposed and Payne appealed, contesting the introduction of damaging evidence and opinions expressed in the VIS. The U.S. Supreme Court upheld Payne's death sentence, holding that VISs do not violate an offender's Eighth Amendment rights. The significance of this case is that it supports and condones the use of VISs against convicted offenders during sentencing hearings. Presently, VISs are considered admissible during the sentencing phase of one's trial.

VISs may sometimes contain factual inaccuracies. Sometimes victims and their families may exaggerate the adverse effects of the offender's actions, particularly where property losses were involved. Some studies have revealed that female offenders are more favorably treated by victims compared with male offenders whenever VISs are provided (Booth 2004).

VISs have additional uses. Further into an offender's processing and imprisonment, VISs may be relied upon by parole boards in determining whether any particular offender should be granted early release. Any written VISs are maintained in an offender's file and used by parole board members whenever an inmate's early-release eligibility occurs. Further, some victims may participate in parole hearings and give additional oral testimony about why the offender should be denied parole (Myers et al. 2004). However, not all victims present oral testimony against their victimizers. In some cases, victims will speak in favor of the offender's early release during parole hearings. While these cases are exceptional, they do occur with some frequency (Booth 2004).

IMPOSING THE SENTENCE

When sentences are imposed by judges, they are guided by information provided in PSIs, the offender's sentencing memorandum, probation officer recommendations, VISs, and their own interpretation and consideration of the offender and the crime's seriousness. Depending upon the sentencing scheme used in each jurisdiction, judges may be bound to sentence offenders in a consistent way. That is, all convicted bank robbers in a given jurisdiction are supposed to receive a specified sentence as punishment, with consideration given to any present aggravating or mitigating circumstances. But judges are permitted latitude under almost every sentencing scheme (Fryling 2005). This is judicial discretion. This discretion sometimes leads to disparities and even discrimination.

Each judge relies upon previous rulings in similar cases and attempts to be fair and impartial when meting out a specific sentence (Austin et al. 1995). Special consideration may be given to one's age in the case of elderly offenders. If an offender is mentally ill, retarded, or in some other way impaired, judges may take these impairments into account for virtually every type of special offender. Judicial sentencing decisions may be challenged, but appellate courts are inclined to assume that the original sentence imposed was the right one. It is difficult to overcome such a presumption on appeal.

SENTENCING DISPARITIES

Race/Ethnicity, Gender, and Socioeconomic Status

Disparity in sentencing refers to differences in incarceration rates or sentence lengths. For instance, in 2008, 93 percent of prisoners in both state and federal prisons were males and male incarceration rates were about 15 times higher than female incarceration rates (Sabol, West, and Cooper 2009); this means there is a clear sex disparity in sentencing. Some disparities are warranted, others are not. Usually, disparities based on extralegal factors such as race/ethnicity, sex, and age are unwarranted because the law does not allow judges to consider demographic characteristics under the law. Does the above statistic mean that judges discriminate against men? Not necessarily, there may be legitimate reasons why there are more men in prison than women. For instance, men often commit more serious offenses for which incarceration is more often warranted. Unwarranted sentencing disparities occur when judges impose different sentences on offenders charged with similar crimes and who have similar backgrounds (McManimon 2005b).

Similarly, blacks and Hispanics may receive harsher sentences compared with whites when the same kinds of offenses are involved. Older offenders may receive less harsh sentences from judges compared with younger offenders even when they have committed the same crimes and have similar backgrounds (McManimon 2005b; Roy 2004).

Promoters of sentencing reforms have been quick to point out these sorts of deficiencies in our sentencing system. Many states have reformed their sentencing systems from an indeterminate structure to a determinate one. Such changes are almost always accompanied by reductions in sentencing disparities attributable to racial, ethnic, gender, or socioeconomic qualities. Sentencing practices under determinate or guidelines-based structures are generally more uniform; however, several research studies have revealed that extralegal disparities are still present in some contexts.

Race and Ethnicity

Different jurisdictions report variations in sentencing attributable to race. Numerous empirical studies have found that race does play a role in sentencing decisions; more recent research has also revealed that ethnicity is also a predictor at the sentencing stage where ethnic minorities (Hispanics) are singled out for harsher treatment. Many researchers have also found that race and ethnicity interact with other variables such as sex and age to produce the harshest sentences for young, black and Hispanic males (Doerner and Demuth 2010; Steffensmeier and Demuth 2000; Steffensmeier, Ulmer, and Kramer 1998). Likewise, Spohn and Holleran (2000) explored sentencing practices in Chicago, Kansas City, and Miami and found that young, black males received the harshest sentences overall but in Chicago, young Hispanic males along with middle-aged, black males received the toughest sentences, in Miami, younger and older Hispanic males received harsher sentences, and in Kansas City, young, white offenders had the highest odds of incarceration. These authors contend that race, ethnicity, gender, and age are in the minds of judges when they make decisions about an appropriate sentence. Further, judges may have stereotypes about which defendants are blameworthy and dangerous that vary according to geography.

Some critics contend that race and ethnicity are especially relevant in homicide cases and capital murder prosecutions where both the race of the offender and the race of the victim factor in the decision-making processes of prosecutors and judges (Walker, Spohn, and Delone 2000). For example, in an investigation of sentencing disparities among 685 white and black women in Alabama during the period 1929–1985, whites who killed blacks were the most likely to have light sentences (of one to five years) compared with blacks who killed whites (Hanke 1995). Besides stereotypes by criminal justice system officials, some have argued that racial and ethnic minorities are less likely to cooperate with criminal justice system officials or that there may be language barriers that hinder plea bargaining opportunities (Mirande 1987).

For example, in a study of 755 defendants in Tucson, Arizona, and El Paso, Texas, Hispanic defendants did not receive sentences that were different from their white counterparts; however, in El Paso, Hispanic defendants were more likely to be convicted at trial and consistently received more severe sentences. Interviews with district attorneys and other officials in both cities indicated that the disparities may be partly attributable to differing language difficulties in the two jurisdictions, differing mechanisms for providing attorneys to indigent defendants, and differences between established Hispanic Americans and less well established Mexican American citizens and Mexican nationals (LaFree 1985). Again, we see race and ethnicity may interact with geography or place to produce divergent outcomes for racial and ethnic minorities.

Despite the increasing attention given to sentencing disparities and the sentencing reforms established to correct such disparate sentences, there is considerable evidence to indicate that racial and ethnic sentencing disparities still exist and are not diminishing (Van Zyl Smit and Ashworth 2004). Blacks are overrepresented at virtually every processing stage in the criminal justice system, and they are increasingly included in incarcerated populations. Hispanics are the fastest growing group of federal prison inmates due to the increasing focus on federal narcotics and immigration offenses (USSC 2010). Table 10-2 displays the race, age, and gender of offenders prosecuted in federal court in fiscal year 2009. As can be seen in the table, young adult, black (ages 21–25 and 26–30) and Hispanic (ages 26–30 and 31–35) males represent large proportions

TABLE 10-2   Age, Race, and Gender of Offenders[a] (Fiscal Year 2009)

Gender and Age	White		Black		Hispanic		Other	
	N	%	N	%	N	%	N	%
Males	17,456	100.0	14,254	100.0	30,685	100.0	2,346	100.0
Under 21	467	2.7	453	3.2	1,325	4.3	85	3.6
21–25	1,959	11.2	2,452	17.2	5,204	17	374	15.9
26–30	2,616	15	3,479	24.4	6,673	21.7	463	19.7
31–35	2,441	14	2,783	19.5	6,320	20.6	342	14.6
36–40	2,394	13.7	2,036	14.3	4,665	15.2	338	14.4
41–50	4,022	23	2,123	14.9	4,865	15.9	442	18.8
Over 50	3,557	20.4	928	6.5	1,633	5.3	302	12.9
Females	3,559	100.0	2,039	100.0	2,772	100.0	543	100.0
Under 21	131	3.7	52	2.6	149	5.4	15	2.8
21–25	528	14.8	308	15.1	443	16	75	13.8
26–30	574	16.1	420	20.6	530	19.1	81	14.9
31–35	472	13.3	360	17.7	478	17.2	87	16
36–40	493	13.9	258	12.7	412	14.9	75	13.8
41–50	799	22.5	414	20.3	547	19.7	126	23.2
Over 50	562	15.8	227	11.1	213	7.7	84	15.2

[a]Of the 81,372 cases, 7,718 were excluded due to one more of the following reasons: missing race (7,688), missing gender (2,052), or missing age (432).

Descriptions of variables used in this are provided in Appendix A.

Source: U.S. Sentencing Commission, 2009 Datafile, USSCFY09.

of those prosecuted in federal court. For females, there seems to be less disparity in the representation of white, black, and Hispanic offenders regardless of age.

Some scholars report that such disproportionate representation of blacks and Hispanics is due to greater offending rates (Blumstein 1982) and lengthier prior criminal histories (Tonry 1996). Others claim, however, that the disproportionate representation of blacks and other minorities in the criminal justice system can be attributed to poverty and unemployment (Spohn 2000). It has been recommended, for instance, that greater use of special circumstances should be exercised by judges when sentencing minority offenders. With more honest sentencing policies, less disproportionate sentencing should occur that is attributable to race or ethnicity (Williams and Holcomb 2004).

Sentencing disparities attributable to race differences are particularly noticeable in the South. It has been shown, for instance, that for 21,169 convicted felons in Georgia for the years 1973–1980, blacks tended to receive longer sentences compared with whites (Clayton 1983). As a matter of fact, blacks received sentences that were on the average 2.5 years longer than sentences for whites convicted for the same crimes. Similar disparities have been observed and are considered pervasive regarding capital cases (Sorensen and Wallace 1995).

Gender

Do women tend to receive more lenient sentences compared with men? Recall above that in 2008, 93 percent of prisoners in state and federal prisons were male. Research has shown that judges may be inclined to be more lenient with female offenders even where they have committed crimes similar to males. If judges do use sex as a criterion in making sentencing decisions, this would be considered discrimination. If sex disparities disappear, however, once the seriousness of offense and prior criminal record are taken into account, this would not be discrimination but warranted disparity. This sex disparity would be warranted because there are increased chances of going to prison and for longer periods due to offense seriousness and the presence of priors. Some scholars have further argued that females may be treated more leniently than males because they are the primary caregivers of children or because they are seen as less blameworthy and culpable, and less likely to recidivate (Daly 1989; Steffensmeier, Kramer, and Streifel 1993).

Finally, some studies conclude that the effect of sex on decision-making practices may depend on the stage in the criminal justice process. Zingraff and Thompson (1984) for instance found that females were treated more leniently at the incarceration decision only. Steffensmeier et al. (1993) examined sex differences in Pennsylvania from 1985 to 1987 and found sex effects may also depend on offense seriousness; female defendants received longer sentences for minor offenses but shorter sentences for serious offenses.

Daly and Bordt (1995) conducted an extensive statistical review of **sentencing disparity** literature to determine whether "sex effects" favoring women over men in sentencing exist. Over half of the 50 studies surveyed indicated that gender effects favoring women over men existed. Both older and more recent data sets reveal similar patterns, where females have received more lenient sentences compared with sentences for male offenders.

Investigations have also been conducted on the relationship between sex and the application of the death penalty in capital cases. Both surveys of citizens and actual patterns of capital punishment use in selected states reveal that females convicted of capital crimes are far less likely to receive the death penalty compared with men convicted of a capital crime under similar circumstances (Vollum, Longmire, and Buffington-Vollum 2004). Further, citizens surveyed tended to favor more lenient treatment for females convicted of capital offenses (i.e., life-without-parole sentences as opposed to death sentences).

One explanation for gender differentiation is the chivalry hypothesis, which is that decision makers or judges tend to treat female offenders with chivalry during sentencing, and further that judges will be inclined to dispense selective chivalry toward white females compared with other females or minorities of either gender (Kakar 2004). Data from 9,866 felony theft cases and 18,176 felony assault cases from California courts in 1988 show that females with no prior record were more likely to receive charge reductions compared with male offenders. Also, female offenders' chances for probation were increased greatly compared with a similar aggregate of male offenders (Champion 2005a).

As more states adopt reforms including presumptive and determinate sentencing systems, fewer sentencing disparities will be observed from one jurisdiction to the next. Also, judges seem to favor greater uniformity in their sentencing practices within the same jurisdictions. The adoption of consistent sentencing standards will gradually eliminate patterns of gender, ethnic, or racial discrimination in sentencing in future years.

Socioeconomic Status

One's socioeconomic status plays a significant part in explaining sentencing disparities. Offenders whose resources are limited cannot afford private counsel, and less-experienced public defenders are often appointed to defend them (Weiss 2004). Further, the sentencing guidelines in many states tend to over-penalize street crimes, which are most often committed by those with lower socioeconomic status (Wooldredge and Griffin 2004).

Evidence of sentencing disparities attributable to one's socioeconomic status is considerable. Empirical studies have shown that poor minorities are disproportionately represented in the criminal justice system and are more likely to be prosecuted for crimes that are subject to mandatory minimums (Caulkins et al. 1998; Mauer 1999; Ogletree 2004; Tonry 1995).

Specifically, research has shown that persons in poverty (Gustafson 2009), or who are from the lowest social strata, receive harsher punishments (Chiricos and Bales 1991).

For example, studies of sentencing patterns in southeastern states have shown that there is an inverse relation between one's socioeconomic status and sentence length (D'Allessio and Stolzenberg 1993). When 2,760 convicted offenders were examined, those of lower socioeconomic status drew longer sentences than those of higher socioeconomic statuses. Thus, it was concluded that this extralegal factor was significant in explaining differential sentence lengths of offenders, controlling for one's criminal history and conviction offense (D'Allessio and Stolzenberg 1993). Other research has supported the idea that those with lower socioeconomic status are disenfranchised by the criminal justice system. However, the influence of socioeconomic status may adversely affect certain persons of higher socioeconomic statuses as well. A survey of white-collar offenders sentenced in seven U.S. District Courts tended to receive imprisonment more often compared with comparable offenders of lower statuses, and furthermore, the sentences imposed on white-collar offenders were longer (Weisburd, Waring, and Wheeler 1990). The general consensus seems to be that lower socioeconomic status offenders will tend to receive harsher and longer sentences compared with offenders of higher socioeconomic statuses, although there are always exceptions. Bernie Madoff's 150-year sentence for securities fraud is an example of this exception.

APPEALS OF SENTENCES

THE PURPOSES OF AN APPEAL   Once defendants have been convicted of crimes, they are entitled to at least one appeal to a higher court. The primary purpose of an appeal is to correct a wrong that may have been committed. These wrongs may be mistakes by police, the prosecution, or the court. Errors may have occurred that influence the trial outcome. Appeals are intended to correct these mistakes and errors.

A secondary purpose of an **appeal** is to render judgment about one or more issues that will influence future cases. Thus, when an appellate court hears a case from a lower trial court, the appellate court's decision becomes a precedent for subsequent similar cases. This is the doctrine of *stare decisis*, meaning that once a higher court has ruled a particular way on a particular issue, lower courts are bound to make rulings consistent with higher court holdings whenever similar cases are heard. However, trial court judges have some discretion in deciding whether certain subsequent cases resemble previous cases where appellate courts have ruled. Thus, trial court judges may decide that although a subsequent case is similar in various respects to previous cases already decided by higher courts, there may be sufficient differences in the cases so that trial judges decide that the higher court rulings do not apply.

APPEALS OF SENTENCES   All death sentences are automatically appealed (Champion 2005b). The appellate process for any case, capital or otherwise, begins by filing an appeal with the most immediate appellate court above the trial court level. When offenders are convicted in federal district courts, for instance, their appeals are directed to one of 13 different circuit courts of appeal. In California, for example, Stacy Koon and Laurence Powell were two police officers convicted in a federal district court of inflicting great bodily harm upon a motorist, Rodney King, under color of their police authority. Under the U.S. Sentencing Guidelines, these former officers were supposed to be sentenced to several years of prison. However, the federal district judge downgraded the seriousness of their offense and sentenced them to time served. The U.S. Attorney's Office in Los Angeles filed an appeal with the Ninth Circuit Court of Appeals, contending that the reasons cited by the federal judge for downgrading their offense were not appropriate. The Ninth Circuit reversed the trial judge and reinstated the original sentence called for under the U.S. Sentencing Guidelines. Koon and Powell appealed, this time to the U.S. Supreme Court, since this is the court of last resort above the circuit courts of appeal.

The Supreme Court ruling in *Koon* overturned the appellate court decision essentially upholding a judge's right to depart from the federal sentencing.

In capital cases originating in state courts, state remedies must be pursued on appeal before the federal system is accessed. For instance, a person convicted of murder in Tennessee and sentenced to death must direct his/her appeal first to the court of criminal appeals. If there is an unfavorable ruling by that appellate court, then the offender can direct an appeal to the Tennessee Supreme Court. If the ruling by this court is unfavorable for the offender, then a direct appeal may be made to the U.S. Supreme Court for relief.

Appellants and Appellees

Appellants are persons who initiate appeals. **Appellees** are those who prevailed in the trial court and argue against reversing the decision of the lower court. Those convicted of capital crimes and sentenced to death are appellants. In most instances, the state is the appellee. Cases are given names to fit the two parties. Thus, we have *Furman v. Georgia*, *Gregg v. Georgia*, *Woodson v. North Carolina*, or *Payne v. Tennessee*. In each of these cases, the appellant is mentioned first and the appellee second. There are many grounds on which to base appeals (Unnever and Cullen 2004). Further, appeals in most death penalty cases drag out over a period of 10–15 years before the appellants are eventually executed (Harmon 2004).

Bases for Appeals

Appeals may be directed to appellate courts on diverse grounds. Appellants may raise questions before appellate courts about how they were originally arrested and processed. They may challenge the admissibility of certain evidence used to convict them. They may claim incompetence or ineffective assistance of counsel (Albonetti and Barron 2004). They challenge the sentence imposed by the judge. Almost every one of these challenges about what happened at different points in their processing as criminal defendants can be included within the scope of a *habeas corpus* petition.

***HABEAS CORPUS* PETITIONS**   *Habeas corpus* means literally produce the body. A *habeas corpus* petition challenges three things: (1) the fact of confinement, (2) the length of confinement, and/or (3) the nature of confinement. The fact of confinement involves every event that led to the present circumstances of the appellant (Belbot et al. 2004). If the appellant is on death row resulting from a capital offense conviction, then any aspect of the justice process leading to the offender's placement on death row is a potential *habeas corpus* target (Westervelt and Cook 2004).

For example, the fact of confinement was challenged in the case of *Preiser v. Rodriguez* (1973). Rodriguez was a state prisoner who was deprived of good-time credits by the New York Department of Correctional Services because of disciplinary proceedings. Rodriguez filed a *habeas corpus* petition. The lower court dismissed the petition, saying that it was not relevant for challenging the fact and duration of one's confinement. However, the U.S. Supreme Court overturned the lower court decision, holding that when state prisoners are challenging the very fact or duration of their physical confinement, and the relief sought is a determination that they are entitled to immediate release from that imprisonment, the sole federal remedy is a writ of *habeas corpus*.

The length of confinement has been challenged numerous times by prisoners who feel that their sentences are too long and disproportionately harsh in relation to the crimes they have committed. In the case of *Hutto v. Davis* (1982), for instance, Roger Davis was a Virginia inmate who had been sentenced to 40 years in prison and a $20,000 fine for a conviction for marijuana possession with intent to distribute. Davis sought *habeas corpus* relief, contending that the 40-year sentence was disproportionate to the crime, and thus, it was cruel and unusual punishment. Ultimately, after considerable hearing and rehearing through the appellate process, the U.S. Supreme Court decided the matter by upholding Virginia authority to mandate sentences for crimes as they see fit without labeling such sentences as cruel and unusual. In Davis's case, the 40-year sentence was legislatively mandated, and thus, the U.S. Supreme Court believed that it would be improper to interfere with state legislative sanctions. Davis's sentence was therefore upheld.

The **conditions of confinement** of jails or prisons are frequent grounds for *habeas corpus* relief. Prisoners who are ordered confined in jails rather than prisons for long periods may object to the lack of facilities and amenities in jails that would ordinarily be found in prisons. A case regarding conditions of confinement was *Hutto v. Finney* (1978). In 1970, the Arkansas prison system was declared unconstitutional on various grounds through a *habeas corpus* petition filed by inmates. The U.S. Supreme Court ruled that the conditions of confinement were cruel and unusual, violative of the Eighth Amendment. Subsequently, a check by federal officials revealed that the reforms to be implemented had not been completed. The Court issued additional orders for prison official compliance. These orders included (1) limiting the number of prisoners who could reasonably be confined in one cell, (2) discontinuing particular types of nonnutritious meals, (3) maximizing the days of **solitary confinement** or **isolation** as punishment to 30, and (4) obligating the state to pay for attorneys' fees and expenses. Hutto, the Arkansas commissioner of corrections, appealed, contending that the 30-day confinement standard was too lenient and that the court had wrongfully assigned attorneys' fees to the state. The U.S. Supreme Court heard the case and upheld the lower court. The 30-day punitive limitation on solitary confinement was upheld as well as the assessment of attorneys' fees against the state.

Sometimes, offender/petitioners allege that the sentencing judge acted inappropriately by making prejudicial remarks in front of the jury. In the case of *Arave v. Creech* (1993), for instance, Creech was convicted of the murder of another inmate while confined in the Idaho Penitentiary. At his trial and sentencing, the judge sentenced him to death and based his decision, in part, on aggravating circumstances. He used the phrase *utter disregard and the cold-blooded pitiless slayer*. Creech appealed the sentence, contending that the phrase *utter disregard* was facially invalid. The U.S. Supreme Court upheld Creech's conviction, holding that the phrase *utter disregard* does not violate any constitutional provisions.

Also, inmates will file *habeas corpus* petitions where they believe prosecutors acted in bad faith or engaged in improper conduct, such as suppressing exculpatory evidence. In the case of *Arizona v. Washington* (1978), for instance, George Washington was convicted of murder, but an Arizona court granted Washington a new trial because the prosecution had withheld exculpatory evidence during discovery. At the beginning of the second trial, defense counsel made various remarks in his opening statement concerning hidden information from the first trial. The prosecutor moved for a mistrial, which was granted. Washington was subsequently convicted in a third trial. However, later as an inmate, Washington filed a *habeas corpus* petition seeking to have his conviction overturned because of the trial judge's decision to declare a **mistrial** in the second trial. Washington contended that the judge's decision to declare a mistrial was erroneous and that this led to his being placed in double jeopardy by a third trial. The U.S. Supreme Court rejected Washington's arguments, holding that the mistrial was properly declared by the judge. Thus, no previous trial had been concluded with an acquittal where Washington was again being tried for the same offense.

Another reason for seeking *habeas corpus* relief is for ineffective assistance of counsel. If convicted offenders believe that they were not properly represented by counsel since they were convicted, they may allege that their counsel was ineffective. Most of these types of petitions are denied by the U.S. Supreme Court. In the case of *Darden v. Wainwright* (1986), Willie Darden was a convicted murderer under sentence of death. He filed a *habeas corpus* petition challenging the exclusion of a juror from his earlier trial, allegedly improper remarks made by the prosecutor during his summation to the jury, and ineffective assistance of counsel. One prospective juror had been excused by the judge when the juror declared a moral and religious opposition to the death penalty, which was one option in Darden's case. Prosecutorial remarks regarded by Darden as improper were references made to Darden's furlough program at the time he committed murder, and that the prosecutor referred to him as an animal. The third allegation involved a one-half hour preparation by Darden's attorney between the trial's guilt phase and the trial's penalty phase. Darden did not believe this time interval gave his attorney sufficient time to prepare an adequate mitigation statement.

The U.S. Supreme Court rejected all of Darden's arguments. The U.S. Supreme Court held that jurors may be excused from death penalty cases where their religious views or moral feelings would render them unable to vote for a death penalty if warranted. Further, the emotional rhetoric from the prosecutor was insufficient to deprive Darden of a fair trial. Finally, evidence showed that the defense counsel spent considerable preparatory time for both the trial and mitigation statement during the penalty phase. Similarly, the Supreme Court in June 2010 in the case of *Holland v. Florida* overturned the Eleventh Circuit Appellate Court's decision to deny a *habeas corpus* petition because it was not filed within the one-year time limit. Holland argued that despite him urging his attorney to file a *habeas corpus* petition, one was never filed. The Eleventh Circuit denied petition because the one-year time limit had passed. The Supreme Court in a 7–2 decision in favor of Holland ruled that the statute of limitations for a federal *habeas corpus* petition could be lifted where extraordinary circumstances exist such as in Holland's case, where his appointed attorney failed to file the petition despite instructions to do so on several occasions.

Additional reasons for *habeas corpus* actions include failure of the court to provide counsel to the offender or to determine whether a guilty plea was indeed voluntary (*Carter v. People of State of Illinois*, 1946); failure of one's counsel to inform the offender of possible sentence enhancements because a firearm was used during the commission of a felony (*Custis v. United States*, 1994); that the search by police was conducted without a **warrant** where the circumstances required the issuance of one before the search would be lawful (*Gerstein v. Pugh*, 1975); and that exposure to cyanide gas is a cruel and unusual punishment (*Gomez v. United States District Court*, 1992).

Over the years, inmates have frequently abused the writ of *habeas corpus* by submitting numerous petitions with frivolous claims. The U.S. Supreme Court has limited such filings in recent years so that inmates and others cannot continue to abuse such petitions. Currently, the use of *habeas corpus* has been severely limited so that inmates must set forth all arguable issues encompassed by *habeas corpus* and not use a separate *habeas corpus* action per issue (*Delo v. Stokes*, 1990). Furthermore, state prisoners must first exhaust all of their state appellate remedies before seeking relief directly from the U.S. Supreme Court (*Duckworth v. Serrano*, 454 U.S. 1 [1981]). The significance of this case is that any petitioner who has been convicted of a state crime must first exhaust all state remedies before attempting to file petitions in federal courts. This is considered a landmark case because it obligates prisoners to direct their *habeas corpus* petitions first to state courts, before they pursue federal remedies. This decision is no doubt calculated to reduce crowded federal court dockets.

New technological developments concerning identification of suspects through DNA testing or **DNA fingerprinting** and other forensic achievements have caused more than a few inmates to be released from prison after they have been determined to be innocent of the crimes for which they were originally convicted (Warden 2004). In order to obtain their release from prison or get new trials, inmates must file *habeas corpus* petitions. But the courts have been reluctant to cause old cases to be reopened, except under the most compelling of circumstances. This is consistent with the general policy change by the U.S. Supreme Court to make it more difficult in recent years for inmates to pursue *habeas corpus* writs without limit (Federman 2004).

Both the number of *habeas corpus* petitions filed by prisoners and the proportion of prisoners filing *habeas corpus* actions are declining steadily. Even in capital cases, *habeas corpus* appeals have declined. This is because of the greater restrictions imposed on such appeals by the U.S. Supreme Court and Congress. This trend is also observed in various states, including California (Atherton 2004).

Writs of *Certiorari*

A writ of *certiorari* is issued by a higher court directing a lower court to prepare the record of a case and send it to the higher court for review. It is also a means of accessing the U.S. Supreme Court in order for a case to be heard. Writs of *certiorari*, especially from those on **death row**, must contain compelling arguments in order for the U.S. Supreme Court to grant them. Most writs of *certiorari* from those sentenced to death are denied. Of those petitions that are heard by the U.S. Supreme Court, only a handful each year result in the death penalty being overturned. Usually, the U.S. Supreme Court may order a new trial if a particularly strong argument is presented showing a flagrant constitutional rights violation.

The Lengthy Process of Appeals

Appeals of any kind, especially death penalty appeals, consume a great deal of time. On the average, it takes about 10 or 11 years for inmates to be executed. In some instances, the appeals process has dragged out over a 15-year period (Maguire and Pastore 2005). One reason for the lengthy appeals process is that prisoners have been allowed to file new petitions with either state or federal courts, under a variety of theories. While *habeas corpus* is the most frequently used type of appeal, there is almost no limit to the number of issues that may be raised by inmates and their counsel that could result in their convictions and/or sentences being overturned.

If an offender's case is reviewed by the U.S. Supreme Court and the Court rules in their favor, often the case is reargued in a new trial. When second or third trials occur, the results are almost always the same as the first trial. However, some evidence exists to show that sentencing judges may abuse their sentencing discretion and punish these offenders with harsher penalties than earlier prescribed. But the U.S. Supreme Court has usually condoned harsher sentences by judges, especially where judges have provided a logical written rationale for the enhanced or harsher sentence. Increased sentences have survived constitutional challenges as violations of double jeopardy, equal protection, and due process without limiting a trial judge's wide sentencing discretion (Wilmot 2002).

Initiating Appeals

Appeals are launched by appellants, or those who lose in the trial court. Most frequently, appellants are convicted offenders. They must first file a **notice of appeal**. A notice of appeal is a written statement of the appellant's intent to file an appeal with a higher court. Such notices are required within a fixed period of time following an offender's conviction.

A copy of the court record or complete transcript of proceedings is forwarded to the appellate court for review. Also, a brief is filed with the appellate court, outlining the principal arguments for the appeal. These arguments may pertain to particular judicial rulings, which are believed to be incorrect. Appellants are required to list the issues that are the substance of the appeal. If the appellant believes that 30 mistakes were committed by the trial judge, or if the prosecutor was believed to have made prejudicial remarks to the jury where such remarks are prohibited, or if the police did not advise the offender of his *Miranda* rights when arrested, all of these mistakes or errors should be listed in the brief or legal argument. These errors or mistakes are considered appealable issues. An offender's first appeal should contain all of these issues, since it is unlikely that courts will consider further appeals concerning omitted issues.

Appellants, or those who succeed in the trial court (usually the prosecution), may file briefs as well, noting why they believe there were no procedural irregularities or errors committed by different actors in the system. Thus, the groundwork is provided for **argument** later before the appellate court.

Most states and the federal government have criminal appellate courts, where offenders direct their appeals. These appellate courts frequently consist of three-judge panels who will hear the legal arguments and decide whether the trial court was in error. Rulings by appellate courts that overturn a lower trial court are rare, however. One reason is that appellate courts assume that whatever transpired during the offender's trial was correct, and that the criminal conviction was valid. This is a difficult presumption for appellants to overcome. They must often present overwhelming evidence of prosecutorial misconduct or judicial indiscretion in order to convince an appellate court to reverse or set aside their conviction. And if a conviction is reversed, this decision does not absolve the offender of any criminal liability. A new trial may be ordered, or a sentencing decision may be modified to be consistent with a higher court ruling.

Presenting the case for the appellant is the defense attorney in most criminal cases, while the district attorney or state prosecutor (the U.S. Attorney or Assistant U.S. Attorney in federal courts) will give the government's position in the matter to be argued. This dispute process is **oral argument**. Once the appellate court has heard the oral argument from both sides and has consulted the trial transcript, it will render an **opinion**. An opinion is a written decision about the issue(s) argued, and a holding as to which side, the appellant or appellee, prevails. If the appellate court holds in favor of the appellant, and if the appellant is a convicted offender, then the case is **reversed and remanded** back to the trial court with instructions for modifying the original decision. Whenever the ruling favors the government, the appellate court is said to **affirm** the holding or judgment against the appellant/offender. When the case against the offender is affirmed by an appellate court, the offender may direct an appeal to the next higher appellate court. In state courts, this higher appellate court is the state supreme court or court of last resort within the state judicial system. If the state supreme court affirms the conviction, the offender may direct an appeal to the U.S. Supreme Court.

In some opinions by appellate courts, not all of the appellate judges agree about the decision rendered. The minority view is sometimes summarized in a **dissenting opinion.** Legal historians value dissenting opinions, because they believe that appellate court policy change can be predicted over time. This is especially true if those rendering dissenting opinions are younger judges on appellate panels. However, the fact is that these minority or dissenting opinions have no impact on the appeal outcome. The majority opinion, however, is the governing opinion in the case and is the more important one. Appellate judges who write the majority opinion also outline the legal rationale for their opinion. These opinions are more or less lengthy.

The Discretionary Powers of Appellate Courts

Appellate courts may or may not decide to hear appeals from lower courts. Their powers in this regard are discretionary. They may choose which cases to review as well as decide which cases not to review. Usually, only a small proportion of cases are reviewed by appellate courts at the state and federal levels annually. For instance, the U.S. Supreme Court receives thousands of appeals from convicted offenders annually. However, only a small fraction, 100 or so cases, are heard each year where written opinions are provided. Most appeals from convicted offenders are denied. The U.S. Supreme Court is also a discretionary body, where their cases to be heard are carefully chosen.

Furthermore, the Rule of Four applies, where at least four or more justices must agree to hear the case. And even if the U.S. Supreme Court consents to hear a case, the sheer volume of scheduled cases may be such that the case may not be heard. This is because the U.S. Supreme Court's time is quite limited. More than a few scheduled cases are not heard each year, because the Court has run out of time. And these cases are not carried over to the next term of the Court. Rather, appellants must refile their appeals with the Court the following term.

Appeals by Indigents

Indigent defendants who are sentenced to death are entitled to counsel on their first nondiscretionary appeals (Harmon 2001). However, more than a few inmates on death rows have filed numerous subsequent appeals, almost always at taxpayer expense, where public defenders have been appointed to assist them. However, as we have seen, the U.S. Supreme Court has limited the number of appeals indigents may file as well as their right to publicly appointed counsel each and every time they launch a new appeal.

Wrongful Convictions and Pardons

The American criminal justice system is not perfect. While no conclusive data are available to dispute the matter one way or another, more than a few innocent persons are sometimes convicted of serious crimes (Gould 2004). This phenomenon is not unique to the United States (Denov and Campbell 2005). There are many reasons for **wrongful convictions** (Burrow 2004). Sometimes there is extensive **circumstantial evidence**, which implicates the defendant and makes him/her appear to be guilty (Burnett 2005). A defendant may have the motive, means, and opportunity to commit particular crimes, but he/she may be unable to account for his/her whereabouts when the crime was committed. Sometimes the simple fact of not being able to explain satisfactorily where you were at a particular time, coupled with other incriminating factors, may make you appear guilty in the eyes of jurors who hear and decide the case.

Some aggressive prosecutors may threaten or intimidate certain defendants with the possibility of charging them with crimes that carry stringent penalties, such as long sentences of incarceration, and even the death penalty. While it is wrong and unethical to engage in such prosecutorial misconduct, some prosecutors threaten and overwhelm certain defendants with very serious charges that have little or no basis in fact. A gray area exists within which prosecutors have great latitude in their charging decisions. Most skillful prosecutors can present only incriminating or inculpatory information to grand juries about criminal suspects and withhold exculpatory information that might exonerate the suspect. Indictments against almost anyone can be obtained, depending upon the prosecutor's wishes (Leo 2005).

But as we have seen, indictments do not mean someone is guilty of a crime. Rather, indictments are simply findings by grand juries that probable cause exists to believe that a crime was committed and a particular suspect named by the prosecutor may have committed the crime. These one-sided proceedings, where defendants and their attorneys are barred from presenting their side or giving exculpatory evidence, frequently overwhelm those indicted for various crimes. Most citizens who read a newspaper article reading, "Federal Grand Jury Indicts James Jones for Six Counts of Burglary," or "The Craig County Grand Jury Indicts Elmer Gantry for Sexual Assault" likely conclude that James Jones or Elmer Gantry are probably guilty of these crimes based on the powerful innuendo of an indictment. But proving the facts alleged in an indictment in court beyond a reasonable doubt may be difficult, particularly if these cases lack direct evidence against particular suspects or are at best circumstantial.

For many suspects, their cases never come to trial. The plea bargaining process circumvents most trials in over 90 percent of all criminal cases. After being overwhelmed by very serious charges, defendants and their attorneys may be approached by "generous" prosecutors who wish to save the government the time and expense of a protracted trial. A compromise is offered, such as a lesser charge. If the defendant pleads guilty to a lesser charge, then probation may be offered instead of jail or prison time that might be imposed if a jury trial were held and the suspect were convicted. Many defense attorneys urge their clients to accept these "generous" offers from prosecutors, especially if these clients have prior criminal records or appear guilty because of the circumstantial evidence the state has compiled. Thus, many defendants relinquish their right to a jury trial as well as other important constitutional rights in an effort to avoid potentially serious punishments if a trial were held and they were convicted.

Then there are cases where innocent defendants go to trial anyway and are convicted, simply because they look guilty to the jury and the state has overwhelmed the jury with extensive circumstantial evidence. These innocent convicted persons spend a great deal of time seeking appeals of their cases by higher courts. But these innocent persons must overcome a powerful presumption that the trial court was correct when the case was originally decided. This is an extremely difficult presumption to overcome, especially if there is little or no hard evidence to substantiate one's claim of innocence.

In recent years there has been greater media attention focused upon very serious cases, particularly death penalty cases, where technology has advanced to the point of conclusively demonstrating one's innocence (Davis 2005). Evidence in most serious criminal cases is carefully preserved for many years following the crime in anticipation of the appeals that will follow. During the 1990s, DNA typing was increasingly used as evidence against suspects (*Technology Review* 2005). But its use also led authorities to exclude certain persons as suspects. By 2005 many of those serving lengthy prison sentences or who were on death rows throughout the United States were demanding reexaminations of blood evidence that was originally used to convict them (Burnett 2005). Law enforcement agencies and correctional institutions are increasingly collecting blood specimens from suspects or convicted offenders and typing these specimens according to unique DNA patterns. Often, a confrontation of the actual perpetrator with DNA evidence may elicit a confession. While prosecutors are reluctant to admitting their mistakes, appellate courts have been persuaded with such DNA evidence and wrongful convictions have been overturned (Boller 2005).

The president of the United States or a state governor may **pardon** certain persons who have been found to be wrongfully convicted of crimes. Pardons are unconditional releases from prison. Pardons are intended to overcome a governmental mistake or right wrongs. They are not extensively invoked, but when they *are* invoked, they frequently have the weight of restoring a person's citizen status, which he/she had prior to being convicted of a crime. Persons may be pardoned from death row if they are subsequently found to be innocent of the crimes for which they were originally convicted. The government may or may not compensate such persons for the time they were incarcerated until pardoned. For instance, North Carolina compensates wrongfully convicted persons $20,000 per year spent in incarceration, while some jurisdictions have no compensation policies.

In 2005, only 37 percent of all wrongfully convicted persons received compensation from various states for the months or years these innocent persons spent in prison. Only 20 states had mechanisms in place and institutional pathways for seeking compensation for wrongful imprisonment or conviction (Scheck and Neufeld 2002). Not all of these states had uniform reimbursement provisions. For instance, Ohio capped awards to wrongfully convicted offenders in 2005 at $25,000 per year of incarceration, while the federal government capped such awards at $100,000 per year (Innocence Project 2005). As of February of 2010, 250 persons had been exonerated of their convictions due to DNA evidence. Further, by 2009, 138 persons had been set free from death rows throughout the United States and classified as actually innocent of their original convictions (Death Penalty Information Center 2010).

Summary

The options available to judges at sentencing usually include incarceration or probation. Capital crimes also have the option of a sentence of death. In the United States, incarceration is almost always an option available to judges especially where the crime is a felony. Probation is also used widely especially where the crime is a misdemeanor. Critics argue that a just system of sentencing should make available more options to judges in between prison and probation; these are referred to as intermediate sanctions.

Victim impact statements (VISs) are a part of the restorative justice philosophy in that victims and others are asked to give statements about how they were affected by the crime either in writing or orally at the sentencing hearing.

Persons who are convicted of serious crimes are subjected to sentencing hearings. These are proceedings where both sides may present evidence and witnesses favoring harsher or more lenient punishments. Aggravating and mitigating circumstances are presented by the prosecutor and defense counsel respectively in an effort to influence the judge in his/her sentencing decision making.

Relevant to sentencing hearings is the presentence investigation report (PSI), which is often prepared by a probation officer. PSIs contain a depiction of the crime committed, the police report, the offender's version of events, background information about the offender, psychiatric reports, a VIS, and other vital information useful to judges and others in making decisions about offenders. Offenders have an opportunity to accept responsibility in such reports in an effort to create a favorable impression on judges and secure some leniency in the sentences imposed.

Even though judges may have information at the sentencing hearing regarding the seriousness of the crime and the defendant's prior criminal record, other factors such as the race/ethnicity, sex, or socioeconomic status of the defendant may affect the sentencing outcome. Because these are legally irrelevant criteria, when a judge bases a sentence even partially due to one of these so-called extralegal factors it leads to disparities in sentencing. If these disparities according to extralegal factors cannot be explained away by some legally relevant criteria, this is discrimination in sentencing.

Some offenders are given shock probation or split sentences. They may be placed in prison or jail for up to 120 days and then brought back before the court to be resentenced to probation. It is believed that the shock of incarceration for some persons at least is sufficiently traumatic to discourage them from committing new crimes. Split sentences involve mixed sentences of probation and confinement, usually in a jail, for short time intervals. Several split sentencing variations have been described.

The death penalty is a special punishment that has evolved its own court protocol over the years. It is incumbent upon criminal courts today to provide bifurcated trials for those facing the death penalty as a possible punishment for capital murder and other crimes, such as terrorist acts or large-scale drug trafficking. A bifurcated trial is a two-part proceeding. The first part is the trial phase, where guilt or innocence of the defendant is determined. If the jury finds the defendant guilty, it must deliberate in a second stage or phase to determine and recommend a punishment, either death, life without the possibility of parole, or life imprisonment. All death sentences are automatically appealed. Most appeals of these sentences are unsuccessful.

The appeals process for any criminal conviction is a lengthy and tedious process. If an offender is convicted, one or more appeals may be launched to the next higher court above the trial court. States have their own court hierarchy, and convicted offenders are expected to follow it when filing appeals. Sometimes offenders may file appeals in federal district courts, under certain circumstances. Ordinarily, state prisoners must exhaust all of their state court appeals remedies before approaching federal courts with their appeals.

The bases for appeals vary, although several types of appeals have been described. Convicted persons may file *habeas corpus* petitions, wherein they challenge the fact, length, and nature of their confinement.

Generally, most appeals from convicted offenders are unsuccessful. A small portion of appeals each year is heard by the U.S. Supreme Court, especially where issues of constitutional significance are involved. U.S. Supreme Court appeals are initiated by writs of *certiorari*.

Questions for Review

1. What is a *habeas corpus* petition? What are three types of issues challenged by such petitions?
2. What is a writ of *certiorari*? Under what circumstances might this type of writ be used?
3. What are some trends regarding the use of *habeas corpus* petitions by jail and prison inmates? What factors seem to account for such trends?
4. Differentiate between shock probation and split sentencing. What are three types of split sentences?
5. What is a sentencing hearing? What are the major functions of such hearings?
6. What is a presentence investigation report? Who prepares it and how is it used to determine an offender's punishment?
7. What is a bifurcated trial? Under what circumstances is it used? What are two significant cases relating to bifurcated trials?
8. What are victim impact statements? Where are such statements found and what purposes do they serve in the sentencing process?
9. Why is the appeals process for death sentences so lengthy?
10. Does disparity in sentencing occur? What does the research reveal about disparities according to race/ethnicity? Sex? Socioeconomic status?

Suggested Readings

1. P. K. Brennan (2006). "Sentencing Female Misdemeanants: An Examination of the Direct and Indirect Effects of Race/Ethnicity." *Justice Quarterly* **23:** 60–94.

2. D. P. Green and D. Winik (2010). "Using Random Judge Assignments to Estimate the Effects of Incarceration and Probation on Recidivism Among Drug Offenders." *Criminology* **48(2):** 357–387.

3. S. E. Barkan and S. F. Cohn (2010). "Contemporary Regional Differences in Support by Whites for the Death Penalty: A Research Note." *Justice Quarterly* **27(3):** 458–471.

4. D. Holleran and C. Spohn (2004). "On the Use of the Total Incarceration Variable in Sentencing Research." *Criminology* **42:** 211–240.

5. J. K. Doerner and S. Demuth (2010). "The Independent and Joint Effects of Race/Ethnicity, Gender, and Age on Sentencing Outcomes in U.S. Federal Courts." *Justice Quarterly* **27(1):**1–27.

6. S. Steen, R. L. Engen, and R. R. Gainey (2005). "Images of Danger and Culpability: Racial Stereotyping, Case Processing, and Criminal Sentencing." *Criminology* **43:** 435–468.

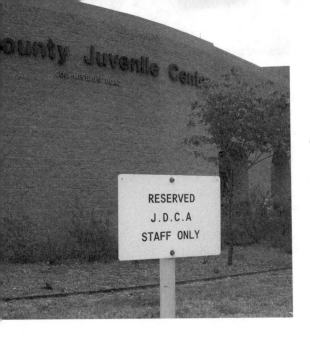

CHAPTER 11

The Juvenile Justice System: Juvenile Rights and Case Processing

CHAPTER OBJECTIVES

As the result of reading this chapter, you will have accomplished the following objectives:

1. Understand the basic components of the juvenile justice system and how juveniles are processed differently from adult offenders.
2. Distinguish between delinquents and status offenders and the reasons for making such distinctions.
3. Describe the influence of due process upon juvenile offender processing, including an examination of the legal rights of juveniles.
4. Describe several key cases in the evolution of juvenile rights and how these rights have affected how juveniles are processed.

KEY TERMS

camp, ranch
case backlog
case processing
chancellors
child savers
children in need of
    supervision (CHINS)
criminalization
curfew violators
deinstitutionalization
deinstitutionalization of
    status offenders (DSO)

direct file
divestiture of jurisdiction
due process
due process courts
English common law
foster home
group home
Illinois Juvenile Court Act
intake
intake hearings
intake officer
Jane Addams

juvenile court
juvenile court jurisdiction
juvenile delinquency
juvenile delinquent
Juvenile Justice and
    Delinquency Prevention
    Act of 1974 (JJDPA)
juveniles
loiterers
Office of Juvenile Justice
    and Delinquency
    Prevention (OJJDP)

parens patriae
prosecutorial waive
reformatory
runaways
Society for the Prevention
    of Pauperism
standard of proof
status offenders
statutory exclusion
stigmas
stigmatize
truants

At a teen peer court in a high school in Los Angeles, defendants literally stand before a jury of their peers. Dorsey high School students mete out sentences to juveniles who are accused of criminal offenses. In one case a student is found guilty of battery and the teen jury sentences him to submit to community service, anger counseling, a curfew, drug testing, and writing a letter of apology to his parents. Teens ending up in this court are usually first-time offenders and the intent is to keep kids out of the criminal justice system and deter them from committing further offenses. The philosophy of these teen courts is that sentences from a jury of other teens rather than adults will have more of an impact on the delinquent teens and their judgments will have a greater deterrent effect. Studies show that close to 90 percent of those sentenced in teen court complete their sanctions and some even go on to serve as teen jurors in other cases. What do you think of teen juries? Might this be a better way to deal with first-time, young offenders rather than formally processing them through the criminal justice system, where they may perhaps come into contact with more serious offenders who will likely not have a positive effect on them?

Source: Adapted from Daniel B. Wood, The Christian Science Monitor, "Teen juries put a new spin on juvenile justice," April 13, 2010.

INTRODUCTION

This chapter examines the juvenile justice system, which is in some ways the analog of the criminal justice system for youthful offenders. Many adults who are processed by the criminal justice system began their criminal offending in their early years as juveniles. Some argue that most persons actually commit some form of delinquent act in their adolescent years and then desist as they become adults (Piquero, Brezina, and Turner 2005), while others persist in committing criminal acts into their adult years. This chapter begins with an overview of the juvenile justice system. It discusses the distinction between juvenile delinquents and status offenders, which is important because juvenile delinquents are those who have committed or are alleged to have committed offenses that would be crimes if adults committed them. By contrast, status offenders commit acts that would not be crimes if adults committed them.

For many decades, the juvenile justice system has not differentiated between these types of offenders, despite the fact that delinquents commit considerably more serious offenses than status offenders and pose greater risks to society. This chapter describes the establishment of the Juvenile Justice and Delinquency Prevention Act of 1974, which contributed much to changing how status offenders are presently treated. In subsequent years, most juvenile courts have divested themselves of their jurisdiction over status offenders, preferring to focus their resources on more serious delinquent offenders. The changes brought about by this act will be described.

Next, the chapter focuses upon the jurisdiction of the juvenile court. Jurisdiction refers to the power of courts to hear particular kinds of cases. A brief history of the juvenile court is presented, and several important contrasts between juvenile and criminal courts are illustrated. The juvenile justice process begins with a referral, which may be made by a parent, guardian, school official, police officer, or neighbor. Over 2 million juveniles annually are referred to the juvenile justice system, although only about half of these are processed eventually by the system in more formal ways. About half of all juveniles who enter the juvenile justice system are there as the result of petitions. Petitions allege that juveniles have committed different acts that juvenile courts must adjudicate.

The process of screening juveniles, intake, is described. Beyond intake, juvenile court prosecutors perform chores relating to juveniles that are quite similar to the tasks performed by criminal court prosecutors. They must decide which cases to pursue and which ones not to pursue. About half a million juveniles or more appear before juvenile court judges annually, and their cases are adjudicated.

The next section discusses the legal rights of juveniles, and several important U.S. Supreme Court cases involving juvenile rights are presented. Their implications for juvenile court treatment are discussed. Several rights conveyed to juveniles by the U.S. Supreme Court include the right to an attorney, the right to a notice of charges, the right to cross-examine one's accuser, the right to give testimony in one's own behalf, the right against self-incrimination, and the right to the beyond a reasonable doubt standard where one's liberty is in jeopardy. Also, juveniles have the right against double jeopardy, which may occur when a juvenile is adjudicated delinquent by the juvenile court and a criminal court subsequently finds him/her guilty of the same charge. This is considered double jeopardy and is thus unconstitutional. Juveniles do not have the right to a jury trial, however, unless provided for by state statutes or by judicial decree. Most juvenile court judges do not allow jury trials for juveniles, inasmuch as this procedure would delay juvenile court processing of youthful offenders considerably.

DELINQUENCY, JUVENILE DELINQUENTS, AND STATUS OFFENDERS

Juvenile Delinquents

JUVENILES   **Juvenile court jurisdiction** is dependent upon established legislative definitions of who **juveniles** are and the offenses they commit. There is considerable variation among the states as to which juvenile offenders are within the purview of juvenile courts. The federal government has no **juvenile court**. Rather, federal cases involving juveniles infrequently are heard in federal district courts, but adjudicated juveniles are housed in state or local facilities if the sentences involve incarceration. Ordinarily, upper and lower age limits are prescribed. However, these age limits are far from uniform among jurisdictions. The common law or **English common law** standard sets the minimum age of juveniles at seven, although no state is obligated to recognize this common law definition. In fact, some states have no lower age limits that would otherwise function to limit juvenile court jurisdiction.

Some states with the lowest maximum age for juvenile court jurisdiction include Connecticut, New York, and North Carolina. The lowest maximum age for juvenile court jurisdiction is 15 in these states. Other states having a low maximum age of 16 for juvenile court jurisdiction are Georgia, Illinois, Louisiana, Massachusetts, Michigan, Missouri, South Carolina, and Texas. All other states and the federal government use age 18 as the minimum age for criminal court jurisdiction (Champion 2007).

In most jurisdictions, youths under the age of seven are often placed in the care of community agencies, such as departments of human services and social welfare. These children frequently have little or no responsible parental supervision or control. In many cases, the parents themselves may have psychological problems or suffer from alcohol or drug dependencies. Youths from such families may be abused and/or neglected, and in need of supervision and other forms of care or treatment. Under common law in those states where common law applies, children under the age of seven are presumed incapable of formulating criminal intent. If a six-year-old child kills someone, for instance, deliberately or accidentally, he/she will likely be treated rather than punished.

JUVENILE DELINQUENCY   **Juvenile delinquency** is the violation of a criminal law of the United States by a person prior to his eighteenth birthday, which would have been a crime if committed by an adult (18 U.S.C., Sec. 5031, 1997). Generally, juvenile delinquency is the violation of any state or local law or ordinance by anyone who has not yet become an adult. Any act committed by a juvenile that would be a crime if an adult committed it is a delinquent act. A **juvenile delinquent** is anyone who has committed juvenile delinquency.

Status Offenders

Status offenders are those who commit offenses that would not be crimes if adults committed them. Typical status offenses are runaway behavior, truancy, and curfew violation. Adults may run away from home, be truant from their classes, and stay out late at night without violating the law. However, juveniles are required to observe these laws that pertain specifically to them (Urban 2005).

RUNAWAYS   According to the Office of Juvenile Justice and Delinquency Prevention (OJJDP), in 2008, the rate of arrest for runaway was 327 per 100,000 juveniles aged 10–17 years (OJJDP 2009). OJJDP also reports that this is 35 percent below the rate of runaway in 1980. Runaways consist of those youths who leave their homes, without permission or their parents' knowledge, and who remain away from home for prolonged periods ranging from several days to several years. Many runaways are eventually picked up by police in different jurisdictions and returned to their homes. Others return of their own free will and choice.

TRUANTS AND CURFEW VIOLATORS   **Truants** are those who absent themselves from school without either school or parental permission. **Curfew violators** are those youths who remain on city streets after specified evening hours when they are prohibited from loitering or not being in the company of a parent or guardian. In 2004, there were 125,000 youths charged with curfew violation in the United States (Bureau of Justice Statistics 2005). Between 1997 and 2008, however, curfew and loitering violations went down about 40 percent (OJJDP 2009).

JUVENILE AND CRIMINAL COURT INTEREST IN STATUS OFFENDERS   Juvenile courts are interested in status offenders who habitually appear before juvenile court judges. Repeated juvenile court appearances may be symptomatic of subsequent adult criminality. The chronicity of juvenile offending seems to be influenced by the amount of contact youths have with juvenile courts. Greater contact with juvenile courts is believed by some experts to **stigmatize** youths and cause them either to be labeled or acquire **stigmas** as delinquents or deviants. Therefore, diversion of certain types of juvenile offenders from the juvenile justice system has been advocated and recommended to minimize stigmatization (McLean, Cocozza, and Skowyra 2004).

One way of removing status offenders from juvenile courts and their stigmatizing effects is to deprive juvenile court judges of jurisdiction over status offenders (Blackmore, Brown, and Krisberg 1988). Another way of minimizing status offender stigmatization is to remove them from custodial institutions where they are housed for various terms, such as industrial schools. These methods are known as **divestiture of jurisdiction** and **deinstitutionalization of status offenders (DSO)** or simply **deinstitutionalization**.

DIVESTING JUVENILE COURTS OF THEIR JURISDICTION OVER STATUS OFFENDERS   Under divestiture, juvenile courts cannot detain, petition, adjudicate, or place youths on probation or in institutions for committing *any* status offense. In lieu of juvenile court intervention, various community agencies and social services are used to care for and place status offenders.

DEINSTITUTIONALIZATION OF STATUS OFFENDERS (DSO)   There is a prevalent belief that institutionalizing status offenders in juvenile industrial schools (e.g., prisons for juveniles) will harden them, thus increasing their likelihood of committing future, more serious offenses. Therefore, in the late 1960s, a movement began to remove status offenders from juvenile penal institutions such as industrial schools. In 1974 the U.S. Congress passed enabling legislation to accomplish this objective on a national basis.

The **Juvenile Justice and Delinquency Prevention Act of 1974 (JJDPA)** (and modified in 1984) was established in response to a national concern about growing juvenile delinquency and youth crime. This act authorized the establishment of the **Office of Juvenile Justice and Delinquency Prevention (OJJDP)**, which has been extremely helpful and influential in matters of disseminating information about juvenile offending and prevention and as a general data source. The JJDPA provides for a state relations and assistance division. The JJDPA has also been modified extensively since its inception in 1974.

THE STATE RELATIONS AND ASSISTANCE DIVISION   This division addresses directly the matter of removing juveniles, especially status offenders, from secure institutions (facilities similar to adult prisons), jails, and lockups. The second division, Research and Program Development, examines how juvenile courts process juvenile offenders.

CHANGES AND MODIFICATIONS IN IHE JJDPA   Congress modified the act in 1977 by declaring the juveniles should be separated by both sight and sound from adult offenders in detention and correctional facilities. Also in 1977, states were given five years to comply with the DSO mandate. Congress prohibited states in 1980 from detaining juveniles in jails and lockups. Congress also directed that states should examine their secure confinement policies relating to minority juveniles and to determine reasons and justification for the disproportionately high rate of minority confinement (Mukoro 2005). In 1992, Congress directed that any participating state would have up to 25 percent of its formula grant money withheld to the extent that the state was not in compliance with each of the JJDPA mandates. Thus, it is clear that state compliance with these provisions of the JJDPA was encouraged and obtained by providing grants-in-aid to various jurisdictions wishing to improve their juvenile justice systems and facilities (Rodriguez 2004).

THE JURISDICTION OF JUVENILE COURTS

THE AGE JURISDICTION OF JUVENILE COURTS   Upper age limits for juveniles have been established in all U.S. jurisdictions (either under 16, under 17, or under 18 years of age). However, presently there is no uniformity concerning applicable lower age limits. Technically, juvenile courts have jurisdiction over three-year-old murderers. However, no juvenile court will adjudicate a three-year-old delinquent and place the child in an industrial school. The type of jurisdictional control over such children by juvenile courts is more care and treatment oriented. This treatment and care may include placement of children or infants in foster homes or under the supervision of community service or human welfare agencies that can meet their needs. Neglected, unmanageable, abused, or other **children in need of supervision (CHINS)** are placed in the custody of these various agencies, at the discretion of juvenile judges. Generally, juvenile courts have broad discretionary powers over most persons under the age of 18.

THE TREATMENT AND PUNISHMENT FUNCTIONS OF JUVENILE COURTS   Not all juveniles who appear before juvenile court judges are delinquents. Many youths in juvenile court have not violated any criminal laws (Feld 2003). Rather, their status as juveniles means that they are within juvenile court control. Several circumstances make these youths susceptible to juvenile court jurisdiction. These circumstances may be the quality of their adult supervision, if any. Other circumstances may be that they run away from home, are truant from school, or loiter on certain city streets during evening hours. Runaways, truants, or **loiterers** are considered status offenders, since their actions would not be criminal ones if committed by adults.

Physically, psychologically, or sexually abused children are within the jurisdictional control of juvenile courts. Many of these juvenile courts are instead called family courts. However, the majority of youthful offenders who appear before juvenile courts are juvenile delinquents. However, in more than a few jurisdictions, a delinquent act is whatever juvenile courts say it is. Thus, juvenile courts have broad discretionary powers over all types of juveniles. Much of this state authority originated under the early English doctrine of ***parens patriae***.

Parens Patriae

PARENS PATRIAE   *Parens patriae* originated with the king of England during the twelfth century. It literally means the father of the country. Applied to juvenile matters, *parens patriae* means that the king is in charge of, makes decisions about, or has responsibility for all matters involving juvenile conduct. Within the scope of early English common law, parental authority was primary in the early upbringing of children. However, as children advanced to age seven and beyond, they acquired some measure of responsibility for their own actions. Accountability to parents was shifted gradually to accountability to the state, whenever youths seven years of age or older violated the law. In the name of the king, chancellors in various districts adjudicated matters involving juveniles and the offenses they committed. Juveniles had no legal rights or standing in any court. They were the sole responsibility of the king or his agents. Their future often depended largely upon decisions made by **chancellors**. In effect, children were wards of the court, and the court was vested with the responsibility to safeguard their welfare.

Since children could become wards of the court and subject to their control, a key concern for many chancellors was for the future welfare of these children. The welfare interests of chancellors and their actions led to numerous rehabilitative and/or treatment measures. Some of these measures included placement of children in foster homes or their assignment to various work tasks for local merchants. Parental influence in these child placement decisions was minimal.

Modern Applications of *Parens Patriae*

Parens patriae is pervasive in all juvenile court jurisdictions, despite that most states have increased the number of juveniles being treated as adults. The pervasiveness of this doctrine is exhibited by the wide range of dispositional options available to juvenile court judges and others involved in earlier stages of offender processing in the juvenile justice system. Most of these dispositional options are either nominal or conditional, meaning that the confinement of any juvenile for most offenses is regarded as a last resort.

The strong treatment or rehabilitative orientation inherent in *parens patriae* is not acceptable to some juvenile justice experts. Contemporary juvenile court jurisprudence stresses individual accountability for one's actions (Champion 2007). Consistent with a growing trend in the criminal justice system toward just deserts and justice, a similar trend is being observed throughout the juvenile justice system (Lawrence and Hesse 2010). This get-tough movement is geared toward providing law violators with swifter, harsher, and more certain justice and punishment than the previously dominant rehabilitative philosophy of American courts.

The *parens patriae* doctrine has been influenced greatly by the changing rights of juveniles. Since the mid-1960s, juveniles have acquired greater constitutional rights commensurate with those enjoyed by adults in criminal courts. Some professionals believe that as juveniles are vested with greater numbers of constitutional rights, a gradual transformation of the juvenile court is occurring toward one of greater **criminalization** (Feld 2000, 2001). Interestingly, as juveniles obtain a greater range of constitutional rights, they become more immune to the influence of *parens patriae*. Quite simply, juvenile judges are gradually losing much of their former, almost absolute, autonomy over juveniles and their life chances.

VARIATIONS IN CRIMINAL AND JUVENILE COURT PROCESSING

Some of the major differences between juvenile and criminal courts are indicated below.

1. Juvenile court proceedings are civil proceedings exclusively designed for juveniles, whereas criminal court proceedings are designed to try adults charged with crimes. The civil–criminal distinction is important because a civil adjudication of a case does not result in a criminal record.
2. Informality characterizes juvenile court proceedings, whereas criminal proceedings are formal. Juvenile court judges frequently address juveniles directly and casually. Formal criminal or evidentiary procedures are not followed rigorously, and hearsay from various sources is considered together with factual evidence.

3. In 39 states, juveniles are not entitled to a trial by jury, unless the juvenile court judge approves. In those jurisdictions that do not provide jury trials for juveniles in special circumstances, judicial approval of a jury trial for juveniles is required.

4. Juvenile court and criminal court proceedings are adversarial.

5. All criminal courts are courts of record, whereas transcripts of most juvenile proceedings are made only if the judge decides. However, some juvenile court judges may have the resources and/or interest to provide for such transcriptions, particularly if serious offenses against certain juveniles have been alleged.

6. The **standard of proof** used for determining one's guilt in criminal proceedings is beyond a reasonable doubt. This same standard is applicable in juvenile courts where violations of criminal laws are alleged and incarceration in a juvenile facility is a possible punishment. However, the less rigorous civil standard of preponderance of evidence is used in most other juvenile court matters where one's loss of liberty is not at issue.

7. Criminal courts have the full range of penalties, including death and life-without-parole options. Juvenile courts have limited jurisdiction, and they can only dispose juveniles to terms that terminate when they reach adulthood.

JUVENILE COURT HISTORY

A BRIEF HISTORY OF JUVENILE COURTS IN THE UNITED STATES   Juvenile courts are primarily an American creation. The first juvenile court was established in Illinois in 1899 under the **Illinois Juvenile Court Act**. This does not mean that other states were unconcerned about juveniles at the time, or that other events had not occurred pertaining to youths, their conduct, and their welfare. In fact, numerous agencies and organizations had been established earlier in other jurisdictions, particularly during the latter half of the 1800s.

REFORMATORIES   The first public **reformatory** for juveniles was the New York House of Refuge. It was established in New York City in 1825 by the Society for the Prevention of Pauperism (Champion 2005b). This house of refuge had several goals relating to juveniles, including providing food, clothing, and lodging for all poor, abused, or orphaned youths. However, the **Society for the Prevention of Pauperism** was comprised, in part, of many benefactors, philanthropists, and religionists, and these individuals sought to instill within the youths they serviced a commitment to hard work, strict discipline, and intensive study. These houses were established in various parts of New York and staffed largely by volunteers who knew little or nothing about individual counseling, group therapy techniques, or other useful interventions that might assist youths in surviving city hazards. Because the organization of these houses was decentralized, there were few, if any, external controls that could regulate the quality of care provided.

CHILD SAVERS   While houses of refuge operated to provide services for misplaced youths, other random efforts led to the creation of child-saving programs. **Child savers** referred to no one in particular, because anyone who wished to be of assistance in helping children and intervening in their lives for constructive purposes could define themselves as child savers. No one knows what child-saving meant, but many persons were involved in providing food, shelter, and other forms of care for needy children.

COMMUNITY-BASED PRIVATE AGENCIES   **Jane Addams** established and operated **Hull House** in Chicago, Illinois, in 1889. This was a settlement home used largely by children from immigrant families in the Chicago area. Many adults worked long hours, and many youths were otherwise unsupervised and wandered about their neighborhoods looking for something to do. Using money from various charities and philanthropists, Addams supplied many children with creative activities to alleviate their boredom and monotony. Addams integrated these activities with moral, ethical, and religious teachings. In her own way, she was hoping to deter these youths from lives of crime with her constructive activities and teaching.

TRUANCY STATUTES   Truancy laws were passed by the Massachusetts state legislature in 1852, where the first compulsory school attendance statutes were established. By 1918, all jurisdictions had truancy statutes. Juveniles who did not attend school were subject to being taken into custody. State homes were used to place such youths, where it could be demonstrated that they had little, if any, adult supervision at home.

THE LACK OF JUVENILE COURT UNIFORMITY   Much variation exists among juvenile court organization and operation in the United States (Champion 2009). Even great variations in juvenile court operations and functions are found within the same state. Some jurisdictions have courts that adjudicate juvenile offenders as well as decide child custody. Thus, while it is true that all jurisdictions presently have juvenile courts, these courts are not always called juvenile courts.

SPECIALIZED JUVENILE COURTS   Most early juvenile court proceedings were different from criminal court proceedings. These proceedings often involved a juvenile charged with some offense; a petitioner claiming the juvenile should be declared delinquent, or dependent, or neglected; and a judge who would decide things. Juveniles had no rights, no attorneys, and were not permitted to call witnesses or testify in their own behalf. Juvenile court judges made decisions about juveniles according to what the judges believed to be in the best interests of the children. Thus, much individualized justice was dispensed by juvenile court judges.

THE CLOSED AND ARBITRARY NATURE OF JUVENILE COURT PROCEEDINGS   Early juvenile court proceedings were closed to the general public in order to protect the identities of the youthful accused. Mere allegations, together with uncorroborated statements and pronouncements from probation officers and others, were sufficient for juvenile court judges to declare any juvenile either delinquent or not delinquent. Penalties imposed ranged from verbal reprimands and warnings to incarceration in a state reform school or industrial school.

THE BUREAUCRATIZATION AND CRIMINALIZATION OF JUVENILE COURTS   Generally, juvenile courts are viewed as **due process courts** rather than traditional courts (Feld 2003). Due process juvenile courts involve more formal case dispositions, a greater rate of intake dismissals, and greater importance attached to offense characteristics and seriousness. Traditional courts are characterized as less formal, with greater use made of secure confinement. Both defense and prosecuting attorneys play more important roles in due process juvenile courts compared with traditional ones (Guevara and Herz 2004).

PUBLIC DEFENDERS FOR JUVENILES   Greater procedural formality in the juvenile justice system has been observed relating to the appointment of public defenders for juvenile indigents. Formerly, a defense counsel for a juvenile often was the juvenile's probation officer or a social caseworker with a vested interest in the case. It is not entirely clear how these officers and workers were able to separate their law enforcement and defense functions to avoid allegations of conflicts of interest. Little public interest was exhibited in the quality of defense of juvenile cases.

In recent years, juvenile court proceedings have become increasingly formalized (Champion 2009). Further, public access to these proceedings in most jurisdictions is increasing. Thus, the presence of defense counsel, an adversarial scenario, a trial-like atmosphere where witnesses testify for and against juvenile defendants, and adherence to Rules of Procedure for Juvenile Courts are clear indicators of greater formalization, bureaucratization, and criminalization. Also with greater formalization, less disparity in dispositional decision making has occurred relating to one's gender, ethnic identity, or race (Charish 2004; Rosay and Myrstol 2004).

THE JUVENILE JUSTICE PROCESS

Referrals and Petitions

REFERRALS   Many juvenile encounters with the juvenile justice system are prompted by referrals from police officers (Champion 2009). Referrals are notifications made to juvenile court authorities that a juvenile requires the court's attention. Referrals may be made by anyone, such as concerned parents, school principals, teachers, neighbors, and others. However, over 90 percent of all referrals to juvenile court are made by law enforcement officers. Some researchers have suggested that disparities in juvenile offender processing begin at this stage and continue throughout the entire juvenile justice system, where factors such as race, ethnicity, gender, and socioeconomic status intervene to affect juveniles in different ways (Ketchum and Embrick 2004). Arrest and being taken into custody is the first of three major processing points that indicate different degrees of entry into the juvenile justice system for juveniles. The other entry points include probation disposition and court disposition. Each of these entry points involves the exercise of discretion from various actors in the juvenile justice system.

PETITIONS   A petition is a legal document filed by interested parties alleging that a juvenile is delinquent, a status offender, or in need of adult supervision. The petition requests that the juvenile court decide whether the allegations are true and determine an appropriate penalty or disposition. When a petition is filed against a particular juvenile, the juvenile is subjected to an intake hearing or simply, intake.

Intake

Intake varies in formality among jurisdictions (Worling 1995). Intake is a screening procedure conducted by a court officer or a probation officer, where one or several courses of action are recommended. Some jurisdictions conduct **intake hearings**, where comments and opinions are solicited from significant others such as the police, parents, neighbors, or victims. These proceedings are important, regardless of their degree of formality.

An **intake officer** is either a court-appointed official who hears complaints against juveniles and attempts early resolutions of them, or more often a juvenile probation officer who performs intake as a special assignment. In many small jurisdictions, juvenile probation officers may perform diverse functions, including intake screenings, enforcement of truancy statutes, and juvenile placements. Intake officers consider youths' attitudes, demeanor, age, offense seriousness, and a host of other factors. If the offenses alleged are serious, what evidence exists against the offender? Should the offender be referred to certain community social service agencies, receive psychological counseling, receive vocational counseling and guidance, acquire educational or technical training and skills, be issued a verbal reprimand, be placed on some type of diversionary status, or be returned to parental custody? Interviews with parents and neighbors may be conducted as a part of an intake officer's information gathering. In most jurisdictions, intake normally results in one of five actions, depending, in part, upon the discretion of intake officers:

1. dismissal of the case, with or without a verbal or written reprimand;
2. remand youths to the custody of their parents;
3. remand youths to the custody of their parents, with provisions for or referrals to counseling or special services;
4. divert youths to an alternative dispute resolution program, if one exists in the jurisdiction;
5. refer youths to the juvenile prosecutor for further action and possible filing of a delinquency petition.

Juvenile Court Prosecutors and Decision Making

Like their criminal court counterparts, juvenile court prosecutors have broad discretionary powers. They may dismiss cases against certain juveniles. They may screen cases by diverting some of the most serious ones to criminal court through waiver, transfer, or certification. A **prosecutorial waiver** is used for this purpose. Some cases are diverted out of the juvenile justice system for informal processing (Feld 2000). Prosecutors may also file petitions or act on the petitions filed by others. These documents assert that juveniles fall within the categories of dependent or neglected, status offender, or delinquent, and the reasons for such assertions are usually provided (Champion 2009). Filing a petition formally places the juvenile before the juvenile court judge in many jurisdictions.

JUVENILE RIGHTS AND STANDARDS OF PROOF

During the mid-1960s and for the next 30 years, significant achievements were made in the area of juvenile rights. Although the *parens patriae* philosophy continues to be somewhat influential in juvenile proceedings, the U.S. Supreme Court has vested youths with certain constitutional rights. These rights do not encompass all of the rights extended to adults who are charged with crimes. But those rights conveyed to juveniles thus far have had far-reaching implications for how juveniles are processed. In the following section, several landmark cases involving juvenile rights will be described.

Landmark Cases in Juvenile Rights

Regardless of the causes, several significant changes have been made in the juvenile justice system and how youths are processed in recent decades. Each of the cases presented below represents attempts by juveniles to secure rights ordinarily extended to adults.

***KENT V. UNITED STATES* (1966)**   Morris A. Kent, Jr., a 14-year-old in the District of Columbia, was apprehended in 1959 as the result of several housebreakings and attempted purse snatchings. He was placed on probation in the custody of his mother. In 1961, an intruder entered the apartment of a woman, took her wallet, and raped her. Fingerprints at the crime scene were later identified as those of Morris Kent, who was fingerprinted when apprehended for housebreaking in 1959. On September 5, 1961, Kent, 16, was taken into custody by police, was interrogated for seven hours, and admitted the offense as well as volunteered information about other housebreakings, robberies, and rapes. Kent was summarily waived to criminal court by the juvenile court judge without a hearing on the waiver, which his attorney had demanded. Kent was later found guilty of six counts of housebreaking by a federal jury, although the jury found him not guilty by reason of insanity on the rape charge. Because of District of Columbia law, it was mandatory that Kent be transferred to a mental institution until such time as his sanity is restored. On each of the housebreaking counts, Kent's sentence was 5–15 years, or a total of 30–90 years in prison. His mental institution commitment would be counted as time served against the 30- to 90-year sentence. The U.S. Supreme Court reversed Kent's conviction on appeal. The Court held that Kent's rights to due process and to the effective assistance of counsel were violated when he was denied a formal hearing on the waiver and his attorneys' motions were ignored. Because of the *Kent* decision, waiver hearings are now considered critical stages requiring an attorney's advice and presence.

***IN RE GAULT* (1967)**   *In re Gault* (1967) is perhaps the most significant of all juvenile rights cases. It is certainly the most ambitious in terms of the rights sought by Gault. The U.S. Supreme Court granted the following rights for all juveniles as the result of the *Gault* decision: (1) the right to a notice of charges, (2) the right to counsel, (3) the right to confront and cross-examine witnesses, and (4) the right to invoke the privilege against self-incrimination.

The facts are that Gerald Francis Gault, a 15-year-old, and a friend, Ronald Lewis, were taken into custody by the Sheriff of Gila County, Arizona, in the morning of June 8, 1964. A verbal complaint had been filed by a neighbor of Gault, Mrs. Cook, alleging that Gault had called her and made lewd and indecent remarks. Gault was picked up while his mother and father were at work. They did not learn of their son's whereabouts until later that evening. Gault was being held at the Children's Detention Home. Gault's parents proceeded to the home and were advised that a petition had been filed against Gault and a hearing was scheduled in juvenile court the following day. No factual basis was provided for the petition, and Gault's parents were not provided with a copy of it in advance of the hearing. When the hearing was held, only Gault, his mother and older brother, probation officers Flagg and Henderson, and the juvenile court judge were present. The original complainant, Mrs. Cook, was not there. No one was sworn at the hearing, no transcript was made of it, and no memorandum of the substance of the proceedings was prepared. The testimony consisted largely of allegations by Officer Flagg about Gault's behavior and prior juvenile record. Gault was adjudicated delinquent by the judge and ordered to serve a six-year term in the Arizona State Industrial School (a juvenile prison). After exhausting their appeals in Arizona state courts, the Gaults appealed to the U.S. Supreme Court. Needless to say, the Court was appalled that Gault's case had been handled in such a cavalier and unconstitutional manner. They reversed the Arizona Supreme Court, holding that Gault did, indeed, have the right to an attorney, the right to confront his accuser (Mrs. Cook) and to cross-examine her, the right against self-incrimination, and the right to have notice of the charges filed against him. Perhaps Justice Black summed up the current juvenile court situation in the United States when he said, "This holding strikes a well-nigh fatal blow to much that is *unique* [emphasis mine] about the juvenile courts in this Nation."

IN RE WINSHIP (1970)   *Winship* was a less complex case compared with *Gault*. But it established an important precedent in juvenile courts relating to the standard of proof used in established defendant guilt. The facts are that Samuel Winship was a 12-year-old charged with larceny in New York City. He purportedly entered a locker and stole $112 from a woman's pocketbook. Under Section 712 of the New York Family Court Act, a juvenile delinquent was defined as a person over 7 and less than 16 years of age who does any act, which, if done by an adult, would constitute a crime. While the juvenile court judge in the case acknowledged that the proof to be presented by the prosecution might be insufficient to establish the guilt of Winship beyond a reasonable doubt, he did adjudicate Winship delinquent and ordered him placed in a training school for 18 months. The U.S. Supreme Court heard Winship's case and reversed the New York Family Court ruling on the basis that an 18-month loss of liberty was substantial enough to warrant a stronger standard of proof such as beyond a reasonable doubt. Since this standard of proof was not used in Winship's case, he was unjustly adjudicated.

MCKEIVER V. PENNSYLVANIA (1971)   The *McKeiver v. Pennsylvania* case is important because the U.S. Supreme Court held that juveniles are not entitled to a jury trial as a matter of right. The facts are that in May 1968, Joseph McKeiver, age 16, was charged with robbery, larceny, and receiving stolen goods. While he was represented by counsel at his adjudicatory hearing and requested a trial by jury, the judge denied his request. McKeiver was adjudicated delinquent. On appeal to the U.S. Supreme Court, McKeiver's adjudication was upheld. The U.S. Supreme Court said that it is the juvenile court judge's decision whether to grant jury trials to juveniles. By 2005 only 12 states legislatively mandated jury trials for juveniles in juvenile courts if they so requested such trials, depending upon the seriousness of the offense(s) alleged.

BREED V. JONES (1975)   This case raised the significant constitutional issue of double jeopardy. The U.S. Supreme Court concluded that after a juvenile has been adjudicated as delinquent on specific charges, those same charges may not be alleged against those juveniles subsequently in criminal courts through transfers or waivers. The facts of the case are that on

February 8, 1971, in Los Angeles, California, Gary Steven Jones was 17 years old, was armed with a deadly weapon, and allegedly committed robbery. Jones was subsequently apprehended and a petition was filed against him. He was adjudicated delinquent. The judge then transferred Jones through a judicial waiver to a criminal court where he could be tried as an adult. In a later criminal trial, Jones was convicted of robbery and committed for an indeterminate period to the California Youth Authority. The California Supreme Court upheld the conviction. When Jones appealed the decision in 1971, the U.S. Supreme Court reversed the robbery conviction. Jones's conviction in criminal court was overturned on the basis that it was a violation of his right against double jeopardy. Jones had already been adjudicated on the same charge in juvenile court. Juveniles cannot be adjudicated on a given charge in juvenile court and then sent to criminal court to face conviction on the same charge.

SCHALL V. MARTIN (1984)   In this case, the U.S. Supreme Court issued juveniles a minor setback regarding the state's right to hold them in preventive detention pending a subsequent adjudication. The Court said that the preventive detention of juveniles by states is constitutional, if judges perceive these youths to pose a danger to the community or an otherwise serious risk if released short of an adjudicatory hearing. This decision was significant, in part, because many experts advocated the separation of juveniles and adults in jails, those facilities most often used for preventive detention. Also, the preventive detention of adults was not ordinarily practiced at that time. [Since then, the preventive detention of adults who are deemed to pose societal risks has been upheld by the U.S. Supreme Court (*United States v. Salerno*, 1987).]

The facts are that 14-year-old Gregory Martin was arrested at 11:30 p.m. on December 13, 1977 in New York City. He was charged with first-degree robbery, second-degree assault, and criminal possession of a weapon. Martin lied to police at the time, giving a false name and address. Between the time of his arrest and December 29 when a fact-finding hearing was held, Martin was detained (a total of 15 days). His confinement was based largely on the false information he had supplied to police and the seriousness of the charges pending against him. Subsequently, he was adjudicated a delinquent and placed on two years' probation. Later, his attorney filed an appeal, contesting his preventive detention as violative of the Due Process Clause of the Fourteenth Amendment. The U.S. Supreme Court eventually heard the case and upheld the detention as constitutional (Rodriguez 2004). Table 11-1 summarizes some of the major rights available to juveniles and compares these rights with selected rights enjoyed by adults in criminal proceedings.

TABLE 11-1   Comparison of Juvenile and Adult Rights Relating to Delinquency and Crime[a]

Right	Adults	Juveniles
1. "Beyond a Reasonable Doubt" standard used in court	Yes	Yes
2. Right against double jeopardy	Yes	Yes
3. Right to assistance of counsel	Yes	Yes
4. Right to notice of charges	Yes	Yes
5. Right to a transcript of court proceedings	Yes	No
6. Right against self-incrimination	Yes	Yes
7. Right to trial by jury	Yes	No in most states
8. Right to defense counsel in court proceedings	Yes	No
9. Right to due process	Yes	No*
10. Right to bail	Yes	No, with exceptions

(continued)

TABLE 11-1   (Continued)

Right	Adults	Juveniles
11. Right to cross-examine witnesses	Yes	Yes
12. Right of confrontation	Yes	Yes
13. Standards relating to searches and seizures:		
a. "Probable cause" and warrants required for searches and seizures	Yes, with exceptions	No
b. "Reasonable suspicion" required for searches and seizures without warrant	No	Yes
14. Right to hearing prior to transfer to criminal court or to a reverse waiver hearing in states with automatic transfer provisions	N/A	Yes
15. Right to a speedy trial	Yes	No
16. Right to *habeas corpus* relief in correctional settings	Yes	No
17. Right to rehabilitation	No	No
18. Criminal evidentiary standards	Yes	Yes
19. Right to hearing for parole or probation revocation	Yes	No
20. Bifurcated trial, death penalty cases	Yes	Yes
21. Right to discovery	Yes	Limited
22. Fingerprinting, photographing at booking	Yes	No, with exceptions
23. Right to appeal	Yes	Limited
24. Waivers of rights:		
a. Adults	Knowingly, intelligently	
b. Juveniles		Totality of circumstances
25. Right to hearing for parole or probation revocation	Yes	No, with exceptions
26. "Equal protection" clause of Fourteenth Amendment applicable	Yes	No, with exceptions
27. Right to court-appointed attorney if indigent	Yes	No, with exceptions
28. Transcript required of criminal/delinquency trial proceedings	Yes	No, with exceptions
29. Pretrial detention permitted	Yes	Yes
30. Plea bargaining	Yes, with exceptions	No, with exceptions
31. Burden of proof borne by prosecution	Yes	No, with exceptions**
32. Public access to trials	Yes	Limited
33. Conviction/adjudication results in criminal record	Yes	No

^aCompiled by the authors.

*Minimal, not full, due process safeguards assured.

**Burden of proof is borne by prosecutor in 23 state juvenile courts, while the rest make no provision or mention of who bears the burden of proof.

Summary

The juvenile justice system is a civil entity that parallels closely the criminal justice system, particularly in how juveniles are processed. Juvenile courts have jurisdiction over all juveniles who commit delinquency, or acts that would be crimes if adults committed them.

Juveniles are any persons who have not reached the age of their majority or adulthood. Juvenile delinquents are distinguished from status offenders, who commit acts that would not be crimes if adults committed them.

Status offenders may be runaways, truants, curfew violators, or those who engage in underage drinking. In more than a few jurisdictions, social welfare agencies and human services have gradually been granted jurisdiction over status offenders because of the nature of their offending.

The juvenile justice process has been influenced largely by the doctrine of *parens patriae*, which originated in England during the 1500s. The king of England utilized chancellors in different shires or English counties to make decisions in his behalf relating to all juveniles who committed various offenses. These decisions were most often influenced by what would be in the children's best interests.

Today juvenile courts make decisions according to these same criteria, although bureaucratization and extended legal rights for juveniles have caused these courts to focus on due process and less on one's best interests. Nevertheless, these courts continue to perpetuate the *parens patriae* doctrine informally, and this practice, the traditional approach to juvenile justice, is largely individualized. Many juvenile courts regard their functions as largely treatment centered rather than punishment centered.

In 1974 the Juvenile Justice and Delinquency Prevention Act was passed, which sought to deinstitutionalize status offenders. At the time, it was customary for juvenile courts to institutionalize both delinquents and status offenders, and some states continue to do so.

But most states have effectively removed status offenders from institutions where they were formerly housed together with qualitatively more serious delinquent offenders. Many juvenile courts have divested themselves of their jurisdiction over status offenders as well, thus giving greater jurisdictional power to social services and social welfare agencies who often supervise those charged with status offenses.

Some similarities and differences between juvenile courts and criminal courts have been described. As previously noted, juvenile courts are civil, while criminal courts process adults who are charged with committing felonies and misdemeanors. The consequences of a conviction in criminal court result in a criminal record, whereas civil consequences from juvenile court adjudications are largely noncriminal and are expunged from one's record upon attaining adulthood. All criminal courts are courts of record and juvenile courts are not. Both types of courts are adversarial, and both use the "beyond a reasonable doubt" standard of proof. Juvenile courts use this standard only when a juvenile is in jeopardy of losing his/her liberty or may be confined for any period of time. Criminal courts have a broader range of punishments, including life without the possibility of parole and the death penalty, which are beyond the scope of a juvenile court's jurisdiction. In most states, jury trials for juveniles are not permitted except with judicial approval. Juvenile court proceedings are generally less formal compared with those of criminal courts, although in recent years, this difference has rapidly diminished.

Juvenile court history is relatively brief. The first juvenile court in the United States was established in 1899 in Illinois under the Juvenile Court Act. By the 1940s, all states had juvenile courts. Prior to 1899, juveniles were subject to a wide variety of sanctions by different bodies, such as children's tribunals. Many juveniles whose parents worked for long hours in factories to earn a living wandered city streets during daytime hours. Some of these juveniles were institutionalized for short periods as a punishment for vagrancy or begging.

Child savers emerged, largely from the middle and upper classes, and these persons often established shelters or temporary homes where idle juveniles could be accommodated safely and removed from the dangers of the streets. During the late 1800s many persons and agencies became concerned and involved with child welfare matters, and the gradual progression to a full-fledged juvenile court was realized.

The juvenile justice process usually commences with a referral from a parent, the police, a guardian, a school official, or a neighbor, and one or more delinquent acts or status offenses are alleged. Juveniles are taken into custody and screened by intake officers, who often are juvenile probation officers. More serious cases are sent to juvenile court prosecutors, where further decision making about them occurs.

Intake officers also have some limited discretionary powers and may defer actions against harmless youthful offenders who seem remorseful and unlikely to reoffend. About half of all juvenile cases are petitioned, where formal documents are filed with juvenile courts. Most petitioned cases result in adjudicatory proceedings before a juvenile court judge who listens and decides each case. If the facts alleged against the juveniles are true, juvenile court judges declare juveniles delinquent or status offenders and impose one of several types of dispositions as punishments.

Several landmark cases involving juveniles have been decided by the U.S. Supreme Court and have vested all juveniles with most due process rights afforded to adults. In *Kent v. United States* (1966), it was declared that all juveniles are entitled to a hearing before they are transferred to criminal court. *In re Gault* (1967) resulted in a juvenile's right to an attorney, the right to confront and cross-examine one's accuser and to give testimony in one's own behalf, the right against self-incrimination, and the right to a notice of charges against the juvenile. *In re Winship* (1970) established the "beyond a reasonable doubt" criminal court standard to prove one's guilt in juvenile court where any juvenile is in danger of losing his/her liberty through secure confinement in a juvenile institution. For cases not involving a possible loss of liberty, the civil standard of the preponderance of evidence continues to be used and governs determinations of whether juveniles have committed certain acts alleged by others in adjudicatory proceedings.

In *McKeiver v. Pennsylvania* (1971), it was decided that juveniles are not entitled to a jury trial in juvenile court as a matter of right. Today juvenile courts provide jury trials for juveniles under special circumstances as a matter of right in 11 states, and juvenile court judges have the discretion to approve jury trials in other jurisdictions if juveniles request one.

In *Breed v. Jones* (1975), it was decided that juveniles cannot be simultaneously adjudicated in juvenile court on a charge and convicted of that same charge in criminal court without violating their right against double jeopardy.

In *Schall v. Martin* (1984), it was decided that juveniles may be held in preventive detention for different periods of time, pending their identification and risk posed if released.

Questions for Review

1. Distinguish between a juvenile delinquent and a status offender. What has the federal government done to keep status offenders out of jails?
2. What is the jurisdiction of juvenile courts?
3. What is the doctrine of *parens patriae*? Why is it significant when investigating the actions of juvenile courts today? In what ways does *parens patriae* influence judicial decision making?
4. What is a referral? Who can make referrals? What are their purposes?
5. Identify three major rights cases involving juveniles. What are the major rights conveyed in the cases you have identified?
6. What is meant by DSO? What was the enabling legislation leading to DSO on the federal level?
7. What are some general differences between criminal courts and juvenile courts?
8. Under what circumstances can juveniles have jury trials in juvenile courts?

Suggested Readings

1. Barry C. Feld (2003). "The Politics of Race and Juvenile Justice: The 'Due Process Revolution' and the Conservative Reaction." *Justice Quarterly* **20**:765–800.
2. Heather Hammer, David Finkelor, and Andrea J. Sedlak (2002). *Runaway/Throwaway Children: National Estimates and Characteristics.* Washington, DC: Office of Juvenile Justice and Delinquency Prevention.
3. B. K. Applegate, R. King Davis, and F. T. Cullen. (2009). "Reconsidering Child Saving: The Extent and Correlates of Public Support for Excluding Youths From the Juvenile Court." *Crime and Delinquency* **55**:51–77.
4. Lynn S. Urban, Jenna L. St. Cyr, and Scott H. Decker (2003). "Goal Conflict in the Juvenile Court: The Evolution of Sentencing Practices in the United States." *Journal of Contemporary Criminal Justice* **19**:454–479.
5. J. L. Viljoen, J. Klaver, and R. Roesch (2005). "Legal Decisions of Preadolescent and Adolescent Defendants: Predictors of Confessions, Pleas, Communications with Attorneys, and Appeals." *Law and Human Behavior* **29**: 253–277.
6. P. E. Tracy, K. Kempf-Leonard, and S. Abramoske-James. (2009). "Gender Differences in Delinquency and Juvenile Justice Processing: Evidence From National Data." *Crime & Delinquency* **55**:171–215.

CHAPTER 12

Juvenile Courts: Adjudication and Disposition

CHAPTER OBJECTIVES

As the result of reading this chapter, you will have accomplished the following objectives:

1. Understand the jurisdiction of juvenile courts and the influence of *parens patriae* on court actions.
2. Examine the role of juvenile court prosecutors and the changing nature of juvenile court proceedings as defense counsels are increasingly used in most jurisdictions.
3. Understand the waiver, transfer, and certification processes, how these procedures move juveniles to criminal court jurisdiction, and the implications of these decisions for juvenile offenders.
4. Understand blended sentencing statutes and how these statutory provisions have changed the nature of juvenile sentencing and rehabilitation.
5. Describe several important trends in juvenile justice that have significance for how juveniles are processed by juvenile courts.

KEY TERMS

adjudicates
adjudication
adjudication hearing
Anchorage Youth Court
automatic waivers
blended sentencing
certification
conditional dispositions
confinement

criminal–exclusive blend
criminal–inclusive blend
custodial dispositions
demand waiver
direct file
discretionary waivers
due process
guardian *ad litem*
judicial waiver

juvenile–contiguous blend
juvenile–exclusive blend
juvenile–inclusive blend
legislative waivers
mandatory transfer
nominal dispositions
nonsecure custody
once an adult/always
   an adult

presumptive waiver
prosecutorial waiver
reverse waiver hearings
secure custody
teen courts
traditional courts
transfer
waiver
waiver hearing

The Supreme Court recently decided that juvenile offenders cannot be sentenced to life in prison without parole. The court in a 5–4 decision ruled that for juveniles who commit murder, an automatic life sentence cannot be imposed because it is a violation of the Eighth Amendment's clause regarding cruel and unusual punishment. The court's decision invalidates laws in over 35 states and gives the opportunity for about 130 juveniles now serving life terms to make the case that they should be given a parole hearing at some point. In the last two decades states have increasingly enacted tougher laws for juveniles who commit serious offenses, often trying them as adults. What do you think? Should juveniles be given a chance to turn their lives around and perhaps be eligible for parole at some point, even if they have committed a murder? Or, do you think that despite their age, courts should be able to sentence juveniles to life in prison? Life expectancy in the U.S. today hovers around 80 years old; should states consider how much it may cost to keep a juvenile in prison for 65–70 years?

Source: Adapted from Joan Biskupic and Martha T. Moore, The USA Today, "Court limits life terms for youths: Ruling against no-parole sentences reflects doubts about state crackdowns," May 18, 2010.

INTRODUCTION

Adjudication is a juvenile court judicial decision that the facts alleged against the juvenile, either by petition or by other means, are true or not true. If judges decide that the facts are true and that the juvenile committed one or more delinquent acts, one of several different kinds of dispositions is imposed. This chapter begins with the different types of dispositions that are available to juvenile court judges. These dispositions are nominal, conditional, and custodial. These dispositions roughly equate respectively with verbal warnings, probation, or incarceration in a secure facility. The adjudicatory process is described, as well as the different types of dispositions imposed on juveniles by juvenile court judges.

Juveniles have the right to due process, which vests them with many of the same rights as adults charged with crimes. All juveniles are entitled to counsel. If the juvenile or the juvenile's family/guardian is indigent, then an attorney will be appointed to represent the juvenile. Cases against juveniles may be plea bargained in much the same way that adult cases are plea bargained. Thus, many juvenile cases are never brought before the juvenile court judge for a formal adjudicatory hearing. At least 11 states make provisions for jury trials for juveniles if they request them. Jury trials for juveniles are not a matter of right, but rather, certain states extend the jury trial privilege to certain juveniles depending on their age, offense seriousness, and other important and relevant criteria.

About 1 percent of all juveniles referred to the juvenile court each year are transferred, waived, or certified to the jurisdiction of criminal courts, where the juveniles are treated as adults. **Transfers**, **waivers**, or **certifications** make it possible for criminal courts to impose harsher sanctions against juveniles, such as the death penalty or life imprisonment. Such sanctions are beyond the jurisdiction of juvenile courts. The waiver process is described, and various positive and adverse implications for juveniles are discussed.

There are four major types of waiver actions. These include judicial waivers, prosecutorial waivers, statutory exclusion or legislative or automatic waivers, and demand waivers. Each of these types of waivers is defined and discussed. All juveniles who are transferred to criminal court jurisdiction are entitled to a hearing before they are waived. The implications of such hearings are described.

In recent decades, most states have evolved blended sentencing statutes. The next section of this chapter examines several types of blended sentencing statutes whereby either juvenile court judges or criminal court judges may hear and decide juvenile cases and impose either juvenile sanctions, criminal sentences, or both, depending upon the jurisdiction. The advantages and disadvantages of blended sentencing statutes will be described. The chapter concludes with an examination of several important trends in juvenile justice and a discussion of the favorable and unfavorable implications of these trends for affected juveniles.

ADJUDICATORY PROCEEDINGS

Most of the physical trappings of criminal courts are present in juvenile courts, including the judge's bench, tables for the prosecution and defense, and a witness stand. Juvenile court judges have almost absolute discretion in how their courts are conducted. Juvenile defendants may or may not be granted a trial by jury, if one is requested. Few states permit jury trials for juveniles in juvenile courts, according to legislative mandates. After hearing the evidence presented by both sides in any juvenile proceeding, the judge decides or **adjudicates** the matter in an **adjudication hearing. Adjudication** is a judgment or action on the petition filed with the court by others. If the petition alleges delinquency on the part of certain juveniles, the judge determines whether the juveniles are delinquent or not delinquent. If the petition alleges that the juveniles involved are dependent, neglected, or otherwise in need of care by agencies or others, the judge decides the matter. If the adjudicatory proceeding fails to support the facts alleged in the petition filed with the court, the case is dismissed and the youth is freed. If the adjudicatory proceeding supports the allegations, then the judge must sentence the juvenile or order a particular disposition (A. Harris 2004).

Dispositions

Twelve dispositions are available to juvenile court judges, if the facts alleged in petitions are upheld. These dispositions may be grouped into (1) nominal, (2) conditional, or (3) custodial options.

NOMINAL DISPOSITIONS   **Nominal dispositions** are the least punitive of the three major courses of action available to juvenile court judges. These are usually verbal warnings or reprimands. Release to the custody of parents or legal guardians completes the juvenile court action.

CONDITIONAL DISPOSITIONS   All **conditional dispositions** are probationary options. Youths are placed on probation and required to comply with certain conditions during the probationary period. Conditional options or dispositions usually provide for an act or acts on the part of juveniles to be fulfilled as conditions of the sentence imposed. If juveniles have been adjudicated as delinquent and if the delinquency involved damage to a victim's property or bodily harm, restitution to victims may be required to pay for the property or medical bills (Wood 2004). Various kinds of community service are performed by juveniles, such as cutting courthouse lawns, cleaning up city parks, and cleaning debris from city highways or public areas. Group or individual therapy may be required of certain juveniles who exhibit psychological or social maladjustment. If some juveniles are alcohol or drug dependent, they may be required to participate in various recovery programs.

CUSTODIAL DISPOSITIONS   **Custodial dispositions** are either **nonsecure custody** or **confinement** or **secure custody.** Nonsecure custody consists of placing certain juveniles into a **foster home, group home**, or **camp, ranch**, or schools. These are temporary measures often designed to make more permanent arrangements for juvenile placement later. Juveniles have freedom of movement, and they can generally participate in school and other youthful activities. For juveniles, secure custody is often the last resort considered by most juvenile court judges. There is a general reluctance among judges to incarcerate youths because of adverse labeling effects. Furthermore, there are increasing numbers of alternatives to incarceration within communities. Judges are increasingly apprised of these programs and are assigning more youths to them in lieu of industrial school placements (Kupchik 2004).

Changing Juvenile Court Practices

MINIMIZING THE CONFIDENTIALITY OF JUVENILE COURT RECORDS AND PROCEEDINGS

Most courts do not allow open hearings in juvenile or family court proceedings to protect the identity of the juvenile. Most states will allow release of the names of the juvenile if he or she is charged with a serious crime or is being transferred to adult court. Most states will release court records to interested parties. In fact, all states currently make available juvenile court records to any party showing a legitimate interest. In such cases, information is ordinarily obtained through a court order. Fingerprinting and photographing of juveniles is conducted routinely in most states. Half the states require registration of all juvenile offenders when they enter new jurisdictions. Also, most states presently have state repositories of juvenile records and other relevant information about juvenile offending. Seventeen states prohibited sealing or expunging juvenile court records after certain dates, such as one's age of majority or adulthood (Champion 2009). Therefore, juveniles today are considerably more likely to have their offenses known to the public in one form or another.

The protections previously enjoyed by juveniles are rapidly disappearing. The greater formality of juvenile proceedings as well as their openness to others may restrict the discretion of juvenile court judges, although this limitation is not particularly an undesirable one. This is because juvenile court judge decision making has often been individualized, and individualized decision making is inherently discriminatory. With more open proceedings, less individualization is evident, thus making due process a greater priority for juvenile court judges. Theoretically, at least, more open proceedings are fairer proceedings.

THE PROSECUTION DECISION

The juvenile justice system has been slow in its **case processing** of juvenile offenders. In fact, delays in filing charges against juveniles and the eventual adjudicatory hearing are chronic in many jurisdictions. Juveniles arrested for various types of offenses may wait a year or longer in some jurisdictions before their cases are heard by juvenile court judges. Juvenile court prosecutors may delay filing charges against particular juveniles for a variety of reasons. The most obvious reasons for delays—court **case backlogs**, crowded court dockets, insufficient prosecutorial staff, too much paperwork—are not always valid reasons. In many instances, the actors themselves are at fault. In short, prosecutors and judges may simply be plodding along at a slow pace, because of their own personal dispositions and work habits. It has been illustrated that in many jurisdictions where prosecutors and judges have aggressively tackled their caseload problems and forced functionaries to work faster, juvenile caseload processing has been greatly accelerated. Thus, the time between a juvenile's arrest and disposition has been greatly shortened because of individual decision making and not because of any organizational constraints or overwork (Champion 2009).

However, in 30 states in 2005, juvenile court prosecutors were at liberty to file charges against juvenile offenders whenever they decided. No binding legislative provisions were applicable to these actors to force them to act promptly and bring a youth's case before the juvenile court. In the meantime, 20 states have established time limits that cannot be exceeded between the time of a juvenile's court referral and the filing of charges by prosecutors.

Defense Counsels as Advocates for Juveniles

ATTORNEYS FOR JUVENILES AS A MATTER OF RIGHT

Juveniles are entitled to attorneys at all stages of juvenile proceedings. Despite this safeguard, attorney representation for juveniles in juvenile courts in most jurisdictions is less than adequate. Feld and Schaefer (2010) cite that even decades after the *Gault* decision, states have failed to set up provisions for adequate defense representation in juvenile cases.

DEFENSE COUNSEL AND ENSURING DUE PROCESS RIGHTS FOR JUVENILES   The manifest function of defense attorneys in juvenile courts is to ensure that **due process** is fulfilled by all participants. Defense attorneys are the primary advocates of fairness for juveniles who are charged with crimes or other types of offenses (Rodriguez and Armstrong 2004). Minors, particularly very young youths, are more susceptible to the persuasiveness of adults.

ARE ATTORNEYS BEING USED MORE FREQUENTLY BY JUVENILE DEFENDANTS?   Yes. However, adequate defense has still not been achieved as fewer than half of juvenile defendants are represented in some states, and juvenile defenders like their adult counterparts have high caseloads which do not allow them to spend much time with clients.

DO DEFENSE COUNSEL FOR JUVENILES MAKE A DIFFERENCE IN THEIR CASE DISPOSITIONS?
Having an attorney to represent you generally makes a difference in the case disposition. But not all dispositions are favorable for juveniles. The presence of attorneys may heighten juvenile court formality. Earlier in the processing of juveniles, attorney presence may cause intake officers to take sterner measures with juveniles who ordinarily would be dismissed from the system. More than a few intake officers, for instance, are intimidated by attorneys, if present. If an intake officer would be inclined to divert a particular case from the juvenile justice system because of his/her judgment that the youth will probably not reoffend, this diversion decision may not be selected if an attorney is present to represent the juvenile's interests. The intake officer may feel that the prosecutor of juvenile court judge should decide the case. However, in an otherwise attorney-free environment, the intake officer would act differently. Thus, an attorney's presence or absence may cause intake officers to react differently and make decisions that are better or worse for juveniles charged with delinquency or status offenses.

DEFENSE COUNSEL AS GUARDIANS *AD LITEM*   Defense counsel perform additional responsibilities as they attempt to ensure that the best interests of their clients are served in ways that will protect children from parents who abuse them (Kupchik 2004; Ward 2004). A **guardian *ad litem*** is a special guardian appointed by the court in which a particular litigation is pending to represent a youth, ward, or unborn person in that particular litigation (Williams, Rodeheaver, and Guerrero 2004). Most juvenile court jurisdictions have guardian *ad litem* programs, where interested persons serve in this capacity. In some cases, defense counsel for youths perform the dual role of defense counsel and the youth's guardians *ad litem.* Guardians *ad litem* are supposed to work in ways that will benefit those they represent, and such guardians provide legal protection from others. Defense counsel working as guardians *ad litem* may act to further the child's best interests, despite a child's contrary requests or demands.

JUVENILE OFFENDER PLEA BARGAINING AND THE ROLE OF DEFENSE COUNSEL   Many juveniles plea bargain with juvenile court prosecutors (Helms et al. 2004). Plea bargaining is an invaluable tool with which to eliminate case backlogs that might occur in some of the larger juvenile courts. Most frequently sought by defense counsel are charge reductions against their clients by prosecutors. Defense counsel are interested in reducing the stigma of a serious, negative juvenile court profile of their youthful clients by seeking reduced charges from prosecutors (Burruss and Kempf-Leonard 2002). Prosecutors benefit because plea agreements would increase case processing time.

Jury Trials for Juveniles

Some states have granted juveniles the right to a jury trial; however, they rarely occur. The National Center for Juvenile Justice investigated various state jurisdictions to determine their present status concerning jury trials and other formal procedures for juveniles. The categories created by this investigation included the following: (1) states providing no right to a jury trial for juvenile delinquents under any circumstances, (2) states providing a right to a jury trial for juvenile delinquents under any circumstances, (3) states not providing a jury trial for juvenile delinquents except under specified circumstances, (4) states providing the right to a jury trial for juvenile delinquents under specified circumstances, and (5) states with statutes allowing juvenile delinquents with a right to jury trial to waive that right (Szymanski, 1997).

STATES NOT PROVIDING JURY TRIALS FOR JUVENILE DELINQUENTS UNDER ANY CIRCUMSTANCES: Alabama, Arizona, Arkansas, California, District of Columbia, Georgia, Hawaii, Indiana, Kentucky, Louisiana, Maryland, Mississippi, Nevada, New Jersey, North Dakota, Ohio, Oregon, Pennsylvania, South Carolina, Tennessee, Utah, Vermont, and Washington.

STATES PROVIDING JURY TRIALS FOR JUVENILES UNDER ANY CIRCUMSTANCES: Alaska, Massachusetts, Michigan, and West Virginia.

STATES NOT PROVIDING JURY TRIALS FOR JUVENILE DELINQUENTS EXCEPT UNDER SPECIFIED CIRCUMSTANCES: Colorado (all hearings, including adjudicatory hearings, shall be heard without a jury; juvenile is not entitled to a trial by jury when petition alleges a delinquent act that is a class 2 or class 3 misdemeanor, a petty offense, a violation of a municipal or county ordinance, or a violation of a court order if, prior to the trial and with the approval of the court, the district attorney has waived in writing the right to seek a commitment to the department of human services or a sentence to the county jail); District of Columbia (probation revocation hearings heard without a jury); Florida (adjudicatory hearings heard without a jury); Louisiana (adjudication hearings heard without a jury); Maine (adjudicatory hearing heard without a jury); Montana (hearing on whether juvenile should be transferred to adult criminal court heard without a jury; probation revocation proceeding heard without a jury); Nebraska (adjudicatory hearing heard without a jury); New Mexico (probation revocation proceedings heard without a jury); North Carolina (adjudicatory hearing heard without a jury); Texas (detention hearing heard without a jury; hearing to consider transfer of child for criminal proceedings and hearing to consider waiver of jurisdiction held without a jury; disposition hearing heard without a jury, unless child in jeopardy of a determinate sentence; hearing to modify a disposition heard without a jury, unless child in jeopardy of a sentence for a determinate term); Wisconsin (no right to a jury trial in a waiver hearing); and Wyoming (probation revocation hearing heard without a jury; [14–6–237]: transfer hearing heard without a jury).

STATES WHERE JUVENILE DELINQUENT HAS A RIGHT TO A JURY TRIAL UNDER SPECIFIED CIRCUMSTANCES: Arkansas (if amount of restitution ordered by the court exceeds $10,000, juvenile has right to jury trial on all issues of liability and damages); Colorado (no right to a jury trial unless otherwise provided by this title; juvenile may demand a jury trial, unless the petition alleges a delinquent act that is a class 2 or class 3 misdemeanor, a petty offense, a violation of a municipal or county ordinance, or a violation of a court order if, prior to the trial and with the approval of the court, the district attorney has waived in writing the right to seek a commitment to the department of human services or a sentence to the county jail; any juvenile alleged to be an aggravated juvenile offender (defined in statute) has the right to a jury trial); Idaho (any juvenile age 14–18 alleged to have committed a violent offense defined in statute or a controlled substance offense has the right to a jury trial); Illinois (any habitual juvenile offender defined in statute has the right to a jury trial); Kansas (any juvenile alleged to have committed an act that would be a felony if committed by an adult has the right to a jury trial); Minnesota (child who is prosecuted as an extended jurisdiction juvenile has the right to a jury trial on the issue of guilt); Montana (any juvenile who contests the offenses alleged in the petition has the right to a jury trial); New Mexico (jury trial on issues of alleged delinquent acts may be demanded when the offenses alleged would be triable by a jury if committed by an adult); Oklahoma (child has the right to a jury trial in an adjudicatory hearing); Rhode Island (child has the right to a jury trial when the court finds the child is subject to certification to adult court); Texas (child has the right to a jury trial at adjudicatory hearing; child has the right to a jury trial at disposition hearing only if the child is in jeopardy of a determinate sentence; child has the right to a jury trial at a hearing to modify the disposition only if the child is in jeopardy of a determinate sentence on the issues of the violation of the court's orders and the sentence); Virginia (if the juvenile indicted, the juvenile has the right to a jury trial; if found guilty of capital murder, the court fixes the sentence with intervention of a jury; where the appeal is taken by the child on a finding that he or she is delinquent and the alleged delinquent act would be a felony if done by an adult, the child is entitled to a jury); and Wyoming (juvenile has right to a jury trial at an adjudicatory hearing).

STATES PROVIDING RIGHT TO A JURY TRIAL FOR JUVENILE DELINQUENTS WHERE JUVENILE DELINQUENTS CAN WAIVE THEIR RIGHT TO A JURY TRIAL: Colorado (unless a jury is demanded, it shall be deemed waived); Illinois (the minor can demand in open court, and with advice of counsel, a trial by the court without a jury); Massachusetts (the child can file written waiver and consent to be tried by the court without a jury; this waiver cannot be received unless the child is represented by counsel or has filed, through his/her parent or guardian, a written waiver of counsel); Montana (in the absence of a demand, a jury trial is waived); Oklahoma (the child has right to waive jury trial); Texas (the trial shall be by jury unless jury is waived); and Wyoming (failure of party to demand a jury no later than ten days after the party is advised of his/her right is a waiver of this right). [*Sources:* Linda A. Szymanski, *Juvenile's Right to a Jury Trial in a Delinquency Hearing (1996 Update).* Pittsburgh: National Center for Juvenile Justice, 1997; updated by author 2005.]

TRANSFERS, WAIVERS, AND CERTIFICATIONS

A **transfer** means changing the jurisdiction over certain juvenile offenders to another jurisdiction, usually from juvenile court jurisdiction to criminal court jurisdiction. A transfer is also known as a **waiver**, referring to a change of jurisdiction from the authority of juvenile court judges to criminal court judges. Prosecutors or juvenile court judges decide that in some cases juveniles should be waived or transferred to the jurisdiction of criminal courts (Bishop et al. 2004).

In Utah, juveniles are waived or transferred to criminal courts through a process known as **certification** (Listwan and Miethe 2004). A certification is a formal procedure whereby the state declares the juvenile to be an adult for the purpose of a criminal prosecution in a criminal court (Sridharan et al. 2004). The results of certifications are the same as for waivers or transfers. Thus, certifications, waivers, and transfers result in juvenile offenders being subject to the jurisdiction of criminal courts where they can be prosecuted as though they were adult offenders. A 13-year-old murderer, for instance, might be transferred to criminal court for a criminal prosecution on the murder charge (Merlo and Benekos 2004).

THE RATIONALE FOR TRANSFERS, WAIVERS, OR CERTIFICATIONS   The basic rationale underlying the use of waivers is that the most serious juvenile offenders will be transferred to the jurisdiction of criminal courts where the harshest punishments, including capital punishment, may be imposed as sanctions (Jordan 2004b). A listing of reasons for the use of transfers, waivers, or certifications includes the following:

1. To make it possible for harsher punishments to be imposed.
2. To provide just deserts and proportionately severe punishments on those juveniles who deserve such punishments by their more violent actions.
3. To foster fairness in administering punishments according to one's serious offending.
4. To hold serious or violent offenders more accountable for what they have done.
5. To show other juveniles who contemplate committing serious offenses that the system works and that harsh punishments can be expected if serious offenses are committed.

6. To provide a deterrent to decrease juvenile violence.

7. To overcome the traditional leniency of juvenile courts and provide more realistic sanctions.

8. To make youths realize the seriousness of their offending and induce remorse and acceptance of responsibility.

THE CHARACTERISTICS OF TRANSFERRED JUVENILES   In 2004, there were 13,200 youths who were transferred to criminal court. Most juveniles transferred were male, with only 625 females (4.7 percent) being waived (Bureau of Justice Statistics 2005). About 7200 (54 percent) of all transferred juveniles were black or other minority, despite the fact that white juveniles comprised about 66 percent of all cases referred to juvenile court. Furthermore, those charged with person offenses and waived to criminal court made up only 41 percent of those transferred (Johnson, Bannister, and Alm 2004). About 44 percent of those charged with property or public order offenses were waived to criminal courts, while about 14 percent of those waived were charged with drug offenses (Bureau of Justice Statistics 2005).

YOUNGEST AGES AT WHICH JUVENILES CAN BE TRANSFERRED TO CRIMINAL COURT   In 1987, all federal districts and 15 states indicated no specified age for transferring juveniles to criminal courts for processing. One state, Vermont, specified age 10 as the minimum age at which a juvenile could be waived. Montana established age 12 as the earliest age for a juvenile waiver. Fourteen states used age 14 as the youngest transfer age, while seven states and the District of Columbia set the minimum transfer age at 15, and seven states used the minimum transfer age of 16. During the 1990s, however, more states moved to have their juvenile age ranges lowered for transfers or waivers. Table 12-1 shows the various states that have modified or enacted changes in their transfer provisions for juveniles during the 1992–1995 period.

TABLE 12-1   States Modifying or Enacting Transfer Provisions, 1996–2005

Type of Transfer Provision	Action Taken (Number of States)	States Making Changes	Examples
Discretionary Waiver	Added crimes (7 states)	DE, KY, LA, MT, NV, RI, WA	Kentucky: 1996 provision permits the juvenile court to transfer a juvenile to criminal court if he/she is 14 years old and charged with a felony committed with a firearm.
	Lowered age limit (4 states)	CO, DE, HI, VA	Hawaii: 1997 provision adds language that allows waiver of a minor at any age (previously 16) if charged with first- or second-degree murder (or attempts) and there is no evidence that the person is committable to an institution for the mentally defective or mentally ill.
	Added or modified prior record provisions (4 states)	FL, HI, IN, KY	Florida: 1997 legislation requires that if the juvenile is 14 at the time of a fourth felony, and certain conditions apply, the state's attorney must ask the court to transfer him or her and certify the child as an adult or must provide written reasons for not making such a request.
Presumptive Waiver	Enacted provisions (2 states)	KS, UT	Kansas: 1996 legislation shifts the burden of proof to the child to rebut the presumption that the child is an adult.

TABLE 12-1 (Continued)			
Type of Transfer Provision	**Action Taken (Number of States)**	**States Making Changes**	**Examples**
Direct File	Enacted or modified (8 states)	AR, AZ, CO, FL, GA, MA, MT, OK	Colorado: 1996 legislation adds vehicular homicide, vehicular assault, and felonious arson to direct file statute.
Statutory Exclusion	Enacted provision (2 states)	AZ, MA	Arizona: 1997 legislation establishes exclusion for 15- to 17-year-olds charged with certain violent felonies.
	Added crimes (12 states)	AL, AK, DE, GA, IL, IN, OK, OR, SC, SD, UT, WA	Georgia: 1997 legislation adds crime of battery if victim is a teacher or other school personnel to list of designated felonies.
	Lowered age limit (1 state)	DE	Delaware: 1996 legislation lowers from 16 to 15 the age for which the offense of possession of a firearm during the commission of a felony is automatically prosecuted in criminal court.
	Added lesser-included offense (1 state)	IN	Indiana: 1997 legislation lists exclusion offenses, including any offenses that may be joined with the listed offenses.

Source: Patricia Torbet and Linda Szymanski, *State Legislative Response to Violent Juvenile Crime: 1996–1997 Update.* Washington, DC: U.S. Department of Justice, 1998:5. Updated 2005 by author.

Inspecting Table 12-1, under **judicial waiver** modifications, 11 states lowered the age limit at which juveniles can be transferred to criminal court. One example of a significant age modification is Missouri, where the minimum age for juvenile transfers was lowered from 14 to 12 for any felony. In the case of Texas, the minimum transfer age was lowered from 15 to 10. Virginia lowered the transfer age from 15 to 14. Table 12-1 also shows that other modifications were made to get tough toward juvenile offenders. Ten states added crimes to the list of those qualifying youths for transfer to criminal courts. In six states, the age of criminal accountability was lowered, while 24 states authorized additional crimes to be included that would automatically direct that the criminal court would have jurisdiction rather than the juvenile court.

Types of Waivers

Four types of waiver actions include (1) prosecutorial waivers, (2) judicial/discretionary waivers, (3) demand waivers, and (4) legislative or automatic waivers.

PROSECUTORIAL WAIVERS   Prosecutorial waivers are also known as **direct file** or concurrent jurisdiction. Thus, under direct file, the prosecutor has the sole authority to decide whether a particular juvenile case will be heard in criminal court or juvenile court. In Florida, one of the states where prosecutors have concurrent jurisdiction, prosecutors may file extremely serious charges (e.g., murder, rape, aggravated assault, robbery) against youths in criminal courts and present cases to grand juries for indictment action. Or prosecutors may decide to file the same cases in the juvenile court.

JUDICIAL OR DISCRETIONARY WAIVERS   The largest numbers of waivers from juvenile to criminal court annually come about as the result of direct judicial action. Judicial waivers give the juvenile court judge the authority to decide whether to waive jurisdiction and transfer the case to criminal court. Known also as **discretionary waivers**, judicial waivers typically involve a juvenile court judge's consideration of various criteria, including the juvenile's age, current offense, criminal history, and amenability to rehabilitation. This particular type of transfer is invoked following a motion by the prosecutor (Champion 2004).

LEGISLATIVE OR AUTOMATIC WAIVERS **Legislative waivers** or **automatic waivers** are statutorily prescribed actions that provide for a specified list of crimes to be excluded from the jurisdiction of juvenile courts, where offending juveniles are within a specified age range, and where the resulting action gives criminal courts immediate jurisdiction over these juveniles. By the mid-1980s, 36 states excluded certain types of offenses from juvenile court jurisdiction. These excluded offenses were either very minor or very serious, ranging from traffic or fishing violations to rape or murder. Also, many state jurisdictions have made provisions for automatic transfers of juveniles to criminal court. Among those states with automatic transfer provisions are Washington, New York, and Illinois (Steiner, Hemmens, and Bell 2004).

Automatic or legislative waivers are also known as **statutory exclusion** or **mandatory transfer**. Statutory exclusion generally refers to provisions that automatically exclude certain juvenile offenders from the juvenile court's original jurisdiction (Champion 2009). An example of statutory exclusion is to simply lower the upper age of original juvenile court jurisdiction from 18 to 17 or 16. States with statutory exclusion make provisions for the statutory exclusion of offenders of particular ages and who are alleged to have committed certain types of serious offenses. For instance, a state may prohibit juvenile courts from hearing any case involving a 15-year-old murderer. The age and offense are combined to create the statutory exclusion.

DEMAND WAIVERS Under certain conditions and in selected jurisdictions, juveniles may submit motions for **demand waiver** actions. Demand waiver actions are requests or motions filed by juveniles and their attorneys to have their cases transferred from juvenile courts to criminal courts. If a juvenile's case is heard in a criminal court, the juvenile is entitled to the full range of rights available to adults charged with crimes.

OTHER WAIVER VARIATIONS Thirteen states, including the District of Columbia, have established **presumptive waiver** provisions, which require that certain offenders should be waived unless they can prove that they are suited for juvenile rehabilitation (Champion 2009). Essentially, a juvenile is considered waived to criminal court unless he/she can prove to be suitable candidates for rehabilitation. This rebuttable presumptive waiver, where the burden of proving one's rehabilitation potential rests with the juvenile and his/her attorney rather than the prosecutor, is used especially in those instances where juveniles have a history of frequent offending or where they have committed serious or violent offenses. It is difficult for any defense attorney to overcome this presumption if the juvenile client has committed an especially serious offense and has a prior record of violent offending.

ONCE AN ADULT/ALWAYS AN ADULT The **once an adult/always an adult** provision is perhaps the most serious and long-lasting for affected juvenile offenders. This provision means that once juveniles at any age have been waived to the criminal court for processing, or once juveniles have been convicted and sentenced for one or more crimes by a criminal court, they are forever after considered adults for the purpose of criminal prosecutions.

Waiver and Reverse Waiver Hearings

All juveniles who are waived to criminal court for processing are entitled to a hearing on the waiver if they request one (Champion 2009). A **waiver hearing** is a formal proceeding designed to determine whether the waiver action taken by the judge or prosecutor is the correct action, and that the juvenile should be transferred to criminal court. Waiver hearings are normally conducted before the juvenile court judge. These hearings are to some extent evidentiary, since a case must be made for why criminal courts should have jurisdiction in any specific instance.

REVERSE WAIVER HEARINGS For those jurisdictions with automatic or legislative waiver provisions, waiver actions may be contested through the use of **reverse waiver hearings**. Reverse waiver hearings are conducted before criminal court judges to determine whether to send the juvenile's case back to juvenile court. Reverse waiver hearings in those jurisdictions with automatic transfer provisions are also conducted in the presence of judges (Champion 2009).

Implications of Waiver Hearings for Juveniles

THE CASE FOR HAVING ONE'S CASE DECIDED IN JUVENILE COURT Among the positive benefits of having one's case heard in juvenile court are the following:

1. Juvenile court proceedings are civil, not criminal; thus, juveniles do not acquire criminal records.
2. Juveniles are less likely to receive sentences of incarceration.
3. Compared with criminal court judges, juvenile court judges have considerably more discretion in influencing a youth's life chances prior to or at the time of adjudication.
4. Juvenile courts are traditionally more lenient than criminal courts.
5. There is considerably more public sympathy extended to those who are processed in the juvenile justice system, despite the general public advocacy for a greater get-tough policy.
6. Compared with criminal courts, juvenile courts do not have as elaborate an information-exchange apparatus to determine whether certain juveniles have been adjudicated delinquent by juvenile courts in other jurisdictions.
7. Life imprisonment and the death penalty lie beyond the jurisdiction of juvenile court judges, and they cannot impose these harsh sentences.

THE CASE AGAINST HAVING ONE'S CASE DECIDED IN JUVENILE COURT Juvenile courts are not perfect, however, and they may be disadvantageous to many youthful offenders (Ward 2004). Some of their major limitations are the following:

1. Juvenile court judges have the power to administer lengthy sentences of incarceration, not only for serious and dangerous offenders, but for status offenders as well.
2. In most states, juvenile courts are not required to provide juveniles with a trial by jury.
3. Because of their wide discretion in handling juveniles, judges may underpenalize a large number of those appearing before them on various charges.
4. Juveniles do not enjoy the same range of constitutional rights as adults in criminal courts.

CRIMINAL COURT PROCESSING OF JUVENILE OFFENDERS

THE CASE FOR AND AGAINST HAVING ONE'S CASE TRIED IN CRIMINAL COURT When juveniles are transferred, waived, or certified to criminal court, then all rules and constitutional guarantees attach for them as well as for adults. The primary benefits for juveniles of being processed in criminal courts are as follows. Positively, depending upon the seriousness of the offenses alleged, a jury trial may be a matter of right. Adversely, periods of lengthy incarceration in minimum, medium, and maximum security facilities with adults become a real possibility. Also negatively, criminal courts in a majority of state jurisdictions may impose the death penalty in capital cases. A sensitive subject with most citizens is whether juveniles should receive the death penalty if convicted of capital crimes (Horton 2005). In recent years, the U.S. Supreme Court has addressed this issue specifically and ruled that in those states where the death penalty is imposed, the death penalty may be imposed as a punishment on any juvenile who was age 18 or older at the time the capital offense was committed (*Roper v. Simmons*, 2005). Positively, one's youthfulness works to the benefit of the defense. Jury sympathy is often evoked for a youth who has committed a horrible crime, since it can be shown that one's home life, sexual or physical abuse, and other factors are to blame for one's present plight. Therefore, a jury often favors leniency for young offenders.

BLENDED SENTENCING STATUTES AND THE GET-TOUGH MOVEMENT

The most significant change in waiver patterns throughout the United States is that between 1992 and 1996, all but ten states had adopted or modified laws making it easier to prosecute juveniles as adults in criminal courts (Champion 2009). Some of the reasons suggested for this tougher stance toward juvenile offending are that (1) juvenile rehabilitation has not been particularly effective at deterring juveniles from further offending, and (2) that the juvenile justice system is simply not punitive enough to impose the nature and types of punishments deserved by an increasingly violent juvenile offender population (Leiber, Fox, and Johnson 2004).

The major ways of making juveniles more amenable to criminal court punishment are to (1) lower the age at which they can be processed by criminal courts as adults, (2) expand the number of crimes that qualify juvenile offenders as adults for criminal court action, and (3) lower the age at which juveniles can be transferred to criminal courts for various offenses.

Blended Sentencing Statutes

Aaron Kupchik (2004) observes that in recent years, many states have legislatively redefined the juvenile court's purpose and role by diminishing the role of rehabilitation and heightening the importance of public safety, punishment, and accountability in the juvenile justice system. One of the most dramatic changes in the dispositional/sentencing options available to juvenile court judges is **blended sentencing**. Blended sentencing refers to the imposition of juvenile and/or adult correctional sanctions to cases involving serious and violent juvenile offenders who have been adjudicated in juvenile court or convicted in criminal court. Blended sentencing options are usually based on age or on a combination of age and offense (Champion 2009).

There are five basic models of blended sentencing. These include (1) juvenile–exclusive blend, (2) juvenile–inclusive blend, (3) juvenile–contiguous blend, (4) criminal–exclusive blend, and (5) criminal–inclusive blend.

The **juvenile–exclusive blend** involves a disposition by the juvenile court judge, which is either a disposition to the juvenile correctional system or to the adult correctional system, but not both. Thus, a judge might order a juvenile adjudicated delinquent for aggravated assault to serve three years in a juvenile industrial school; or the judge may order the adjudicated delinquent to serve three years in a prison for adults. The judge cannot impose *both* types of punishment under this model, however. In 1996, only one state, New Mexico, provided such a sentencing option for its juvenile court judges.

The **juvenile–inclusive blend** involves a disposition by the juvenile court judge, which is both a juvenile correctional sanction and an adult correctional sanction. In cases such as this, suppose the judge had adjudicated a 15-year-old juvenile delinquent on a charge of vehicular theft. The judge might impose a disposition of two years in a juvenile industrial school or reform school. Further, the judge might impose a sentence of three additional years in an adult penitentiary. However, the second sentence to the adult prison would typically be suspended, unless the juvenile violated one or more conditions of his/her original disposition and any conditions accompanying the disposition. Usually, this suspension period would run until the youth reaches age 18 or 21. If the offender were to commit a new offense or violate one or more program conditions, he/she would immediately be placed in the adult prison to serve the second sentence originally imposed.

The **juvenile–contiguous blend** involves a disposition by a juvenile court judge that may extend beyond the jurisdictional age limit of the offender. When the age limit of the juvenile court jurisdiction is reached, various procedures may be invoked to transfer the case to the jurisdiction of adult corrections. States with this juvenile–contiguous blend include Colorado, Massachusetts, Rhode Island, South Carolina, and Texas. In Texas, for example, a 15-year-old youth who has been adjudicated delinquent on a murder charge can be given an incarcerative term of from 1 to 30 years. At the time of the disposition in juvenile court, the youth is sent to the Texas Youth Commission and incarcerated in one of its facilities (similar to reform or industrial schools). By the time the youth reaches age 17½, the juvenile court must hold a transfer hearing to determine whether the youth should be sent to the Texas Department of Corrections. At this hearing, the youth may present evidence in his/her favor to show why he/she has become rehabilitated and no longer should be confined. However, evidence of institutional misconduct may be presented by the prosecutor to show why the youth should be incarcerated for more years in a Texas prison. This hearing functions as an incentive for the youth to behave and try to improve his/her behavior while confined in the juvenile facility.

The **criminal–exclusive blend** involves a decision by a criminal court judge to impose either a juvenile court sanction or a criminal court sanction, but not both. For example, a criminal court judge may hear the case of a 15-year-old youth who has been transferred to criminal court on a rape charge. The youth is convicted in a jury trial in criminal court. At this point, the judge has two options: The judge can sentence the offender to a prison term in an adult correctional facility, or the judge can impose an incarcerative sentence for the youth to serve in a juvenile facility. The judge may believe that the 15-year-old would be better off in a juvenile industrial school rather than an adult prison. The judge may impose a sentence of adult incarceration, but he/she may be inclined to place the youth in a facility where there are other youths in the offender's age range.

The **criminal–inclusive blend** involves a decision by the criminal court judge to impose both a juvenile penalty and a criminal sentence simultaneously. Again, as in the juvenile court–inclusive blend model, the latter criminal sentence may be suspended depending upon the good conduct of the juvenile during the juvenile punishment phase. For example, suppose a 12-year-old boy has been convicted of attempted murder. The boy participated in a drive-by shooting and is a gang member. The criminal court judge sentences the youth to a term of six years in a juvenile facility, such as an industrial school. At the same time, the judge imposes a sentence of 20 years on the youth to be spent in an adult correctional facility, following the 5-year sentence in the juvenile facility. However, the adult portion of the sentence may be suspended, depending upon whether the juvenile behaves or misbehaves during his 6-year industrial school incarceration. There is an additional twist to this blend. If the juvenile violates one or more conditions of his confinement in the juvenile facility, the judge has the power to revoke that sentence and invoke the sentence of incarceration in an adult facility. With good behavior, the youth can be free of the system following the period of juvenile confinement; the adult portion of the sentence is suspended if the youth deserves such leniency. Arkansas has the revocation power and ability to place youths in adult correctional facilities (Champion 2007).

TEEN COURTS

Increasing numbers of jurisdictions are using **teen courts** as an alternative to juvenile court for determining one's guilt and punishment. Teen court proceedings are informal jury proceedings, where jurors consist of teenagers who hear and decide minor cases. First-offender cases, where status offenses or misdemeanors have been committed, are given priority in a different type of court setting involving one's peers as judges. Judges may divert minor cases to these teen courts. Adults function only as presiding judges, and these persons are often retired judges or lawyers who perform such services voluntarily and in their spare time. The focus of teen courts is upon therapeutic jurisprudence, with a strong emphasis upon rehabilitation (Reed 2004). One objective of such courts is to teach empathy to offenders. Victims are encouraged to take an active role in these courts. Youths become actively involved as advisory juries (Peterson 2005).

Teen courts are also known as youth courts, peer courts, and student courts (Preston and Roots 2004). In 1997 there were 78 active teen courts. By 2005 there were over 1000 youth court programs operating in juvenile justice systems, schools, and community-based organizations throughout the United States, with an anticipated 2000 youth courts being established over the next few years (Peterson 2005). The American Probation and Parole Association has recognized the significance and contributions of teen courts by establishing September as National Youth Court Month to highlight the activities of youth courts and their contributions to the youth justice system (APPA Perspectives 2004a, 8).

The Use of Teen Courts

Among the first cities to establish teen courts were Seattle, Washington, and Denver, Colorado (Rasmussen 2004). Subsequently, teen courts have been established in many other jurisdictions, including Odessa, Texas. In Odessa, for instance, juveniles are referred to teen courts for class C misdemeanors and minor traffic violations. Defendants range in age from 10 to 16. Traffic citation cases result in teen court referrals by municipal judges, who give youths the option of paying their fines or having their cases heard by the teen court. If youths select the teen court for adjudication, then they do not acquire a juvenile record. The teen court listens to all evidence and decides the matter (Peterson 2005).

Teen court dispositions are always related closely to community service as well as jury service (Karp 2001, 2004). Thus, juveniles who are found guilty by teen courts may, in fact, serve on such juries in the future, as one of their conditional punishments (Rasmussen 2004). Or they may be required to perform up to 22 hours of community service, such as working at the animal shelter, library, or nursing home; picking up trash in parks or ball fields; or working with various community agencies. The teen court program in Odessa has been very successful. Prior to using teen courts, the recidivism rate for all juvenile offenders in the city was between 50 and 60 percent. However, teen court adjudications all but eliminated this recidivism figure. Interestingly, juveniles who are tried by the teen court often develop an interest in the legal system. Teen courts place a high priority on educating young people about their responsibilities of being individuals, family members, and citizens (Roberts 2003). As a part of one's diversion, conditional options such as restitution, fines, or community service may be imposed in those cases where property damage was incurred as the result of the juvenile's behavior (Chapman 2005). Juvenile court judges must exercise considerable discretion and impose dispositions that best meet the juvenile's needs and circumstances.

Constructive dispositions are the objective of teen courts in Kentucky. In September, October, and November 1992, teen jurors in a Kentucky teen court heard case details in nine different cases (Williamson, Chalk, and Knepper 1993). Referrals to teen court were made from the regular juvenile court, a division of the state's district court. If juveniles are found guilty by the teen court, then the court imposes constructive dispositions involving community service hours. It should be noted that these teen courts do not determine one's guilt or innocence—rather, they convene and recommend appropriate dispositions. Teenagers act as prosecutors, defense attorneys, clerks, bailiffs, jury forepersons, and jurors as they carry out roles similar to those of their counterparts in criminal courts. The Kentucky teen court variety is interesting because accused and judged teens are themselves recruited subsequently to serve as teen jurors. Thus, all defendants are assigned to jury duty following their teen court appearances. When this study was conducted, no youth had been returned to the teen court for noncompliance. Perhaps seeing how the process works from the other side, as jurors, made these teenagers understand the seriousness of what they had done themselves as victimizers in the past. One example of a teen court is the Anchorage, Alaska Youth Court.

By 2005, there were over 1000 teen courts established in most states (Peterson 2005). These courts are not always known as teen courts. In Anchorage, Alaska, for instance, a teen court program was established in 1989 and exists today as the **Anchorage Youth Court**. Subsequently, 14 other youth courts have been established in various Alaska cities and modeled after the Anchorage Youth Court (AYC) (Anchorage Youth Court 2005). Funding for youth courts in Alaska varies. AYC receives a third of its funds from federal block grants, United Way, and program fees; a third from fundraising and donations; and a third from the Anchorage Assembly. The AYC targets first-time offenders and makes extensive use of volunteers from the community.

Blue Earth County Teen Court

A contrast to the AYC is the Blue Earth County Teen Court (BECTC), in Makato, Minnesota (Blue Earth County 2005). According to BECTC officials, teen court is an alternative to the district court that handles very serious juvenile offenses. The BECTC is a collaborative effort that involves Blue Earth County officials and citizens. Juveniles are held accountable for their actions by a jury of their peers, and the rights of victims, if any, are respected. BECTC is also an opportunity for teens and adult volunteers to have an active, positive role in the juvenile justice system. The overall goal is to reduce the number of juvenile offenders who offend in Blue Earth County. Targeted are juveniles who commit petty offenses and choose to appear in the BECTC rather than in district court. These youths may have already participated in the Blue Earth County Youth Diversion Program as a result of a prior offense.

The goals of the BECTC are to (1) hold juvenile petty offenders accountable in a timely manner, (2) respect and maintain victims' rights, (3) reduce the number of petty offenses and less serious cases in district court, (4) educate all participants about the court system and other agencies involved in the teen court process, and (5) promote an awareness of the importance of community civic participation.

A teen jury asks juveniles questions about the offenses they committed. Victims will also have the opportunity to be heard and present any pertinent information. All juveniles appearing in the BECTC have already admitted their guilt. The BECTC jury will decide the consequences for the juvenile's behaviors. Since these are largely petty offenses, juveniles are not entitled to representation by public defenders or any other attorneys. Examples of petty offenses heard by the BECTC include shoplifting, alcohol offenses, smoking, curfew violations, and criminal damage to property or vandalism. Some possible consequences as punishments include community service hours, restitution to victims, fines, completion of offense-related educational programming, and service on teen court juries in the future. BECTC officials believe that it is quite useful for former offenders to sit in judgment of subsequent offenders, since this gives them insights into their own prior conduct.

There is a dress code for juveniles who appear before the BECTC jury. No shorts, tank tops, hats or caps, or inappropriate T-shirts are permitted. Jeans are okay if they are neat and clean. All BECTC clients pay a $25 fine. They qualify for the BECTC by being under age 18. They must admit guilt to the petty offense(s) alleged. The BECTC does not determine one's guilt or innocence. It decides the punishments and consequences of one's actions. Youths who admit their guilt will automatically be placed on probation for six months. If they successfully complete the terms of the probation program, then the charges against them will be dropped or dismissed. While on probation, they must (1) perform community service, (2) pay a fine, (3) apologize to the victim(s), (4) see a counselor, (5) write an essay, (6) attend other teen groups/sessions, and (7) serve on the teen court at a later date.

If some youths fail to complete the terms of their probation successfully, then they will be referred back to the district court for processing. They must appear before a judge for violating the BECTC's rules. There is the possibility that more serious consequences will be imposed on such juveniles by presiding judges.

It is important to note that the BECTC is totally voluntary. Youths who do not wish to participate in it can have their cases heard in the district court. There are obvious benefits to youths for keeping their cases away from district courts, however. The principal benefit is that they will not acquire a juvenile record if they complete the terms of their program successfully. This is a strong incentive to remain law-abiding and conform to all rules imposed by the BECTC.

Teen Court Variations

Several variations of teen courts have been described (Champion 2007). Four courtroom models of teen courts include (1) adult judge, (2) youth judge, (3) peer jury, and (4) tribunal.

ADULT JUDGE TEEN COURT MODEL Adult judge teen courts use adult judges to preside over all actions. The judge is responsible for managing all courtroom dynamics. Generally, a youth volunteer acting as the prosecutor presents each case against a juvenile to a jury comprised of one's peers. This is similar to a prosecutor in the adult system presenting a case against a defendant in a grand jury action. A juvenile defense counsel offers mitigating evidence, if any, that the jury may consider. The jury is permitted to ask the youthful defendant any question in an effort to determine why the offense was committed and any circumstances surrounding its occurrence. Subsequently, the jury deliberates and determines the most fitting punishment. This is a recommendation only. The suitability of the recommended punishment, which is most often some form of community service and/or victim compensation or restitution, is decided by the judge. About half of all teen courts in the United States use the adult judge model.

YOUTH JUDGE MODEL The youth judge variation of teen courts uses a juvenile judge instead of an adult judge. Youths are used as prosecutors and defense counsel as well. This teen court variation functions much like the adult judge teen court model. Again, a sentence is recommended by a jury, and the appropriateness of the sentence is determined by the juvenile judge. About a third of all teen courts use this model.

This model is used by the Elko (Nevada) Teen Court (ETC). The ETC uses teens as judges, prosecutors, and defense counsels. The proceedings are conducted in real trial courtrooms. The procedures emulate adult proceedings as much as possible. The average teen court hearing lasts about 20–30 minutes. During the ETC proceedings, the jury is sworn in by a court clerk. The court clerk states to the jury the charge and the plea of guilty entered by the youthful defendant. The prosecutor summarizes the police report, or facts in the case, for the jury. The defense counsel calls one or more witnesses, including the defendant. The defendant's parents may also be called. The prosecutor can cross-examine witnesses. Both the prosecutor and defense counsel make closing arguments to the jury who then receives jury instructions from the judge and retires to reach a verdict. The verdict is returned. The objective of this proceeding is to heighten offender accountability, not deal with the guilt or innocence of the defendant. The teen jury determines the consequences of the juvenile's actions. The jury can require juvenile detention center tours, community service, educational classes, apology letters, and written reports (Elko Teen Court 2005).

PEER JURY MODEL In the peer jury model, an adult judge presides, while a jury hears the case against the defendant. There are no youth prosecutors or defense counsels present. After hearing the case, which is usually determined through jury questioning of the defendant directly, the jury deliberates and decides the sentence, which the judge must approve. This model is used by the BECTC example in Minnesota.

TRIBUNAL MODEL Under the tribunal model, one or more youths act as judges, while other youths are designated as prosecutors and defense counsels. The prosecution and defense present their side of the case against the youthful defendant to the judges who subsequently deliberate and return with a sentence. All sentences may be appealed. Again, the sentences usually involve restitution or some form of victim compensation, community service, or a combination of punishments depending upon the circumstances. This tribunal model is the one featured in the AYC example.

Each of these models is summarized below:

	Judge	Youth Attorneys	Jury/Role of Jury
Adult Judge Model	Adult	Yes	Recommend sentence
Youth Judge Model	Youth	Yes	Recommend sentence
Peer Jury Model	Adult	No	Questions defendant, recommends sentence
Tribunal Model	Youths (1–3)	Yes	No jury present

The Successfulness of Teen Courts

The growing popularity of teen courts as alternatives to formal juvenile court actions attests to their successfulness in sanctioning first-time low-risk youthful offenders (Patrick et al. 2004). Being judged by one's peers seems to be an effective method of imposing sanctions. Youths who function as judges, prosecutors, and defense counsels usually receive a certain number of hours of training to perform these important roles (Carrington and Schulenberg 2004). In New York, for instance, an average of 16–20 hours of training is required of youth court juvenile officials (Champion 2009). In some instances, written tests are administered following one's training. These are the equivalent of bar exams for youths, to ensure that they understand some basic or fundamental legal principles.

Several national youth court guidelines have been articulated. These guidelines have been developed for (1) program planning and community mobilization, (2) program staffing and funding, (3) legal issues, (4) identified respondent population and referral process, (5) volunteer recruitment and sentencing options, (6) volunteer training, (7) youth court operations and case management, and (8) program evaluation.

Recidivism rates of teen courts have not been studied consistently throughout all jurisdictions. However, available information suggests that the recidivism rates among youthful defendants who have gone through the teen court process are very low, less than 20 percent. One positive consequence that is reported in many jurisdictions is that processed youth emerge with a greater appreciation for the law, a greater understanding of it, and a greater respect for authority figures. They appear to be more law-abiding compared with youths adjudicated in more traditional ways through juvenile courts (Champion 2009). A majority of states have adopted teen court models of one type or another, and many are in the process of considering legislation to establish them (Chapman 2005).

States vary in terms of the eligibility age limits and types of offenses that youth courts may consider. Mostly first-offense, low-level misdemeanors or status offenses are included. More serious offenses are usually passed along to the juvenile court beyond the intake stage. The accountability of participating youths is heightened considerably inasmuch as youths must admit guilt before participating in teen courts (Champion 2009). Furthermore, they must waive their confidentiality rights in most jurisdictions.

TRENDS AND IMPLICATIONS FOR JUVENILE OFFENDERS

A Summary of Juvenile Justice Trends

The trends discussed in this section pertain to (1) the legal rights of juveniles; (2) law enforcement; (3) the prosecution of juveniles and juvenile courts; (4) diversion, probation, and intermediate punishments; and (5) juvenile corrections and aftercare.

1. The juvenile justice system will experience greater reforms in the area of juvenile rights commensurate with those enjoyed by adult offenders.
2. Attaining constitutional rights commensurate with adult offenders. Currently, there are no speedy trial provisions for juvenile offenders.
3. Greater accountability and responsibility expected from juvenile offenders.
4. The deinstitutionalization of status offenders. As we have seen, there is a general trend toward DSO as a means of diverting less serious offenders from the jurisdiction of juvenile courts.
5. Greater attention to preventing short-term detention of juveniles with adult offenders after arrest.
6. Greater use of transfers and waivers to adult criminal courts.
7. The juvenile court will become increasingly adversarial, in many respects paralleling the adult system.
8. Greater formality of juvenile courts (Guevara and Herz 2004).

9. The increased use of transfers of juveniles to criminal courts will continue, especially for serious offenses including rape, robbery, and murder.
10. Greater concern for juvenile rights.
11. More stringent standards relating to the admissibility of evidence in juvenile proceedings.
12. Greater use of plea bargaining.
13. Greater use of diversion.
14. Greater innovations in juvenile offender management, including electronic monitoring and/or home confinement (Rodriguez 2004).
15. Greater emphasis on victim restitution and community service.

Summary

Dispositions in juvenile court are like sentences in adult court, in that they involve nominal or verbal warnings, conditional punishments such as probation, or custodial sanctions, including incarceration in a juvenile facility for various lengths of time.

Relatively few juveniles are actually incarcerated, and the terms of their incarceration are short compared with time served by convicted adults who are incarcerated.

The juvenile justice process has become increasingly legalistic, particularly since the 1960s, when the U.S. Supreme Court commenced hearing juvenile cases and extending various rights to juveniles.

Defense counsels for juveniles attempt to ensure that their due process rights are respected. Many juvenile cases are plea bargained similar to criminal cases. Defense counsels perform many of the same functions for juveniles as they do for adults, including representing them in adjudicatory proceedings.

In those states where jury trials for juveniles are permitted, defense counsels are advocates for juveniles in every respect, seeking their acquittal of charges against them.

Approximately 1 percent of all juveniles referred to the juvenile justice system each year are transferred, waived, or certified as adults and processed by criminal courts. These transferred juveniles are not always the most serious offenders, despite the fact that the intent of transfers or waivers is to make it possible for criminal courts to impose more serious punishments, which are beyond the jurisdiction of juvenile courts.

States vary in the youngest ages at which juveniles may be transferred to criminal court to be processed as though they were adults. Different types of waivers include judicial waivers, where judges on their own waive particular juveniles to the jurisdiction of criminal courts; prosecutorial waivers or concurrent jurisdiction or direct file, where prosecutors decide whether to prosecute juveniles in criminal or juvenile courts; and legislative or automatic waivers, also known as statutory exclusion, where juveniles are automatically waived to the jurisdiction of criminal courts for processing as adults.

All juveniles are entitled to hearings on waiver actions. For those subject to legislative or automatic waivers, these juveniles may obtain hearings to have their cases placed back into juvenile courts for adjudication. These types of actions are known as reverse waiver hearings.

Some juveniles may also initiate transfer proceedings through demand waiver actions. Thus, they ask juvenile courts to transfer jurisdiction over them to criminal courts.

The implications of transfers are several and diverse. Not all transferred juveniles are the most serious offenders. About 60 percent of all transferred juveniles are persistent or chronic property offenders or drug users. About 40 percent are violent offenders who are supposedly the most vulnerable to being transferred or waived. About 50 percent of all juvenile cases transferred to criminal court result in dismissals or the charges are downgraded, and probation is usually imposed through plea bargaining.

Even where the remaining cases come to trial, the result for nearly another 40 percent of these offenders is probation. Only 12 percent or fewer juveniles ever serve time as the result of transfers and subsequent convictions in criminal courts. Thus, the transfer process does not necessarily achieve its manifest goals, and this general failure of the waiver process is repeated annually with uncanny similarity.

Since the early 1990s, increasing numbers of states have designed blended sentencing statutes that authorize either juvenile court or criminal court judges to impose either juvenile sanctions or criminal penalties or both on juvenile offenders. These blended sentencing statutes afford juveniles the full range of constitutional rights, including a trial by jury.

But the transfer process is bypassed. Blended sentencing statutes include the juvenile–inclusive blend, the juvenile–exclusive blend, the juvenile–contiguous blend, the criminal–inclusive blend, and the criminal–exclusive blend. Inclusive blends for both juvenile and criminal courts authorize judges to impose both juvenile and criminal punishments.

Several trends in juvenile justice include greater reforms in juvenile justice processing; greater emphasis on due process issues; greater accountability among juveniles in terms of sanctions imposed; greater use of waivers and transfers for more serious juvenile offenders; increasingly adversarial juvenile court proceedings; more stringent evidentiary standards; less use of secure confinement; greater use of plea bargaining; greater use of diversion and probation; greater use of innovations in offender supervision, including electronic monitoring, home confinement, and intensive supervised probation with conditions; and greater emphasis upon victim compensation, restitution, and restorative justice as sanctioning options.

Questions for Review

1. Identify four types of waivers. Which types of waivers are made by judges? Which types of waivers are made by legislatures?
2. Can juveniles contest waivers? How can these waiver actions be reversed? Describe several methods to accomplish this task.
3. What is a blended sentencing statute? How does it relate to the get-tough movement?
4. What are several important trends relating to juveniles and juvenile court processing of juveniles?
5. What are teen courts or youth courts? How do they work?
6. What was the significance of the *in re Gault* case? Are most juveniles represented by defense counsel? Why or why not?
7. Do most states allow jury trials for juveniles? What has the Supreme Court said about this?
8. What are some arguments for a juvenile having his/her case heard in adult court? Arguments against?

Suggested Readings

1. Alex Escarcega (2004). "Working Collaboratively: Addressing the Needs of Federally Sentenced Juvenile Offenders." *Corrections Today* **66**:20–22.
2. James Gondles (2004). "Kids are Kids, Not Adults." *Corrections Today* **66**:6–7.
3. Daniel P. Mears (2002). "Sentencing Guidelines and the Transformation of Juvenile Justice in the 21st Century." *Journal of Contemporary Criminal Justice* **18**:6–19.
4. Gerard A. Rainville and Steven K. Smith (2003). *Juvenile Felony Defendants in Criminal Courts*. Washington, DC: U.S. Department of Justice.
5. B. C. Feld. (2009). "Violent Girls or Relabeled Status Offenders?: An Alternative Interpretation of the Data." *Crime & Delinquency* **55**:241–265.

CHAPTER 13

Diversion, Alternative Dispute Resolution, and Specialty Courts

CHAPTER OBJECTIVES

As a result of reading this chapter, you will have accomplished the following objectives:

1. Understand the options that judges have at sentencing and that these vary by type of crime and jurisdiction.
2. Understand the decriminalization process.
3. Examine alternative dispute resolution, including its applications, advantages, and disadvantages.
4. Understand the role and participation of victims in alternative dispute resolution and victim–offender reconciliation projects.
5. Describe pretrial diversion, its implications for divertees, and the advantages and disadvantages of diversion.

6. Describe several sanctioning options available to judges, including community service, fines, restitution to victims, and various types of victim compensation programs.
7. Understand specialty and problem solving courts and the underlying focus on treatment and rehabilitation of the offender rather than punishment of the offense.
8. Describe therapeutic justice and its relationship to problem solving courts.
9. Describe several different types of specialty courts such as drug courts, mental health courts, veterans courts, domestic violence courts, and youth courts.

KEY TERMS

alternative dispute resolution (ADR)
community service
community service orders
Comprehensive Crime Control Act of 1984
decriminalization
diversion
diversion programs
drug courts

financial/community service model
fines
impartial arbiters
mediation
mental health courts
pretrial diversion
problem solving courts
reparations
restitution
restorative justice

specialty courts
stigmatization
teen courts
veterans courts
victim
victim compensation
victim compensation programs
victim impact statement
victim–offender mediation model

victim–offender reconciliation
Victim–Offender Reconciliation Project (VORP)
victim/reparations model
Victims of Crime Act of 1984
youth courts

Recently various states have been looking for ways to reduce their prison populations due to the economic downturn and state budget shortfalls. Another recent phenomenon has been the return of hundreds of thousands of veterans from Iraq and Afghanistan. Texas, for instance, has seen over 150,000 veterans return from Iraq and Afghanistan, many of whom face difficulties adjusting back to normal life. The death, destruction, grief, and sorrow that these soldiers have encountered overseas often lead to drug and alcohol addiction and abuse as well as crime. The Texas legislature recently authorized counties to use programs designed to defer prosecution and get the veterans the treatment and counseling that they might need. Bexar County, which is home to over 10,000 veterans, has implemented a veterans court in San Antonio similar to the many drug courts around the state and nation which are designed to focus on the offender rather than the offense. Veterans who can prove that their criminal behavior or drug use is stemming from their combat experiences would be eligible to enter the program designed to treat their underlying conditions rather than send them to jail or place them on probation with no counseling or treatment. Some district attorneys are in opposition to these types of specialty court programs which divert offenders away from the court without prosecuting and sentencing them. Those who advocate for these types of courts say that if the goal is crime prevention, treating the underlying conditions that veterans are facing which led to the criminal activity is the most practical and cost-effective method. They also argue that those who have risked their lives serving the country deserve to be treated better and deserve a second chance to get their lives back to normal. What do you think? Do veterans who have served their country deserve to get a second chance and counseling and treatment rather than jail if their behavior is stemming from problems related to stress and trauma from combat?

Source: Adapted from *The Texas Tribune*, "Courts for Accused Veterans Prioritize Treatment," May 17, 2010.

INTRODUCTION

Several jurisdictions around the country over the past two decades have sought to dispose of certain types of cases using methods other than those traditionally used by the criminal justice system. More state and local court authorities today are using alternative sanctions to deal with certain types of crimes or offenders. Some of these alternative methods of disposing of cases include alternative dispute resolution or ADR, pretrial diversion or community-based corrections, and specialty, or problem solving, courts.

ADR uses informal processes to dispose of certain types of cases, especially where there is some type of dispute between the offender and victim. This sometimes involves victim–offender mediation or victim–offender reconciliation and has the goal of removing less serious offenders from criminal court jurisdiction and to alleviate the number of these cases in criminal courts. Offenders who agree to participate in ADR do not usually get criminal records and victims are usually compensated for their losses or injuries. Some of these programs may be referred to as restorative justice processes because they aim to achieve justice by restoring or repairing the harm that was done between offender and victim. Advocates say that ADR is beneficial because court dockets are eased, prosecutor caseloads are lessened, and the community may benefit if community service is involved. Some also believe that community service and restitution heighten offender accountability by obligating offenders to pay for the damages they have caused to property, or for the loss of wages if victims are injured.

Pretrial diversion is another option that prosecutors may use to divert cases from the criminal justice process, at least temporarily. Diversion is the temporary stopping of prosecution of someone, who then is required to participate in one or more community programs. If these persons, known as divertees, complete their periods of diversion successfully, they often have the charges against them dismissed and the records of the arrest expunged. There are many functions of diversion that will be discussed in this chapter.

Other types of noncriminal or pretrial sanctions include community service, victim compensation, and restitution. The forms of community service vary from jurisdiction to jurisdiction. Victim compensation is a way of offsetting the damages caused to victims. The nature of victim compensation may also vary; different programs will be described in this chapter including the financial/community service model, the victim–offender mediation model, the victim/reparations model, and repaying victims through restitution.

Specialty courts are also known as **problem solving courts** and are alternative methods of dealing with certain types of offenders. Specialty courts have a philosophy of therapeutic jurisprudence and are focused on rehabilitating the offender rather than simply punishing them for an offense. Certain specialty courts, such as domestic violence courts, also focus on victims to ensure their safety. Drug courts are the most prevalent of the problem solving courts, but others also include youth or teen courts, mental health courts, and more recently veterans courts.

DECRIMINALIZATION, ALTERNATIVE DISPUTE RESOLUTION (ADR), DIVERSION, AND RESTORATIVE JUSTICE: EXPLORING ALTERNATIVES TO CRIMINAL PROSECUTION

It is important to understand that once a criminal case is placed into the criminal justice system, this doesn't necessarily mean that the case will proceed throughout the entire system and be processed fully. Several factors operate to determine whether specific cases will move further into the system or whether they will be removed from it. There is a great deal of pressure on prosecutors to resolve increasing numbers of cases expeditiously. Unfortunately, prosecutor's offices throughout the United States do not have sufficient person power or resources to prosecute all cases brought to their attention. Therefore, prosecutors must often prioritize cases and arrange them from the most to least serious. The most serious cases will likely receive the full attention of prosecutors and move forward. However, there are a massive number of less serious criminal cases that are relegated to lower priority for prosecution.

Several solutions have been devised or proposed to resolve these less serious cases and not consume valuable court time. For instance, a large number of cases involve possession of marijuana and/or recreational drug use. Some cases involve assault and battery or spousal abuse, where persons married or otherwise have physically injured one another. Subsequently, one or both parties have been arrested by police who have intervened. It is clear that while criminal laws have been violated, prosecutors do not always regard these types of offenses with the same degree of seriousness as armed robbery, rape, and murder.

In the case of illegal drug use, some persons have advocated legalizing certain drugs, thus rendering their possession as a noncriminal act. This doesn't mean that prosecutors don't think drug use is harmless. But they might inquire as to whether the criminal justice system is the best place to deal with illicit drug use and punish it. Should drug users be treated rather than punished? No one knows the answer to this question. Certainly there are strong opinions favoring and opposing the legalization of certain drugs.

Accordingly, some types of assault and battery as well as spousal abuse may be regarded as less serious crimes. Again, this doesn't mean that prosecutors are insensitive to the needs of persons who have been assaulted, or that they condone spousal abuse. These are serious offenses deserving of some form of punishment. But should some of these crimes receive the same amount of attention and court time compared with murder, rape, and armed robbery? Again, there are no easy answers to this question. The following section, therefore, explores several strategies devised by legislators and others to reduce the caseloads of prosecutors and accelerate the justice process by focusing on the most serious cases. These strategies for reducing the sheer numbers of criminal cases confronting overworked prosecutor's offices include (1) decriminalization, (2) alternative dispute resolution, and (3) diversion.

Decriminalization

Decriminalization is removing an act from the category of crime (Sheehy 2004). Decriminalization might occur, for instance, in marijuana use (Jones 2003). Some states, such as Oregon and Washington, have entertained legislation that would legalize marijuana. California decriminalized marijuana use for medical purposes in the mid-1990s. When crimes are decriminalized, they may be shifted to civil courts for noncriminal resolution (Coomber, Oliver, and Morris 2003). Thus, a fight at a football game between overly enthusiastic fans may be shifted from criminal court to some type of civil resolution which entails a process which can restore or repair the harm done. Some of these alternative methods have been referred to as restorative processes or restorative justice. **Restorative justice** is gaining more ground as a popular alternative to traditional criminal justice responses; the underlying assumption is that all persons involved or affected by the crime (offender, victim, victim's family, and community) should play a part in the response to it (Ventura Miller 2008). At the same time that decriminalization is occurring with certain acts, however, criminalization is occurring with other acts, such as certain types of domestic violence and substance abuse (Sridharan et al. 2004).

Alternative Dispute Resolution

An increasingly used option to settle minor criminal cases is **alternative dispute resolution (ADR)**. ADR is a community-based, informal dispute settlement between offenders and their victims. Most often targeted for participation in these programs are first-time, low-level, or misdemeanor offenders. Some overly excited persons at a football game may get into a fight. One person may assault another, causing physical injuries and broken teeth. While criminal charges may be filed against the aggressor, these cases often consume considerable and valuable court time. However, if the offenders and victim agree, ADR may be used to conclude these cases quickly and informally to the mutual satisfaction of all parties involved. Victim–offender mediation or ADR programs originated in the midwestern United States (Schiff and Bazemore 2004). Umbreit (1994, 25) notes that in most victim–offender programs, the process consists of four phases:

1. Case intake from referral sources.
2. Preparation for mediation, during which the mediator meets separately with the offender and the victim.
3. The mediation session, which consists of a discussion of what occurred and how people felt about it, followed by negotiation of a restitution agreement.
4. Follow-up activities such as monitoring restitution completion.

Umbreit found in a cross-site study that 79 percent of the victims were satisfied with the results of the mediation, 87 percent of the offenders were satisfied, and 83 percent of all parties believed that the mediation process was fair for both the victims and the offenders. Examples of the volume of referrals in specific mediation agencies are 591 mediations in 1991 in Albuquerque, New Mexico; 903 mediations in Minneapolis, Minnesota in 1991; 541 mediations in Oakland, California in 1991; and 1,107 mediations in Austin, Texas in 1991 (Umbreit 1994, 28).

Restorative Justice

Another name for ADR is **restorative justice** (Braithwaite 2002). Restorative justice seeks to produce a civil remedy between victims and their victimizers (Strang 2004). The roots of restorative justice can be traced to aboriginal courts in other countries, such as Australia and South Africa (Gallinetti, Redpath, and Sloth-Nielsen 2004; M. Harris 2004).

Restorative justice programs or processes emphasize reparation and reintegration (Ventura Miller 2008).

The intent of restorative justice is not simply to restore to victims that which was lost or the value of services or lost wages due to injuries suffered. An additional objective is to heighten the accountability of the offender by requiring him/her to enter into a bilateral agreement with the victim in an effort to reach a compromise that will be mutually satisfying for both parties (Lemley 2004). Thus, although a criminal case has been transformed into a civil one, ADR involves the direct participation of the victim and offender, with the aim of mutual accommodation for both parties. The emphasis of ADR is upon restitution rather than punishment (Jones 2003). There are small costs associated with it compared with trials, and criminal **stigmatization** is avoided (Tishler et al. 2004; Tshehla 2004). Many criminal cases are being diverted from the criminal justice system through ADR (Hayes 2004). **Mediation** is increasingly used. ADR is recognized increasingly as a means by which differences between criminals and their victims can be resolved through civil means (Karp, Bazemore, and Chesire 2004). These usually involve face-to-face meetings between victims and offenders. The model program started in Canada (Grace 2010) but has expanded throughout the United States for both adults and juvenile offenders (Bakker 1994). Mediation services help relieve congested criminal and civil courts. Often volunteers from the community are used as mediators.

States vary in their use of ADR (Tifft 2004); however, ADR programs are operating in every state in some way, shape, or form. That is not to say that these programs are operating extensively and in all corners of every state, but that there are programs in each state. How extensively and exactly the different types of programs are being piloted or implemented, however, is a difficult thing to measure (National Center for State Courts 2010). ADR is most frequently used to settle misdemeanor cases.

ADVANTAGES AND DISADVANTAGES OF ADR   ADR has the following advantages:

1. Offenders do not acquire a criminal record following a successful resolution of the dispute.
2. Victims have the satisfaction of seeing punishment imposed for the criminal act committed.
3. Court dockets are eased because of the diversion of disputes to ADR.
4. Prosecutor caseloads are alleviated.
5. The community benefits where community service orders are issued to perpetrators.
6. Accountability is heightened, since victim compensation and restitution are required of offenders. (Palumbo, Musheno, and Hallett 1994)

The disadvantages of ADR include the following:

1. Offenders who have committed crimes escape criminal convictions. Some persons regard this as unjust and believe that if you commit a crime, you should receive a criminal conviction as a result.
2. ADR is insufficient as a punishment and causes some persons to flaunt the law, knowing that they will not be harshly treated if caught. ADR is perceived as too lenient.
3. Reoffending may occur if perpetrators believe that they can get away with crimes with only civil sanctions being imposed.
4. The criminal justice system image is tainted by excessive leniency from ADR programs.
5. The proportionate punishment is not the same as a criminal conviction and the record an offender would acquire as a result.

IMPARTIAL ARBITERS AND THEIR QUALIFICATIONS

WHO ARE THE IMPARTIAL ARBITERS?   **Impartial arbiters** in ADR programs may be retired judges, attorneys, or interested citizens. Depending on the jurisdiction, ADR arbiters are appointed on the basis of their fairness and integrity (Deukmedjian 2003). There are no special qualifications for arbiters. They do not have to have a precise and extensive knowledge of the law. Their actions are designed to be fair, and the resolutions they negotiate must be agreeable to both the offender and the victim. In the event that the arbiters cannot settle cases, then prosecutors can always reinstitute criminal charges against defendants and take these cases to court for resolution.

VICTIM PARTICIPATION AND INPUT

Victim involvement in offender sentencing and punishments has increased dramatically in recent years in both criminal and juvenile proceedings (Booth 2004; Carr, Logio, and Maier 2003). Testimony from victims can add much emotional appeal to formal proceedings. Victim feedback through direct participation in such proceedings is not always negative. In more than a few cases, victims have spoken on behalf of perpetrators and made requests for leniency (Hayes 2004). However, in ADR, victim participation ensures that all aspects of the offense and its results are brought to the attention of the arbiter. When prosecutors decide to divert cases to ADR, every effort is made to reconcile the dispute between victims and offenders. When victims have such input, often it is in the form of a **victim impact statement**, or a written and/or oral summary of the damages or injuries suffered from actions of the perpetrator (Roberts and Erez 2004). When the perpetrator and victim agree on the proposed punishment, under the supervision of an impartial arbiter, then **victim compensation** is discussed (Rojek, Coverdill, and Fors 2003). This is usually a monetary award to be paid by the perpetrator to the victim for the loss of property or work time. Many jurisdictions have **victim compensation programs** to provide guidelines about how much perpetrators should pay for the suffering and losses they have caused to victims (Myers et al. 2004).

Victim–Offender Reconciliation

Victim–offender reconciliation is another version of ADR (Lightfoot and Umbreit 2004; Presser, Hamilton, and Gaarder 2004). Roy, Sudipto, and Brown (1992) report that victim–offender reconciliation is a specific form of conflict resolution between the victim and the offender. Face-to-face encounter is the basic element in this process. Elkhart County, Indiana, has been the site of the **Victim–Offender Reconciliation Project (VORP)** since 1987. The primary aims of VORP are to (1) make offenders accountable for their wrongs against victims, (2) reduce recidivism among participating offenders, and (3) heighten responsibility of offenders through victim compensation and repayment for damages inflicted (Roy, Sudipto, and Brown 1992).

VORP was established in Kitchener, Ontario, in 1974 and was subsequently replicated as PACT, or Prisoner and Community Together, in northern Indiana near Elkhart, Indiana (Bakker 1994). Subsequent replications in various jurisdictions have created different varieties of ADR, each variety spawning embellishments, additions, or program deletions deemed more or less important by the particular jurisdiction (Lightfoot and Umbreit 2004). The Genesee County (Batavia), New York, Sheriff's Department established a VORP in 1983, followed by programs in Valparaiso, Indiana; Quincy, Massachusetts; and Minneapolis, Minnesota in 1985. In Quincy, for instance, the program was named EARN-IT and was operated through the Probation Department (Lightfoot and Umbreit 2004). ADR programs in other jurisdictions have been evaluated, and the results of these evaluations suggest that most victims and offenders are satisfied with the fairness of these proceedings. A high rate of restitution by offenders has been reported by many participating jurisdictions (Lightfoot and Umbreit 2004). But criticisms have been lodged against VORPs that allege both victims and offenders do not benefit in ways originally conceived by this type of programming (Tifft 2004). VORPs are not unique to the United States. Other countries, such as Chile, England, Australia, and Italy, have experimented with such programs in recent years with positive results (Stanley 2004).

PRETRIAL DIVERSION

Pretrial diversion or simply **diversion** is the process where criminal defendants are either diverted to a community-based agency for treatment or assigned to a counselor for social and/or psychiatric assistance. Pretrial diversion may involve education, job training, counseling, or some type of psychological or physical therapy (Minor, Wells, and Jones 2004). Diversion officially halts or suspends criminal proceedings against a defendant (Ulrich 2002). The thrust of diversion is toward an informal administrative effort to determine (1) whether nonjudicial processing is warranted; (2) whether treatment is warranted; (3) if treatment is warranted, which one to use; and (4) whether charges against the defendant should be dropped or reinstated (Peters et al. 2004).

Most likely targeted for pretrial **diversion programs** are first-time petty offenders. If these programs are completed successfully, then the charges against these defendants are either downgraded or dismissed outright. The totality of circumstances of the offender's crime is ascertained by the prosecutor and the court, and a decision about diversion is made. Each case is evaluated and decided on its own merits. Persons charged with possessing marijuana may be diverted and required to attend counseling classes or sessions where drug abuse discussions are featured. Diverted defendants usually pay monthly fees during the period of their diversion in order to defray a portion of the expenses for their supervision (Maxwell and Morris 2002).

The History and Philosophy of Diversion

Diversion originated in the United States through the early juvenile courts in Chicago and New York in the late 1800s. Strong efforts were made by religious groups and reformers to keep children from imprisonment of any kind, since children over eight years of age were considered eligible for adult court processing. Cook County, Illinois, implemented a diversion program for youthful offenders in 1899 (National Association of Pretrial Services Agencies 1995).

The philosophy of diversion is community reintegration and rehabilitation (Proulx 2003). The objective is that offenders can avoid the stigma of incarceration and public notoriety. In most state courts where diversion is condoned, diversion does not entirely remove offenders from court processing, since the court usually must approve prosecutorial recommendations for diversion in each case. Since these approvals are often conducted in less publicized hearings, a divertee's crimes are less likely to be scrutinized publicly.

Functions of Diversion

The functions of diversion are as follows:

1. To permit divertees the opportunity of remaining in their communities where they can receive needed assistance or treatment, depending upon the nature of the crimes charged.
2. To permit divertees the opportunity to make restitution to their victims where monetary damages were suffered and property destroyed.
3. To permit divertees the opportunity of remaining free in their communities to support themselves and their families, and to avoid the stigma of incarceration.
4. To help divertees avoid the stigma of a criminal conviction.
5. To assist corrections officials in reducing prison and jail overcrowding by diverting less serious cases to nonincarcerative alternatives.
6. To save the courts the time, trouble, and expense of formally processing less serious cases and streamlining case dispositions through informal case handling.
7. To make it possible for divertees to participate in self-help, educational, or vocational programs.
8. To preserve the dignity and integrity of divertees by helping them avoid further contact with the criminal justice system and assisting them to be more responsible adults capable of managing their own lives.
9. To preserve the family unit and enhance family solidarity and continuity.

Factors Influencing Pretrial Diversion

Excluded from diversion programs are recidivists with prior records of violent offending. Also, if offenders have drug or alcohol dependencies, they may be excluded from diversion programs. Probation and parole violators are also excluded. In view of these restrictive criteria, diversion is most often granted for low-risk, first-time property offenders. While recidivism rates among property offenders are not particularly different from those of violent offenders and drug traffickers, property offenders pose less public risk and are less dangerous compared with these other types of criminals. Relevant criteria operating in most jurisdictions where diversion exists as an option include the following:

1. The age of the offender.
2. The residency, employment, and familial status of the offender.
3. The prior record of the offender.
4. The seriousness of the offense.
5. Aggravating or mitigating circumstances associated with the commission of the offense.

One's residency, employment, and familial status are important considerations because they are indicators of one's stability. More stable persons are more likely to complete diversion programs successfully. Most diversion programs require at least some regular contact with probation agencies operated by state or local authorities. Unemployed and transient offenders are more likely to flee from the jurisdiction contrasted with those offenders who are gainfully employed and have families in the area.

Criticisms of Diversion

1. Diversion is the wrong punishment for criminals. Criminals ought to be convicted of crimes and sent to jail or prison. Diverting them to community programs is wrong.
2. Diversion assumes guilt without a trial. If prospective divertees accept diversion in lieu of a trial, this is regarded as their admission that they are guilty of the offenses alleged.
3. Diversion leads to net-widening. When diversion programs exist in communities, there is a tendency for prosecutors to assign persons to these programs who otherwise would not be prosecuted because of case backlogs and crowded court dockets.
4. Diversion excludes female offenders. In the 1990s this criticism is no longer a valid one, since many female offenders are diverted from criminal prosecutions.
5. Diversion ignores due process. When a case is diverted, the defendant is deprived of his/her right to a trial by jury, a mechanism where guilt must be established beyond a reasonable doubt. Diversion frustrates due process by avoiding a trial.
6. Diversion is too lenient with criminals. (Mackay and Moody 1996)

OTHER NONCRIMINAL OR CRIMINAL SANCTIONS

Community Service

Community service sentencing is one way of achieving offender accountability (Lo and Harris 2004). Community service is different from restitution in that usually, though not always, offenders perform services for the state or community. The nature of community service to be performed is discretionary with the sentencing judge or paroling authority (Teske and Zhang 2005). Judges may also impose **fines** as a part of an offender's sentence for almost any crime, but in many jurisdictions, fines are imposed only about a third of the time. Also, when fines are imposed, not all offenders pay them. The Victim and Witness Protection Act of 1982 made restitution to victims a mandatory part of one's sentence. Victim advocates strongly urge that restitution to victims be an integral feature of the sentencing process (Xenos 2003).

IS COMMUNITY SERVICE A PUNISHMENT?   Community service is considered a punishment and is court-imposed. Many types of projects are undertaken by offenders as community service. Usually, these projects are supervised by probation office staff, although supervisors may be recruited from the private sector. Some amount of offender earnings is allocated to victims as well as to the state or local public or private agencies that provide supervisory services (McCold 2003). Restitution to victims may be through periodic payments from offender earnings while on work release, probation, or parole. Sometimes, restitution takes nonmonetary forms, where offenders rebuild or restore property destroyed earlier by their crimes (Ruback 2002).

IS COMMUNITY SERVICE EFFECTIVE? Because many offenders are released into their communities for the purpose of performing community service, it raises a public risk issue for some people, although those offenders ordinarily selected for community service are low-risk and nonviolent (Ruback 2002). Other criticisms relate to the personal philosophies of judicial and correctional authorities, the offender eligibility and selection criteria used among jurisdictions, organizational arrangements, the nature of supervision over offenders performing community services, and how such services are evaluated. Most researchers regard community service and restitution as just and fitting punishments to accompany whatever incarcerative sentence is imposed by judges.

Restitution and Victim Compensation

Restitution is also a victim-initiated action. Restitution is the practice of requiring offenders to compensate crime victims for damages offenders may have inflicted. If the victim fails to notify the court of financial losses or medical expenses, the restitution order may be neglected. Currently, there are no reliable statistics concerning the proportion of convictions where restitution orders are imposed, nor are there statistics showing the extent to which probationers and parolees must make restitution as a part of their probation or parole programs (Ruback 2002). Several models of restitution have been described. These include the following models.

THE FINANCIAL/COMMUNITY SERVICE MODEL   The **financial/community service model** stresses the offender's financial accountability and community service to pay for damages inflicted upon victims and to defray a portion of the expenses of court prosecutions. It is becoming more commonplace for probationers and divertees to be ordered to pay some restitution to victims *and* to perform some type of community service. Community service may involve clean-up activities in municipal parks, painting projects involving graffiti removal, cutting courthouse lawns, or any other constructive project that can benefit the community. These community service sentences are imposed by judges. Probation officers are largely responsible for overseeing the efforts of convicted offenders in fulfilling their community service obligations. These sentencing provisions are commonly called **community service orders**.

Community service orders involve redress for victims, less severe sanctions for offenders, offender rehabilitation, reduction of demands on the criminal justice system, and a reduction of the need for vengeance in a society, or a combination of these factors (Lutz 1990). Community service orders are found in many different countries and benefit the community directly. Further, where convicted offenders are indigent or unemployed, community service is a way of paying their fines and court costs. Some of the chief benefits of community service are that (1) the community benefits because some form of restitution is paid, (2) offenders benefit because they are given an opportunity to rejoin their communities in law-abiding responsible roles, and (3) the courts benefit because sentencing alternatives are provided (Jaffe and Crooks 2004).

THE VICTIM–OFFENDER MEDIATION MODEL   The **victim–offender mediation model** focuses upon victim–offender reconciliation. ADR is used as a mediating ground for resolving differences or disputes between victims and perpetrators (Lightfoot and Umbreit 2004).

THE VICTIM/REPARATIONS MODEL   The **victim/reparations model** stresses that offenders should compensate their victims directly for their offenses. Many states have provisions that provide **reparations** or financial payments to victims under a U.S. Victims of Crime Act (VOCA). VOCA is a federally financed program of reparations to persons who suffer personal injury and to dependents of persons killed as the result of certain criminal conduct. In many jurisdictions, a specially constituted board determines, independent of court adjudication, the existence of a crime, the damages caused, and other elements necessary for reparation.

REPAYING VICTIMS AND SOCIETY THROUGH RESTITUTION   President Ronald Reagan signed Public Law 98-473 on October 12, 1984, which established the Comprehensive Crime Control Act. Chapter 14 of this act is known as the **Victims of Crime Act of 1984** or the **Comprehensive Crime Control Act of 1984**. Currently, all states and the federal government have victim compensation programs. As a part of offender work release requirements, a certain amount of their earned wages may be allocated to restitution and to a general victim compensation fund. In fact, in the federal system, the Federal Victim/Witness Protection Act of 1982 created a statute whereby federal judges should order restitution to the victim in all cases in which the victim has suffered a financial loss, unless they state compelling reasons for a contrary ruling on the record. Thus, fines, restitution, and some form of community service have become common features of federal sentencing (18 U.S.C. Sec. 3563(a)(2), 2005; Keller and Spohn 2005).

SPECIALTY COURTS

Specialty Courts sometimes referred to as **problem solving courts** have increased rapidly around the country as jurisdictions attempt to find alternative methods of dealing with certain types of offenders. Specialty courts often spring up in jurisdictions where traditional criminal justice processing practices have been ineffective at solving certain types of problematic crimes or behaviors. Drug courts are the most popular and prevalent type of specialty court, but others include domestic violence courts, DWI courts, youth or teen courts, mental health courts, and more recently veterans courts. These different types of specialty courts are more focused on the offender, or in the case of domestic violence courts, the victim, rather than on the offense that has been committed in order that the offender gets the help he/she needs to prevent him/her from committing future offenses.

Problem solving courts take a different approach; the courts and courtroom actors look at cases as problems to be solved. Berman and Feinblatt (2005, 5–7) outline five elements underlying the problem solving court agenda:

1. Tailoring justice to the needs of each case—this involves disaggregating the cases to identify the special problems of each and tailoring the courts' approach to better meet these needs.
2. Partnering with other agencies—problem solving courts work with other agencies not normally involved in the justice process such as community groups, social service agencies, treatment providers, and vocational programs utilizing the expertise of each to help offenders rehabilitate and reintegrate into a normal productive life. This lessens the reliance on the incarcerative and supervisory probation role of the courts.
3. Making informed decisions—problem solving courts through the above-mentioned methods provide judges and other courtroom actors with more information about offenders' personal background and treatment needs as well as progress so that they may make better informed decisions about sanctions and or future treatment.
4. Accountability—problem solving courts often monitor offenders very aggressively requiring them to be in front of the judge on a weekly basis, show up for treatment or services, and comply with court orders. Offenders in these programs often sign contracts with the court giving up Fourth Amendment rights, meaning their persons, belongings, or residences can be searched at any time for contraband. If offenders miss a court appearance, do not show up for

services they need, or are found in the possession of illegal substances, the court has the power to use graduated sanctions such as a specific period in jail. Some say this type of accountability is more effective than regular probation or even a jail sentence.

5. Focusing on results—because problem solving courts tailor services and sanctions to the need of the individual, they are more focused on results than on punishment. This means getting input from a number of sources about offenders' progress and continuing supervision until the offenders are not at risk to relapse or reoffend.

These elements of problem solving courts make them very successful at lowering recidivism rates and getting offenders the help they need. Some studies also show that these methods are more cost effective in the long run than incarceration and continuing the revolving door of justice. Advocates of these courts say they also provide the benefit of turning offenders into taxpayers again instead of a tax burden on the state which has long-term immeasurable benefits (Alonso 2009).

Drug Courts

In a growing number of jurisdictions, **drug courts** are being used to process offenders charged with various types of drug offenses (Veneziano 2005b). Drug courts are specialized courts that hear and decide exclusively drug-related charges against defendants who may be either users or traffickers. There is a therapeutic milieu associated with drug courts (Maahs 2005). Often, judges will attempt to place drug abusers into programs where their drug problems can be remedied. These persons receive counseling and other forms of therapy, including drugs of use in assisting them to withdraw from highly addictive substances, such as heroin and methamphetamine (Atkins 2005; Veneziano 2005a). Thus, many drug offenders are more likely to be treated rather than punished, compared with more traditional offender processing in conventional criminal courts (Maahs 2005). These drug courts seem successful in assisting many offenders to overcome and deal with their addiction problems.

The first drug court began in Dade County (Miami) in 1989; today there are somewhere around 2,500 drug courts across the United States (Alonso 2009). Drug courts take the stance that addiction is at the heart of the offender's criminal activity (Berman and Feinblatt 2005). The Office of Justice Programs (1998) states that the reason the drug court movement has been so powerful is due to the human element involved; many of the participants are polydrug users, many have never had drug treatment, and most have not experienced the supervision, care, and concern that the drug court judges, attorneys, and treatment and service providers will exhibit.

The results that drug courts and other problem solving courts have produced are unparalleled by any other approach. Berman and Feinblatt (2005) point out a few of these results including reduced drug use and abuse, reductions in recidivism rates, enhanced services, stringer familial ties, and improved confidence by the public in the justice process. The Office of Justice Programs (1998) likewise states that beyond reduced recidivism and drug use rates, drug courts have resulted in hundreds of families being reunified, the regaining of custody of hundreds of children by parents, increases in educational and job training, and fewer babies born to addicted parents. It is likely that due to the results of drug courts and reduced costs to jurisdictions in the long run drug courts are here to stay and the numbers of them across the country will likely continue to increase.

Domestic Violence Courts

In the 1990s, many jurisdictions implemented specialized courts to deal with domestic violence because of the problems these types of cases cause for courts regarding both the offenders and victims (Buzawa and Buzawa 1996; Labriola et al. 2009). The goals of domestic violence courts revolve around providing consistent responses to cases of domestic violence, coordinating services and advocacy for the victim, and providing accountability for the offender as well as close supervision and monitoring (Labriola et al. 2009).

Traditional criminal justice system approaches to domestic violence have been criticized that they do not reduce domestic violence between the offender and the victim; often the victim (wife) is the person who bails the offender (her husband) out of jail, and the problems associated with court processing and legal fees cause increased domestic violence among the couple. Other criticisms to traditional criminal justice system approaches include that the criminal justice system does a poor job at protecting the victim from further abuse by making it easy to get protection orders (even when protection orders are granted, they are often violated with little response from the court), and that the court has been reluctant to get formally involved in domestic and familial matters, providing only cursory responses to domestic disputes (Tsai 2000). As Ostrom (2006) points out, the traditional approaches of arrest and conviction do nothing to reduce violence. These courts therefore utilize therapeutic jurisprudence to place more attention on the victim, offender, and community to reduce levels of domestic violence (OStrom 2006).

Youth Courts

Today there are well over a thousand **youth courts** operating in jurisdictions around the country. Youth courts are also referred to as teen courts, peer courts, or student courts (Preston and Roots 2004). These jurisdictions are utilizing youth courts as an alternative to traditional juvenile court processing. Youth court proceedings are informal, where other youth act as jurors. These courts usually only hear and decide minor cases. Usually, where a youth has committed a status offense or a misdemeanor, a judge will divert the case to a youth court. The focus of these courts is therapeutic jurisprudence, with a strong emphasis upon rehabilitation (Judith Reed 2004) and teaching empathy to offenders. Youth courts are explained much more in depth in Chapter 12.

Mental Health Courts

Problems with mentally ill prisoners is not new to United States' prisons and jails (American Bar Association 1989; Mattick 1975). Prisoners with mental health issues present particularly problematic issues for prison administrators, as well as guards and inmates (Henderson 1998; Steadman and Veysey 1997). The most fundamental problem is that prisons, and specifically jails, are ill equipped to deal with these prisoners by providing adequate mental health services (Wolff 1998). According to James and Glaze (2006) over half of persons in jail and prison have some type of mental health problem; this means there are over 700,000 mentally ill persons in state prison, close to 79,000 mentally ill persons in federal prison, and roughly 480,000 persons with mental health problems in jails. These statistics portray that mental health issues are a clear problem for individuals who come into contact with the courts as well as the difficulties that might be encountered by the criminal justice system in dealing with these offenders.

The extent of mental health problems for criminal defendants has prompted calls for the court to do more regarding defendants with mental illnesses. Mental health courts are specialized courts designed to deal with defendants who have diagnoses of mental illness to provide them with a wide range of services in order to stop the cycle of contact with the criminal justice system and help them to be functional, participating members of the community again (Harraiz 2005). These offenders, as opposed to mentally stable offenders, cause numerous problems for criminal courts. Controlling and supervising jail and prison populations in order to ensure the safety of both prisoners and guards is crucial to corrections officials. The presence of mentally ill prisoners in the nation's jails and prisons, coupled with overcrowding problems, makes supervision and safety increasingly difficult (Goldcamp and Irons-Guynn 2000). First, offenders may not realize the rights that they have as defendants in a court of law, and second, they may not understand the consequences of their actions or the severity of the sanctions they are facing. Often these offenders have dual diagnoses.

Common features among mental health courts include the following: some eligibility requirements for participation (a demonstrable mental health issue), preventing incarceration of the mentally ill and instead providing some form of community-based corrections facilities, ensuring public safety through careful screening and acceptance only of low-level offenders without histories of violent behavior, and early intervention through identification of eligible participants within a short period after their arrest (Goldcamp and Irons-Guynn 2000). By 2005, there were just over 100 mental health courts operating in the United States (Harraiz 2005). As jurisdictions continue to struggle with the best and most cost-effective ways to resolve criminal cases involving defendants with mental health issues, the number of mental health courts being implemented is likely to increase.

Veterans Courts

As the number of veterans who are returning from Iraq and Afghanistan with severe depression and posttraumatic stress disorder increases, courts are seeking new ways to deal with those who commit crimes or are addicted to and abuse drugs (Haughney 2010). The first veterans court was set up in Buffalo, New York, in 2008, and the number of them being implemented around the country continues to grow. Veterans courts like other specialty courts are run from a therapeutic justice approach. These courts similarly have certain goals and objects in dealing with and treating their clients, U.S. veterans. Some of these include eligibility for participation related to service in the armed forces and some type of illness related to combat; the court acting as a liaison with the criminal justice system and the Veterans Affairs (VA); treatment, supervision, advocacy, and support for veterans struggling with addiction, depression, and other illnesses related to reintegration back into society after combat (Schaffer 2010).

Unfortunately today veterans are overrepresented in statistics relating to "substance abuse, driving under the influence (DUI)...assaults, intimate partner violence (IPV), family conflicts, homelessness episodes, suicides, PTSD, and other problems" (Schaffer 2010, 22). Veterans are also more likely to commit suicide; these chances might increase if they are incarcerated (Wortzel 2009). As more and more veterans return from Iraq and Afghanistan and as some of them have difficulties adjusting back to civilian life, veterans courts will become an increasingly important aspect of the criminal justice system in helping those who have served their country to get the help they need (Haughney 2010).

Not every veteran returning from war will have problems adjusting to life back at home, or turn to alcohol, drugs, or crime to deal with their adjustment. Transitioning back to civilian life, however, may be difficult for some veterans returning from war, especially those who have seen a lot of combat time. The nation's courts, VA, and our prison systems are often lacking resources to adequately deal with offenders who suffer from some of the problems that returning vets will face (Schaffer 2010). Jurisdictions that set up veterans courts to provide a holistic approach to dealing with substance abuse and other crime problems such as domestic violence will give those who have served their country a fighting chance to reintegrate back into society and civilian life.

Summary

Several states have sought to decriminalize various laws seeking to lessen the number of defendants charged with minor crimes. Decriminalization means to remove a particular act from the classification of misdemeanor and/or felony.

Often when certain crimes are decriminalized, some of these acts, which were previously crimes, fall within civil jurisdiction and are resolved through civil courts.

Another pretrial option is to use alternative dispute resolution, or ADR. ADR is an informal process of dispute settlement between an offender and a victim, under the supervision of a third party. Sometimes known as restorative justice or victim–offender mediation or victim–offender reconciliation, ADR seeks to remove less serious offenses from the jurisdiction of criminal courts and decrease their case volumes.

When ADR is used, offenders ordinarily do not acquire criminal records; victims are compensated for their losses or injuries; court dockets are eased; prosecutor caseloads are alleviated; the community benefits in various ways; and one's accountability is heightened through the restitution process.

Some disadvantages are that ADR permits many persons to escape prosecution as criminals; it may be an insufficient punishment and deterrent to future offending; reoffending may be encouraged if offenders think their crimes will only result in civil resolutions; excessive leniency may be alleged by an increasingly critical public; and the proportionality of punishment may be questioned. Several victim–offender reconciliation projects (VORPs) have been used as the basis for experiments designed to heighten offender accountability, reduce offender recidivism, and provide adequate compensation to victims for their losses.

Pretrial diversion is another option that prosecutors may use to divert cases from the criminal justice process, at least temporarily. Diversion is the temporary cessation of a prosecution against someone, usually a low-risk first offender, who may be required to participate in one or more community programs and complete different types of activities for periods of six months or longer.

If persons, known as divertees, complete their periods of diversion successfully, they often have the charges against them dismissed and the records of the arrest expunged.

There are many functions of diversion. These include permitting offenders to remain in their communities and continue earning a living and supporting their dependents; making restitution to victims if appropriate; avoiding the stigma of a criminal conviction; reducing jail and prison overcrowding; making it possible for offenders to participate in self-help programs and to receive possible individual or group counseling for certain problems they may have; and preserving family unity.

Criticisms of diversion are that it sends a leniency message to offenders that they can get away with violating the law and have their records expunged as a result; guilt is assumed without a trial; net-widening is encouraged; some gender bias results, as proportionately greater numbers of men are placed on diversion compared with women; due process is ignored; and the policy of diversion is too lenient.

Other types of noncriminal or pretrial sanctions include community service, victim compensation, and restitution. The forms of community service vary from maintaining public parks, cutting courthouse lawns, and picking up highway litter, to participating in youth leagues or assisting the elderly in their residences or group homes.

Restitution heightens offender accountability by obligating offenders to pay for the damages they have caused to property or for the loss of wages if victims are injured.

Victim compensation is a way of offsetting the damages caused to victims. The nature of victim compensation may vary. Different victim compensation programs have been described. These include the financial/community service model, the victim–offender mediation model, the victim/reparations model, and repaying victims through restitution. Each of these models offers victims some form of compensation or restitution, and perpetrator involvement in such programs is mandatory. Offender accountability is heightened.

Specialty courts are also known as problem solving courts and are alternative methods of dealing with certain types of offenders. Specialty courts have a philosophy of therapeutic jurisprudence and are focused on rehabilitating the offender rather than punishment for an offense. Certain specialty courts, such as domestic violence courts, also focus on victims to be sure of their safety and getting them the help they may also need. Drug courts are the most prevalent of these problem solving courts, but others also include domestic violence courts, youth or teen courts, mental health courts, and more recently veterans courts.

Questions for Review

1. What are four types of victim–offender mediation? Describe each briefly.
2. Distinguish between diversion and alternative dispute resolution.
3. What is meant by decriminalization?
4. What are the advantages of alternative dispute resolution? Disadvantages?
5. What is victim–offender mediation? Where did it start and for what type of crime?
6. What is restorative justice? How is it different from traditional methods of criminal case processing?
7. What is special about specialty or problem solving courts? What is the focus of these courts?
8. Where was the first ever drug court begun? How extensive are drug courts today?
9. List the ways in which specific specialty courts are focused on the offender or victim rather than on the offense.

Suggested Readings

1. Jeremy Prichard (2010). "Net-Widening and the Diversion of Young People From Court: A Longitudinal Analysis With Implications for Restorative Justice." *Australian and New Zealand Journal of Criminology* **43:**112–129.

2. Jacqueline Lewis (2010). "Shifting the Focus: *Restorative Justice* and Sex Work." *Canadian Journal of Criminology and Criminal Justice* **52:**285–301.

3. Maggie T. Grace (2010). "Criminal Alternative Dispute Resolution: Restoring Justice, Respecting responsibility, and Renewing Public Norms." *Vermont Law Review* **34:**563–595.

4. Richard D. Schneider (2010). "Mental Health Courts and Diversion Programs: A Global Survey." *International Journal of Law and Psychiatry* **33:**201–206.

5. Eric J. Miller (2009). "Drugs, Courts, and the New Penology." *Stanford Law and Policy Review* **20:**417–461.

6. Greg Berman and John Feinblatt (2005). *Good Courts: The Case for Problem-Solving Justice.* New York: The New Press.

CHAPTER 14

Courts, Media, and the Litigation Explosion

CHAPTER OBJECTIVES

As a result of reading this chapter, you will have accomplished the following objectives:

1. Understand how the media have been instrumental in shaping our perceptions of justice, and that the courts and the media are at odds with each other because of competing interests.
2. Describe the history of media and the courts from before the 1800s up until today and the idea of cameras in courtrooms.
3. Describe the current status of the access granted to media by the courts in the various jurisdictions throughout the United States.
4. Describe pretrial publicity and the effect it has on trials.

5. Understand the types of information that potential jurors consider to be prejudicial including case-specific and general pretrial publicity.
6. Describe the different ways in which pretrial publicity can be minimized including gag orders, jury instructions, change of venues, and jury sequestration.
7. Understand the litigation explosion and the reasons why America has become more litigious including the emergence of industrial capitalism, changing legal doctrines, and the transformation of scholarly legal thought.
8. Describe the different arguments for tort reform such as the fact that the number of tort cases has dramatically increased, and the belief that juries are unable to handle tort cases because they are usually sympathetic to the plaintiff and hand out excessive awards.

KEY TERMS

case-specific pretrial publicity
change of venue
court of public opinion
doctrine of assumptive risk

doctrine of contributory negligence
doctrine of last clear chance
doctrine of *res ipsa loquitur*
fellow servant rule

gag order
general pretrial publicity
judicial instructions
jury selection
litigation explosion

pretrial publicity
tort actions
tort reform
torts
vice principal doctrine

From the Lindbergh baby kidnapping to the Marv Albert sexual assault case, the O. J. Simpson murder trial, and more recent cases like baby Jessica, the media play a very important role in our perceptions about the facts of the case and ultimately justice. Nancy Grace is one of many commentators in the media who offer speculation about the victims, offenders, and any possible evidence. In several recent examples of missing children cases, experts are called upon to offer comment and speculate upon statements and actions made by police, friends, and family. Do you believe this media scrutiny affects the outcome of these cases? Are potential jurors tainted by the constant media attention given to these cases? What should be the role of the media in high-profile court cases?

Mancini, a female police lieutenant, received a New Jersey jury award of $1.5 million for being subjected to offensive cartoons, magazines, and comments, and she had been demoted in retaliation for filing a sex discrimination suit. (*Mancini v. Township of Teaneck, et al.,* JVR No. 801654, 2000 WL 33125820, Hudson Co.)

In the mid-1990s a blind man was given the gift of a seeing-eye dog. When the man went to a shopping mall in Bradenton, Florida, his seeing-eye dog allegedly stepped on the foot of a woman, who became distressed. When she learned that the blind man had no money, she filed a lawsuit against Southeastern Guide Dogs, Inc. for "loss of earning capacity and mental pain and suffering" resulting from the dog stepping on her foot. The case was "Susan Faith and Reverend Ian Faith, Plaintiffs, v. Southeastern Guide Dogs, Inc., Defendant." Kimberly Marlow, Southeastern Guide Dogs, Inc.'s development director, said that the nonprofit group had to gather extensive documents in preparation for the trial. But the case never made it to court. After being ridiculed in newspapers and on television, the plaintiffs dropped the suit. In fact, the plaintiff's law firm donated $1,000 to Southeastern Guide Dogs.

Source: Adapted from Robert Trigaux and the *St. Petersburg Times,* St. Petersburg, FL, 2005.

INTRODUCTION

These awards and many others like them every year are given to plaintiffs by juries in civil cases. They seem exorbitant or out of proportion compared with the harm done in the case. The U.S. society is characterized as being too litigious, so much so that doctors, coaches, teachers, and even ministers have a fear of being sued. It is the reason insurance premiums in some professions are excessive, the reason why some cities have to cut funding to public services, and the reason why the average citizen when wanting to have something as simple as a garage sale has to put up a sign saying that they are not responsible for accidents.

Do these things happen every day? Should we be fearful of litigation against us? Or is the media blowing these things out of proportion by focusing on what constitutes an infinitesimal number of cases? According to the American system of justice, this media coverage of trials is supposedly irrelevant and should not be viewed by jurors. Jurors take an oath that they will remain impartial and objective. They are obliged to refrain from listening to, reading about, or watching anything related to the trial. In reality, however, many jurors keep in close touch with trial events and media coverage of them. And most people, including jurors, are affected by what they see and hear. We are in the midst of an era of media news frenzy, and in diverse ways almost everyone is influenced by the media and its news reports and characterizations.

Since the early 1900s, the courts have had an antagonistic relationship with the media. Increasing numbers of courtrooms are permitting limited or extensive television coverage. Such permissiveness is consistent with the public's right to know, about public access to the courts, and about the freedom of speech. However, the media has almost always sought to dramatize court events in different ways so as to stimulate listeners, readers, and viewers. *Court TV* and *CNN Headline News* shows pioneered creative and innovative court reporting through the use of experts and panels of experts who debate, criticize, and overanalyze information bits from trial testimony and events. No court actor has escaped the intensive scrutiny of television cameras or the opinions, reactions, and interpretations of events through the eyes and ears of courtroom observers. Hourly reporting of who has testified, what the judge thought or seemed to think about the testimony, juror reactions, and other courtroom banter has riveted millions of television viewers. If the courtroom news has not been sufficiently dramatic, these shows will often create their own news by giving less newsworthy events fictitious spins for audience consumption. Conjectures from guests and "what ifs" from news commentators or legal experts and analysts are often passed off as factual information, when in fact they may simply be their opinion.

Today the public seems discontent with simple news reporting. Generally, judicial decisions are reported only when they seem newsworthy. When television producers or newspaper reporters determine that a judge has imposed a lenient sentence, or that a jury has failed to convict a guilty-appearing defendant, or if an unusually large monetary award is made in a civil case by a jury, these outcomes are reported on the evening news or in daily newspapers. The selection of the news events to report is not particularly random. Rather, the news selection process is carefully calculated to yield the greatest public impact. The more sensational the news and the way it is reported, the greater the interest and viewership.

The police and prosecutors often have a symbiotic relationship with the media. In exchange for confidential information from the police or district attorney's offices, reporters will slant their stories in ways favorable to police conclusions and prosecutorial theorizing about the crime, how it was committed, and who probably committed it. Seldom is equal time allocated to defendants so that they can give their version of events or their side of the story. The courts have increasingly relied upon media technology to assist in processing cases. In many jurisdictions, initial appearances and arraignments are held by means of closed-circuit television. The defendant remains at the jail and enters a plea before the judge across town in the courthouse through closed-circuit television monitoring systems. Jurisdictions have adopted this alternative to minimize security problems and the costs of transporting defendants to and from their jails for short court appearances.

This chapter examines two important issues that shape our perceptions about the American court system. The first issue is the nature of the interplay between the courts and the media. This interplay has prompted much public discourse, especially as the direct result of several high-profile trials during the 1990s. The O. J. Simpson trial focused national attention both on court protocol and on the various personalities involved in the trial. All relevant actors were scrutinized, including the judge, the prosecution and defense counsel, jury members, and witnesses. All persons watching the courtroom drama were active participants who critiqued the actions of the witnesses, attorneys, and the judge.

The second issue is our definition of justice as portrayed by the media. Has the legitimacy of the court system been undermined because our ideals of justice are inconsistent with courtroom reality delivered by the media into our homes through radio or television? Have the courts been effective and acted responsibly in their use of media technology? How has the media shaped our perceptions of the "litigation explosion"? We have witnessed seemingly outlandish jury judgments in civil cases extended to persons who have filed lawsuits that appear frivolous. We have seen an array of courtroom tactics used successfully by plaintiff's attorneys against big businesses and corporate giants. The mentality of juries and the racial and ethnic composition of jurors have been analyzed extensively by the media, and we are inclined to view the average juror in a criminal or civil case in disparaging ways. Jurors are perceived both as pawns of the legal system and as self-styled vigilantes with their own political and social agendas. The buzzword of the 1990s was jury nullification, where juries disregard the facts in favor of some alternative and contrary verdict that satisfies political ends rather than legal ones.

This chapter is organized as follows. First, a brief history is provided of the media and its uneasy association with the American justice system. Technological change has modified greatly the nature of courtroom intrusion by the media. Newspapers, radio, and television innovations have been significant in influencing what happens in courtrooms throughout the nation. Increasingly clear is the fact that the behaviors of courtroom actors have undergone a metamorphosis of sorts as courtrooms have been subjected to greater public scrutiny. The implications of these behavioral changes for the justice process are explored.

Several highly visible trials are described, together with the nature of media attention given to each. The media has been instrumental in promoting a defendant's guilt or innocence, depending on the specific case. Accordingly, jurors have been responsive to particular types of media coverage, such that it is questionable whether justice has been served in certain cases. Indeed, some jury verdicts have been reversed by the U.S. Supreme Court because of the undue influence of media trial coverage. Often, media coverage has been passed off and labeled as the court of public opinion. The media has magnified the popularity of this term over time, and many citizens accept media opinion as factually based and give considerable credence to it.

Next, pretrial publicity is described. Pretrial publicity is almost always prejudicial for the defense or prosecution. Sensationalized coverage of both spectacular and heinous crimes has created an emotionally charged milieu for more than a few defendants. In certain cases, defense counsels have sought to change the site of a trial because of extensive adverse pretrial publicity. The trials of Timothy McVeigh and Terry Nichols were transferred from Oklahoma City, Oklahoma, to Denver, Colorado, because it was believed that the amount of pretrial publicity indicated that they could not receive a fair trial in Oklahoma. This section will also explore the factors that determine whether the prejudice generated by pretrial publicity is sufficient to jeopardize one's right to a fair and impartial trial. Several ways for minimizing the prejudicial effects of pretrial publicity are described.

Besides criminal trials, many civil trials have generated a considerable amount of publicity and media coverage. Often these trials involve tort actions, where monetary damages are sought instead of convictions. **Tort actions** may highlight negligence, wrongful death, or product liability. The litigation explosion is also depicted, where the volume of civil cases has burgeoned in recent decades. The media has labeled our society as litigious, emphasizing quite appropriately the increasing interest of persons in seeking monetary awards from their employers or from large corporations. The bases of these increasing numbers of lawsuits may be sexual harassment, product liability, or wrongful death. Many lawsuits are labeled by judges as frivolous and dismissed. Others are decided in civil courtrooms by juries. Again, the media is present and pervasive to assess and interpret what is going on and why. The chapter concludes with a discussion of tort reforms.

TRIALS AND THE COURT OF PUBLIC OPINION

The media has been instrumental in shaping our perceptions of justice. The media and the courts are often at odds because of their competing interests. The courts operate in a methodical fashion, following specific criminal or civil protocols that may at times frustrate the observer. A great deal of time is consumed over seemingly trivial details of events, although we are reminded by the experts on television talk shows that the most trivial details have profound importance in shaping trial outcomes. Verdicts are rendered only after juries have given careful review to factual details, expert witness testimony, and an intricate inspection of all relevant evidence. While the case proceeds at a snail's pace, the media has its story to tell. The most innocuous details of a case are given great weight. Thus, an otherwise boring media story is converted into an exciting one by creative media spins. The viability of a network television show is critically dependent upon the nature of sensational coverage given to the most mundane courtroom events.

There has been considerable debate about the role and influence of the media and the courts. The O. J. Simpson case brought all the arguments for and against media access to the courts into the public discourse. For instance, before the O. J. Simpson murder case, the presiding judge, Lance Ito, was initially reluctant to permit television cameras in his courtroom. Judge Ito believed that the presence of television cameras would undermine the justice process and cause viewers to misunderstand the proceedings. He also believed that tabloidization of the judicial process would occur. In retrospect, Judge Ito was right, although he permitted television cameras to cover most aspects of the trial anyway.

Judge Ito's reservations about the intrusion of television cameras and media representatives into his courtroom were well-founded and grounded in scientific research. Several scholars and legal experts have provided compelling arguments both for and against television cameras in courtrooms (Hoskins, Ruth, and Ruback 2004). While these arguments are inconclusive and inconsistent, the general sentiment is that television coverage of courtroom drama does influence what goes on in the courtroom. There is extensive debate about whether this influence jeopardizes one's right to a fair trial, however. Media representatives emphasize that their interest in covering courtroom events is based on the public's right to be present inside courtrooms as public events. Thus, a judge's refusal to allow the media into courtrooms is perceived as a violation of the First Amendment. Technological change and the advent of television and closed-circuit broadcasting have done much to change the definition of public access to courtroom activities, however. In order to understand how the definition of public courtroom access has changed, we must first examine the early vestiges of courtroom coverage by the media.

HISTORY OF MEDIA AND THE COURTS

Court reaction to media intrusion has gradually changed with changing media technology. In the 1800s, trial outcomes or happenings were relayed by word of mouth. This information dissemination shifted from word of mouth to the printed page with the advent of newspapers. By the 1850s, trial events and court decisions were transmitted throughout the country by use of the telegraph. Those eager to hear the results would often gather at the local telegraph office and wait for the trial results to be announced. The most widely acknowledged example of this process was the murder trial of Harry Thaw. He had killed millionaire Stanford White over the affections of a very young Evelyn Nesbit, also known as the "girl in the red velvet swing."

Soon courtroom photographers and newsreel cameras were common occurrences in the most high-profile cases. The Tennessee trial of teacher John Scopes, known as the "monkey trial," was the first to be broadcast over the radio. Attorneys Clarence Darrow and William Jennings Bryan were well aware of the impact of the media presence and structured their trial tactics not only for the benefit of the jury but also for the benefit of the larger national audience. In fact, compared with today's standards, the media seemed to intrude on court proceedings by making requests similar to those from a movie director to an actor rather than to court officers. For instance, media representatives have often made requests for the attorneys and judges to position themselves so that their cameras could get better picture angles.

The problems created by the media during the murder trial of Bartolomeo Vanzetti and Nicola Sacco in 1921 and during the trial of Richard Loeb and Nathan Leopold Jr. in 1924 prompted the American Bar Association to review the issue of news reporting and the courts. It took another "trial of the century" to force the courts to come to terms with the impact of the media on court proceedings.

The trial involved Bruno Hauptmann, a German immigrant. Hauptmann was accused of kidnaping and murdering the baby of Charles Lindberg. The trial started with over 700 representatives of the media, with 120 being cameramen. The trial was chaos. Witnesses were barraged by reporters and blinded by flashbulbs reminiscent of an opening at a Hollywood movie premiere. Hauptmann appealed his conviction, alleging that the extensive media coverage prevented him from receiving a fair trial. He lost his appeal, but the trial prompted the American Bar Association to review their position on camera access to court proceedings. They ultimately ruled in 1937 that photographing and broadcasting court proceedings should be prohibited. Most states adopted the position of the American Bar Association and forbid photographing and broadcasting trials and trial participants. In 1952, the American Bar Association extended the media ban to include television coverage of court proceedings.

Texas was one of the states that ignored the recommendation of the American Bar Association and allowed cameras into the courtroom at the discretion of the judge. In 1962, Texas provided the case that served as the basis for denying cameras into the courtroom. Billie Sol Estes,

---

BOX 14.1

The First Trial of the Century

The Girl in the Red Velvet Swing

Stanford White was one of the brightest stars in New York society at the turn of the century. As an architect he was a visionary. Many of the new millionaires of the Industrial Revolution flocked to White to have him design their mansions. His talent was recognized by officials of the city and he was hired to design the New York Public Library and Madison Square Garden. White's appetite for design was only matched with his desire for young women. He had several apartments throughout Manhattan where young girls were often accompanied by White. At the turn of the century, the newest sensation in New York was 16-year-old Evelyn Nesbit. Nesbit had arrived in New York from Pittsburgh with her mother, a widowed seamstress. Evelyn was slim and beautiful and soon found work as an artist's model and later landed a role in a Broadway musical. She was an instant sensation. Soon many admirers were waiting for her after the show. One of the hopeful suitors was Stanford White.

In 1901, White convinced Nesbit to have lunch with him. This was the beginning of an affair that would last for five years. Nesbit was raped by White while she was intoxicated with champagne drunk at White's apartment during one of their meetings. She did not seem to be fazed by this development and continued their relationship. Nesbit eventually fell in love with White and made frequent visits to his apartment, where he encouraged her to swing on his red velvet swing—preferably naked.

Evelyn's mother knew a long-term financially secure future with White was not possible. White was married with children. Therefore, she encouraged her daughter to see other men. One of the men who met her mother's expectations was Harry Thaw, who stood to inherit $40 million from the Pittsburgh Railroad fortune. Thaw courted Evelyn with antics like sending her roses individually wrapped in $50 bills. Thaw and Stanford White had more in common than an interest in Evelyn. Earlier White had blackballed Thaw from many of New York's social clubs. Thaw deeply resented this. During the courtship of Nesbit and Thaw, she told Thaw how White had taken advantage of her by getting her drunk and raping her. Upon hearing this Thaw became furious. A short time later during a trip to Europe, he tied her up and beat her with a whip until she was covered with welts. Six months later she married him because she believed he was the only rich man who would propose to her.

On June 25, 1906 Stanford White sat on the rooftop Madison Square Garden theater enjoying a production when Harry Thaw walked up and shot him three times, proclaiming "I did it because he ruined my wife." At the trial, Nesbit testified about White's sexual behavior in an effort to "save a husband I didn't love from the chair." Thaw's mother went to considerable effort to demonstrate her son's insanity. She even went to the extreme of testifying that the entire Thaw family was crazy. The initial jury could not reach a verdict and the second jury found Thaw not guilty by reason of insanity. For what reasons does the media seem to present us with a new "trial of the century" every decade? Do you feel if this offense were to happen today the nation would be transfixed on the case? Are these types of cases good measures of how the criminal justice system operates?

Source: Adapted from "Stanford White and Evelyn Nesbit," _People Weekly_, February 12, 2006, **45**:79–80.

a friend of President Lyndon B. Johnson, was charged with swindling persons out of large sums of cash. The trial judge decided to allow television cameras into the courtroom, but they were restricted to the back of the courtroom in a specially constructed booth. Like Hauptmann 30 years earlier, Estes argued that the media coverage deprived him of a fair trial. The Texas Court of Appeals declared that his due process rights had not been violated, and Estes appealed to the U.S. Supreme Court. In a 5–4 decision, the U.S. Supreme Court reversed Estes's conviction. In the decision of the majority, the Court held that although no prejudice was actually shown, the circumstances of the case were suspect. Furthermore, Justice Clark believed that the presence of the cameras in the courtroom had a harmful effect on all of those involved in the trial. In its decision, the U.S. Supreme Court did not address the issue of whether the First Amendment extended to the media to broadcast from the courtroom (*Estes v. Texas*, 1965).

After the *Estes* decision, states continued to experiment with media coverage. Judges were generally given the discretion to allow cameras. For the next 12 years, courts individually struggled with the decision to allow cameras. In 1977, the Florida Supreme Court approved a one-year pilot study that allowed the electronic media to cover all of cases in Florida state courts without the consent of the participants. The crucial case that emerged during this year involved a 15-year-old boy who was charged with murdering an elderly neighbor while he and some friends burglarized the victim's house. The circumstances of the offense were not unusual. What attracted the media to the trial was the unusual defense of involuntary television intoxication, which was offered by the boy and his attorneys. The defense alleged that Zamora (the boy) did not know what he was doing because of the massive amounts of crime and violence he had watched on television. The local media broadcast segments of the trial on the nightly news and the worldwide audience was estimated at several million viewers. At the conclusion of the trial, Judge Paul Baker submitted a report including his observations about the effect of the media on the trial. He believed that the equipment did not produce any distracting noises or light flashes. By contrast, during the Estes trial, the camera and lighting equipment created various distractions. In the years between these cases, media and camera technology had changed significantly, and ultimately it became less intrusive in the courtroom and seemed to have little impact on the courtroom actors.

Judge Baker spoke with jurors about their reactions to the presence of the media. The jurors believed that the presence of the cameras caused only slight distractions. Yet the actions of the media did not hinder or distract the jurors from following the testimony, arguments of counsel, and judicial instructions. The judge also found no support for the assertion that judges would alter the way that they conduct business with the presence of the cameras.

Considering this information as well as the evidence from other cases, in 1979 the Florida Supreme Court permanently allowed cameras in the courts with the approval of the presiding judge. The new provisions were put to the test with the Ted Bundy murder trial. Ted Bundy defended himself and appeared to enjoy playing to the cameras. However, the trial judge believed that the rules in place were effective and the cameras did not hamper the court process. The court acknowledged that publicity could undermine a defendant's right to a fair trial. However, this risk did not allow for an absolute ban on news reporting and the broadcasting of trials. Essentially, the U.S. Supreme Court left the decision up to the individual states whether to allow the media into their courtrooms.

CURRENT STATUS OF MEDIA ACCESS TO THE COURTS

As of 2006, only three states did not allow cameras into their different courtrooms. Table 14-1 shows states that permit cameras in certain courtrooms, and under particular conditions. Most states have allowed cameras in their courtrooms on either an experimental or a permanent basis. States that have allowed cameras in the courtroom have developed guidelines for their usage. In most states, the consent of the presiding judge is required. Many states require a written application submitted in advance of the trial. Furthermore, in some states, if the defendant objects, cameras will not be permitted to record the trial proceedings.

Most states do not allow television coverage of cases involving juveniles, and coverage is limited where victims of sex crimes are involved or where cases involve trade secrets of business organizations. Fewer states limit coverage of jurors and the *voir dire* process. And all states ban the coverage of pretrial conferences or sidebars between the judge, prosecutor, and defense counsel in court. States have also developed guidelines that regulate media equipment and personnel. Courts specify which types of cameras are allowed and limit the movement and number of media personnel in the court.

TABLE 14-1   Current Status of the Use of Media in U.S. Courtrooms*
States that allow the most coverage; presiding judge has broad discretion:
California, Colorado, Florida, Georgia, Idaho, Kentucky, Michigan, Montana, Nevada, New Hampshire, New Mexico, North Dakota, South Carolina, Tennessee, Vermont, Virginia, Washington, West Virginia, Wisconsin, Wyoming
States with restrictions prohibiting coverage of important types of cases, or prohibiting coverage of all or large categories of witnesses who object to coverage of their testimony:
Alaska, Arizona, Connecticut, Hawaii, Iowa, Kansas, Massachusetts, Missouri, North Carolina, New Jersey, Ohio, Oregon, Rhode Island, Texas, Virginia
States that allow appellate coverage only, or that have such restricting trial coverage rules essentially preventing coverage:
Alabama, Arkansas, Delaware, Illinois, Indiana, Louisiana, Maine, Maryland, Minnesota, Mississippi, Nebraska, New York, Oklahoma, Pennsylvania, South Dakota, Utah
States that prohibit trial and appellate coverage entirely:
District of Columbia

*Compiled by the authors.

PRETRIAL PUBLICITY

One of the primary concerns of those who study the relationship between the court and the media is the effect of **pretrial publicity**. Within this area there are two different issues. The first is that the extensive pretrial publicity will make it difficult if not impossible to locate jurors who have not heard of the cases and developed some preconceived notions about the defendant's guilt or innocence. The second is that the jurors, as the result of the pretrial publicity, will recognize that their decision will be scrutinized by friends, family, neighbors, and the larger community. This pressure will ultimately influence them to vote on the basis of how their own lives will be affected rather than the actual facts of the case. In the *Estes* decision, this was probably the issue that concerned the U.S. Supreme Court the most. The Court wrote that the potential impact of television on the jurors is perhaps of the greatest significance. They are the nerve center of the fact-finding process. And we must remember that realistically it is only the notorious trial that will be broadcast, because of the necessity of the paid sponsorship. The conscious or unconscious effect that this may have on the juror's judgment cannot be evaluated, but experience indicates that it is not only possible but probable that it will have a direct bearing on his/her vote as to guilt or innocence. Where pretrial publicity of all kinds has created intense public feeling that is aggravated by the telecasting or picturing of the trial, the televised jurors cannot help but feel the pressure of knowing that friends or neighbors have their eyes upon them. If the community is hostile to an accused, then a televised juror, realizing he/she must return to neighbors who saw the trial themselves, may well be led "not to hold the balance nice, clear and true between the State and the accused" (*Estes v. Texas*, 1965:545).

Some persons have argued that juror concerns over the impact of their decisions should not allow for their identity to be concealed. In fact juror anonymity should only be allowed in the rarest of cases. In fact jurors in high-profile cases should be regarded as citizen-soldiers in the quest for justice.

It may be that the pretrial publicity placed in the context of day-to-day operations of the court should not be a concern. Daily, the courts process thousands of cases, usually in empty courtrooms. Some persons might assert that rather than having a problem with pretrial publicity, the larger problem facing the court is public apathy. When somebody wanders into a courtroom merely to watch the proceedings, the courtroom actors take notice. They assume that the observer must be a defendant, and when this is not the case, they wonder why this person doesn't have

---

BOX 14.2

Television in the Courtroom?

Court TV   was able to cover the trial of an incestuous cult leader and much of the Scott Peterson murder trial. But in 2005 *Court TV* was in court itself seeking admission into New York criminal courts under the First Amendment. New York courts have consistently refused to allow televised coverage of their criminal trials since 1952, when a state law banning cameras in courtrooms was passed. *Court TV* alleges that New York courts should allow cameras in the courtroom, since to ban them would infringe a basic First Amendment right of citizens to see justice in action literally. In 2005, a total of 43 states approved the use of cameras in courtrooms to televise proceedings. Those states where it is banned, including New York, oppose cameras on grounds having to do with undue influence of court officers. New York officials say that admitting cameras into criminal proceedings would have a negative effect on those proceedings, causing lawyers, judges, and witnesses to be intimidated and act unnaturally These claims have never been proven in the states where cameras have been used to cover trials.

Court TV and other broadcasting organizations say that televised court proceedings would give the public a valuable education on the workings of the justice system. That would have been especially useful during the volatile legal proceedings like those surrounding the shooting death of Amadou Diallo by New York City police officers. The educational benefit could be even greater in the nation's highest court. However, the U.S. Supreme Court has typically been opposed to televising their work, just as Congress at one time balked at having cameras cover their proceedings. But today, programs such as those on C-Span have given millions of Americans a better understanding of how their laws are made. The public also deserves to see how the courts carry out and interpret the law. Sometimes, however, what the public sees isn't especially what the courts want them to see. Lawyers, judges, and others may act in ways that cast unfavorable images of themselves and hold them up to public ridicule. The New York governor, the New York State Bar Association, American Civil Liberties Union, and other organizations favor cameras in the courtroom and support legislation to make that happen in New York and the other states where cameras are presently banned.

Should all courts allow cameras in the courtroom? Shouldn't all persons be allowed to see their appointed and elected officials, including the U.S. Supreme Court, in action firsthand? What harm would cameras cause, if any? What do you think?

Source: Adapted from the Associated Press, "Allow Cameras in New York Courts and the U.S. Supreme Court," April 18, 2005.

---

anything better to do than watch courtroom proceedings. Researchers have estimated that only 7 percent of felony arrests are covered by the press (Champion 2005b).

The concern over pretrial publicity only occurs when there is a high-profile case. The common assumption is that pretrial publicity almost always favors the prosecution and therefore limits the defendant's ability to receive a fair and impartial trial. Researchers have disclosed that most courtroom actors do not believe that pretrial publicity does not significantly affect juror behavior. Judges believe that the *voir dire* process is an effective method for removing jurors who have been prejudiced by the media. Prosecutors acknowledge that pretrial publicity usually works in their favor. Simon and Eimermann (1971), for example, found that 65 percent of those exposed to pretrial publicity had pro-prosecution attitudes compared to 45 percent of those not exposed to pretrial publicity. As prosecutors contend, whether defense attorneys can overcome this bias depends on the type of information prospective jurors are exposed to prior to the trial. Defense attorneys are most inclined to believe that pretrial publicity adversely affects their

---

BOX 14.3

Case Law on Pretrial Publicity

Sheppard v. Maxwell 384 U.S. 333, 86 S.Ct. 1507 (1966)

Sheppard claimed that someone unknown to him entered his home in Bay Village, Ohio, and hit him on the head. When he awakened, he saw his wife had been injured and was sitting in a chair, bleeding, and not moving. Early in the case, police suspected Sheppard of killing his wife and later diverted attention from himself to so-called unknown assailants. The police made known their views to the media, which dramatized the event, as Sheppard was a well-respected physician in the community. Front-page headlines in the local newspapers created a media frenzy, with Sheppard at its center. During his subsequent trial, Sheppard was subjected to considerable media attention, and cameras and other media agents and apparatuses were admitted into the courtroom to witness the proceedings. This action by the court further intensified the media frenzy. In this milieu, Sheppard was convicted of murder. He appealed, and the U.S. Supreme Court overturned his murder conviction, holding that the failure of the state trial judge to protect Sheppard from inherently prejudicial publicity, which saturated the community, and to control disruptive influences in court had deprived Sheppard of a fair trial consistent with due process.

Dobbert v. Florida 432 U.S. 282, 97 S.Ct. 2290 (1977)

Dobbert was convicted of first-degree murder, second-degree murder, child torture, and child abuse and sentenced to death. He appealed, alleging that changes in the jury decision to recommend mercy instead of the death penalty without review by a trial judge had jeopardized his chances of receiving a life sentence. Further, he claimed that there was no death penalty "in effect" in Florida at the time he was convicted, because an earlier death-penalty statute had been held to be invalid when *Furman v. Georgia* (1972) had been decided. Dobbert also claimed that excessive pretrial publicity denied him the right to a fair trial. The U.S. Supreme Court rejected all of his arguments, saying that changes in the death-penalty statute were simply procedural, and thus there was no rights violation. Further, new statutes provided convicted offenders with *more* procedural safeguards rather than fewer of them. Dobbert's equal-protection rights under the Fourteenth Amendment were not violated either, because the new statute did not deny him such protection. Finally, the pretrial publicity, in view of the "totality of circumstances," was insufficient to conclude that he was denied a fair trial. The U.S. Supreme Court upheld his conviction and sentence.

Mu'Min v. Virginia 500 U.S. 415, 111 S.Ct. 1899 (1991)

Mu'Min was charged with and convicted of a murder while he was out on a prison work detail (where he was serving a term on another charge). There was considerable news publicity surrounding the killing, and when the case came to trial, Mu'Min's attorney made a motion for the judge during *voir dire* to ask whether any specific jurors had any knowledge of the pretrial publicity and if so, what effect it would have on their ability to hear and decide the case fairly. The judge denied the motion, and Mu'Min was subsequently convicted. He appealed, alleging that his right to an impartial jury as provided by the Sixth Amendment had been violated. The U.S. Supreme Court upheld his conviction, holding that the refusal of the judge to question jurors about specific contents of news reports to which they had been exposed had not violated Mu'Min's Sixth or Fourteenth Amendment rights to due process.

---

clients. However, it is believed that pretrial publicity is an insignificant problem. Surveys of the public reveal that while pretrial publicity may affect juror attitudes about the case, they still believe that despite this information, they could render objective and impartial judgments and base their decisions on the facts presented at trial.

WHAT TYPES OF INFORMATION DO POTENTIAL JURORS CONSIDER PREJUDICIAL?

Researchers have identified two ways that jurors are affected by prejudicial information. The first is **case-specific pretrial publicity** (Greene 1990). This is information about a specific case where jurors must make a determination of one's guilt or innocence. An example of case-specific pretrial publicity might come from the Rodney King state and federal cases. Most Americans were repeatedly exposed to the videotape showing police officers beating King as he lay on the ground. Jurors asked to serve in that case were probably exposed to that videotape numerous times prior to the trial. Their perceptions of the event were only relevant to this individual case.

The second type of pretrial publicity is **general pretrial publicity**. This includes information about crime, criminals, and the criminal justice system that is constantly in the media and shapes our perceptions when we are asked to serve as jurors. For example, most of us have probably developed an opinion about the insanity defense based on several cases and stories about the insanity defense presented to us in the media. Jurors with these vague perceptions may have already formed an opinion about whether they might accept insanity as a valid defense before hearing any relevant evidence or testimony about one's sanity in an actual trial. Many jurors may still believe that if they find the defendant guilty but mentally ill, he/she will escape punishment or receive a light sentence.

Research has revealed that when jurors were exposed to pretrial publicity revealing a confession or a prior lengthy criminal record of a particular defendant, they were more likely to believe that the defendant was guilty. Furthermore, when information was released prior to the trial about the defendant failing a lie detector test, jurors were more likely to infer guilt from this event.

Uncovering the effects of general pretrial publicity is more difficult. The best research comes from conducting experiments with mock juries. Greene and Loftus (1984) compared three groups of mock jurors. The first group read newspaper stories about a defendant who was mistakenly identified and convicted of rape. The second group was asked to read stories about how the testimony of an eyewitness led to the conviction of a mass murderer. The final group was exposed to no pretrial publicity and acted as the control group. All three groups were then asked to make a decision about guilt or innocence for the cases involving an alleged armed robbery and murder. The prosecution's case consisted primarily of the testimony of an eyewitness. The first group had a significantly higher acquittal rate than either of the other two groups. From this evidence, we might infer that the story about the miscarriage of justice influenced the jurors and made them more skeptical of law enforcement and increased the probability of acquittal.

Research has also indicated that the entertainment media influences individual's perceptions of criminality and the criminal justice system. Jurors may expect the courtroom to be an exciting and dramatic place if they have watched crime dramas such as *L.A. Law*, *Law and Order*, *Judge Judy*, or *Perry Mason*. These shows do not accurately portray what happens in real courtrooms. Court proceedings are typically routine and bland. There are no riveting revelations or courtroom confessions. Jurors are more likely to struggle to find ways to overcome boredom.

HOW TO MINIMIZE THE EFFECTS OF PRETRIAL PUBLICITY

Trial judges can minimize the effects of pretrial publicity by various methods. The most radical and least-used approach is to issue a **gag order**. This is the most controversial approach because it raises serious First Amendment questions. Gag orders usually require that the media cannot publish or broadcast any prejudicial information about a case. Sometimes gag orders are extended to include the attorneys involved in the case. When a gag order includes attorneys, they are under court order not to talk about the case; this means that they are prohibited from giving television interviews or appearing on talk shows while the trial is in progress.

Another possible remedy to minimize pretrial publicity is to grant a **change of venue**. A change of venue would shift the trial from one location to another. The objective is that jurors selected from the new trial location have not been exposed to the same degree of pretrial publicity as the potential jurors in the original jurisdiction. This remedy is rarely used because it is quite costly. All the people who have been called to testify have to travel great distances to the new jurisdiction. Family and friends of the victim and the accused have to travel to the new jurisdiction as well, and this hardship increases their emotional and financial stability. Granting continuances is another method judges use to lessen the effect of pretrial publicity. Most high-profile cases only capture the public's and media attention for a brief period. It is a short time before something new has attracted media attention. Similar to our fleeting attention, memories also fade with time. This allows judges to grant short trial delays in the hope of selecting a jury who has forgotten the media stories about a particular case.

Another method used to minimize pretrial publicity is the use of **judicial instructions**. During the O. J. Simpson trial, Judge Ito gave the jury detailed judicial instructions about what they could and could not do. The question is, do jurors abide by the judge's wishes and follow these judicial instructions? This is one area where much research points to the same conclusion. Judicial warnings do relatively little or nothing to change juror behavior. In fact, judicial warnings seem to make matters worse.

Many attorneys and judges believe that they can eliminate jurors who have been affected by pretrial publicity through **jury selection**. They assume that an intensive *voir dire* will unmask those prospective jurors who have been unduly influenced by the media. In cases where the publicity has reached most of the potential jurors, lawyers may have to permit some jurors to be seated who have been exposed to stories about the case, although they argue that such media information can be disregarded and an impartial verdict can be rendered. While their intentions may be honorable, research does not support their assertion. Jurors exposed to pretrial publicity and who argue that such publicity will not influence their ability to evaluate the facts are much more likely to convict defendants than those who have not been exposed to any pretrial publicity.

Legal scholars have suggested that juries can police themselves during jury deliberations. The belief is that once juries are in the jury room, anyone who begins to depart from the judicial instructions and introduces information that was not presented during trial will be censured by the other members of the jury. The evidence on the jury's ability to police itself has been inconsistent. Some evidence has shown that when jury members who have particular biases join with others with similar biases, this makes the group's determination stronger such that it has a more profound impact on the decision rather than the opinions of any particular juror. When reinforced, individual biases of the group are difficult for juries to overcome. Therefore, it seems that jury deliberations strengthen rather than weaken juror biases.

Overall, these investigations of juror conduct indicate that eliminating biased jurors during *voir dire* is ineffective. The jury is unable to eliminate bias during its deliberations, and judicial instructions simply go unheeded. The most effective option available to judges is granting a continuance until the media fascination with the case has disappeared and people forget case details.

THE LITIGATION EXPLOSION

Like many children, Denise Richie was afraid of monsters and demons. However, Denise Richie's demons were real. For five years until she ran away from home, she was sexually abused by her father. As a result of the abuse at the hands of her father, she spiraled downwards into depression, emotional distress, and several subsequent suicide attempts. Finally, when she was able to pull herself together, she brought criminal charges against her father who was convicted and sent to jail for the sexual abuse. For Denise the legal battle was not over. At the urging of her attorneys, she filed a lawsuit against her mother. Was the lawsuit against her mother because, for a year, she had turned a blind eye to the abuse of her daughter and two other family members? In a word, no. Denise had sued the Richie household because of an insurance policy covering negligence. Detractors argue that Denise did not sue to garnish wages from her father's paycheck. Instead, she went for the "deep pockets" of the insurance company. And she argued that her mother was negligent in her failure to respond to her suspicions regarding her husband's sexual abuse. A jury agreed and awarded $1 million against Mr. Richie in punitive damages and $1.4 million against Mrs. Richie in a negligence lawsuit ultimately paid by the insurance company. The Richie family seem to have overcome their differences because at the same time Denise was in court suing her mother, she was also in criminal court urging the judge to be lenient so that her father could keep his job and support her mother and younger brother.

BOX 14.4

Journalism v. The Courts: A Compromise

Journalists, judges, and legal experts have debated the limitations and merits of allowing cameras in the courts. At the heart of the matter is a conflict between the First and Sixth Amendments. Judges and lawyers argue that often the press limits a defendant's Sixth Amendment right for a fair trial. However, journalists argue that free press and free speech protections are equally as important under the First Amendment.

The press has argued that journalists should have more access to court proceedings. "The presumption of openness should be the first presumption," says Paul Masters, Freedom Forum First Amendment ombudsman. "When we increase the amount of secrecy, we increase the amount of suspicion and erode confidence in the system," Masters adds.

Legal scholars and lawyers believe that camera access to the courtroom may serve to erode public confidence in legal system. Peter Arenella, professor of UCLA Law School, believes that this occurs when the public acting as the thirteenth juror sees the testimony and other coverage, often reaching a different verdict from the jury. Ira Reiner, former Los Angeles district attorney and NBC commentator, believed that some coverage would shed light on courtroom weaknesses. Reiner has declared, "Live TV...revealed the single greatest weakness in the court system: inadequate judicial management of criminal trials."

Ten recommendations have been developed by the judges, journalists, legal scholars, and lawyers attending the conference.

1. Encourage and establish continuing interdisciplinary educational opportunities and dialogue for judges, journalists, and lawyers to foster an understanding of each other's roles through journalism schools, law schools, and the National Judicial College.
2. Assume accuracy in all court proceedings and records and place the burden of proof for closure on the entity seeking secrecy. Privacy issues may overcome the presumption in appropriate cases.
3. Refrain from imposing gag orders on the news media or attorneys. The court should seek other remedies in lieu of gag orders except in extraordinary cases.
4. Establish and or support bench bar media committees that will meet regularly in every community to address issues of mutual concern.
5. Establish guidelines for trial-press management in high-profile cases. Court officials should confer and consult with media representatives to avoid unanticipated problems and understand each other's legal constraints.
6. Adopt professional standards for journalists that are nonbinding and encourage industry-administered certification.
7. Assume that cameras should be allowed in the courtroom, including the federal system, and that such access should be limited or excluded for only the strongest of reasons.
8. Encourage judges to explain, on the record, the reasons for their rulings.
9. Develop a national model to determine when it may be appropriate to compel reporters to testify or produce notes and tapes, with the understanding that the media cannot serve as an arm of law enforcement.
10. Encourage media organizations to develop an ombudsman system to hear recommendations from the courts and public wherever feasible.

Source: Adapted from Steve Geiman, "Journalism v. Courts," *The Quill,* July–August 1996:46–48.

Another example involves Texas attorney Joe Jamails. Jamails likes civil litigation. In his office he proudly displays the $3 billion bank deposit slip that was his part of the $10.5 billion award to Pennzoil against Texaco. He often urges companies to settle their case rather than to face him in court and suffer the same fate as Texaco. Tort cases have spread the wealth to other attorneys in the Houston area. In fact five of the highest-paid trial attorneys in the United States reside in the Beaumont suburb of Houston, Texas. In 1994 these attorneys collectively made a total of $188 million. They specialize in product liability cases, primarily breast implants and asbestos. There is no end in sight for such litigation and the enormous financial awards that follow. Jamails is estimated to be worth $600 million, and many other attorneys are looking forward to working out similar settlements with tobacco companies.

Within the last decade there has been a concerted effort to limit tort litigation. The impetus for this movement has been fueled by allegations that the tort system is careening out of control. The arguments for reform revolve around two central themes. First, there has been a dramatic increase in the number of tort cases. Second, juries are handing out excessive awards. A public opinion poll conducted for the Aetna Life and Casualty Insurance Company revealed that 59 percent of the American population believed that the number of lawsuits has been growing faster than the population. Sixty-eight percent of Americans polled believe that more people originate lawsuits than they should, and that many of these lawsuits are frivolous. Over half of the Americans polled believe that the sizes of awards have risen faster than inflation. And 45 percent of the Americans polled are convinced that the size of jury awards in personal injury cases has been excessive (Taylor, Kagay, and Leichenko 1987).

Referendums to reform the tort system and the litigation explosion extend back in time for many decades. For instance, it has been argued that the current trend in litigation will force the collapse of the court system. This sentiment was echoed in the popular press. *Newsweek* magazine (2003) revealed that Americans from all walks of life are being buried under an avalanche of lawsuits. Doctors are being sued by patients. Lawyers are being sued by clients. Teachers are being sued by students. Merchants, manufacturers, and all levels of government and even cities themselves are being sued by all sorts of persons. The fear of being sued is ubiquitous and no profession is insulated from it.

Even Chief Justice Burger has warned that one reason our courts have become overburdened is that Americans are increasingly turning to the courts for relief from a range of personal distresses and anxieties. Remedies for personal wrongs were once considered the responsibilities of institutions other than the courts. But now damages for personal wrongs are boldly asserted as legal entitlements. The courts have been expected to fill the void created by the decline of church, family, and neighborhood unity (Burger 1982).

TORTS

The emergence and development of **torts** and tort law in America can be attributed to three diverse but ultimately related phenomena. These are (1) the emergence of industrial capitalism, (2) changing legal doctrine and legislative intervention, and (3) a transformation of scholarly legal thought. In the following section, a brief description of each of these phenomena is provided.

Industrial Capitalism

Prior to industrial capitalism, interaction and transactions among strangers were governed by contract law. Upon entering into a contract, each individual had a responsibility to uphold his/her obligation or the contract would be declared null and void. This form of law was well suited for governing obligations that occurred between a small number of people. However, the emergence of industrial capitalism greatly reduced face-to-face interaction between producers and consumers. Consumers were inundated with an unprecedented array of products created by an ever-increasing number of manufacturers. Furthermore, because production became more

---

BOX 14.5

On Pirate's Booty and Jack Asses

Meredith Berkman filed a $50 million lawsuit against *Pirate's Booty*, a snack food. *Pirate's Booty* is basically flavored puffed rice, containing 147 calories and 8.5 grams of fat, while the label says it contains 120 calories and 2.5 grams of fat, according to a Good Housekeeping Institute inspection and analysis of the product. Berkman alleges in her anti-fat lawsuit that based on the stated amounts of calories and fat, she consumed too much *Pirate's Booty* and gained considerable weight, for which she now has various health problems and has had to rigorously diet and exercise to lose the gained weight. Following Berkman's lawsuit, the manufacturer of *Pirate's Booty*, Robert's American Gourmet Foods, a subsidiary of Keystone Foods, blamed the problem on the manufacturing process and immediately recalled the product from store shelves. Berkman went on to allege that because of this "false advertising," many consumers ruined their diets and had to spend more time at the gym because they ate mislabeled *Pirate's Booty*. Berkman claims she has suffered from extreme emotional distress and weight gain, mental anguish, outrage, and indignation.

Jack Ass, a Montana resident, has sued media giant, Viacom, contending that their MTV show, *Jackass*, plagiarized his name, infringed on his trademark and copyright of his name, and defamed his good character. Jack Ass, whose earlier name was Bob Craft, had his name changed to "Jack Ass" in 1997 in order to raise awareness about the dangers of drunken driving. Subsequently, MTV aired *Jackass*, which premiered in 2000 and features a group of guys performing ludicrous and sometimes dangerous stunts. It was made into a movie in 2002. In his suit against Viacom, Jack Ass claims the organization is liable for injury to his reputation that he has built and defamation of the character, which he has tried so hard to create. He is seeking $10 million in damages. He claims that Viacom committed "trademark and copyright infringement on his legal name and on a cartoon character, called Andi Ass, who he created to help spread his message."

How should courts respond to frivolous lawsuits such as these? Should such suits be allowed to be filed? What limitations, if any, should be set in place to protect the courts from frivolous lawsuits? Should filers of such suits be held liable for wasting valuable court time? What do you think?s

---

Sources: Adapted from the Associated Press, "A Little Too Much Booty," June 1, 2006; adapted from CNN, " 'Jackass' Sued By Real Jack Ass," March 5, 2006.

---

efficient through mechanization, producers were able to sell larger numbers of products to consumers. Capitalism also increased stranger interaction because it increased urbanization. Richard Abel explains why this is problematic when he says that the frequency of interaction among strangers is significant because strangers, unlike acquaintances or intimates, have less incentive to exercise care not to injure one another inadvertently and find it more difficult to resolve differences that arise when such injury occurs (Abel 1990). Industrialization also has the dubious distinction of being directly related to increasing the number of personal injuries. Machines of the Industrial Revolution have had a marvelous capacity for smashing the human body. Increasing the number of accidents is a natural result of increasing the number of persons working with and around dangerous machinery. Because contract law was not developed to deal with these new forms of personal injury, an increasing number of injured persons began to demand some alternative legal solution (Abel 1990).

Changing Legal Doctrine and Legislative Intervention

Initial tort claims brought against organizations in the emerging Industrial Revolution were usually unsuccessful. This was because legal doctrines were generally more supportive of industry than of individuals. Also, the courts were hesitant to support claims that could possibly cause irreparable harm to fledgling industries. Friedman says about this process that lawsuits and damage might injure the health of precarious enterprise. The machines were the basis for economic growth, for national wealth, and for the greater good of society (Friedman 1985, 468).

Doctrines that have guided American legal decisions had their origins in common law. According to Friedman, this occurred because England had experienced initial forms of the Industrial Revolution prior to those occurring in America. The initial doctrines that guided legal decisions regarding tort law were the doctrine of contributory negligence, the fellow servant rule, and the doctrine of assumptive risk.

The **doctrine of contributory negligence** essentially held that the defendant was not negligent if the plaintiff was in any degree responsible for his/her own injury. This doctrine was initially developed in England in 1809, and was transplanted in American law to deal with railroad cases. The courts believed that if a person crossing the tracks had any degree of negligence in relation to his/her injury, the railroad could not be held liable.

The **doctrine of assumptive risk** was equally as problematic for plaintiffs. This doctrine generally held that a person could not recover any damages if he/she willingly placed himself/herself in danger. Initially, this doctrine does not seem restrictive but in reality, it offered no satisfactory remedy for persons who knowingly worked in hazardous occupations.

The first two new legal doctrines that began to chip away at existing legal rules were the doctrines of last clear chance and *res ipsa loquitur* (Friedman 1985). The **doctrine of last clear chance** was developed in England in the case of *Davies v. Mann* (1842). This doctrine allowed some degree of negligence on the part of plaintiffs while holding defendants responsible for their actions if they had the slightest chance of avoiding the injury. In the *Davies* case, Mann failed to hobble his donkey and it wandered into the path of Davies's approaching wagon, which smashed into the donkey and killed it. It is clear that Mann contributed to the death of his own animal because he failed to control it, but the court ruled that Davies was also negligent because he had the "last clear chance" to avoid hitting the animal but failed to do so. The **doctrine of *res ipsa loquitur*** or "the thing speaks for itself" originated in *Byrne v. Boadle* (1863). This case is important because it shifted the burden of responsibility from the plaintiff to the defendant where negligence was alleged and damages were sought.

Developing simultaneously with the notion of assumptive risk was the **fellow servant rule**. The fellow servant rule was the largest obstacle that faced injured plaintiffs. However, as the number of industrial accidents increased, so did the number of injured parties bringing suit against organizations rather than specific individuals. The courts began to realize that the plight of the injured worker could not be ignored. This rule held that a servant or employee could not sue his/her master or employer for injuries caused by the negligence of another employee (Friedman 1985, 472). The doctrine essentially left no recourse for employees who were injured in the workplace. They had the option of bringing a lawsuit against the fellow employee who caused the injury. However, this was often a futile effort because the negligent employee was equally as impoverished as the employee bringing suit.

In the 1840s and throughout the 1860s, these doctrines were relatively unchallenged. However, by the 1890s labor had obtained a collective voice and there was diverse judicial opinion concerning personal injury cases. Furthermore, political and legislative intervention began to erode previously existing legal doctrines. One of the original legal rules that limited the fellow servant rule was the **vice principal doctrine**. This doctrine has been described by Friedman (1985), who says that an employee could sue his/her employer in tort if the careless fellow servant who caused the injury was a supervisor or a boss, more properly compared to an employer than a fellow servant.

Employer immunity for tort law has also been limited by federal and state legislatures. As early as the 1850s, statutes were established that outlined safety regulations for railroads. These regulations forced railroads to ring bells prior to passing through railroad crossings, and railroads were also responsible for any fires caused by their locomotives and had to compensate ranchers for any cattle that were killed by their trains.

The Influence of Legal Scholars

Originating and continuing through the middle of the eighteenth century, prominent legal scholars began to rethink the role and purposes of law. Prior to this period, law was believed to have naturalistic and religious origins. These religious foundations seemed less applicable to a world that was experiencing radical social transformations caused by the Industrial Revolution. Consequently, only a few legal scholars believed that order and law had to be based on these new principles. White (1999) explains this process when he indicates that in general, post–Civil War intellectuals were interested in restoring a sense of order and unity that had characterized eighteenth-century thought, but they rejected efforts to derive order and unity from "mythologic" religious principles. A particular interest of the intellectuals in the quarter of century after the war was the conceptualization and the transformation of data into theories of universal applicability.

The two leading proponents of this legal reconceptualization were Nicholas St. John Green and Oliver Wendel Holmes, Jr. These scholars rejected the notion that law was static and bound by religious or naturalistic rules. Rather, they believed that law should be evolutionary. Holmes and Green were convinced that life was in constant flux and that laws and the legal system must adapt in order to address these social changes. It is precisely because contract law and the writ system were unable to adequately address the changing social structure that Holmes and Green advocated the expansion of tort law.

More recent expansions of tort law, specifically enterprise liability, were profoundly influenced by twentieth-century legal scholars. In fact, Priest (1985) has rejected the argument that tort expansion was significantly influenced by industrialization, urbanization, mechanization, and expanding intervention of the federal government. Instead, Priest believes that the current form of tort law classified as enterprise liability was the handiwork of three legal scholars: Flemming James, Friedrich Kessler, and William Prosser. The literary and oratory confluence of James's notion of "risk distribution," Kessler's conviction that contract law was inadequate for monopolized capitalism, and Prosser's synthesis of contract and tort law gave rise to the current conception of enterprise liability. Presently, many legal scholars, businesses, and interest groups believe that tort law has expanded too far and is in need of substantial legislative reform.

ARGUMENTS FOR TORT REFORM

Advocates of **tort reform** argue for its necessity because (1) in the last few years the number of tort cases has increased dramatically, and this event can be attributed to the increased litigiousness of American society; and (2) juries are incompetent to handle tort cases because they are sympathetic to plaintiffs and consistently dole out large awards. In the following section each of these arguments will be examined.

A Dramatic Increase in the Number of Tort Cases

Until the mid-1960s, most courts never kept records concerning the number and types of cases that they decided. Consequently, gathering statistics for a longitudinal study of American litigiousness is extremely difficult. Within the last two decades a handful of agencies have emerged that compile statistics on litigation rates. These include the National Center for State Courts, the Administrative Office of the U.S. Courts, and the Rand Corporation's Institute for Civil Justice. When investigations are conducted to determine whether we have experienced a litigation explosion, researchers at the Institute for Civil Justice have found that, overall, tort filings in state courts have increased between 2.3 percent and 3.9 percent annually. Federal courts experienced a similar annual increase of 4 percent. Galenter's analysis of tort filings in federal district courts between 1975 and 1984 has shown that these courts had a 46 percent increase during that nine-year period.

This percentage may be misleading because the absolute percent increase of tort cases in this nine-year period was only 8.2 percent. During this same time interval, federal government suits against individuals for overpayments comprised 31.6 percent of the entire federal caseload (Galenter 1986).

More recent statistics reveal that civil cases may be decreasing. In 2001, there were 11,908 civil cases in the 75 largest counties, which represents a 47 percent decline from the 22,451 cases in the same counties in 1992. Federally, from 1985 to 2003, tort cases decreased 79 percent (Cohen 2004).

It should be noted that statistics reveal as much as they conceal. The above analyses would suggest that tort litigation has increased from 1979 to 1984, and then decreased from 1985 to 2003. However, several interesting results are disclosed when we control for the actual type of tort filing. For example, it may be that the number of people injured by unsafe products has increased, thus causing the rise in the litigation rate. Perhaps large toxic torts, where a large number of claims are processed in a short time period, have caused the litigation rate to be exaggerated. And perhaps this increased rate is an anomaly of the federal system and should not be used as evidence of a litigation explosion, since federal courts handle only 5 percent of all tort cases. Also, if we disaggregate the statistics across the years from 1985 to 2003, we find that cases were actually increasing until about 1990 and then began to decline but spiked again around the year 2000. Several other factors have been given for the recent decline. For instance, the federal system increased its use of alternative dispute resolution, steering a number of cases away from the courts. Another reason may be that it has become increasingly complex and costly to take a civil case to trial (Cohen 2004).

BOX 14.6

Are Jury Awards Out of Control?

Betty Bullock, Newport Beach, California

A $28 billion award was given by a jury to Betty Bullock, 64, of Newport Beach, California. A lawsuit was filed against Philip Morris, Inc. for fraud and negligence. Bullock alleged that Philip Morris had failed to warn her about the possible cancer-causing ingredients of the cigarettes they marketed, and that over the years, Bullock contracted lung and liver cancer as the result of the cigarettes she smoked.

Source: Adapted from Henry Weinstein and the *Los Angeles Times*, October 5, 2002.

The largest award in aviation history was given to James Cassoutt, his wife, Cindy, and a passenger, Judy Kealey, who were flying in a Cessna 185 airplane that crashed in 1989. The verdict included $400 million in punitive damages and $80 million in compensatory damages. The plaintiffs claimed that the crash was caused by a defective seat latching mechanism. The suit claimed that the pilot's seat suddenly slid back as he was attempting to land the plane and caused the nose to pitch up because he had the control yoke in his grasp. The single-engine Cessna 185 then crashed and burned in a small clearing amid thick woods 75 yards from the runway at Coastal Airport, a small Pensacola landing strip. Cessna's lawyers claimed that the seat did not slip, and they denied that the locking mechanisms were defective. They blamed the crash on pilot error, since James Cassoutt had little experience or instruction on flying the Cessna 185. Cindy Cassoutt suffered third-degree burns over half of her body. Her husband and Kealey were burned less seriously, but Kealy also suffered a broken back.

Source: Adapted from the Associated Press, "Cessna Fined $480M," August 17, 2001.

There were almost twice as many $1 million awards in 2002 as in 2001 by juries in Michigan, according to a survey. Juries in Michigan awarded a record $101 million to various plaintiffs. The largest was a $22.5 million verdict against McLaren Regional Medical Center in Genesee Circuit Court, one of two medical malpractice verdicts. Other big verdicts included a $13 million wrongful death verdict against Garden City with a construction company that it hired to make water main and streetscape improvements. Also $12 million was awarded in a verdict against a Wayne County car dealership that allowed a prospective buyer to use its vehicle without first transferring the title. The prospective buyer's negligent driving killed a teenager.

Source: Adapted from David Shepardson and *The Detroit News,* "Jury Awards Set Record in 2002," January 14, 2003.

When Scott Peterson's trial occurred in San Mateo County in 2004, news teams from across the country converged on the Redwood City courthouse, where the trial was held. Only a limited amount of sidewalk space was available to accommodate these numerous news teams, and San Mateo County officials determined that television stations must pay a monthly rental fee of $8,500 for sidewalk space. It was estimated that during the Peterson trial, television stations would each pay $51,000 to reserve a coveted spot next to the courthouse. County officials indicated that the trial, which was estimated to last six months, would cost $255,000 to the county just for providing services to the media. An additional indoor media center was to be made available at a cost of $582 per month for space in a large room with audio feeds from the trial. With 20 outlets available to interested media networks and publications, the operating costs to the county would be defrayed. The county officials declared also that if not enough media outlets agreed to pay the required fees, the audio feed room would be closed and the county will discontinue sidewalk services provided to television outlets, such as generators, portable toilets, and security.

Source: Adapted from the Associated Press, "Media Fees for Peterson Trial Coverage Reduced," February 10, 2004.

Juries Delivering Excessive Awards

When arguing about whether juries deliver excessive awards, both proponents and opponents of tort reform seem to have the relevant statistics to support their respective positions. This does not mean that one group's statistics are wrong, but rather, they may be the result of applying incorrect statistical techniques. When analyzing data that are extremely skewed (e.g., jury awards), it is inappropriate to use the mean or arithmetic average because a few large cases can severely skew the results. Therefore, it is more appropriate to use the median, or the midpoint of the data, when analyzing jury awards and trends. Using data from San Francisco and Cook County, Illinois, the Institute for Civil Justice has conducted a study of jury awards. Between 1960 and 1979 the median jury award for all tort cases was approximately $30,000. However, in 1979 the awards in Cook County decreased dramatically, while in San Francisco the awards increased dramatically.

The awards declined in Cook County because of a shift to comparative negligence, which may have increased attorney propensity to bring cases involving smaller damage amounts to trial. Conversely, the awards in San Francisco increased because a mandatory arbitration program eliminated most of the smaller cases from reaching courts. When the median tort awards are disaggregated, the median award for auto claims ranges from $5000 to $40,000. Meanwhile, in product liability cases, the juries award between $180,000 and $200,000 per case. This represents an increase from $70,000 to $150,000 since 1960. When arithmetic means are used as indicators of the average tort award, the picture is quite different. In 1960, for instance, the average award for all tort cases ranged from $50,000 to $75,000. By 1984 this number had increased to between $250,000 and $300,000. When the average award is disaggregated, the data reveal that malpractice awards average about $1.2 million. Average awards for San Francisco automobile accidents and personal injury awards were $150,000 and $250,000, respectively.

More recent statistics reveal that federally, from 1985 to 2003 the number of tort trials in U.S. District Courts has declined, and median awards for plaintiff winners in 2003 were around $200,000 (Cohen 2004). Also in the 75 largest counties in the United States, the median award decreased from $65,000 in 1992 to around $37,000 in 2001, yet approximately $4 billion in damages were awarded to plaintiffs in 2001 (Cohen 2004).

Proponents of tort reform have utilized mean awards to support their position that juries are delivering excessive awards and that legislative limits should be placed on the amount of these awards, especially in malpractice suits. In this regard, they have been relatively successful because as of 2003, 24 states had passed legislation that limited maximum awards courts would approve. Furthermore, state legislatures have become convinced that tort law is out of control and is in need of reform. In fact, by 2005 about two-thirds of states had passed some form of legislation limiting the amount of awards against the state. There is little doubt that these reforms have significantly altered the tort system. But scholars are beginning to ask whether these reforms are a benefit to citizens or to businesses.

Who Benefits from Tort Reform?

If reform measures were supportive of citizen's interests, we might assume that when reform measures were passed, insurance availability would increase and insurance premiums would decrease. Research has revealed several instances where reform measures have had no appreciable impact on the availability or affordability of insurance. For example, Florida, Minnesota, Washington, Wisconsin, and Ontario, Canada, have passed legislative reform measures. Despite these reforms, all locations have experienced increased insurance premiums, and many locations are unable to locate any insurance carriers. In fact, allegations by manufacturers and the medical community that reform was necessary because their rates were too high have no basis in fact. Abel (1990) has said that product, occupier, and general liability costs or insurance premiums plus damage payments have totaled less than 0.2 percent of sales; in the manufacturing sector where these costs were highest (e.g., rubber and plastic manufacture), they constituted only 0.58 percent; even among hospitals, these costs were only 2.35 percent of gross income.

BOX 14.7

Medical Malpractice Lawsuits and Jury Awards

It happened in Cody, Wyoming. Chad Ooten, a Cody resident, underwent surgery for a back injury in 2000. But Dr. Stephen Emery removed the wrong cervical disc from Ooten's spine, requiring three follow-up surgeries. Ooten filed a lawsuit against the doctor and hospital where the surgery was originally performed, alleging medical malpractice. A jury awarded Ooten a total of $1 million for economic and noneconomic damages, and his wife was given $175,000. Wyoming Medical Society president Dr. Robert Monger of Cheyenne criticized the verdict. He says that it will increase the state's medical malpractice insurance considerably and make the state's doctor shortage even worse than it presently is. The plaintiff's attorney, Todd Hambrick, said that the insurance industry is to blame for failing to agree to settle on such claims when the doctor clearly is at fault.

It happened in Madison, Wisconsin. Jessica Greenfield, 33, underwent surgery in 2000 for acid reflux. However, the surgery went awry and left her stomach and intestines unable to function properly. No subsequent surgery has been successful to remedy the problem. Following the original surgery, Greenfield has had to receive nutrition through a feeding tube. Ms. Greenfield filed suit against the surgeon and hospital, alleging negligence in performing the surgery. She alleged substantial pain and suffering and lost wages. Additionally, her son joined the lawsuit with one of his own, alleging loss of companionship with his mother. The jury awarded $4.13 million to Ms. Greenfield for economic damages, lost wages, and medical expenses, as well as $4.25 million for pain and suffering. An award of $82,000 was made to her son for loss of companionship with his mother. Wisconsin recently removed caps on damages awarded by juries for medical malpractice suits.

Janice Bird, a daughter of Nita Bird, was at the Los Angeles County Hospital one evening, where her mother was undergoing outpatient surgery. Janice was soon joined by one of her sisters. However, something went wrong with the surgical procedure, and hospital personnel rushed Mrs. Bird to the emergency surgery room. Janice Bird and her sister happened to be standing in the hallway when hospital personnel rushed their mother by on a gurney. Janice Bird and her sister claim that her mother was bright blue and that her head was almost touching the floor. This caused them so much emotional distress, they claim, that they decided to sue the hospital for several million dollars. The daughters sued, not for malpractice, but for the emotional distress to them, not their mother.

Stephen Roel got drunk at the Las Vegas Hilton and Mandalay Hotel and Casino. While intoxicated, he claimed to gamble away over $1 million. When he sobered up, he sued the casino and hotel for damages, claiming that they permitted him to gamble despite his drunken condition. He had established a $50,000 credit line with the casino and had played there for 15 years. In exchange for his gambling, the casino always permitted him to stay free at the hotel, and they paid for his roundtrip flights to Las Vegas, meals, and other incidentals. However, the casino allowed him to go over his limit on that particular evening. In the days following his loss, he sobered up and sued the casino for unspecified damages in excess of $2 million, alleging negligence and other improper behaviors on the part of casino staff. Hotel authorities wanted to know that if he had won $1 million in his drunken state, would he have given it back?

Should states and the federal government put limits on monetary awards for lawsuits against physicians, hospitals, and others? If so, what should be these limits? What do you think?

Sources: Adapted from the Associated Press, "Jury Awards $1.2 Million for Botched Surgery, Largest Award in Years," May 25, 2006; adapted from the Associated Press, "Jury Awards $8.4 Million in Medical Malpractice Case," March 13, 2006; adapted from the Associated Press, "Birds of a Feather Sue Together," May 12, 2006; adapted from the Associated Press, "A Million Dollar Gamble," March 1, 2005.

The research that focuses on the efficacy of jurors would contradict the notions of jurors portrayed by tort reformers. These reforms allege that juries are sympathetic to plaintiffs simply because they deliver large cash awards. However, research focusing on jury behavior finds the opposite is true. Some jurors are extremely careful and often frugal when deciding cash awards. Sometimes jurors make very precise calculations of medical expenses, repair bills, and other costs when determining awards in order to ensure that the plaintiffs got no more than they were entitled to receive. Furthermore, such careful accounting, particularly in the case of tragic dimensions, contrasts sharply with the common view of juries as overgenerous and free spending.

Legislators are convinced that litigation has increased at a dramatic rate and reform measures (e.g., alternative dispute resolution) might control this problem. Increased litigation rates would indeed be a problem if an increasing number of litigants were bringing frivolous cases while the injury rate remained the same. However, research has revealed the contrary. Abel summarizes research reporting that among those who suffered major permanent partial disability as a result of medical malpractice, less than 17 percent filed claims, and only 6.5 percent received any payment (Abel 1990, 785–788). Regarding workplace injury claims, only 37 percent of the injured workers made worker's compensation claims. These results indicate that contrary to the perception of a litigious public, the majority of persons who have a legitimate injury fail to make a claim. These results seem to indicate that tort reform measures are not intended to help the average citizen. In each of the examples cited, the reform measures have limited the recourse of injured individuals and benefitted insurance companies, businesses, and interest groups.

Summary

This chapter has examined some of the major issues that are facing the American court system. The first is the relationship between the courts and the media. The media and the courts have had a relationship dating back to the 1800s. The media has always had a desire to report about certain cases that involve celebrities or are bizarre or unique in some respect. The courts, on the other hand, operate in a more methodical manner, following specific criminal or civil rules of procedure that at times can be very boring. A large amount of trial time is spent on the facts of the case, and specific detail of the events that occurred. Verdicts are rendered only after juries have carefully reviewed all the facts presented in trial, and expert and witness testimony. While this attention to detail and legal procedures may drag out for an extended period of time, the media wants to tell the story now. The media may focus on the most trivial aspects of a trial that are not even relevant legally, like the defendant's demeanor, the defendant's appearance or clothing, or missteps that the prosecution has made. Therefore, a boring, drawn-out trial is converted into an exciting media story. The coverage of the trial may even be sensationalized in order to obtain greater viewership. When the ratings of a network are dependent upon the nature of sensational coverage given, the most mundane courtroom events will be blown out of proportion.

During the 1900s there have been many "trials of the century," including the trial of Stanford White, Bruno Hauptmann, Sacco and Vanzetti, John and Lorena Bobbit, and O. J. Simpson. In each of these cases the media and the courts have battled to balance the power of the media with the objectives of justice. In most cases the court has had to determine whether the defendant can have a fair trial because of pretrial publicity generated by the media. Several methods are used to limit pretrial publicity from gag orders to sequestration of the jury. However, with technological advances and the idea of cameras in the courtrooms, there has been some contention about balancing the fact that trials are public with affording the defendant a fair trial by an impartial jury. For instance, in the 1800s, verdicts were relayed by word of mouth. This changed with the advent of newspapers, where verdicts were given on printed page. By the 1850s, the telegraph was used to transmit trial events and court decisions. Soon courtroom photographers and newsreel cameras became the plague of the most high-profile cases. The Scopes trial was the first to be broadcast over the radio. Attorneys became aware of the impact the media presence could have and used trial tactics that were not only intended for the jury but for the larger national audience. Media representatives have even made requests for the attorneys and judges to position themselves so that their cameras could get better picture angles. It was during the Hauptmann trial that the court realized the media was not going to go away. Soon the American Bar Association would rule that photographing and broadcasting court proceedings should be prohibited. Most states adopted the position of the American Bar Association and forbid photographing and broadcasting trials and trial participants. In 1952, the American Bar Association extended the media ban to include television coverage of court proceedings. Today, most states allow cameras in their courtrooms but have developed guidelines for their usage. In most states, the consent of the presiding judge is a requirement, and many states require a written application submitted in advance of the trial. Finally, in some states, if the defendant objects to cameras in the courtroom, they will not be permitted.

The primary concern of the relationship between the court and the media is the effect of pretrial publicity. Two different issues emerge here—the first is that pretrial publicity will make the process of finding jurors who have not heard of the case very difficult; the second is that because of the pretrial publicity, the jurors will realize their decision could be analyzed by the community, and this will influence them to vote on how their lives will be affected in the aftermath rather than on the facts of the case. A concern is that the effect of pretrial publicity on a juror's decision cannot be known. It should be mentioned, however, that the majority of cases are not subject to media scrutiny and usually it is only the high-profile cases that get coverage. Some research has shown that most courtroom actors say pretrial publicity does not significantly affect juror behavior because they believe that the *voir dire* process is effective at removing those jurors who have been prejudiced by the media.

There are two basic ways in which jurors can be affected by pretrial publicity. The first is case specific, which is information about a specific case, and the second is general pretrial publicity, which includes information about crime, criminals, and the criminal justice system that may shape the perceptions of those asked to serve as jurors. This pretrial publicity can be minimized in several ways. The least used method is probably for the judge to issue a gag order. Gag orders usually say that the media cannot publish or broadcast any prejudicial information about a case, which borders on fundamentally free speech issues. Another method would be to grant a change of venue, which would change the location of the trial, the idea being that jurors from the new location have not had the same exposure to pretrial publicity as the jurors in the original jurisdiction. Change of venue is, however, rarely used because of the cost involved. Granting continuances can be another method for the judge to minimize pretrial publicity; most cases only get media attention for short periods. In this way, a judge can implement short trial delays in the hope that the jury will have forgotten the media attention for a case. The use of judicial instructions can also minimize the effect of pretrial publicity. Using this method, the judge gives the jury detailed instructions about what they can and cannot do. Lastly, the most common form of eliminating pretrial publicity is through jury selection. This process should reveal those prospective jurors who are no longer impartial because of media publicity. Legal scholars believe that juries also police themselves, and anyone who tries to depart from judicial instructions or uses information that was not presented at trial will be criticized by the other jury members.

Another issue facing the courts is the perception that juries are out of control and awarding excessive damage awards in civil cases. The evidence suggests that this is more myth than reality. The amount of litigation spikes up and down from year to year but appears to actually be on the decline as of 2003. Because of the greater time and monetary resources needed to take a case to trial or the increase in the use of alternative dispute resolution, caseloads do not appear to be overwhelming, and the awards juries are handing out also seem to be declining, although they vary depending on the type of tort. Furthermore, excessive jury awards have been reduced on appeal in more than a few instances. One side believes that due to the emergence of industrial capitalism, changing legal doctrine, legislative intervention, and a legal scholarly thought, torts and litigation have inevitably increased. The other side believes that if we delve into the statistics, litigation is actually on the decline. The increased use of alternative dispute resolution by the federal system and the complexity and costliness of taking a civil case to trial have been a couple of reasons proffered for the steering of a number of cases away from the courts.

Several states have, however, started implementing legislation placing caps on monetary damages especially where medical malpractice is concerned. Whether this is because state legislators believe awards given by juries in these cases are out of control, or that medical insurance premiums have skyrocketed, is not known. The media, however, does seem to be still perpetuating a myth that the litigiousness of U.S. society is excessive. One fact that does remain is that doctors, teachers, and state and city officials will continue to be the aim of litigation due to the very nature of the jobs that they hold, and that disputes will arise from human interaction.

Questions for Review

1. What is meant by "trials of the century"? What is the relation between the court and the media in so-called trials of the century?
2. How much pretrial publicity is necessary for a change of venue?
3. What are some of the advantages and disadvantages of allowing the media into courtrooms?
4. What are some opposing views regarding frivolous lawsuits and excessive jury awards? Should defendants be allowed millions of dollars in damages for minor injuries or mental suffering? Why or why not?
5. What is tort reform? Who benefits from tort reform?
6. What is a change in venue?
7. What types of circumstances suggest that pretrial publicity is unfavorable to defendants?
8. What is the litigation explosion? Why do you believe that it has occurred?
9. What is a gag order? Why do judges impose gag orders on jurors and other participants in legal actions?
10. Do media representatives have a constitutional right to enter and record what is going on in U.S. courtrooms? What are your opinions on this issue?

Suggested Readings

1. Janet Cotterill (2002). *Language in the Legal Process.* New York: Palgrave Macmillan.
2. Steve Kroll-Smith (2004). "Toxic Torts and Environmental Justice." *Law and Policy* **26:**177–307.
3. *Newsweek* (2003). "Civil Wars." *Newsweek*, December 15, 43.
4. Joanne Terrell and Karen M. Staller (2003). "Buckshot's Case: Social Work and Death Penalty Mitigation in Alabama." *Qualitative Social Work Research and Practice* **2:**7–23.
5. Neil Vidmar (2002). "Case Studies of Pre- and Midtrial Prejudice in Criminal and Civil Litigation." *Law and Human Behavior* **26:**73–105.

GLOSSARY

ABA Model Code of Professional Responsibility American Bar Association standards of behavior, which are voluntary and intended as self-regulating for lawyer conduct in the courtroom and between lawyers and clients.

Acceptance of responsibility A genuine admission or acknowledgment of wrongdoing. In federal presentence investigation reports, for example, convicted offenders may write an explanation and apology for the crime(s) they committed. A provision that may be considered in deciding whether leniency should be extended to offenders during the sentencing phase of their processing.

Accused Person alleged to have committed a crime; the defendant in any criminal action.

Acquittal Any judgment by the court, considering a jury verdict or a judicial determination of the factual basis for criminal charges, where the defendant is declared not guilty of the offenses alleged.

Action, actions at law A court proceeding; either civil, to enforce a right, or criminal, to punish an offender. Court litigation where opposing parties litigate an issue involving an alleged wrongdoing; may be for the protection of a right or for the prevention of a wrong.

Addams, Jane (circa 1860–1910) Founded Hull House in the 1890s in Chicago, a shelter for runaways and others who were in need of housing, food, and clothing.

Adjudicates To judge, decide a case, conclude a matter.

Adjudication Legal resolution of a dispute; when a juvenile is declared delinquent or a status offender, the matter has been resolved; when an offender has been convicted or acquitted, the matter at issue (guilt or innocence) has been concluded by either a judge or jury.

Adjudication hearing Formal proceeding involving a prosecuting attorney and a defense attorney where evidence is presented and a juvenile's status or condition is determined by the juvenile court judge.

Administrative law The body of laws, rules, orders, and regulations created by an administrative agency.

Administrative Office of United States Courts Organization that hires federal probation officers to supervise federal offenders. Also supervises pretrial divertees; probation officers prepare presentence investigation reports about offenders at the request of a district judge.

Admissible An evidentiary term designating testimony or physical evidence that may be presented to the finders of fact (juries or judges) in criminal proceedings. Restrictions and conditions are usually articulated in federal and state rules of evidence.

Admission A confession; a concession as to the truthfulness of one or more facts, usually associated with a crime that has been committed. May also apply to tort actions.

Admit A plea of guilty, an acknowledgment of culpability, accuracy of the facts alleged in either an adult or a juvenile proceeding.

Adversarial proceedings Opponent-driven court litigation, where one side opposes the other; prosecution seeks to convict or find defendants guilty, while defense counsel seeks to defend its clients and seeks their acquittal.

Adversary system Legal system involving a contest between two opposing parties under a judge who is an impartial arbiter.

Affidavit A statement in writing given under oath before someone who is authorized to administer an oath.

Affirm To uphold the opinion or decision of a lower trial court; usually an action by an appellate court.

Affirmation In courts, an oath, or declaration in place of an oath for persons whose religious beliefs prohibit oaths, to tell the truth and nothing but the truth when giving testimony.

Affirmative defenses Responses to a criminal charge where the defendant bears the burden of proof (e.g., automatism, intoxication, coercion, duress, mistake), which go beyond simple denial of facts and gives new facts in favor of the defendant, if facts in the original complaint are true.

Affirmative registration Action on the part of women to actively seek to be included on juries, which were formerly comprised exclusively of men.

Age of majority Chronological date when one reaches adulthood, usually either 18 or 21; when juveniles are no longer under the jurisdiction of the juvenile courts, but rather the criminal courts; also age of consent.

Aggravating circumstances Events about crime that may intensify the severity of punishment, including bodily injury, death of victim, or the brutality of the act.

Alibi Defense to a criminal allegation that places an accused individual at some place other than the crime scene at the time the crime occurred.

Allegation Assertion or claim made by a party to a legal action.

Allege To aver, assert, claim; usually a prosecutor will allege certain facts in developing a case against a criminal defendant.

Alternate jurors Jurors who have been selected to replace any of the regular jurors who may become ill and cannot attend the full trial proceeding; these jurors have been vested with the same tasks as regular jurors who will hear and decide cases.

Alternative dispute resolution (ADR) Procedure whereby a criminal case is redefined as a civil one and the case is decided by an impartial arbiter, where both parties agree to amicable settlement. Usually reserved for minor offenses.

Amendment A modification, addition, deletion.

American Bar Association (ABA) National organization of U.S. lawyers headquartered in Chicago, Illinois.

Amicus curiae A friend of the court. Persons may initiate petitions on behalf of others, perhaps for someone who is in prison. Such *amicus* briefs are designed to present legal arguments or facts on behalf of someone else. Person allowed to appear in court or file a brief even though the person has no right to participate in the litigation otherwise.

Answer A written response in relation to a filed complaint prepared by a litigant or defendant.

Appeal, appeal proceedings Any request by the defense or prosecution directed to a higher court to contest a decision or judgment by a lower court.

Appearance Act of coming into a court and submitting to the authority of that court.

Appellants Persons who initiate an appeal.

Appellate courts Courts hearing appeals emanating from lower courts. These courts typically do not try criminal cases.

Appellate jurisdiction Authority to rehear cases from lower courts and alter, uphold, or overturn lower court decisions.

Appellate review A comprehensive rehearing of a case in a court other than the one in which it was previously tried.

Appellees Parties who prevailed in lower court, who argue on appeal against reversing the lower court's decision.

Argument Any rationale provided by the defense or prosecution to support their position in court; any oral persuasion attempted before a jury.

Arraignment Official proceeding in which defendant is formally confronted by criminal charges and enters a plea; trial date is established.

Arrest Taking persons into custody and restraining them until they can be brought before court to answer the charges against them.

Arrestees Persons who have been arrested by police for suspicion of committing a crime.

Assigned counsel system Program wherein indigent clients charged with crimes may have defense attorneys appointed for them; these defense attorneys may be private attorneys who agree to be rotated to perform such services for a low rate of reimbursement from the city, county, or state.

Assistant state's attorneys Prosecutors who serve under other prosecutors in local or state jurisdictions; government prosecutors.

Assistant U.S. attorneys (AUSAs) Government prosecutors who are subordinate to the U.S. attorney who heads the prosecutor's office for each federal district.

Attorney–client confidentiality and privilege Relation between a counsel and his/her client wherein any information exchanged between parties will not be disclosed to others, such as prosecutors; attorneys are protected from disclosing information about the clients they represent because of this privilege.

Attorney competence Standards for determining whether clients are fairly and intelligently represented by their lawyers when they are charged with crimes.

Attorney general Senior U.S. prosecutor in each federal district court. A cabinet member who heads the Justice Department.

Attorney, lawyer, counsel Anyone trained in the law who has received a law degree from a recognized university and who is authorized to practice law in a given jurisdiction.

Automatic waivers Jurisdictional laws that provide for automatic waivers of juveniles to criminal court for processing; legislatively prescribed directive to transfer juveniles of specified ages who have committed especially serious offenses to jurisdiction of criminal courts.

Automatism A set of actions taken during a state of unconsciousness.

Backdooring hearsay evidence Action by prosecutor where prosecutor comments about or mentions information that is otherwise inadmissible in court; remarks made in front of a jury for their emotional and persuasive effects, which are otherwise barred because of the inadmissibility of evidence.

Backlog Number of impending cases that exceeds the court's capacity that cannot be acted upon because the court is occupied in acting upon other cases.

Bail Surety provided by defendants or others to guarantee their subsequent appearance in court to face criminal charges. Available to anyone entitled to it (not everyone is entitled to bail); is denied when suspects are considered dangerous or likely to flee. *See also* preventive detention and *United States v. Salerno* in list of cases.

Bail bond A written guarantee, often accompanied by money or other securities, that the person charged with an offense will remain within the court's jurisdiction to face trial at a time in the future.

Bail bond companies Any organization established for the purpose of posting bail for criminal suspects.

Bail bondsperson, bail bondsman Person who is in the business of posting bail for criminal suspects. Usually charges a percentage of whatever bail has been set.

Bail recovery agents Persons who seek to take into custody a fugitive or someone who has jumped bail by fleeing the jurisdiction before trial; also persons who seek to recover the amount of bail from a fugitive from justice.

Bail Reform Act Original act passed in 1966 to assure that bail practices would be revised to ensure that all persons, regardless of their financial status, shall not needlessly be detained to answer criminal charges.

Bail Reform Act of 1984 Revision of original 1966 Bail Reform Act where changes in bail practices were implemented to assure that all persons, regardless of their financial status, shall not needlessly be detained to answer criminal charges; gave judges and magistrates greater autonomy to decide conditions under which bail would be granted or denied. Does not mean that all persons are entitled to bail regardless of their alleged offense.

Bailiff Court officer who maintains order in the court while it is in session. Bailiff oversees jury during a trial proceeding, sometimes has custody of prisoners while they are in the courtroom. Also known as messengers.

Bar Aggregate denoting all attorneys admitted to practice law in every jurisdiction.

Bench trial Tribunal where guilt or innocence of defendant is determined by the judge rather than a jury.

Beyond a reasonable doubt Standard used in criminal courts to establish guilt of criminal defendant.

Bifurcated trial Tribunal in capital cases where jury is asked to make two decisions. First decision is to determine guilt or innocence of defendant; if guilty, jury meets to decide punishment, which may include the death penalty.

Bill of Rights First ten amendments to the U.S. Constitution setting forth certain freedoms and guarantees to U.S. citizens.

Bind over Following a finding of probable cause that a crime has been committed and the defendant has committed it, a court action to cause the defendant to be tried on the charges later in a criminal court.

Blaming A step in the dispute process whereby the victim singles out someone as a potential target for legal action.

Blaming the victim The stereotypical practice of charging the socially and psychologically handicapped with the lack of motivation. An attitude or belief that the adverse conditions and negative characteristics of a group, often of minorities, are the group's own fault.

Blended sentencing Any type of sentencing procedure where either a criminal or juvenile court judge can impose both juvenile and/or adult incarcerative penalties.

Blue-ribbon jury A jury considered by either side, prosecution or defense, to be ideal because of its perceived likelihood of rendering a verdict favorable to that side; jurors often are selected because of their higher educational level and intellectual skills.

Bond Written document indicating that defendants or sureties assure the presence of these defendants at a criminal proceeding; if not, then the bond will be forfeited.

Booking Process of making written report of arrest, including name and address of arrested persons, the alleged crimes, arresting officers, place and time of arrest, physical description of suspect, photographs, sometimes called "mug shots," and fingerprints.

Bounties, bounty hunters Monetary rewards offered for capture of persons who escape prosecution from a given jurisdiction. Often, such persons have posted a bond with a bonding company and the bonding company hires a bounty hunter (person who earns living by apprehending these persons) to track them down so that monies deposited with the courts by the bonding company can be recovered.

Brady materials Exculpatory materials must be disclosed through discovery to defense counsel by the prosecution when the defendant is to be tried for a crime. *See Brady v. Maryland* (1963).

Brady violation Violation of discovery rules when prosecutor fails to turn over exculpatory materials acquired during a criminal investigation to defense counsel. Violation occurs whenever three conditions are met: (1) the evidence at issue must be favorable to the accused, either because it is exculpatory or because it is impeaching; (2) the evidence must have been suppressed by the state, either willfully or inadvertently; and (3) prejudice must have ensued.

Bribery Crime of offering, giving, requesting, soliciting, receiving something of value to influence a decision of a public official.

Brief A document filed by a party to a lawsuit to convince the court of the merits of that party's case.

Burden of proof The requirement to introduce evidence to prove an alleged fact or set of facts.

Bureaucracy Organizational model that vests individuals with authority and spheres of competence in a predetermined hierarchy with abstract rules and selection by test.

Camp, ranch Any of several types of similar correctional confinement facilities for adults or juveniles, usually located in rural areas.

Canons of Professional Ethics Part of ABA Model Code of Professional Responsibility formulated in 1908; nine canons pertain to representing clients in a competent way; improving the legal system; avoiding the appearance of impropriety; and observing client confidences.

Capacity Mental state of being legally responsible; having the mental acuity to know the difference between right and wrong and to realize and appreciate the nature and consequences of particular actions.

Capital punishment Imposition of the death penalty for the most serious crimes. May be administered by electrocution, lethal injection, gas, hanging, or shooting.

Career criminals Those offenders who make their living through crime. Usually offenses occur over the lifetime of the offender.

Case Incident investigated by law enforcement officers. A single charging document under the jurisdiction of a court. A single defendant.

Case backlogs Crowded court dockets in either juvenile court or criminal court; a massive buildup of cases, where judges cannot hear all cases in a timely fashion.

Case law Legal opinions having the status of law as enunciated by the courts (e.g., U.S. Supreme Court decisions become case law and governing cases when identical or very similar cases are subsequently heard in lower courts).

Case processing The speed with which cases are heard in either criminal or juvenile court.

Case-specific pretrial publicity Direct familiarity with actual events that transpired in particular cases where persons are to serve as jurors; example is the Rodney King case, where millions of viewers watched the privately recorded videotape of the Rodney King beating by police on national television newscasts.

Cash bail bond Cash payment for situations in which charges are not serious and the scheduled bail is low. Defendants obtain release by paying in cash the full amount, which is recoverable after the required court appearances are made.

Centralization Limited distribution of power among a few top staff members of an organization.

Certification (juvenile) *See* waiver.

Certiorari, **writ of** A writ issued by a higher court directing a lower court to prepare the record of a case and send it to the higher court for review; a means of accessing the U.S. Supreme Court in order for a case to be heard.

Challenge *See* peremptory challenge.

Challenge for cause In jury selection, the method used by either the prosecution or defense attorneys to strike or remove prospective jurors from the available jury pool because of prejudices they might have, either toward the defendant or prosecution. Prospective jurors may also be excused from jury duty because of being law enforcement officers, relatives of law enforcement officers, court officers, or relatives of court officers. Any obvious bias for or against a defendant may result in the exclusion of the biased prospective juror.

Challenges of jurors Questions raised of jurors by the judge, prosecutor, and/or defense attorney relating to their qualifications as impartial finders of fact; a determination of juror bias one way or another for or against the defendant.

Chambers Usually a judge's office in a courthouse.

Chancellors King's agents used to settle disputes between neighbors in his behalf, such as property boundary issues, trespass allegations, and child misconduct. Early equivalent of the chancellor with similar duties and responsibilities was the justice of the peace, dating back to about 1200 A.D.

Chancery court Tribunal of equity rooted in early English common law where civil disputes are resolved. Also responsible for juvenile matters and adjudicating family matters such as divorce. Has jurisdiction over contract disputes, property boundary claims, and exchanges of goods disputes.

Change of venue A change in the place of trial, usually from one county or district to another. Changes of venue are often conducted to avoid prejudicial trial proceedings, where it is believed that a fair trial cannot be obtained in the specific jurisdiction where the crime was alleged to have been committed.

Charge A formal allegation filed against some defendant in which one or more crimes are alleged.

Charge reduction bargaining, charge bargaining Negotiation process between prosecutors and defense attorneys involving dismissal of one or more charges against defendants in exchange for a guilty plea to remaining charges, or in which the prosecutor downgrades the charges in return for a plea of guilty.

Chief justice The presiding or principal judge of a court, possessing nominal authority over the other judges (e.g., the chief justice of the U.S. Supreme Court).

Child savers Groups who promoted rights of minors during the nineteenth century and helped create a separate juvenile court.

Their motives have been questioned by modern writers who see their efforts as a form of social control and class conflict.

Children in need of supervision (CHINS) Typically unruly or incorrigible children who cannot be supervised well by their parents. Also includes children from homes where parents are seldom present. State agencies exist to find housing for such children.

Chronic offenders Habitual offenders; repeat offenders; persistent offenders; youths who commit frequent delinquent acts.

Chronic recidivists Persons who continue to commit new crimes after being convicted of former offenses.

Circuit courts Originally, courts that were held by judges who followed a circular path, hearing cases periodically in various communities. The term now refers to courts with several counties or districts within their jurisdiction. In the federal court organization, there are 13 federal circuit courts of appeal, having jurisdiction over U.S. District Courts within specified states.

Circuit riders Judges who rode from jurisdiction to jurisdiction in remote locations of states or federal territories to hold trials on a regular basis, such as once a month or once every six months.

Circumstantial evidence Material provided by a witness from which a jury must infer a fact.

Citation Any document issued by a law enforcement or court officer directing one to present oneself in court on a specific date and time.

Cite, citation Any legal reference in which a point of law is made. In law enforcement, a summons.

Civil action Any lawsuit brought to enforce private rights and to remedy violations thereof.

Civil law All state and federal law pertaining to noncriminal activities, also referred to as municipal law. Laws pertain to private rights and remedies. A body of formal rules established by any society for its self-regulation.

Civil liability In tort law, the basis for a cause of action to recover damages.

Claiming The process in a dispute where a grievance is expressed and a cause of action is cited.

Class action, class action suit Any lawsuit on behalf of a segment of the population with specific characteristics, namely that they are victims of whatever wrongs are alleged. The class of persons may persist over time and change, but the action is for all current and future members of the class.

Coconspirator Another party besides the defendant who is alleged to have committed the same crime in concert with the defendant.

Code A systematic collection of laws.

Code of ethics Regulations formulated by major professional societies that outline the specific problems and issues that are frequently encountered in the types of research carried out within a particular profession. Serves as a guide to ethical research practices.

Codefendants Two or more defendants charged with the same crime and tried in the same judicial proceeding.

Coercion Affirmative defense similar to duress, wherein defendants allege that they were made or forced to commit an illegal act.

Common law Authority based on court decrees and judgments that recognize, affirm, and enforce certain usages and customs of the people. Laws determined by judges in accordance with their rulings.

Community service An alternative sanction requiring offenders to work in the community at such tasks as cleaning public parks or working with handicapped children in lieu of an incarcerative sentence. Restitution involves paying back a victim through money received from one's work.

Community service orders Judicially imposed restitution for those convicted of committing crimes; some form of work must be performed to satisfy restitution requirements.

Complaint Written statement of essential facts constituting the offense alleged, made under oath before a magistrate or other qualified judicial officer.

Comprehensive Crime Control Act of 1984 Significant act that authorized establishment of U.S. Sentencing Commission, instituted sentencing guidelines, provided for abolition of federal parole, and devised new guidelines and goals of federal corrections.

Concession givers Judges who make plea agreement offers to criminal defendants, wherein the defendants will plead guilty to a criminal charge in exchange for judicial leniency in sentencing.

Conclusive evidence Any compelling evidence that is so strong that it cannot be disputed or discounted. Proof establishing guilt beyond a reasonable doubt.

Concurrent jurisdiction Situation in which offender may be held accountable in several different jurisdictions simultaneously. Courts in the same jurisdiction.

Conditional dispositions Decisions by juvenile court judge authorizing payment of fines, community service, restitution, or some other penalty after an adjudication of delinquency has been made.

Conditions of confinement The nature of jail or prison incarceration; refers to heat and humidity, cleanliness of one's cell and surroundings, and general treatment; often is basis for legal action filed as *habeas corpus* petitions.

Confidentiality Any privileged communication between a client and an attorney.

Confidentiality privilege Right between defendant and his/her attorney where certain information cannot be disclosed to prosecutors or others because of the attorney–client relation; for juveniles, records have been maintained under secure circumstances with limited access, and only then accessed by those in authority with a clear law enforcement purpose.

Conflict stage Either a pretrial or alternative dispute resolution phase where a plaintiff and a defendant confront one another and an accusation is made; a confrontation where the victim faces an alleged victimizer or defendant; may involve a third-party arbiter.

Constitutional rights Rights guaranteed to all U.S. citizens by the U.S. Constitution and its amendments.

Contract system Providing counsel to indigent offenders by having an attorney under contract to the county to handle some or all of these types of cases.

Conviction State of being judged guilty of a crime in a court, either by the judge or jury.

Corroboration Evidence that strengthens the evidence already given.

Cost–benefit analysis Method of analyzing the costs associated with particular policies and determining whether the benefits or value derived from those policies are justified on the basis of the results.

Court Public judiciary body that applies the law to controversies and oversees the administration of justice.

Court administrator Any individual who controls the operations of the court in a particular jurisdiction. May be in charge of scheduling, juries, judicial assignment.

Court-appointed counsel Attorneys who are appointed to represent indigent defendants.

Court calendar Docket; the schedule of events for any judicial official.

Court clerk Court officer who may file pleadings, motions, or judgments, issue process, and may keep general records of court proceedings.

Court of last resort The last court that may hear a case. In the United States the Supreme Court is the court of last resort for many kinds of cases.

Court of limited jurisdiction *See* trial court of limited jurisdiction.

Court of public opinion Informal reactions to legal cases by unofficial pollsters and media broadcasters who cover high-profile cases on television and in the newspapers; independent reactions to court events by persons who may have only a passing interest in cases.

Court order Any judicial proclamation or directive authorizing an officer to act on behalf of the court.

Court reporter Court official who keeps a written word-for-word and/or tape-recorded record of court proceedings. *See also* transcript.

Courtroom work group The phrase denoting all parties in the adversary process who work together cooperatively to settle cases with the least amount of effort and conflict.

Courts of general jurisdiction Any court having the power to hear diverse types of cases, both civil and criminal.

Courts of last resort Either state or federal supreme courts that function as the final stage for appeals from lower courts; the ultimate court of last resort is the U.S. Supreme Court.

Courts of record Any legal proceedings where a written record is kept of court matters and dialogue.

Crime Act or omission prohibited by law, by one who is held accountable by that law. Consists of legality, *actus reus*, *mens rea*, consensus, harm, causation, and prescribed punishment.

Crime Bill of 1994 Legislation supported by President Bill Clinton designed to increase crime prevention measures and put more police officers on city streets; also established truth-in-sentencing laws to maximize the amount of time inmates must serve in relation to their maximum sentences.

Crime prevention Any overt activity conducted by individuals or groups to deter persons from committing crimes. May include "target hardening" by making businesses and residences more difficult to burglarize; neighborhood watch programs, in which neighborhood residents monitor streets during evening hours for suspicious persons or automobiles and equipping homes and businesses with devices to detect crime.

Criminal courts Tribunals handling criminal cases. May also handle civil cases, and are then called criminal courts only in reference to the criminal cases that they handle.

Criminal–exclusive blend Form of sentencing by a criminal court judge where either juvenile or adult sentences of incarceration can be imposed, but not both.

Criminal history One's prior convictions, indictments, and arrests.

Criminal–inclusive blend Form of sentencing by a criminal court judge where both juvenile and adult sentences can be imposed simultaneously.

Criminal informations Written accusations made by a public prosecutor against a person for some criminal offense, usually restricted to minor crimes or misdemeanors, without an indictment.

Criminal law Body of law that defines criminal offenses and prescribes punishments (substantive law) and that delineates criminal procedure (procedural law).

Criminal trial An adversarial proceeding within a particular jurisdiction, in which a judicial determination of issues can be made, and in which a defendant's guilt or innocence can be decided impartially.

Criminalization Transformation of civil proceedings into criminal proceedings; the juvenile court has undergone a transformation toward greater criminalization as juveniles have acquired almost the same number of legal rights as adults.

Critical legal studies Movement involving an examination of the entire legal system; recognizes that law is subjective rather than objective.

Cross-examination Questioning of one side's witnesses by the other side's attorney, either the prosecution or defense.

Culpable, culpability State of mind of persons who have committed an act that makes them liable for prosecution for that act.

Curfew violators Persons under the legal age of adulthood who roam city streets beyond times when they are supposed to be in their homes; a type of status offender.

Custodial dispositions Outcomes by juvenile judge following adjudication of juvenile as delinquent. Includes nonsecure custody (in a foster home, community agency, farm, camp) or secure custody (in a detention center, industrial, reform school).

Damages Monetary sums awarded to prevailing litigants in civil actions.

De novo Anew, afresh, as if there had been no earlier decision.

Death penalty *See* capital punishment.

Death row Arrangement of prison cells where inmates who have been sentenced to death are housed.

Decriminalization, decriminalize Legislative action whereby an act or omission, formerly criminal, is made noncriminal and without punitive sanctions.

Defendant Person against whom a criminal proceeding is pending.

Defendant dispositions Any one of several adjudication and dispositional options available to a judge at various places during a criminal proceeding, ranging from dismissal of the case to long-term imprisonment.

Defendant's sentencing memorandum Version of events leading to conviction offense in the words of the convicted offender. Memorandum may be submitted together with victim impact statement.

Defense A response by defendants in criminal law or civil cases. May consist only of a denial of the factual allegations of the prosecution (in a criminal case) or of the plaintiff (in a civil case). If defense offers new factual allegations in an effort to negate the charges, this is called an affirmative defense.

Defense attorney, counsel A lawyer who represents a client accused of a crime.

Defense of property Affirmative defense to justify illegal conduct, wherein defendants claim that they broke one or more laws to safeguard their property or possessions or the property or possessions of others.

Defense strategy Approach taken by defense counsel for defending his/her client; usually involves a particular defense to criminal charges.

Deferred prosecution Temporary halting of a prosecution against a defendant while he/she is subjected to a program with particular requirements for a short period. *See also* diversion.

Deinstitutionalization Providing programs in community-based settings instead of institutional ones.

Deinstitutionalization of status offenders (DSO) Movement to remove nondelinquent juveniles from secure facilities by eliminating status offenses from the delinquency category and removing juveniles from or precluding their confinement in juvenile correction facilities. Process of removing status offenses from jurisdiction of juvenile court.

Demand waiver Request by juveniles to have their cases transferred from juvenile courts to criminal courts.

Demonstrative evidence Material related to a crime that is apparent to the senses, in contrast to material presented by the testimony of other persons.

Deponents Persons who give testimony through a deposition. If someone cannot physically attend a trial and give testimony under oath, then a deposition is taken and read into the court record.

Derivative evidence Information obtained as the result of previously discovered evidence (e.g., residue from an automobile tire may suggest that a crime was committed in a part of the city where such residue is found and police discover subsequent "derivative" evidence by investigating that area).

Determinate sentencing Sanctioning scheme in which court sentences offender to incarceration for fixed period, and which must be served in full and without parole intervention, less any good time earned in prison.

Deterrence, general or specific Actions that are designed to prevent crime before it occurs by threatening severe criminal penalties or sanctions. May include safety measures to discourage potential lawbreakers such as elaborate security systems, electronic monitoring, and greater police officer visibility; influencing by fear, where fear is of apprehension and punishment.

Differential discretion View that sentencing disparities are more likely to occur during informal charge reduction bargaining than in the final sentencing process following trial and the sentencing hearing.

Direct evidence Evidence offered by an eyewitness who testifies to what was seen or heard.

Direct examination Questioning by attorney of one's own (prosecution or defense) witness during a trial.

Direct file Prosecutorial waiver of jurisdiction to a criminal court; an action taken against a juvenile who has committed an especially serious offense, where that juvenile's case is transferred to criminal court for the purpose of a criminal prosecution.

Directed verdict of acquittal Order by court declaring that the prosecution has failed to produce sufficient evidence to show defendant guilty beyond a reasonable doubt.

Discovery Procedure where prosecution shares information with defense attorney and defendant. Specific types of information are made available to defendant before trial, including results of any tests conducted, psychiatric reports, transcripts or tape-recorded statements made by the defendant. Also known as "Brady materials" after a specific court case.

Discretionary waivers Transfers of juveniles to criminal courts by judges, at their discretion or in their judgment; also known as judicial waivers.

Disposition Action by criminal or juvenile justice court or agency signifying that a portion of the justice process is completed and jurisdiction is relinquished or transferred to another agency or signifying that a decision has been reached on one aspect of a case and a different aspect comes under consideration, requiring a different kind of decision.

Disposition hearing Hearing in juvenile court, conducted after an adjudicatory hearing and a finding of delinquency, status offender, dependent/neglected, to determine the most appropriate punishment/placement/treatment for the juvenile.

Disputants Opposing sides in a civil action or case.

Dispute resolution Civil action intended to resolve conflicts between two parties, usually a complainant and a defendant.

Dispute stage Public revelation of a dispute by filing of a legal action.

Dissenting opinion Any judicial opinion disavowing or attacking the decision of a collegial court.

District attorneys City, county, and state prosecutors who are charged with bringing offenders to justice and enforcing the laws of the state.

District court Trial courts at the state or federal level with general and original jurisdiction. Boundaries of their venue do not conform to standard political unit boundaries, but generally include several states or counties.

Diversion Removing a case from the criminal justice system, while a defendant is required to comply with various conditions (e.g., attending a school for drunk drivers, undergoing counseling, performing community service). May result in expungement of record. Conditional removal of the prosecution of a case prior to its adjudication, usually as the result of an arrangement between the prosecutor and judge.

Diversion programs One of several programs preceding formal court adjudication of charges against defendants; defendants participate in therapeutic, educational, and other helping programs. *See also* diversion.

Divestiture of jurisdiction Juvenile court relinquishment of control over certain types of juveniles, such as status offenders.

DNA fingerprinting Deoxyribonucleic acid (DNA) is an essential component of all living matter, which carries hereditary patterning. Suspects can be detected according to their unique DNA patterning, as each person has a different DNA pattern. Similar to fingerprint identification, in which no two persons have identical fingerprints.

Docket A court record of the cases scheduled to appear before the court.

Doctrine of assumptive risk Theory holding that plaintiffs who engage in dangerous enterprises must accept some or all of the responsibility when accidents happen to them.

Doctrine of contributory negligence Theory holding that a plaintiff by his/her own actions has brought about injuries for which he/she seeks relief from a defendant.

Doctrine of last clear chance Theory holding that when an accident occurs, the responsibility lies largely with the party who has the last clear chance to avoid the accident; example is a person standing on a railroad track who is subsequently struck by the train; the person is more in the position of avoiding the train than the train is of avoiding the person, even if the train engineer sees the person on the tracks before striking him/her.

Doctrine of *res ipsa loquitur* "The thing speaks for itself"; blame in a legal action lies on the part of the defendant, since the instrument(s) bringing about the injury to a plaintiff was within the control of the defendant.

Document Any written paper, official or unofficial, having potential evidentiary importance.

Double jeopardy Subjecting persons to prosecution more than once in the same jurisdiction for the same offense, usually without new or vital evidence. Prohibited by the Fifth Amendment.

Dual court system A system consisting of a separate judicial structure for each state in addition to a national structure. Each case is tried in a court of the same jurisdiction as that of the law or laws broken.

Due process Basic constitutional right to a fair trial, presumption of innocence until guilt is proven beyond a reasonable doubt, the opportunity to be heard, to be aware of a matter that is pending, to make an informed choice whether to acquiesce or contest, and to provide the reasons for such a choice before a judicial official. Actual due process rights include timely notice of a hearing or trial that informs the accused of charges, the opportunity to confront one's accusers and to present evidence on one's own behalf before an impartial jury or judge, the presumption of innocence under which guilt must be proved by legally obtained evidence and the verdict must be supported by the evidence presented, the right of accused persons to be warned of their constitutional rights at the earliest stage of the criminal process, protection against self-incrimination, assistance of counsel at every critical stage of the criminal process, and the guarantee that individuals will not be tried more than once for the same offense.

Due process courts Juvenile courts where the emphasis is upon punishment and offender control rather than individualized treatments and assistance.

Due process of law A right guaranteed by the Fifth, Sixth, and Fourteenth Amendments of the U.S. Constitution, and generally understood to mean the due course of legal proceedings according to the rules and forms that have been established for the protection of private rights. *See also* due process.

Duress Affirmative defense used by defendants to show lack of criminal intent, alleging force, psychological or physical, from others as stimulus for otherwise criminal conduct.

Early release *See* parole board.

Electronic monitoring The use of electronic devices (usually anklets or wristlets) which emit electronic signals to monitor offenders, probationers, and parolees. The purpose of their use is to monitor an offender's presence in a given environment where the offender is required to remain or to verify the offender's whereabouts.

En banc "In the bench." Refers to a session of the court, usually an appellate court, where all of the judges assigned to the court participate.

English common law *See* common law.

Entrapment Activity by law enforcement officers that suggests, encourages, or aids others in the commission of crimes, which would ordinarily not have occurred without officer intervention. Defense used by defendants to show otherwise criminal act would not have occurred without police intervention, assistance, and/or encouragement.

Equal protection Clause of Fourteenth Amendment of U.S. Constitution guaranteeing to all citizens equal protection of the law, without regard to race, color, gender, class, origin, or religion.

Equity The concept that the relationships between men, women, and society should be just and fair and in accordance with contemporary morality.

Ethical code Canons of professional responsibility articulated by professional associations such as the American Bar Association.

Evarts Act Introduced in 1891 and sponsored by New Jersey lawyer William M. Evarts, this act created circuit courts of appeal to hear appeals emanating from the U.S. District Courts.

Evidence All materials or means admissible in a court of law to produce in the minds of the court or jury a belief concerning the matter at issue.

Evidence, corroborating Any collateral evidence that enhances the value of other evidence.

Evidence-driven jury Jury that decides to consider all evidence presented as relevant rather than selected evidence based on juror interest or preferences.

Evidentiary Pertaining to the rules of evidence or the evidence in a particular case.

Ex parte A hearing or examination in the presence of only one party in the case.

Examination, direct and cross *See* direct examination and cross-examination.

Exception An objection to a ruling, comments made by the judge or attorneys.

Excessive bail Any bail amount that so grossly exceeds the proportionality of the seriousness of the offense so as to be prohibited by the Eighth Amendment.

Exclusionary rule Rule providing that where evidence has been obtained in violation of the privileges guaranteed by the U.S. Constitution, such evidence may be excluded at the trial.

Exclusive jurisdiction Specific jurisdiction over particular kinds of cases. The U.S. Supreme Court has authority to hear matters involving the diplomats of other countries who otherwise enjoy great immunity from most other courts. Family court may have exclusive jurisdiction to hear child custody cases.

Exculpate, exculpatory Tending to exonerate a person of allegations of wrongdoing.

Exculpatory evidence Any information that exonerates a person of allegations of wrongdoing; any information that reflects favorably upon the accused and shows that they are innocent of the crimes with which they are charged.

Expert testimony Any oral evidence presented in court by someone who is considered proficient and learned in a given field where such evidence is relevant. Testimony provided by an expert witness.

Expert witnesses Witnesses who have expertise or special knowledge in a relevant field pertaining to the case at trial. Witnesses who are qualified under the Federal Rules of Evidence to offer an opinion about the authenticity or accuracy of reports, who have special knowledge relevant to the proceeding. Sometimes called "hired guns."

Expunge, expungement Deletion of one's arrest record from official sources. In most jurisdictions, juvenile delinquency records are expunged when one reaches the age of majority or adulthood.

Extralegal factors Any element of a nonlegal nature. In determining whether law enforcement officers are influenced by particular factors when encountering juveniles on the streets, extralegal factors might include juvenile attitude, politeness, appearance, dress. Legal factors might include age and specific prohibited acts observed by the officers. In reference to adult offenders, these refer to factors not legally relevant to case processing decisions such as race, ethnicity, and sex.

Eyewitnesses Persons who testify in court as to what they saw when the crime was committed.

Fact A true statement. An actual event.

Fact-finders Juries who hear cases, criminal or otherwise.

Factual basis for the plea Evidence presented to the judge by the prosecutor that would have been used if a plea-bargained case had gone to trial; evidence of one's guilt beyond a reasonable doubt to substantiate a plea bargain agreement.

Failure to appear When defendants fail to present themselves for trial or some other formal proceeding, such as arraignment or a preliminary hearing/examination.

Federal district courts Basic trial courts for the federal government that try all criminal cases and have extensive jurisdiction. District judges are appointed by the president of the United States with the advice, counsel, and approval of the Senate. Cases from these courts are appealed to particular circuit courts of appeal.

Federal misdemeanor Any federal crime where the maximum punishment is less than one year in prison or jail.

Federal Rules of Criminal Procedure Contained in Title 18 of the U.S. Code, all protocols and regulations that must be followed during offender processing, from arrest to conviction.

Federal Rules of Evidence Official rules governing the introduction of certain types of evidence in U.S. District Courts.

Fellow servant doctrine Theory holding employer responsible for actions of employees.

Felony Crime punishable by incarceration, usually in a state or federal prison, for periods of one year or longer.

Felony property offending Any crime punishable by more than one year in prison or jail and causes property loss or damage (e.g., burglary, larceny/theft, vehicular theft).

Feminist legal studies View that women use a different type of logic than men when interpreting the law, favoring less litigation and more mediation.

Filing The commencement of criminal proceedings by entering a charging document into a court's official record.

Financial/community service model Restitution model for juveniles that stresses the offender's financial accountability and community service to pay for damages.

Finding A holding or ruling by the court or judge.

Finding of fact Court's determination of the facts presented as evidence in a case, affirmed by one party and denied by the other.

Fines Financial penalties imposed at time of sentencing convicted offenders. Most criminal statutes contain provisions for the imposition of monetary penalties as sentencing options.

Flat term A specific, definite term for a conviction, not necessarily known in advance of sentencing.

Flat time Actual amount of time required to be served by a convicted offender while incarcerated.

Foster home Dwelling including family where child is placed, usually where such child is from an abusive household or without parents or legal guardians; foster home parents are responsible for proper upbringing of child for a period of time.

Frivolous lawsuits Legal actions commenced by one or more parties where there is little hope of a successful outcome; often groundless legal actions without sufficient bases.

Fruits of the poisonous tree doctrine A U.S. Supreme Court decision in *Wong Sun v. United States* (1963) holding that evidence that is spawned or directly derived from an illegal search or an illegal interrogation is generally inadmissible against a defendant because of its original taint.

Fugitive recovery agents One who seeks to return to a jurisdiction a person who has been charged with a crime and has jumped bail or fled the jurisdiction before trial.

Fundamental fairness Legal doctrine supporting the idea that so long as a state's conduct maintains the basic elements of fairness, the Constitution has not been violated.

Gag order Official declaration by the judge in a trial proceeding that all parties in the action, including the jurors, must refrain from discussing the case with the media.

General jurisdiction Power of a court to hear a wide range of cases, both civil and criminal.

General pretrial publicity Information about a legal case involving general details, including names of suspects, how the crime was committed, names of victims and alleged perpetrators, covered by the news media.

General sessions courts Tribunals in particular states with limited jurisdiction to hear misdemeanor cases and some low-level felony cases.

General trial courts Any one of several types of courts, either civil or criminal, with diverse jurisdiction to conduct jury trials and decide cases.

Geographic jurisdiction The power to hear particular kinds of cases depending upon the legally defined boundaries of cities, counties, or states.

Get-tough movement General orientation toward criminals and juvenile delinquents that favors the maximum penalties and punishments for crime and delinquency; any action toward toughening or strengthening sentencing provisions or dispositions involving adults or juveniles.

Going rate Local view of the appropriate sentence or punishment for a particular offense, the defendant's prior record, and other factors; used in implicit plea bargaining.

Good time, good-time credit An amount of time deducted from the period of incarceration of a convicted offender, calculated as so many days per month on the basis of good behavior while incarcerated. Credits earned by prisoners for good behavior. Introduced in early 1800s by British penal authorities, including Alexander Maconochie and Sir Walter Crofton.

Grand jury Investigative bodies whose numbers vary among states. Duties include determining probable cause regarding commission of a crime and returning formal charges against suspects. *See also* true bill and no true bill.

Grievance, grievance procedure Formalized arrangements, usually involving a neutral hearing board, whereby institutionalized individuals have the opportunity to register complaints about the conditions of their confinement.

Group home Facilities for juveniles that provide limited supervision and support. Juveniles live in homelike environment with other juveniles and participate in therapeutic programs and counseling. Considered nonsecure custodial. *See also* foster home.

Guardian *ad litem* A court-appointed attorney who protects the interests of children in cases involving their welfare and who works with the children during the litigation period.

Guidelines-based sentencing *See* sentencing guidelines.

Guilty plea A defendant's formal affirmation of guilt in court to charges contained in a complaint, information, indictment claiming that they committed the offenses listed.

Habeas corpus Writ meaning "produce the body"; used by prisoners to challenge the nature and length of their confinement.

Habeas corpus petition Writ filed, usually by inmates, challenging the legitimacy of their confinement and the nature of their confinement. Document commands authorities to show cause why an inmate should be confined in either a prison or jail. Also includes challenges of the nature of confinement. A written order by the court to any person, including a law enforcement officer, directing that person to bring the named individual before the court so that it can determine if there is adequate cause for continued detention.

Habitual offenders Persons who have been convicted of two or more felonies and may be sentenced under the habitual offender statute for an aggravated or longer prison term.

Habitual offender statutes Statutes vary among states. Generally provide life imprisonment as a mandatory sentence for chronic offenders who have been convicted of three or more serious felonies within a specific time period.

Harmful errors Errors made by judges that may be prejudicial to a defendant's case. May lead to reversals of convictions against defendants and to new trials.

Harmless error doctrine Errors of a minor or trivial nature and not deemed sufficient to harm the rights of parties in a legal action. Cases are not reversed on the basis of harmless errors.

Hearing Any formal proceeding in which the court hears evidence from prosecutors and defense and resolves a dispute or issue.

Hearing, probable cause A proceeding in which arguments, evidence, or witnesses are presented and in which it is determined whether there is sufficient cause to hold the accused for trial or whether the case should be dismissed.

Hearsay evidence Evidence that is not firsthand but is based on an account given by another.

Hearsay rule Courtroom precedent that hearsay cannot be used in court. Rather than accepting testimony on hearsay, the trial process asks that persons who were the original source of the hearsay information be brought into court to be questioned and cross-examined. Exceptions to the hearsay rule may occur when persons with direct knowledge are either dead or otherwise unable to testify.

Hierarchical jurisdiction Distinction between courts at different levels, where one court is superior to another and has the power to hear appeals from lower court decisions.

Holding The legal principle drawn from a judicial decision. Whatever a court, usually an appellate court, decides when cases are appealed from lower courts. When an appellate court "holds" a particular decision, this may be to uphold the original conviction, set it aside, overturn in part, and uphold in part.

Home confinement Housing of offenders in their own homes with or without electronic monitoring devices. Reduces prison overcrowding and prisoner costs. Sometimes an intermediate punishment involving the use of offender residences for mandatory incarceration during evening hours after a curfew and on weekends. Also called "house arrest."

Hung jury Jury that cannot agree on a verdict.

Illinois Juvenile Court Act Legislation establishing first juvenile court in United States in 1899.

Impartial arbiters Persons such as judges, attorneys, or prominent citizens who are called upon to be objective and neutral third parties in disputes between perpetrators and their victims under conditions of restorative justice or alternative dispute resolution.

Impeachment Proceeding for the removal of a political officer, such as a governor, president, or judge.

Implicit plea bargaining Occurs when defendant pleads guilty with the expectation of receiving a more lenient sentence. *See also* plea bargaining.

In re "In the matter of." Refers to cases being filed for juveniles who must have an adult act on their behalf when filing motions or appeals.

Inadmissible Evidentiary term used to describe something that cannot be used as evidence during a trial.

Incapacitation, isolation Philosophy of corrections espousing loss of freedom proportional to seriousness of offense. Belief that the function of punishment is to separate offenders from other society members and prevent them from committing additional criminal acts.

Inculpatory evidence Any information that places the defendant in an unfavorable light and increases the likelihood of his/her guilt.

Incumbents Political officers who are currently in power, but who are seeking to be re-elected or reappointed.

Indeterminate sentencing Sentencing scheme in which a period is set by judges between the earliest date for a parole decision and the latest date for completion of the sentence. In holding that the time necessary for treatment cannot be set exactly, the indeterminate sentence is closely associated with rehabilitation.

Indictments Charges or written accusations found and presented by a grand jury that a particular defendant probably committed a crime.

Indigent defendants Poor persons; anyone who cannot afford legal services or representation.

Ineffective assistance of counsel Standard for determining whether client is defended in a competent way; guidelines for determining counsel's effectiveness articulated in case of *Strickland v. Washington* (1984), which include (1) whether counsel's behavior undermined the adversarial process to the degree that the trial outcome is unreliable; and (2) the counsel's conduct was unreasonable to the degree that the jury's verdict would have been different otherwise.

Informations Written accusations made by a public prosecutor against a person for some criminal offense, without an indictment. Usually restricted to minor crimes or misdemeanors. Sometimes called criminal informations.

Initial appearance Formal proceeding during which the judge advises the defendant of the charges, including a recitation of the defendant's rights and a bail decision.

Insanity Degree of mental illness that negates the legal capacity or responsibility of the affected person.

Insanity defense Defense that seeks to exonerate accused persons by showing that they were insane at the time they were believed to have committed a crime.

Insanity plea A plea entered as a defense to a crime. The defendant admits guilt but assigns responsibility for the criminal act to the condition of insanity presumably existing when the crime was committed.

Intake Review of a case by a court (juvenile or criminal) official. Screening of cases includes weeding out weak cases. In juvenile cases, intake involves the reception of a juvenile against whom complaints have been made. Decision to proceed or dismiss the case is made at this stage.

Intake hearings Proceedings, usually presided over by an intake officer, where determinations are made about whether certain juveniles should undergo further processing by the juvenile justice system; a screening mechanism for juvenile offenders.

Intake officer Officer who conducts screening of juveniles. Dispositions include release to parents pending further juvenile court action, dismissal of charges against juvenile, detention, treatment by some community agency.

Intake screening A critical phase where a determination is made by a juvenile probation officer or other official whether to release juveniles to their parent's custody, detain juveniles in formal detention facilities for a later court appearance, or release them to parents pending a later court appearance.

Intensive supervised probation Varies from standard probation and includes more face-to-face visits between probation officers and probationers under community supervision.

Intent A state of mind, the *mens rea*, in which a person seeks to accomplish a given result, such as a crime, through a given course of action.

Interim judges Temporary judge who is appointed following the death, resignation, or retirement of another judge, usually to complete the original judge's term; after the interim judge serves, a new judge is appointed or elected according to the rules of judicial selection in the particular jurisdiction.

Intermittent sentencing Imposed punishment where offender must serve a portion of sentence in jail, perhaps on weekends or specific evenings. Considered similar to probation with limited incarceration. *See also* split sentencing.

Intoxication The state of being incapable of performing certain tasks legally, such as operating motor vehicles or boats. Can be induced through consumption of alcoholic beverages, inhaling toxic fumes from petroleum products, or consumption of drug substances. May also be a defense to criminal conduct, although the courts often rule that it is voluntary.

Ipso facto "By the mere fact." By the fact itself (e.g., "We can assume, *ipso facto*, that if the defendant was observed beating another person in a bar by ten witnesses, then he is likely guilty of the beating inflicted on the victim.").

Isolation A sentencing philosophy seeking to remove the offender from other offenders when confined by placing prisoner in a cell with no communication with others. Also known as solitary confinement, which originated in the Walnut Street Jail in Philadelphia, Pennsylvania in the late 1700s. Another usage of this term is to segregate offenders from society through incarceration.

Jail as a condition of probation Sentence in which judge imposes limited jail time to be served before commencement of probation. *See also* split sentencing.

Jencks materials Discoverable materials available from either the prosecutor or defense counsel prior to trial. *See Jencks v. United States* (1957).

Judge A political officer who has been elected or appointed to preside over a court of law, whose position has been created by statute or by constitution and whose decisions in criminal and juvenile cases may only be reviewed by a judge or a higher court and may not be reviewed *de novo*.

Judgment Final determination of a case. A proclamation stating one's guilt or innocence in relation to criminal offenses alleged. In tort law, a finding in favor of or against the plaintiff. The amount of monetary damages awarded in civil cases.

Judicial activism U.S. Supreme Court's use of its power to accomplish social goals.

Judicial appointments Selections of judges by political figures, such as governors or presidents.

Judicial conduct commission Investigative body created in California in 1960, comprised of other judges, attorneys, and prominent citizens; task was to investigate allegations of judicial misconduct, incompetence, and unfairness.

Judicial instructions Specific admonitions to jurors, prosecutors, and defense counsels to do or refrain from doing different things.

Judicial misconduct Departure of a judge from accepted modes of conduct after becoming a judicial official; forms of misconduct are accepting bribes in exchange for money or services; making biased decisions favoring one side or the other during a trial; engaging in behaviors (e.g., drunkenness, driving while intoxicated, perjury) while serving on the bench.

Judicial plea bargaining Recommended sentence by judge who offers a specific sentence and/or fine in exchange for a guilty plea. *See also* plea bargaining.

Judicial powers Court jurisdiction to act in certain cases and decide punishments.

Judicial privilege Power of judges to change plea bargain agreements and substitute their own punishments; the power to override prosecutors and defense counsel concerning the agreed upon terms of plea agreements.

Judicial process The sequence of procedures designed to resolve disputes or conclude a criminal case.

Judicial review The authority of a court to limit the power of the executive and legislative branches of government by deciding whether their acts defy rights established by the state and federal constitutions.

Judicial waiver Decision by juvenile judge to waive juvenile to jurisdiction of criminal court.

Judiciary Act of 1789 A congressional act that provided for three levels of courts: (1) 13 federal district courts, each presided over by a district judge; (2) 3 higher circuit courts of appeal, each comprising 2 justices of the Supreme Court and 1 district judge; and (3) a Supreme Court, consisting of a chief justice and 5 associate justices.

Jumping bail Act by defendant of leaving jurisdiction where trial is to be held. Attempt by defendant to avoid prosecution on criminal charges.

Jurisdiction The power of a court to hear and determine a particular type of case. Also refers to territory within which court may exercise authority such as a city, county, or state.

Juror misconduct Any impropriety by a juror; acceptance of illegal gratuities in exchange for a favorable vote for or against the defendant; sleeping during the trial; reading newspaper accounts, listening or watching newscasters voice their opinions about the case, and then relating this information to other jurors in attempt to persuade them one way or another for or against the defendant.

Jury *See* petit jury.

Jury deliberations Discussion among jury members concerning the weight and sufficiency of witness testimony and other evidence presented by both the prosecution and defense. An attempt to arrive at a verdict.

Jury misconduct Any impropriety exhibited by one or more jurors, such as sleeping during a trial; attempting to bias other jurors for or against a particular defendant by illegal means;or accepting bribes or gratuities from persons interested inthe case.

Jury nullification Jury refuses to accept the validity of evidence at trial and acquits or convicts for a lesser offense (e.g., although all of the elements for murder are proved, a jury may acquit defendants who killed their spouses allegedly as an act of mercy killing).

Jury panel A list of jurors summoned to serve on possible jury duty at a particular court. From the jury panel, the petit jury is selected.

Jury poll A poll conducted by a judicial officer or by the clerk of the court after a jury has stated its verdict but before that verdict has been entered into the record of the court, asking each juror individually whether the stated verdict is his or her own verdict.

Jury pool Aggregate of persons from which a jury is selected; use of voter registration lists, driver's licenses, home ownership records, and other public documents to create such pools; also known as a *venire* or venireman list.

Jury selection The process whereby a jury is impaneled for either a civil or criminal trial proceeding.

Jury sequestration The process of isolating a jury from the public during a trial; the objective is to minimize the influence of media publicity and exposure, which might otherwise influence juror opinions about the guilt or innocence of the defendant.

Jury size Traditional 12-member jury at federal level and many state and local levels; may vary between 6-member jury and 12-member jury at state and local levels.

Jury trial Proceeding by which guilt or innocence of defendant is determined by jury instead of by the judge.

Jury waiver system Occurs when defendants waive their constitutional right to a jury trial and enter into a plea bargain agreement with the prosecutor.

Juvenile–contiguous blend Form of blended sentencing by a juvenile court judge where the judge can impose a disposition beyond the normal jurisdictional range for juvenile offenders; for example, a judge may impose a 30-year term on a 14-year-old offender, but the juvenile is entitled to a hearing when he/she reaches the age of majority to determine whether the remainder of the sentence shall be served.

Juvenile court Formal adjudicatory hearing to determine whether one is a juvenile delinquent, a status offender, or in need of supervision.

Juvenile court jurisdiction Power of juvenile courts to hear cases involving persons under the legal age of adulthood.

Juvenile–exclusive blend Blended sentencing form where a juvenile court judge can impose either adult or juvenile incarceration as a disposition and sentence but not both.

Juvenile–inclusive blend Form of blended sentencing where a juvenile court judge can impose *both* adult and juvenile incarceration simultaneously.

Juvenile court A term for any court with original jurisdiction over persons statutorily defined as juveniles and alleged to be delinquents, status offenders, or dependents.

Juvenile delinquency The violation of criminal laws by juveniles. Any illegal behavior or activity committed by persons who are within a particular age range; subjects them to the jurisdiction of a juvenile court or its equivalent.

Juvenile delinquent Any minor who commits an offense that would be a crime if committed by an adult.

Juvenile Justice and Delinquency Prevention Act of 1974 Act passed by Congress in 1974 and amended numerous times, including 1984, encouraging states to deal differently with their juvenile offenders. Promotes community-based treatment programs and discourages incarceration of juveniles in detention centers, industrial schools, or reform schools.

Juvenile justice system, process The system through which juveniles are processed, sentenced, and corrected after arrests for juvenile delinquency.

Juveniles Persons who have not as yet achieved their eighteenth birthday or the age of majority.

Kales Plan The 1914 version of Missouri Plan, in which a committee of experts creates a list of qualified persons for judgeships and makes recommendations to governor. *See also* Missouri Plan.

Labeling theory, labeling Theory attributed to Edwin Lemert that persons acquire self-definitions that are deviant or criminal. Persons perceive themselves as deviant or criminal through labels applied to them by others; thus the more people are involved in the criminal justice system, the more they acquire self-definitions consistent with the criminal label.

Law The body of rules of specific conduct, prescribed by existing, legitimate authority in a particular jurisdiction and at a particular point in time.

Law in action Procedural law.

Law in books Substantive law.

Legal realism View that law and society are constantly evolving and that law should be the means to a social end rather than an end in itself.

Legislative waivers Provisions that compel juvenile court to remand certain youths to criminal courts because of specific offenses that have been committed or alleged.

Lex talionis The law of retaliation or retribution. A form of revenge dating back to the Apostle Paul and used up until the Middle Ages.

Lie detectors Apparatuses that record one's blood pressure and various other sensory responses and plot one's reactions by means of a moving pencil and paper. Designed to determine whether one is telling the truth during an interrogation. Also known as polygraphs. Results of tests are not admissible in court.

Life imprisonment Any sentence involving lengthy incarceration, presumably for the life expectancy of the convicted offender; however, life imprisonment in the United States averages about seven years.

Life-without-parole sentence Penalty imposed as maximum punishment in states that do not have death penalty; provides for permanent incarceration of offenders in prisons, without parole eligibility; early release may be attained through accumulation of good-time credits.

Limited jurisdiction Court is restricted to handling certain types of cases such as probate matters or juvenile offenses. Also known as special jurisdiction.

Litigation Civil prosecution in which proceedings are maintained against wrongdoers, as opposed to criminal proceedings.

Litigation explosion Sudden increase in inmate suits against administrators and officers in prisons and jails during late 1960s and continuing through 1980s. Suits usually challenge nature and length of confinement or torts allegedly committed by administration, usually seek monetary or other forms of relief.

Loiterers Persons who stand around idly, hanging around. Loitering is a term often used as a provocation by police officers to stop and question citizens who appear suspicious, to describe vagrants, persons who are in public places with no visible means of support.

Magistrate A judge who handles cases in pretrial stages. Usually presides over misdemeanor cases. An officer of the lower courts.

Magistrate courts Courts of special jurisdiction, usually urban.

Malfeasance Misconduct by public officials. Engaging in acts that are prohibited while serving in public office.

Malicious prosecution Prosecutorial action against someone without probable cause or reasonable suspicion.

Mandamus See writ of *mandamus*.

Mandatory sentencing, mandatory sentence Sentencing where court is required to impose an incarcerative sentence of a specified length, without the option for probation, suspended sentence, or immediate parole eligibility.

Mandatory transfer Automatic waiver of certain juveniles to criminal court on the basis of (1) their age and (2) the seriousness of their offense; for example, a 17-year-old in Illinois who allegedly committed homicide would be subject to mandatory transfer to criminal court for the purpose of a criminal prosecution.

Material witness Any witness who has relevant testimony about a crime.

Mediation Informal conflict resolution through the intervention of a trained negotiator who seeks a mutually agreeable resolution between disputing parties.

Mens rea Intent to commit a crime. Guilty mind.

Merit selection Reform plan in which judges are nominated by a committee and appointed by the governor for a given period. When the term expires, the voters are asked to signify their approval or disapproval of the judge for a succeeding term. If judge is disapproved, the committee nominates a successor for the governor's appointment.

Miranda **warning, rights** Warning given to suspects by police officers advising suspects of their legal rights to counsel, to refuse to answer questions, to avoid self-incrimination, and other privileges. Named after landmark case of *Miranda v. Arizona* (1966).

Misdemeanor Crime punishable by fines and/or imprisonment, usually in a city or county jail, for periods of less than one year.

Misdemeanor Trial Law Action by New York City passed in 1985 permitting low-level misdemeanor cases involving incarceration of six months or less to be disposed of by bench trials rather than jury trials; a time-saving strategy for more rapid criminal case processing.

Missouri Plan Method of selecting judges in which merit system for appointments is used. Believed to reduce political influence in the selection of judges.

Mistake Affirmative defense that alleges an act was not criminal because the person charged did not know the act was a prohibited one.

Mistake of fact Unconscious ignorance of a fact or the belief in the existence of something that does not exist.

Mistake of law An erroneous opinion of legal principles applied to a given set of facts. A judge may rule on a given court issue and the ruling may be wrong because the judge misunderstands the meaning of the law and how it should be applied.

Mistrial A trial that cannot stand, is invalid. Judges may call a mistrial for reasons such as errors on the part of prosecutors or defense counsel, the death of a juror or counsel, or a hung jury.

Mitigating circumstances Factors about a crime that may lessen the severity of sentence imposed by the judge. Cooperating with police to apprehend others involved, youthfulness or old age of defendant, mental instability, and having no prior record are considered mitigating circumstances.

Mittimus An order by the court to an officer to bring someone named in the order directly to jail.

Mixed sentencing Two or more separate sentences imposed after offenders have been convicted of two or more crimes in the same adjudication proceeding. *See also* split sentencing.

Motion for a bill of particulars An action before the court asking that the details of the state's case against a defendant be made known to the defense. *See also* discovery.

Motion for a change of venue Action requested by either the prosecutor or defense counsel seeking to change the trial site to a different jurisdiction or geographical location, possibly because of extensive pretrial publicity and the belief that prospective jurors might be biased one way or another toward the defendant.

Motion for continuance An action before the court asking that the trial or hearing or proceeding be postponed to a later date.

Motion for determination of competency Action requested by defense counsel where the court is asked to order a psychiatric examination of the defendant to determine whether the defendant is competent to stand trial for a crime.

Motion for discovery Action initiated by either prosecutor or defense counsel entitling either side to certain discoverable evidence, such as police reports and defendant interviews, and any other relevant evidentiary items that might be useful as the basis for case arguments at trial later.

Motion for dismissal of charges Action requested by defense counsel to have charges against the defendant dismissed because of an insufficiency of evidence presented by the prosecutor.

Motion for intention to provide alibi Defense-initiated motion to indicate the intention to use an alibi witness or witnesses, evidence, or some type of rationale to show cause for why defendant was not at the scene of the crime(s) alleged and for which the defendant is being tried.

Motion for severance Action requested by either the prosecutor or defense counsel to have separate trial proceedings for different persons charged with the same offense and who are accused of acting in concert with one another to effect a crime.

Motion for summary judgment Request granted by judges who have read the plaintiff's version and defendant's version of events, and a decision is reached holding for the defendant.

Motion for suppression of evidence Action initiated by prosecutor or defense counsel asking the judge to bar the admission of certain evidence from the trial proceeding.

Motion to dismiss An action before the court requesting that the judge refuse to hear a suit. Usually granted when inmates who file petitions fail to state a claim upon which relief can be granted.

Motion to suppress An action before the court to cause testimony or tangible evidence from being introduced either for or against the accused.

Motions Oral or written requests to a judge asking the court to make a specific ruling, finding, decision, or order. May be presented at any appropriate point from an arrest until the end of a trial.

Motions *in limine* A pretrial motion, generally to obtain judicial approval to admit certain items into evidence that might otherwise be considered prejudicial or inflammatory.

Municipal courts Courts of special jurisdiction whose jurisdiction follows the political boundaries of a municipality or city.

Naming Identifying a party in a legal action as the target of that action.

Narrative A portion of a presentence investigation report prepared by a probation officer or private agency, which provides a description of offense and offender. Culminates in and justifies a recommendation for a specific sentence to be imposed on the offender by judges.

Necessity A condition that compels someone to act because of perceived needs. An affirmative defense (e.g., when someone's automobile breaks down during a snowstorm and an unoccupied cabin is nearby, breaking into the cabin to save oneself from freezing to death is acting out of "necessity" and would be a defense to breaking and entering charges later).

Negligence Liability accruing to prison or correctional program administrators and probation or parole officers as the result of a failure to perform a duty owed to clients or inmates or the improper or inadequate performance of that duty. May include negligent entrustment, negligent training, negligent assignment, negligent retention, or negligent supervision (e.g., providing probation or parole officers with revolvers and not providing them with firearms training).

Negotiated guilty pleas Pleas of guilty entered in exchange for some form of sentencing leniency during plea bargaining.

New trial Tribunal *de novo*. After a hung jury or a case is set aside or overturned by a higher court, a new trial is held to determine one's guilt or innocence.

New York House of Refuge Established in New York City in 1825 by the Society for the Prevention of Pauperism; school that managed largely status offenders; compulsory education provided; strict prison-like regimen was considered detrimental to youthful clientele.

No bill *See* no true bill.

No true bill Grand jury decision that insufficient evidence exists to establish probable cause that a crime was committed and a specific person committed it.

Nolle prosequi An entry made by the prosecutor on the record in a case and announced in court to indicate that the specified charges will not be prosecuted. In effect, the charges are thereby dismissed.

Nolo contendere Plea of "no contest" to charges. Defendant does not dispute facts, although issue may be taken with the legality or constitutionality of the law allegedly violated. Treated as a guilty plea. Also known as "Alford plea" from leading case of *North Carolina v. Alford* (1970).

Nominal dispositions Juvenile court outcome in which juvenile is warned or verbally reprimanded, but returned to custody of parents.

Nonpartisan elections Voting process in which candidates who are not endorsed by political parties are presented to the voters for selection.

Nonsecure custody, confinement A facility that emphasizes the care and treatment of youths without the need to place constraints to ensure public protection.

Notice An official document advising someone of a proceeding that usually requires his/her attendance.

Notice of appeal Filing a formal document with the court advising the court that the sentence is to be appealed to a higher court or appellate court.

Objections Actions by either the prosecutor or defense requesting that certain questions not be asked of witnesses or that certain evidence should or should not be admitted.

Office of Juvenile Justice and Delinquency Prevention (OJJDP) Established by Congress under the Juvenile Justice and Delinquency Prevention Act of 1974; designed to remove status offenders from jurisdiction of juvenile courts and dispose of their cases less formally.

Once an adult/always an adult Provision that once a juvenile has been transferred to criminal court to be prosecuted as an adult, regardless of the criminal court outcome, the juvenile can never be subject to the jurisdiction of juvenile courts in the future; in short, the juvenile, once transferred, will always be treated as an adult if future crimes are committed, even though the youth is still not of adult age.

Open court Any court where spectators may gather.

Opening statement Remarks made by prosecution and defense attorneys to the jury at the commencement of trial proceedings. Usually these statements set forth what each side intends to show by evidence to be presented.

Operation Greylord FBI undercover investigation of corruption among judges in Cook County (Chicago), Illinois, in 1978; results of investigation disclosed numerous instances of judicial corruption.

Opinion The official announcement of a court's decision and the reasons for that decision. In research methods, the verbal expression of an attitude.

Opinion of the court Opinion summarizing the views of the majority of judges participating in a judicial decision; a ruling or holding by a court official.

Oral argument Verbal presentation made to an appellate court by the prosecution or the defense in order to persuade the court to affirm, reverse, or modify a lower court decision.

Order Any written declaration or proclamation by a judge authorizing officials to act.

Original jurisdiction First authority over a case or cause, as opposed to appellate jurisdiction.

Overrule To reverse or annul by subsequent action (e.g., judges may overrule objections from prosecutors and defense attorneys in court, nullifying these objections; lower court decisions may be overruled by higher courts when the case is appealed).

Parens patriae "Parent of the country." Refers to doctrine that the state oversees the welfare of youth, originally established by the king of England and administered through chancellors.

Parole board, paroling authority Body of persons either appointed by governors or others or elected, which determines whether those currently incarcerated in prisons should be granted parole or early release.

Partisan elections Elections in which candidates endorsed by political parties are presented to the voters for selection.

Per diem "By the day." The cost per day, for example, the daily cost of housing inmates.

Per se "By itself." In itself (e.g., the death penalty is not unconstitutional *per se*, but a particular method of administering the death penalty may be unconstitutional in some states).

Peremptory challenge Rejection of a juror by either the prosecution or the defense in which no reason needs to be provided for excusing the juror from jury duty. Each side has a limited number of these challenges. The more serious the offense, the more peremptory challenges are given each side.

Perjury Lying under oath in court.

Persistent felony offenders Habitual offenders who commit felonies with a high recidivism rate.

Persistent offender statutes Any law prohibiting someone from being a habitual offender or someone who has been convicted of several serious crimes.

Petit jury The trier of fact in a criminal case. The jury of one's peers called to hear the evidence and decide the defendant's guilt or innocence. Varies in size among states.

Petition A document filed in juvenile court alleging that a juvenile is a delinquent, a status offender, or a dependent and asking that the court assume jurisdiction over the juvenile or that the juvenile transferred to a criminal court to be prosecuted as an adult.

Petitioner Person who brings a petition before the court.

Petty offenses Minor infractions or crimes, misdemeanors. Usually punishable by fines or short terms of imprisonment.

Philadelphia Experiment Study conducted involving setting bail guidelines in Philadelphia, Pennsylvania, during 1981–1982 and the use of release on one's own recognizance (ROR); experiment led to greater equity in bail decision making for persons of different socioeconomic statuses.

Pickpocketing The theft of money or valuables directly from the garments of the victim.

Plea Answer to charges by defendant. Pleas vary among jurisdictions. Not guilty, guilty, *nolo contendere*, not guilty by reason of insanity, and guilty but mentally ill are possible pleas.

Plea, guilty A defendant's formal answer in court to the charges in a complaint, information, or an indictment where the defendant states that the charges are true and that he or she has committed the offense(s) as charged.

Plea, initial The first plea entered in response to a given charge entered in a court record by or for a defendant.

Plea, not guilty A defendant's formal answer in court to the charges in a complaint or information or indictment, in which the defendant states that he or she has not committed the offense(s) as charged.

Plea agreement hearing Meeting presided over by a trial judge to determine the accuracy of a guilty plea and acceptability of general conditions of a plea bargain agreement between the prosecution and defense attorneys.

Plea bargain agreement Formal agreement between prosecutor and defense counsel wherein the defendant enters a guilty plea to one or more criminal charges in exchange for some form of sentencing leniency.

Plea bargaining A preconviction deal-making process between the state and the accused in which the defendant exchanges a plea of guilty or *nolo contendere* for a reduction in charges, a promise of sentencing leniency, or some other concession from full, maximum implementation of the conviction and sentencing authority of the court. Includes implicit plea bargaining, charge reduction bargaining, sentence recommendation bargaining, and judicial plea bargaining.

Plea bargains Formal agreements between the prosecutors and defense concerning the defendant offering a guilty plea in exchange for some form of sentencing leniency.

Plea negotiation *See* plea bargaining.

Plea *nolo contendere* *See nolo contendere*.

Plead To respond to a criminal charge.

Polling jurors A direct method of asking jurors to state whether they have voted in a particular way.

Polygraph tests *See* lie detectors.

Postconviction relief Term applied to various mechanisms whereby offenders may challenge their conviction after other appeal attempts have been exhausted.

Pound's model Plan of court organization with three tiers: supreme court, major trial court, and minor trial court.

Precedent Principle that the way a case was decided previously should serve as a guide for how a similar case currently under consideration ought to be decided.

Pre-conflict stage Perception by individuals or groups that they are involved in a conflict situation where a legal resolution is sought.

Preliminary examinations *See* preliminary hearings.

Preliminary hearings, preliminary examinations Hearings by magistrate or other judicial officer to determine if person charged with a crime should be held for trial. Proceedings to establish probable cause. They do not determine guilt or innocence.

Preponderance of the evidence Civil standard whereby the weight of the exculpatory or inculpatory information is in favor of or against the defendant; the greater the weight of information favoring the defendant, the greater the likelihood of a finding in favor of the defendant.

Presentence investigation reports, presentence reports (PSI) Reports filed by probation or parole officer appointed by the court containing background information, socioeconomic data, and demographic data relative to defendant. Facts in the case are included. Used to influence the sentence imposed by the judge and by the parole board considering an inmate for early release.

Presentment An accusation, initiated by the grand jury on its own authority, from jurors' own knowledge or observation, which functions as an instruction for the preparation of an indictment.

Presiding judge The title of the judicial officer formally designated for some period as the chief judicial officer of the court.

Presumption of innocence Premise that a defendant is innocent unless proven guilty beyond a reasonable doubt. Fundamental to the adversary system.

Presumptive sentencing, presumptive sentences Statutory sentencing method that specifies normal sentences of particular lengths with limited judicial leeway to shorten or lengthen the term of the sentence.

Presumptive waiver Type of judicial waiver where burden of proof shifts from the state to the juvenile to contest whether youth is transferred to criminal court.

Pretrial conference A meeting between opposing parties in a lawsuit or criminal trial, for purposes of stipulating things that are agreed upon and thus narrowing the trial to the things that are in dispute, disclosing the required information about witnesses and evidence, making motions, and generally organizing the presentation of motions, witnesses, and evidence.

Pretrial diversion *See* diversion.

Pretrial motions *See* motions *in limine.*

Pretrial publicity Any media attention given to a case before it is tried in court.

Prima facie case A case for which there is as much evidence as would warrant the conviction of defendants if properly proved in court. A case that meets the evidentiary requirements for a grand jury indictment.

Pro se Acting as one's own defense attorney in criminal proceedings. Representing oneself.

Probable cause Reasonable suspicion or belief that a crime has been committed and that a particular person committed it.

Probation officer Professional who supervises probationers.

Procedural law Rules that specify how statutes should be applied against those who violate the law. Procedures whereby the substantive laws may be implemented.

Process A summons requiring the appearance of someone in court.

Process of law Procedural law.

Proof beyond a reasonable doubt Standard of proof to convict in criminal case.

Prosecuting attorney *See* prosecutor.

Prosecution Carrying forth of criminal proceedings against a person, culminating in a trial or other final disposition such as a plea of guilty in lieu of trial.

Prosecution agency, prosecutorial agency Any local, state, or federal body charged with carrying forth actions against criminals. State legal representatives, such as district attorneys or U.S. attorneys and their assistants, who seek to convict persons charged with crimes.

Prosecutor Court official who commences civil and criminal proceedings against defendants. Represents state or government interest, prosecuting defendants on behalf of state or government.

Prosecutorial bluffing Attempt by prosecution to bluff the defendant into believing the case is much stronger than it really is. Used to elicit a guilty plea from a defendant to avoid a lengthy trial where the proof of a defendant's guilt may be difficult to establish.

Prosecutorial discretion The decision-making power of prosecutors based upon the wide range of choices available to them in the handling of criminal defendants, the scheduling of cases for trial, and the acceptance of bargained pleas. The most important form of prosecutorial discretion lies in the power to charge or not to charge a person with an offense.

Prosecutorial misconduct Any deliberate action that violates ethical codes or standards governing the role of prosecutors; usually the action is intended to injure defendants and illegally or unethically strengthen the case of prosecutors.

Prosecutorial waiver Authority of prosecutors in juvenile cases to have those cases transferred to the jurisdiction of criminal court.

Public defender system Means whereby attorneys are appointed by the court to represent indigent defendants.

Punishment Any sanction imposed for committing a crime; usually a sentence imposed for being convicted of either a felony or misdemeanor.

Reasonable doubt Standard used by jurors to decide if the prosecution has provided sufficient evidence for conviction. Jurors vote for acquittal if they have reasonable doubt that the accused committed the crime.

Reasonable suspicion Warranted suspicion (short of probable cause) that a person may be engaged in criminal conduct.

Recall election Special election called to remove a politician or judge from his/her office.

Recognizance Personal responsibility to return to court on a given date and at a given time.

Re-cross-examination Opposing counsel further examines an opposing witness who has already testified.

Re-direct examination Questioning of a witness following the adversary's questioning under cross-examination.

Referral Any citation of a juvenile to juvenile court by a law enforcement officer, interested citizen, family member, or school official; usually based upon law violations, delinquency, or unruly conduct.

Reformatory Detention facility designed to change criminal behavior or reform it.

Rehabilitation, rehabilitative ideal Correcting criminal behavior through educational and other means, usually associated with prisons.

Reintegration Punishment philosophy that promotes programs that lead offenders back into their communities. Reintegrative programs include furloughs, work release, and halfway houses.

Release on their own recognizance (ROR) Arrangement where defendants are able to be set free temporarily to await a later trial without having to post a bail bond; persons released on ROR are usually well known or have strong ties to the community and have not been charged with serious crimes.

Remand To send back (e.g., the U.S. Supreme Court may remand a case back to the lower trial court where the case was originally tried).

Remedy Any declared solution to a dispute between parties (e.g., if someone is found guilty of slashing another's automobile tires, the remedy may be to cause the convicted offender to compensate the victim with money for the full value of the destroyed tires).

Reparations Damages assigned to be paid by a defendant found liable in a civil action; may include restitution to victims; usually follow trial showing liability or culpability of defendant in lawsuit filed by plaintiff who is seeking damages.

Respondent A person asked to respond in a lawsuit or writ.

Responsible Legally accountable for one's actions and obligations.

Restitution Stipulation by the court that offenders must compensate victims for their financial losses resulting from crime. Compensation to the victim for psychological, physical, or financial loss. May be imposed as a part of an incarcerative sentence.

Restorative justice Mediation between victims and offenders whereby offenders accept responsibility for their actions and agree to reimburse victims for their losses; may involve community service and other penalties agreeable to both parties in a form of arbitration with a neutral third party acting as arbiter.

Reverse waiver hearings Formal proceedings, usually conducted by a criminal court judge, to determine whether a transferred juvenile should be sent back to be tried for his/her crimes in juvenile court rather than criminal court.

Reversed and remanded Decision by the appellate court to set aside or overturn the verdict of a lower trial court with instructions to the trial court to rehear the case with suggested modifications.

Reversible errors Mistakes committed by judges during a trial that may result in reversal of convictions against defendants.

Review The procedure whereby a higher court examines one or more issues emanating from a lower court on an appeal by the prosecution or defense.

Rights of defendant Constitutional guarantees to all persons charged with crimes. Includes representation by counsel at various critical stages, such as being charged with crimes, preliminary hearings, arraignments, trial, and appeals.

Right to counsel Right to be represented by an attorney at critical stages of the criminal justice system. Indigent defendants have the right to counsel provided by the state.

ROR See release on their own recognizance.

Rule of Four U.S. Supreme Court rule whereby the Court grants *certiorari* only on the agreement of at least four justices.

Rule of law Describes willingness of persons to accept and order their behavior according to rules and procedures that are prescribed by political and social institutions.

Rules of Criminal Procedure Rules legislatively established by which a criminal case is conducted. Law enforcement officers, prosecutors, and judges use rules of criminal procedure in discretionary actions against suspects and defendants.

Runaways Juveniles who abscond from their homes or residences without parental permission; often these youths seek a free life in another city away from parental control; a type of status offender.

Scientific jury selection Applying the scientific method to select jurors who it is believed will render favorable decisions for or against defendants.

Screening Process of jury selection by attempting to remove biased jurors and select only the most competent and objective ones.

Screening cases Procedure used by prosecutor to define which cases have prosecutive merit and which ones do not. Some screening bureaus are made up of police and lawyers with trial experience.

Seal To close from public inspection any record of an arrest, judgment, or adjudication, either criminal or juvenile.

Secure custody, confinement Incarceration of juvenile offender in a facility that restricts movement in the community. Similar to an adult penal facility involving total incarceration.

Selective chivalry View that judges tend to favor white females in their sentencing decisions compared with females of other races or ethnicities or males.

Self-defense Affirmative defense in which defendants explain otherwise criminal conduct by showing necessity to defend themselves against aggressive victims.

Self-incrimination The act of exposing oneself to prosecution by answering questions that may demonstrate involvement in illegal behavior. Coerced self-incrimination is not allowed under the Fifth Amendment. In any criminal proceeding, the prosecution must prove the charges by means of evidence other than the testimony of the accused.

Self-representation See pro se.

Sentence Penalty imposed upon a convicted person for a crime. May include incarceration, fine, both, or some other alternative. See also mandatory sentencing, presumptive sentencing, indeterminate sentencing, determinate sentencing.

Sentence disparity See sentencing disparity.

Sentence hearing See sentencing hearing.

Sentence recommendation bargaining Negotiation in which the prosecutor proposes a sentence in exchange for a guilty plea. See also plea bargaining.

Sentencing Process of imposing a punishment on a convicted person following a criminal conviction.

Sentencing disparity Inconsistency in sentencing of convicted offenders, in which those committing similar crimes under similar circumstances are given widely disparate sentences by the same judge. Usually based on gender, race, ethnic, or socioeconomic factors.

Sentencing guidelines Instruments developed by the federal government and various states to assist judges in assessing fair and consistent lengths of incarceration for various crimes and past criminal histories. Referred to as presumptive sentencing in some jurisdictions.

Sentencing hearing Optional hearing held in many jurisdictions in which defendants and victims can hear contents of presentence investigation reports prepared by probation officers. Defendants and/or victims may respond to the report orally, in writing, or both. This hearing precedes the sentence imposed by the judge.

Sentencing memorandum Court decision that furnishes ruling or finding and orders to be implemented relative to convicted offenders. Does not necessarily include reasons or rationale for the sentence imposed.

Sentencing Reform Act of 1984 Act that provided federal judges and others with considerable discretionary powers to provide alternative sentencing and other provisions in their sentencing of various offenders.

Sequester, sequestration The insulation of jurors from the outside world so that their decision making cannot be influenced or affected by extralegal factors.

Sequestered jury A jury that is isolated from the public during the course of a trial and throughout the deliberation process.

Serious felonies Any crime punishable by more than a year in prison or jail that causes substantial property loss or fraud; may include some crimes against persons, such as robbery.

Severance Separation of related cases so that they can be tried separately in different courts.

Sexual predator laws Somewhat ambiguous laws enacted in various states to identify and control previously convicted sex offenders; may include listing such persons in public announcements or bulletins, or some other form of community notification.

Shock incarceration *See* shock probation.

Shock parole *See* shock probation.

Shock probation Sentencing offenders to prison or jail for a brief period, primarily to give them a taste or "shock" of prison or jail life, and then releasing them into the custody of a probation or parole officer through a resentencing project.

Sides Opposing parties in an adversarial relation, usually in the courtroom; prosecutors and defense counsel are considered "sides" in the adversarial system of U.S. justice.

Social change Process whereby ideas and/or practices are modified either actively or passively or naturally.

Social control Informal and formal methods of getting members of society to conform to norms, folkways, and mores.

Society for the Prevention of Pauperism Philanthropic society that established first public reformatory in New York in 1825, the New York House of Refuge.

Sociological jurisprudence View that holds that part of law should be devoted to making or shaping public policy and social rules.

Solitary confinement *See* isolation.

Speedy trial Defined by federal law and applicable to federal district courts, where a defendant must be tried within 100 days of an arrest. Every state has speedy trial provisions that are within reasonable ranges of the federal standard. Originally designed to comply with the Sixth Amendment of the U.S. Constitution. The longest state speedy trial provision is in New Mexico, which is 180 days.

Speedy Trial Act of 1974 (amended 1979, 1984) Compliance with Sixth Amendment provision for a citizen to be brought to trial without undue delay of 30–70 days from date of formal specification of charges, usually in arraignment proceeding.

Spirit of the law Efforts by police officers to exhibit leniency where law violations are observed. Usually first offenders may receive leniency because of extenuating circumstances.

Split sentencing Procedure whereby a judge imposes a sentence of incarceration for a fixed period, followed by a probationary period of a fixed duration. Similar to shock xprobation.

Standard of proof Norms used by courts to determine validity of claims or allegations of wrongdoing against offenders; civil standards of proof are "clear and convincing evidence" and "preponderance of evidence," while criminal standard is "beyond a reasonable doubt."

Standing A doctrine mandating that courts may not recognize a party to a suit unless that person has a personal stake or direct interest in the outcome of the suit.

Stare decisis Legal precedent. Principle whereby lower courts issue rulings consistent with those of higher courts, where the same types of cases and facts are at issue. The principle of leaving undisturbed a settled point of law or particular precedent.

State bar associations Professional organizations of lawyers bound to observe the laws of the various states where they reside; state affiliate organizations in relation to national American Bar Association.

State's attorneys Government prosecutors.

Status offenders Juveniles who have committed an offense that would not be considered a crime if committed by an adult (e.g., a curfew violation would not be criminal action if committed by an adult, but such an act is a status offense if engaged in by a juvenile).

Status offense Any act committed by a juvenile that would not be a crime if committed by an adult.

Statute of limitations Period of time after which a crime that has been committed cannot be prosecuted. No statute of limitations exists for capital crimes.

Statutes Laws passed by legislatures. Statutory definitions of criminal offenses are embodied in penal codes.

Statutory exclusion Provisions that automatically exclude certain juveniles and offenses from the jurisdiction of the juvenile courts; for example, murder, aggravated rape, armed robbery.

Statutory law Authority based on enactments of state legislatures. Laws passed by legislatures.

Stigmas The result of the process of being labeled as a delinquent or unruly child by others.

Stigmatization Social process whereby offenders acquire undesirable characteristics as the result of imprisonment or court appearances. Undesirable criminal or delinquent labels are assigned to those who are processed through the criminal and juvenile justice systems.

Stigmatize The process of labeling someone as a delinquent or a criminal on the basis of their exhibited behavior.

Strike for cause *See* challenge for cause.

Subject matter jurisdiction Term applied when certain judges have exclusive jurisdiction over particular crimes.

Subornation of perjury The crime of procuring someone to lie under oath.

Subpoena Document issued by a judge ordering a named person to appear in court at a particular time to either answer to charges or to testify in a case.

Substantive criminal law Legislated rule that governs behaviors that are required or prohibited. Usually enacted by legislatures. Such law also specifies punishments accompanying such law violations.

Substantive law Body of law that creates, discovers, and defines the rights and obligations of each person in society. Prescribes behavior, whereas procedural law prescribes how harmful behavior is handled.

Summary judgment Any granted motion following the presentation of a case against a defendant in a civil court. Any argument countering the plaintiff's presented evidence. Usually the result of failing to state a claim upon which relief can be granted.

Summation Conclusionary remarks made by the prosecutor and defense counsel at the end of a trial before the jury.

Summons Same form as a warrant, except it commands a defendant to appear before the magistrate at a particular time and place.

Superior courts The courts of record or trial courts.

Supreme Court The federal court of last resort as specified by the U.S. Constitution; at the state level, any court of last resort in most kinds of cases.

Surety bond A sum of money or property that is posted or guaranteed by a party to ensure the future court appearance of another person. *See also* bail bond.

Sustain To uphold (e.g., the conviction was sustained by a higher appellate court).

Sworn in The process whereby persons who offer testimony in court swear to tell the truth and nothing but the truth, usually by oath upon the Bible.

Teen courts Courts where proceedings are conducted by youths who try other youths for nonserious misdemeanors such as shoplifting or mischief; punishments are nonincarcerative and usually involve restitution of some form of victim compensation of community service; an adult supervises the proceedings and the decisions by youths and juries of youths are valid and enforceable.

Texas model Also known as the "traditional" model of state court organization. Two "supreme" courts, one for civil appeals, one for criminal appeals. Has five tiers of district, county, and municipal courts.

Three-strikes-and-you're-out Legislation designed to prevent offenders from becoming recidivists; provides that persons who commit three or more serious felonies are in jeopardy of being incarcerated for life terms.

Three-strikes-and-you're-out policies A crime prevention and control strategy that proposes to incarcerate those offenders who commit and are convicted of three or more serious or violent offenses; usual penalty is life imprisonment or the life-without-parole option. Intent is to incarcerate high-rate offenders to reduce crime in society. *See also* habitual offender statutes.

Tiers Different floor levels in prisons and jails where inmates are housed; usually, different tiers house different types of offenders according to their conviction offenses and offense seriousness.

Tort actions Any legal proceeding where a plaintiff is seeking damages from a defendant for a civil wrong.

Tort reform Any action taken by an individual or group to revise existing rules governing tort actions in courts, including limiting monetary awards for prevailing in lawsuits.

Torts Private or civil wrongs or injuries, other than breach of contract, for which the court will provide a remedy in the form of an action for damages. A violation of a duty imposed by law. Existence of a legal duty to plaintiff, breach of that duty, and damage as a result of that breach.

Totality of circumstances Exception to exclusionary rule, whereby officers may make warrantless searches of property and seizures of illegal contraband on the basis of the entire set of suspicious circumstances; sometimes applied to bail decision making, where the entire set of circumstances is considered for persons considered bail-eligible.

Traditional courts Courts where juvenile proceedings are characterized by individualized treatments and proscriptions for assistance; the opposite of due process courts.

Transcript A written record of a trial or hearing.

Transfer Proceeding to determine whether juveniles should be certified as adults for purposes of being subjected to jurisdiction of adult criminal courts, where more severe penalties may be imposed. Also known as "certification" or "waiver."

Transfers Proceedings where the jurisdiction over juvenile offenders shifts from the juvenile court to criminal court.

Trial An adversarial proceeding within a particular jurisdiction, in which a judicial examination and determination of issues can be made, and in which a criminal defendant's guilt or innocence can be decided impartially by either a judge or jury. *See also* bench trial, jury trial.

Trial by the court *See* bench trial.

Trial by the judge *See* bench trial.

Trial courts Courts where guilt or innocence of defendants is established; may be criminal or civil, depending on the nature of the charge; criminal courts try defendants charged with crimes; civil courts seek to resolve disputes between plaintiffs, who seek damages, against named defendants who claim they should not be held liable.

Trial court of general jurisdiction Criminal court that has jurisdiction over all offenses, including felonies, and may in some states also hear appeals from lower courts.

Trial court of limited jurisdiction Criminal court where trial jurisdiction either includes no felonies or is limited to some category of felony. Such courts have jurisdiction over misdemeanor cases, probable-cause hearings in felony cases, and sometimes, felony trials that may result in penalties below a specific limit.

Trial delays Any one of several legitimate reasons that may contribute to delaying or prolonging the occasion that a trial commences; may be due to crowded court dockets; requests from the defense or prosecution for more time in case preparation; or the health of different courtroom actors, such as the prosecutor, defense counsel, or defendant.

Trial judge *See* judge.

Trial jury *See* petit jury.

Tribunal A court. A place where judges sit. A judicial weighing of information leading to a decision about a case.

Truants Juveniles who absent themselves from school during school hours and without excuse of parental or school consent; a type of status offender.

True bills Grand jury decisions that sufficient evidence exists that a crime has been committed and that a specific suspect committed it.

Truth in sentencing Policy of imposing a sentence, most of which must be served in prison or jail; maximizing one's incarceration under the law.

Truth-in-sentencing laws Any legislation intended to maximize one's sentence and time served for committing a crime; intent is to compel offenders to serve at least 80 or 90 percent of their maximum sentences before they become eligible for parole or early release.

Typicality hypothesis View that judges give women greater consideration than men during sentencing, but only when their criminal charges are consistent with stereotypes of female offenders.

United States attorneys Officials responsible for the prosecution of crimes that violate the laws of the United States. Appointed by the president and assigned to a U.S. District Court jurisdiction.

United States Attorney's Office Chief prosecuting body affiliated with each U.S. District Court in the federal court system.

United States Circuit Courts of Appeal Appellate courts from which U.S. District Court decisions are appealed; cases appealed from the U.S. Circuit Courts of Appeal are appealed directly to the U.S. Supreme Court; there are 13 circuit courts of appeal.

United States Courts of Appeal The federal circuit courts of appellate jurisdiction. As of 1996, there were 13 circuit courts of appeal zoned throughout the United States and its territories.

United States District Courts The basic trial courts for federal civil and criminal actions.

United States magistrates Judges who fulfill the pretrial judicial obligations of the federal courts. Formerly, United States commissioners.

United States Sentencing Commission Body of persons originating from Sentencing Reform Act of 1984 and promulgated sentencing guidelines for all federal crimes.

United States sentencing guidelines Rules implemented by federal courts in November 1987 obligating federal judges to impose presumptive sentences on all convicted offenders. Guidelines are based upon offense seriousness and offender

characteristics. Judges may depart from guidelines only by justifying their departures in writing.

United States Supreme Court Court of last resort; final and highest court that decides particular issues, usually issues with constitutional significance.

Vacate To annul, set aside, or rescind.

Vacated sentence Any sentence that has been declared nullified by action of a court.

***Venire*, vereman list, veniremen** List of prospective jurors made up from registered voters, vehicle driver's licenses, tax assessors' records. Persons must reside within the particular jurisdiction where the jury trial is held. Persons who are potential jurors in a given jurisdiction.

Venue Area over which a judge exercises authority to act in an official capacity. Place where a trial is held.

Venue, change of Relocation of a trial from one site to another, usually because of some pretrial publicity making it possible that a jury might be biased and that a fair trial will be difficult to obtain.

Verdict Decision by judge or jury concerning the guilt or innocence of a defendant.

Verdict-driven jury Jury that decides guilt or innocence first without considering adequately the relevant evidence in the case; jurors are polled initially to see to what extent they agree or disagree among themselves; if most or all of the jurors vote the same way, then they conclude their deliberations without further consideration of the evidence.

Verdict, guilty In criminal proceedings, the decision made by a jury in a jury trial, or by a judicial officer in a bench trial, that defendants are guilty of the offense(s) for which they have been tried.

Verdict, not guilty In criminal proceedings, the decision made by a jury in a jury trial, or by the judge in a bench trial, that defendants are not guilty of the offense(s) for which they have been tried.

Vice principal doctrine Theory holding that someone may be sued by another if he/she is a supervisor or boss, and not necessarily the owner of an organization.

Victim Person who has either suffered death or serious physical or mental suffering, or loss of property resulting from actual or attempted criminal actions committed by others.

Victim compensation Any financial restitution payable to victims by either the state or convicted offenders.

Victim compensation programs Any plans for assisting crime victims in making social, emotional, and economic adjustments.

Victim impact statement Information or version of events filed voluntarily by the victim of a crime, appended to the presentence investigation report as a supplement for judicial consideration in sentencing the offender. Describes injuries to victims resulting from convicted offender's actions.

Victim–offender mediation model Meeting between criminal and person suffering loss or injury from criminal whereby third-party arbiter, such as a judge, attorney, or other neutral party decides what is best for all parties. All parties must agree to decision of third-party arbiter. Used for both juvenile and adult offenders.

Victim–offender reconciliation Any agreement between the victim and the perpetrator concerning a satisfactory arrangement for compensation for injuries or financial losses sustained.

Victim–Offender Reconciliation Project (VORP) Form of alternative dispute resolution, whereby a civil resolution is made by mutual consent between the victim and an offender; objectives are to provide restitution to victims, hold offender accountable for crime committed, and to reduce recidivism.

Victim/reparations model Restitution model for juveniles in which juveniles compensate their victims directly for their offenses.

Victim-witness assistance programs Plans available to prospective witnesses to explain court procedures and inform them of court dates, and to assist witnesses in providing better testimony in court.

Victims of Crime Act of 1984 Also known as the Comprehensive Crime Control Act of 1984, includes sanctions against offenders such as victim compensation, community service, and/or restitution.

Violent felonies Any crime that is punishable by more than one year in a prison or jail and causes serious bodily injury or death (e.g., rape, aggravated assault, murder, armed robbery).

Voir dire "To speak the truth." Interrogation process whereby prospective jurors are questioned by either the judge or by the prosecution or defense attorneys to determine their biases and prejudices.

Voluntariness Willingness of defendant to enter a plea or make an agreement in a plea bargain proceeding. Judges must determine the voluntariness of the plea to determine that it was not coerced.

Waiver, waiver of jurisdiction Made by motion, the transfer of jurisdiction over a juvenile to a criminal court where the juvenile is subject to adult criminal penalties. Includes judicial, prosecutorial, and legislative waivers. Also known as "certification" or "transfer."

Waiver hearing Motion by prosecutor to transfer juvenile charged with various offenses to a criminal or adult court for prosecution, making it possible to sustain adult criminal penalties.

Warrant A written order directing a suspect's arrest and issued by an official with the authority to issue the warrant. Commands suspect to be arrested and brought before the nearest magistrate.

Warrant, arrest Document issued by a judge that directs a law enforcement officer to arrest a person who has been accused of an offense.

Warrant, bench Document issued by a judge directing that a person who has failed to obey an order or notice to appear be brought before the court without undue delay.

Warrant, search Any document issued by a judicial official, based upon probable cause, directing law enforcement officers to conduct an inspection of an individual, automobile, or building with the intent of locating particular contraband or incriminating evidence as set forth in the document.

With prejudice To dismiss charges, but those same charges cannot be brought again later against the same defendant.

Without prejudice To dismiss charges, but those same charges can be brought again later against the same defendant.

Without undue delay or unnecessary delay Standard used to determine whether suspect has been brought in a timely manner before a magistrate or other judicial authority after arrested. Definition of undue delay varies among jurisdictions. Circumstances of arrest, availability of judge, and time of arrest are factors that determine reasonableness of delay.

Witnesses Persons who have relevant information about the commission of a crime; persons who have seen or heard inculpatory or exculpatory evidence that may incriminate or exonerate a defendant.

Writ A document issued by a judicial officer ordering or forbidding the performance of a specific act.

Writ of *certiorari* An order of a superior court requesting that the record of an inferior court (or administrative body) be brought forward for review or inspection. Literally, "to be more fully informed."

Writ of *habeas corpus* *See habeas corpus.*

Writ of *mandamus* An order of a superior court commanding that a lower court, administrative body, or executive body perform a specific function. Commonly used to restore rights and privileges lost to a defendant through illegal means.

Wrongful convictions Adjudications of guilt by either a judge or jury and where the convicted offender is actually innocent of the charges alleged.

REFERENCES

Aas, Katja Franko (2004). "Sentencing Transparency in the Information Age." *Journal of Scandinavian Studies in Criminology and Crime Prevention* **5**:48–61.

Abel, Richard (1990). "A Critique of Torts." *UCLA Law Review* **37**:785–831.

Abrams, Stan (1995). "False Memory Syndrome vs. Total Repression." *Journal of Psychiatry and Law* **23**:283–293.

Adamson, Hoebel E. (1954). *The Law of Primitive Man: A Study in Comparative Legal Dynamic*. Cambridge, MA: Harvard University Press.

Adler, Stephen J. (1995). *The Jury: Disorder in the Court.* New York: Doubleday.

Ajzenstadt, Mimi, and Odeda Steinberg (2001). "Never Mind the Law: Legal Discourse and Rape Reform in Israel." *Affilia* **16**:337–259.

Albonetti, Celesta A., and Chana Barron (2004). "On the Way to Settled Law: An Examination of Law Making and Law Finding in Federal Appellate Decisions." Unpublished paper presented at the annual meeting of the American Society of Criminology, November (Nashville, TN).

Alfini, James J. (1981). "Mississippi Judicial Selection: Election, Appointment, and Bar Anointment." In *Courts and Judges,* James A. Cramer (ed.). Beverly Hills, CA: Sage.

Alexander, R. (2004). "The United States Supreme Court and the Civil Commitment of Sex Offenders." *The Prison Journal* **84**:33–54.

Alonso, Alfonso (2009). "Best Practices for Drug Courts." Unpublished thesis, University of Nevada at Reno.

Ambos, Kai (2003). "International Criminal Procedure: 'Adversarial,' 'Inquisitorial,' or Mixed?" *International Criminal Law Review* **3**:1–27.

American Bar Association (1989). *Criminal Justice Mental Health Standards*. Washington, DC. American Bar Association.

Anchorage Youth Court (2005). "Youth Courts Strive for Sustainability." *Gavel* **16**:1–4.

APPA Perspectives (2004a). "APPA Resolves Support for Youth Courts." *APPA Perspectives* **28**:8.

Arpey, Andrew W. (2003). *The William Freeman Murder Trial: Insanity, Politics and Race*. Syracuse, NY: Syracuse University Press.

Arrigo, B. A., and M. C. Bardwell (2000). "Law, Psychology, and Competency to Stand Trial: Problems with and Implications for High-profile Cases." *Criminal Justice Policy Review* **11**:16–43.

Asch, Solomon E. (1966). "Effect of Group Pressure Upon the Modification and Distortion of Judgments." *Group Dynamics* **14**:189–199.

Associated Press (1998). "Judge Who Drank after Trial Quits." *Minot (N.D.) Daily News,* April 8, 1998:A2.

Atherton, Matthew (2004). "Study of Hispanic Outcomes in U.S. Federal Courts." Unpublished paper presented at the annual meeting of the American Society of Criminology meeting, November (Nashville, TN).

Atkins, Holly (2005). "Evaluation of a Large Urban Drug Court." Unpublished paper presented at the annual meeting of the Academy of Criminal Justice Sciences, March (Chicago).

Auerhahn, Kathleen (2004). "Homicide Sentencing and the Behavior of Law." Unpublished paper presented at the annual meeting of the American Society of Criminology, November (Nashville, TN).

Austin, James et al. (1995). *National Assessment of Structured Sentencing*. Washington, DC: U.S. Bureau of Justice Statistics.

Bakker, Mark William (1994). "Repairing the Breach and Reconciling the Discordant: Mediation in the Criminal Justice System." *North Carolina Law Review* **71**:1479–1483.

Ball, Jeremy D. (2005). "Does Race Matter? Assessing Racial and Ethnic Bias." Unpublished paper presented at the annual meeting of the Academy of Criminal Justice Sciences, March (Chicago).

Barrile, Leo G., and Neal Slone (2005). "Punishing Environmental Criminals: Extra Legal Factors and the Sentencing Guidelines." Unpublished paper presented at the annual meeting of the Academy of Criminal Justice Sciences, March (Chicago).

Beechen, Paul D. (1974). "Can Judicial Elections Express the People's Choice?" *Judicature* **57**:242–256.

Beger, Randall R. (2003). "The Worst of Both Worlds: School Security and the Disappearing Fourth Amendment Rights of Students." *Criminal Justice Review* **28**:336–354.

Belbot, Barbara et al. (2004). "Legal Issues in Corrections." *Prison Journal* **84**:287–410.

Bell, Bernard P. (1983). "Closure of Pretrial Suppression Hearings: Resolving the Fair Trial/Free Press Conflict." *Fordham Law Review* **51**:1297–1316.

Bensinger, Gad J. (1988). "Operation Greylord and Its Aftermath." *International Journal of Comparative and Applied Criminal Justice* **12**:111–118.

Berman, Greg, and John Feinblatt (2005). *Good Courts: The Case for Problem Solving Justice*. New York: Free Press.

Birzer, Michael L., and Ronald Tannehill (2003). "Criminal Justice Practitioners' Perceptions of Themselves, Each Other, and Selected Criminal Justice Practices." *Journal of Crime and Justice* **26**:77–100.

Bishop, Donna M. et al. (2004). "Prosecutorial Charging Decisions in Transfer Cases." Unpublished paper presented at the annual meeting of the American Society of Criminology, November (Nashville, TN).

Black, Donald (1973). "The Mobilization of Law." *The Journal of Legal Studies* **2:**125–149.

Black, Henry Campbell (1990). *Black's Law Dictionary*. St. Paul, MN: West Publishing Company.

Blackmore, John, Marci Brown, and Barry Krisberg (1988). *Juvenile Justice Reform: The Bellwether States*. Ann Arbor, MI: University of Michigan.

Blackwell, Kevin R. (2004). "Is There a Penalty for Going to Trial in Federal Court?" Unpublished paper presented at the annual meeting of the American Society of Criminology, November (Nashville, TN).

Blankenship, Michael B., Jerry B. Sparger, and W. Richard Janikowski (1994). "Accountability v. Independence: Myths of Judicial Selection." *Criminal Justice Policy Review* **6:**69–79.

Blue Earth County (2005). *Blue Earth County Teen Court*. Mankato, MN: Blue Earth County Teen Court.

Blumstein, Alfred (1982). "Racial Disproportionality of U.S. Prison Populations Revisited." *University of Colorado Law Review* **64:**743–760.

Boari, Nicola, and Gianluca Fiorentini (2001). "An Economic Analysis of Plea Bargaining: The Incentives of the Parties in a Mixed Penal System." *International Review of Law and Economics* **21:**213–231.

Boller, Kelley G. (2005). "Wrongful Convictions: Theoretical Explanations for the Differing Perceptions of Criminal Justice Actors." Unpublished paper presented at the annual meeting of the Academy of Criminal Justice Sciences, March (Chicago).

Booth, Tracey (2004). "Homicide, Family Victims and Sentencing: Continuing the Debate about Victim Impact Statements." *Current Issues in Criminal Justice* **15:**253–257.

Boyle, Robert, Donna R. Newman, and Sam A. Schmidt (2003). "Center for Professional Values and Practice Symposium: Criminal Defense in the Age of Terrorism." *New York Law School Law Review* **48:**3–384.

Bradfield, A., and D. E. McQuiston (2004). "When Does Evidence of Eyewitness Confidence Inflation Affect Judgments in a Criminal Trial?" *Law and Human Behavior* **28:**369–387.

Braithwaite, John (1998). "Restorative Justice." In *The Handbook of Crime and Punishment*, Michael Tonry (ed.). New York, NY: Oxford University Press.

Braithwaite, John (2002). *Restorative Justice and Responsive Regulation*. Oxford, UK: Oxford University Press.

Breckenridge, Sophonisba P. (1906). "Legislative Control of Women's Work." *Journal of Political Economy* **14:**115–120.

Brocke, Michaela et al. (2004). "Attitudes Toward the Severity of Punishment: A Conjoint Analytic Approach." *Psychology, Crime and the Law* **10:**205–219.

Bullock, Jennifer Leslie (2002). "Involuntary Treatment of Defendants Found Incompetent to Stand Trial." *Journal of Forensic Psychology Practice* **2:**1–34.

Bureau of Justice Statistics (2005). *Annual Reports*. Washington, DC: U.S. Department of Justice, Bureau of Justice Statistics.

Burger, Warren (1982). "Isn't There a Better Way?" *American Bar Association Journal* **68:**274–275.

Burnett, Cathleen (2005). "Restorative Justice and Wrongful Capital Convictions." *Journal of Contemporary Criminal Justice* **21:**272–289.

Burrow, John D. (2004). "The Death of Innocence: Factual and Procedural Errors that Result in Wrongful Convictions." Unpublished paper presented at the annual meeting of the American Society of Criminology, November (Nashville, TN).

Burruss, George W., and Kimberly Kempf-Leonard (2002). "The Questionable Advantage of Defense Counsel in Juvenile Court." *Justice Quarterly* **19:**37–67.

Buzawa, Eve S., and Carl G. Buzawa (2003). *Domestic Violence: The Criminal Justice Response*. Thousand Oaks, CA: Sage.

Carey, Bryan A. (2001). "Should American Courts Listen to What Foreign Courts Hear? The Confrontation and Hearsay Problems of Prior Testimony Taken Abroad in Criminal Proceedings." *American Journal of Criminal Law* **29:**29–58.

Carr, Patrick J., Kim A. Logio, and Shana Maier (2003). "Keep Me Informed: What Matters for Victims as They Navigate the Juvenile Criminal Justice System in Philadelphia." *International Review of Victimology* **10:**117–136.

Carrington, Peter J., and Jennifer L. Schulenberg (eds.) (2004). "The Youth Criminal Justice Act." *Canadian Journal of Criminology and Criminal Justice* **46:**219–389.

Carter, Linda E. (2001). "The Sporting Approach to Harmless Error in Criminal Cases: The Supreme Court's 'No Harm, No Foul' Debacle in *Neder v. United States*." *American Journal of Criminal Law* **28:**229–246.

Caulkins, Jonathan P., C. Peter Rydell, William L. Schwabe, and James Chiesa (1998). "Are Mandatory Minimum Drug Sentences Cost Effective?" *Corrections Management Quarterly* **2:**8–73.

Ceci, Stephen J., and Maggie Bruck (1995). *Jeopardy in the Courtroom: A Scientific Analysis of Children's Testimony*. Washington, DC: American Psychological Association.

Chambers, Rex L. (1989). "Comparative Performance of Women in Law School." *Excelsior Law Review* **22:**196–222.

Champion, Dean J. (2004). "Juvenile Felons and Waivers, 1990–1999: Bursting the 'Get Tough' Bubble." Unpublished paper presented at the annual meeting of the American Society of Criminology, November (Nashville, TN).

Champion, Dean J. (2005a). "Plea Bargaining in Texas 2000–2001: A View from Prosecutors." Unpublished paper presented at the annual meeting of the Academy of Criminal Justice Sciences, March (Chicago).

Champion, Dean J. (2005b). *Probation, Parole, and Community Corrections* (5th ed.). Upper Saddle River, NJ: Prentice-Hall.

Champion, Dean J. (2007). *The Juvenile Justice System: Delinquency, Processing and the Law* (5th ed.). Upper Saddle River, NJ: Prentice Hall/Pearson.

Champion, Dean J. (2009). *The Juvenile Justice System: Delinquency, Processing and the Law*. Upper Saddle River, NJ: Prentice Hall.

Chapman, Yvonne K. (2005). "Teen Courts and Restorative Justice." Unpublished paper presented at the annual meeting of the Academy of Criminal Justice Sciences, Chicago (March).

Charish, Courtney L. (2004). "Gender Effects on Juvenile Justice System Processing." Unpublished paper presented at the annual meeting of the American Society of Criminology, November (Nashville, TN).

Chiricos, T., and B. Bales (1991). "Unemployment and Punishment: An Empirical Assessment." *Criminology* **29**:701–724.

Church, Thomas (1976). "Plea Bargains, Concessions and the Courts: Analysis of a Quasi-Experiment." *Law and Society Review* **10**:377–401.

Clark, James D. (2004a). "Racial, Ethnic, and Citizenship Disparity in Sentencing Under Federal Sentencing Guidelines: A Comparison of Two Judicial Districts." Unpublished paper presented at the annual meeting of the American Society of Criminology, November (Nashville, TN).

Clark, John W. III (2004b). "The Utility of Jury Consultants in the Twenty-First Century." Unpublished paper presented at the annual meeting of the American Society of Criminology, November (Nashville, TN).

Clayton, Obie Jr. (1983). "Reconsideration of the Effects of Race in Criminal Sentencing." *Criminal Justice Review* **8**:15–20.

Cohen, Thomas H. (2004). "The Impact of Bench Trial Convictions on Sentencing." Unpublished paper presented at the annual meeting of the American Society of Criminology, November (Nashville, TN).

Connell, Nadine M. (2004). "The Power of the Prosecutor: Understanding Prosecutorial Discretion in a Social Network Analysis Framework." Unpublished paper presented at the annual meeting of the American Society of Criminology, November (Nashville, TN).

Cook, Alison, Jamie Arndt, and Joel D. Lieberman (2004). "Firing Back at the Backfire Effect: The Influence of Mortality Salience and Nullification Beliefs on Reactions to Inadmissible Evidence." *Law and Human Behavior* **28**:389–410.

Coomber, Ross, Michael Oliver, and Craig Morris (2003). "Using Cannibis Therapeutically in the United Kingdom: A Qualitative Analysis." *Journal of Drug Issues* **33**:325–356.

Correctional Association of New York (1993). *Court Case Processing in New York: Problems and Solutions*. New York: Correctional Association of New York.

Cossins, Anne (2003). "Saints, Sluts, and Sexual Assault: Rethinking the Relationship Between Sex, Race, and Gender." *Social and Legal Studies* **12**:77–103.

Crow, Matthew S. (2004). "The Impact of Sentencing Guidelines Policy Reform: Florida's 1994 Sentencing Guidelines." Unpublished paper presented at the annual meeting of the American Society of Criminology, November (Nashville, TN).

Cunningham, Mark D., and Mark P. Vigen (1999). "Without Appointed Counsel in Capital Postconviction Proceedings: The Self-Representation Competency of Mississippi Death Row Inmates." *Criminal Justice and Behavior* **26**:293–321.

Cummingham, Scott (2005). "Perspectives on Prosecutors, Community Prosecution, and Collective Bargaining Issues." Unpublished paper presented at the annual meeting of the Academy of Criminal Justice Sciences, March (Chicago).

Dabney, Dean, Sue Carter Collins, and Volkan Topalli (2004). "Statutory Provisions and Legal Precedents in the Area of Bail Bondsmen and Bail Recovery Agents: Assessing a Fringe Element of the Criminal Justice System." Unpublished paper presented at the annual meeting of the American Society of Criminology, November (Nashville, TN).

D'Allessio, Stewart J., and Lisa Stolzenberg (1993). "Socioeconomic Status and the Sentencing of the Traditional Offender." *Journal of Criminal Justice* **21**:61–77.

Daly, Kathleen (1989). "Neither Conflict Nor Labeling Nor Paternalism Will Suffice: Intersections of Race, Ethnicity, Gender, and Family in Criminal Court Decisions." *Crime & Delinquency* **35**:136–168.

Daly, Kathleen, and Rebecca L. Bordt (1995). "Sex Effects and Sentencing: An Analysis of the Statistical Literature." *Justice Quarterly* **12**:141–175.

Davis, Jacqueline (2005). "Texas Landmark Cases: An Analysis and Comparison of *Ruiz v. Estelle* and *Morales v. Turman*." Unpublished paper presented at the annual meeting of the Academy of Criminal Justice Sciences, March (Chicago).

Davis-Frenzel, Erika, and Cassia Spohn (2004). "Questioning the Measurement of the Dependent Variable Used in Sex Disparity Research." Unpublished paper presented at the annual meeting of the American Society of Criminology, November (Nashville, TN).

Davies, Graham M. et al. (1995). "Seminar: A New Look at Eyewitness Testimony: Papers presented at the BAFS Joint Seminar on 12 October 1994." *Medicine Science and the Law* **35**:95–149.

Death Penalty Information Center (2010). *The Death Penalty in 2010: Year End Report*. Washington, DC: Death Penalty Information Center.

DeLone, Miriam A., and Keith A. Wilmot (2004). "Minnesota Sentencing Guidelines Revisited: Does Race Matter for Native American Offenders?" Unpublished paper presented at the annual meeting of the American Society of Criminology, November (Nashville, TN).

Demuth, Stephen (2003). "Racial and Ethnic Differences in Pretrial Release Decisions and Outcomes: A Comparison of Hispanic, Black, and White Felony Arrestees." *Criminology* **41**:873–907.

Denov, Myriam S., and Kathryn M. Campbell (2005). "Understanding the Causes, Effects, and Responses to Wrongful Conviction in Canada." *Journal of Contemporary Criminal Justice* **21**:224–249.

Dent, Helen, and Rhona Flin (eds.) (1992). *Children as Witnesses*. Chichester, UK: Wiley.

Deukmedjian, John Edward (2003). "Reshaping Organizational Objectives in Canada's National Police Force: The Development of the RCMP Alternative Dispute Resolution." *Policing and Society* **13:**331–348.

DiCristina, Bruce (2004). "Durkheim's Theory of Homicide and the Confusion of the Empirical Literature." *Theoretical Criminology* **8:**57–91.

Ditton, Paula M., and Doris James Wilson (1999). *Truth in Sentencing in State Prisons*. Washington, DC. U.S. Department of Justice, Bureau of Justice Statistics.

Doerner, Jill K., and Stephen Demuth (2010). "The Independent and Joint Effects of Race/Ethnicity, Gender, and Age on Sentencing Outcomes in US Federal Courts." *Justice Quarterly* **27:**1–27.

Dubois, Philip L. (1990). "Voter Responses to Court Reform: Merit Judicial Selection on the Ballot." *Judicature* **73:**238–247.

Dynia, Paul A. (1987). *Misdemeanor Trial Law Study: Final Report*. New York: New York City Criminal Justice Agency.

Dynia, Paul A. (1990). *Misdemeanor Trial Law: Is It Working?* New York: New York City Criminal Justice Agency.

Elko Teen Court (2005). *Elko, Nevada Teen Court*. Elko, NV: Elko Teen Court.

Emmelman, Deborah S. (2003). *Justice for the Poor: A Study of Criminal Defense Work*. Burlington, VT: Ashgate Publishing Company.

Enriquez, Roger (2005). "Courts and Juries." Unpublished paper presented at the annual meeting of the Academy of Criminal Justice Sciences, March (Chicago).

Enriquez, Roger, and John W. Clark (2005). "The Relationship Between Personality and Jury Selection: An Exploratory Study of Jurors in Bexar County, Texas." Unpublished paper presented at the annual meeting of the Academy of Criminal Justice Sciences, March (Chicago).

Erez, Edna, and Peter R. Ibarra (2004). "Making Your Home a Shelter: The Electronic Monitoring of Domestic Violence Cases." Unpublished paper presented at the American Society of Criminology, November (Nashville, TN).

Fearn, Noelle (2004). "The Main and Conditioning Effects of Community Characteristics on Sentencing: A Multilevel Analysis." Unpublished paper presented at the annual meeting of the American Society of Criminology, November (Nashville, TN).

Federman, C. (2004). "Who Has the Body? The Paths to Habeas Corpus Reform." *The Prison Journal* **84:**317–339.

Feld, Barry C. (2000). *Cases and Materials on Juvenile Justice Administration*. St. Paul, MN: West Group.

Feld, Barry C. (2001). "Race, Youth Violence, and the Changing Jurisprudence of Waiver." *Behavioral Sciences and the Law* **19:**3–22.

Feld, Barry C. (2003). "The Constitutional Tension Between *Apprendi* and *McKeiver*: Sentence Enhancements Based on Delinquency Convictions and the Quality of Justice in Juvenile Courts." *Wake Forest Law Review* **38:**1111–1224.

Feld, Barry C., and Shelly Schaefer (2010). "The Right to Counsel in Juvenile Court: Law Reform to Deliver Legal Services and Reduce Justice by Geography." *Criminology and Public Policy* **9:**327–256.

Felstiner, William, Richard Abel, and Austin Sarat (1980). "The Emergence of Disputes: Naming, Blaming, and Claiming." *Law and Society Review* **15:**631–634.

Ferdinand, Theodore (1992). *Boston's Lower Criminal Courts, 1814–1850*. Newark, DE: University of Delaware Press.

Finn, Peter, and B. Lee (1985). "Collaboration with Victim-Witness Assistance Programs: Payoffs and Concerns for Prosecutors." *Prosecutor* **18:**27–36.

Findlay, Mark, and Peter Duff (eds.) (1988). *The Jury Under Attack*. Sydney, Australia: Butterworths.

Fischer, Gloria J. (1997). "Gender Effects on Individual Verdicts and on Mock Jury Verdicts in a Simulated Acquaintance Rape Trial." *Sex Roles: A Journal of Research* **36:**491–502.

Fisher, George (2000). "Plea Bargaining's Triumph." *Yale Law Journal* **109:**868–1086.

Fisher, Jim (1999). *The Ghosts of Hopewell: Setting the Record Straight in the Lindbergh Case*. Carbondale, IL: Southern Illinois University Press.

Fletcher, George P. (2004). "Black Hole in Guantanamo Bay." *Journal of International Criminal Justice* **2:**121–132.

Florida Joint Legislative Management Committee (1992). *An Empirical Examination of the Application of Florida's Habitual Offender Statute*. Tallhassee, FL: Florida Joint Legislative Management Committee Economic and Demographic Research Division.

Foley, Michael A. (ed.) (2003). *The Supreme Court, the Constitution, and the Death Penalty*. Westport, CT: Praeger.

Forst, Brian (2004). "Minimizing Errors of Justice: The Role of the Prosecutor." Unpublished paper presented at the annual meeting of the American Society of Criminology, November (Nashville, TN).

Freedman, Eric M. (2001). *Habeas Corpus: Rethinking the Great Writ of Liberty*. New York: New York University Press.

Friedman, Lawrence (1985). *History of American Law* (2nd ed.). New York: Simon and Schuster.

Fryling, Tina M. (2005). "Mitigating and Aggravating Factors in Death Penalty Cases: A Review of State Law." Unpublished paper presented at the annual meeting of the Academy of Criminal Justice Sciences, March (Chicago).

Galenter, Marc (1986). "The Day After the Litigation Explosion." *Maryland Law Review* **46:**3–39.

Gallinetti, J., J. Redpath, and J. Sloth-Nielsen (2004). "Race, Class and Restorative Justice in South Africa: Achilles Heel, Glass Ceiling, or Crowning Glory?" *South African Journal of Criminal Justice* **17:**17–40.

Gants, Earl III (2005). "Why Do You People Always Think About Race? Historically African-Americans and Courts." Unpublished paper presented at the annual meeting of the Academy of Criminal Justice Sciences, March (Chicago).

Geoghagan, Angel D. (2004). "Race and Gender Disparities in Criminal Justice Treatment." Unpublished paper presented at the annual meeting of the American Society of Criminology, November (Nashville, TN).

Gerwitz, Marian (1987). *Court-Ordered Releases—November 1983.* New York: New York City Criminal Justice Agency.

Gilbertson, D. Lee (2005). "Gangs in the Law." *Journal of Gang Research* **13:**1–16.

Glaze, Lauren E., and Thomas P. Bonczar (2009). *Probation and Parole in the United States in 2009.* Washington, DC: United States Department of Justice, Bureau of Justice Statistics.

Glick, Henry R., and Craig F. Emmert (1987). "Selection Systems and Judicial Characteristics: The Recruitment of State Supreme Court Judges." *Judicature* **70:**228–235.

Goldkamp, John S., and Michael R. Gottfredson (1984). *Judicial Guidelines for Bail: The Philadelphia Experiment.* Washington, DC: U.S. Government Printing Office.

Goldkamp, John S., and Cheryl Irons-guynn (2000). Emerging Judicial Strategies for the Mentally Ill in the Criminal Caseload: Mental Health Courts in Fort Lauderdale, Seattle, San Bernardino, and Anchorage. Washington, DC: Bureau of Justice Statistics.

Goldman, Sheldon et al. (2003). "George W. Bush Remaking the Judiciary: Like Father Like Son?" *Judicature* **86:**282–309.

Goodman, John C., and Philip Porter (2002). "Is the Criminal Justice System Just?" *International Review of Law and Economics* **22:**25–39.

Gottlieb, Barbara (1984). *Public Danger as a Factor in Pretrial Release: Summaries of State Danger Laws.* Washington, DC: Toborg.

Gould, Jon B. (2004). "A First Try: The Innocence Commission for Virginia." Unpublished paper presented at the annual meeting of the American Society of Criminology, November (Nashville, TN).

Grace, Maggie T. (2010). "Criminal Alternative Dispute Resolution: Restoring Justice, Respecting, Responsibility, and Renewing Public Norms." *Vermont Law Review* **34:**563–595.

Graham, Michael H. (1985). *Witness Intimidation: The Law's Response.* Westport, CT: Quorum.

Greene, J. (1990). "Media Effects on Jurors." *Law and Human Behavior* **14:**439–450.

Greene, J., and C. Loftus (1984). "What's News in the News? The Influence of Well-Publicized News Events on Psychological Research and Courtroom Trials." *Basic and Applied Social Psychology* **5:**123–135.

Greenstein, Marla N., and Kate Sampson (2004). *A National Symposium on Sentencing: Report and Policy Guide.* Des Moines, IA: American Judicature Society.

Greenstein, Steven C. (1994). *The Impact of Restrictions on Post-Indictment Plea Bargaining in Bronx County: The Processing of Indictments Already Pending.* Albany, NY: New York State Division of Criminal Justice.

Gubanski, Jakub (2004). "Comparative Criminal Justice: Special Investigation Techniques During the Criminal Trial: Disclosure Issues in Polish and American Legal Systems." *Crime, Law, and Social Change: An Interdisciplinary Journal* **41:**15–32.

Guevara, Lori, and Denise C. Herz (2004). "Race, Gender, and Juvenile Justice: Differences in Dispositional Outcomes." Unpublished paper presented at the annual meeting of the American Society of Criminology, November (Nashville, TN).

Gustafson, Kaaryn (2009). "Criminal Law: The Criminalization of Poverty." *Journal of Criminal Law and Criminology* **99:**643–716.

Hack, Peter (2003). "The Roads Less Traveled: Post-Conviction Relief Alternatives and the Antiterrorism and Effective Death Penalty Act of 1996." *American Journal of Criminal Law* **30:**171–223.

Hanke, Penelope J. (1995). "Sentencing Disparities by Race of Offender and Victim: Women Homicide Offenders in Alabama, 1929–1985." *Sociological Spectrum* **15:**277–297.

Harmon, Talia Roitberg (2000). *Overturned Convictions in Capital Cases.* Ann Arbor, MI: University Microfilms International.

Harmon, Talia Roitberg (2001). "Guilty Until Proven Innocent: An Analysis of Post-*Furman* Capital Errors." *Criminal Justice Policy Review* **12:**113–139.

Harmon, Talia Roitberg (2004). "Close Calls: Exonerations in Capital Cases in the Post-*Furman* Era." Unpublished paper presented at the annual meeting of the American Society of Criminology, November (Nashville, TN).

Harris, Alexes (2004). "The Institutional Careers of Juvenile Delinquents: Offending and Processing Patterns of a Sample of Violent and Chronic Offenders." Unpublished paper presented at the annual meeting of the American Society of Criminology, November (Nashville, TN).

Harris, M. (2004). "From Australian Courts to Aboriginal Courts in Australia: Bridging the Gap?" *Current Issues in Criminal Justice: Journal of the Institute of Criminology* **16:**26–41.

Harris, Victoria, and Christos Dagadakis (2004). "Length of Incarceration: Was There Parity for Mentally Ill Offenders?" *International Journal of Law and Psychiatry* **27:**387–393.

Hartley, Richard D. (2008). "Sentencing Reforms and the War on Drugs: An Analysis of Sentencing Outcomes for Narcotics Offenders Adjudicated in U.S. District Courts on the Southwest Border." *Journal of Contemporary Criminal Justice* **24:**437–461.

Hartley, Richard D., Holly V. Miller, and Cassia Spohn (2010). "Do You Get What You Pay For? Type of Counsel and Its Effect on Criminal Court Outcomes." *Journal of Criminal Justice* 38:1063–1070.

Haughney, Kathleen (2010). Senate Report Suggests Veterans Court. The St. Augustine Record, October 20.

Hayes, Hennessey D. (2004). "Effectiveness of Restorative Justice." Unpublished paper presented at the annual meeting of the American Society of Criminology, November (Nashville, TN).

Haynes, Andrew (2000). "The Struggle Against Corruption: A Comparative Analysis." *Journal of Financial Crime* **8**:123–135.

Helms, Michael et al. (2004). "Waiver of Counsel among Young Offenders: Variability Between the Juvenile and Criminal Justice Systems." Unpublished paper presented at the annual meeting of the American Society of Criminology, November (Nashville, TN).

Hemenway, David (2004). *Private Guns, Public Health.* Ann Arbor, MI: University of Michigan Press.

Hermida, Julian (2005). "Comparative Analysis of the Theory of Offense in Common Law and Civil Law Criminal Justice Systems." Unpublished paper presented at the annual meeting of the Academy of Criminal Justice Sciences, March (Chicago).

Henderson, D. (1998). "Gender Appropriate Mental Health Services for Incarcerated Women: Issues and Challenges." *Family Community Health* **21**:42–53.

Herzog, Sergio (2003). "The Relationship Between Public Perceptions of Crime Seriousness and Support for Plea Bargaining in Israel: A Factorial-Survey Approach." *Journal of Criminal Law and Criminology* **94**:103–131.

Herzog, Sergio (2004). "Plea Bargaining Practices: Less Covert, More Public Support?" *Crime & Delinquency* **50**:590–614.

Hewitt, William E. (1995). *Court Interpretation: Model Guides for Policy and Practice in the State Courts.* Williamsburg, VA: National Center for State Courts.

Hodge, John L. (1986). "Deadlocked Jury Mistrials, Lesser Included Offenses, and Double Jeopardy: A Proposal to Strengthen the Manifest Necessity Requirement." *Criminal Justice Journal* **9**:9–44.

Hollander, Jocelyn A. (2004). " 'I Can Take Care of Myself': The Impact of Self-Defense Training on Women's Lives." *Violence Against Women* **10**:205–235.

Holmes, Malcolm D. et al. (1992). "Plea Bargaining Policy and State District Court Caseloads: An Interrupted Time Series Analysis." *Law and Society Review* **26**:139–159.

Holmes, Oliver Wendell (1897). *Courts and the Law.* New York: Knopf.

Horton, Candace L. (2005). "America's Stance." Unpublished paper presented at the annual meeting of the Academy of Criminal Justice Sciences, March (Chicago).

Hoskins, Stacy N., Gretchen R. Ruth, and R. Barry Ruback (2004). "Courtroom Workgroups: A Quantitative Description and Analysis of Their Effect on Sentencing." Unpublished paper presented at the annual meeting of the American Society of Criminology, November (Nashville, TN).

Hospers, John (1977). "Punishment, Protection and Rehabilitation." In *Justice and Punishment*, J. Cederblom and W. L. Blizek (eds.). Cambridge, MA: Ballinger.

Hunzeker, Donna (1985). "Habitual Offender Statutes." *Corrections Compendium* **10**:1–15.

Illinois Supreme Court (1993). *Final Report.* Chicago: Illinois Supreme Court Special Commission on the Administration of Justice.

Inciardi, James A. et al. (2004). "Sentencing Drug Offenders." *Criminology and Public Policy* **3**:397–492.

Innocence Project (2005). *An Act Concerning Claims for Wrongful Conviction and Imprisonment: Model Legislation 2005 State Legislative Sessions.* Washington, DC: Innocence Project.

Institute for Court Management (1983). *Evaluation of Telephone Conferencing in Civil and Criminal Court Cases.* Denver: Prepared for the National Institute of Justice and the National Science Foundation; American Bar Association Action Commission to Reduce Court Costs and Delay.

Jacoby, Joseph E., and Eric F. Bronson (2004). "More Executions, Less News, Little Public Knowledge: News Coverage and Public Awareness of Executions in the U.S., 1977–2003." Unpublished paper presented at the annual meeting of the American Society of Criminology, November (Nashville, TN).

Jaffe, P. G., and C. V. Crooks (2004). "Partner Violence and Child Custody Cases: A Cross-National Comparison of Legal Reforms and Issues." *Violence Against Women* **10**:917–934.

James, D. J., and L. E. Glaze (2006). *Mental Health Problems of Prison and Jail Inmates.* Washington, DC: United States Department of Justice, Bureau of Justice Statistics.

Johnson, Brian D. (2004). "Judges on Trial: The Impact of Judge Characteristics Across Modes of Conviction." Unpublished paper presented at the annual meeting of the American Society of Criminology, November (Nashville, TN).

Johnson, Brian, Jeff Ulmer, and John Kramer (2008). "The Social Context of Guideline Circumvention: The Case of Federal District Courts." *Criminology* **44**:259–298.

Johnson, Deborah L., Debra Bannister, and Michelle Alm (2004). "The Violent Youth Offender and Juvenile Transfer to the Adult Criminal Court." Unpublished paper presented at the annual meeting of the American Society of Criminology, November (Nashville, TN).

Jones, Marilyn J. (2003). "Jamaica: Marijuana Decriminalization Conundrum." *Canadian Journal of Law and Society* **18**:91–114.

Jordan, C. E. (2004a). "Intimate Partner Violence and the Justice System: An Examination of the Interface." *Journal of Interpersonal Violence* **19**:1412–1434.

Jordan, Kareem L. (2004b). "Youth in Adult Court: Examining the Predictors of Juvenile Decertification." Unpublished paper presented at the annual meeting of the American Society of Criminology, November (Nashville, TN).

Jordan, Kareem L., and David L. Meyers (2003). "Attorneys, Psychiatrists, and Psychologists: Predictors of Attitudes Toward the Insanity Defense." *Criminal Justice Studies* **16**:77–86.

Kakar, Suman (2004). "Causes of Disproportionate Minority Representation: A Pilot Study." Unpublished paper presented at the annual meeting of the American Society of Criminology, November (Nashville, TN).

Kales, Albert H. (1914). *Unpopular Government in the United States*. Chicago: University of Chicago Press.

Kalven, Harry Jr., and Hans Ziesel (1966). *The American Jury*. Chicago: University of Chicago.

Karp, David R. (2001). "Harm and Repair: Observing Restorative Justice in Vermont." *Justice Quarterly* 18:727–757.

Karp, David R. (2004). "Teen Courts." *APPA Perspectives* 28:18–20.

Karp, David R., G. Bazemore, and J. D. Cheshire (2004). "The Role and Attitudes of Restorative Board Members: A Case Study of Volunteers in Community Justice." *Crime & Delinquency* 50:487–515.

Katz, Charles M., and Cassia Spohn (1995). "The Effect of Race and Gender on Bail Outcomes: A Test of an Interactive Model." *American Journal of Criminal Justice* 19:161–184.

Kauder, Neal B., and Brian J. Ostrom (2008). *State Sentencing Guidelines: Profiles and Continuum*. Williamsburg, VA: National Center for State Courts.

Kaufman, Whitley (2004). "Is There a 'Right' to Self-Defense?" *Criminal Justice Ethics* 23:20–32.

Keil, K. Douglas et al. (1994). "Election, Selection, and Retention." *Judicature* 77:290–321.

Keller, Elizabeth M. (2005). "Security and Prosecution Issues." Unpublished paper presented at the annual meeting of the Academy of Criminal Justice Sciences, March (Chicago).

Keller, Elizabeth M., and Cassia Spohn (2005). "Focal Concerns in Federal Sentencing Decisions." Unpublished paper presented at the annual meeting of the Academy of Criminal Justice Sciences, March (Chicago).

Kellough, Gail, and Scot Wortley (2002). "Remand for Plea: Bail Decisions and Plea Bargaining as Commensurate Decisions." *The British Journal of Criminology* 42:186–210.

Kerr, Norbert L. (1994). "The Effects of Pretrial Publicity on Jurors." *Judicature* 78:120–127.

Kerr, Norbert L., and Robert J. MacCoun (1985). "The Effects of Jury Size and Polling Method on the Process and Product of Jury Deliberation." *Journal of Personality and Social Psychology* 48:349–363.

Ketchum, Paul Robert, and David Geronimo Embrick (2004). "Where Are All the White Kids? An Analysis of the Effects of Race in Juvenile Court." Unpublished paper presented at the annual meeting of the American Society of Criminology, November (Nashville, TN).

Kirschner, Stuart M., and Gary J. Galperin (2001). "Psychiatric Defenses in New York County: Pleas and Results." *Journal of the American Academy of Psychiatry and the Law* 29:194–201.

Klein, Richard, and Robert Spangenberg (1993). *The Indigent Defense Crisis*. Washington, DC: Section of Criminal Justice, American Bar Association.

Kleinig, John (ed.) (1989). "Ethics in Context: The Selling of Jury Deliberations." *Criminal Justice Ethics* 8:26–34.

Knab, Karen M. (ed.) (1977). *Courts of Limited Jurisdiction: A National Survey*. Washington, DC: U.S. National Institute of Law Enforcement and Criminal Justice.

Kramer, John H., and Brian D. Johnson (2004). "Guideline Revisions and Courtroom Actor Decision-Making: Assessing the Influence of Legislative Changes in Pennsylvania, 1991–2000." Unpublished paper presented at the annual meeting of the American Society of Criminology, November (Nashville, TN).

Kramer, John H., and Jeffrey T. Ulmer (1996). "Sentencing Disparities and Guidelines Departures." *Justice Quarterly* 13:401–426.

Kremling, Janine (2004). "An Empirical Analysis of the Role of Mitigation on Capital Sentencing in North Carolina Before and After *McKoy v. North Carolina* (1990)." Unpublished paper presented at the annual meeting of the American Society of Criminology, November (Nashville, TN).

Kuckes, N. (2004). "The Useful, Dangerous Fiction of Grand Jury Independence." *American Criminal Law Review* 41:1–66.

Kupchik, Aaron (2004). "The Negotiated Balance of Care and Control in the Juvenile Court." Unpublished paper presented at the annual meeting of the American Society of Criminology, November (Nashville, TN).

Labriola, Melissa, Sarah Bradley, Chris S. O'Sullivan, Michael Rempel, and Samantha Moore (2009). *A National Portrait of Domestic Violence Courts*. Washington, DC: National Institute of Justice, Center for Court Innovation.

Lafferty, Elaine (1994). "Now, a Jury of His Peers." *Time*, November 14, 1994.

LaFree, Gary D. (1985). "Official Reactions to Hispanic Defendants in the Southwest." *Journal of Research in Crime & Delinquency* 22:213–237.

Langton, Lynn, and Donald Farole (2010). State Public Defender Programs, 2007. Bureau of Justice Statistics Special Report. USDOJ

Lawrence, Richard, and Marop Hesse (2010). *Juvenile Justice: The Essentials*. Thousand Oaks, CA: Sage.

Leiber, Michael J., Kristan Fox, and Joe Johnson (2004). "Race, Gender, and Juvenile Justice: Differences in Disposition Outcomes." Unpublished paper presented at the annual meeting of the American Society of Criminology, November (Nashville, TN).

Lemley, Ellen C. (2004). "Restorative and Perceived Fairness: A Gateway Variable." Unpublished paper presented at the annual meeting of the American Society of Criminology, November (Nashville, TN).

Leo, Richard A. (1994). "Police Interrogation and Social Control." *Social and Legal Studies* 3:93–120.

Leo, Richard A. (2005). "Rethinking the Study of Miscarriages of Justice: Developing a Criminology of Wrongful Conviction." *Journal of Contemporary Criminal Justice* 21:201–223.

Levenson, J. S. (2004). "Reliability of Sexually Violent Predator Civil Commitment Criteria in Florida." *Law and Human Behavior* 28:357–368.

Levin, Martin H. (1988). "The Jury in a Criminal Case: Obstacles to Impartiality." *Criminal Law Bulletin* **24:**492–520.

Levine, James P. (2005). "Race, American Courts and Their Quest for Equal Protection." Unpublished paper presented at the annual meeting of the Academy of Criminal Justice Sciences, March (Chicago).

Levine, James P., and J. Petitt (2005). "The Impact of Excluding Convicted Felons from Jury Service on the Racial Composition of Juries." Unpublished paper presented at the annual meeting of the Academy of Criminal Justice Sciences, March (Chicago).

Liptak, Adam (2008). "Inmate Count in US Dwarfs Other Nations." *New York Times,* April 23.

Listwan, Shelley Johnson, and Terance D. Miethe (2004). "Adult Certification and Juvenile Justice: A Comparative Analysis of Differential Treatment." Unpublished paper presented at the annual meeting of the American Society of Criminology, November (Nashville, TN).

Litwack, Thomas R. (2003). "The Competency of Criminal Defendants to Refuse, for Delusional Reasons, a Visible Insanity Defense Recommended by Counsel." *Behavioral Sciences and the Law* **21:**135–156.

Llewellyn, Karl (1931). "Some Realism about Realism: Responding to Dean Pound." *Harvard Law Review* **44:**1222–1235.

Lo, T. Wing, and Robert J. Harris (2004). "Community Service Orders in Hong Kong, England, and Wales: Twins or Cousins?" *International Journal of Offender Therapy and Comparative Criminology* **48:**373–388.

Lobo-Antunes, M. J. (2004). "Racial and Gender Discrimination in Federal Court Pretrial Processing." Unpublished paper presented at the annual meeting of the American Society of Criminology, November (Nashville, TN).

Loftus, Elizabeth F. (1996). *Eyewitness Testimony.* Cambridge, MA: Harvard University Press.

Lovrich, Nicholas P. Jr., and Charles H. Sheldon (1994). "Is Voting for State Judges a Flight or Fancy or a Reflection of Policy and Value Preferences?" *Justice System Journal* **16:**57–71.

Lutz, R. (1990). *Community Service Orders and Restitution.* Washington, DC: U.S. Government Printing Office.

Ma, Yue (2002). "Prosecutorial Discretion and Plea Bargaining in the United States, France, Germany, and Italy: A Comparative Analysis." *International Criminal Justice Review* **12:**23–52.

Maahs, Jeff (2005). "Evaluation of a Large Urban Drug Court." Unpublished paper presented at the annual meeting of the Academy of Criminal Justice Sciences, March (Chicago).

Mackay, Robert E., and Susan R. Moody (1996). "Diversion of Neighbourhood Disputes in Community Mediation." *Howard Journal of Criminal Justice* **35:**299–313.

Maguire, Kathleen, and Ann L. Pastore (2005). *Sourcebook of Criminal Justice Statistics 2004.* Albany, NY: The Hindelang Criminal Justice Research Center.

Martin, Jamie S., and Jennifer Roberts (2005). "To Die or Not To Die: Factors Influencing Death Sentences." Unpublished paper presented at the annual meeting of the Academy of Criminal Justice Sciences, March (Chicago).

Mason, Mary Ann (1991). "A Judicial Dilemma: Expert Witness Testimony in Child Sex Abuse Cases." *Journal of Psychiatry and Law* **19:**185–219.

Matthews, Roger, Catherine Pease, and Ken Pease (2001). "Repeated Bank Robbery: Theme and Variations." In *Repeat Victimization,* Graham Farrell and Ken Pease (eds.). Monsey, NY: Criminal Justice Press.

Mattick, H. (1975). "The Contemporary Jails of the United States." In *handbook of Criminology*, Daniel Glaser (ed.). Chicago, IL: Rand McNally.

Mauer, Marc (1999). *Race to Incarcerate.* New York, NY: The New Press.

Maxwell, Christopher D., Steven B. Dow, and Sheila Royo Maxwell (2004). "The Impact of Defense Counsel on the Processing and Disposition of Felony Court Cases." Unpublished paper presented at the annual meeting of the American Society of Criminology, November (Nashville, TN).

Maxwell, Gabrielle, and Allison Morris (2002). "Restorative Justice and Reconviction." *Contemporary Justice Review* **5:**133–146.

McCart, Samuel W. (1964). *Trial by Jury: A Complete Guide to the Jury System.* New York: Chilton Books.

McCold, Paul (2003). "An Experiment in Police-Based Restorative Justice: The Bethlehem Pennsylvania Project." *Police Practice and Research* **4:**379–390.

McConville, Mike, and Chester Mirsky (2005). *Jury Trials and Plea Bargaining: A True History.* Oxford, UK: Hart.

McDonald, William F. (1985). *Plea Bargaining: Critical Issues and Common Practices.* Washington, DC: U.S. National Institute of Justice by the Institute of Criminal Law and Procedure, Georgetown University.

McGough, Lucy S. (1994). *Fragile Voices in the American Legal System.* New Haven, CT: Yale University Press.

McKimmie, B. M. et al. (2004). "Jurors' Responses to Expert Witness Testimony: The Effects of Gender Stereotypes." *Group Processes and Intergroup Relations* **7:**131–143.

McLean, Sarah J., Joseph Cocozza, and Kathy Skowyra (2004). "Understanding the Diversity of Juvenile Diversion Programs." Unpublished paper presented at the annual meeting of the American Society of Criminology, November (Nashville, TN).

McManimon, Patrick F. (2005a). "Effects of Truth-in-Sentencing on Inmate Conduct: The Good-Time Myth." Unpublished paper presented at the annual meeting of the Academy of Criminal Justice Sciences, March (Chicago).

McManimon, Patrick F. (2005b). "The Role of Sentencing Policy in the Corrections System." Unpublished paper presented at the annual meeting of the Academy of Criminal Justice Sciences, March (Chicago).

McSherry, B. (2004). "Criminal Responsibility: Fleeting States of Mental Impairment, and the Power of Self-Control." *International Journal of Law and Psychiatry* **27**:445–457.

Menkel-Meadow, Carrie (1986). "The Comparative Sociology of Women Lawyers." *Osgood Law Journal* **24**:897–918.

Merlo, Alida V., and Peter J. Benekos (2004). "The Constitution and the Death Penalty for Juveniles: Assessing Standards of Decency." Unpublished paper presented at the annual meeting of the American Society of Criminology, November (Nashville, TN).

Miller, Holly Ventura. (2008). "Restorative Justice: From Theory to Practice." *Sociology of Crime Law and Deviance*, Vol. 11. Bingley, UK: Emerald/ JAI Press.

Minor, Kevin I., James B. Wells, and Brandi Jones (2004). "Staff Perceptions of the Work Environment in Juvenile Group Home Settings: A Study of Social Climate." *Journal of Offender Rehabilitation* **38**:17–30.

Mirande, Alfredo (1987). *Gringo Justice.* Notre Dame, IN: University of Notre Dame Press.

Mitchell, Edward W. (2003). *Self-Made Madness: Rethinking Illness and Criminal Responsibility.* Aldershot, UK: Ashgate.

Morgan, Thomas D. (1983). *Legal Ethics.* Chicago: Harcourt Brace Jovanovich Legal and Professional Publications, Inc.

Morris, Norval, and Michael Tonry (1990). *Between Prison and Probation: Intermediate Punishments in a Rational Sentencing System.* New York, NY: Oxford University Press.

Mukoro, Saliba D. (2005). "Disproportionate Minority Confinement: What Way Forward?" Unpublished paper presented at the annual meeting of the Academy of Criminal Justice Sciences, March (Chicago).

Mulford, Carrie Fried et al. (2004). "Legal Issues Affecting Mentally Disordered and Developmentally Delayed Youth in the Justice System." *International Journal of Forensic Mental Health* **3**:3–22.

Myers, Bryan et al. (2004). "Victim Impact Statements and Mock Juror Sentencing: The Impact of Dehumanizing Language on a Death Qualified Sample." *American Journal of Forensic Psychology* **22**:39–55.

Myers, Laura B., and Sue Titus Reid (1995). "The Importance of County Context in the Measurement of Sentence Disparity." *Journal of Criminal Justice* **23**:223–241.

Nadeau, Sarah, Melissa W. Burek, and Marian R. Williams (2005). "Quit Mocking Me: An Examination of Racial Composition of Juries on Non-Capital Felony Case Outcomes." Unpublished paper presented at the annual meeting of the Academy of Criminal Justice Sciences, March (Chicago).

Nader, Laura (1979). "Disputing within the Force of the Law." *Yale Law Journal* **88**:998–1043.

Nader, Laura, and Harry F. Todd (eds.) (1978). "Introduction." In *The Disputing Process: Law in Ten Societies.* New York: Columbia University Press.

National Association of Pretrial Services Agencies (1995). *Performance Standards and Goals for Pretrial Release and Diversion.* Frankfort, KY: National Association of Pretrial Services Agencies.

National Center for State Courts (2010). Alternative Dispute Resolution. Available online at: http:// www. ncsconline.org/WC/Publications/ADR/default.htm.

National Center for Victims of Crime (1996). *Statutory and Constitutional Protection of Victim's Rights: Implementation and Impact on Crime Victims, Final Report.* Arlington, VA.

Newsweek (2003). "Lawsuits Out of Control in Major Cities." Editorial, *Newsweek,* November 3, 2003:61.

Nicholson, Marlene Arnold, and Bradley Scott Weiss (1986). "Funding Judicial Campaigns in the Circuit Court of Cook County." *Judicature* **70**:17–25.

Nunn, Samuel (2003). "Seeking Tools for the War on Terror: A Critical Assessment of Emerging Technologies in Law Enforcement." *Policing* **26**:454–473.

Office of Justice Programs (1998). *Looking at a Decade of Drug Courts.* Washington, DC: United States Department of Justice.

Ogletree, C. (2004). "Discriminatory Impact of Mandatory Minimum Sentences in the United States." *Federal Sentencing Reporter* **18**:273–278.

OJJDP (2009). *Juveniles Arrest Rate Trends.* Washington, DC: Office of Juvenile Justice and Delinquency Prevention.

O'Rourke, W. (1972). *The Harrisburg 7 and the New Catholic Left.* New York: Thomas Y. Crowell.

Ostrom, Brian J. (2006). "Domestic Violence Courts." *Criminology and Public Policy* **3**:105–108.

O'Sullivan, Julie R. (2001). *Federal White Collar Crime: Cases and Materials.* St. Paul, MN: West Group.

Palermo, George B. (2004). "Tattooing and Tattooed Criminals." *Journal of Forensic Psychology Practice* **4**:1–25.

Palumbo, Dennis J., Michael Musheno, and Michael Hallett (1994). "The Political Construction of Alternative Dispute Resolution and Alternatives to Incarceration." *Evaluation and Program Planning* **17**:197–203.

Park, Mirang (2005). "Racial Disparity in Drug Sentencing: Focusing on Hispanic." Unpublished paper presented at the annual meeting of the Academy of Criminal Justice Sciences, March (Chicago).

Patrick, Steven et al. (2004). "Control Group Study of Juvenile Diversion Programs." *Social Science Journal* **41**:129–135.

Penrod, Steven D., Solomon M. Fulero, and Brian L. Cutler (1995). "Expert Psychological Testimony on Eyewitness Reliability Before and After Daubert: The State of the Law and Science." *Behavioral Sciences and the Law* **13**:229–259.

Peters, Roger H. et al. (2004). "Co-Occurring Disorders and the Criminal Justice System." *Behavioral Sciences and the Law* **22**:427–610.

Peterson, Scott (2005). *The Growth of Teen Courts in the United States.* Washington, DC: Office of Juvenile Justice and Delinquency Prevention.

Phillips, Amy K. (1997). "Thou Shalt Not Kill Any Nice People: The Problem of Victim Impact Statements in Capital Sentencing." *American Criminal Law Review* **35**:93–118.

Pickles, James (1987). *Straight from the Bench*. London, UK: Dent and Sons.

Pinello, Daniel R. (1995). *The Impact of Judicial Selection Method on State Supreme Court Policy: Innovation, Reaction, and Atrophy*. Westport, CT: Greenwood Press.

Piquero, A. R., T. Brezina, and M. G. Turner (2005). "Testing Moffit's Account of Delinquency Abstention." *Journal of Research in Crime & Delinquency* **42**:27–54.

Piquero, N. L., and J. L. Davis (2004). "Extralegal Factors and the Sentencing of Organizational Defendants: An Examination of the Federal Sentencing Guidelines." *Journal of Criminal Justice* **32**:643–654.

Pohlman, H. L. (1995). *Constitutional Debate in Action: Criminal Justice*. New York: HarperCollins College Publishers.

Posey, Amy J., and Lisa M. Dahl (2002). "Beyond Pretrial Publicity: Legal and Ethical Issues Associated with Change of Venue Surveys." *Law and Human Behavior* **26**:107–125.

Pound, Roscoe (1912). "The Scope and Purpose of Sociological Jurisprudence." *Journal of Political Economy* **25**:489–500.

Prentice, Melissa A. (2001). "Prosecuting Mothers Who Maim and Kill: The Profile of Munchausen Syndrome by Proxy Litigation in the Late 1990s." *American Journal of Criminal Law* **28**:373–412.

President's Commission on Law Enforcement (1967). *President's Commission on Law Enforcement and the Administration of Justice*. Washington, DC: U.S. Government Printing Office.

Presser, Lis, Cynthia Hamilton, and Emily Gaarder (2004). "Power Dynamics of Victim-Offender Mediation." Unpublished paper presented at the annual meeting of the American Society of Criminology, November (Nashville, TN).

Preston, Frederick W., and Roger I. Roots (eds.) (2004). "When Laws Backfire: Unintended Impacts of Public Policy." *American Behavioral Scientist* **47**:1371–1466.

Priest, George (1985). "The Invention of Enterprise Liability: A Critical History of the Intellectual Foundations of Modern Tort Law." *Journal of Legal Studies* **14**:461–527.

Proulx, Craig (2003). *Reclaiming Aboriginal Justice, Identity, and Community*. Saskatoon, Canada: Purich Publishing.

Rasmussen, A. (2004). "Teen Court Referral, Sentencing, and Subsequent Recidivism: Two Proportional Hazards Models and a Little Speculation." *Crime & Delinquency* **50**:615–635.

Read, J. Don, John C. Yuille, and Patricia Tollestrup (1992). "Recollections of a Robbery: Effects of Arousal and Alcohol Upon Recall and Person Identification." *Law and Human Behavior* **16**:425–446.

Reed, Gary (2004). "Therapeutic Communities in Restorative Justice." Unpublished paper presented at the annual meeting of the American Society of Criminology, November (Nashville, TN).

Reed, Judith (2004). *Teen Courts*. Albuquerque, NM: Youth Development and Diagnostic Center.

Roberts, Albert R. (ed.) (2003). *Critical Issues in Crime and Justice* (2nd ed.). Thousand Oaks, CA: Sage.

Roberts, Julian V., and Edna Erez (2004). "Communication in Sentencing: Exploring the Expressive Function of Victim Impact Statements." *International Review of Victimology* **10**:223–244.

Roberts, Melinda, Jacinta M. Gau, and David C. Brody (2004). "Eligible Jurors' Knowledge, Information Sources, and Attitudes About the Jury System." Unpublished paper presented at the annual meeting of the American Society of Criminology, November (Nashville, TN).

Robinson, Paul H., and J. M. Darley (2004). "Does Criminal Law Deter? A Behavioral Science Investigation." *Oxford Journal of Legal Studies* **24**:173–205.

Rockwell, P., and A. E. Hubbard (2004). "The Effect of Attorneys' Nonverbal Communication on Perceived Credibility." *Polygraph* **33**:102–114.

Rodriguez, Nancy (2004). "Examining the Influence of Community Racial/Ethnic Composition in Juvenile Detention Decisions: The Mediating Role of Community Characteristics in Juvenile Court." Unpublished paper presented at the annual meeting of the American Society of Criminology, November (Nashville, TN).

Rodriguez, Nancy, and Gaylene S. Armstrong (2004). "The Relationship Between Offense Type and Attorney Presence in Juvenile Court Disposition Decisions." Unpublished paper presented at the annual meeting of the American Society of Criminology, November (Nashville, TN).

Rogers, Patrick, Sharon Cotliar, and Steve Erwin (2000). "Judgment Day." *People,* November 6, 2000:87–91.

Rojek, Dean G., James E. Coverdill, and Stuart W. Fors (2003). "The Effect of Victim Impact Panels on DUI Rearrest Rates: A Five-Year Follow-up." *Criminology* **41**:1319–1340.

Rosay, Andre B., and Brad A. Myrstol (2004). "Gender Effects in the Alaska Juvenile Justice System." Unpublished paper presented at the annual meeting of the American Society of Criminology, November (Nashville, TN).

Rose-Ackerman, Susan (2002). "Corruption and the Criminal Law." *Forum on Crime and Society* **2**:3–21.

Ross, David Frank, J. Don Read, and Michael P. Toglia (1994). *Adult Eyewitness Testimony: Current Trends and Developments*. Cambridge: Cambridge University Press.

Rottman, David B., Carol R. Flango, Melissa Cantrell, Randall Hansen, and Neil LaFountain (2000). *State Court Organization, 1998*. Washington, DC: Bureau of Justice Statistics.

Rottman, David B., and Shauna M. Strickland (2006) *State Court Organization, 2004*. Washington, DC: United States Department of Justice, Bureau of Justice Statistics.

Roy, Dina (2004). "Age Disparity in Criminal Court Sentencing." Unpublished paper presented at the annual meeting of the American Society of Criminology, November (Nashville, TN).

Roy, Sudipto, and Michael Brown (1992). "Victim-Offender Reconciliation Project for Adults and Juveniles: A Comparative Study in Elkhart County, Indiana." Unpublished paper presented at the annual meetings of the American Society of Criminology, November (San Francisco, CA).

Ruback, R. Barry (2002). *Restitution in Pennsylvania: A Multimethod Investigation.* Erie, PA: Pennsylvania Commission on Crime and Delinquency.

Sabelli, Martin, and Stacey Leyton (2000). "Train Wrecks and Freeway Crashes: An Argument for Fairness and Against Self-Representation in the Criminal Justice System." *Journal of Criminal Law and Criminology* **91**:161–235.

Sabol, W. J., H. C. West, and M. Copper (2009). *Prisoners in 2008.* Washington, DC: U.S. Department of Justice, Office of Justice Programs, Bureau of Justice Statistics.

Sacks, Stanley, and Frank S. Pearson (2003). "Co-Occurring Substance Use and Mental Disorders in Offenders: Approaches, Findings, and Recommendations." *Federal Probation* **67**:32–39.

Saltzburg, Stephen A., and Kenneth R. Redeen (1994). *Federal Rules of Evidence Manual.* Charlottesville, VA: Michie.

Schaffer, B. (2010). "Veterans Courts and Diversion Alternatives." *American Jails*, January/February 2010:21–24.

Schauffler, Richard Y., Robert C. LaFountain, Neal B. Kauder, and Shauna M. Strickland (2004). *Examining the Work of State Courts, 2004.* Washington, DC: Bureau of Justice Statistics.

Scheb, John M. II (1988). "State Appellate Judges' Attitudes Toward Judicial Merit Selection and Retention: Results of a National Survey." *Judicature* **62**:170–174.

Scheck, Barry, and Peter Neufeld (2002). "Toward the Formation of Innocence Commissions in America." *Judicature* **86**:98–105.

Schiff, Mara F., and Gordon Bazemore (2004). "Why Restorative Justice Works: Building and Testing Intervention Theories." Unpublished paper presented at the annual meeting of the American Society of Criminology, November (Nashville, TN).

Schmid, Karl H. (2002). "Journalist's Privilege in Criminal Proceedings: An Analysis of United States Courts of Appeals' Decisions from 1973–1999." *American Criminal Law Review* **39**:1441–1499.

Schoenfeld, Heather (2005). "Violated Trust: Conceptualizing Prosecutorial Misconduct." *Journal of Contemporary Criminal Justice* **21**:250–271.

Schram, Pamela J., Barbara A. Koons-Witt, and Merry Morash (2004). "Management Strategies When Working with Female Prisoners." *Women and Criminal Justice* **15**:25–50.

Schulman, William L. (2005). "Videotaping the Process: Technology in America's Jails and Courtrooms." Unpublished paper presented at the annual meeting of the Academy of Criminal Justice Sciences, March (2005).

Schwelme, Barbara (2008). "Legislative, Executive and Judicial Officials: Process for Adjusting Pay and Current Salaries." **CRS** *Report for Congress.*

Sheehy, Elizabeth (2004). "Advancing Social Inclusion: The Implications for Criminal Law and Policy." *Canadian Journal of Criminology and Criminal Justice* **46**:73–95.

Simon, Rita J., and Thomas Eimermann (1971). "The Jury Finds Not Guilty: Another Look at Media Influence on the Jury." *Journalism Quarterly* **48**:343–344.

Smith, Alisa (2004). *Law, Social Science, and the Criminal Courts.* Durham, NC: Carolina Academic Press.

Smith, Steven K., and Carol J. DeFrances (1996). *Indigent Defense.* Washington, DC: U.S. Department of Justice.

Sorensen, Jonathan R., and Donald H. Wallace (1995). "Arbitrariness and Discrimination in Missouri Capital Cases: An Assessment Using the Barnett Scale." *Journal of Crime and Justice* **18**:21–57.

Spangenberg, Robert L. et al. (1999). *Indigent Defense and Technology: A Progress Report.* Washington, DC: Bureau of Justice Assistance.

Spohn, Cassia C. (2000). *Thirty Years of Sentencing Reform: The Quest for a Racially Neutral Sentencing Process.* Washington, DC: National Institute of Justice, Criminal Justice.

Spohn, Cassia C. (2002). *How Do Judges Decide? The Search for Fairness and Justice in Punishment.* Thousand Oaks, CA: Sage.

Spohn, Cassia C. (2004). "Sentencing Decisions in Three U.S. District Courts: Testing the Assumption of Uniformity in the Federal Sentencing Process." Unpublished paper presented at the annual meeting of the American Society of Criminology, November (Nashville, TN).

Spohn, Cassia C. (2005). "Sentencing Decisions in Three U.S. District Courts: Testing the Assumption of National Uniformity in the Federal Sentencing Process." *Justice Research and Policy* **7**:1–28.

Spohn, Cassia C. (2009). *How Do Judges Decide: The Search for Fairness and Justice in Punishment.* Thousand Oaks, CA: Sage.

Spohn, Cassia C., and David Holleran (2000). "The Imprisonment Penalty Paid by Young, Unemployed Black and Hispanic Male Offenders." *Criminology* **38**:281–306.

Spohn, Cassia C., and Elizabeth Keller (2005). "U.S. Attorneys and the Federal Sentencing Process: A Test of Inter-Prosecutor Disparity." Unpublished paper presented at the annual meeting of the American Society of Criminology, November (Toronto, CAN).

Sridharan, S. et al. (2004). "Juvenile Transfer." *Criminology and Public Policy* **3**:599–649.

Stacey, Lynn R., and P. E. Dayton (1988). *Jury Deliberations and Judicial Opinions.* Washington, DC: U.S. Department of Justice.

Stalans, Loretta J. et al. (2004). "Identifying Three Types of Violent Offenders and Predicting Violent Recidivism While on Probation: A Classification Tree Analysis." *Law and Human Behavior* **28**:253–271.

Stalmaster, Irvin (1931). *What Price Jury Trials?* New York: Penguin.

Stanley, Steve (2004). " 'What Works'? Revisiting the Evidence in England and Wales." *Journal of Community and Criminal Justice* **51**:7–20.

Steadman, Henry J. and Bonita M. Veysey (1997). *Providing Services for Jail Inmates with Mental Disorders.* Washington, DC: National Institute of Justice.

Steelman, David C., and Samuel D. Conti (1987). *Representation of Indigent Criminal Defendants in the Courts of Hamilton County, Ohio.* North Andover, MA: National Center for State Courts.

Steffensmeier, D., and S. Demuth (2000). "Ethnicity and Sentencing Outcomes in U.S. Federal Courts: Who is Punished More Harshly?" *American Sociological Review* **65**:705–729.

Steffensmeier, D., J. Kramer, and C. Steifel (1993). "Gender and Imprisonment Decisions." *Criminology* **31**:411–446.

Steffensmeier, D., J. T. Ulmer, and J. H. Kramer (1998). "The Interaction of Race, Gender, and Age in Criminal Sentencing: The Punishment Cost of Being Young, Black, and Male." *Criminology* **36**:763–797.

Steiner, Benjamin, Craig Hemmens, and Valerie Bell (2004). "Legislative Waiver Reconsidered: An Examination of General Deterrence." Unpublished paper presented at the annual meeting of the American Society of Criminology, November (Nashville, TN).

Stemen, Donald (2004). "Policies of Imprisonment: The Adoption of Determinate Sentencing and Sentencing Guidelines in the United States, 1975–2002." Unpublished paper presented at the annual meeting of the American Society of Criminology, November (Nashville, TN).

Stemen, Donald, James A. Wilson, and Andres Rengifo (2004). "Of Fragmentation and Ferment: The Impact of Sentencing Policies on State-Level Incarceration Rates and Admissions to Prison, 1970–2002." Unpublished paper presented at the annual meeting of the American Society of Criminology, November (Nashville, TN).

Stephenson-Lang, Juli (2005). "Tipping the Scales of Justice: The Importance of Proportionality in a Balanced Sentencing Scheme." Unpublished paper presented at the annual meeting of the Academy of Criminal Justice Sciences, March (Chicago).

Stith, Kate, and Jose A. Cabranes (1998). *Fear of Judging Sentencing Guidelines in Federal Court.* Chicago: University of Chicago Press.

Strang, Heather (2004). "Effectiveness in Restorative Justice: First Doing No Harm." Unpublished paper presented at the annual meeting of the American Society of Criminology, November (Nashville, TN).

Suggs, David, and Bruce Sales (1981). "Juror Self-Disclosure in the Voir Dire: A Social Science Analysis." *Indiana Law Journal* **56**:245–271.

Swain, F. W. (1985). *Of God and His Conscience: Judicial Selection in Louisiana.* Baton Rouge, LA: Louisiana State Legislature.

Szymanski, L. (1997). "Juvenile Delinquent's Right to a Jury Trial." *NCJJ Snapshot* **2**(4). Pittsburgh, PA: National Center for Juvenile Justice.

Tague, Peter W. (1999). "Representing Indigents in Serious Criminal Cases in England's Crown Court: The Advocates' Performance and Incentives." *American Criminal Law Review* **36**:171–222.

Tappan, Christy (2005). "The New Face of Prosecution: Structural Characteristics and Outcomes Associated with Community Prosecution." Unpublished paper presented at the annual meeting of the Academy of Criminal Justice Sciences, March (Chicago).

Taylor, Humphrey, Michael Kagay, and Stuart Leichenko (1987). *Public Attitudes Toward the Civil Justice System and Tort Law Reform.* New York: Louis Harris and Associates for Aetna Life and Casualty Insurance Company.

Technology Review (2005). "The DNA Defense." *Technology Review* **108**:20.

Teske, Raymond H. C. Jr., and C. Zhang (2005). "Disposition of Defendants Charged with Felony-Level Violation of Protective Orders in Harris County, Texas." Unpublished paper presented at the annual meeting of the Academy of Criminal Justice Sciences, March (Chicago).

The Center for Public integrity (2003). Harmful Error: Investigating America's Local Prosecutors.

Thomas, Wayne (1976). *Bail Reform in America.* Berkeley: University of California Press.

Thomas, Wayne (1977). *National Evaluation Program: Pretrial Release Programs.* Washington, DC: Law Enforcement Assistance Administration.

Thompson, R. Alan (2005). "Results of the 2004 Mississippi Crime Poll." Unpublished paper presented at the annual meeting of the Academy of Criminal Justice Sciences, March (Chicago).

Tifft, Larry (2004). "A Critique of Restorative Justice Evaluation Research." Unpublished paper presented at the annual meeting of the Academy of Criminal Justice Sciences, November (Nashville, TN).

Tishler, C. L. et al. (2004). "Is Domestic Violence Relevant? An Exploratory Analysis of Couples Referred for Mediation in Family Court." *Journal of Interpersonal Violence* **19**:1042–1062.

Tomasi, Timothy B., and Jess A. Velona (1987). "All the President's Men: A Study of Ronald Reagan's Appointments to the U.S. Courts of Appeals." *Columbia Law Review* **87**:766–793.

Tonry, Michael (1995). *Malign Neglect.* New York, NY: Oxford University Press.

Tonry, Michael (1996). *Sentencing Matters.* New York, NY: Oxford University Press.

Tonry, Michael (2004). *Punishment and Politics: Evidence and Emulation in the Making of English Crime Control Policy.* Cullompton, Devon, UK: Willan Publishing.

Tsai, B. (2000). "The Trend Toward Specialized Domestic Violence Courts: Improvements on an Effective Innovation." *Fordham Law Review* **68**:1285–1327.

Tshehla, B. (2004). "The Restorative Justice Bug Bites the South African Criminal Justice System." *South African Journal of Criminal Justice* **17**:1–16.

Ueckert, Edwin (2005). "The Issue of Civil Commitment of Habitual Violent Offenders." Unpublished paper presented at the annual meeting of the Academy of Criminal Justice Sciences, March (Chicago).

Ulmer, Jeffery T. (2004). "Differences in Guideline Departures and Sentencing among Seven Federal District Courts." Unpublished paper presented at the annual meeting of the American Society of Criminology, November (Nashville, TN).

Ulmer, Jeffery T. (2005). "The Localized Uses of Federal Sentencing Guidelines in Four U.S. District Courts: Evidence of Processual Order." *Symbolic Interaction* **28**:255–279.

Ulmer, Jeffery T., and Keri B. Burchfield (2004). "Charge Manipulation and Relevant Conduct in Federal Criminal Case Processing." Unpublished paper presented at the annual meeting of the American Society of Criminology, November (Nashville, TN).

Ulrich, Thomas E. (2002). "Pretrial Diversion in the Federal Court System." *Federal Probation* **66**:30–37.

Umbreit, Mark S. (1994). "Victim Empowerment through Mediation." *APPA Perspectives* **18**:25–28.

Umbreit, Mark S., and Elizabeth Lightfoot (2004). "An Analysis of State Statutory Provisions for Victim-Offender Mediation." *Criminal Justice Policy Review* **15**:418–436.

United States Sentencing Commission (2010). *Demographic Differences in Federal Sentencing Practices: An Update of the Booker Report's Multivariate Regression Analysis.* Washington, DC: Author.

U.S. Advisory Commission on Intergovernmental Relations (1971). *For a More Perfect Union—Court Reform.* Washington, DC: U.S. Government Printing Office.

U.S. Department of Justice (2005). *Justice Statistics.* Washington, DC: U.S. Department of Justice, Bureau of Justice Statistics.

U.S. Department of Justice (2010). *Crime in the United States, 2009: Offenses Cleared.* United States Department of Justice, Federal Bureau of Investigation.

U.S. Office of Personnel Management (2010). Personal Communication.

U.S. Sentencing Commission (2003). *Downward Departures from the Federal Sentencing Guidelines.* Washington, DC: U.S. Sentencing Commission.

Unnever, James D., and Francis T. Cullen (2004). "Readdressing the Racial Divide in Support for Capital Punishment." Unpublished paper presented at the annual meeting of the American Society of Criminology, November (Nashville, TN).

Urban, Lynn S. (2005). "The Effect of a Curfew Check Program on Juvenile Opportunities for Delinquent Activity." Unpublished paper presented at the annual meeting of the Academy of Criminal Justice Sciences, Chicago (March).

Vago, Steven (2006). *Law and Society* (6th ed.). Upper Saddle River, NJ: Prentice Hall.

van Koppen, Peter J., and Steven D. Penrod (2003). *Adversarial Versus Inquisitorial Justice: Psychological Perspectives on Criminal Justice Systems.* New York: Kluwer.

Van Zyl Smit, D., and A. Ashworth (2004). "Disproportionate Sentences as Human Rights Violations." *Modern Law Review* **67**:541–560.

Vaughn, Michael S., Volkan Topalli, and Sarah Pierre (2004). "Legal Issues Involving Show-Ups, Line-Ups, and Photographic Identification." Unpublished paper presented at the annual meeting of the American Society of Criminology, November (Nashville, TN).

Veneziano, Carol (2005a). "An Evaluation of a Rural Drug Court Program." Unpublished paper presented at the annual meeting of the Academy of Criminal Justice Sciences, March (Chicago).

Veneziano, Carol (2005b). "Evaluating Drug Courts." Unpublished paper presented at the annual meeting of the Academy of Criminal Justice Sciences, March (Chicago).

Vidmar, Neil (2000). "Juries and Expert Evidence." *Brooklyn Law Review* **66**:1121–1180.

Villanova Law Review (1982). "Judicial Selection in Pennsylvania: A Proposal." *Villanova Law Review* **27**:1163–1178.

Vincent, Barbara S., and Paul J. Hofer (1994). *The Consequences of Mandatory Minimum Prison Terms: A Summary of Recent Findings.* Washington, DC: U.S. Government Printing Office.

Vito, Gennaro F. (1984). "Developments in Shock Probation: A Review of Research Findings." *Federal Probation* **48**:22–27.

Volcansek, Mary L., Maria Eisabetta DeFranciscis, and Jacqueline Lucienne Lafron (1996). *Judicial Misconduct: A Cross-National Comparison.* Gainesville, FL: University Press of Florida.

Vollum, S., Dennis R. Longmire, and J. Buffington-Vollum (2004). "Confidence in the Death Penalty and Support for Its Use: Exploring the Value-Expressive Dimension of Death Penalty Attitudes." *Justice Quarterly* **21**:521–546.

Walker, Sam, Cassia Spohn, and Miriam DeLone (2000). *The Color of Justice: Race, Ethnicity and Crime in America.* Belmont, CA: Wadsworth.

Wanamaker, John L. (1978). "Computers and Scientific Jury Selection: A Calculated Risk." *Journal of Urban Law* **55**:345–370.

Ward, Geoff (2004). "Custody Against Care in the Concept of Accountability: Shifting Policies and Stubborn Priorities in Juvenile Court Organizations." Unpublished paper presented at the annual meeting of the American Society of Criminology, November (Nashville, TN).

Warden, Rob (2004). "DNA and Justice." *Newsfeed.* Evanston, IL: Northwestern University, May 3, 2004.

Weinberg, S., N. Gordon, and B. Williams (2005). *Harmful Error: Investigating America's Local Prosecutors.* Washington, DC: Center for Public Integrity.

Weisburd, David, Elin Waring, and Stanton Wheeler (1990). "Class, Status, and the Punishment of White-Collar Criminals." *Law and Social Inquiry* **15**:223–243.

Weiss, Michael Scott (2004). "Public Defenders' Pragmatic Motivations: A Qualitative and Inductive Study." Unpublished paper presented at the annual meeting of the American Society of Criminology, November (Nashville, TN).

Wely, Theodore (1904). *Hygiene of Occupation*. New York: Jena.

Westervelt, Saundra D., and Kimberly J. Cook (2004). "Life After Death: Life Histories of Innocents Released from Death Row." Unpublished paper presented at the annual meeting of the American Society of Criminology, November (Nashville, TN).

Wettstein, Robert M. (ed.) (1992). "Cults and the Law." *Behavioral Sciences and the Law* **10**:1–140.

Wheeler, R. (2010). *Judicial Nominations in the First Fourteen Months of the Obama and Bush Administrations*. Washington, DC. The Brookings Institution.

Whitcomb, Debra et al. (1994). *The Child Victim as a Witness*. Washington, DC: U.S. Office of Juvenile Justice and Delinquency Prevention.

White, E.W. (1999). *History of Law in American Society*. New York: Cakewalk Books.

White, Welsh S. (2002). "Curbing Prosecutorial Misconduct in Capital Cases: Imposing Prohibitions on Improper Penalty Trial Arguments." *American Criminal Law Review* **39**:1147–1185.

Williams, James J., Daniel G. Rodeheaver, and Felicia Guerrero (2004). "Processing Offenders in Texas Juvenile Courts: Trends and Patterns." Unpublished paper presented at the annual meeting of the American Society of Criminology, November (Nashville, TN).

Williams, L. Susan, Delores E. Craig-Moreland, and A. Elizabeth Cauble (2004). "Chivalry Revisited: The Case of Girls in Rural Areas." Unpublished paper presented at the annual meeting of the American Society of Criminology, November (Nashville, TN).

Williams, M. R., and J. E. Holcomb (2004). "The Interactive Effects of Victim Race and Gender on Death Penalty Disparity Findings." *Homicide Studies* **8**:350–376.

Williamson, Deborah, Michelle Chalk, and Paul Knepper (1993). "Teen Court: Juvenile Justice for the 21st Century?" *Federal Probation* **57**:54–58.

Wilmot, Keith Alan (2002). *Prosecutorial Discretion and Real Offense Sentencing Under the Federal Sentencing Guidelines: An Analysis of Relevant Conduct*. Ann Arbor, MI: University Microfilms International.

Wilmot, Keith Alan, and Cassia C. Spohn (2004). "Prosecutorial Discretion and Real-Offense Sentencing: An Analysis of Relevant Conduct Under the Federal Sentencing Guidelines." *Criminal Justice Policy Review* **15**:324–343.

Winston, Norma A., and William E. Winston (1980). "The Use of Sociological Techniques in the Jury Selection Process." *National Journal of Criminal Defense* **6**:79–97.

Wolff, N. (1998). "Interactions Between Mental Health and Law Enforcement Systems: Problems and Prospects for Cooperation." *Journal of Health, Politics, Policy and Law* **23**:133–174.

Wood, William R. (2004). "Defining Success in Juvenile Restorative Justice: A Community Based Approach in Clark County, WA." Unpublished paper presented at the annual meeting of the American Society of Criminology, November (Nashville, TN).

Wooldredge, John, and Tim Griffin (2004). "Neighborhood Level Disparities in Court Dispositions Before and After the Implementation of Sentencing Guidelines in Ohio." Unpublished paper presented at the annual meeting of the American Society of Criminology, November (Nashville, TN).

Worden, Alissa Pollitz (1995). "The Judge's Role in Plea Bargaining: An Analysis of Judges' Agreement with Prosecutor's Sentencing Recommendations." *Justice Quarterly* **12**:257–278.

Worling, James R. (1995). "Adolescent Sex Offenders Against Females: Differences Based on the Age of Their Victims." *International Journal of Offender Therapy and Comparative Criminology* **39**:276–293.

Wortzel, H. S., L. A. Binswanger, C. A. Anderson, and L. E. Adler (2009). "Suicide Among Incarcerated Veterans." *Journal of American Academy of Psychiatry and the Law* **37**:82–91.

Xenos, Nicholas (ed.) (2003). "Restorative Justice." *Polity* **36**:1–90.

Zalman, Marvin (2004). "The Adversary Jury Trial and Wrongful Conviction." Unpublished paper presented at the annual meeting of the American Society of Criminology, November (Nashville, TN).

Zaragoza, Maria S. (1995). *Memory and Testimony in the Child Witness*. Thousand Oaks, CA: Sage.

Zingraff, Matthew, and Randall Thompson (1984). "Differential Sentencing of Women and Men in the USA." *International Journal of the Sociology of Law* **12**:401–413.

CASES CITED INDEX

NAME INDEX

SUBJECT INDEX

Note: The locators followed by b, f, and t are referred to boxes, figures, and tables respectively.